FOURTH EDITION

Managing Risk in Information Systems

Chuck Easttom
PhD², DSc, MEd, MS, MBA

JONES & BARTLETT
LEARNING

jblearning:\cybersecurity+IT™

World Headquarters
Jones & Bartlett Learning
25 Mall Road
Burlington, MA 01803
978-443-5000
info@jblearning.com
www.jblearning.com

Jones & Bartlett Learning books and products are available through most bookstores and online booksellers. To contact Jones & Bartlett Learning directly, call 800-832-0034, fax 978-443-8000, or visit our website, www.jblearning.com.

Substantial discounts on bulk quantities of Jones & Bartlett Learning publications are available to corporations, professional associations, and other qualified organizations. For details and specific discount information, contact the special sales department at Jones & Bartlett Learning via the above contact information or send an email to specialsales@jblearning.com.

31643-8

Production Credits
Vice President, Innovative Learning and Assessment Solutions: Ada Woo
Senior Director, Content Production and Delivery: Christine Emerton
Director, Product: Melissa Kleeman-Moy
Manager, Content Development: Carol Brewer Guerrero
Content Manager: Sara Holloway
Content Coordinator: Rachelle Soden
Manager, Intellectual Properties and Content Production: Kristen Rogers
Content Production Manager: Belinda Thresher
Senior Intellectual Property Specialist (eBook): Angela Dooley
Product Marketing Manager: Elizabeth Ward
Director, Product Fulfillment: Aaron McKinzie
Purchasing Manager: Wendy Kilborn
Composition: XBP Global
Project Management: XBP Global
Cover Design: MPS Limited
Text Design: MPS Limited
Media Developer: Faith Brosnan
Intellectual Property Specialist: Lisa Passmore
Cover Image (Title Page, Part Opener, Chapter Opener): © Yuichiro Chino/Moment/Getty Images
Printing and Binding: Gasch Printing

Library of Congress Cataloging-in-Publication Data
Library of Congress Cataloging-in-Publication Data unavailable at time of printing.

LCCN: 2026005967

6048

Printed in the United States of America

30 29 28 27 26 10 9 8 7 6 5 4 3 2 1

I would like to dedicate this book to my wife, Teresa, who is so supportive and patient through all my work.

Brief Contents

Preface xix

About the Author xxiii

PART ONE Risk Management Business Challenges 1

CHAPTER 1 Risk Management Fundamentals 3

CHAPTER 2 Managing Risk: Threats, Vulnerabilities, and Exploits 29

CHAPTER 3 Understanding and Maintaining Compliance 59

CHAPTER 4 Developing a Risk Management Plan 89

PART TWO Mitigating Risk 115

CHAPTER 5 Defining Risk Assessment Approaches 117

CHAPTER 6 Performing a Risk Assessment 143

CHAPTER 7 Identifying Assets and Activities to Be Protected 171

CHAPTER 8 Identifying and Analyzing Threats, Vulnerabilities, and Exploits 197

CHAPTER 9 Identifying and Analyzing Risk Mitigation Security Controls 225

CHAPTER 10 Planning Risk Mitigation Throughout an Organization 253

CHAPTER 11 Turning a Risk Assessment Into a Risk Mitigation Plan 281

PART THREE Risk Mitigation Plans 309

CHAPTER 12 Mitigating Risk With a Business Impact Analysis 311

CHAPTER 13 Mitigating Risk With a Business Continuity Plan 335

CHAPTER 14 Mitigating Risk With a Disaster Recovery Plan 361

CHAPTER 15 Mitigating Risk With a Computer Incident Response Team Plan 389

APPENDIX A Answer Key 419

APPENDIX B Standard Acronyms 421

Glossary 425

Index 433

Contents

Preface xix
About the Author xxiii

PART ONE Risk Management Business Challenges 1

CHAPTER 1 Risk Management Fundamentals 3

What Is Risk? 4
Compromise of Business Functions 5
Threats, Vulnerabilities, Assets, and Impact 6
Classify Business Risks 10
Risks Posed by People 10
Risks Posed by a Lack of Process 12
Risks Posed by Technology 13
Risk Identification Techniques 15
Identifying Threats 15
Identifying Vulnerabilities 16
Assessing Impact and Likelihood 18
Risk Management Process 20
Cost-Benefit Analysis 21
Profitability Versus Survivability 22
Risk-Handling Strategies 23
Avoiding 24
Sharing or Transferring 24
Mitigating 24
Accepting 25
Residual Risk 25
CHAPTER SUMMARY 26
KEY CONCEPTS AND TERMS 26
CHAPTER 1 ASSESSMENT 27

CHAPTER 2 Managing Risk: Threats, Vulnerabilities, and Exploits 29

Understanding and Protecting Assets 30

Understanding and Managing Threats 30

Uncontrollable Nature of Threats 31
Unintentional Threats 31
Intentional Threats 32
Best Practices for Managing Risk Within an IT Infrastructure 34
EY Global Information Security Survey 2025 36

Understanding and Managing Vulnerabilities 37

Threat/Vulnerability Pairs 37
Vulnerabilities Can Be Mitigated 38
Mitigation Techniques 38
Best Practices for Managing Vulnerabilities Within an IT Infrastructure 42

Understanding and Managing Exploits 42

What Is an Exploit? 42
How Do Perpetrators Initiate an Exploit? 45
Where Do Perpetrators Find Information About Vulnerabilities and Exploits? 47
Mitigation Techniques 48
Best Practices for Managing Exploits Within an IT Infrastructure 49

U.S. Federal Government Risk Management Initiatives 50

National Institute of Standards and Technology 50
Department of Homeland Security 52
National Cybersecurity and Communications Integration Center 52
U.S. Computer Emergency Readiness Team 53
The MITRE Corporation and the CVE List 54

CHAPTER SUMMARY 56

KEY CONCEPTS AND TERMS 56

CHAPTER 2 ASSESSMENT 57

CHAPTER 3 **Understanding and Maintaining Compliance** 59

U.S. Compliance Laws 60

Federal Information Security Modernization Act 61
Health Insurance Portability and Accountability Act 61
Gramm-Leach-Bliley Act 64
Sarbanes-Oxley Act 64
Family Educational Rights and Privacy Act 64
Children's Internet Protection Act 65
Children's Online Privacy Protection Act 66
Computer Fraud and Abuse Act 67
California Consumer Privacy Act 67

Regulations Related to Compliance 68

Securities and Exchange Commission 68
Federal Deposit Insurance Corporation 68
Department of Homeland Security 69
Federal Trade Commission 69
State Attorneys General 70
U.S. Attorney General 70

Organizational Policies for Compliance 71

Standards and Guidelines for Compliance 72

Payment Card Industry Data Security Standard 73
National Institute of Standards and Technology 75
Generally Accepted Information Security Principles 75
Control Objectives for Information and Related Technologies 76
International Organization for Standardization 77
International Electrotechnical Commission 79
Information Technology Infrastructure Library 79
Capability Maturity Model Integration 82
General Data Protection Regulation 83
Department of Defense Information Assurance Certification and Accreditation Process 84

CHAPTER SUMMARY 85

KEY CONCEPTS AND TERMS 85

CHAPTER 3 ASSESSMENT 86

CHAPTER 4 **Developing a Risk Management Plan** 89

Objectives of a Risk Management Plan 90

Objectives Example: Website 91
Objectives Example: HIPAA Compliance 92

Scope of a Risk Management Plan 93

Scope Example: Website 95
Scope Example: HIPAA Compliance 95

Assigning Responsibilities 95

Responsibilities Example: Website 96
Responsibilities Example: HIPAA Compliance 97

Describing Procedures and Schedules for Accomplishment 98

Procedures Example: Website 99
Procedures Example: HIPAA Compliance 100

Reporting Requirements 100

Presenting Recommendations 101
Documenting Management Response to Recommendations 105
Documenting and Tracking Implementation of Accepted Recommendations 106

Plan of Action and Milestones 106

Charting the Progress of a Risk Management Plan 108

Milestone Plan Chart 108
Gantt Chart 109
Critical Path Chart 110

Steps of the NIST Risk Management Framework 111

Cautionary Tales 111

CHAPTER SUMMARY 112

KEY CONCEPTS AND TERMS 112
CHAPTER 4 ASSESSMENT 113

PART TWO Mitigating Risk 115

CHAPTER 5 Defining Risk Assessment Approaches 117

Understanding Risk Assessments 118
Importance of Risk Assessments 119
Purpose of a Risk Assessment 120
Critical Components of a Risk Assessment 121
Identifying Scope 121
Identifying Critical Areas 122
Identifying Team Members 123
Types of Risk Assessments 123
Quantitative Risk Assessments 124
Qualitative Risk Assessments 126
Comparing Quantitative and Qualitative Risk Assessments 133
Risk Assessment Challenges 134
Using a Static Process to Evaluate a Moving Target 135
Availability of Resources and Data 135
Data Consistency 136
Estimating Impact Effects 138
Providing Results That Support Resource Allocation and Risk Acceptance 138
Best Practices for Risk Assessment 139
CHAPTER SUMMARY 140
KEY CONCEPTS AND TERMS 140
CHAPTER 5 ASSESSMENT 141

CHAPTER 6 Performing a Risk Assessment 143

Selecting a Risk Assessment Methodology 145
Defining the Assessment 145
Reviewing Previous Findings 148
Identifying the Management Structure 149
Identifying Assets and Activities Within Risk Assessment Boundaries 150
System Access and Availability 151
System Functions 151
Hardware and Software Assets 152
Personnel Assets 152
Data and Information Assets 152
Facilities and Supplies 153

Identifying and Evaluating Relevant Threats 154
Reviewing Historical Data 154
Performing Threat Modeling 155
Performing Threat Intelligence 155
Identifying and Evaluating Relevant Vulnerabilities 156
Vulnerability Assessments 156
Exploit Assessments 158
Identifying and Evaluating Controls 158
In-Place and Planned Controls 158
Control Categories 159
Another Approach to Categorizing Controls 162
Selecting a Methodology Based on Assessment Needs 162
Quantitative Method 162
Qualitative Method 164
Developing Mitigating Recommendations 165
Threat/Vulnerability Pairs 165
Estimate of Cost and Time to Implement 165
Estimate of Operational Impact 166
Cost-Benefit Analysis 167
Presenting Risk Assessment Results 167
Best Practices for Performing Risk Assessments 168
CHAPTER SUMMARY 168
KEY CONCEPTS AND TERMS 169
CHAPTER 6 ASSESSMENT 169

CHAPTER 7 Identifying Assets and Activities to Be Protected 171
System Access and Availability 172
System Functions: Manual and Automated 174
Manual Methods 175
Automated Methods 175
Hardware Assets 176
Software Assets 177
Personnel Assets 179
Data and Information Assets 180
Organization 181
Customer 182
Intellectual Property 183
Data Warehousing and Data Mining 184

Asset and Inventory Management Within the Seven Domains of a Typical IT Infrastructure 185

User Domain 187
Workstation Domain 187
LAN Domain 187
LAN-to-WAN Domain 188
WAN Domain 188
Remote Access Domain 189
System/Application Domain 189

Identifying Facilities and Supplies Needed to Maintain Business Operations 190

Mission-Critical Systems and Applications Identification 190
Business Impact Analysis Planning 191
Business Continuity Planning 192
Disaster Recovery Planning 193
Business Liability Insurance Planning 194
Asset Replacement Insurance Planning 194

CHAPTER SUMMARY 195

KEY CONCEPTS AND TERMS 195

CHAPTER 7 ASSESSMENT 195

CHAPTER 8 **Identifying and Analyzing Threats, Vulnerabilities, and Exploits 197**

Threat Assessments 198

Techniques for Identifying Threats 201
Best Practices for Threat Assessments Within the Seven Domains of a Typical IT Infrastructure 205

Vulnerability Assessments 206

Review of Documentation 208
Review of System Logs, Audit Trails, and Intrusion Detection and Prevention System Outputs 208
Vulnerability Scans and Other Assessment Tools 210
Audits and Personnel Interviews 211
Process Analysis and Output Analysis 211
System Testing 212
Best Practices for Performing Vulnerability Assessments Within the Seven Domains of a Typical IT Infrastructure 215

Exploit Assessments 216

Identifying Exploits 217
Mitigating Exploits With a Gap Analysis and Remediation Plan 220
Implementing Configuration or Change Management 221
Verifying and Validating the Exploit Has Been Mitigated 221
Best Practices for Performing Exploit Assessments Within an IT Infrastructure 221

CHAPTER SUMMARY 222

KEY CONCEPTS AND TERMS 222
CHAPTER 8 ASSESSMENT 223

CHAPTER 9 Identifying and Analyzing Risk Mitigation Security Controls 225

In-Place Controls 226
Planned Controls 226
Control Categories 227
NIST Control Families 227
Procedural Control Examples 230
Policies and Procedures 230
Security Plans 232
Insurance and Bonding 235
Background and Financial Checks 235
Data Loss Prevention Program 236
Education, Training, and Awareness 237
Rules of Behavior 237
Software Testing 238
Technical Control Examples 238
Logon Identifier 239
Session Time-Out 239
System Logs and Audit Trails 240
Data Range and Reasonableness Checks 241
Firewalls and Routers 241
Encryption 243
Public Key Infrastructure 244
Physical Control Examples 246
Locked Doors, Guards, Access Logs, and Closed-Circuit Television 246
Fire Detection and Suppression 248
Water Detection 248
Temperature and Humidity Detection 249
Electrical Grounding and Circuit Breakers 250
Best Practices for Risk Mitigation Security Controls 250
CHAPTER SUMMARY 251
KEY CONCEPTS AND TERMS 251
CHAPTER 9 ASSESSMENT 251

CHAPTER 10 Planning Risk Mitigation Throughout an Organization 253

Where Should an Organization Start With Risk Mitigation? 254
What Is the Scope of Risk Management for an Organization? 255
Critical Business Operations 256
Customer Service Delivery 257
Mission-Critical Business Systems, Applications, and Data Access 258

Seven Domains of a Typical IT Infrastructure 261
Information Systems Security Gap 265

Understanding and Assessing the Impact of Legal and Compliance Issues on an Organization 266

Legal Requirements, Compliance Laws, Regulations, and Mandates 267
Assessing the Impact of Legal and Compliance Issues on an Organization's Business Operations 269

Translating Legal and Compliance Implications for an Organization 273

Assessing the Impact of Legal and Compliance Implications on the Seven Domains of a Typical IT Infrastructure 274

Assessing How Security Countermeasures, Controls, and Safeguards Can Assist With Risk Mitigation 275

Understanding the Operational Implications of Legal and Compliance Requirements 275

Identifying Risk Mitigation and Risk Reduction Elements for the Entire Organization 276

Performing a Cost-Benefit Analysis 277

Best Practices for Planning Risk Mitigation Throughout an Organization 278

CHAPTER SUMMARY 279

KEY CONCEPTS AND TERMS 279

CHAPTER 10 ASSESSMENT 279

CHAPTER 11 **Turning a Risk Assessment Into a Risk Mitigation Plan 281**

Reviewing the Risk Assessment for the IT Infrastructure 282

Overlapping Countermeasures 283
Risk Assessments: Understanding Threats and Vulnerabilities 284
Identifying Countermeasures 285

Translating a Risk Assessment Into a Risk Mitigation Plan 287

Cost to Implement 287
Time to Implement 291
Operational Impact 294

Prioritizing Risk Elements That Require Risk Mitigation 295

Using a Threat Likelihood/Impact Matrix 295
Prioritizing Countermeasures 296

Verifying Risk Elements and How They Can Be Mitigated 298

Performing a Cost-Benefit Analysis on the Identified Risk Elements 299

Calculating the CBA 299
A CBA Report 300

Implementing a Risk Mitigation Plan 301

Staying Within Budget 301
Staying on Schedule 302

Following Up on the Risk Mitigation Plan 303

Ensuring Countermeasures Have Been Implemented 304
Ensuring Security Gaps Have Been Closed 305

Best Practices for Enabling a Risk Mitigation Plan from the Risk Assessment 306

CHAPTER SUMMARY 307

KEY CONCEPTS AND TERMS 307

CHAPTER 11 ASSESSMENT 308

PART THREE Risk Mitigation Plans 309

CHAPTER 12 Mitigating Risk With a Business Impact Analysis 311

What Is a Business Impact Analysis? 312

Collecting Data 313
Varying Data Collection Methods 314

Defining the Scope of the Business Impact Analysis 314

Objectives of a Business Impact Analysis 316

Identifying Critical Business Functions 317
Identifying Critical Resources 318
Identifying the MAO and Impact 320
Identifying Recovery Requirements 322

Steps of a Business Impact Analysis Process 324

Identifying the Environment 325
Identifying Stakeholders 325
Identifying Critical Business Functions 326
Identifying Critical Resources 326
Identifying the MAO 327
Identifying Recovery Priorities 327
Developing the BIA Report 328

Identifying Mission-Critical Business Functions and Processes 329

Mapping Business Functions and Processes to IT Systems 330

Best Practices for Performing a BIA for an Organization 331

CHAPTER SUMMARY 332

KEY CONCEPTS AND TERMS 332

CHAPTER 12 ASSESSMENT 332

CHAPTER 13 Mitigating Risk With a Business Continuity Plan 335

What Is a Business Continuity Plan? 336

Elements of a BCP 337

Purpose 338
Scope 338
Assumptions and Planning Principles 339
System Description and Architecture 341
Responsibilities 345
Notification and Activation Phase 348
Recovery Phase 351
Reconstitution Phase (Return to Normal Operations) 352
Plan Training, Testing, and Exercises 354
Plan Maintenance 356

How Does a BCP Mitigate an Organization's Risk? 358

Best Practices for Implementing a BCP for an Organization 358

CHAPTER SUMMARY 359

KEY CONCEPTS AND TERMS 359

CHAPTER 13 ASSESSMENT 359

CHAPTER 14 Mitigating Risk With a Disaster Recovery Plan 361

What Is a Disaster Recovery Plan? 363

Need for a DRP 364
Purpose of a DRP 365
Eight Tiers of Disaster Recovery 365

Critical Success Factors 366

What Management Must Provide 366
What DRP Developers Need 366
Primary Concerns 368
Disaster Recovery Financial Budget 375

Elements of a DRP 376

Purpose 377
Scope 377
Disaster/Emergency Declaration 378
Communications 378
Emergency Response 379
Activities 379
Recovery Procedures 380
Critical Operations, Customer Service, and Operations Recovery 382
Restoration and Normalization 383
Testing 383
Maintenance and DRP Update 384

How Does a DRP Mitigate an Organization's Risk? 385

Best Practices for Implementing a DRP for an Organization 385

CHAPTER SUMMARY 386

KEY CONCEPTS AND TERMS 387

CHAPTER 14 ASSESSMENT 387

CHAPTER 15 Mitigating Risk With a Computer Incident Response Team Plan 389

What Is a Computer Incident Response Team Plan? 390

Purpose of a CIRT Plan 392

Elements of a CIRT Plan 394

CIRT Members 394
CIRT Policies 397
Incident Handling Process 399
Communication Escalation Procedures 407
Incident Handling Procedures 408

How Does a CIRT Plan Mitigate an Organization's Risk? 414

Best Practices for Implementing a CIRT Plan for an Organization 414

CHAPTER SUMMARY 415

KEY CONCEPTS AND TERMS 415

CHAPTER 15 ASSESSMENT 415

APPENDIX A Answer Key 419

APPENDIX B Standard Acronyms 421

Glossary 425

Index 433

Preface

Purpose of This Text

This text is part of the *Information Systems Security & Assurance Series* from Jones & Bartlett Learning (https://www.jblearning.com/science-technology/computing/issa-series). Designed for courses and curriculums in IT security, cybersecurity, information assurance, and information systems security, this series features a comprehensive, consistent treatment of the most current thinking and trends in this critical subject area. The textbooks in this series deliver fundamental information security principles packed with real-world applications and examples. Authored by well-qualified cybersecurity experts, they deliver comprehensive information on all aspects of information security. Reviewed word for word by leading technical experts in the field, these textbooks are not just current, but also forward thinking, putting you in the position to solve the cybersecurity challenges not just of today, but of tomorrow as well.

This text provides a comprehensive view of managing risk in information systems. It covers the fundamentals of risk and risk management and includes in-depth details on more comprehensive risk management topics in three major parts.

Part One, Risk Management Business Challenges, addresses many of the issues relevant to present-day businesses. It covers details of risks, threats, and vulnerabilities. Topics help students understand the importance of risk management in the organization, including many of the techniques used to manage risks. Several current laws are presented with clear descriptions of how they are relevant in organizations. It also includes a chapter describing the contents of a risk management plan.

Part Two, Mitigating Risk, focuses on risk assessments. Topics presented include risk assessment approaches, including the overall steps in performing a risk assessment. It covers the importance of identifying assets and then identifying potential threats, vulnerabilities, and exploits against these assets. Chapter 9 covers the types of controls that can be used to mitigate risk. The last two chapters in this part identify how to plan risk mitigation throughout the organization and convert the risk assessment into a risk management plan.

Part Three, Risk Mitigation Plans, covers the many elements of risk mitigation plans, such as a business impact analysis and a business continuity plan. The last two chapters cover disaster recovery and computer incident response team plans.

Learning Features

The writing style of this text is practical and conversational. Step-by-step examples of information security concepts and procedures are presented throughout the text. Each chapter begins with a statement of learning objectives. Illustrations are used to clarify the material and vary the presentation. The text is sprinkled with Notes, Tips, FYIs, and sidebars to alert the reader to additional and helpful information related to the subject under discussion. Chapter Assessments appear at the end of each chapter, with solutions provided in the back of the textbook.

Chapter summaries are included in the text to provide a rapid review or preview of the material and to help students understand the relative importance of the concepts presented.

Audience

The material is suitable for undergraduate or graduate computer science or information science majors, students at a 2-year technical college or community college who have a basic technical background, or readers who have a basic understanding of IT security and want to expand their knowledge. This text can also be useful for professionals in the field.

New to This Edition

This text has been broadly updated to include new and emerging concepts in the expanding field of information systems and cybersecurity, in particular risk management. Concepts are more appropriately defined and explained; for example, the definition of *risk* references *assets* as a critical component of the totality of risk. Risk management and assessment topics have been updated throughout the text with references to threat sources, for example, advanced persistent threats. Included are updated references and examples of threat-likelihood impacts and how organizations compute risk loss scenarios. Explanations of business continuity plans, minimum business continuity objectives, disaster recovery plans, and recovery sites are updated. Several new guidelines have been introduced in the text to reflect advances in the field of cybersecurity. In particular, federal guidelines from the National Institute of Standards and Technology (NIST) and the Department of Homeland Security have been updated, with the inclusion of new NIST Special Publications: 800-183; 800-154; 800-153; 800-150; 800-84; 800-63 a, b, and c; 800-53 Rev. 5; 800-34; and 800-37.

The text includes updated references to the current organizational state of affairs in the field of cybersecurity, such as surveys of executives in the field, and references to the new and emerging topics of cloud computing, analytics, mobile computing, artificial intelligence, machine learning, robotic process automation, and blockchain. Besides updated information on the NIST Risk Management Framework, updates to the Common Vulnerabilities and Exposures (CVE) are included. The textbook now has updated references to U.S. and international compliance laws, including the Federal Information Security Modernization Act (FISMA), Health Insurance Portability and Accountability Act (HIPAA), Gramm-Leach-Bliley Act (GLBA), and the EU's General Data Protection Regulation (GDPR). The Children's Online Privacy Protection Act (COPPA) is introduced as well as the Equifax data breach. The text includes updated references to ISACA's Control Objectives for Information and Related Technologies (COBIT) 2019. Updated end-of-chapter questions are also included in the text. Newer threats such as deep fakes are discussed in the text. Recent breaches are included as case studies to illustrate specific risks and appropriate risk management.

Cloud Labs

This text is accompanied by Cybersecurity Cloud Labs. These hands-on virtual labs provide immersive mock IT infrastructures whereby students can learn and practice foundational cybersecurity skills as an extension of the lessons in this textbook. For more information or to purchase the labs, visit go.jblearning.com/easttom_4e.

About the Author

Dr. Chuck Easttom is the author of 45 books, including several on computer security, forensics, and cryptography. He is also an inventor with 27 patents and the author of over 80 research papers. He holds a PhD in computer science, a PhD in Nanotechnology, and a Doctor of Science in Cybersecurity, and four master's degrees (one in applied computer science, one in education, one in Strategic and Defense studies, and one in systems engineering). He is a senior member of both the IEEE and the ACM. He is also a Distinguished Speaker of the ACM and a Distinguished Visitor of the IEEE. Dr. Easttom is currently an adjunct professor for Georgetown University and for Vanderbilt University. He is also a member of the American Institute Of Aeronautics and Astronautics and the American Physical Society.

PART ONE

Risk Management Business Challenges

CHAPTER 1 Risk Management Fundamentals 3

CHAPTER 2 Managing Risk: Threats, Vulnerabilities, and Exploits 29

CHAPTER 3 Understanding and Maintaining Compliance 59

CHAPTER 4 Developing a Risk Management Plan 89

CHAPTER 1

Risk Management Fundamentals

MUCH OF MODERN cybersecurity begins with risk management. Without a clear understanding of risk, one cannot properly create policies, conduct penetration tests, perform security audits, or even select mitigation controls. In essence, all of security, physical or cyber, is an implementation of risk management.

Effective risk management starts with understanding the assets that require protection and the threats and vulnerabilities that might affect them. A person builds on this knowledge by identifying ways to mitigate the risks. Risks can be mitigated by reducing vulnerabilities or the impact of the risks. Then, customized plans to mitigate risks in different areas of the company can be created. A company typically has several risk mitigation plans in place; however, it is important to note that risks cannot be completely eliminated.

This text will help the student build a solid foundation in risk management as it relates to information systems and cybersecurity. It serves as an introduction to a career in this field. Many of the topics presented in just a few paragraphs in this text can fill entire chapters or books. The more the student learns, the closer they will be to becoming an expert whom others seek out to solve their problems.

Chapter 1 Topics

This chapter covers the following topics and concepts:

- What risk is and its relationship to threat, vulnerability, and asset loss
- What the major components of risk to an IT infrastructure are
- What risk management is and how important it is to the organization
- What some risk identification techniques are

Chapter 1 Goals

When you complete this chapter, you will be able to:

- Define risk
- Identify the major components of risk

- Describe the relationship among threats, vulnerabilities, assets, and impact of loss
- Define risk management
- Describe risk management's relationship with profitability and survivability
- Explain the relationship between the cost of loss and the cost of risk management
- Describe how risk is perceived by different roles within an organization
- Identify threats
- List the different categories of threats
- Describe techniques to identify vulnerabilities
- Identify and define risk management techniques
- Describe the purpose of a cost-benefit analysis (CBA)
- Define residual risk

What Is Risk?

Risk is the likelihood or probability that something negative is going to occur. Certainly, unexpected positive things can occur, but these don't typically require risk management. This is often phrased as the probability of a risk being *realized*. You probably do this on a daily basis. When you operate a motor vehicle, you must take into account the various risks involved such as mechanical failure or a collision. You probably don't perform formal risk calculations, but you do consider, at least in a casual manner, what the risks are and what steps you can take to mitigate those risks. Given that motor vehicle collisions are not at all uncommon, you probably rate this risk high and take multiple mitigation measures. Conversely, you most likely view the probability of a meteor crashing through the roof of your home as very low, and take few if any measures to mitigate this threat. Estimating risk is something we do automatically and on a regular basis.

Risk management is the practice of identifying, assessing, controlling, and mitigating risks. In this discussion, the key terms that a person will need to be familiar with are shown in the following list. Each term will be discussed in detail later in the chapter.

NOTE

Threats and vulnerabilities are explored in much more depth later in this chapter.

- **Threat**—A **threat** is any activity that represents a possible danger.
- **Vulnerability**—A **vulnerability** is a weakness.

- **Asset**—An **asset** is a thing of value worth protecting.
- **Impact of loss**—**Impact of loss** is a loss resulting in a compromise to business functions or assets.

Risks to a business can result in a loss that negatively affects the business and its core business functions. A business commonly tries to limit, or control, its exposure to risks. The overall goal is to reduce as much as possible the impact of losses that can occur from risk.

> **NOTE**
>
> NIST Special Publication 800-37 Rev. 2 provides a definition of risk: "Risk is a measure of the extent to which an entity is threatened by a potential circumstance or event. Risk is also a function of the adverse impacts that arise if the circumstance or event occurs, and the likelihood of occurrence. Types of risk include program risk; compliance/regulatory risk; financial risk; legal risk; mission/business risk; political risk; security and privacy risk (including supply chain risk); project risk; reputational risk; safety risk; strategic planning risk." NIST Special Publication 800-37 Rev. 2 is entitled "Risk Management Framework for Information Systems and Organizations: A System Life Cycle Approach for Security and Privacy," Revision 2, published in December 2018. NIST SP 800-37 Rev. 2 provides comprehensive guidance on applying the Risk Management Framework (RMF) to federal information systems and organizations.

Compromise of Business Functions

Business functions are the activities a business performs to sell products or services. If any of these functions are negatively affected, the business won't be able to sell as many products or services. The business will earn less revenue, resulting in an overall loss.

Here are a few examples of business functions and possible compromises:

- Salespeople regularly call or email customers. If the capabilities of either phones or email are reduced, sales are reduced or in fact temporarily halted. This will also affect technical support operations.
- An organization receives excessive inbound traffic that is unrelated to business objectives. This could be a flood of network packets or emails. This is called a **denial of service (DoS) attack**. When a DoS attack comes from multiple sources, it is called a **distributed denial of service (DDoS) attack**.
- A website sells products on the internet. If the website is attacked and fails, sales are lost.
- Authors write articles that must be submitted by a deadline to be published. If the author's computer becomes infected with a virus, the deadline passes, and the article's value is reduced.
- Analysts compile reports used by management to make decisions. Data is gathered from internal servers and internet sources. If network connectivity fails, analysts won't have access to current data. Management could make decisions based on inaccurate information.
- A warehouse application is used for shipping products that have been purchased. It identifies what has been ordered, where the products need to be sent, and where the products are located. If the application fails, products aren't shipped on time.
- A person calls an organization pretending to have a legitimate purpose and attempts to trick someone in the organization into divulging personal or protected information. This form of impersonation, known as **social engineering**, can compromise the organization's business functions and lead to losses.

Demystifying Social Engineering

Social engineering is the art of manipulating people into performing actions or divulging confidential information, often by exploiting psychological vulnerabilities rather than technical weaknesses. Some people refer to this as 'human hacking'. One way this can be done is through pretexting. In pretexting the attacker invents a scenario (pretext) to obtain information (e.g., pretending to be IT support). Phishing can also use social engineering. In 2024 a criminal group used deep fake videos coupled with fake news featuring celebrities promoting cryptocurrency schemes[1]. Investors were promised high returns on their investment. The criminals scammed $35 million.

This is, of course, a rather extreme example of social engineering. A more common scenario would be an attacker calling someone in a company and pretending to be from tech support. The attacker will then try to get the person to install something, click a link, or give information. Sophisticated criminals will first learn as much as they can about the target organization in order to make the call sound legitimate. For example, if a company has multiple offices in New York, with technical support based in Queens, and the manager of technical support is someone named John Smith, the attacker might call stating something such as "Hello, I am Shelly, I work for John Smith over in the Queens office . . ." Using real-world information increases the chances of the victim believing the attacker.

Social engineering attacks are often part of larger attacks. They may be used for initial access or reconnaissance. Ultimately, all attacks can lead to a loss of some business functions. Even if the loss is only temporary, it generally has a deleterious effect on the business.

Because compromises to any of these business functions can result in a loss of revenue, all of them represent a risk. One of the tasks when considering risk is identifying the important functions for a business and ensuring that organizations provide necessary employee training to reduce their weakest links (i.e., people with limited knowledge of technology and security).

The importance of any business function is relative to the business. In other words, the failure of a website for one company may be catastrophic if all products and services are sold through the website. Another company may use its website only to provide hours of operation to its customers; therefore, the website's failure will have less impact on the business.

Threats, Vulnerabilities, Assets, and Impact

Earlier, key terms related to risk were introduced. Their relationship can now be seen. When a threat exploits a vulnerability to gain access to an asset, the threat could potentially result in a loss if the asset is compromised. The impact of the threat identifies the severity of that loss. It is important to note that not all assets have the same value. The greater the value attached to an asset, the greater the severity of the loss will be, making the need to put controls in place to prevent the loss from being greater.

---

[1] Simon Goodley, Zoe Wood, Pamela Duncan, and Michael Goodier, "Revealed: The Scammers Who Conned Savers out of $35m Using Fake Celebrity Ads," *The Guardian*, March 5, 2025, https://www.theguardian.com/money/2025/mar/05/revealed-the-scammers-who-conned-savers-out-of-35m-using-fake-celebrity-ads.

Threats

A threat is any circumstance or event with the potential to cause a loss. A threat can also be thought of as any activity that represents a possible danger. Threats are always present and cannot be eliminated, but they can be controlled.

Threats have independent probabilities of occurring that often are unaffected by an organization's action. As an example, an attacker may be an expert in attacking web servers hosted on Apache. There is very little a company can do to stop this attacker from trying to attack. However, the company can reduce or eliminate vulnerabilities to reduce the attacker's chances of success.

Threats can be thought of as attempts to exploit vulnerabilities that result in the loss of **confidentiality**, **integrity**, or **availability** of a business asset. The protection of confidentiality, integrity, and availability is a common security objective for information systems.

FIGURE 1-1 shows these three security objectives as a protective triangle. If any side of the triangle is breached or fails, security fails. In other words, risks to confidentiality, integrity, or availability represent potential loss to an organization. Because of this, a significant amount of risk management is focused on protecting these resources.

- **Confidentiality**—Preventing unauthorized disclosure of information. Data should be available only to authorized users. Loss of confidentiality occurs when data is accessed by someone who should not have access to it. Data is protected using access controls and encryption technologies.
- **Integrity**—Ensuring data or an IT system is not modified or destroyed unless authorized. If data is modified or destroyed, it loses its value to the company. Hashing is often used to ensure integrity.
- **Availability**—Ensuring data and services are available when needed. IT systems are commonly protected using fault tolerance and redundancy techniques. Backups are used to ensure the data is retained even if an entire building is destroyed.

NOTE

Confidentiality, integrity, and availability are often referred to as the *security triad*, or the *C-I-A triad.* A more advanced version, called The McCumber Cube, was developed by John McCumber in 1991. The McCumber Cube is a conceptual model used to understand and evaluate information assurance and security. It provides a three-dimensional framework for analyzing the effectiveness of security measures across a wide range of environments. This is shown in **FIGURE 1-1A**.

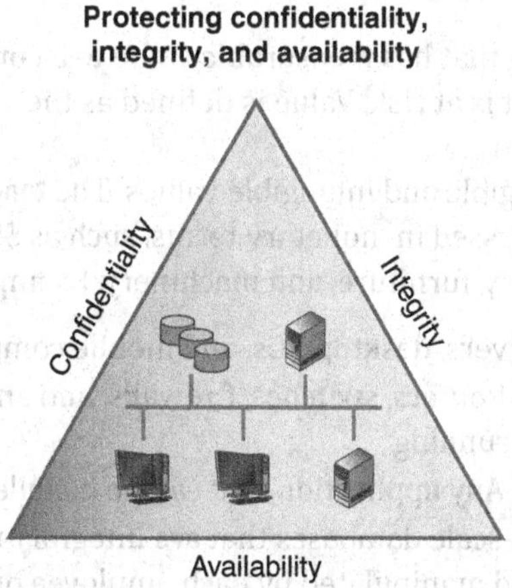

FIGURE 1-1

Security objectives for information and information systems.

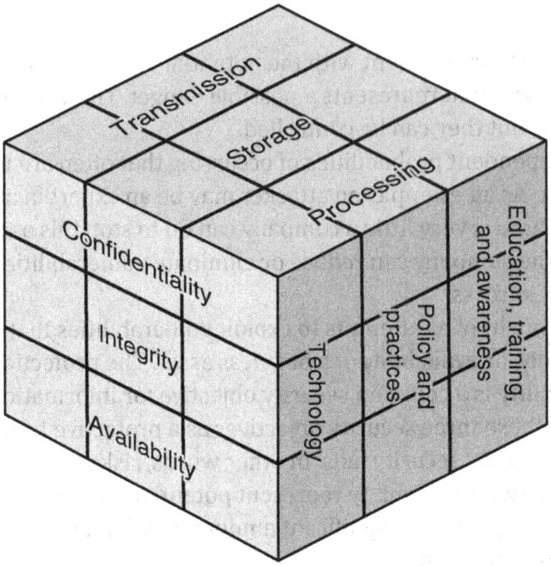

FIGURE 1-1A

The McCumber Cube.

Reproduced from McCumber, J. (2004). Assessing and managing security risk in IT systems: A structured methodology. CRC Press.

> **TIP**
> The method used to take advantage of a vulnerability can also be referred to as an **exploit**.

Vulnerabilities

A vulnerability is a weakness. It could be a procedural, technical, or administrative weakness. It could be a weakness in physical, technical, or operational security. Just as all threats don't result in a loss, all vulnerabilities don't result in a loss. A loss to an asset occurs only when an attacker is able to exploit the vulnerability.

Vulnerabilities may exist because they've never been corrected. They can also exist if security is weakened either intentionally or unintentionally.

Considering a locked door used to protect a server room; a technician could intentionally unlock it to make it easier to access. If the door doesn't shut tight on its own, it could accidentally be left open. Either way, the server room and its contents become vulnerable.

Assets

A business asset is anything that has measurable value to a company. If an asset has the potential to lose value, it is at risk. Value is defined as the worth of an asset to a business.

Assets can have both tangible and intangible values. The **tangible value** is the actual cost of the asset and can be expressed in monetary terms, such as $5,000. The tangible assets of a business include its inventory, furniture, and machinery. Examples of tangible IT assets are:

- **Computer systems**—Servers, desktop PCs, and mobile computers
- **Network components**—Routers, switches, firewalls, and any other components necessary to keep the network running
- **Software applications**—Any application that can be installed on a computer system
- **Data**—Includes the large-scale databases that are integral to many businesses; also includes the data used and manipulated by each employee or customer

The **intangible value** is value that cannot be measured by cost, such as client confidence or company reputation. Generally acceptable accounting principles (GAAP) refer to client confidence as **goodwill**.

For example, a company sells products via a website, and it earns $5,000 an hour in revenue. The web server hosting the website fails and is down for two hours. The cost to repair it totals $1,000. What is the tangible loss?

- **Lost revenue**—$5,000 times two hours equals $10,000
- **Repair costs**—$1,000
- **Total tangible value**—$11,000

The intangible value isn't as easy to calculate but is still important. For example, a customer with an urgent need tried to make a purchase when the website was down. If the same product is available somewhere else, they may choose to purchase the product elsewhere. That experience may damage the organization's reputation in the eye of that customer, and, if the customer's experience with the other business is positive, the customer may go directly to the second company the next time they want to purchase this product. The loss of this future business cannot be measured, which makes it intangible.

Intangible value includes:

- **Future lost revenue**—Any additional purchases customers make with another company are a loss to the company whose website was down.
- **Cost of gaining the customer**—Large sums of money are invested in attracting customers. A repeat customer is much easier to sell to than acquiring a new customer. If a company loses a customer, the company's investment is lost.
- **Customer influence**—Customers have friends, families, and business partners. They commonly share their experience with others, especially if the experience is exceptionally positive or negative.
- **Reputation**—Customers share their negative experience with others, so one customer's bad experience could potentially influence other current or potential customers to avoid future business transactions.

One of the early steps in risk management is associated with identifying the assets of a company and the assets' associated costs. This data is used to prioritize risks for different assets. Once a risk has been prioritized, identifying risk management processes to protect the asset becomes easier.

Impact

The impact is the amount of the loss, which can be expressed in monetary terms, such as $5,000. The value of hardware and software is often easy to determine. If a laptop is stolen, the purchase or replacement value can be used to determine the value of the stolen laptop. However, some losses aren't easy to determine. If that same laptop held data, the value of the data is hard to estimate.

Descriptive terms, instead of monetary terms, can be used to explain the impact of a loss. For example, losses can be described in relative terms, such as high, medium, or low, which helps an organization quantify the loss by describing the potential harm. The harm might be to operations, such as the inability to perform critical business functions; assets, such as hardware or facilities; individuals, such as loss of personal information, injury, or loss of life; other organizations, resulting in financial losses or damaged relationships; or the nation, affecting government operations or national security.

Published by the National Institute of Standards and Technology, the "Guide for Conducting Risk Assessments" (NIST SP 800-30) includes the following scale for assessing the impact of threats to a business's assets:

- **Very high**—Indicates multiple severe or catastrophic adverse effects. *Severe* or *catastrophic* indicates a loss of critical business functions. This loss might result in major financial losses or serious injuries to personnel.
- **High**—Indicates a severe or catastrophic adverse effect. Note that *high* indicates one adverse effect. *Very high* indicates multiple adverse effects.
- **Moderate**—Indicates a serious adverse effect. *Serious* indicates critical business functions are significantly degraded. The organization might still be able to operate but not as effectively as normal. The resulting damage can be significant.
- **Low**—Indicates a limited adverse effect. *Limited* indicates critical business functions are degraded. The resulting damage is minor.
- **Very low**—Indicates a negligible adverse effect. *Negligible* indicates the impact on critical business functions is small and unnoticeable.

Classify Business Risks

The way in which individuals and businesses use their assets varies across all industries. If a person looks at risk and its impact to the organization, they could quickly become overwhelmed trying to create a comprehensive list of all the possible threats and vulnerabilities that affect the company. Luckily, there are several techniques that can help direct this activity. The following method achieves this by focusing the task on the risks posed by the people, process, and technology of the organization.

Risks Posed by People

Ideally, all personnel in an organization should readily understand the threat to a company's health if risk is not managed. Unfortunately, risks and risk management are often perceived quite differently. Personnel often tend to be the weakest link when it comes to security threats to an organization.

One of the challenges with effective risk management of IT resources is achieving a proper balance between security and usability. **FIGURE 1-2** shows a diagram. In the diagram, on the left, the computers are completely locked down with such a high level of security that the controls may prevent users from adequately performing their jobs. On the right, the computers are easy to use, but security is being neglected. In the middle, a balance between the two has been achieved.

Balanced security rarely satisfies everyone. Security personnel want to lock systems down tight, whereas end users find those security controls inconvenient and want more usability.

FIGURE 1-2

Balancing security and usability in an organization.

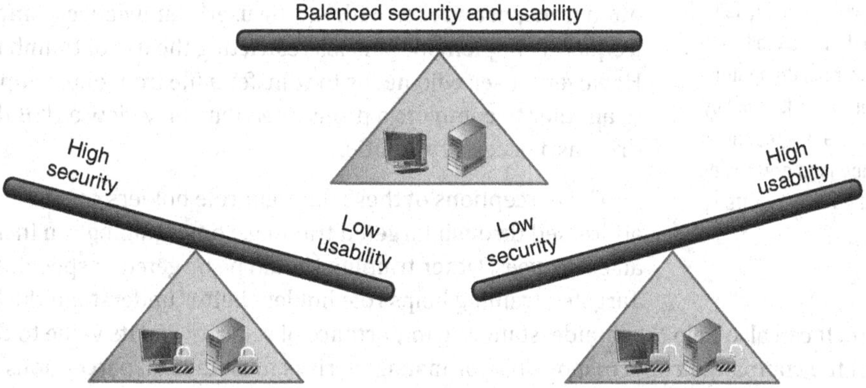

It is common for individuals in the following roles to have different perceptions of risk:

- **Leaders and managers**—Leaders and managers are concerned mostly with profitability and survivability. Because attacks can result in loss of C-I-A, leaders are willing to spend money to mitigate risks. However, their view of risk is typically based on costs associated with the risk and the controls. Managers need accurate facts to make decisions regarding which controls to implement to protect company assets.
- **System administrators**—System administrators are responsible for protecting IT systems. When they understand the risks, they often want to lock systems down as tight as possible. Administrators are often highly technical individuals. Sometimes, they lose sight of the need to balance security costs with profitability. Some organizations have administrators, often Tier 1, who serve as the first line of defense for IT support. These administrators are given limited administrative permissions. They often view the security controls as hindrances to performing their job and don't always recognize the importance of the controls. For example, the need to use a change management process isn't always understood. A well-meaning technician may bypass a change management process to solve one problem but unintentionally create another problem. These unapproved changes can result in business losses.
- **Developer**—Some companies have in-house application developers. They write applications that can be used in-house or sold as part of the company's product offerings. Many developers have adopted a secure computing mindset. They realize that security needs to be included beginning at the design stage and going all the way through to the release stage. When developers haven't adopted a security mindset, they often try to patch security holes at the end of the development cycle. This patching mindset rarely addresses all problems and results in the release of vulnerable software. Ideally, security needs to be an integral step in the life cycle of software or application development.
- **End user**—End users simply want the computer to work for them. They are most concerned with usability and often don't understand the reason for the security controls

> **TIP**
>
> The use of thumb drives can be restricted through a written policy telling people not to use them as well as by using technical controls. Computer users can easily ignore a written policy, but they can't easily bypass a technical control. A best practice is to create and enforce both types of policies, written and technical.

and restrictions. Instead, security is viewed as an inconvenience. Well-meaning users often try to circumvent controls so they can accomplish their job. For example, because USB thumb drives often transport viruses without the user's knowledge, companies frequently implement policies restricting the use of thumb drives. However, a user who needs to transfer a file from one computer to another to complete a project deadline may view a USB thumb drive as a necessary solution.

The perceptions of these different role holders can be addressed through targeted training. Some training can include all employees. Other training should be targeted to specific roles. Targeted training helps role holders better understand the big picture. It can also help them understand the importance of security and its value to the success of the company. People responsible for managing risks must take all perceptions into account. This is especially true if any of the controls can be bypassed. For example, theft of laptops is a common problem for some companies. An employee can leave a laptop to take a break at a conference only to come back and find the laptop gone. This risk can almost be eliminated if the company purchases hardware locks, which can secure the laptop to a desk or other furniture. However, if users don't perceive the risk as valid, they may simply not use the lock; therefore, they must be trained to understand the controls and the consequences (to the company and themselves) for not complying with the controls.

Risks Posed by a Lack of Process

Process represents the actions taken to reach a desired outcome. A lack of formal process is a contributor to risk in any organization. Without a process for creating recipes and training cooks, a bakery, for example, could not produce consistently delicious cupcakes, and risks income loss. Without a process for inventory control, a sales company may risk loss of customers from lack of supply. For many organizations, these processes take the form of **policies**, **standards**, and **guidelines**. The following list describes some of the processes associated with IT resources:

- **Policies**—Policies are formal statements that are issued directly by an organization's leaders, such as an acceptable use policy, which describes both acceptable and unacceptable behavior when using company-owned computers and network resources.
- **Standards**—Standards are mandatory rules written to support or at least provide some direction to policies. For example, a password standard could follow an acceptable use policy.
- **Guidelines**—Guidelines are not mandatory but provide guidance on specific behavior. For example, guidelines are written on how to create a strong password.

Ideally all organizations should have a general information security policy and may have specific policies in place to define how the business will handle access control, remote access, email usage, incident response, **disaster recovery**, business continuity, and other risk situations.

FIGURE 1-3

The seven domains of a typical IT infrastructure.

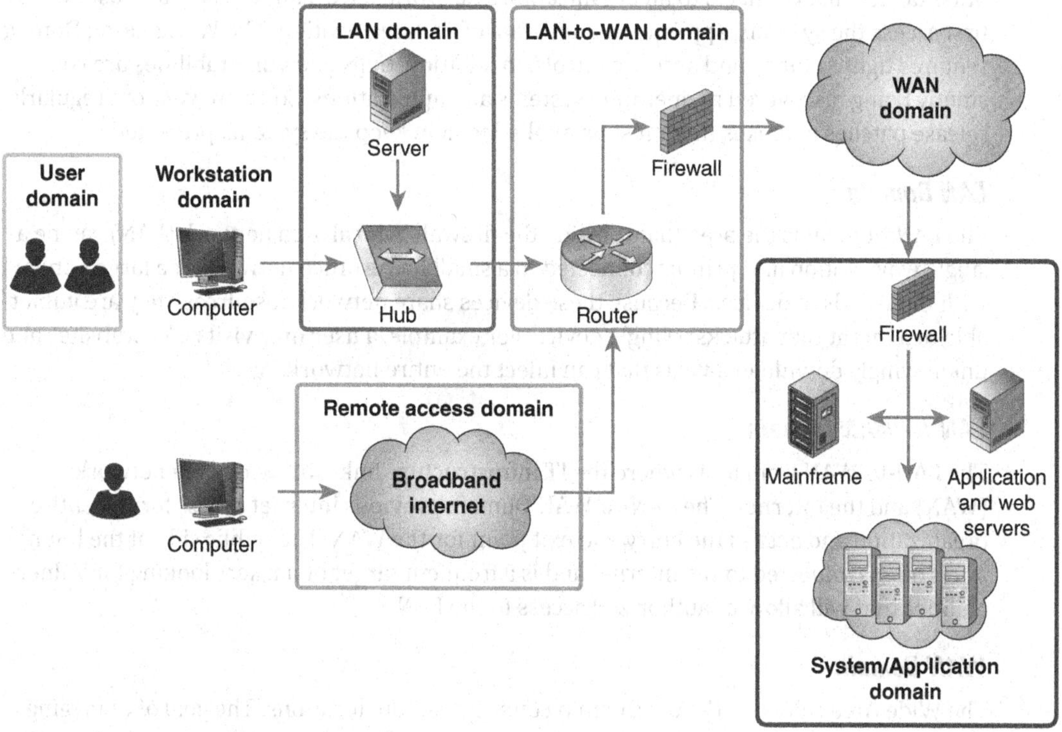

Risks Posed by Technology

Whether in a small business, large government body, or publicly traded corporation, most IT infrastructures consist of the seven domains shown in **FIGURE 1-3**: User, Workstation, LAN, LAN-to-WAN, WAN, Remote Access, and System/Application. Each domain poses its own set of risks. One method for identifying the risks posed by technology is to review each domain, concentrating on the threats, vulnerabilities, and impact of a loss.

The following examples describe *some* of the risks for each domain; more risks exist than are described for each domain. Businesses must provide protection in each of the domains. A weakness in any one of the domains can be exploited by an attacker even if the other six domains have no vulnerabilities.

User Domain

The User Domain defines the way in which people interact with an organization's information system. They can be customers, employees, contractors, or consultants. The old saying that a chain is only as strong as its weakest link applies to IT security too. People are often the weakest link in IT security. For example, an organization may require strong, complex passwords that can't be easily cracked, but an employee may write their password on a sticky note, leaving the organization vulnerable to unauthorized access.

Workstation Domain

A workstation can be a desktop or a laptop computer, a special-purpose terminal, or any other device that connects to an organization's network; a workstation is where users first access the systems, applications, and data of the organization. The Workstation Domain requires tight security and access controls. In addition, bugs and vulnerabilities are constantly being discovered in operating systems and applications. Software vendors regularly release patches and fixes that must be applied to help keep the systems protected.

LAN Domain

The LAN Domain is the area that is inside the firewall. A local area network (LAN) can be a single workstation and printer connected to a small home office network or a large network with thousands of devices. Because these devices share network resources, they are vulnerable to a threat that attacks a single device. For example, a user may visit risky websites and unknowingly download a virus that can infect the entire network.

LAN-to-WAN Domain

The LAN-to-WAN Domain is where the IT infrastructure links to a wide area network (WAN) and the internet. The LAN-to-WAN Domain provides internet access for the entire organization and acts as the entry and exit point for the WAN. The public side of the boundary is often connected to the internet and is a frequent target of hackers looking for vulnerabilities that will allow unauthorized access to the LAN.

WAN Domain

The Wide Area Network (WAN) Domain connects remote locations. The goal of managing the WAN Domain is to allow users the most access possible while making sure that what goes in and out is safe. A significant amount of security is required to keep hosts in the WAN Domain safe. Risks associated with this domain include eavesdropping and unauthorized access because most traffic in this domain is sent in cleartext, which means that hackers can access usernames and passwords. In addition, data is subject to corruption and malicious attacks.

Remote Access Domain

The Remote Access Domain connects remote users to the organization's IT infrastructure. Remote access is critical for staff members who work in the field or from home, for example, outside sales reps, technical support specialists, or healthcare professionals. Wi-Fi hotspots make it easy for users to connect to a virtual private network (VPN) to access email and other business applications, but it also poses risks to the organization's proprietary data if the employee's device is stolen or left unsecured.

> **NOTE**
>
> VPN connections use tunneling protocols to reduce the risk of data being captured. A tunneling protocol encrypts the traffic sent over the network, which makes it more difficult for attackers to capture and read data.

System/Application Domain

The System/Application Domain is where the organization's data is stored. This data can be private customer data, intellectual property, or national security information. Data is what attackers seek deep within an IT system. Loss of this data, whether by attack, disaster, or negligence, is the greatest threat in the System/Application Domain.

> **TIP**
> A server should be locked down using the specific security requirements needed by the hosted application. In other words, an email server requires one set of protections, which is different from that required for a database server.

Risk Identification Techniques

Risk and losses were presented earlier in this chapter. Risk is the likelihood or probability that something unexpected is going to occur. Some risks lead to losses. Losses occur when a threat exposes a vulnerability and harms an asset. To identify risks, these three steps need to be followed:

1. Identifying threats
2. Identifying vulnerabilities
3. Estimating the likelihood of a threat exploiting a vulnerability to harm an asset

The following sections explore these concepts.

Identifying Threats

A threat is any circumstance or event with the potential to cause a loss. Said another way, it is any activity that represents a possible danger. The loss or danger is directly related to one of the following:

- **Loss of confidentiality**—Someone sees a person's password or a company's "secret formula."
- **Loss of integrity**—An email message is modified in transit, a virus infects a file, or someone makes unauthorized changes to a website.
- **Loss of availability**—An email server is down so no one has email access, or a file server is down so data files aren't available.

Threat identification is the process of creating a list of threats. Companies should attempt to identify *all* possible threats to an organization, which is no small task. The list can be extensive.

To compile this list of threats, businesses often consider threats in the following categories:

- **External or internal**—External threats are outside the boundary of the organization. They can also be thought of as risks that are outside the control of the organization. Internal threats are within the boundary of the organization. They could be related to employees or other personnel who have access to company resources. Internal threats can be related to any hardware or software controlled by the business.
- **Natural or man-made**—Natural threats are often related to weather, such as hurricanes, tornadoes, and ice storms. Earthquakes and tsunamis are also natural threats. A human, or man-made, threat is any threat from a person. Any attempt to sabotage resources is a man-made threat. Fire could be man-made or natural, depending on how the fire is started.

- **Intentional or accidental**—Any deliberate attempt to compromise confidentiality, integrity, or availability is intentional. Employee mistakes or user errors are accidental threats. A faulty application that corrupts data could be considered accidental.

One method used to identify threats is through a brainstorming session. In a brainstorming session, participants throw out anything that pops into their heads. All ideas are written down without any evaluation. This creative process helps bring up ideas that may be missed when a problem is analyzed only logically.

Examples of threats to an organization include:

- An unauthorized employee trying to access data
- Any type of malware
- An attacker defacing a website
- Any DoS or DDoS attack
- An external attacker trying to access data
- Any loss of data
- Any loss of services
- A social engineer tricking an employee into revealing a secret
- Earthquakes, floods, or hurricanes
- A lightning strike
- Electrical, heating, or air-conditioning outages
- Fires

All these threats represent possible risks if they expose vulnerabilities and potentially harm assets.

Of course, threats and vulnerabilities will be identified that are particular to an organization. In fact, a business with multiple locations may have some threats and vulnerabilities unique to each location.

Identifying Vulnerabilities

That a vulnerability is a weakness was presented earlier in the chapter. Vulnerabilities become apparent when threats exploit them. Ideally, the weaknesses would be identified before threats exploit them. Luckily, most organizations have many sources that can help a person do this.

Some of the sources that can be used are:

- **Audits**—Many organizations are regularly audited. Systems and processes are checked to verify that a company complies with existing rules and laws. Auditors document their findings in reports, which list findings that directly relate to weaknesses.
- **Certification and accreditation records**—Several standards exist to examine and certify IT systems. If the system meets the standards, the IT system can be accredited. The entire process includes detailed documentation. This documentation can be reviewed to identify existing and potential weaknesses.
- **System logs**—Many types of computer system logs can be used to identify threats. Audit logs can determine whether users are accessing sensitive data. Firewall logs can

identify traffic that is trying to breach the network and computers taken over by malware and acting as zombies. Domain Name System (DNS) logs can identify unauthorized transfer of data.

- **Prior events**—Previous security incidents are excellent sources of data. As evidence of risks that already occurred, they help justify controls. They show the problems that have occurred and can show trends. Ideally, weaknesses from a security incident will be resolved right after the incident. In practice, sometimes, employees are eager to put the incident behind them and forget it as soon as possible. Even if documentation doesn't exist on the incident, a few key questions can uncover the details.
- **Trouble reports**—Most companies use databases to document trouble calls. These databases can contain a wealth of information. With a little analysis, they can be used to identify trends and weaknesses.
- **Incident response teams**—Some companies have incident response teams. These teams will investigate all the security incidents within the company. Team members can be interviewed to get a wealth of information because they are often eager to help reduce risks.

> **TIP**
>
> Some malware can take control of multiple computers and control them as robots. The controlling computer issues attack commands, and the computers attack. The individual computers are referred to as *zombies*. The network of controlled computers is called a *botnet*.

As you will see throughout this book, there are many standards that one can use to guide their organization in managing risk. NIST SP 800-30 Rev. 1, "Guide for Conducting Risk Assessments," was first released in September 2012. This guide is part of NIST's series of security publications and provides a structured approach for conducting risk assessments of federal information systems and organizations. It supports broader frameworks such as the Risk Management Framework (RMF) outlined in NIST SP 800-37, "Risk Management Framework for Information Systems and Organizations." This guide is meant to assist organizations in the following tasks:

- Identify and assess risks to their operations, assets, individuals, and other organizations.
- Make informed decisions about how to allocate resources to mitigate those risks.
- Integrate risk assessments into the system development life cycle (SDLC) and organizational risk management strategies.

Using the Seven Domains of a Typical IT Infrastructure to Identify Weaknesses

Another way of identifying weaknesses is by examining the seven domains of a typical IT infrastructure, which were presented earlier in this chapter. Each domain can be examined individually. Further, each domain can be examined by experts in that domain. The following list provides examples of vulnerabilities in each of these domains:

- **User Domain**—Social engineering represents a big vulnerability. For example, Sally gets a call: "Hi, this is Bob from the help desk. We've identified a virus on your computer." Bob then attempts to walk Sally through a long, detailed process and then says, "Why don't I just fix this for you so you can get back to work? All I need is your password."
- **Workstation Domain**—Computers that aren't patched can be exploited. If they don't have antivirus software, they can become infected.

- **LAN Domain**—Any data on the network that is not secured with appropriate access controls is vulnerable. Weak passwords can be cracked. Permissions that aren't assigned properly allow unauthorized access.
- **LAN-to-WAN Domain**—If users are allowed to visit malicious websites, they can mistakenly download malicious software. Firewalls with unnecessary ports open allow access to the internal network from the internet.
- **WAN Domain**—Any public-facing server is susceptible to DoS and DDoS attacks. A File Transfer Protocol (FTP) server that allows anonymous uploads can host warez from black-hat hackers.
- **Remote Access Domain**—Remote users may be infected with a virus but not know it. When they connect to the internal network via remote access, the virus can infect the network.
- **System/Application Domain**—Database servers can be subject to SQL injection attacks. In an SQL injection attack, the attacker can read the entire database. SQL injection attacks can also modify data in the database.

> **TIP**
>
> *Warez* (pronounced "wares") is a term that describes pirated files. Examples include pirated games, MP3 files, and movies. A warez site often includes hacking tools, which anyone can download, including hackers.

> **TIP**
>
> An *SQL injection attack* tries to access data from websites. SQL statements are entered into text boxes. If the website isn't programmed defensively, these SQL statements can be executed against a database. Programs are available that can launch an SQL injection attack and retrieve an entire database.

This section does not represent a complete list; it couldn't. The number of vulnerabilities discovered in IT systems is constantly growing. The MITRE Corporation catalog **Common Vulnerabilities and Exposures (CVE)** currently includes more than 40,000 items.

Assessing Impact and Likelihood

The third step when identifying risks is to estimate the likelihood of a threat exploiting a vulnerability to harm an asset. Threats are matched to existing vulnerabilities to determine the impact of the threat to the organization.

Several threats are listed under the earlier section Identifying Threats. **TABLE 1-1** takes a few of those threats and matches them to vulnerabilities to identify the impact of possible losses.

The following formula is often used when pairing threats with vulnerabilities:

$$\text{Risk} = \text{Threat} \times \text{Vulnerability}$$

However, this isn't a true mathematical formula. Threat and vulnerability don't always have numerical values. Instead, the formula shows the relationship between the two.

If the value of the asset can be identified, the formula is slightly modified to:

$$\text{Total risk} = \text{Threat} \times \text{Vulnerability} \times \text{Asset value}$$

Balancing Risk and Cost

The costs to manage the risk must be balanced against the impact value. The costs can be measured in actual monetary values if they are available. The costs can also be balanced by using relative values, such as *low*, *medium*, and *high*.

TABLE 1-2 shows an example of how the relative values can be assigned. Likelihood values are shown vertically, and impact values are shown horizontally. If a threat has a

TABLE 1-1 Assessing the impact of a threat

THREAT	VULNERABILITY	IMPACT
An unauthorized employee tries to access data hosted on a server.	The organization doesn't use adequate authentication and access controls.	The possible loss would depend on the sensitivity of the data and how it's used. For example, if the unauthorized employee accessed salary data and freely shared it, morale and productivity could be impacted.
Any type of malware, such as viruses or worms, enters the network.	Antivirus software doesn't detect the virus.	The virus could be installed on systems. Viruses typically result in loss of confidentiality, integrity, or availability.
An attacker modifies or defaces a website.	The website isn't protected.	Depending on how the attacker modifies the website, the credibility of the company could be affected.
A social engineer tricks an employee into revealing a password.	Users aren't adequately trained.	Passwords could be revealed. An attacker who obtains a password could take control of the user's account.

0 to 10 percent likelihood of occurring, it is assigned a value of low. If the value is between 11 and 50 percent, the value is medium. If the value is between 51 and 100, the value is high. Similarly, the impact can be ranked as low, medium, and high.

Sometimes, the potential for risks to occur and their impact are very high, which presents an easy choice. For example, systems without antivirus software will become infected. The threat is common. The likelihood is high. If or when it happens, an infected system can result in the compromise or destruction of all the business's data. The impact is also high. This risk needs to be mitigated. The cost of antivirus software is far less than the impact costs. Therefore, antivirus software is commonly used in business.

Other times, the likelihood is low, but the impact is high. For example, the risk of fire in a data center is low. However, the impact is high. A business will often have fire detection and suppression equipment to prevent the impact should a fire occur. Insurance is also purchased to reduce the impact if a fire does cause damage.

TABLE 1-2 A threat-likelihood–impact matrix

	LOW IMPACT (0%–10%)	MEDIUM IMPACT (11%–50%)	HIGH IMPACT (51%–100%)
High-threat likelihood—100% (1.0)	10 × 1 = 10	50 × 1 = 50	100 × 1 = 100
Medium-threat likelihood—50% (.50)	10 × .50 = 5	50 × .50 = 25	100 × .50 = 50
Low-threat likelihood—10% (.10)	10 × .10 = 1	50 × .10 = 5	100 × .10 = 10

Reasonableness

With so many risks threatening a company's business, realizing that the company doesn't need to manage every possible risk should be good news. Some risks are reasonable to manage, whereas others are not.

Reasonableness is a test that can be applied to risk management to determine whether the risk should be managed. The test is derived from the reasonable-person standard in law. In short, this question should be answered: "Would a reasonable person be expected to manage this risk?"

Risks that don't meet the reasonableness test are accepted. For example, the threat of nuclear war exists. A company could spend resources on building bomb shelters for all employees and stocking them with food and water to last 30 years. However, this scenario just isn't reasonable.

As another example, consider a company located on the east coast of Florida. Hurricanes are a very real threat and should be considered. However, the likelihood of a major earthquake hitting the east coast of Florida is relatively minor and doesn't need to be addressed. A business in San Francisco, however, has different concerns. An earthquake there is a real threat but not a hurricane. So, for San Francisco, the risk of a hurricane is readily accepted, whereas the risk of an earthquake is not.

Another standard of reasonableness is to focus on the vulnerabilities only within the organization or the system being evaluated. External vulnerabilities are often not addressed. For example, a server will likely fail if the air-conditioning fails. This situation would be addressed when vulnerabilities for a server room were being identified. This vulnerability wouldn't be addressed for each of the 50 servers in the server room. Similarly, the commercial power may fail. This situation may be addressed by having uninterruptible power supplies (UPSs) and generators. However, alternatives don't need to be identified for the commercial power company.

> **TIP**
>
> A more detailed threat-likelihood–impact matrix can be created. For example, instead of assigning values of low, medium, or high for the threat likelihood, actual percentages can be assigned. Also, more categories can be used, instead of just three. Using more categories allows greater separation between them. Similarly, any number within a range can be assigned to the impact. The matrix in Table 1-2 uses a range of 10, 50, and 100, but any numbers between 1 and 100 could be used.

Risk Management Process

Earlier in this chapter, risk management was defined as the practice of identifying, assessing, controlling, and mitigating risks. Identifying the threats and vulnerabilities that are relevant to the organization is an important step, just as knowing the worth of an asset can help determine the impact of its loss. With this information, action can then be taken to reduce potential losses to assets from these risks.

Realizing that risk management is not the same as risk elimination is important. Risk elimination isn't a reasonable goal. Instead, risk management attempts to identify the risks that can be minimized at a reasonable cost and implements controls to do so. Risk management includes several elements:

- **Assessing risks**—Risk management starts with a **risk assessment**, or risk analysis. There are several steps to developing a risk assessment:

- **Identifying the assets of an organization and their value**—When focused on IT, these assets can include data, hardware, software, services, and the components of the IT infrastructure itself.
- **Identifying threats and vulnerabilities to the assets**—Prioritize the threats and vulnerabilities.
- **Identifying the likelihood of a vulnerability being exploited by a threat**—These vulnerabilities are the risks.
- **Identifying the impact of a risk**—Risks with higher impacts should be addressed first.

> **TIP**
>
> Risk management **controls** are any actions or changes put into place to reduce a weakness or potential loss. NIST Special Publication 800-37 Rev. 2 identifies three classes of controls: technical, administrative, and physical. More will be learned about controls later in this text.

- **Identifying a risk response**—Risks can be avoided, shared or transferred, mitigated, or accepted. That decision is often based on the likelihood of the risk's occurring, the impact it would have if it does occur, and the cost to implement a sufficient control.
- **Selecting controls**—After the risks have been identified, control methods can be identified and selected. Control methods are also referred to as *countermeasures*. Controls are primarily focused on reducing vulnerabilities and impacts.
- **Implementing and testing controls**—Once the controls have been implemented, they can be tested to ensure they provide the expected protection.
- **Evaluating controls**—Risk management is an ongoing process. Implemented controls should regularly be evaluated to determine whether they still provide the expected protection. Evaluation is often done by performing regular vulnerability assessments.

> **TIP**
>
> Controls are often referred to as either preventive or detective. **Preventive controls** attempt to prevent the risk from occurring. Examples include increasing physical security and training personnel. **Detective controls** try to detect activity that may result in a loss. Examples include antivirus software and intrusion detection systems.

Cost-Benefit Analysis

After risks have been identified, steps can be taken to reduce or manage them, often by implementing controls, or countermeasures. Managing risks comes at a cost. If too much money is spent on reducing risks, the business's overall profit will be reduced. If too little money is spent on reducing risks, a loss could result from an easily avoidable threat and/or vulnerability. Ideally, organizations should never spend more on controls than the value of the asset. For example, an organization should not spend $10,000 in controls for an asset that is worth only $5,000. The amount spent on controls should be proportional to the risk, which is known as the **principle of proportionality**.

Risks can be measured based on the value of the asset. A **cost-benefit analysis (CBA)** can be performed to help determine which controls, or countermeasures, to implement. If the benefits outweigh the costs, the control is often selected.

A CBA compares the business impact with the cost to implement a control. For example, the loss of data on a file server may represent the loss of $1 million worth of research. Implementing a backup plan to ensure the availability of the data may cost $10,000. In other words, $10,000 would be spent to save $1 million, which makes sense.

Starting a CBA begins by gathering data to identify the costs of the controls and benefits gained if they are implemented:

- **Cost of the control**—Cost of the control includes the purchase costs plus the operational costs over the lifetime of the control.
- **Projected benefits**—Projected benefits include the potential benefits gained from implementing the control. These benefits are identified by examining the costs of the loss and how much the loss would be reduced if the control were implemented.

A control doesn't always eliminate the loss. Instead, the control reduces it. For example, annual losses for a current risk may average $100,000. If a control is implemented, these losses may be reduced to $10,000. Thus, the benefit of the control is $90,000.

The following formula can be used to determine whether the control should be used:

$$\text{Loss before control} - \text{Loss after control} = \text{Cost of control}$$

For example, the company lost $100,000 last year without any controls implemented. If the control is implemented, a loss of $12,000 a year is estimated. The cost of the control is estimated at $7,000. The formula is:

$$\$100{,}000 - \$7{,}000 \text{ (Cost of control)} - \$12{,}000 \text{ (Expected residual loss)} = \$81{,}000$$

Implementing the control represents a benefit of $81,000.

One of the biggest challenges when performing a CBA is getting accurate data. Although current losses are often easily available, future costs and benefits need to be estimated. Costs are often underestimated, and benefits are often overestimated.

The immediate costs of a control are often available. However, sometimes, the ongoing costs are hidden. Some of the hidden costs may be:

- Costs to train employees
- Costs for ongoing maintenance
- Software and hardware renewal costs, such as subscription costs

Following the principle of proportionality, if the costs outweigh the benefits, the organization might choose not to implement the control. Instead, it might choose to accept, share or transfer, or avoid the risk.

Profitability Versus Survivability

Both **profitability** and **survivability** must be considered when evaluating the cost of risk management:

- **Profitability**—Profitability is the ability of a company to make a profit. It is calculated as revenues minus costs.
- **Survivability**—Survivability is the ability of a company to survive a loss due to a risk. Some losses, such as fire, can be disastrous and will cause the business to fail.

In terms of profitability, a loss can ruin a business. In terms of survivability, a loss may cause a company never to earn a profit. The costs associated with risk management don't contribute directly to revenue gains. Instead, these costs help to ensure that a company can continue to operate even if it incurs a loss.

Regarding profitability and survivability, the following items should be considered:

- **Out-of-pocket costs**—The cost to reduce risks comes from existing funds.
- **Lost opportunity costs**—Money spent to reduce risks can't be spent elsewhere, which may result in lost opportunities if the money could be used for other purposes.
- **Future costs**—Some countermeasures require ongoing or future costs. These costs could be for renewing hardware or software. Future costs can also include the cost of employees to implement the countermeasures.
- **Client and stakeholder confidence**—The value of client and stakeholder confidence is also important. If risks aren't addressed, clients and stakeholders may lose confidence when a threat exploits a vulnerability, resulting in a significant loss to the company.
- **Total cost of security**—The total cost of security includes one-time costs, for example, spending money on an IDS, and ongoing, or recurring, costs, for example, the cost of an antivirus software subscription. This cost can be quite high, and the money spent reduces the company's overall profit. But what's the alternative? If these protections are not taken, the entire business could grind to a halt. If this happens too often or for too long, the business could fail.

Data is often one of the most valuable assets a business owns. It can include customer data; accounting data, such as accounts payable and accounts receivable; and employee data. The list could go on and on. This data is integral to the success of a business, so it is often backed up regularly.

For example, a business spends $15,000 a year on data backups, a cost that will not increase revenue or profits. In a full year's time, data is never lost, and the backups are never needed. If profitability is the only consideration, management may decide to eliminate this cost. Backups are stopped, but the next year, data could be lost, causing the company to fail and go bankrupt.

The cost does need to be considered against profitability, though. For example, if a company earns only $10,000 a year in profit, the company's spending $15,000 a year to protect its data doesn't make sense.

On the other hand, for example, a company has $100,000 in annual profits. It chooses not to spend the $15,000 on backups, but then a virus spreads through the enterprise, destroying all customer and accounting data. The company no longer has reliable records of accounts receivable, and no one has access to the customer base. Such a scenario can be a business-ending catastrophe.

Risk-Handling Strategies

Risk management can also be thought of as handling risk. Remembering that risk management is not risk elimination is important. A business that is unwilling to take any risks doesn't stay in business for long because the cost to eliminate all risks would consume all the profits.

The ultimate goal of risk management is to protect the organization. It helps ensure a business can continue to operate and earn a profit. Risk management includes several steps:

- Identifying risks
- Assessing risks
- Determining which risks will be handled and which risks will be accepted
- Taking steps to reduce risks to an acceptable level

A risk can be avoided, shared or transferred, mitigated, or accepted. Each of these techniques is explained in the following sections.

Avoiding

One of the ways risks can be managed is by simply avoiding them. The primary reason for **avoiding** a risk is when the impact of the risk outweighs the benefit of the asset.

An organization can avoid risk by:

- **Eliminating the source of the risk**—The company can stop the risky activity. For example, a company may have a wireless network that is vulnerable to attacks. The risk could be avoided by removing the wireless network, which can be done if the wireless network isn't an important asset in the company.
- **Eliminating the exposure of assets to the risk**—The company can move the asset. For example, a data center could be at risk because it is located where earthquakes are common. It could be moved to an earthquake-free zone to eliminate this risk, but the cost to move the data center would be high. However, if the risk is unacceptable and the value of the data center is high, it makes sense.

Sharing or Transferring

Sharing or **transferring** risk means shifting responsibility to another party. Transferring risk shifts the entire responsibility or liability. Sharing risk shifts a portion of the responsibility or liability. Organizations can outsource part or all of the activity.

- **Insurance**—A company can purchase insurance to protect it from a loss. If a loss occurs, the insurance covers it. Many types of insurance are available, including fire insurance.
- **Outsourcing the activity**—For example, a company may want to host a website on the internet. The company can host the website with a web-hosting provider. The company and the provider can agree on who assumes responsibility for security, backups, and availability.

Mitigating

Risk is reduced by reducing vulnerabilities. The primary strategy in this process is **mitigating** risks. Mitigating risks is also known as *risk reduction*.

Implementing controls, or countermeasures, reduces vulnerabilities. The cost of a control should not exceed the benefit. Determining costs and benefits often requires a CBA, which was covered earlier in this chapter.

Examples of mitigation steps are:

- **Alter the physical environment**—Replace hubs with switches. Locate servers in locked server rooms.
- **Change procedures**—Implement a backup plan. Store a copy of backups off-site, and test the backups.
- **Add fault tolerance**—Use RAIDs for important data stored on disks. Use failover clusters to protect servers.
- **Modify the technical environment**—Increase security on the firewalls. Add IDSs. Keep antivirus software up to date.
- **Train employees**—Train technical personnel on how to implement controls. Train end users on social engineering tactics.

Often, the goal is not to eliminate the risk but, instead, to make it too expensive for the attacker. Here are two formulas:

- **Attacker's cost < Attacker's gain**—When this is true, attacking is appealing to the attacker.
- **Attacker's cost > Attacker's gain**—When this is true, the attacker is less likely to pursue the attack.

Cryptography is one of the ways to increase the attacker's cost. If a company sends data across the network in cleartext, the data can be captured and analyzed. If the company encrypts the data, an attacker must decrypt it before analyzing it. The goal of the encryption isn't to make it impossible to decrypt the data. Instead, the goal is to make it too expensive or time-consuming for the attacker to crack it.

Accepting

Accepting a risk is another choice. A company can evaluate a risk, understand the potential loss, and choose to accept it, which is commonly done when the cost of the control outweighs the potential loss.

> **NOTE**
>
> A simple failover cluster could include two servers. One server provides the service to users, and the other server acts as a spare. If the online server fails, the spare server can sense the failure and automatically take over.

For example, a company hosts a web server used for e-commerce. The web server generates about $1,000 per month in revenue. The server could be protected using a failover cluster. However, estimates indicate that a failover cluster will cost approximately $10,000. If the server goes down, it may be down for only one or two hours, which equates to less than $3 (Revenue per hour = $1,000 × 12 / 365 / 24 = $1.37).

Residual Risk

Residual risk is the risk that remains after controls have been applied. Eliminating all risks is not feasible. Instead, steps are taken to reduce the risk to an acceptable level. The risk that's left is residual risk.

Earlier in this chapter, the following two formulas were given for risk:

$$\text{Risk} = \text{Threat} \times \text{Vulnerability}$$

$$\text{Total risk} = \text{Threat} \times \text{Vulnerability} \times \text{Asset value}$$

The following formula can be used to calculate residual risk:

$$\text{Residual risk} = \text{Total risk} - \text{Controls}$$

Senior managers are responsible for losses due to residual risk. They decide whether a risk should be avoided, shared or transferred, mitigated, or accepted. They also decide which controls to implement. Any resulting loss due to their decisions falls on their shoulders.

CHAPTER SUMMARY

Risks occur when threats exploit vulnerabilities and result in a loss. The loss can compromise assets and core business functions. The impact of losses can be seen in business costs. The steps in risk management are to identify threats and vulnerabilities, which can then be paired to help determine the impact of the risk. By implementing controls, vulnerabilities can be reduced. The amount spent on controls should be proportional to the risk.

By choosing one of four techniques, avoiding, sharing or transferring, mitigating, or accepting, risks can be managed. The primary risk management technique is mitigating risk, which is also known as risk reduction or risk treatment. Deciding to accept a loss becomes easier if a CBA has been completed.

KEY CONCEPTS AND TERMS

accepting
asset
availability
avoiding
audits
business functions
Common Vulnerabilities and Exposures (CVE)
confidentiality
controls
cost-benefit analysis (CBA)
denial of service (DoS) attack
detective controls
disaster recovery
distributed denial of service (DDoS) attack
exploit
goodwill
guideline
impact of loss
intangible value
integrity
mitigating
policies
preventive controls
principle of proportionality
profitability
reasonableness
residual risk
risk
risk assessment
risk management
sharing
social engineering
standard
survivability
tangible value
threat
transferring
vulnerability

CHAPTER 1 ASSESSMENT

1. Which one of the following properly defines risk?
   A. Threat × Mitigation
   B. Vulnerability × Controls
   C. Controls – Residual risk
   D. Threat × Vulnerability
2. Which one of the following properly defines total risk?
   A. Threat – Mitigation
   B. Threat × Vulnerability × Asset value
   C. Vulnerability – Controls
   D. Vulnerability × Controls
3. The best bet is to reduce risk to a level that can be accepted.
   A. True
   B. False
4. Which of the following are accurate pairings of threat categories? (Select two.)
   A. External and internal
   B. Natural and supernatural
   C. Intentional and accidental
   D. Computer and user
5. A loss of client confidence or public trust is an example of a loss of ________.
6. A ________ is used to reduce a vulnerability.
7. As long as a company is profitable, it does not need to consider survivability.
   A. True
   B. False
8. What is the primary goal of an information security program?
   A. To eliminate losses related to employee actions
   B. To eliminate losses related to risk
   C. To reduce losses related to residual risk
   D. To reduce losses related to loss of confidentiality, integrity, and availability
9. The ________ is an industry-recognized standard list of common vulnerabilities.
10. Which of the following is a goal of risk management?
    A. To identify the correct cost balance between risk and controls
    B. To eliminate risk by implementing controls
    C. To eliminate the loss associated with risk
    D. To calculate value associated with residual risk
11. If the benefits outweigh the cost, a control is implemented. Costs and benefits are identified by completing a ________.
12. A company decides to reduce losses of a threat by purchasing insurance, which is known as risk ________.
13. What can be done to manage risk? (Select three.)
    A. Accept it
    B. Transfer it
    C. Avoid it
    D. Mitigate it
14. After controls to minimize risk in the environment have been applied, what is the remaining risk called?
    A. Remaining risk
    B. Mitigated risk
    C. Managed risk
    D. Residual risk
15. Who is ultimately responsible for losses resulting from residual risk?
    A. End users
    B. Technical staff
    C. Senior managers
    D. Security personnel

CHAPTER 2

Managing Risk: Threats, Vulnerabilities, and Exploits

ORGANIZATIONAL ASSETS include far more than just tangible items. Information is a valuable commodity. Recent data breaches wherein data was subsequently sold on the dark web illustrate this fact. The following is a quote from a March 2024 news article: "AT&T has determined that AT&T data-specific fields were contained in a data set released on the dark web approximately two weeks ago."[1] And this is not an unusual event. It is common now for a ransomware attack to involve first exfiltrating data then threatening to release the data if the victim does not pay. This illustrates the value of information. When considering assets to be protected, an organization should certainly consider information, ranging from personally identifiable information (PII) to trade secrets, as important assets to protect.

The U.S. federal government has done much in the information security space, including developing frameworks to help understand and manage risks regarding organizational assets. One example of a framework is the Risk Management Framework (RMF) from the National Institute of Standards and Technology (NIST). The NIST RMF 800 special publications series provides a set of policies and standards that cover the life cycle of risk activities. These publications are freely available on the NIST.gov website. Additionally, the Department of Homeland Security (DHS) oversees several other initiatives related to information technology (IT) security. Throughout this book there will be frequent references to NIST documents.

Chapter 2 Topics

This chapter covers the following topics and concepts:

- What assets are and why they need to be managed
- What threats are and how they can be managed
- What vulnerabilities are and how they can be managed
- What exploits are and how they can be managed
- What the value of the risk management initiatives that the U.S. federal government sponsors is

[1] AT&T, "AT&T Addresses Recent Data Set Released on the Dark Web," AT&T, Published March 30, 2024, https://about.att.com/story/2024/addressing-data-set-released-on-dark-web.html.

Chapter 2 Goals

When you complete this chapter, you will be able to:

- Explain what assets are and why they need to be protected
- Describe the uncontrollable nature of threats
- List unintentional and intentional threats
- Identify best practices for managing threats
- Identify threat/vulnerability pairs
- Define *mitigation*
- List and describe methods used to mitigate vulnerabilities
- Identify best practices for managing vulnerabilities
- Define *exploit*
- Describe the perpetrator's role in vulnerabilities and exploits
- Identify mitigation techniques
- Identify best practices for managing exploits
- Identify the purpose of U.S. federal government risk management initiatives

Understanding and Protecting Assets

An asset represents anything of value that needs to be protected. In the IT world, assets include data, processes, and technology systems. The processes that the organization has developed, such as policies, standards, and guidelines, are important assets worth protecting, just like the data in the technology systems are. Weaknesses in any of these areas can be exploited by threats to harm these assets. Organizations need to protect their assets; otherwise, the businesses become far more difficult to manage or even cease to exist.

Understanding and Managing Threats

A threat is any activity that represents a possible danger to an asset. Threats include any circumstances or events with the potential to adversely impact confidentiality, integrity, or availability of a business's assets. Certainly, malicious attacks are threats, but so are natural disasters and economic instability.

Threats are a part of the equation that creates risk:

$$\text{Risk} = \text{Threat} \times \text{Vulnerability} \times \text{Asset}$$
$$\text{R} = \text{TVA}$$

Note, this equation is commonly used. However, you may notice it does not take into account the probability of the threat occurring. That probability is taken into account with other formulas we will see a bit later. Any attempt to manage risk requires thorough knowledge of threats. This section includes the following topics:

- Uncontrollable nature of threats
- Unintentional threats
- Intentional threats
- Best practices for managing threats within an IT infrastructure

Uncontrollable Nature of Threats

Realizing a few basic facts about threats is important:

- Threats can't be eliminated.
- Threats are always present.
- Sometimes, threats can persist. Some threats remain undetected in an asset, such as a network, for a long period of time.
- Action can be taken to reduce the potential for a threat to occur.
- Action can be taken to reduce the impact of a threat.

For example, a thief can't be stopped from wanting to break into a computer lab to steal computers or the data they contain. However, steps can be taken to either enhance or reduce the threat against the computer lab. To decrease the chances of a thief breaking into the computer lab, locks can be provided on the doors, computers can be attached to desks, security cameras can be added, and access to the computer lab can be controlled. While this is a physical security example, the principles apply to both physical and cybersecurity. One must first identify the threat, then select specific methods to mitigate that threat. It should also be noted that physical security is part of cybersecurity.

Threats to IT software are similar. Malicious actors seek to exploit software. Software developers make mistakes that lead to vulnerabilities attackers will try to take advantage of. This threat is pervasive. It is not realistic to stop the threat entirely, but there are certainly steps that can be taken to mitigate it. These steps are varied. You can perform rigorous testing to find and correct vulnerabilities. One can also apply secure coding standards to reduce the number of errors and vulnerabilities in software.

Unintentional Threats

Unintentional threats are threats that don't have a perpetrator; they don't occur because someone is specifically trying to attack. Such things as natural events and disasters, human errors, and simple accidents are considered unintentional.

There are four primary categories of unintentional threats:

- **Environmental**—Threats affecting the environment. They include weather events, such as floods, tornadoes, and hurricanes. Earthquakes are also environmental threats. Illnesses or an epidemic can cause a loss to the labor force and reduce the availability of systems. Unfortunately, we actually saw this in action in the COVID-19 pandemic.

- **Human**—Errors caused by people. A simple keystroke error can cause incorrect or invalid data to be entered. A user may forget to enter key data. A technician could fail to follow a backup procedure that results in an incomplete backup. An administrator might write incomplete or incorrect backup procedures. Undiscovered software bugs can also cause serious problems.
- **Accidents**—Anything from a minor mishap to a major catastrophe. A backhoe digging a new trench for new cables can accidentally cut power or data cables. An employee might accidentally start a fire in a break room.
- **Failures**—Equipment problems. A hard drive can crash, a server can fail, or a router can stop routing traffic. The air-conditioner might stop blowing cool air, causing multiple systems to overheat and fail. Any of these failures can result in the loss of availability of data or services.

Although these threats are unintentional, they can be addressed with a risk management plan. Here are some common methods:

- **Managing environmental threats**—Insurance can be purchased to reduce the impact of many environmental threats. A business might decide to move to reduce the threat; for example, a business in an area prone to hurricanes. Additionally, an organization can take steps such as operating from a building that has a structure that is resistant to certain threats (high winds, small earthquakes, etc.). Organizations frequently have fire suppression equipment to mitigate the threat of fire.
- **Reducing human errors**—Automation and input validation are common methods used to reduce errors. Any process that can be automated will consistently run the same way. Input validation checks data to ensure it is valid before it is used. For example, if a program expects a first name, the input validator checks whether the data looks like a valid name. Rules for a valid first name may be no more than 20 characters, no numbers, and only specific special characters. Input validation can't check to ensure that data is accurate, but it can ensure that data is valid.
- **Preventing accidents**—To prevent common accidents, safety should be stressed. Physical risk is a part of cyber risk management. As an example, if a server room catches fire, the servers are in danger, as is the data on the servers.
- **Avoiding failures**—Fault-tolerant and redundant systems can be used to protect against the immediate impact of failures. A redundant array of independent disks (RAID) system helps ensure data availability, and failover clusters help ensure that users can access servers at all times.

Intentional Threats

Intentional threats are acts that are hostile to an organization. One or more perpetrators are involved in carrying out the threat. Perpetrators are generally motivated by one of the following:

- **Greed**—Many attackers want to make money through the attacks. Attackers steal data and use it to perform acts of fraud. They steal customer data from databases and commit identity theft. Criminals steal proprietary data from competitors. Social engineers try to trick users into giving up passwords for financial sites. And both criminals and social engineers utilize ransomware to extract financial gain by holding victim data hostage. Financially motivated cyberattacks are on the rise.

- **Anger**—When anger is the motivator, the attacker often wants the victim to pay a price. Anger can result in attempts to destroy assets or disrupt operations. These threats often result in a loss of availability. A disgruntled former employee may lash out at an organization.
- **Desire to damage**—Some attackers just want to cause damage. The result is the same as an attacker being motivated by anger. The damage can result in a loss of availability.
- **Ideology**—Some attackers believe they are justified in attacking an organization based on ideological issues. For example, someone might believe a cyberattack on a company is justified because they feel the company's policies are unethical. It should be noted that such attacks are still illegal.

> **TIP**
>
> The U.S. government's Cybersecurity & Infrastructure Security Agency maintains a website that provides common threats and their descriptions. The website can be accessed at https://www.cisa.gov/topics/cyber-threats-and-advisories. The U.S. Federal Bureau of Investigation at also maintains a cyberthreat website https://www.fbi.gov/investigate/cyber

The threat landscape changes over time. For example, in recent years ransomware has changed such that now ransomware attackers tend to perform a double extortion. Double extortion is a cyberattack strategy increasingly used in ransomware attacks, where attackers apply two layers of pressure on victims to coerce them into paying a ransom. This method significantly raises the stakes compared to traditional ransomware, which only encrypts data. Before encryption, the attacker steals sensitive data from the victim's systems. They then threaten to leak, sell, or publish this data online if the ransom is not paid—even if backups are available. This was not a common form of attack even a few years ago. This is why it is important to keep up to date on current threats.

Some of the more common attackers today are:

- **Criminals**—Opportunities to make money from online attacks have resulted in a growth in criminal activity. Furthermore, criminal activity is far more organized today than ever before. This activity includes fraud and theft. For example, *rogueware* tricks users into installing bogus antivirus software. Then, they must pay to get it removed. Criminals have extorted millions of dollars using rogueware. More recently, rogueware has morphed into *ransomware.* Criminals restrict access to the system and display messages to the user demanding ransoms to get access to their computer and/or files. Another common attack by criminals is *formjacking*. This type of attack uses malicious JavaScript codes to steal customers' personal financial details, such as credit card information, at the checkout stage of an e-commerce site.
- **Advanced persistent threats (APTs)**—These attackers focus on a specific target and have high levels of expertise and almost unlimited resources. Nation-states or terrorist groups often sponsor them. An example of a nation-state-sponsored APT group is APT43. APT43, also known as the Kimsuky group (also known as Black Banshee), specializes in cyber espionage, initially targeted individuals and organizations related to South Korean affairs, foreign policy, and international relations, but now its targets are global. This group is also referred to as Velvet Chollima. The word 'Chollima' is a Korean word

referring to a mythological flying horse. It should be noted that Velvet Chollima refers to APT43/Kimsuky, whereas Silent Chollima refers to the Andariel threat actor group. After the Korean War, the country required rebuilding to function again. In order to expedite the construction, President Kim Il-Sung devised the slogan "rush as the speed of chollima". Today, the Chollima in North Korea is synonymous with great speed and progress in the DPRK. It is not surprising to see the term Chollima throughout many North Korean threat actor groups.

- **Vandals**—Some attackers are intent on doing damage. They damage just for the sake of damaging something. Their targets are often targets of opportunity.
- **Saboteurs**—A saboteur commits sabotage. The sabotage could be against a competing company or another country. The primary goal is to cause a loss of availability.
- **Disgruntled employees**—Disgruntled employees often present significant threats to a company. Countless reasons exist for why an employee might be disgruntled; for example, not receiving a pay raise. Employees with a great deal of access can cause so much damage.
- **Activists**—Occasionally, activists present a threat to a company. They often operate with a mindset of the end justifies the means. In other words, if the company does something the activist doesn't approve of, the activist considers it acceptable to attack. Sometimes, these attacks happen at a national level with nonstate actors motivated by the desire for some form of change in a country's policies or decisions.
- **Hackers**—Hackers attempt to breach systems. Depending on the goal of the hacker, the motivation may range from innocent curiosity to malicious intent.

> **TIP**
>
> A technical difference exists between a hacker and a cracker. *Hackers* have historically been known as white-hat hackers or ethical hackers, the good guys. They hack into systems to learn how it can be done but not for personal gain. For example, penetration testers can be hired by organizations to try to hack the system in order to locate security flaws. *Crackers* have been known as black-hat hackers or malicious hackers, the bad guys. They hack into systems to damage, steal, or commit fraud. The term cracker has fallen into disuse in recent years, and many people simply refer to black-hat hackers. Many black-hat hackers present themselves as white-hat hackers, claiming that their actions are innocent. However, most mainstream media often refer to hackers as simply cybercriminals. The general perception is that all hackers are bad guys.

Best Practices for Managing Risk Within an IT Infrastructure

Many steps can be taken to manage risk within an IT infrastructure. The following list represents steps that IT security professionals consider best practices:

- **Creating a security policy**—Senior managers identify and support the role of security and create a **security policy**, which provides a high-level overview of the goals of security but not the details of how to implement the security techniques. Managers use this policy to identify resources and create plans to implement the policy. Security policies are an important first step in reducing the impact from threats. Once the security policy has been approved, it needs to be implemented and enforced.
- **Purchasing insurance**—Companies purchase insurance to reduce the impact of threats. They commonly purchase insurance for fire, theft, and losses due to environmental events.

> **TIP**
>
> A security policy may include several individual policies. For example, it could include a password policy, an acceptable use policy, and a firewall policy.

Cyberthreat insurance has become more common in recent years. One important principle to consider here is the:

- Principle of proportionality—The amount spent on mitigating a risk, such as buying insurance, should be proportional to the risk. For example, a $100,000 insurance policy should not be bought to protect a $50,000 asset.

- **Using access controls**—Users should be required to authenticate and granted access to only what they need. Using access controls includes the following two principles:
  - Principle of least privilege—The **principle of least privilege** involves granting users only the rights and permissions they need to perform their job and no more. By doing this, users are prevented from accidentally or intentionally causing problems. This is a fundamental cornerstone of security. If you do not implement the principle of least privilege, it will undermine all of your other security measures.
  - Principle of need to know—The **principle of need to know** involves granting users access only to the data they need to perform their job and no more. For example, a person may have a security clearance for Secret data. However, that person doesn't automatically receive access to all Secret data. Instead, the person is granted access only to what he or she needs for the job. This helps prevent abuse of unnecessary access.

NOTE

Privileges include rights and permissions. *Rights* refers to actions users can perform on objects. For example, a user might have the right to change the system time. *Permissions* refers to object access. For example, a user might have permission to read and modify a file. The *principle of least privilege* includes both rights and permissions. The *principle of need to know* focuses on data permissions.

- **Using automation**—Processes should be automated as much as possible to reduce human errors.
- **Including input validation**—To determine whether data is valid, it should be tested before any applications use it. There are a number of widespread vulnerabilities such as SQL injection which would be eliminated with proper input validation. Anytime data enters your system it should be validated to ensure it has the appropriate data type, size, and does not contain any symbols used in attacks such as SQL injection and cross-site scripting.
- **Providing training**—Training can be used to increase safety awareness and reduce accidents as well as to increase security awareness to reduce security incidents.
- **Using antivirus software**—Antivirus software should be installed on all systems, and virus definition updates should be scheduled to occur automatically.
- **Protecting the boundary**—A firewall, at a minimum, should be used to protect the boundary between the intranet and the internet. Intrusion detection systems (IDSs) can also be used for an added layer of protection.
  - Defense in depth—Protecting the boundary is important, but it is not the end of security. In fact, it is just the beginning. You should always employ defense in depth. As an example, consider a firewall. Yes, you should have one at the boundary, but also have one at each switch or router in your network, and running on individual computers.

EY Global Information Security Survey 2025

Ernst & Young, a professional services firm, completes regular surveys that identify many of the trends related to IT security. The 2025 report[2] includes responses from security executives and professionals in numerous organizations.

Some of the notable findings in this report are:

- Generative AI (GenAI) is now being used in some way by nearly every company (93%), and many report that they have plans to use GenAI to improve cybersecurity by helping companies identify potential cyber risk.
- More than two-thirds of breaches include some involvement by company workers through phishing, behavior manipulation, or other methods to obtain and exploit employee credentials.
- In 2023 the FBI saw a 10% increase in complaints and a 22% increase in losses suffered—now $12.5b per year. Nearly a third (32%) of these incidents involve some type of extortion scheme, such as ransomware.
- Of respondents, approximately 40% of organizations reported that their organization's cybersecurity budget stayed about the same compared to the previous year and about 15% plan to increase their cybersecurity budget by over 25%. Only 1 percent of organizations surveyed reported a 25% cybersecurity budget decrease.
- Of respondents, approximately 17% reported customer information as the most valuable information to cybercriminals, and another 12% reported financial information and strategic plans. Approximately 22% reported phishing as the biggest cyberthreat, and 20% reported malware as their biggest cyberthreat.
- Respondents reported that the biggest source of vulnerabilities (34%) is with careless/unaware employees, and 26% indicated the source is from outdated security controls.
- Respondents indicated that organizations need to spend on relatively new technologies, such as cloud computing, cybersecurity analytics, mobile computing, artificial intelligence, machine learning, robotic process automation, and blockchain.
- The respondents agreed on the need for governance, indicating that cybersecurity needs to be in the DNA of the organization and must be included in the business strategy.

In 2024, state legislatures have introduced 132 bills and considered over 250 bills (including bills that carried over from 2023) related to cybersecurity. Twenty-seven bills were signed into law, including measures requiring insurers to investigate and notify the insurance commissioner of cybersecurity events, protecting election systems and electronic grids, providing for security measures in procurement, and funding for cybersecurity training and education. Bills have been enacted in Alaska, Arizona, California, Florida, Indiana, Iowa, Kansas, Louisiana, Maryland, Massachusetts, Minnesota, Mississippi, New York, Ohio, Oklahoma, Pennsylvania, Rhode Island, South Dakota, Tennessee, Utah, Virginia, Washington, and West Virginia.

---

2 https://www.ey.com/en_us/board-matters/cyber-disclosure-trends

Understanding and Managing Vulnerabilities

A vulnerability can be a weakness in an asset or the environment. A weakness can also be considered as a flaw in any system or business process.

A vulnerability may lead to a risk, although by itself it does not become a loss. The loss occurs when a threat exploits the vulnerability, which is also referred to as a threat/vulnerability pair.

FIGURE 2-1 shows the flow of a threat to a loss. Mitigation techniques can be used to reduce the vulnerability, the loss, or both.

This section presents the following topics:

- Threat/vulnerability pairs
- Mitigating vulnerabilities
- Mitigation techniques
- Best practices for managing vulnerabilities within an IT infrastructure

Threat/Vulnerability Pairs

A **threat/vulnerability pair** occurs when a threat exploits a vulnerability. The vulnerabilities provide a path for the threat that results in a harmful event or a loss. That both the threat and the vulnerability must come together to result in a loss is important to know.

Vulnerabilities depend on the organization. For example, if the organization hosts public-facing servers, the servers have several potential weaknesses. However, if the organization doesn't have any public-facing servers, the vulnerabilities for the organization are limited only to internal employees without proper authorization. Thus, the risk may be minimal compared to having people external to the organization having access to the server.

TABLE 2-1 shows examples of threat/vulnerability pairs and the potential losses. This table only scratches the surface. The list of vulnerabilities for any single network can be quite extensive.

FIGURE 2-1

The flow of threat/vulnerability pairs.

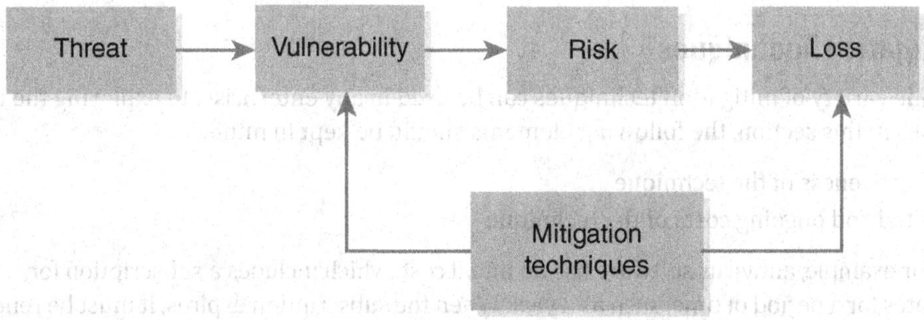

TABLE 2-1 Examples of Threat/Vulnerability Pairs and Potential Losses

THREAT	VULNERABILITY	HARMFUL EVENT OR LOSS
Fire	Lack of fire detection and suppression equipment	Can be total loss of business
Human	Unlocked computer laboratory	Loss of equipment and data
Malware	Lack of antivirus software Outdated definitions	Infection (impact of loss determined by payload of malware)
Equipment failure	Data not backed up	Loss of data availability (impact of loss determined by value of data)
Stolen data	Access controls not properly implemented	Loss of confidentiality of data
Denial of service (DoS) or distributed denial of service (DDoS) attack	Public-facing servers not protected with firewalls and IDSs	Loss of service availability
Users	Weak passwords	Loss of confidentiality
Social engineer	Lack of security awareness and education	Loss depends on the goals and success of attacker

Vulnerabilities Can Be Mitigated

Mitigating or reducing vulnerabilities reduces potential risk. The risk reduction comes from one or a combination of the following:

- Identifying and prioritizing vulnerabilities
- Reducing the exposure of the vulnerabilities
- Reducing the rate of occurrence
- Reducing the impact of the loss
- Providing security education, training, and awareness

A threat's being completely eliminated is rare. Instead, more commonly, the risk is reduced to an acceptable level. The remaining risk is referred to as the *residual risk*. **TABLE 2-2** matches the threat/vulnerability pairs from Table 2-1 with possible mitigation steps.

Mitigation Techniques

A wide variety of mitigation techniques can be used in any enterprise. In exploring the techniques in this section, the following elements should be kept in mind:

- Effectiveness of the technique
- Initial and ongoing costs of the technique

For example, antivirus software has an initial cost, which includes a subscription for updates for a period of time, such as a year. When the subscription expires, it must be renewed.

TABLE 2-2 Common Threat/Vulnerability Pairs and Possible Mitigation Steps

THREAT	VULNERABILITY	MITIGATION
Fire	Lack of fire detection and suppression equipment	Install fire detection and suppression equipment Purchase insurance
Hurricane, earthquake, tornado	Location	Purchase insurance Designate alternate sites
Malware	Lack of antivirus software Outdated definitions	Install antivirus software Update definitions at least weekly
Equipment failure	Data not backed up	Back up data regularly Keep copies of backup off-site
Stolen data	Access controls not properly implemented	Implement both authentication and access controls Use principle of need to know
DoS or DDoS attack	Public-facing servers not protected with firewalls and IDSs	Implement firewalls Implement IDSs Monitor web server regularly
Users	Weak passwords	Implement both authentication and access controls Create strong passwords
Social engineer	Lack of security awareness	Provide training Raise awareness through posters, occasional emails, and mini-presentations

When estimating the value and cost of any of these techniques, the value of the resource and the impact of the loss can be considered. For example, training in basic social engineering tactics may cost $10,000 a year. However, if users don't receive the training, the company may lose $100,000. The value of the training is thus $90,000.

However, there are other variables to consider when estimating the value of a mitigation technique. A company may have lost $100,000 last year. If people are trained, the company estimates it will lose only $5,000 this year. Thus, the training would be valued at $85,000. Here is the calculation:

Last year's loss – Training cost – This year's loss
$100,000 – $10,000 – $5,000 = $85,000

The following list identifies many common mitigation techniques that can be used in any enterprise:

- **Policies and procedures**—Written policies and procedures provide standards. The standards make it clear what should be implemented and how. Many organizations start by creating a security policy, as mentioned earlier. Policies and procedures should be reviewed on a regular basis. One could argue that a written policy does not guarantee compliance, and that is true. However, not having a policy leaves employees with nothing to comply with.

- **Documentation**—Documentation is useful in a large number of areas. Up-to-date documentation of networks makes problems easier to troubleshoot. Once problems occur, they can be repaired more quickly, which results in improved availability times. As the network and systems change, updated documentation is necessary.
- **Training**—Training helps employees understand that security is everyone's responsibility. Some training is geared to all users, and other training must be targeted to specific users. For example, all end users should be trained about social engineers, administrators should be trained on current threats and vulnerabilities, and managers should be trained on risk management strategies. Training is an ongoing event; as things change, updated training classes should be offered.
- **Separation of duties**—The **separation of duties** principle, also referred to as segregation of duties, ensures that no single person controls all the functions of a critical process. The principle is designed to prevent fraud, theft, and errors. For example, accounting separates accounts receivable from accounts payable. One division accepts and pays bills, and the other division accepts payments from customers. Separation of duties also helps prevent conflicts of interest.
- **Configuration management**—When system configuration is standardized, systems are easier to troubleshoot and maintain. One method of **configuration management** is to use baselines. For example, a system is configured and then a system image is created. The image can be deployed to 100 other systems so every system is identical. Maintenance of each of these systems is the same. When technicians learn one system, they learn them all. Without a baseline, the systems may be configured 100 different ways, making it necessary for technicians to learn how each system is configured before they can provide effective support. Images are updated as the configuration changes. Configuration management also ensures that systems are not improperly modified. Most organizations have change management processes in place, which ensure that only authorized changes are made. Compliance auditing is done to ensure that unauthorized changes don't occur.

> **NOTE**
>
> Symantec's Ghost, now known as Broadcom Ghost Suite[3], is a common tool used to image and deploy desktops, laptops, tablets, and servers. Ghost allows a quick and easy migration to the latest operating systems, configuring updates and releasing software to multiple platforms and operating systems.

- **Version control**—When several people work on the same document or application, data can be lost or corrupted. **Version control** systems are commonly used with the development of applications. They track all changes and can reduce wasted time and effort, especially if changes need to be reversed. The process requires programmers to check out modules or files before modifying them. After the file has been modified, it can be checked in, and someone else can modify the file. Some version control software allows multiple changes to be merged into a single file.

[3] Broadcom, "GHOST® Solution Suite," https://www.broadcom.com/products/cybersecurity/endpoint/management/ghost-solutions-suite.

- **Patch management**—Over time, bugs may be discovered in software. Software bugs are vulnerabilities that can be exploited. When the bugs are discovered, they are patched by vendors; however, attackers also find out about the bugs. Systems that aren't patched are vulnerable to attack. A comprehensive **patch management** policy governs how patches are understood, tested, and rolled out to systems and clients. The policy should include compliance audits to verify that clients are current. Patch management can also include the ability to quarantine unpatched clients. Patch management is an almost continuous process.

> **NOTE**
> Microsoft releases patches on the second Tuesday of every month, which has become known as **Patch Tuesday**. When the patches aren't deployed, attackers can exploit the bugs. For example, a Zero Day attack can happen when a vulnerability in a software is exploited. The hackers release a malware before the software developer has the opportunity to create a patch to fix the vulnerability.

- **Intrusion detection system**—An **intrusion detection system (IDS)** is designed to detect threats, not prevent threats. A passive IDS will log the event and may provide an alert. An active IDS may modify the environment to block the attack after it has been detected. Many IDS systems use definitions the way antivirus software uses signatures. A network-based IDS (NIDS) provides overall network protection. A host-based IDS (HIDS) can protect individual systems.
- **Incident response**—When a company is prepared and able to respond to an incident, it has a better chance of reducing the impact. An important step when responding to an incident is containment, which ensures the incident doesn't spread to other systems. Incident response teams try to identify what happened. They look for the vulnerabilities that allowed the incident and then seek ways to reduce the vulnerability in the future. On the other hand, some companies would like to quickly put the incident behind them. They try to fix the immediate issue without addressing the underlying problem. The underlying problems must be addressed to reduce the chance of recurring incidents for the same issue.
- **Continuous monitoring**—Security work is never finished. **Continuous monitoring** is necessary. Controls are implemented and then checked and audited to ensure the controls are still in place. Patches are deployed, and, later, through compliance audits, all systems are verified to be patched. Through access controls, systems and data are locked down. Later, they are checked to ensure they haven't been modified. A wide range of activity is recorded in logs, and then the logs are monitored for trends and suspicious events. Luckily, many tools are available that can be used to audit and monitor systems within a network. The tools are the basis of *security analytics,* which is a method used to proactively analyze security data for patterns so that anything unusual can be caught and acted on.
- **Technical controls—Technical controls** are measures that use technology to reduce vulnerabilities. IT professionals implement the controls, and computers enforce them. For example, after an IT professional installs antivirus software, the software prevents infections. Other examples of technical controls include IDSs, access controls, and firewalls. As new vulnerabilities are discovered, new technical controls can be implemented.
- **Physical controls—Physical controls** are measures that prevent unauthorized personnel from having physical access to areas or systems. For example, servers should be located in server rooms and the server room doors kept locked. Network devices should be placed in wiring closets and the wiring closet doors kept locked. Physical security can also include guards, cameras, and other monitoring equipment. For mobile equipment, such as laptops, cable or hardware locks can be used.

Best Practices for Managing Vulnerabilities Within an IT Infrastructure

Vulnerabilities are the portion of the threat/vulnerability pair that can be controlled. Therefore, steps need to be taken to manage vulnerabilities. Here are some of the best practices that can be used to do this:

- **Identifying vulnerabilities**—Several tools are available that can be used to identify vulnerabilities. For example, audits and system logs help identify weaknesses. All the available tools should be used, and all seven domains of the typical IT infrastructure should be examined.
- **Matching the threat/vulnerability pairs**—The vulnerabilities that should be addressed first are the ones that have matching threats. Some vulnerabilities may not have a matching threat, and, if so, the weakness may not need to be addressed. For example, a company may have an isolated network used for testing that does not have access to the internet. Weaknesses that can be exploited only from internet threats can't reach this network and may be ignored.
- **Using as many of the mitigation techniques as feasible**—Several mitigation techniques were listed in this section, and all of these techniques could possibly be used. Depending on the IT infrastructure, more may be used. With multiple techniques in place, multiple layers of security are created.
- **Performing vulnerability assessments**—Vulnerability assessments can help identify weaknesses. They can be performed internally, or external experts can be hired to perform them.
- **Using security analytical tools**—Analytical tools enable the continuous monitoring and detection of vulnerabilities and threats and their near real-time mitigation.

Understanding and Managing Exploits

Losses occur when threats exploit vulnerabilities. To reduce losses from risks, having a good understanding of what exploits are and how to manage them is necessary. This section covers the following topics:

- What an exploit is
- How perpetrators initiate an exploit
- Where perpetrators find information about vulnerabilities and exploits
- What mitigation techniques are
- What best practices for managing exploits within an IT infrastructure are

What Is an Exploit?

An **exploit** is the act of taking advantage of a vulnerability. The exploit takes advantage of a vulnerability by executing a command or program against an IT system to take advantage of a weakness. The result is a compromise to the system, an application, data, or people. An exploit can also be thought of as an attack executed by code or even humans. A social engineering attack takes advantage of an employee's lack of knowledge about a threat.

In the context of code, an exploit primarily attacks a public-facing server. In other words, it attacks servers that are available on the internet. Common internet servers are:

- Web servers
- Simple Mail Transfer Protocol (SMTP) email servers
- File Transfer Protocol (FTP) servers

FIGURE 2-2 shows how these public-facing servers are often configured in a network. They are placed within two firewalls configured as a **demilitarized zone (DMZ)**. A DMZ is also known as a *buffer area* or a *perimeter zone*. The firewall connected to the internet allows access to these public-facing servers. The firewall connected to the internal network restricts traffic from the internet. Most modern gateway routers have a built-in DMZ.

Because the servers in the DMZ are public-facing, they are accessible to anyone with a public internet protocol (IP) address, which includes attackers or black-hat hackers.

Although internal servers are susceptible to attacks from employees, an employee's using an exploit to attack an internal server is not common. Employees can attack and cause damage; however, stealing data or performing acts of sabotage is much easier for them. An insider usually won't take the time to write a program to attack an internal system. Insiders have the advantage of at least some basic employee privileges and internal knowledge. Commonly, the internal network is trusted, so the company pays less attention to exploits on the internal network.

A **buffer overflow** is a common type of exploit. It can occur when an attacker sends more data or different data than a system or application expects. The vulnerability exists when the system or application is not prepared to reject it, which can cause the system to act unreliably. Additionally, if the exploit's creator is especially skilled, the exploit will run extra instructions, gaining the attacker additional privileges on a system.

FIGURE 2-2

Public-facing servers in a DMZ bounded by two firewalls.

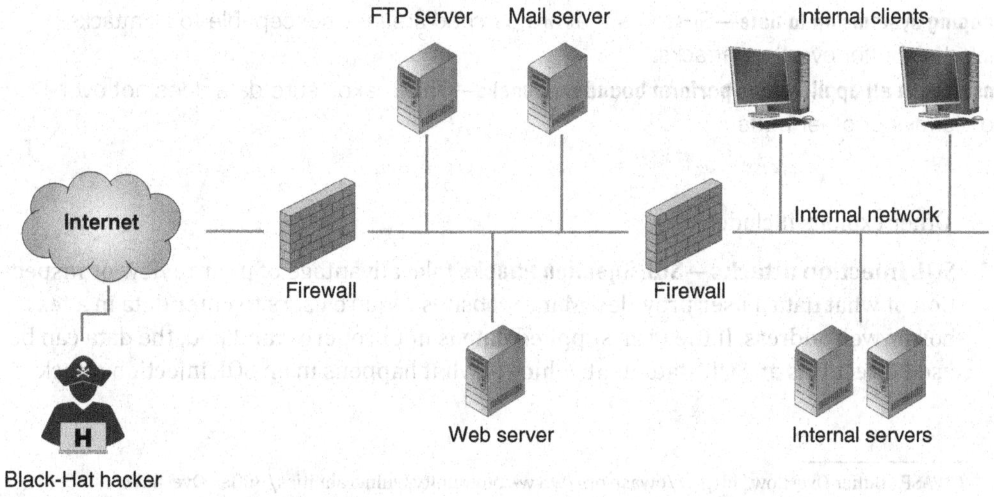

2

Managing Risk: Threats, Vulnerabilities, and Exploits

Normally, the system will validate and reject data that isn't expected. Occasionally, a bug allows invalid data to be used.

For example, here's a simple validation calculation: X / Y = Z. The program expects the value of X and Y to be provided. It will then divide the two to calculate the value of Z. However, if zero is given as the value of Y, Z cannot be calculated. Zero can't divide anything. If the program didn't check to ensure that X and Y were valid numbers, the program could fail when a user enters zero. If the error isn't handled gracefully, an attacker may be able to exploit the failure.

NOTE

Although a divide-by-zero error is simple to explain, its causing a problem today is unlikely. Most applications will detect the problem and never try to divide by zero. However, there are many more advanced errors that aren't predicted.

Buffer overflow errors allow attackers to insert additional data, which is often in the form of an unexpected command to be run immediately. The command could insert a worm that spreads through the network or causes the server to shut down and no longer be able to reboot, or it could be code that seeks and destroys data on the system.

When a vendor finds buffer overflow vulnerabilities, it patches the code to prevent the error in the future. This patch should be downloaded and applied to plug the hole.

OWASP Buffer Overflow

The Open Web Application Security Project (OWASP) says the following about buffer overflows: "A buffer overflow condition exists when a program attempts to put more data in a buffer than it can hold or when a program attempts to put data in a memory area past a buffer. In this case, a buffer is a sequential section of memory allocated to contain anything from a character string to an array of integers. Writing outside the bounds of a block of allocated memory can corrupt data, crash the program, or cause the execution of malicious code."[4] There are some common ways to mitigate buffer overflow.

- **Reducing the attack surface of servers**—Unneeded services and protocols should not be running or listening. If they are installed, they should be removed. This is helpful for mitigating all attacks.
- **Keeping systems up to date**—Systems that are patched are less susceptible to all attacks, including buffer overflow attacks.
- **Ensure that all applications perform boundary checks**—This makes sure data does not overflow arrays or other buffers.

Other exploits include:

- **SQL injection attacks—SQL injection attacks** take advantage of poor review or inspection of what data a user provides. Many websites require users to enter data in a text box or web address. If the user-supplied data is not properly validated, the data can be used directly as an SQL statement, which is what happens in an SQL injection attack.

[4] OWASP, "Buffer Overflow," https://owasp.org/www-community/vulnerabilities/Buffer_Overflow.

Typically, at the end of giving the data that's expected, an SQL command is added. This injection attack performs a different string of SQL code. This different code can compromise the database. SQL injection attacks are easy to avoid by using parameters and stored procedures that first review the code before allowing it to affect the system. However, all database developers aren't aware of the risks.

> **NOTE**
>
> Structured Query Language (SQL) is the language used to query and modify databases. It has specific rules that must be followed. SQL Injection (SQLi) is a type of security vulnerability that allows an attacker to interfere with the queries that an application makes to its database. It is one of the most common and dangerous web vulnerabilities, often resulting from improper validation or sanitization of user input. When a web application uses input from a user in an SQL query without properly filtering or escaping it, an attacker can manipulate the query by injecting malicious SQL code.

- **Denial of service (DoS) attacks**—**Denial of service (DoS) attacks** are designed to prevent a system from providing a service. For example, a **SYN flood attack** is common. Normally, Transmission Control Protocol (TCP) uses a three-way handshake to start a connection. A host sends a packet with the synchronize (SYN) flag set. The server responds with the SYN and acknowledge (ACK) flags set. The host then responds with the ACK flag set to complete the handshake. In the SYN flood attack, the host never responds with the third packet. This scenario can be likened to the host and server sticking out their hands to shake, but then the host pulls its hand away, leaving the server's hand hanging. When this is repeatedly done in a short time period, it consumes the server's resources and can cause it to crash.
- **Distributed denial of service (DDoS) attacks**—**Distributed denial of service (DDoS) attacks** are initiated from several clients at the same time. For example, many criminals and attackers run botnets from a command and control center. A botnet controls multiple hosts as *clones* or *zombies*. These clones can be given a command at any time to attack, and they all attack at the same time. The attack could be as simple as constantly pinging the same server. If thousands of clients are pinging a server at the same time, it can't respond to other requests as easily.

How Do Perpetrators Initiate an Exploit?

Most exploits are launched by programs developed by attackers. The attackers create and run the programs against vulnerable computers.

Script kiddies are attackers with little or limited knowledge of computers and sometimes are young teenagers. However, they can download scripts and small programs from the internet and then launch attacks. They don't have to be intelligent about computers or even about the potential harm they can do. Some programs are so simple that the script kiddie can simply enter an IP address and click Go to launch an attack.

However, the attackers that most companies are worried about are much more sophisticated. They have programming skills, know how to target specific servers, and know methods to infiltrate networks. They erase evidence to cover their tracks. They are professional attackers.

Imagine a country with extensive computer expertise that is hostile to the United States. For example, we have heard about attacks from Russia and how it purportedly meddled in U.S. elections. A hostile country can create an internal secret department with separate divisions. Each division can be assigned specific jobs or tasks, and the divisions can work together to launch exploits as soon as they become known. This department could have the following divisions:

- **Public server discovery**—Every system on the internet has a public IP address. This division can use ping scanners to identify systems that are operational with public IP addresses. IP addresses are assigned geographically, so servers can also be mapped to geographic locations.
- **Server fingerprinting**—This division can use several methods to learn as much about the discovered server as possible. A ping can be used to identify whether systems are running UNIX or Microsoft operating systems. This division can use port scans to identify which ports are open. Based on the ports that are open, it can identify the running protocols. For example, port 80 is the well-known port for Hypertext Transfer Protocol (HTTP). So, if port 80 is open, HTTP is probably running. If HTTP is running, the server is probably a web server. The department can use other techniques to determine whether the server is an Apache or IIS web server.
- **Vulnerability discovery**—Investigators and hackers in this division are constantly on the lookout for new weaknesses. They can try new things to see what can be done or lurk on newsgroups to hear about new bugs that aren't widely known. They may subscribe to professional journals or read blogs by IT security experts, and, if they discover a vulnerability, they can pass it on to programmers or attackers to exploit.
- **Programmers**—After vulnerabilities have been discovered, programmers can write code or applications to exploit them. A few lines of code are embedded into a webpage and downloaded when a user visits the website. A virus can be released to exploit the weakness, or an application can be installed on zombie computers waiting for the botnet command to attack. Some of these programmers are black-hat hackers.
- **Attackers**—Attackers initiate an exploit. For example, attackers may discover a new vulnerability for Apache servers. They may want to target servers in Washington, DC. They can obtain from other divisions a list of servers in DC running Apache and then launch an attack on those servers. This group might regularly launch legacy attacks, which current patches block. Most systems will be patched, but, if group members find an unpatched system, they can exploit it. For example, they launch an attack on 10,000 computers. Even if they have only a 1% success rate, they've exploited 100 computers.

NOTE

Attackers often use diversion when launching attacks. Instead of launching the attack from their own computer, they take control of one or more other computers on the internet. They then direct the attack from that remote-controlled computer.

This secret department in a hostile country is presented as fictitious. However, cyberattacks from one country against another are not fiction. The news reports cyberattacks regularly. APT43(mentioned previously in this chapter) is one recent example. If someone wanted to commit cyberwarfare against a hostile country, how would they do that? Possibly, they would design a similar department with similar divisions.

Even if a single perpetrator launches an attack, the steps listed previously would be separated. The attacker would take the time to learn as much about a target as possible through reconnaissance and might even develop a program to automate the attack. Regardless, the actual attack is usually quick.

Realizing that attackers often spend 100% of their work time on attacks is important. Because their attacks often return significant amounts of money, they aren't shy about working more than 40 hours a week. They take the time to discover targets, identify weaknesses, and plan the attacks. When the opportunity presents itself, they swoop in and attack, just as quickly as an owl attacks a field mouse.

Where Do Perpetrators Find Information About Vulnerabilities and Exploits?

A surprising number of sources are available for perpetrators to learn about vulnerabilities and exploits. A primary source is security professionals sharing information with each other.

Of course, when security professionals write about or discuss an exploit, the danger is that they are educating the enemy. Because of this possibility, some people say that the weaknesses shouldn't be discussed at all. However, when nothing is said, systems are attacked without IT professionals having a clue about the vulnerabilities.

The general mindset that currently prevails is that the vulnerabilities should be discussed with a focus on mitigation. In other words, publicly sharing the details on how to exploit a vulnerability is not advised, but freely sharing the details on how to prevent the vulnerability is warranted.

Even sharing details about how to prevent a vulnerability provides the attackers with information. They can use this information to learn about the weakness and then exploit it. However, the alternative is worse. If information on how to reduce the weakness isn't shared, more systems will be wide open.

The following list identifies some of the sources that attackers can use to gain information:

- **Blogs**—Many security professionals regularly blog about their findings. When they suspect vulnerabilities, they often discuss them. Many full-time security professionals are cautious about what they post because they realize that they have a mixed audience and they try to avoid giving too many details.
- **Forums**—IT and security professionals often share ideas on various forums. Sometimes, users have problems they don't understand, so they post their problems on the forum. Some of these problems expose vulnerabilities that can be exploited.
- **Security newsletters**—Many security newsletters are regularly released to anyone on the email list, and anyone can sign up. Although companies use newsletters to advertise and promote their products, the newsletters also provide valuable content. Such content includes information about threats and vulnerabilities. Attackers can even use the newsletters published by the U.S. government. Some of these newsletters are discussed later in this chapter, including how to subscribe to them.
- **Common Vulnerabilities and Exposures (CVE) list**—The CVE is discussed in more detail later in this chapter. When someone discovers a vulnerability, they can submit it to the MITRE Corporation for inclusion in this list. The entry about the vulnerability will include information on resources for more details.
- **Vulnerability Websites**—Sites like Shodan (https://www.shodan.io/) provide a search engine for vulnerabilities. Shodan can be seen in the following image:

Reproduced from Shodan. https://www.shodan.io/

- **Reverse engineering**—Patch Tuesday was mentioned earlier as the day that Microsoft releases patches, which is the second Tuesday of every month. The day after is known by some attackers as **Exploit Wednesday**. They often reverse-engineer the patches to discover the vulnerability. Once the weakness is understood, exploits are written to attack the weakness.
- **The dark web**—The **dark web** represents a part of the World Wide Web accessible only by using special software. Professional hackers use the dark web to share vulnerabilities and ways to exploit applications. Some examples of dark web sites include The Hidden Wiki, SoylentNews, ProPublica, DuckDuckGo, and Galaxy3. If individuals with little knowledge of cybersecurity are considering accessing these sites, they should do so using a virtual private network (VPN) connection.

NOTE

The dark web is often used for illegal activities. The **deep web** consists of normal web pages, but they are not indexed by any search engine. The dark web has content that is not found in a typical search engine, such as Google. It is accessed anonymously and only by using special hidden software networks.

A good philosophy to adopt is, if a vulnerability exists, a bad guy knows about it, and it takes only one bad guy who knows about the vulnerability to attack an unprotected system. All the systems must be protected to stay protected.

Mitigation Techniques

Mitigation techniques are the individual steps necessary to protect systems that are vulnerable. Together, these steps are often referred to as **hardening a server**. Hardening a server makes it more secure than the default installation.

Some of the specific mitigation techniques that can be taken to protect public-facing servers are:

- **Removing or changing defaults**—If an operating system or application has defaults, ensure they are removed or changed as soon as the system is installed. As an example, change default passwords to secure passwords. Commonly, changing the name of privileged accounts, such as the Administrator account, is also done. Doing so thwarts attempts to guess the password.
- **Reducing the attack surface**—The **attack surface** refers to how many services can be attacked on a server. For example, if 10 services are running on a server but only 7 are needed, then the attack surface can be reduced by disabling the 3 unneeded services. To reduce the overall attack surface and therefore the risk, all unneeded services and protocols should be removed.
- **Keeping systems up to date**—A patch management system should be used to ensure that vulnerabilities are patched, and the patches should be applied as quickly as possible after they have been released. Every hour that passes without the patch gives attackers more time to reverse-engineer the patch and begin their attacks. Compliance audits ensure that patches are consistently applied to all systems.
- **Enabling firewalls**—Firewalls filter traffic coming into a network, and DMZs use firewalls to create network buffer areas. Host-based firewalls can also be enabled on each server as an added layer of protection.
- **Enabling IDS**—An active IDS can detect attacks and take steps to stop them.
- **Enabling an intrusion prevention system**—An **intrusion prevention system (IPS)** is placed in-line with traffic. It detects and blocks malicious traffic to prevent attacks from reaching the internal network.
- **Installing antivirus software**—Antivirus software should be installed on all systems, including servers, before they are connected to the network. Many servers require different versions of antivirus software. For example, a Microsoft Exchange mail server needs a specialized version of antivirus software so the mail stores can be examined.

Best Practices for Managing Exploits Within an IT Infrastructure

Several best practices can be used to reduce the risk from exploits. Many of these techniques are directly related to basic risk management practices:

- **Hardening servers**—Methods for hardening servers were mentioned in the previous section. They include basic steps such as reducing the attack surface and keeping systems up to date.
- **Using configuration management**—Systems should be configured with consistent security settings and security baselines used to ensure systems are configured the same way. A security baseline can come from an image created with a tool, such as Broadcom Ghost. A security baseline can also be achieved by applying settings to all systems with technology, such as Microsoft's Group Policy. Compliance audits should be performed to ensure that systems stay configured the same way.

- **Performing risk assessments**—Learning about relevant threats and vulnerabilities can be enabled by performing risk assessments. Then, countermeasures can be identified and evaluated.
- **Performing vulnerability assessments**—Vulnerability assessments were mentioned earlier in this chapter. They can also be used as a best practice to manage exploits.
- **Using security information and event management (SIEM) tools**—SIEM tools provide real-time analysis of security alerts to systems from the data of security events and activities gathered on the systems.

U.S. Federal Government Risk Management Initiatives

The U.S. federal government has taken many steps to help companies manage IT risks. The initiatives covered in this section are:

- National Institute of Standards and Technology (NIST)
- Department of Homeland Security (DHS)
- National Cybersecurity and Communications Integration Center (NCCIC)
- United States Computer Emergency Readiness Team (US-CERT)
- MITRE Corporation and the CVE list

FIGURE 2-3 shows the relationships among many of these organizations. There are two primary paths, under the U.S. Department of Commerce or the DHS.

NIST is directly under the Department of Commerce. The Information Technology Laboratory (ITL), which is part of NIST, issues special publications. The DHS includes the Office of Cybersecurity and Communications.

Within the Office of Cybersecurity and Communications is the NCCIC. The Office of Cybersecurity and Communications provides funding for the civilian MITRE Corporation. MITRE maintains the CVE list. The US-CERT is located within the NCCIC.

National Institute of Standards and Technology

The **National Institute of Standards and Technology (NIST)** is a division of the U.S. Department of Commerce. NIST's mission is to promote U.S. innovation and industrial competitiveness. It does this by advancing measurement science, standards, and technology.

NIST includes the ITL, which develops standards and guidelines. The goal is improved security and privacy of information on computer systems.

The Special Publication 800 (SP 800) series includes several reports that document ITL's work. It includes research, guidance, and outreach efforts in computer security and is intended to be a collaborative effort combining the work of industry, government, and academic organizations. Many of the publications in the SP 800 series are available on the internet. NIST has revised many of these documents, so the number might not reflect the relative date of the current version.

NOTE

ITL and ITIL are two different programs. The Information Technology Infrastructure Library (ITIL) was developed by the United Kingdom (UK). It is managed by the UK Office of Government Commerce (OGC). ITIL is a collection of books that provide guidance and best practices for the successful operation of IT. The ITL, managed by NIST, is a U.S. program.

FIGURE 2-3

Relationships among organizations involved in the U.S. federal government risk management initiatives.

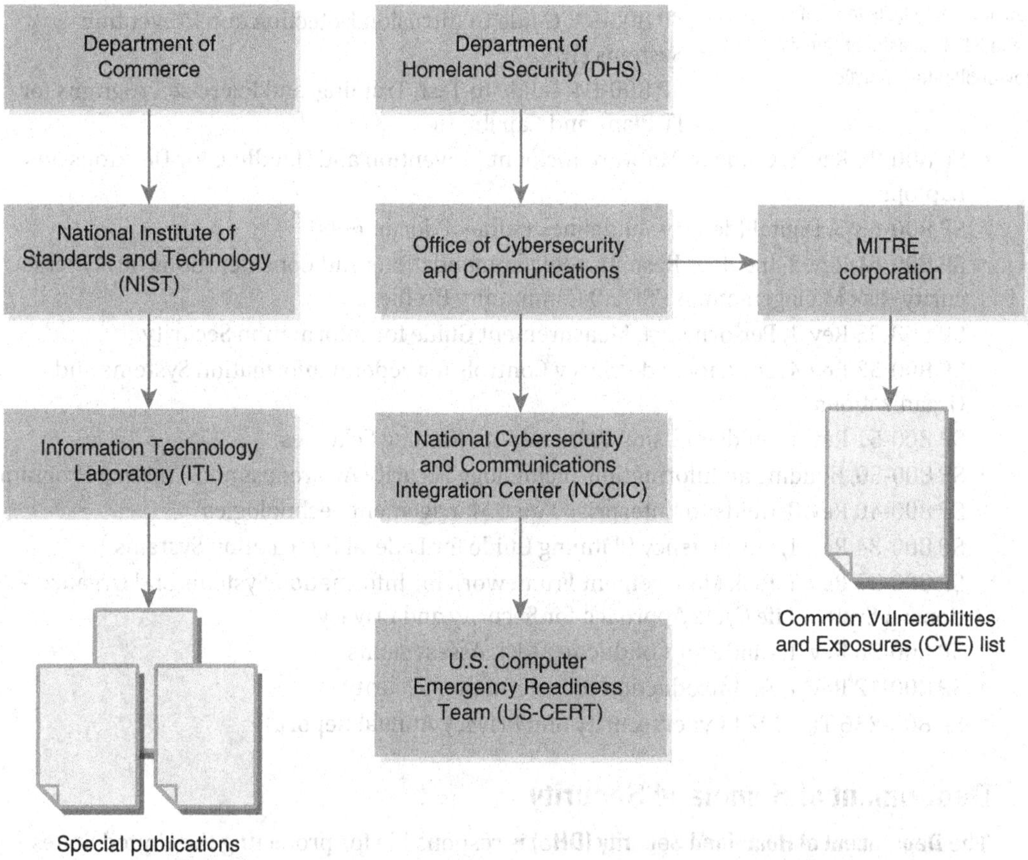

The following list includes some of these publications. You can find a complete list at[5]:

- SP 800-183, Networks of 'Things'
- SP 800-154, Guide to Data-Centric System Threat Modeling
- SP 800-153, Guidelines for Securing Wireless Local Area Networks (WLANs)
- SP 800-150, Guide to Cyber Threat Information Sharing
- SP 800-124 Rev. 1, Guidelines for Managing the Security of Mobile Devices in the Enterprise
- SP 800-123, Guide to General Server Security
- SP 800-122, Guide to Protecting the Confidentiality of Personally Identifiable Information (PII)
- SP 800-121 Rev. 2, Guide to Bluetooth Security
- SP 800-119, Guidelines for the Secure Deployment of IPv6

[5] NIST, "Computer Security Resource Center, Search Results for SP 800 Series," https://csrc.nist.gov/publications/sp800.

NOTE

The full list of Special Publications can be accessed, including links to all of them, from the NIST website at https://csrc.nist.gov/publications/sp800.

- SP 800-115, Technical Guide to Information Security Testing and Assessment
- SP 800-100, Information Security Handbook: A Guide for Managers
- SP 800-94, Guide to Intrusion Detection and Prevention Systems (IDPS)
- SP 800-84, Guide to Test, Training, and Exercise Programs for IT Plans and Capabilities
- SP 800-83 Rev. 1, Guide to Malware Incident Prevention and Handling for Desktops and Laptops
- SP 800-63-3, Digital Identity Guidelines (suite of documents)
- SP 800-61 Rev. 3, Incident Response Recommendations and Considerations for Cybersecurity Risk Management: A CSF 2.0 Community Profile
- SP 800-55 Rev. 1, Performance Measurement Guide for Information Security
- SP 800-53 Rev. 4, Security and Privacy Controls for Federal Information Systems and Organizations
- SP 800-51 Rev. 1, Guide to Using Vulnerability Naming Schemes
- SP 800-50, Building an Information Technology Security Awareness and Training Program
- SP 800-40 Rev. 3, Guide to Enterprise Patch Management Technologies
- SP 800-34 Rev. 1, Contingency Planning Guide for Federal Information Systems
- SP 800-37 Rev. 2, Risk Management Framework for Information Systems and Organizations: A System Life Cycle Approach for Security and Privacy
- SP 800-30 Rev. 1, Guide for Conducting Risk Assessments
- SP 800-12 Rev. 1, An Introduction to Information Security
- SP 800-236 The 2024 Cybersecurity and Privacy Annual Report

Department of Homeland Security

The **Department of Homeland Security (DHS)** is responsible for protecting the United States from threats and emergencies, including terrorist attacks. DHS is also responsible for responding to natural disasters, such as hurricanes and earthquakes.

Congress passed the Homeland Security Act of 2002 in November 2002, in which the DHS was established. Both the Homeland Security Act of 2002 and the DHS were created in response to the terrorist bombings of September 11, 2001.

The DHS includes many agencies. Some of them are:

- U.S. Secret Service
- U.S. Coast Guard
- U.S. Immigration and Customs Enforcement
- Federal Emergency Management Agency

National Cybersecurity and Communications Integration Center

The **National Cybersecurity and Communications Integration Center (NCCIC)** operates within the DHS. It works together with private, public, and international parties to secure cyberspace and America's cyber assets.

Previously, cybersecurity was scattered in different departments. Today, the NCCIC serves as the central point of contact. The NCCIC oversees several programs:

- **National Cyber Awareness System**—This is an email alert system that allows a person to subscribe to various emails.
- **United States Computer Emergency Readiness Team (US-CERT) Operations**—This division is tasked with analyzing and reducing cyberthreats and vulnerabilities. As issues become known, US-CERT disseminates information and coordinates incident response activities. See the following section for more information about US-CERT.
- **Industrial Control Systems Cyber Emergency Response Team (ICS-CERT)**—This group works to reduce risks to critical infrastructure sectors. Such infrastructures include roads, water, communications, energy, and more.

> **NOTE**
> One of the great benefits of the National Cyber Awareness System is that its emails don't include advertisements. Also, because they are from the U.S. government, the information is not slanted to sell or promote specific products.

U.S. Computer Emergency Readiness Team

The **United States Computer Emergency Readiness Team (US-CERT)** is a part of the NCCIC. US-CERT's primary mission is to provide response support and defense against cyberattacks. Its focus is on providing support for the federal civil executive branch of government, which includes all sites with a .gov domain name. However, US-CERT also collaborates and shares information with several other entities, including:

- State and local governments
- International partners
- Other federal agencies
- Other public and private sectors

Information gathered by US-CERT is shared with the public through the National Cyber Awareness System. This system includes a website, mailing lists, and Really Simple Syndication (RSS) channels.

A person can sign up to receive emails and alerts from US-CERT from this link: http://www.us-cert.gov/mailing-lists-and-feeds/. A person can also sign up for the following feeds:

- **Alerts**—These alerts include timely information about current security issues, vulnerabilities, and exploits and are released as needed. They are written for system administrators and experienced users. Past alerts can be viewed at http://www.us-cert.gov/ncas/alerts.
- **Bulletins**—These bulletins provide weekly summaries of security issues and vulnerabilities from the previous week. They are written for system administrators and experienced users. Past bulletins can be viewed at http://www.us-cert.gov/ncas/bulletins.
- **Current activity**—These emails provide information about high-impact types of security activity. Depending on current

> **NOTE**
> *Cyber* generally refers to any computer assets but usually refers to assets on the internet. The global network of computers on the internet is commonly referred to as *cyberspace*. *Cyberwarfare*, or cyberwar, refers to the attacks and counterattacks carried out against countries or companies by other countries or companies.

threats, they can be sent several times a day or several times a week. Past updates can be viewed at http://www.us-cert.gov/ncas/current-activity/.

The MITRE Corporation and the CVE List

The MITRE Corporation manages four **Federally Funded Research and Development Centers (FFRDCs)**. The FFRDCs conduct research for several major departments of the U.S. government.

The MITRE Corporation maintains the CVE list. MITRE is the editor of the list and is responsible for assigning numbers. The DHS sponsors the CVE.

The CVE is an extensive list of known vulnerabilities and exposures. As new discoveries are made, they are submitted as candidates for the list. The primary benefit of the list is standardized naming and descriptions.

Before the CVE existed, one company may have addressed a problem as Exploit234a. The same problem could have been addressed by another company as X42A. Both companies may have published papers regarding the same problem, but determining whether one problem was different from the other was difficult.

The CVE provides one name for any single vulnerability or exposure. The format is CVE-yyyy-nnnnnn, where *yyyy* is the year the vulnerability was added to the list and *nnnnnn* is a unique sequence number for that year. Effective January 1, 2014, the format of the sequence number was expanded to accommodate more digits as needed. Previously, only four digits were allowed, limiting the number of vulnerabilities to 9,999 CVE IDs. With six digits, MITRE could assign up to 999,999 CVE IDs for that year. The entries include a brief description of the vulnerability and one or more references users can access for more information about the vulnerability. The following example shows a CVE entry from 2018:

- **Name**—CVE-2018-1999046
- **Description**—An exposure of sensitive information vulnerability exists in Jenkins 2.137 and earlier, 2.121.2, and earlier in Computer.java that allows attackers with Overall/Read permission to access the connection log for any agent.
- **References**—URL: https://www.cvedetails.com/cve/CVE-2018-1999046/

NIST uses the CVE names and descriptions in the National Vulnerability Database (NVD). The NVD listings include the same information as in the CVE, but impact and severity scores are added. The page at http://cve.mitre.org/cve/ (The current site is cve.org) includes links to search for the entry on MITRE's CVE list or on NIST's NVD list.

> **NOTE**
>
> MITRE is not an acronym, contrary to many claims you may read online. Many of the original employees came from the Massachusetts Institute of Technology (MIT). These employees work on research and engineering (RE). However, MITRE is not a part of MIT.

The CVE is considered the standard for information security vulnerability names. CVE describes its founding as follows: "The original concept for what would become the CVE List was presented by the co-creators of CVE, The MITRE Corporation's David E. Mann and Steven M. Christey, as a white paper entitled, Towards a Common Enumeration of Vulnerabilities (PDF, 0.3MB), at the 2nd Workshop on Research with Security Vulnerability Databases on January 21-22, 1999 at Purdue University in West Lafayette,

Indiana, USA."[6] MITRE launched the CVE in 1999, and it was quickly embraced. Some of the relevant milestones are:

- **Year 2000**—Over 40 products were declared compatible with CVE. CVE is used by 29 organizations.
- **Year 2001**—Over 300 products and services were declared compatible. CVE is used by more than 150 companies.
- **Year 2002**—NIST recommends the use of CVE by U.S. agencies. NIST SP 800-51, Use of the Common Vulnerabilities and Exposures (CVE) Vulnerability Naming Scheme, is released. SP 800-51 was updated and renamed in 2011. The current name is Guide to Using Vulnerability Naming Schemes.
- **Year 2003**—The CVE Compatibility process is started. This process allows products and services to achieve official compatibility status.
- **Year 2004**—The U.S. Defense Information Systems Agency (DISA) requires use of products that use CVE identifiers. Also that same year, use of CVE by U.S. agencies was recommended by the National Institute of Standards and Technology (NIST) in "NIST Special Publication (SP) 800-51, Use of the CVE Vulnerability Naming Scheme."
- **Year 2007**—NVD implemented several upgrades to the CVE-based database. These upgrades increased usability and improved the scoring system. Many other entities have since adopted the NVD, which has increased the use of the CVE as a standard.
- **Year 2008**—CVE provides major updates to multiple cross-site scripting (XSS) vulnerabilities. CVE was mentioned in a December 29, 2008, article entitled "Microsoft Denies Vulnerability in Windows Media Player" on SCMagazine.com.
- **Year 2009**—The database is updated to include major security vulnerabilities across several media and search engines. CVE celebrates 10 years with more than 38,000 vulnerabilities catalogued.
- **Year 2010**—CVE expands reach and recognition. CVE was mentioned in an article entitled "Securing Voice Over Internet Protocol (VoIP)" in the June 2010 issue of Hacking.
- **Year 2011**—CVE is mentioned in the December 12, 2011, release of the DHS's "Blueprint for a Secure Cyber Future: The Cybersecurity Strategy for the Homeland Security Enterprise" on the DHS website.
- **Year 2012**—CVE gains new recognition. CVE, Common Weakness Enumeration, and the CWE/SANS Top 25 Most Dangerous Software Errors are mentioned in an article entitled "Supply Chain Risk Management" in the March/April 2012 issue of *CrossTalk: The Journal of Defense Software Engineering*.
- **Year 2013**—CVE revamped its numbering format for identified vulnerabilities. The MITRE Corporation announced that the CVE list will start to publish data using the Common Vulnerability Reporting Framework (CVRF). The CVE list is a dictionary of common names for publicly known information security vulnerabilities in software.
- **Year 2014**—CVE is cited in numerous major advisories, posts, and news media references related to the recent Network Time Protocol vulnerability affecting Apple and Linux operating systems.

[6] The MITRE Corporation, "History," CVE, https://www.cve.org/about/history.

- **Year 2015**—CVE is included in a September 2015 technical report entitled "Security in Telecommunications and Information Technology 2015" on the International Telecommunication Union (ITU) website.
- **Year 2017**—CVE celebrates providing common identifiers for publicly known cybersecurity vulnerabilities, including everything from relatively minor flaws, such as missing HttpOnly flags, all the way to headline-hitting exploits, such as EternalBlue.
- **Year 2018**—CVE list passes 100,000 entries.
- **Year 2019**—CVE is now 20 years running.
- **Year 2024**—CVE Program Workshop, Autumn 2024. CVE is now 25 years old.

The FBI/SANS Top 20 List of the Most Critical Internet Security Vulnerabilities also references the CVE list.

CHAPTER SUMMARY

Threats are always present and can't be eliminated. The potential for a threat to do harm or the impact of a threat can be reduced but not the threat itself. However, many steps can be taken to reduce vulnerabilities. The most important vulnerabilities are those that are likely to match up as a threat/vulnerability pair. Once the likely threat/vulnerability pairs have been identified, mitigation techniques can be implemented.

The U.S. federal government has many resources that organizations can use to manage risk. The National Institute of Standards and Technology (NIST) has published several Special Publications. The SP 800 series includes many publications targeted for IT security. The Department of Homeland Security also has many divisions focused on IT security. Its resources are freely available to IT and security professionals.

KEY CONCEPTS AND TERMS

attack surface
buffer overflow
configuration management
continuous monitoring
dark web
deep web
demilitarized zone (DMZ)
denial of service (DoS) attacks
Department of Homeland Security (DHS)
distributed denial of service (DDoS) attacks
exploit
Exploit Wednesday
Federally Funded Research and Development Centers (FFRDCs)
hardening a server
Industrial Control Systems Cyber Emergency Response Team (ICS-CERT)
intentional threat
intrusion detection system (IDS)
intrusion prevention system (IPS)
National Cybersecurity and Communications Integration Center (NCCIC)
National Institute of Standards and Technology (NIST)
patch management
Patch Tuesday
physical controls
principle of least privilege

principle of need to know
script kiddie
security policy
separation of duties
SQL injection attack
SYN flood attack
technical controls
threat/vulnerability pair
unintentional threats
United States Computer Emergency Readiness Team (US-CERT)
version control

CHAPTER 2 ASSESSMENT

1. What is a security policy?
   A. A document with a rigid set of rules created so that people follow it explicitly to be effective and avoid technical problems
   B. A technical control used to enforce security
   C. A physical control used to enforce security
   D. A document created by senior managers that identifies the role of security in the organization and is used as a defense mechanism to protect the assets of the organization

2. What should be used to ensure that users are granted only the rights to perform actions required for their jobs?
   A. Principle of least privilege
   B. Principle of need to know
   C. Principle of limited rights
   D. Separation of duties

3. What should be used to ensure that the amount spent on mitigating a risk (such as buying insurance) is proportional to the risk?
   A. Principle of least privilege
   B. Principle of proportionality
   C. Principle of limited rights
   D. Principle of limited permissions

4. Which of the following security principles divides job responsibilities to reduce fraud?
   A. Need to know
   B. Least privilege
   C. Separation of duties
   D. Mandatory vacations

5. What can be used to ensure that unauthorized changes are not made to systems?
   A. Input validation
   B. Patch management
   C. Version control
   D. Configuration management

6. What are two types of intrusion detection systems?
   A. Intentional and unintentional
   B. Natural and man-made
   C. Host-based and network-based
   D. Technical and physical

7. A technical control prevents unauthorized personnel from having physical access to a secure area or secure system.
   A. True
   B. False

8. What allows an attacker to gain additional privileges on a system by sending unexpected code to the system?
   A. Buffer overflow
   B. MAC flood
   C. Input validation
   D. Spiders

9. What is hardening a server?
   A. Securing it from the default configuration
   B. Ensuring it cannot be powered down
   C. Locking it in a room that is hard to access
   D. Enabling necessary protocols and services

10. Which of the following steps could be taken to harden a server?
    A. Removing unnecessary services and protocols
    B. Keeping the server up to date
    C. Changing defaults
    D. Enabling local firewalls
    E. E. All of the above

11. Which government agency includes the Information Technology Laboratory and publishes SP 800-30?
    A. NIST
    B. DHS
    C. NCCIC
    D. US-CERT

12. Which of the following is a Risk Management Framework for Information Systems and Organizations: A System Life Cycle Approach for Security and Privacy?
    A. SP 800-34
    B. SP 800-35
    C. SP 800-37
    D. SP 800-84

13. Which U.S. government agency regularly publishes alerts and bulletins related to security threats?
    A. NIST
    B. FBI
    C. US-CERT
    D. MITRE Corporation

14. The CVE list is maintained by _____.

15. What is the standard used to create information security vulnerability names?
    A. CVE
    B. MITRE
    C. DISA
    D. CSI

CHAPTER 3

Understanding and Maintaining Compliance

LEGISLATION, UNFORTUNATELY is often lagging behind technology. However, there are numerous laws that provide guidance on information security. With e-commerce, cloud resources, and other technology that spans national boundaries, international laws and regulations take on more importance.

After gaining an idea of which laws and regulations apply, IT security personnel can then dig deeper to ensure their organization is in compliance. The cost of not complying can be expensive. Fines can be in the hundreds of thousands of dollars, and some offenses can result in jail time. For companies, the public shame of not complying can lead to a bad reputation, which can cost them their business.

Chapter 3 Topics

This chapter covers the following topics and concepts:

- What U.S. compliance laws exist
- What some relevant regulations related to compliance are
- What organizational policies for compliance should be considered
- What standards and guidelines for compliance exist

Chapter 3 Goals

When you complete this chapter, you will be able to:

- Define *compliance*
- Describe the purpose of the Federal Information Security Management Act (FISMA)
- Identify the purpose and scope of the Health Insurance Portability and Accountability Act (HIPAA)
- Describe the Gramm-Leach-Bliley Act (GLBA) and the Sarbanes-Oxley Act of 2002 (SOX) and their impact on IT
- Describe the purpose of the Family Educational Rights and Privacy Act (FERPA)

- Identify the purpose and scope of the Children's Internet Protection Act (CIPA)
- List federal entities that control regulations related to IT
- Describe the purpose of the Payment Card Industry Data Security Standard (PCI DSS)
- Describe the contents of SP 800-30, Guide for Conducting Risk Assessments
- Describe the purpose of the Control Objectives for Information and Related Technologies (COBIT)
- Describe the purpose of the International Organization for Standardization (ISO) and identify relevant security standards
- Identify the purpose of the Information Technology Infrastructure Library (ITIL)
- Identify the purpose of Capability Maturity Model Integration (CMMI)
- Describe the purpose of the General Data Protection Regulation (GDPR)

U.S. Compliance Laws

Many laws exist in the United States related to information technology (IT) and security. Companies affected by the laws are expected to comply with the laws, which is commonly referred to as **compliance**. These laws are important to organizations as they develop a comprehensive risk management plan to guide their operations internally and to stay compliant externally.

Many organizations have internal programs in place to ensure they remain in compliance with relevant laws and regulations. These programs commonly use internal audits, and the organizations will frequently reference organizational governance processes that are in place. The organizations can also use certification and accreditation programs. When compliance is mandated by law, external audits are often done. These external audits provide third-party verification that the requirements are being met.

An old legal saying is "ignorance is no excuse." In other words, a person can't break the law and then say "I didn't know." The same goes for laws that apply to organizations. Knowing what the relevant laws and regulations are is important for organizations.

Organizations are not expected to be experts on these laws. However, managers and executives should be aware of them. The relevant laws and regulations can be rolled into a compliance program for more detailed checks.

This section covers the following U.S. laws:

- Federal Information Security Modernization Act (FISMA), 2014
- Health Insurance Portability and Accountability Act (HIPAA), 1996
- Gramm-Leach-Bliley Act (GLBA), 1999
- Sarbanes-Oxley Act (SOX), 2002
- Family Educational Rights and Privacy Act (FERPA), 1974
  - Children's Internet Protection Act (CIPA), 2000

- California Consumer Privacy Act (CCPA)
- Computer Fraud and Abuse Act (CFAA)

Federal Information Security Modernization Act

The **Federal Information Security Modernization Act (FISMA)** of 2014 was initially passed in 2002 as the Federal Information Security Management Act. Its purpose is to ensure that federal agencies protect their data by assigning specific responsibilities to them. The 2014 update made significant changes to the original law.

First, the 2014 law authorizes the Secretary of the Department of Homeland Security (DHS) to assist the Office of Management and Budget (OMB) Director in administering the implementation of agency information and security practices for federal information systems. Second, the law changes the agency reporting requirements by modifying the scope of reportable information from primarily policies and financial information to specific information about threats, security incidents, and compliance with security requirements. Third, the update addresses cyberbreach notification requirements. Fourth, within one year of the passing of the updated law, the OMB Director is required to revise budget circular A-130 to remove inefficient reporting.

Agencies are responsible for:

- **Protecting systems and data**—Agency heads are responsible for all the systems and data in their agencies.
- **Complying with all elements of FISMA**—FISMA includes details on how to protect systems and data. Systems must be inventoried and risk assessments done to categorize systems and data. Different security controls can be used based on risk levels. Systems must go through a certification and accreditation process.
- **Integrating security in all processes**—Security must be used throughout the agency, and continuous monitoring must be done to ensure the systems stay secure.

FISMA requires annual inspections. Each year, agencies must have an independent evaluation of their program. The goal is to determine the effectiveness of the program. These evaluations are to include:

- **Testing for effectiveness**—A representative sample of policies, procedures, and practices are to be tested. The sample chosen should be realistic based on the expectations of the organization.
- **Issuing an assessment or report**—The report identifies and lists the agency's compliance with FISMA as well as compliance with other standards and guidelines.

Health Insurance Portability and Accountability Act

The **Health Insurance Portability and Accountability Act (HIPAA)** was passed in 1996. It ensures that health information data is protected. The passage of HIPAA has led to improved security of personal medical information, which was previously lax and often misused. There are three major areas that HIPAA covers in terms of compliance: administrative (ways to protect patient data and ensure that it can be accessed only by authorized parties), physical (ways to prevent physical theft and unauthorized access to systems with protected data), and technical (using technology to protect computer networks and devices from threats).

The Healthcare Information and Management Systems Society (HIMSS) Cybersecurity Survey of 2024[1] identifies many of the trends in IT security. Some of this data helps to show the impact of HIPAA. The following data was gathered from survey respondents:

- About 65% of respondents were in the health services industry.
- More than 85% of respondents had to comply with HIPAA.
- HIPAA applies more than any other law or regulation.

NOTE

A link exists between these laws and IT corporate governance in organizations. IT corporate governance comprises a system of rules, practices, and processes that are essential to minimizing IT risks in organizations. Depending on the type and location of the organization, compliance requirements differ, such as those enumerated in FISMA, HIPAA, GLBA, or GDPR. An organization must account for corporate governance as part of developing a comprehensive IT risk management plan.

If an organization handles health information, HIPAA applies, which makes the definition of health information important. HIPAA defines *health information* as any data that:

- Is created or received by:
  - Healthcare providers
  - Health plans
  - Public health authorities
  - Employers
  - Life insurers
  - Schools or universities
  - Healthcare clearinghouses
- And relates to the health of an individual, including:
  - Past, present, or future health
  - Physical health, mental health, or condition of an individual
  - Past, present, or future payments for health care

Title II of HIPAA includes a section titled Administrative Simplification. This section includes the requirements and standards of HIPAA for IT:

- **Security standards**—Every organization that handles health information must protect that information. Companies must also protect systems that handle the information, including all the health data the organization creates, receives, or sends. Specific standards are to be used for:
  - Storing data
  - Using data
  - Transmitting data
- **Privacy standards**—Data must not be shared with anyone without the express consent of the patient. A person who has gone to a doctor's office or hospital has probably signed a consent form. The form also notifies patients of practices used to keep their health information private.

---

[1] HIMSS, "2024 HIMSS Healthcare Cybersecurity Survey," 2025, https://www.himss.org/resources/himss-healthcare-cybersecurity-survey/.

- **Penalties**—Penalties can be levied if the rules aren't followed. Such penalties differ according to how culpable or neglectful the organization was:
  - **"No knowledge" mistakes**—Fines range from $100 to $50,000 per violation, with a maximum of $50,000 per year.
  - **Reasonable cause**—Penalties range from $1,000 to $50,000, with a maximum of $100,000 per year.
  - **Willful neglect but corrected**—Penalties range from $10,000 to $50,000, with a maximum of $250,000 per year.
  - **Willful neglect and not corrected since discovery**—Penalties are $50,000 per violation, with a maximum of $1.5 million per year.

NOTE

Title I of HIPAA relates to insurance portability and identifies rules for insurance plans. For example, when employees change jobs, HIPAA helps them retain insurance. Title I rules aren't related to IT compliance. Only Title II of HIPAA covers the protection of data, in particular the first of five rules, the Privacy Rule, which covers protected health information (PHI).

If an organization includes data covered by HIPAA, the organization must have a compliance plan. **FIGURE 3-1** shows the process of creating a HIPAA compliance plan:

- **Assessment**—An assessment helps to identify whether an organization is covered by HIPAA. If it is, then what data needs to be protected must be identified.
- **Risk analysis**—A risk analysis helps to identify the risks. In this phase, how the organization handles data is analyzed. For example, is data only stored electronically or is it also transferred electronically?
- **Plan creation**—After the risks have been identified, a plan is created. This plan includes methods to reduce the risk.
- **Plan implementation**—The plan is implemented.
- **Continuous monitoring**—Security in depth requires continuous monitoring. Regulations and risks should be monitored for changes, and the plan should be monitored to ensure it is still used.
- **Assessment**—Regular reviews must be conducted. These reviews ensure that the organization remains in compliance.

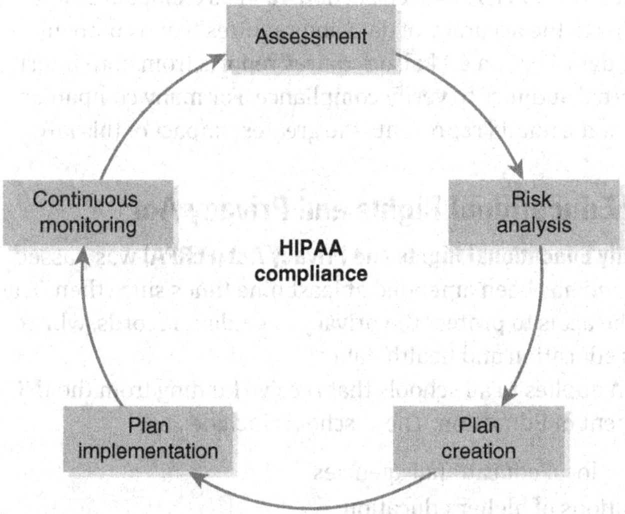

FIGURE 3-1
HIPAA compliance.

Gramm-Leach-Bliley Act

The **Gramm-Leach-Bliley Act (GLBA)**, also known as the Financial Services Modernization Act, was passed in 1999. GLBA is broad in scope. Most of it relates to how banking and insurance institutions can merge. However, two parts of GLBA are relevant to IT security and apply to financial institutions in the United States. They are:

- **Financial Privacy Rule**—This rule requires companies to notify customers about their privacy practices. Anyone who has a bank account has probably received such a notification from the bank. Anyone who has a credit card has received one from the credit card company. It explains how the bank or company collects and shares data.
- **Safeguards Rule**—Companies must have a security plan to protect customer information, which should ensure data isn't released without authorization and ensure data integrity. Companies are responsible for ensuring risk management plans are used. All employees must be trained on security issues. The Federal Trade Commission (FTC) proposed updates to the Safeguards Rule in April 2019, which are currently in review.

Sarbanes-Oxley Act

The **Sarbanes-Oxley Act (SOX)** was passed in 2002. This law applies to all companies that are publicly traded. It is designed to hold company executives and board members personally responsible for financial data. If the data is not accurate, these people can be fined and sent to jail.

The goal is to reduce fraud. Because individuals can be held liable, there is more pressure to ensure the reported data is accurate. Chief executive officers (CEOs) and chief financial officers (CFOs) must be able to:

- Verify accuracy of financial statements
- Prove the statements are accurate

Most of SOX is outside the direct scope of IT. However, Section 404 has elements that are directly related. Section 404 pertains to the accuracy of data and requires that a company use internal controls to protect the data. Section 404 also requires reports from both internal and external auditors to verify compliance. For many companies, the cost of the audits represents the greatest impact of this law.

NOTE

SOX was passed in response to several large scandals. In these scandals, executives deliberately misled the public, and investors lost billions of dollars. For example, Enron was reportedly worth over $100 billion in 2000, but it went bankrupt in 2001. Later, the failure was determined to be caused by fraud and corruption. Many senior officers and board members were directly involved.

Family Educational Rights and Privacy Act

The **Family Educational Rights and Privacy Act (FERPA)** was passed in 1974 and has been amended at least nine times since then. The goal of the act is to protect the privacy of student records, which includes education and health data.

FERPA applies to all schools that receive funding from the U.S. Department of Education. These schools include:

- State or local educational agencies
- Institutions of higher education

- Community colleges
- Schools or agencies that offer a preschool program
- All other education institutions

FERPA grants rights to parents of students under 18. The parent can inspect records and request corrections. When the student reaches 18, these rights pass to the student.

All Personally identifiable information (PII) about the student must be protected. Schools usually need permission from either the parent or the student to release PII.

There are a few exceptions to when PII can be accessed or released:

NOTE

Personally identifiable information (PII) is a common term used with information security. PII is all data that can be used to identify a person. Such data can be a name, a Social Security number, biometric data, or other data used to identify a person. Several laws and regulations specify that PII must be protected. PII in information security is synonymous with PHI in HIPAA.

- Some school officials may view records.
- Data can be transferred to a new school if the student is transferred.
- Data can be transferred when some types of financial aid are used.
- Accrediting organizations can access data.
- Data can be accessed when required by a court.
- Data can be accessed for health and safety emergencies.

Children's Internet Protection Act

The **Children's Internet Protection Act (CIPA)** was passed in 2000 and is designed to limit access to offensive content from school and library computers. All schools and libraries that receive funding from the E-Rate program are covered under CIPA. More information on the E-Rate program is available at https://www.fcc.gov/consumers/guides/universal-service-program-schools-and-libraries-e-rate.

CIPA requires that schools and libraries:

- Block or filter Internet access to pictures that are:
  - Obscene
  - Child pornography
  - Harmful to minors (if the computers are accessed by minors)
- Adopt and enforce a policy to monitor online activity of minors
- Implement an Internet safety policy addressing:
  - Access by minors to inappropriate content
  - Safety and security of minors when using email and chat rooms
  - Unauthorized access
  - Unlawful activities by minors online
  - Unauthorized use of minors' personal information
  - Measures restricting minors' access to harmful materials

NOTE

The E-Rate program is under the Federal Communications Commission. It provides discounts to most schools and libraries for internet access, ranging from 20 to 90% of the actual costs.

Some of these terms are difficult to define, such as what is obscene or harmful to minors. CIPA includes a definitions section that identifies other specific sections of U.S. code where some of these terms are defined.

Children's Online Privacy Protection Act

The **Children's Online Privacy Protection Act (COPPA)**, which is managed by the FTC, was passed in 1998 and took effect in 2000. The act was designed to protect the privacy of children under 13.

Using Proxy Servers to Limit Content

Most organizations use proxy servers as gateways to access the internet. An organization configures its computers to use the proxy server. The proxy receives the request, retrieves the webpage from the internet, and then serves the page to the client.

Proxy servers improve the level of service to clients. They can also be used to filter content. If an organization doesn't want employees to access certain content, the proxy server can block the requests to specific websites.

Third-party companies maintain lists of websites based on their content. They then sell subscriptions to these lists to organizations that want them. For example, a company may want to restrict access to gambling sites from a work computer. The gambling list can be purchased and installed on the proxy server. The company can then block attempts to access these sites.

Proxy servers also have the ability to log attempts by users to access unapproved sites. When a site is blocked, the user will often see a message such as "Warning. Access to this site is restricted by the acceptable use policy. Your activity is being monitored."

Similarly, schools and libraries can use proxy servers to filter content. The technology is widely available.

The act specifies the following:

- Sites must require parental consent for the collection or use of all personal information of young website users.
- The contents of a privacy policy, including the requirement that the policy itself be posted everywhere data is collected.
- When and how to seek verifiable consent from a parent or guardian.
- The responsibility of a website operator regarding children's privacy and safety online, including restrictions on the types and methods of marketing that targets those under 13.

Although COPPA does not define the process to gain parental consent, the FTC shares guidelines to help website operators. Some of these requirements are:

- Consent forms that can be easily downloaded and mailed or faxed to the operator must be clearly displayed.
- A parent must use a credit card to authenticate age and identity.
- A parent must call a toll-free phone number.
- Accepting an email from a parent that includes a digital signature.

CIPA was challenged on freedom of speech grounds. The U.S. Supreme Court upheld the law in June 2003. All libraries were given until early 2004 to comply. At this point, all schools and libraries accepting E-Rate funds are expected to be compliant with CIPA.

Computer Fraud and Abuse Act

The Computer Fraud and Abuse Act (CFAA) is a U.S. federal law enacted in 1986 to address and combat various forms of cybercrime and unauthorized access to computer systems. It has been amended multiple times to adapt to the changing landscape of technology and cyberthreats. Originally part of the Comprehensive Crime Control Act of 1984, it was officially enacted in 1986. There are key provisions that are often cited in computer crime cases:

Unauthorized Access (§1030(a)(2))

Criminalizes accessing a computer without authorization or exceeding authorized access to obtain information from:

- Financial records
- Government records
- Any protected computer

Fraud and Related Activity (§1030(a)(4))

- Prohibits accessing a protected computer with intent to defraud and obtaining value through such access.

Damage to Computer Systems (§1030(a)(5))

- Covers the transmission of code or commands (e.g., viruses, malware) that cause damage to protected computers.

Trafficking in Passwords (§1030(a)(6))

- Criminalizes the trafficking of passwords or similar information when it affects interstate or foreign commerce or U.S. government computers.

Extortion Involving Computers (§1030(a)(7))

- Outlaws threats to damage a protected computer to extort money or other benefits.

California Consumer Privacy Act

The California Consumer Privacy Act of 2018 is a landmark state privacy law that significantly enhances privacy rights and consumer protection for residents of California. It represents one of the most comprehensive privacy regulations in the United States and has influenced similar legislation across the country. This law applies to businesses that collect personal information from California residents and meet certain thresholds. This law was expanded by the California Privacy Rights Act (CPRA), which was passed in November 2020 and took effect on January 1, 2023.

Regulations Related to Compliance

In addition to laws, several regulations have created different U.S. entities. Most of these entities operate at the federal level.

Some of these entities have a direct impact on IT initiatives for most companies. Others are related only to companies engaged in specific activities. Organizations covered in this section are:

- Securities and Exchange Commission (SEC)
- Federal Deposit Insurance Corporation (FDIC)
- Department of Homeland Security (DHS)
- Federal Trade Commission (FTC)
- State Attorneys General (AG)
- U.S. Attorney General (U.S. AG)

Securities and Exchange Commission

The **Securities and Exchange Commission (SEC)** is a federal agency. It is charged with regulating the securities industry, which includes all sales or trades of securities. Securities include stocks, bonds, and options.

If a company is involved with the sale or trade of securities, then IT security personnel should be aware of these laws:

- Securities Act of 1933
- Securities Exchange Act of 1934
- Trust Indenture Act of 1939
- Investment Company Act of 1940
- Investment Advisors Act of 1940
- Sarbanes-Oxley Act of 2002
- Dodd-Frank Act of 2010

Many of these laws also apply if the company is a *publicly traded* company, which is any company that has stock that outside investors can buy and sell.

Federal Deposit Insurance Corporation

The **Federal Deposit Insurance Corporation (FDIC)** is a federal agency created in 1933. The primary goal is to promote confidence in U.S. banks. The FDIC was created as a direct result of the bank failures that occurred in the 1920s and early 1930s, which led to the Great Depression.

Funds in all banks insured by the FDIC are guaranteed, meaning depositors will not lose their money, even if the bank goes bankrupt. The purpose is to prevent a run on a bank, which is when many depositors rush to withdraw their money.

Currently, funds for individual depositors are insured up to $250,000. The National Credit Union Administration (NCUA) covers credit unions, and it also insures deposits up to $250,000.

Department of Homeland Security

The Department of Homeland Security (DHS) is a federal agency. It is responsible for protecting the United States from terrorist attacks and is charged with responding to natural disasters.

The DHS was formed in 2002 as a direct response to the terrorist attacks of September 11, 2001. It includes several divisions that are related to IT, which include:

- Office of Cybersecurity and Communications
- National Cybersecurity and Communications Integration Center (NCCIC)
- United States Computer Emergency Readiness Team (US-CERT)

Federal Trade Commission

The **Federal Trade Commission (FTC)** is a federal agency. It was created in 1914, with the current primary goal being to promote consumer protection, but that goal was different in the past.

When the FTC was first created, its primary goal was to prevent unfair methods of competition. At that time, there were many special trusts in existence. These trusts were often engaged in anticompetitive practices, such as:

- Business monopolies
- Restraining trade
- Fixing prices

The creation of the FTC was one of many steps taken to "bust the trusts." Over the years, Congress has passed several consumer protection laws that the FTC enforces. These laws grant the FTC authority to address consumer protection and unfair competition issues.

At this point, the original trusts are gone. However, the FTC is still in existence, and the focus has shifted to promote consumer protection.

FIGURE 3-2 shows the hierarchy of the FTC. As indicated in the figure, the FTC has three primary bureaus. These bureaus perform the following actions:

- **Bureau of Consumer Protection**—This bureau tries to protect consumers against unfair, deceptive, or fraudulent practices. The bureau enforces many consumer protection laws and trade regulation rules.
- **Bureau of Competition**—This bureau is the FTC's antitrust arm. It seeks to prevent anticompetitive actions. These actions include anticompetitive mergers and anticompetitive business practices.
- **Bureau of Economics**—This bureau helps the FTC evaluate the economic impact of FTC actions. It provides economic analysis for different investigations and evaluates the economic impact of government regulations.

The FTC also has several supporting offices that perform additional work in support of the FTC.

FIGURE 3-2

The Federal Trade Commission.

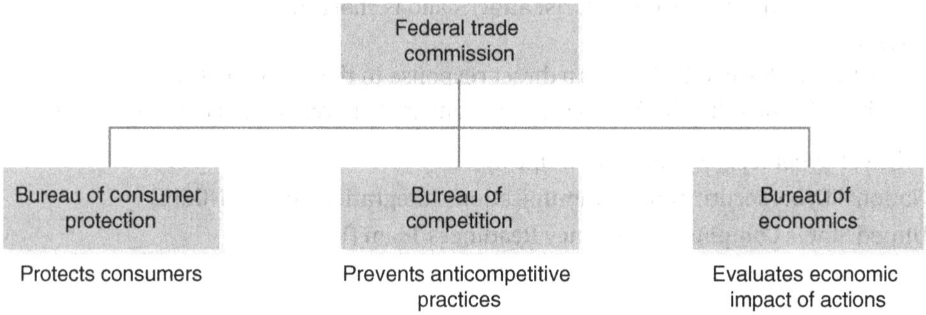

State Attorneys General

Every state has a state **attorney general (AG)**. The AG is the primary legal advisor for the state, and, for many states, the AG is also the chief law enforcement officer. Although all states have an AG, the specific responsibilities can vary from state to state. For example, in some states, the AG is tasked with specific IT issues, such as preventing identity theft.

Following are some of the responsibilities that can be assigned to an AG:

- Representing the state in all legal matters
- Defending the laws of the state
- Providing legal advice to all state entities
- Performing criminal investigations and prosecuting crimes as the chief law enforcement officer
- Reviewing all deeds, leases, and contracts for the state
- Protecting consumers by fighting identity theft and online scams
- Proposing legislation

Some AGs are elected, and others are appointed by the governor or other state officials. A state AG is a person who is granted the authority to represent the state in all legal matters, which is similar to how a general power of attorney is used. A state AG can be thought of as a person granted a general power of attorney for the state.

U.S. Attorney General

The **U.S. Attorney General (U.S. AG)** is the head of the United States Department of Justice (DOJ). The president of the United States nominates the U.S. AG.

Specific responsibilities of the DOJ include:

- Enforcing the law
- Defending the interests of the United States according to the law
- Ensuring public safety against threats
- Providing federal leadership in preventing and controlling crime

- Seeking just punishment for those guilty of unlawful behavior
- Ensuring fair and impartial justice for all Americans

Many actions that the U.S. AG takes fall into the arena of IT. For example, the U.S. AG announced an intellectual property task force in February 2010. Companies, organizations, and governments often transfer data using intellectual property systems and networks. The goal is to address intellectual property crimes on the national and international level. Many government leaders agree that the theft of intellectual property does significant harm to the economy.

Power of Attorney

A power of attorney can be given to any individual to grant certain rights. For example, a person can give a friend a power of attorney to sell their car in their absence. The friend can then legally act for that person in the sale of the car.

A general power of attorney can also be granted. A general power of attorney allows one person to act for another for legal issues and sometimes is used if someone becomes mentally incapacitated.

FYI

Intellectual property (IP) is any intangible property that is the result of creativity and is produced by a person or company. Specific rights are granted to the owner of the creation. IP includes music, programs, books, movies, trademarks, trade secrets, and more. The creator and owner should be able to reap the profits from the creation. However, when IP rights are ignored, others benefit at the expense of the creator.

Organizational Policies for Compliance

Organizations often implement policies to ensure they remain compliant with laws and regulations. These policies can contain multiple elements. However, in the context of this chapter, the most important element is **fiduciary responsibility**.

Fiduciary refers to a relationship of trust. A fiduciary could be a person who is trusted to hold someone else's assets. The trusted person has the responsibility to act in the other person's best interests. They should avoid conflicts of interest.

Once someone trusts a fiduciary, a fiduciary responsibility exists. Notice that this relationship requires two separate entities. The fiduciary responsibility can take many forms. Examples of fiduciary responsibilities are:

- **An attorney and a client**—The client trusts the attorney to act in the best interests of the client.
- **A CEO and a board of directors**—The board trusts the CEO to act in the best interests of the company.
- **Shareholders and a board of directors**—Shareholders trust the board to act in the best interests of the shareholders.

A great deal of trust is granted in a fiduciary responsibility. Because of this, the fiduciary is expected to take extra steps to uphold this trust. Two steps that can be taken are **due diligence** and **due care**:

- **Due diligence**—The fiduciary takes a reasonable amount of time and effort to identify risks. It investigates risks so they are understood. Failure to exercise due diligence can be considered negligence.
- **Due care**—If a risk is known, the fiduciary needs to take reasonable steps to protect against the risks. Failure to take due care to protect assets can also be considered negligence.

Exercising due care and due diligence doesn't mean that all risks should be eliminated. Residual risk is the amount of risk that remains after controls have been applied, which is also referred to as acceptable risk.

A fiduciary is expected to understand and weigh the risks. By exercising due care and due diligence, the fiduciary is less likely to be accused of acting recklessly or being negligent.

Other elements of an organizational policy could include:

- **Mandatory vacations**—Employees may be required to take an annual vacation of at least five consecutive days. The purpose of a **mandatory vacation** is to reduce fraud or embezzlement. If an employee is required to be out of the office, someone else must perform the duties, which increases the likelihood of discovering the illegal activities.
- **Job rotation**—Employees may be rotated through different jobs. When an employee is transferred into a new job, past transactions are often reviewed and examined. This oversight can uncover suspicious activity. **Job rotation** helps prevent or reduce fraudulent activity. It is also done for cross-training to expand the skills of employees.
- **Separation of duties**—Separation of duties ensures that no single person controls an entire process. It helps prevent fraud, theft, errors, and conflicts of interest.
- **Acceptable use**—An **acceptable use policy (AUP)** defines acceptable use for IT systems and data. Companies often inform employees of acceptable use when they are hired. Some companies use banners and login screens to remind personnel of the policy.

Standards and Guidelines for Compliance

Several standards and guidelines exist that can be used to assess and improve security. Most of these standards are optional. However, some are mandatory for certain sectors. For example, the PCI DSS is required for merchants using specific credit cards.

The standards and guidelines covered in this section include:

- Payment Card Industry Data Security Standard (PCI DSS)
- National Institute of Standards and Technology (NIST)
- Generally Accepted Information Security Principles (GAISP)
- Control Objectives for Information and Related Technologies (COBIT)
- International Organization for Standardization (ISO)
- International Electrotechnical Commission (IEC)
- Information Technology Infrastructure Library (ITIL)

- Capability Maturity Model Integration (CMMI)
- General Data Protection Regulation (GDPR)
- Department of Defense Information Assurance Certification and Accreditation Process (DIACAP)

Payment Card Industry Data Security Standard

The **Payment Card Industry Data Security Standard (PCI DSS)** is an international security standard. The purpose is to enhance security of credit card data. It was created by the PCI Security Standards Council with input from several major credit card companies. These companies include:

- American Express
- Discover Financial Services
- JCB International
- MasterCard Worldwide
- Visa Inc. International

The goal is to thwart theft of credit card data. Fraud can occur if a thief gets certain data. The key pieces of data are:

- Name
- Credit card number
- Expiration date
- Security code

Theft becomes easy if a thief has all of this information.

This data is often transmitted to and from the merchant. It can travel wirelessly from point-of-sale machines and from the merchant's computer to an approval authority. It can be intercepted any time it's transmitted and easily read if it is not encrypted.

For example, data from as many as 100 million credit cards was intercepted from a large retail chain between July 2005 and December 2006. Losses on Visa cards alone were close to $83 million. Millions of customers sued and the banks that issued the cards sued the retailer. Other examples include the Equifax data breach of 2017, which affected about 40% of Americans and exposed the personal information of 147 million people. A 2019 data breach involving Capital One exposed the records of almost 106 million people. All these problems could have been prevented with basic security.

The PCI DSS is built around six principles. Each of these principles has between one to three requirements. The principles and requirements are:

- **Build and Maintain a Secure Network**
  - Requirement 1: Install and maintain a firewall.
  - Requirement 2: Do not use defaults, such as default passwords.
- **Protect Cardholder Data**
  - Requirement 3: Protect stored data.
  - Requirement 4: Encrypt transmissions.

- **Maintain a Vulnerability Management Program**
  - Requirement 5: Use and update antivirus software.
  - Requirement 6: Develop and maintain secure systems.
- **Implement Strong Access Control Measures**
  - Requirement 7: Restrict access to data.
  - Requirement 8: Use unique logins for each user. Don't share usernames and passwords.
  - Requirement 9: Restrict physical access.
- **Regularly Monitor and Test Networks**
  - Requirement 10: Track and monitor all access to systems and data.
  - Requirement 11: Regularly test security.
- **Maintain an Information Security Policy**
  - Requirement 12: Maintain a security policy.

Merchants using credit cards are required to comply with PCI DSS. Compliance is monitored by the acquirer, which is the company that authenticates the transactions.

Compliance with PCI DSS is a three-step continuous process. This process is shown in **FIGURE 3-3:**

- **Assessing**—The merchant inventories IT assets and processes used for credit card data. It identifies existing cardholder data and then analyzes data and processes for vulnerabilities.
- **Remediating**—The merchant corrects vulnerabilities. It stores data only when necessary.
- **Reporting**—The merchant submits compliance reports to the acquiring banks.
- This process is repeated at different times.

Although PCI DSS compliance helps prevent losses, it isn't foolproof. For example, attackers stole credit card data on 40 million customers in a major attack against Target Corporation in late 2013. Attackers also stole personal information on up to 70 million more customers in the same attack. In 2019, personal data from over 106 million customers was stolen from Capital One. Target was certified as PCI DSS compliant during the attack. The same attack compromised 1.1 million cards at Neiman Marcus. Michael Kingston, CIO at Neiman Marcus, stated that the company's security measures exceeded PCI standards.

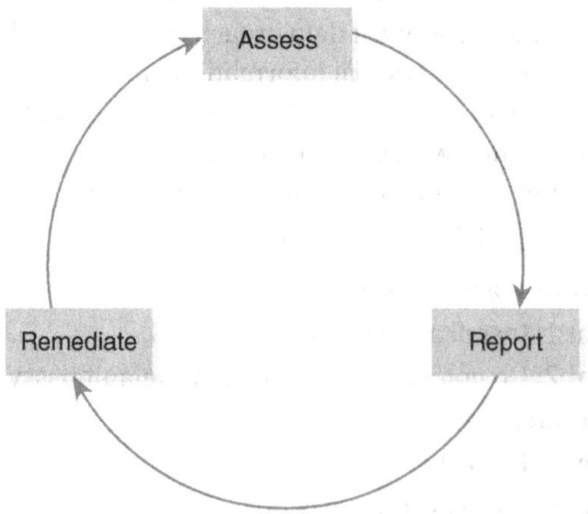

FIGURE 3-3
PCI compliance process.

A PCI DSS investigation might reveal a problem missed by the PCI DSS assessments that certified these companies. In the past, PCI compliance has been retroactively revoked, which allows the certifying agencies to state that "no PCI compliant organization has ever been breached." However, many security experts suggest that it is time to update PCI DSS.

National Institute of Standards and Technology

The National Institute of Standards and Technology (NIST) is a division of the U.S. Department of Commerce. The mission of NIST is to promote U.S. innovation and competitiveness.

NIST hosts the Information Technology Laboratory (ITL). The ITL develops standards and guidelines related to IT. They are published as special publications whose titles have a prefix of SP. SP 800-30, Guide for Conducting Risk Assessments, is valuable when studying risk management.

SP 800-30 includes three chapters:

- **Introduction**—This short chapter identifies the objectives and gives some references.
- **The Fundamentals**—This chapter discusses the importance of risk assessment. It includes definitions for many key risk terms. It also presents models used to assess risk.
- **The Process**—This chapter describes the process of risk assessments. It includes information on how to prepare for and conduct the assessment. It also provides detailed information on how to perform six key risk assessment tasks. The tasks are:
    - Identifying relevant threat sources
    - Identifying potential threat events related to the threat sources
    - Identifying vulnerabilities threats can exploit
    - Determining the likelihood threats will occur and can succeed
    - Determining the adverse impact if a threat exploits a vulnerability
    - Determining the risk by combining the likelihood and impact

Generally Accepted Information Security Principles

The Generally Accepted Information Security Principles (GAISP) is an older standard that evolved from the Generally Accepted System Security Principles (GASSP), which was created in 1992. GAISP was an update to GASSP.

GAISP version 3 was released in August 2003 and was adopted by the Information Systems Security Association (ISSA). However, GAISP is no longer mentioned on the ISSA website. Additionally, the gaisp.org website is no longer maintained.

GAISP includes two major sections:

- **Pervasive principles**—These principles provide general guidance. The goal is to establish and maintain information security.
- **Broad functional principles**—These principles are derived from the pervasive principles. They represent broad goals of information security (IS).

Control Objectives for Information and Related Technologies

Control Objectives for Information and Related Technologies (COBIT) is a set of practices that apply to IT management and governance. **Information technology governance (ITG)** refers to the processes that ensure IT resources are enabling the organization to achieve its goals. Further, ITG processes help ensure the effectiveness and efficiency of these resources. COBIT helps link business goals with IT goals.

The IT Governance Institute (ITGI) worked with ISACA to develop COBIT. ISACA was previously known as the Information Systems Audit and Control Association. However, it now uses only the acronym. Many of the free COBIT resources can be accessed from ISACA's website at https://www.isaca.org/resources/cobit.

ISACA recently published COBIT 2019. COBIT 2019 is a leading framework for the governance and management of IT resources throughout an enterprise.

> The overall goal of COBIT 2019 is to get the most value from IT assets. Organizations do this by maintaining a balance between benefits, risk, and asset use. COBIT 2019 replaced COBIT 5 with an expanded definition of information and technology governance, including updating COBIT principles. The 2019 version also introduced the COBIT core model and 40 governance and management objectives. Other updates include new processes for data, projects, and compliance; updates to cybersecurity and privacy; and updates to regulations, guidelines, and best practices that organizations could employ in their governance activities. As of 2025, COBIT 2019 is still the current version. NOTE: Even though GASSP and GAISP are no longer active, references to them may still be seen in documentation.

The five principles are:

1. **Meeting stakeholder needs**—A stakeholder is an entity affected by activity. In this case, stakeholders are typically decision makers who benefit from IT resources.
2. **Covering the enterprise end to end**—All areas of responsibility are included.
3. **Applying a single integrated framework**—COBIT 2019 uses an expanded and robust integrated framework. The integrated framework avoids conflicts when using multiple frameworks.
4. **Enabling a holistic approach**—A holistic approach ensures that the organization is examined as a whole.
5. **Separating governance from management**—Governance includes evaluating, directing, and monitoring. Management includes planning, building, running, and monitoring.

FIGURE 3-4 shows the seven COBIT components. The following bullets describe them:

1. **Principles, policies, and frameworks**—These components translate desired behavior into practical guidance.
2. **Processes**—Processes are the practices and activities performed within the organization. They help an organization reach its IT-related goals.

FIGURE 3-4

The seven COBIT components.

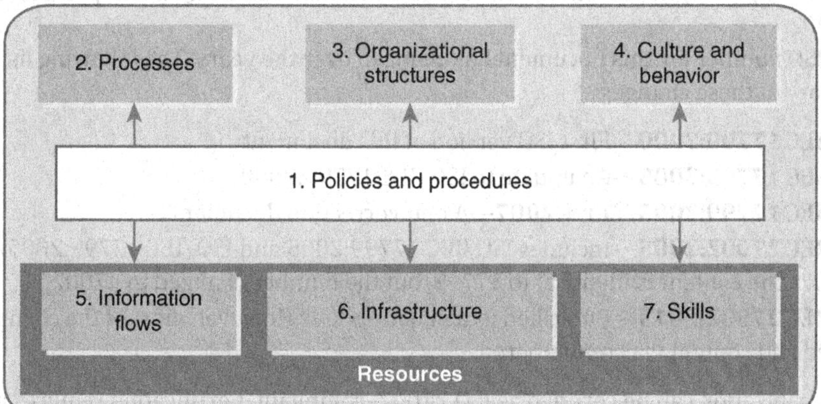

3. **Organizational structures**—Organizational structures refer to the entities making key decisions. Many organizations define these entities in organization charts.
4. **Culture, ethics, and behavior**—The success of individuals within the organization and the entire organization itself depends on these factors.
5. **Information**—Organizations rely on accurate information, which is true for both operations and governance.
6. **Services, infrastructure, and applications**—Organizations rely on the IT processing and services provided by these elements.
7. **People, skills, and competencies**—Successful completion of activities is dependent on these components.

International Organization for Standardization

The **International Organization for Standardization (ISO)** develops and publishes standards. Its members are from 164 countries, and its main office is in Geneva, Switzerland.

ISO works with the International Electrotechnical Commission (IEC). Many of the standards are published as ISO/IEC standards; however, commonly, the standards are identified as only ISO. For example, the ISO/IEC 27002 standard is frequently shortened to ISO 27002.

ISO has published many standards that are relevant to risk and IT. Three important standards are:

1. ISO 27002 Security Techniques
2. ISO 31000 Principles and Guidelines on Implementation
3. ISO 73 Risk Management—Vocabulary

Documentation for these standards can be purchased from the ISO website at http://www.iso.org.

ISO 27002 Information Technology Security Techniques

ISO 27002 is a set of guidelines and principles that are used for security management. The current version is ISO 27002:2013. This version was derived from the British Standard (BS) 7799, which was a well-respected standard and important precursor to ISO 27002.

The ISO number for this document has changed over the years. The following list shows the history of these changes:

- **ISO/IEC 17799:2000**—First ISO version of this document
- **ISO/IEC 17799:2005**—An update to ISO/IEC 17799:2000
- **ISO/IEC 17799:2005/Cor 1:2007**—A one-correction document
- **ISO/IEC 27002:2005**—Includes ISO/IEC 17799:2005 and ISO/IEC 17799:2005/Cor 1:2007. The content is identical to 17799, but the number changed to 27002.
- **ISO/IEC 27002:2013**—Published as a major update. However, most of the changes just moved and content was renumbered.

An organization can be certified as ISO 27002–compliant. Certification requires a two-step process. First, the organization must implement certain best practices, and, second, an outside source must evaluate the practices.

These best practices are related to:

- Security policy
- Organization of information security
- Asset management
- Human resources security
- Physical and environmental security
- Access control
- Incident management
- Business continuity
- Compliance

ISO 31000 Risk Management Principles and Guidelines

ISO 31000:2009 provides generic guidance on risk management. In other words, it applies to other than IT. An organization can use the principles and guidelines throughout its life and apply them to all types of risk.

No certification process exists for ISO 31000. For comparison, an organization can become ISO 27002–certified but not ISO 31000–certified.

Two supplementary documents associated with ISO 31000 are:

- ISO 73 Risk Management—Vocabulary
- IEC 31010 Risk Management—Risk Assessment Techniques

ISO 73 Risk Management—Vocabulary ISO 73:2009 is a list of terms that are related to risk management. The goal of this list is to provide common definitions for terms used in risk management.

Definitions can be used by:

- Anyone managing risks
- Anyone involved in ISO and IEC activities
- Developers of other risk management standards and guides

> **NOTE**
>
> The ISO 73:2009 standard replaced the ISO/IEC 73:2002 standard.

ISO 73 refers to ISO 31000:2009 for principles and guidelines on risk management. ISO 73:2009 and ISO 31000:2009 were released at the same time.

IEC 31010 Risk Management—Risk Assessment Techniques This generic risk management standard supports ISO 31000 and also guides the selection and application of techniques considered systematic for the assessment of risks.

International Electrotechnical Commission

The **International Electrotechnical Commission (IEC)** is an international standards organization. It prepares and publishes standards for electrical, electronic, and related technologies. The overall objectives of the IEC are to:

- Meet the requirements of the global market
- Ensure maximum use of its standards
- Assess and improve products and services covered by its standards
- Aid in interoperability of systems
- Increase the efficiency of processes
- Aid in improvement of human health and safety
- Aid in protection of the environment

The IEC published IEC 31010 Risk Management—Risk Assessment Techniques, which is a supporting standard for ISO 31000.

Information Technology Infrastructure Library

The **Information Technology Infrastructure Library (ITIL)** is a group of five books developed by the United Kingdom's Office of Government Commerce (OGC). ITIL has been around since the 1980s and has improved and matured since then. The OGC released ITIL 2011 in July 2011. It replaces ITIL 2007, which was previously called ITIL v3. The differences between ITIL 2007 and ITIL 2011 are minor. Instead, the books have been updated for clarity.

The UK recognized that some companies that were using IT were succeeding and others using similar technologies were failing. One of the goals of ITIL was to document the differences. Early versions of ITIL identified best practices, which were proven activities or processes that were successful in many organizations.

> **NOTE**
>
> One of the drawbacks to ITIL is the affordability of the books. The five ITIL books together have a retail cost of $300 or more.

ITIL later renamed *best practice* to *good practice*. A good practice is a proven, generally accepted practice. It isn't required in every organization. However, good practices are implemented whenever possible. ITIL recommends the use of several frameworks as good practices. Two of the frameworks recommended by ITIL are:

- Control Objectives for Information and Related Technologies (COBIT), mentioned earlier in this section.
- Capability Maturity Model Integration (CMMI), mentioned later in this section.

The five books of the ITIL focus on its life cycle. They are:

- **ITIL Service Strategy**—This book helps an organization identify the services it should provide.
- **ITIL Service Design**—This book details how identified services can be implemented.
- **ITIL Service Transition**—This book focuses on introducing the services and also includes modifying or changing services. Most companies have learned the hard way that, if changes aren't managed, they can take systems down. Change management has become important for many companies.
- **ITIL Service Operation**—This book focuses on day-to-day operations.
- **ITIL Continual Service Improvement**—This book focuses on methodologies used to improve the services.

FYI

ITIL is centered on services. A service is a means of delivering value to customers, to give customers what they want. Having the service doesn't require the customer to take ownership of the costs and risks of service delivery. For example, email is a service, and most customers want to be able to send and receive emails. However, most customers don't want to own and manage the email servers. In this context, email can be provided to employees from the IT department. The employees are the customers, and the IT department is the service provider.

FIGURE 3-5 shows the relationships among the five phases of the ITIL life cycle. Any service implemented and managed within an IT organization will go through several phases, and each phase has its own concerns and requirements.

For an example of email as a provided service, a company was moving from outsourced email to an internal email server. The company could use the ITIL life cycle for each phase of the implementation:

- **Service Strategy phase**—Services are evaluated to determine whether they have value to the organization. Email could provide value with improved sales and improved productivity due to better communication. If the determination is made that internal email will provide value, the process continues to the next phase.
- **Service Design phase**—IT designs services for use within the organization. In this phase, IT would design the company's email solution. For example, the company's IT network

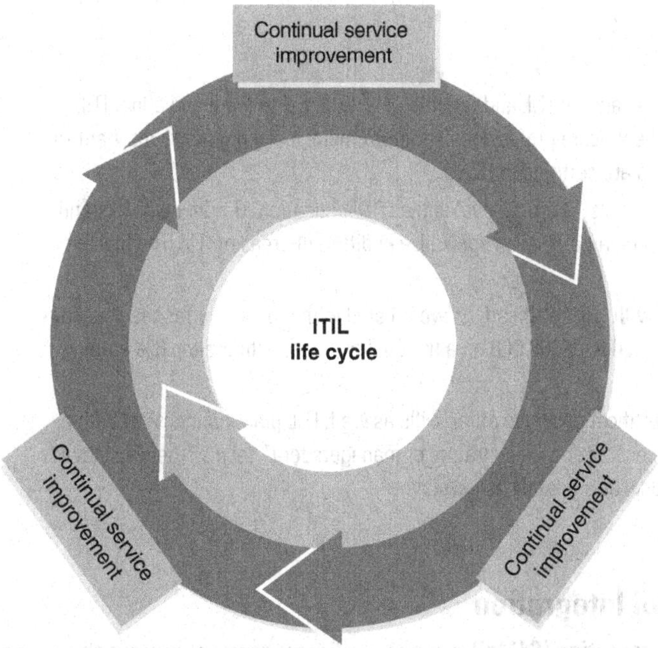

FIGURE 3-5
ITIL life cycle.

may be a Microsoft Windows domain, so IT would design a Microsoft Exchange solution. How many servers to add and any changes needed in the network to support the servers would be identified.

- **Service Transition phase**—This phase includes adding, modifying, and removing obsolete services. A primary goal of this phase is to ensure the transition does not cause an outage. Adding a Microsoft Exchange email solution, for example, would include several elements. The Active Directory schema would need to be modified, and global catalog servers might need to be added. Microsoft Exchange servers would need to be built and applications installed on users' computers. Everyone from end users to technicians maintaining the new servers would need to be trained.
- **Service Operation phase**—Daily operations and support of any service are handled at this stage. For email, these services can include regular maintenance and handling incidents that impact the service. They would also include performing backups and test restores. The goal here is to ensure that the end users have access to their email when they expect to have it.
- **Continual Service Improvement phase**—This phase focuses on measuring and monitoring services and processes. The goal is to determine areas where services can be improved, which can include regular monitoring and performance tuning of the email servers. Analysis can be used to identify problem areas before they become actual problems and provide insight into areas that can be improved.

ITIL resources can be accessed at https://www.itlibrary.org.

ITIL Certifications

More and more organizations are recognizing the value of ITIL and requiring IT personnel to learn and adopt ITIL practices. Just as people would want certified healthcare professionals to treat them, many organizations want to ensure that a certain percentage of IT employees are certified in ITIL.

ITIL certifications validate knowledge at various levels. The first level is the ITIL Foundation. IT administrators and managers often pursue this knowledge. From there, a person can specialize in different areas of ITIL. The highest level is ITIL Master Qualification.

ZipRecruiter did a salary survey in 2019. Those with ITIL certifications were listed in the top salary ranges. Individuals with the basic ITIL Foundation certificate earned over $88,000 on a national average, with the top 6% earning between $146,000 and $158,000 a year.

It should be noted that most people with ITIL certifications have other skills as well. ITIL practitioners start with a solid foundation in IT, which may lead them to become IT administrators or managers for IT teams. The ITIL knowledge helps them ensure that the IT network works as smoothly as possible.

Capability Maturity Model Integration

The **Capability Maturity Model Integration (CMMI)** is a process improvement approach to management. It uses different levels to determine the maturity of a process.

CMMI can be used in three primary areas of interest:

- **Product and service development**—CMMI is often used with software development to help ensure that the final product meets the original goals and the product is completed within budget and time constraints.
- **Service establishment, management, and delivery**—CMMI can be used to measure the effectiveness of services, one of which is security. Security helps ensure confidentiality, integrity, and availability of data and systems.
- **Product and service acquisition**—This area of CMMI can be used to ensure that what is needed is consistently bought and what is paid for is received.

FIGURE 3-6 shows the six levels of the CMMI, which are also referred to as CMMI characteristics. These levels can be used to determine the effectiveness of security within an organization. The following list identifies the levels and how they can be used to evaluate security. Although Level 0 is listed here, sometimes, it is omitted:

- **Level 0: Nonexistent**—Security controls are not in place. There is no recognition of a need for security.
- **Level 1: Initial**—Sometimes, this level is referred to as ad hoc, or as needed. Risks are considered after a threat exploits a vulnerability.
- **Level 2: Managed**—The organization recognizes risks and the need for security. However, it performs controls out of intuition, rather than from detailed plans. Responses are reactive.

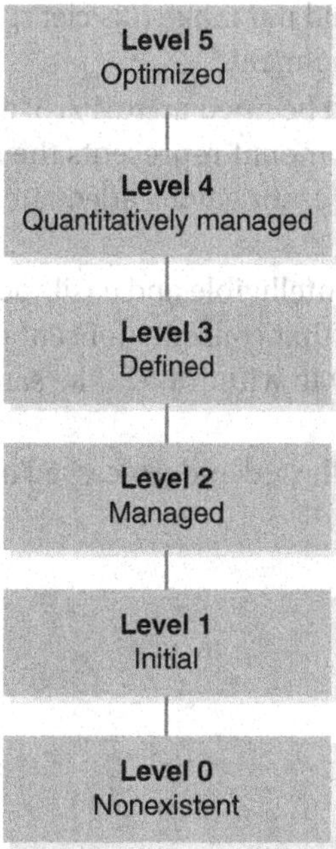

FIGURE 3-6
CMMI characteristics.

- **Level 3: Defined**—The organization has security policies in place. It has some security awareness, and action is proactive.
- **Level 4: Quantitatively Managed**—The organization measures and controls security processes. It has formal policies and standards in place and performs regular risk and vulnerability assessments.
- **Level 5: Optimized**—The organization has formal security processes in place throughout. It monitors security on a continuous basis and focuses on process improvement. This level shows the highest degree of maturity.

General Data Protection Regulation

The **General Data Protection Regulation (GDPR)** is part of European Union (EU) law. The regulation replaced the Data Protection Directive 95/46/ec in 2018 as the primary law regulating how companies protect the personal data of EU citizens. It was designed as a legal framework that sets guidelines to collect and process the personal information of individuals who live in the EU and the European Economic Area (EEA). The regulation applies to all businesses that deal with the personal data of individuals living in the EU or EEA, no matter where the companies are located. All companies, including those that were previously compliant, must comply with the 2018 GDPR directive or otherwise face stiff penalties and fines. Listed below are key changes under the GDPR and how they differ from the previous regulation:

- **Increased territorial scope (extraterritorial applicability)**—GDPR applies to all companies that process personal data of individuals living in the EU or EEA, no matter where the companies are located. The previous directive did not make this clear; instead, it referred to data processing "in context of an establishment."

- **Penalties**—Companies in breach of the GDPR could be fined up to 4% of annual global turnover or $22 million, whichever is greater. This amount represents the maximum amount that a company can be liable for, for example, not having adequate customer consent to process data or violating privacy principles.
- **Consent**—Companies must provide consent in an intelligible and easily accessible form, stating the purpose for data processing attached to that consent. Consent must be clear and distinguishable from other matters and be easy to withdraw in the same way it was given.
- **Data subject rights**—Individuals whose data is collected and processed have a number of rights governed by the following principles:
  - Breach notification
  - Right to access
  - Right to be forgotten
  - Data portability
  - Privacy by design
  - Data protection officers

Department of Defense Information Assurance Certification and Accreditation Process

The **Department of Defense Information Assurance Certification and Accreditation Process (DIACAP)** is a risk management process that applies to IT systems used by the U.S. Department of Defense (DoD). It is fully documented in DoD instruction 8510.1.

DIACAP details specific phases that IT systems must go through. The core goal is to ensure that systems are in compliance with requirements. These phases are:

- **Phase 1: Initiate and Plan**—Register the system with DIACAP. Assign information assurance (IA) controls. Create a DIACAP team. Develop a DIACAP strategy. Begin the IA plan.
- **Phase 2: Implement and Validate**—Implement the IA plan. Update the IA plan if needed. Perform validation activities to verify compliance of the system. Document validation results.
- **Phase 3: Make Certification and Accreditation Decisions**—Analyze residual risk. Review documentation to verify certification. A decision is then made whether to accredit the system. Once the system has been accredited, it receives an authorization to operate (ATO).
- **Phase 4: Maintain ATO/Review**—Maintain the system. The goal is to ensure it stays in compliance with the requirements of the ATO. Periodically review the system for compliance.
- **Phase 5: Decommission**—Decommission the system. Dispose of DIACAP data.

NOTE

DIACAP replaced DITSCAP in 2007. DITSCAP was an acronym for DoD Information Technology Security Certification and Accreditation Process.

(ISC)[2] offers a civilian-based certification that can be used for DoD 8570.1. It is called Certification and Accreditation Professional (CAP). It requires two years' experience in the certification and accreditation field, and an exam must be passed with a score of at least 700.

NOTE

(ISC)[2] sponsors several certifications. One of them is the Systems Security Certified Practitioner (SSCP), and another one is the Certified Information Systems Security Professional (CISSP), which is a higher-level certification than the SSCP.

CHAPTER SUMMARY

IT systems and data need to be protected. For the organizations that won't do this on their own, there are now many laws in place, several of which are designed to ensure that IT systems and data are protected.

Beyond the laws, there are also many regulations that apply to specific sectors, and a wide assortment of standards and guidelines related to IT are in place. Many of these standards and guidelines any organization can use to help it assess and improve its own security.

KEY CONCEPTS AND TERMS

acceptable use policy (AUP)
attorney general (AG)
Capability Maturity Model Integration (CMMI)
Children's Internet Protection Act (CIPA)
Children's Online Privacy Protection Act (COPPA)
compliance
Control Objectives for Information and Related Technologies (COBIT)
Department of Defense Information Assurance Certification and Accreditation Process (DIACAP)
due care
due diligence
Family Educational Rights and Privacy Act (FERPA)
Federal Deposit Insurance Corporation (FDIC)
Federal Information Security Modernization Act (FISMA)
Federal Trade Commission (FTC)
fiduciary responsibility
General Data Protection Regulation (GDPR)
Gramm-Leach-Bliley Act (GLBA)
Health Insurance Portability and Accountability Act (HIPAA)
information technology governance (ITG)
Information Technology Infrastructure Library (ITIL)
intellectual property (IP)
International Electrotechnical Commission (IEC)
International Organization for Standardization (ISO)
job rotation
mandatory vacation
Payment Card Industry Data Security Standard (PCI DSS)
Sarbanes-Oxley Act (SOX)
Securities and Exchange Commission (SEC)
U.S. Attorney General (U.S. AG)

CHAPTER 3 ASSESSMENT

1. ISMA requires federal agencies to protect IT systems and data. How often should compliance be audited by an external organization?
   A. Never
   B. Quarterly
   C. Annually
   D. Every three years
2. Which law applies to organizations handling healthcare information?
   A. SOX
   B. GLBA
   C. FISMA
   D. HIPAA
3. CEOs and CFOs can go to jail if financial statements are inaccurate. Which law is this from?
   A. SOX
   B. GLBA
   C. FISMA
   D. HIPAA
4. Which law requires schools and libraries to limit offensive content on their computers?
   A. FERPA
   B. HIPAA
   C. CIPA
   D. SSCP
5. Employees in some companies are often required to take an annual vacation of at least five consecutive days. The purpose is to reduce fraud and embezzlement. What is this called?
   A. Job rotation
   B. Mandatory vacation
   C. Separation of duties
   D. Due diligence
6. Fiduciary refers to a relationship of trust.
   A. True
   B. False
7. Merchants that handle credit cards are expected to implement data security. Which standard should they follow?
   A. GAISP
   B. CMMI
   C. COBIT
   D. PCI DSS
8. NIST published Special Publication 800-30. What does this cover?
   A. Risk assessments
   B. Maturity levels
   C. A framework of good practices
   D. Certification and accreditation
9. The COBIT framework refers to IT governance. Of the following choices, which *best* describes IT governance?
   A. IT-related laws
   B. IT-related regulations
   C. Processes to manage IT resources
   D. Processes to manage IT-related laws and regulations
10. This standard is focused on maintaining a balance between benefits, risk, and asset use and is based on five principles and comprises seven components. Which standard is described?
    A. COBIT
    B. ITIL
    C. GAISP
    D. CMMI
11. Which of the following ISO standards can be used to verify that an organization meets certain requirements? Part I identifies objectives and controls, and part II is used for certification.
    A. ISO 73 Risk Management—Vocabulary
    B. ISO 27002 Information Technology Security Techniques
    C. ISO 31000 Risk Management Principles and Guidelines
    D. IEC 31010 Risk Management—Risk Assessment Techniques

12. Which of the following ISO documents provides generic guidance on risk management?

A. ISO 73 Risk Management—Vocabulary
B. ISO 27002 Information Technology Security Techniques
C. ISO 31000 Risk Management Principles and Guidelines
D. IEC 31010 Risk Management—Risk Assessment Techniques

13. Which law aims to protect the privacy data for citizens in the EU and EEA?

A. GLBA
B. HIPAA
C. GDRP
D. GDPR

14. In the CMMI, level _____ indicates the highest level of maturity.

15. The DIACAP is a risk management process applied to IT systems. What happens after a system has been accredited?

A. It is certified.
B. It is decommissioned.
C. It is validated.
D. It receives authority to operate.

CHAPTER 4

Developing a Risk Management Plan

A RISK MANAGEMENT PLAN is a specialized type of project management. Many of the same techniques are applied to risk management that would be applied when managing any project. At the core is the need to plan. As the old saying goes, if you fail to plan, you plan to fail. Without a risk management plan, failure is much more likely than success. A number of industry standards require a risk management plan.

A well-documented risk management plan helps ensure that the desired goals are reachable. Primarily, a risk management plan is created to mitigate risks. This plan is helpful in identifying the risks and choosing the best solutions. It also helps with the tracking of the solutions to ensure they are implemented on budget and on schedule. A fully implemented plan will include a plan of action and milestones (POAM), which can also be used to track the project. The Risk Management Framework from the **National Institute of Standards and Technology (NIST)** is a useful guide to use when implementing a risk management plan. In this chapter we will refer to this framework frequently; it can be found at https://csrc.nist.gov/Projects/risk-management.

Chapter 4 Topics

This chapter covers the following topics and concepts:

- What the objectives of a risk management plan are
- What the scope of a risk management plan is
- How to assign responsibilities in a risk management plan
- How procedures and schedules are described in the risk management plan
- What the reporting requirements are
- What a plan of action and milestones (POAM) is
- How to chart the progress of a risk management plan
- What the steps of the NIST Risk Management Framework are

Chapter 4 Goals

When you complete this chapter, you will be able to:

- Describe the objectives of a risk management plan
- Describe the purpose of a plan's scope
- Identify the components of a risk management plan
- Identify the importance of assigning responsibilities
- Describe the purpose of the procedures list in a risk management plan
- List reporting requirements of a risk management plan
- Document findings of a risk management plan
- Create a plan of action and milestones (POAM)
- Identify a milestone plan chart
- Identify a Gantt chart and define a critical path chart
- Identify the steps of the NIST Risk Management Framework

Objectives of a Risk Management Plan

One of the important first steps for a risk management plan is to establish the objectives. The objectives become the foundation for the plan. They help identify where the plan is going and, just as important, help in knowing when the plan has been achieved. Objectives should be established for the plan as early as possible. Objectives also need to be specific. Generalized comments such as 'reduce risk' are not objectives.

The objectives identify the goals of the project. These objectives outline what should be included in the plan. Some common objectives for a risk management plan are:

- Specific threats to mitigate
- Vulnerabilities that must be remediated
- An acceptable risk level
- Costs associated with risks
- A list of recommendations to reduce the risks
- Costs associated with recommendations
- A cost-benefit analysis (CBA)
- Standards that need to be complied with

The more specific the objectives are, the better they can be used to guide risk management planning. Note the objective of acceptable risk level. Ideally this would be something quantitative, but frequently it is not. Simply, identifying if the organization's goals include an aggressive risk appetite, or are very risk-averse, can guide risk management planning.

The next phase of the risk management plan covers implementation of the plan. Implementation involves the following tasks:

- Documenting management decisions
- Documenting and tracking implementation of accepted recommendations
- Creating a POAM

Throughout this chapter, two examples are used. They show how a risk management plan can be created for actual projects. The two examples are:

- **Website**—A company, Acme Widgets, hosts a website that is used to sell widgets on the internet. The website is hosted on a web server owned and controlled by Acme Widgets. The website was recently attacked and went down for two days, and the company lost a large amount of money. Additionally, the company lost the goodwill of many customers. This was the second major outage for this website in the past two months, and only two of the many outages in the past three years.
- **Health Insurance Portability and Accountability Act (HIPAA) compliance**—A company recently purchased Mini Acme. Mini Acme has not complied with HIPAA. Managers want to identify the risks associated with this noncompliance and to ensure that issues are corrected as soon as possible.

> **NOTE**
>
> The Health Insurance Portability and Accountability Act (HIPAA) was passed in 1996 to ensure protection of health information data. Title II of HIPAA covers the protection of health data. The Health Information Technology for Economic and Clinical Health (HITECH) Act, enacted in 2009, is a federal law that expands upon the HIPAA regulations to promote the adoption and meaningful use of electronic health records (EHRs) and enhance privacy and security of protected health information (PHI).

In this chapter, examples are used to show how a portion of the plan could be created. The examples aren't intended to show the only possible way to create a plan. Plans vary based on the needs of the company.

Objectives Example: Website

The Acme Widgets website has suffered outages. These outages have resulted in unacceptable losses. The losses could have been prevented by managing website threats and risks. The risk management plan can be used to identify these risks.

The objectives of the plan are:

- **Identifying threats**—This means any threats that directly affect the website. These threats may include:
  - Attacks from the internet
  - Hardware or software failures
  - Loss of internet connectivity
- **Identifying vulnerabilities**—Vulnerabilities are weaknesses and may include:
  - Lack of protection from a firewall
  - Lack of protection from an intrusion detection system
  - Lack of antivirus software
  - Lack of updates for the server
  - Lack of updates for the antivirus software

NOTE

A **firewall** filters traffic. Firewall rules are configured to specifically allow certain traffic. Most firewalls block all traffic that is not specifically allowed. Both network and host-based firewalls can be used. A network firewall usually consists of both hardware and software and filters traffic for the network. Individual systems can have a software firewall that filters traffic for a single system. There are also specialized firewalls for specific applications. The most notable example is the Web Application Firewall (WAF).

- **Identifying assets**—Assets are the important things that the company can lose if there is an attack and may include:
  - Potential losses quantified in terms of sales
  - Potential losses in terms of loss of goodwill or reputation
- **Assigning responsibilities**—Responsibilities are assigned to specific departments for collecting data, which will be used to create recommendations. Later, in the plan, responsibilities will be assigned to departments to implement and track the plan.
- **Identifying the costs of an outage**—Both direct and indirect costs are included. The direct costs are the lost sales during the outage. The amount of revenue lost if the server is down for 15 minutes or longer will come from sales data. Indirect costs include the loss of customer goodwill and the cost to recover the goodwill.
- **Providing recommendations**—A list of recommendations to mitigate the risks is included. The recommendations may reduce the weaknesses. They may also reduce the impact of the threats. For example, a hardware failure threat could be addressed by recommending hardware redundancy. A lack of updates could be addressed by implementing an update plan.
- **Identifying the costs of recommendations**—The cost of each recommendation is identified and listed.
- **Providing a CBA**—A CBA for each recommendation is included. The CBA will compare the cost of the recommendation against the benefit to the company of implementing the recommendation. The benefit can be expressed in terms of income gained or the cost of the outage reduced.
- **Documenting accepted recommendations**—Managers will choose which recommendations to implement. They can accept, defer, or modify recommendations. These choices will then be documented in the plan.
- **Tracking implementation**—The plan will track the choices and their implementation.
- **Creating a POAM**—A POAM that assigns responsibilities is included. Managers will use the POAM to track and follow up on the project.

Objectives Example: HIPAA Compliance

A company recently acquired Mini Acme. An inspection of Mini Acme's records indicates that health information isn't protected. The acquiring company is therefore not in compliance with HIPAA, and noncompliance can result in fines and jail time.

The purpose of this plan is to ensure compliance with HIPAA. The objectives of the plan are:

- **Identifying threats**—Threats could be both internal and external.
- **Identifying vulnerabilities**—Vulnerabilities are weaknesses. They may include:
  - Lack of policies preventing information sharing
  - Lack of protection when the data is stored
  - Lack of protection when the data is transmitted

- **Assigning responsibilities**—Responsibilities are assigned to specific departments to identify threats and vulnerabilities. This data will be used to identify corrective actions. Later, responsibilities can be assigned to departments to implement and track the plan.
- **Identifying the costs of noncompliance**—Costs include the legal fines associated with noncompliance. Additional costs may result from lawsuits or the loss of customer confidence.
- **Providing recommendations**—A list of recommendations is created. This list may include procedural changes, protecting the data with access controls, and encrypting the data during transmissions.
- **Identifying the costs of recommendations**—The cost of each recommendation is identified and listed.
- **Providing a CBA**—A CBA is completed for each recommendation. It will compare the cost of the recommendation against the cost of the outage.
- **Documenting accepted recommendations**—Managers will choose which recommendations to implement. They can accept, defer, or modify recommendations. These choices will be documented in the plan.
- **Tracking implementation**—The plan will track the choices and their implementation.
- **Creating a POAM**—A POAM that assigns responsibilities is created. Managers will use it to track and follow up on the project.

Scope of a Risk Management Plan

In addition to the objectives, identifying the **scope** of a risk management plan is also important. The scope identifies the boundaries of the plan. The boundaries can include the entire organization or a single system or process. Without defined boundaries, the plan can get out of control.

A common problem with many projects is **scope creep**. Scope creep comes from uncontrolled changes. As the changes creep in, the scope of the project grows. Changes bring in additional requirements, and uncontrolled changes result in cost overruns and missed deadlines.

For example, in the HIPAA compliance example mentioned earlier, the objective of this project is to bring Mini Acme into compliance with HIPAA. Suppose more unprotected data, such as financial data, research data, or user data, is found.

If this data is rolled into the project, it would expand the project because threats and vulnerabilities would need to be identified, the costs of the data loss would need to be calculated, and additional recommendations and their costs would need to be identified. Doing all of this would take more time and money.

To say that the scope of a project should never change is unrealistic. The key is to control the changes. A risk management project manager should work with stakeholders to identify which changes are acceptable. These changes would ideally go through a change control board (CCB), a committee that includes discipline experts and project stakeholders who evaluate such changes and then decide whether to accept the changes.

A **stakeholder** is an individual or a group that has a stake, or interest, in the success of a project. A key stakeholder is one who has authority to make decisions about the project, including the ability to grant additional resources. Examples of key stakeholders would be a company executive, such as a chief information officer or chief financial officer; a vice president who will "own" the project upon completion; or a chief compliance officer who is an expert in a particular discipline, for example, HIPAA compliance.

Stakeholders should be involved in drafting a scope statement. Their involvement can be anything from drafting the statement to approving it. Stakeholders should have ownership of the project, which is also referred to as buy-in for the project.

A true stakeholder has a vested interest in the project and wants to see it succeed. On the other hand, a stakeholder named as a figurehead without a stake in the project sees it as a nuisance. A project without a true stakeholder will often die from lack of support: Resources aren't allocated, decisions aren't made, and team members realize the project is not supported and eventually stop contributing.

For example, from the HIPAA example regarding finding unprotected data unrelated to HIPAA, if a risk management team discovered unprotected financial data, the team could present its concerns to the project manager (PM). The PM can evaluate the data and determine that none of it is HIPAA related but realize it is important. The PM can pass the information on to a stakeholder as an issue of concern. A stakeholder may direct the PM to include the data in the plan. At that point, it is a controlled change.

NOTE

Companies typically have C-level executives, such as CCOs, CEOs, CFOs, CIOs, CSOs, and CTOs. CCO is short for chief compliance officer, CEO is short for chief executive officer, CFO is short for chief financial officer, CIO is short for chief information officer, CSO is short for chief security officer (also referred to as a CISO, chief information security officer), and CTO is short for chief technology officer. Recent years have expanded the number of C-Level titles you may encounter. Some of these newer titles include: chief knowledge officer (CKO), chief marketing officer (CMO), chief rand officer (CBO), chief risk officer, and chief privacy officer (CPO).

Scope Creep in Application Development

Scope creep is a common problem in application development. Programmers often see how a program can be improved by tweaking it a little here or there. Although the programmers are well intentioned, sometimes these changes can have far-reaching effects.

In one project, a programmer added an additional capability to a program, which allowed the user to search through data. This change was clearly outside the scope of the project, and the change was not evaluated and authorized by a CCB. However, programming it didn't take much time, and the change was added without notice to anyone. The application was then shipped to the customer with the new capability.

The customer used the program successfully for a few months. Later, the format of the data was changed. The change of the format didn't affect the primary purpose of the program; it still worked as required. However, the additional search feature no longer worked.

Who's responsible for fixing the problem? The application developer is responsible.

A change that originally looked like added value actually became added liability. Even though the search capability was outside the scope of the project, it became part of the application. This added capability would have to be maintained just as any other part of the application would need to be maintained. The developer didn't have much choice. If the developer refused to fix the problem, the perceived usability of the program would be affected.

At this point, the added capability wasn't easy to remove. It looked and behaved like a feature. Although it would not have been missed if it had never been added, it would now be missed if it were removed.

Examples of scope statements for the website and HIPAA compliance projects are provided in the following sections.

Scope Example: Website

The purpose of the risk management plan is to secure the Acme Widgets website. The scope of the plan includes:

- Security of the server hosting the website
- Security of the website itself
- Availability of the website
- Integrity of the website's data

Stakeholders for this project include:

- Vice president of sales
- Information technology (IT) support department head

Written approval is required for all activities outside the scope of this plan.

Scope Example: HIPAA Compliance

The purpose of the risk management plan is to ensure compliance with HIPAA for Mini Acme's data. The scope of the plan includes:

- Identifying all health data
- Storing health data
- Using health data
- Transmitting health data

Stakeholders for this project include:

- CIO
- Human resources (HR) department head

Written approval is required for all activities outside the scope of this plan.

Assigning Responsibilities

The risk management plan specifies responsibilities, which provides accountability. If responsibilities are not assigned, tasks can easily be missed. Responsibilities can be assigned to:

- Risk management PM
- Stakeholders
- Departments or department heads
- Executive officers, such as the CIO or CFO

Ensuring that any entity that is assigned a responsibility has the authority to complete the task is important. This is especially important for the PM.

NOTE

A risk management PM is sometimes called a risk management coordinator. The skills required of a successful risk management PM are the same skills required of a successful project manager for almost any project.

For example, team members may not work directly for the PM. Technicians, for example, might work in the IT department. They can be assigned as team members for a project. However, they may still report directly to supervisors in the IT department. So their task assignments from the IT department and from the PM may compete with each other. If the PM doesn't have the authority to resolve these problems, the success of the project can be affected. At the very least, the PM should have access to stakeholders to resolve problems.

The PM is responsible for the overall success of the plan. Some of the common tasks of a PM are:

- Ensuring costs are controlled
- Ensuring quality is maintained
- Ensuring the project stays on schedule
- Ensuring the project stays within scope
- Tracking and managing all project issues
- Ensuring information is available to all stakeholders
- Raising issues and problems as they become known
- Ensuring others are aware of their responsibilities and deadlines

Individual responsibilities could be assigned for the following activities:

- **Identifying risk**—This responsibility includes identifying threats and vulnerabilities. The resulting lists of potential risks can be extensive.
- **Assessing risk**—This responsibility entails identifying the likelihood and impact of each risk. A threat matrix is a common method used to assess risks.
- **Identifying risk mitigation steps**—This responsibility encompasses identifying steps that can be taken to reduce weaknesses as well as steps to reduce the impact of the risk.
- **Reporting**—This responsibility entails reporting the documentation created by the plan to management. The PM is often responsible for compiling reports.

TIP

Consider creating a threat-likelihood–impact matrix. A percentage from 10 to 100 is assigned for each likelihood. The impact severity is assigned a value between 10 and 100. The risk level value is then calculated by multiplying the likelihood and impact values. Higher values indicate risks that should be addressed first. Lower values indicate risks that may be accepted.

Examples of responsibility statements for the website and HIPAA compliance scenarios are presented in the following two sections.

Responsibilities Example: Website

The CFO will provide funding to the IT department to hire a security consultant who will assist the IT department.

The IT department is responsible for providing:

- A list of threats
- A list of vulnerabilities

- A list of recommended solutions
- Costs for each of the recommended solutions

The sales department is responsible for providing:

- Direct costs of all outages that last 15 minutes or longer
- Indirect costs of all outages that last 15 minutes or longer

The CFO will validate the data provided by the IT and sales departments. The CFO will then complete a CBA.

Responsibilities Example: HIPAA Compliance

The HR department is responsible for identifying all health information held by Mini Acme. The HR department is responsible for providing:

- A list of all health information sources
- Inspection results for all data sources regarding their compliance with HIPAA:
  - How the data is stored
  - How the data is protected
  - How the data is transmitted
- A list of existing HIPAA policies used by Mini Acme
- A list of needed HIPAA policies
- A list of recommended solutions to ensure compliance with HIPAA
- Costs for each of the recommended solutions
- Costs associated with noncompliance

Using Affinity Diagrams

Although assigning responsibility is easy, identifying the tasks may not be so easy. One of the challenges is to generate lists of realistic threats, vulnerabilities, and recommendations. An affinity diagram can help with these tasks. An **affinity diagram** is created in four basic steps:

1. **Identifying the problem**—A basic problem statement is created. For example, consider the website problem. The problem could be stated as "Website outages result in lost sales."
2. **Generating ideas**—The more the better. The ideas can be about any elements of the problem. They can include threats and vulnerabilities and recommended solutions. **Brainstorming** is one method that can be used. In a brainstorming session, participants are encouraged to mention anything that comes to mind. All ideas are written down without judgment. The creative process can often bring out a wealth of ideas.
3. **Gathering ideas into related groups**—After the ideas have been generated, they are grouped together. For a risk management plan, the groups will usually fit into categories of threats, vulnerabilities, and recommendations. Some of these categories may include subcategories. For example, vulnerabilities could be divided into network and server weaknesses.

4. **Creating an affinity diagram**—**FIGURE 4-1** shows an example of an affinity diagram. It groups all the ideas together.

In an actual scenario, the affinity diagram is likely to be much larger. Threats could be divided into external and internal. The list of vulnerabilities could be almost endless.

FIGURE 4-1
Affinity diagram.

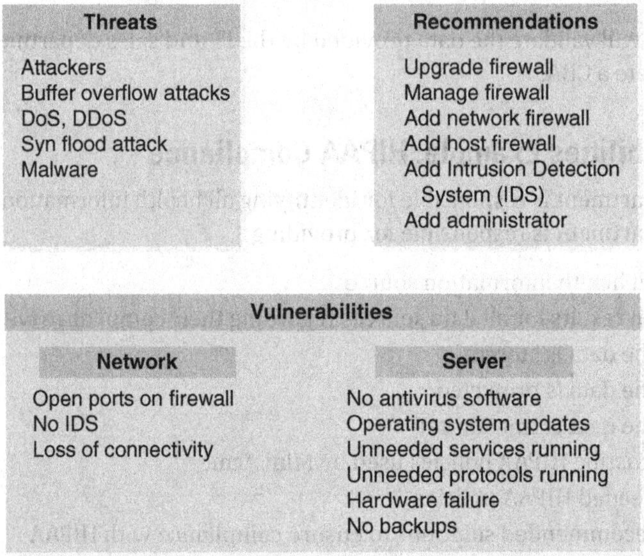

The IT department is responsible for providing:

- Identification of access controls used for data
- A list of recommended solutions to ensure compliance with HIPAA
- Costs for each of the recommended solutions

The CFO will validate the data provided by the IT and sales departments and then complete a CBA.

Describing Procedures and Schedules for Accomplishment

This part of the risk management plan is created after the project has started. A recommended solution is included for threats or vulnerabilities, with the goal of mitigating the associated risk. Though a solution can be summarized in a short phrase, the solution itself will often include multiple steps.

For example, an existing firewall may expose a server to multiple vulnerabilities. The solution could be to upgrade the firewall. This upgrade can be broken down into several steps, such as:

- Determining what traffic should be allowed
- Creating a firewall policy

NOTE

MITRE provides a guideline for selecting risk management tools: https://www.mitre.org/our-impact/mitre-labs/systems-engineering-innovation-center/selecting-risk-management-tools.

- Purchasing a firewall
- Installing the firewall
- Configuring the firewall
- Testing the firewall
- Implementing the firewall

Each of these steps can be described in further detail. In addition, a timeline can be included for completion of each of the steps.

There are a few things to remember at this point:

- Management is responsible for choosing the controls to implement.
- Management is responsible for residual risk.
- Firewall configuration will need to be monitored and perhaps updated over time.

Because management has not reviewed the recommendations yet, this schedule will usually not include dates. Instead, the schedule will list how long it may take to complete the recommendations.

For example, a single recommendation may include five tasks. The time required can be listed for each of these tasks. Start and end dates can be added later.

Partial listings of procedures for the website and HIPAA examples are given in the following sections.

Procedures Example: Website

The website is vulnerable to denial of service (DoS) attacks from the internet. This risk cannot be eliminated. However, several tasks can be completed to mitigate the risk:

> **NOTE**
> A DoS (Denial of Service) attack is any attack designed to prevent a system from providing a service. A distributed DoS (DDoS) attack is a DoS attack launched from multiple systems at the same time. DDoS attacks often include zombie computers controlled in a botnet.

- **Recommendation**—Upgrade the firewall.
- **Justification**—The current firewall is a basic router. It filters packets but does not provide advanced firewall capabilities.
- **Procedures**—The following steps can be used to upgrade the new firewall:
  1. **Starting firewall logging**—This log can be used to determine what ports are currently being used. Logs should be collected for at least one week.
  2. **Creating a firewall policy**—A **firewall policy** identifies what traffic to allow past the firewall. It is a written document and is based on the content of the firewall logs.
  3. **Purchasing a firewall appliance**—A **firewall appliance** provides a self-contained firewall solution. It includes both hardware and software that provide protection for a network. Firewall appliances range from $200 to more than $10,000.
  4. **Installing the firewall**—The firewall could be installed in the server room. Existing space and power are available there.
  5. **Configuring the firewall**—Technicians will use the firewall policy to configure the firewall.

6. **Testing the firewall before going live**—Testing will ensure normal operations are not impacted. Technicians can complete testing in one week.
7. **Bringing the firewall online**—Technicians can complete this step within a week after completing tests.

FYI

Firewalls labeled as appliances are intended to be easy to use. The implication is that, to get them to work, they only need to be plugged in so that being an expert in how they work is not necessary. They are like a toaster. The bread goes in and the toast comes out. Users don't have to know how the toaster works to make toast. Similarly, being an expert on firewalls is not necessary to use a firewall appliance. And just as a toaster offers a knob to lighten or darken the output, firewall appliances offer simplified approaches to help tune to your specific needs.

Procedures Example: HIPAA Compliance

Employees of Mini Acme are not aware of HIPAA. They don't understand the requirements of the law, nor do they understand the consequences of noncompliance. The following tasks can be completed to mitigate the risk of noncompliance:

- **Recommendation**—Increase awareness of HIPAA.
- **Justification**—Make clear that noncompliance can result in fines totaling $25,000 a year for mistakes.
- **Procedures**—Use the following steps to increase awareness:
  1. **Requiring all employees to read and comply with HIPAA policies**—Employees will read and acknowledge HIPAA policies currently in place. This can be accomplished in 30 days.
  2. **Providing training to all employees on HIPAA compliance**—Training will include what data is covered by HIPAA. It will also include consequences of noncompliance. If approved, it will take approximately 60 days to create training materials. Training can be completed in 30 days. However, there are also third-party HIPAA training companies that may have existing training material.
  3. **Online Training**—Offer online self-paced training courses. These are meant to augment regularly scheduled training, not to replace it.

Reporting Requirements

After data on the risks and recommendations have been collected, the data needs to be included in a report. This report will then be presented to management. The primary purpose of the report is to allow management to decide on what recommendations to use. Note these are internal reports to management, not the required HIPAA reports of a cyberbreach.

There are four major categories of reporting requirements:

- **Presenting recommendations**—These recommendations are the risk response recommendations.

- **Documenting management response to recommendations**—Management can accept, modify, or defer any of the recommendations.
- **Documenting and tracking implementation of accepted recommendations**—This process becomes the actual risk response plan.
- **Creating a POAM**—The POAM tracks the risk response actions.

Presenting Recommendations

The collected data is compiled into a report, which will include the lists of threats, vulnerabilities, and recommendations. This report is then presented to management. Management will use this data to decide what steps to take.

Remembering the overall goal of the risk management plan is important at this stage. The goal is to identify the risks and recommend strategies to reduce them. Most of the risks won't be eliminated, but, instead, they will be reduced to an acceptable level. Every risk identified will be accompanied by a recommendation to reduce the risk.

This report should include the following information:

- Findings
- Recommendation cost and time frame
- CBA

Findings

The findings list the facts. Remember that losses from risks occur when a threat exploits a vulnerability. Risk management findings need to include threats, vulnerabilities, and potential losses. The findings are described as cause, criteria, and effect:

- **Cause**—The cause is the threat. For example, an attacker may try to launch a DoS attack. In this case, the threat is the attacker. Identifying the root cause is also important. A successful attack is dependent on an attacker having access and the system being vulnerable. Risk management attempts to reduce the impact of the cause or reduce the vulnerabilities.
- **Criteria**—The criteria that will allow the threat to succeed are identified, which are the vulnerabilities. For example, a server would be susceptible to a DoS attack if the following criteria are met:
  - **Inadequate manpower**—If manpower isn't adequate to perform security steps, the site is vulnerable.
  - **Unmanaged firewall**—Each open port represents a vulnerability. If ports are not managed on a firewall, unwanted traffic can be allowed in.
  - **No intrusion detection system (IDS)**—Depending on the type of IDS, it not only detects intrusions, but also responds to intrusions and changes in the environment.
  - **Operating system not updated**—Applying patches to the system as they are released and tested is imperative. If updates are not applied, the system is vulnerable to new exploits.
  - **Antivirus software not installed and updated**—Antivirus software can detect malware. The software should be updated with definitions to ensure it will detect new malware.
- **Effect**—The effect is often an outage of some type. For example, the effect on a website could be that the website is not reachable anymore.

FIGURE 4-2

Website cause and effect diagram.

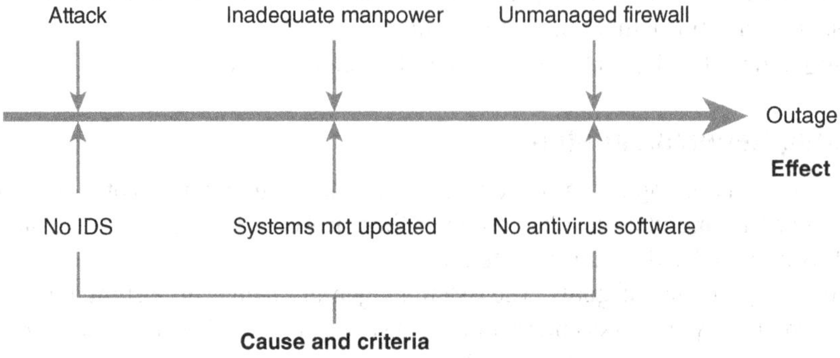

An important consideration as findings are documented is resource availability. Possibly, all the discovered issues were previously known. However, money may not have been allocated to purchase the solutions in the past. Also, possibly, manpower wasn't adequate to implement the solutions.

When adequate manpower isn't available, security is often sacrificed for ease of use. Consider the website example. The first goal may be to ensure the website is operational. Once it's up, resources may be used for other jobs. The website may still not be secure, backups may not be made, or other security issues may still exist.

A **cause and effect diagram** can be used to discover and document the findings. **FIGURE 4-2** shows an example of a cause and effect diagram for the website scenario. In this diagram, the primary cause is an attack. The remaining items are contributing factors that allow the attack to succeed. The effect is an outage.

Using a cause and effect diagram has several advantages. It can help guide discussions during the discovery process and help visualize the relationships between causes and effects in documentation. Cause and effect diagrams can be used for any problem.

A cause and effect diagram starts by creating the line and the ultimate effect. In Figure 4-2, the effect is the outage. Then, additional items are added (the causes), making the diagram look similar to a fishbone. The diagram can be expanded for any of the elements. For example, "attack" could be expanded to include specific types of attacks. Attacks may include malware, DoS, buffer overflow, or other types of attacks.

> **NOTE**
>
> The cause and effect diagram is also called an *Ishikawa diagram*, or a *fishbone diagram*. It is used to link problems with causes.

When creating a cause and effect diagram, running out of ideas or focus on a single topic might happen. To balance the diagram, the following five elements can be considered, but not all of them need to be included. However, any of them can be used to help identify causes:

- **Methods**—What methods could contribute to an outage?
- **Machinery**—What machinery issues could contribute to an outage?
- **Manpower**—What manpower issues could contribute to an outage?

FIGURE 4-3

HIPAA compliance cause and effect diagram.

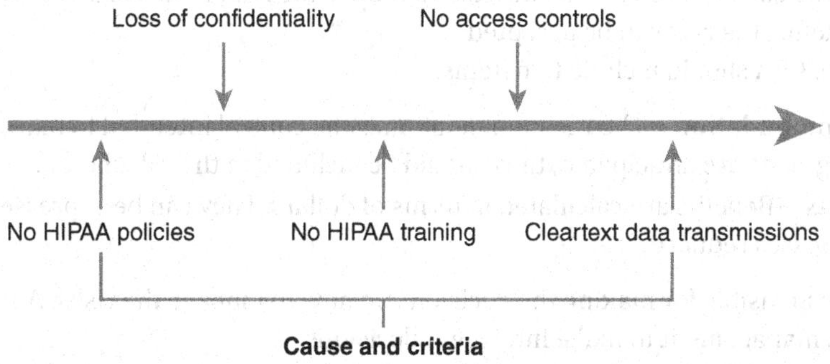

- **Materials**—What material issues could contribute to an outage?
- **Environment**—What environmental issues could contribute to an outage?

FIGURE 4-3 shows another example of a cause and effect diagram. In this example, the cause is loss of confidentiality. The remaining items show the criteria that can allow the loss of data. For HIPAA, the effect can be substantial fines or criminal charges such as jail time.

Recommendation Cost and Time Frame

In addition to the findings, the report will include a list of recommendations. These recommendations will address the potential causes and criteria that can result in the negative effect.

NOTE

The individual ongoing costs may be small, but the cumulative requirements may be more. In this example, the time required to maintain these solutions may justify an additional administrator.

Each item should include the cost required to implement it. The timeline should also be included to implement the solution. Management will use this data to decide whether the solution should be applied.

For example, the following partial list of recommendations could be included in the website risk management plan:

- **Upgrading firewall**—Initial cost: $4,000. Ongoing costs: $1,000 annually. The initial cost will cover the purchase of the firewall. The ongoing costs are related to training and maintenance. The firewall should be purchased and installed within 30 days of approval.
- **Purchasing and installing IDS**—Initial cost: $1,500. Ongoing costs: negligible. The IDS should be purchased and installed within 30 days of approval.
- **Creating a plan to keep the system updated**—Initial cost: manpower. Ongoing costs: manpower. The system should be purchased and installed within 30 days of approval.
- **Installing antivirus software on server**—Initial cost: $75. Ongoing costs: negligible. The software should be purchased and installed within 30 days of approval.
- **Updating antivirus software**—Initial cost: negligible. Ongoing costs: negligible. Antivirus software for automatic updates should be configured after installation.
- **Adding one IT administrator**—Cost: negotiated salary. Because of the ongoing maintenance requirements of these recommendations, an additional administrator is required.

Cost-Benefit Analysis

The CBA is a process used to determine how to manage a risk. If the benefits of a control outweigh the costs, the control can be implemented to reduce the risk. If the costs are greater than the benefits, the risk can be accepted.

In this context, the CBA should include two items:

- **Cost of the recommendation**—The recommendation is the control intended to manage the risk. If ongoing costs are anticipated, they should be included in the calculation.
- **Projected benefits**—Benefits are calculated in terms of dollars. They can be expressed as money earned or losses reduced.

Management is responsible for making the decisions on how to manage the risks. An accurate CBA allows management to make intelligent decisions.

Here is an example of a CBA for a website recommendation:

- **Recommendation**—Install antivirus software on the web server.
- **Cost of the recommendation**—$75.
- **Background**—Antivirus software was not installed on the web server in the past because of performance concerns. Malware infected the web server several times in the past year, which caused multiple outages on the web server. The total downtime was 5 hours. The web server generates approximately $500 per 15 minutes of uptime, or $2,000 per hour. Antivirus software is expected to prevent 90% of infections.
- **Loss before antivirus software**—$30,000. Outages resulted in $10,000 of direct loss of revenue ($2,000 × 5 hours). Indirect losses are estimated to be $20,000, which includes the advertising costs to bring back lost customers.
- **Expected loss with antivirus software**—$3,000. The antivirus software is expected to reduce the losses by 90% [$30,000 − ($30,000 × .9) = $3,000].
- **Benefit of antivirus software**—$27,000 ($30,000 × .9 = $27,000).
- **CBA**—$26,925. The CBA is calculated as:
  - Loss before antivirus software − Loss after antivirus software − Cost of antivirus software
  - $30,000 − $3,000 − $75 = $26,925

The importance of accurate data can't be overestimated. The key to completing an accurate CBA is starting with accurate data. Again, sometimes, accurate data is difficult to get. Finding accurate data often requires digging below the surface to determine costs.

Probing questions can often uncover flaws in the data. Following are scenarios and questions to be considered:

- If a control is said to reduce losses by 90%, ask, "How did you arrive at 90%?"
- If the cost of a control is given, ask, "Does this include any ongoing costs?"

Probing questions don't need to be accusatory. The goal isn't to create a conflict. Instead, the goal is to validate the data. Questions should be asked with a tone of "help me understand." If the data is flawed, the presenter can easily get defensive. On the other hand, if the data is valid, the presenter can answer questions with facts to support the claims.

Cost Estimate Accuracy

Because a CBA is only as accurate as its cost estimates, acquiring accurate data is important. However, doing so can be difficult. Understanding how data can be skewed is important.

Costs for solutions are often underestimated. For example, ongoing costs may not be included in the initial cost estimates. A product that looks easy to manage may require expensive training.

The success of a solution can be overestimated. A solution may be expected to reduce incidents by 90%, but, in practice, the reduction may be closer to 50%.

Sometimes, personnel don't have a vested interest in providing accurate information. For example, sales personnel interested in an initial sale may gloss over ongoing costs. They can also be expected to stress the most positive aspects of their products.

Risk Statements

Reports are often summarized in **risk statements**. Risk statements are used to communicate a risk and the resulting impact. They are often written using "if/then" statements. The "if" part of the statement identifies the elements of the risk, and the "then" portion of the statement identifies the effect. For example, the following risk statement could be used for the website:

- If antivirus software is not installed on the web server, then the likelihood that the server will become infected is high. The web server has a constant connection to the internet.
- If the server is infected, then an outage is likely to occur. Any outage will result in $500 of lost sales for every 15 minutes of downtime.

The risk statements should be able to be matched to the scope and objectives of the project. If the statement isn't within the scope or objectives, the risk assessment may be off track, which means the findings or the recommendation need to be focused.

Documenting Management Response to Recommendations

After the recommendations have been presented to the managers, they will decide what to do. They can either accept, defer, or modify recommendations:

- **Accept**—Management can approve the recommendation. Approved recommendations are funded and implemented. They will then be added to a POAM for tracking.
- **Defer**—Management can defer a recommendation. The recommendation may still be implemented at a later time. However, the recommendation is not included in the list of accepted recommendations.
- **Modify**—Management can modify a recommendation. For example, a firewall may be recommended, but management decides to install two firewalls to implement a demilitarized zone (DMZ). On the other hand, a $4,000 firewall may be recommended, but management decides to purchase an $800 firewall instead.

NOTE

A demilitarized zone (DMZ) is commonly used to protect internet-facing servers. It usually consists of two firewalls. One firewall filters traffic from the internet to the DMZ, and the other firewall filters traffic from the internal network to the DMZ.

Documenting and Tracking Implementation of Accepted Recommendations

Documenting the decisions made by management is important. As time passes, the decisions can become distorted if they are not documented, which is especially true if the recommendations are deferred or modified.

For example, in managing the risk management plan for the website, the plan recommended purchase of antivirus software, but this recommendation was deferred. Three months later, the system is infected with malware. A four-hour outage results in losses exceeding $8,000. The question may be asked why the software wasn't purchased.

If the decisions had been documented, this would be a simple matter to address. Without documentation, the result may be uncomfortable finger-pointing.

The documentation doesn't need to be extensive. It could be a simple document listing the recommendation and the decision. It could look similar to this:

- **Recommendation to purchase antivirus software**—Accepted. Software is to be purchased as soon as possible.
- **Recommendation to hire an IT administrator**—Deferred. IT department needs to provide clearer justification for this. In the interim, the IT department is authorized to use overtime to ensure security requirements are met.
- **Recommendation to purchase SS75 firewall**—Modified. Two SS75 firewalls are to be purchased as soon as possible. These two firewalls will be configured as a DMZ.

Plan of Action and Milestones

A **plan of action and milestones (POAM)** is a document used to track progress. POAMs are used in many types of project management. A POAM is used to assign responsibility and to allow management to follow up:

- **Assigning responsibility**—The POAM makes it clear who is responsible for each task. When a task is not completed on schedule, it also makes clear whom to hold accountable.
- **Management follow-up**—PMs and upper-level management can use the POAM to follow up on a project. The POAM allows managers to quickly determine the status of any project. When project management tools are used, the source of the problem is often easy to identify.

POAMs are also useful for audited projects. For example, HIPAA requires regular reviews. The POAM can show the progress the company has made to become compliant. If a company is not 100% compliant but can show it has made significant progress, fines may be waived or reduced. If a company doesn't have any documentation indicating progress, maximum fines could be assessed.

A POAM does not require a specific format. One company may create a POAM in a Microsoft Excel spreadsheet with 15 columns for every item. Another company may create a POAM in a Microsoft Word document.

NOTE

A POAM is also abbreviated as POA&M.

The POAM is a living document. It is not a report that is created once and is complete. Instead, the POAM should be updated throughout the life cycle of a project. Additionally, the POAM may look different depending on the phase of the project. Early in the project, the POAM may be generic, but later in the project, it could be more specific.

For example, in the website risk management plan, the website has been attacked. It has suffered two major outages in the past two months. The cause of these two incidents is probably well known. However, all the threats and vulnerabilities are probably not known. The initial POAM might have the following generic items:

- Approve risk management plan: Assigned to ______ Due by ______
- Identify threats: Assigned to ______ Due by ______
- Identify vulnerabilities: Assigned to ______ Due by ______
- Identify potential solutions: Assigned to ______ Due by ______
- Prepare risk management plan report: Assigned to ______ Due by ______
- Approve risk response plan: Assigned to ______ Due by ______
- Begin implementation of plan: Assigned to ______ Due by ______
- Complete implementation of plan: Assigned to ______ Due by ______

Later, when management approves the specific recommendations, a POAM can be created for the approved and modified recommendations. Each recommendation within the POAM could have multiple line items. For example, the task of upgrading the firewall could be a major milestone. When all of the tasks have been completed, the milestone is met.

- Log current firewall activity: Assigned to ______ Due by ______
- Purchase two SS75 firewalls: Assigned to ______ Due by ______
- Create firewall policy: Assigned to ______ Due by ______
- Test firewalls: Assigned to ______ Due by ______
- Implement external firewall: Assigned to ______ Due by ______
- Implement internal firewall: Assigned to ______ Due by ______
- Move web server to DMZ: Assigned to ______ Due by ______

NOTE

A **milestone** is a scheduled event. It indicates the completion of a major task or group of tasks. Milestones are commonly used in project management to verify how the project is doing. When milestone dates are missed, the project is behind schedule.

Each line item could include the following details:

- Task name
- Associated threat or vulnerability
- Risk level (low, medium, or high)
- Step or milestone name
- Assignment of responsibility
- Point of contact
- Estimated cost
- Actual cost
- Estimated person-hours to complete task
- Actual person-hours to complete task
- Scheduled start date
- Actual start date
- Milestone due date
- Current status

Project Management Software

Many versions of project management software are available. One example is Microsoft Office Project, which includes different versions, such as Microsoft Office Project Standard and Project Professional.

Project software includes tools that can be used to create charts. Charting tools provide a graphic representation of the project and can automatically detect the status of a project.

Some software will indicate the status of a project with colors, such as green, yellow, or red. Green could indicate on schedule and on budget, yellow could indicate a danger of going overschedule or overbudget, and red could indicate overschedule or overbudget.

A PM can enter data as the risk management project progresses, and these charts will automatically be updated. A server can be used to host data on multiple projects so that managers can access reports on any of the projects via a web browser.

- Scheduled completion date
- Actual date of completion
- Comments

Different tools can be used to assist in tracking the POAM. These tools don't replace the POAM but instead provide graphic representations of the POAM and its progress. These tools include:

- Milestone plan chart
- Gantt chart
- Critical path chart

Charting the Progress of a Risk Management Plan

Managers often use charts to show the progress of a risk management plan. The risk management plan should include a risk register, where the following items are documented: (1) identified risks, (2) when risks are assessed/evaluated, (3) the chosen risk responses/mitigating actions, and (4) the reassessed or residual risk. Charts provide a graphic representation of key information. As the saying goes, "a picture is worth a thousand words." Similarly, a chart is worth a thousand words. The following sections cover some of the common charts managers use to track a plan's progress.

Milestone Plan Chart

A **milestone plan chart** is a simple graphic representation of major milestones, showing them laid out in a graphic format. If dependencies exist between the milestones, this chart will show them. In other words, if milestone 2 can't begin until milestone 1 has been completed, this chart will show this dependency.

Commonly, actual start and end dates are included in the chart. **FIGURE 4-4** shows an example of a milestone plan chart.

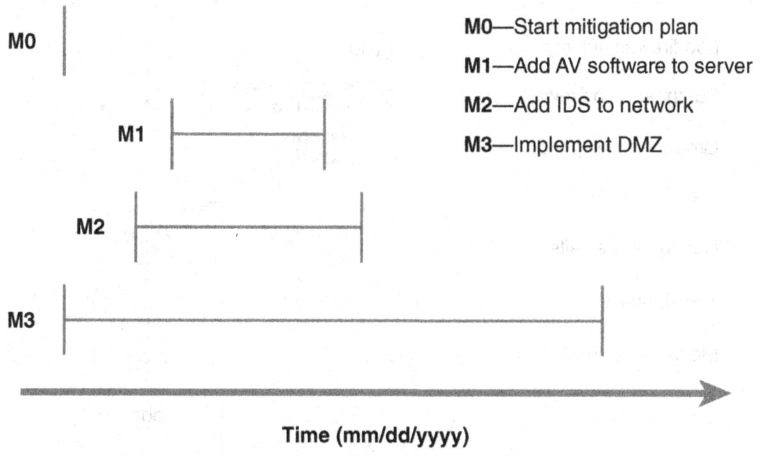

FIGURE 4-4
Milestone plan chart.

The milestone plan chart can also help allocate resources. For example, the tasks in Figure 4-4 aren't dependent on one another, as indicated in the chart by the staggered tasks, thus allowing each task to start at the same time. However, if the same person or department will be performing all the tasks, starting each one at the same time may not be possible.

In this case, the task milestone that will take the longest time to complete should be started first. In Figure 4-4, the M3 milestone will implement a DMZ and will take the longest. Once the firewalls have been ordered, another task can be started while waiting for the firewalls to arrive. M2 can start at that point. Once the IDS software has been ordered, milestone M1 can be started.

This chart can also help management change the priority of any of the milestones. The installation of antivirus software may be considered the most important first step. Figure 4-4 shows that M1 is being delayed so that M3 can start first. This can be changed so M1 starts first with an accepted delay in the implementation of the DMZ.

Gantt Chart

A **Gantt chart** shows a project schedule. Gantt charts are commonly used in project management. The primary difference between the milestone plan chart and the Gantt chart is that the Gantt chart shows more detail.

FIGURE 4-5 shows an example of a Gantt chart. The shaded items show the tasks that have been completed. Notice that the Gantt chart is showing the detailed steps for the implementation of the DMZ.

The Gantt chart allows managers to quickly view the progression and status of the project. In Figure 4-5, all the tasks that were supposed to have been completed before today have been completed. The PM needs only to focus on the tasks in progress or future tasks.

NOTE

The Gantt chart was developed by Henry Gantt, who worked with the Army Bureau of Ordnance during World War I. He realized that processes could be controlled more easily if they were broken down into smaller elements. As the often-repeated saying goes, "How do you eat an elephant? One bite at a time."

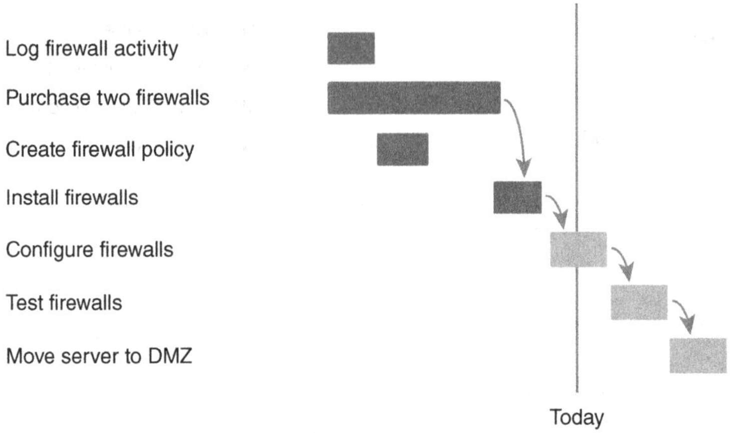

FIGURE 4-5
Gantt chart.

On the other hand, if previous tasks weren't completed, the PM can quickly identify where to focus attention. For example, if the firewalls weren't installed yet, the Install Firewalls task would not be shaded. The PM could see this element is past due and address the issue.

Most project management software automates the creation of Gantt charts. Additionally, as the tasks in the project are completed, the chart will automatically indicate completion in the chart. Before computers were popular, these charts would be filled in by hand.

Critical Path Chart

Some tasks within a project can be delayed without impacting the project's finish date. Other tasks must be completed on time. A **critical path chart** shows a list of project tasks that must be completed on time. If tasks in the path are delayed, the overall project will be delayed.

For example, a firewall cannot be installed until the firewall has been purchased. If the purchase is delayed, the installation will be delayed. These two items would be in the critical path. On the other hand, creating a log of current firewall activity can be delayed. As long as the delay isn't too long, the delay won't impact the overall schedule.

FIGURE 4-6 shows an example of a critical path chart for the firewall project. Compare Figures 4-5 and 4-6. Notice that two tasks are missing in Figure 4-6, Log Firewall Activity and

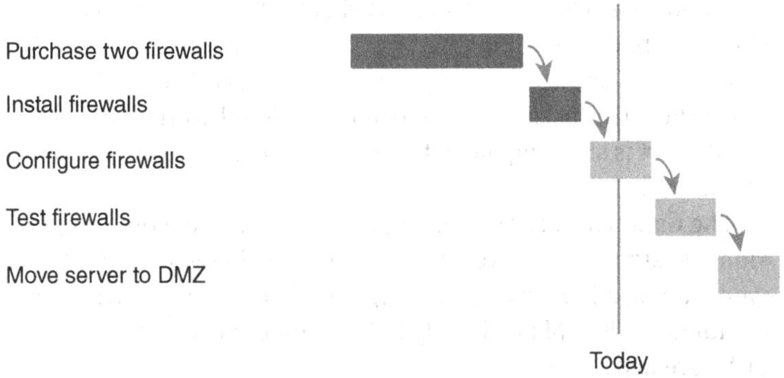

FIGURE 4-6
Critical path chart.

Create Firewall Policy. If these two tasks are slightly delayed, they will not delay the entire project. The only requirement is that they be completed before the Install Firewalls task starts.

Steps of the NIST Risk Management Framework

The **National Institute of Standards and Technology Risk Management Framework (RMF)** (NIST SP 800-37 Rev. 2) is an informative guide to use when implementing a risk management plan. The RMF is a process that combines security and risk management as part of a systems development life cycle. It follows seven steps:

1. **Prepare Step**—Includes all the required activities that help prepare an organization to manage its security and privacy risks
2. **Categorize Step**—Involves categorizing the system and any information processed, stored, and transmitted
3. **Select Step**—Involves the setup of an initial set of baseline controls for the system, based on the security categorization
4. **Implement Step**—Implements the security controls and documents how the controls are used within the system of operation
5. **Assess Step**—Pertains to assessing the security controls using appropriate methods to determine the extent to which they were implemented and checking to ensure the controls work as intended and with the correct outcomes
6. **Authorize Step**—Authorizes the operation of the system based on a determination of the risk to the organization's operations and assets, people, technology, other organizations, and the nation to ensure that the risk is acceptable to them
7. **Monitor Step**—Focuses on continually monitoring and assessing the selected security controls, assessing the effectiveness of the security controls, documenting changes to the system's operation, conducting security impact analyses of the changes, and reporting the security state of the system

Cautionary Tales

Obviously, a desire to protect your customers' confidential data is a strong motivation to protect data. However, if that is insufficient to convince upper management to allocate appropriate budget for risk management, a few cautionary tales may help.

Shields Health Care is an ambulatory surgical center in Massachusetts that was the victim of a breach in 2022. They were sued over the breach and ended up settling for $15.3 million[1]. The lawsuit had alleged that Shields Health Care had failed to implement reasonable and appropriate data security measures.

Hospital Sisters Health System (HSHS) which operates in Illinois and Wisconsin is facing multiple class action lawsuits over a 2023 data breach. A forensic investigation determined that the attackers accessed specific files between August 16 and 27, 2023, resulting in several days of downtime for HSHS's systems. The information that may have been

[1] Steve Alder, "Shields Health Care Agrees to $15.35 Million Settlement to Resolve Data Breach Litigation," The HIPAA Journal, May 23, 2025, https://www.hipaajournal.com/shields-health-care-data-breach-settlement/

compromised includes names, addresses, dates of birth, medical record numbers, treatment information, Social Security numbers, and driver's license numbers.[2]

UnitedHealth is also facing litigation over a cyberbreach. Plaintiffs allege that UnitedHealth and its subsidiary Change failed to secure the personal identifiable information and protected health information of consumers during a February 2024 data breach. The plaintiff's specifically allege that UnitedHealth failed to take "reasonable, timely and appropriate" measures to protect against the "foreseeable, catastrophic cyberattack."[3]

These are just a few examples. You should use your favorite search engine and simply type in 'data breach lawsuit'. Or if you wish to narrow that down to a specific sector you may use a search such as 'healthcare data breach lawsuit'. It is quite common for a lawsuit to be filed subsequent to any significant data breach. And the costs of litigation far exceed the costs of risk management.

CHAPTER SUMMARY

A risk management plan is a specific type of project plan. The project is to identify and mitigate risks and is started by creating objectives and a project scope. Risks are then identified. Finally, a response plan is created as recommendations to mitigate the risks. Management can then choose to accept, defer, or modify the recommendations. A risk management plan should include a risk register.

The recommendations are then implemented. A primary tool used to track the recommendations is a plan of action and milestones (POAM). The POAM is a living document that is updated throughout the project. Various charting tools can be used to supplement the POAM to ease project management tasks. The NIST RMF (SP 800-37 Rev. 2) is an effective guide that can be used when implementing a risk management plan.

KEY CONCEPTS AND TERMS

affinity diagram
brainstorming
cause and effect diagram
critical path chart
firewall
firewall appliance
firewall policy
Gantt chart
milestone
milestone plan chart
National Institute of Standards and Technology (NIST)
National Institute of Standards and Technology Risk Management Framework (RMF)
plan of action and milestones (POAM)
risk statement
scope
scope creep
stakeholder

---

[2] "Class Action Lawsuits Pile Up After Healthcare Data Breach," The HIPAA E-Tool, February 11, 2025, https://thehipaaetool.com/class-action-lawsuits-pile-up-after-healthcare-data-breach/

[3] "UnitedHealthcare data breach leads to class action lawsuit," Top Class Actions, April 30, 2024, https://topclassactions.com/lawsuit-settlements/privacy/data-breach/unitedhealthcare-data-breach-leads-to-class-action-lawsuit/

CHAPTER 4 ASSESSMENT

1. What are valid contents of a risk management plan?
   A. Objectives
   B. Scope
   C. Recommendations
   D. POAM
   E. All of the above
2. What should be included in the objectives of a risk management plan?
   A. A list of threats
   B. A list of vulnerabilities
   C. Costs associated with risks
   D. Cost-benefit analysis
   E. All of the above
3. What will the scope of a risk management plan define?
   A. Objectives
   B. POAM
   C. Recommendations
   D. Boundaries
4. What problem can occur if the scope of a risk management plan is not defined?
   A. Excess boundaries
   B. Stakeholder loss
   C. Scope creep
   D. SSCP
5. What is a stakeholder?
   A. A mark that identifies critical steps
   B. An individual or a group that has an interest in the project
   C. A critical process or procedure
   D. Another name for the risk management plan project manager
6. A key stakeholder should have authority to make decisions about a project, including authority to provide additional resources.
   A. True
   B. False
7. A risk management plan project manager oversees the entire plan. What is the project manager responsible for? (Select two.)
   A. Ensuring costs are controlled
   B. Ensuring the project stays on schedule
   C. Ensuring stakeholders have adequate funds
   D. Ensuring recommendations are adopted
8. A risk management plan includes steps to mitigate risks. Who is responsible for choosing what steps to implement?
   A. The project manager
   B. Management
   C. The risk management team
   D. The POAM manager
9. A risk management plan includes a list of findings in a report. The findings identify threats and vulnerabilities. What type of diagram can document some of the findings?
   A. Gantt chart
   B. Critical path chart
   C. POAM diagram
   D. Cause and effect diagram
10. What three elements should be included in the findings of the risk management report?
    A. Causes, criteria, and effects
    B. Threats, causes, and effects
    C. Criteria, vulnerabilities, and effects
    D. Causes, criteria, and milestones
11. What is a primary tool used to identify the financial significance of a mitigation tool?
    A. Ishikawa diagram
    B. Fishbone diagram
    C. CBA
    D. POAM
12. A fishbone diagram can link causes with effects.
    A. True
    B. False

13. A fishbone diagram is also known as a(n):
    A. Risk management framework
    B. Program management tool
    C. Ishikawa diagram
    D. NIST core plan

14. What is the NIST Risk Management Framework?
    A. The planning phase of the systems life cycle
    B. A process that combines security and risk management as part of a systems development life cycle
    C. A record of project milestones
    D. POAM

15. A POAM is used to track the progress of a project. What type of chart is commonly used to assist with tracking?
    A. Fishbone chart
    B. Cause and effect chart
    C. Gantt chart
    D. POAM chart

PART TWO

Mitigating Risk

CHAPTER 5 Defining Risk Assessment Approaches 117

CHAPTER 6 Performing a Risk Assessment 143

CHAPTER 7 Identifying Assets and Activities to Be Protected 171

CHAPTER 8 Identifying and Analyzing Threats, Vulnerabilities, and Exploits 197

CHAPTER 9 Identifying and Analyzing Risk Mitigation Security Controls 225

CHAPTER 10 Planning Risk Mitigation Throughout an Organization 253

CHAPTER 11 Turning a Risk Assessment Into a Risk Mitigation Plan 281

CHAPTER 5

Defining Risk Assessment Approaches

A RISK ASSESSMENT IS PERFORMED to identify risks and to rank them in order of severity and probability of occurrence. Risk management techniques include avoiding, sharing or transferring, mitigating, or accepting risks. The risk assessment allows for the prioritization of the risks. The high-priority risks are managed, and the low-priority risks are accepted. The risk assessment also helps to identify the best methods to control the risks, which helps to ensure that the controls that are purchased provide the best benefits.

There are two primary methods used to create a risk assessment: quantitative and qualitative. The quantitative method can be used with predefined formulas. For example, the annual loss expectancy (ALE) can be calculated by multiplying the annual rate of occurrence (ARO) by the single loss expectancy (SLE), which is expressed as ALE = ARO × SLE. Note, this is only one formula, albeit a quite common one; you will learn other formulas in this chapter.

The qualitative method can also be used. In the qualitative method, values or words are assigned to the probability of a risk occurring and the impact of a risk if it occurs. Both methods are important to understand so they can be applied in different scenarios.

Risk itself is generally given by the following formula:

Risk = Threat × Vulnerability × Impact

Obviously, it is preferrable to have quantitative data for each of the inputs into this formula (Threat, Vulnerability, and Impact). However, that is not always possible and one may have to use qualitative data instead.

Chapter 5 Topics

This chapter covers the following topics and concepts:

- What risk assessment is
- What the critical components of a risk assessment are
- What types of risk assessments are available
- Which risk assessment challenges should be addressed
- What best practices for risk assessments are

Chapter 5 Goals

When you complete this chapter, you will be able to:

- Define risk assessment
- Describe the importance of a risk assessment
- Explain when a risk assessment should be performed
- Explain the purpose of a risk assessment and a risk assessment scope
- Explain what is meant by identifying critical areas for a risk assessment
- Identify the main types of risk assessments
- Describe the elements of a quantitative and a qualitative risk assessment
- Identify the differences between quantitative and qualitative risk assessments
- Identify the benefits and limitations of quantitative and qualitative risk assessments
- List the challenges with risk assessments
- Describe the importance of data consistency and the use of uncertainty levels
- Identify how to provide useful results for a risk assessment
- List best practices associated with risk assessments

Understanding Risk Assessments

A risk assessment, also referred to as a *risk analysis*, is a process used to identify and evaluate risks. Risks are then ranked based on their importance or impact severity and the probability of the risk being realized. These risks are then prioritized. With this understanding, the ranking process should become somewhat easier. If a risk has a high severity and high probability of occurring, that would obviously be ranked high. A risk with low severity and low probability would be ranked low. The ranking becomes more nuanced when probability and severity seem to balance each other instead of factoring together. For example, consider a risk that has a moderate severity, but a high probability of occurring. This can be more difficult to properly rank. As a general rule, if one must err, err on the side of caution.

Risk assessments are a major part of an overall risk management program. They help identify which risks are most important. A major difference between a risk assessment and a risk management program is that the risk assessment is created for a moment in time, whereas a risk management program is a continuous process.

> **NOTE**
>
> Companies must consider profitability and survivability. A risk assessment helps a company maintain a proper balance between these two goals.

A risk assessment helps identify which safeguards to implement. **Safeguards** are also known as controls. They are used to control or reduce risk. A control may reduce the probability of a vulnerability being discovered or exploited, or reduce the impact from a threat. Either way, the control reduces the risk.

Clearly, budget constraints affect how much can be spent on cybersecurity, including on risk management. One reason for doing a risk assessment is to ensure the most serious risks are addressed first. In this way, if some risk cannot be addressed, or is only addressed with minimal mitigation, then one can at least be confident that this particular risk is less serious.

Another method of prioritizing risk management and cybersecurity expenditures is to start with regulatory requirements. For example, a health care–related organization must first consider HIPAA and HITECH requirements. After those are addressed, other issues can be addressed. Similarly, a company that processes credit cards should always begin with PCI-DSS (Payment Card Industry Data Security Standard) requirements. But do keep in mind, that even if one is entirely compliant with a given standard, that does not denote one is secure. Standards and regulatory requirements should be considered as a baseline for mitigating risks. Put another way, once one has achieved compliance, one has a good foundation to begin exploring additional security measures. Too often organizations equate regulatory compliance with being secure, and that is not accurate. However, recall the cautionary tales given at the end of Chapter 4. One defense against litigation is whether or not the organization took reasonable steps. Complying with regulatory requirements and industry standards is one demonstration of having taken reasonable steps to secure data.

NOTE

HIPAA and HITECH govern the control of health-related data. SOX governs the accuracy of financial data. PCI-DSS governs the handling of credit card–related information. For those in Europe or doing business in Europe, GDPR (General Data Protection Regulation) has a major impact on the handling of individuals' personal data.

Importance of Risk Assessments

Risk assessments are an important part of the risk management process. Without a risk assessment, determining how much resources to apply to securing what systems becomes difficult and how to protect them remains unclear. However, a risk assessment will help to identify the most important systems to protect and provide insight into what controls will provide the most value.

A risk assessment should be completed:

- **When evaluating risk**—Risk assessments are part of the overall risk management process. They are useful any time risk management is being used, which is especially true if the risks need to be prioritized.
- **When evaluating a control**—A risk assessment can be used to evaluate the usefulness of a control. Managers can't approve all controls. A risk assessment helps managers decide which controls to adopt.
- **Periodically after a control has been implemented**—A risk assessment is a point-in-time document. However, risks don't stand still. Attackers are constantly upgrading their techniques and tactics. Risk assessments should be scheduled on a regular basis after a control has been implemented. The goal is to determine whether the control is still useful.

- **When assessing security policies**—Determining if a given security policy adequately addresses a particular risk is very important.

Purpose of a Risk Assessment

Risk assessments are important tools to assist management. They help management quantify risks and identify and evaluate the effectiveness of controls. Risk assessments tend to:

- **Support decision making**—A risk assessment prioritizes risks, which helps decision makers determine which risks should be reduced. As a reminder, not all risks have to be reduced. Risks can be avoided, shared or transferred, mitigated, or accepted. High-priority risks should be mitigated, but lower-priority risks may be accepted.
- **Guide budgeting**—Cybersecurity, like any other expense, must be done within budget constraints. Risk assessments assist in budgeting cybersecurity expenses in a manner that has optimal efficacy.

Developing a risk assessment involves many steps. It isn't a task that can be completed in a single sitting, a single day, or even a single week. When done properly, developing a risk assessment involves the input of several key players. Steps involved in developing a risk assessments are as follows:

1. **Identifying assets**—Before one can analyze threats and vulnerabilities, one must first understand what assets are being protected. This includes valuation of said assets, appreciating what assets may be deemed critical to the organization.
2. **Identifying threats and vulnerabilities**—Losses occur when a threat exploits a vulnerability. Organizations can reduce the losses if they've identified likely threats and vulnerabilities. This process includes the use of cyberthreat intelligence.
3. **Identifying the likelihood that a risk will occur**—This process can be based on historical data or opinions. For example, a risk occurred an average of four times in the past three years. If no steps are taken to reduce the risk, it will probably occur four times next year. If historical data isn't available, experts can provide opinions on the likelihood of the risk's occurring.
4. **Determining the impact of a risk**—This process can also be based on historical data or opinions. For example, a risk resulted in losses averaging $20,000 a year in the past three years. If no steps are taken to reduce the risk, it will probably result in a loss of about $20,000 next year. If historical data isn't available, experts can provide opinions on the impact of the risk's occurring.
5. **Determining the efficacy of a control**—Controls reduce the risk or the risk's impact. Some controls will be more effective than others. A risk assessment helps determine which ones to implement. Typically, multiple different controls can be applied to the same risk.

A risk assessment identifies threats and vulnerabilities against the current system. It assumes current controls are working as expected. Another way of saying this is that a risk assessment is performed at a moment in time based on current conditions, whereas risk management is a continuous process.

Critical Components of a Risk Assessment

Three critical steps should be completed early in the risk assessment process. These steps identify major components of the risk assessment and will directly impact its success. These steps are:

- Identifying scope
- Identifying critical areas
- Identifying team members

The following sections explore each of these steps in depth.

Identifying Scope

The scope identifies the boundary of the risk assessment. When participants understand the scope, they are less likely to change it. Identifying the scope of the risk assessment helps keep it on track. In contrast, uncontrolled changes result in scope creep. Scope creep causes cost overruns and missed deadlines. You may think that a risk assessment should assess every system in an organization. In an ideal world, that would be correct. However, that is often not feasible for both time and budget constraints. This is why it is important to identify the scope of the assessment very early in the process.

For example, **FIGURE 5-1** shows a web server configured in a network. The server hosts a website that is accessible from the internet. Customers can access the website and purchase products. The web server hosts the website application. The back-end database server hosts data.

The scope could be set to focus only on the web server. Alternatively, the scope could include the web server and the database server. Both of the firewalls in the demilitarized zone (DMZ) could also be included. The range of items included can vary based on a number of factors. One factor is the reason for the risk assessment. For example, if the risk assessment is in response to either some breach, or to cyberthreat intelligence regarding some potential breach, then the scope may be limited to those areas most relevant to the breach/potential breach.

FIGURE 5-1

Network diagram with web and database servers.

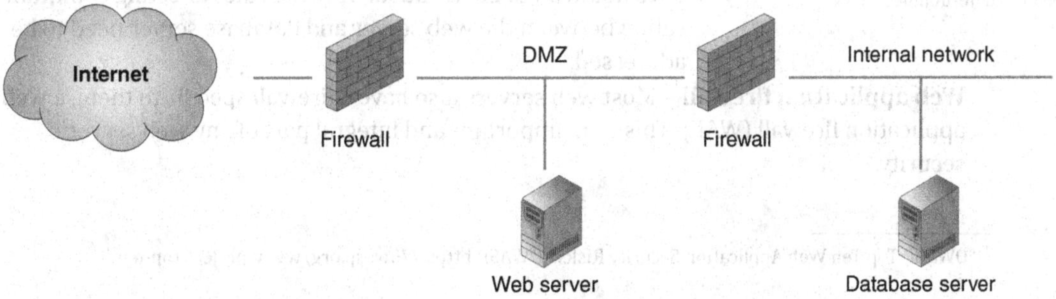

NOTE

Cyberthreat intelligence is the process of getting information on current threats and vulnerabilities that are likely to affect your systems. This includes issues that are happening in your industry, or that are relevant to the systems you use. This text is not a cyberthreat intelligence textbook, but you will see references to cyberthreat intelligence, along with specific tools, throughout the book.

Consider the scenario wherein a web server was attacked several times in the past year. Some of these attacks resulted in the website crashing or the web server failing. However, existing controls protected the data on the database server, and it was not accessed inappropriately or lost. In this example, the database server might not be included. Also, the database server could be included just to ensure the existing controls will protect against current risks.

Obviously setting the scope is an important step. If you define the scope too narrowly you may miss relevant systems/subsystems. Considering the previous web server example, if you don't include the web application firewall (WAF) you are probably defining the scope too narrowly. Conversely, if you define the scope too broadly you may waste time and resources analyzing systems that are not pertinent to your current objectives.

Identifying Critical Areas

Once scope has been determined, the next step is to identify critical areas within that scope that should be included. Identifying these critical areas helps the risk assessment team focus on what's important. For example, a scope could include a web server, a database server, and a firewall. The risk assessment could then identify the following critical areas:

- **Web server**—Addressing all elements of the web server includes hardware, the operating system, and the website application. For hardware, any single point of failure could be the focus. A **single point of failure (SPOF)** is any piece of hardware whose failure can take down the website. A process that regularly updates the operating system should be considered as well as applying best practices to prevent attacks on the website application, which include those for buffer overflow and SQL injection attacks.
- **Database server**—The database server hosts about 20 databases. The risk assessment should include only the databases accessed by the web server through the firewall. SQL injection attacks should definitely be considered. However, the primary protection from SQL injection attacks will be implemented in the website application.
- **Internal firewall**—The internal firewall controls all traffic to and from the internal network. All traffic in the risk assessment does not need to be included. Only the rules affecting communication between the web server and database server need to be addressed.
- **Web application firewall**—Most web servers also have a firewall specific to them, a web application firewall (WAF). This is an important and integral part of any web server's security.

NOTE

Buffer overflow and SQL injection attacks are common attacks for internet-facing web servers. Both have continually been listed in the OWASP (Open Web Application Security Project) top 10 list of vulnerabilities[1].

[1] "OWASP Top Ten Web Application Security Risks," OWASP, https://owasp.org/www-project-top-ten/

When critical areas are identified, areas that are most critical to the business should be the main focus. Profitability and survivability were mentioned previously in this chapter. The risk assessment needs to balance potential profits and losses. Losses that threaten an organization's survivability are critical.

Some data is critical, such as financial and customer data. Other data, such as public data, doesn't need the same level of protection. Similarly, some servers or IT services are critical, whereas other servers and services are less critical.

Although including only critical areas certainly makes sense, the risk assessment team may not understand what is critical to management. The team should stay focused on what management considers important.

TIP

Commonly, the scope is focused on who owns the system, which makes implementing the recommendations easier. For example, imagine a risk assessment that includes three servers. Each of the three servers is owned by a different department. The departments may have conflicting goals and interests that prevent the recommendations from being easily implemented. In this case, a separate risk assessment should be created for each department.

Identifying Team Members

Risk assessment team personnel should not be the same people who are responsible for correcting deficiencies, which helps avoid a conflict of interest.

For example, an administrator is responsible for implementing controls on a web server. Their input may be biased by their desire to implement the control. If disinterested parties provide the input, chances are better of getting accurate, objective data.

Regardless, input should be obtained from the responsible department. Its staff probably has excellent insight into the problems and how to fix them. However, when prioritizing risks and determining the usefulness of controls, input from the people who correct deficiencies should not be the deciding factor.

Types of Risk Assessments

When considering a risk assessment, which method to use must first be identified. The two primary methods used in the IT field are:

- **Quantitative**—The quantitative method is objective. It uses numbers, such as actual dollar values. A quantitative risk assessment requires a significant amount of data. Gathering this data often takes time. If the data is available, this type of risk assessment becomes a simple math problem with the use of formulas.
- **Qualitative**—The qualitative method is subjective. It uses relative values based on opinions from experts. Experts provide their input on the probability and impact of a risk. A qualitative risk assessment uses words, such as *low*, *medium*, and *high*, instead of numbers. It can be completed relatively quickly.

Both of these methods are explored in greater depth in the following sections.

That neither method is superior to the other is important to keep in mind. They both have benefits and limitations. However, one method works better than the other in specific situations. Being aware of the options makes choosing the right method for the right situation easier.

Quantitative Risk Assessments

A **quantitative risk assessment** uses numbers, such as dollar values. Data is gathered and then entered into standard formulas. The results can help identify the priority of risks. The results can also be used to determine the effectiveness of controls.

Some of the key terms associated with quantitative risk assessments are:

- **Single loss expectancy**—The total loss expected from a single incident is the **single loss expectancy (SLE)**. An incident occurs when a threat exploits a vulnerability. The loss is expressed as a dollar value, such as $5,000. The dollar value of the loss includes the value of hardware, software, and data. The asset value (AV) multiplied by the **exposure factor (EF)** equals SLE. The EF describes the loss that will happen to the asset as a result of the threat, which is expressed as a percentage value. Hence, $SLE = AV \times EF$. For example, if AV is $10,000 and EF is 0.5 (i.e., 50% exposure to a threat), then SLE is $5,000.
- **Annual rate of occurrence (ARO)**—The number of times an incident is expected to occur in a year is the **annual rate of occurrence (ARO)**. If an incident occurred once a month in the past year, the ARO is 12. Assuming nothing changes, the incident's occurring 12 times next year is likely.
- **Annual loss expectancy**—The expected loss for a year is the **annual loss expectancy (ALE)**. ALE is calculated by multiplying $SLE \times ARO$. Because SLE is given as a dollar value, ALE is given as a dollar value. For example, if the SLE is $5,000 and the ARO is 12, the ALE is $60,000.
- **Safeguard value**—The cost of a control is the **safeguard value**. Controls are used to mitigate risk. For example, antivirus software could have an average cost of $50 for each computer. Therefore, the safeguard value of 100 computers is $5,000.

> **TIP**
>
> Understanding the types of risk assessments for the (ISC)² Systems Security Certified Practitioner (SSCP) and Certified Information Systems Security Professional (CISSP) exams is important. Having a good understanding of quantitative and qualitative methods is necessary, which includes all the associated terms of quantitative methods.

In this scenario, a company issues laptop computers to employees. The value of each laptop is $2,000, which includes the hardware, software, and data. About 100 laptops are being used at any time. In the past 2 years, the company has lost an average of one laptop per quarter. These laptops were stolen when systems were left unattended. With this information, the following questions can be answered:

- What's the SLE?
- What's the ARO?
- What's the ALE?

> **FYI**
>
> A hardware lock is a metal cable that can attach a laptop computer to furniture. The cable is looped around a desk or chair and then connected to the laptop. Once the lock, which is usually a combination lock, is secured, the combination needs to be entered to remove the lock from the laptop. Even though a thief could use bolt cutters to cut the cable or could carry the laptop out with the desk, both actions would look suspicious.

Because the value of each laptop is $2,000, the SLE is $2,000. One laptop is lost each quarter, resulting in an ARO of 4. The ALE is calculated as $2,000 × 4, or $8,000.

The ALE can then be used to determine the usefulness of a control. For example, the company could purchase hardware locks for the laptops in bulk at a cost of $10 each. The safeguard value is $10 × 100 laptops, or $1,000. The estimation is that, if the locks are purchased, the ARO will decrease from 4 to 1. Should the company purchase these locks?

The effectiveness of the control can be determined using the following calculations:

- Current ALE = $8,000 (ARO of 4 × $2,000)
- ARO with control = 1
- ALE with control = $2,000 (ARO of 1 × $2,000)
- Savings with control = $6,000 (Current ALE of $8,000 − ALE with control of $2,000)
- Safeguard value (cost of control) = $1,000 ($10 × 100)
- Realized savings = $5,000 (Savings with control of $6,000 − Safeguard value of $1,000)

In this example, the savings in the first year is $5,000, which provides a cost-benefit analysis (CBA) and clearly indicates the locks should be purchased. If nothing is done, the company will likely lose $8,000. However, by purchasing the locks at a cost of $1,000, the company will lose only $2,000. In other words, the company is spending $1,000 to save $6,000.

Another tool in quantitative risk analysis is the FAIR model. The FAIR model (Factor Analysis of Information Risk) is a quantitative risk analysis framework that provides a structured, repeatable method for evaluating cyber and information risk in financial terms. The basic formula is given here: Risk = Loss Event Frequency (LEF) × Probable Loss Magnitude (PLM).

Each of these inputs requires some explanation. Loss event frequency (LEF) is number of times a threat agent is expected to act against an asset in a year, and succeed. The probable loss magnitude (PLM) is the expected financial impact of a loss event. There is a formula for PLM:

$$\text{PLM} = \text{Primary Loss} + \text{Secondary Loss}$$

Primary loss consists of direct costs from the incident (e.g., hardware replacement, legal fees, immediate business interruption). Secondary losses are indirect or consequential costs (e.g., reputational damage, fines, customer churn, long-term productivity drops).

> **NOTE**
>
> These formulas typically look at a single year. The calculations can become quite complex if other costs are included. Depreciation, maintenance, and replacement costs for follow-on years are usually not included in the calculations.

Benefits

One of the primary benefits of a quantitative risk assessment is that it becomes a simple math problem, which is especially true if tools that automate the assessment are used. For example, applications are available that allow the SLE, ARO, and safeguard values to be plugged in. The application then calculates the results and provides a recommendation. Because the application performs the calculations, the data is often more accurate.

Another big benefit of a quantitative risk assessment is that it provides a CBA. When the SLE, ARO, and safeguard values are accurate, a CBA can also be calculated, which was discussed in the previous section.

NOTE
Some quantifiable data related to incidents and vulnerabilities in your industry can be found in common cybersecurity reports. Verizon publishes a Data Breach Investigations Report (DBIR) every year[2]. CrowdStrike also publishes an annual cybersecurity report[3]. These can help you determine items such as annual rate of occurrence in your industry.

Management is often familiar with quantitative assessment terminology. For example, a quantitative assessment uses dollar terms to express losses. Because of this, it becomes easy for management to grasp the details of the assessment and its recommendations.

Last, the formulas use verifiable and objective measurements. If a website makes $2,000 in revenue an hour, it will lose that revenue if it is down for one hour, which is a verifiable fact.

Limitations

Using a quantitative analysis has its limitations. One of the biggest limitations is that accurate data isn't always available, which is especially true when identifying ARO reductions. The accuracy of these estimates can be difficult to verify.

For example, an earlier example stated that, if hardware locks were purchased, the ARO would decrease from 4 to 1. In other words, instead of four laptops being stolen each year, only one laptop would be stolen. Decreasing the ARO from 4 to 1 sounds good, but is it true? This difficulty is also a vulnerability when reporting to skeptical or unsupportive managers.

Another limitation is ensuring that people use the control as expected. Hardware locks were mentioned in the example to protect the laptops. As long as everyone uses the hardware locks, they will work. However, users may consider them inconvenient. Just because the organization purchased the locks doesn't mean employees will use them.

NOTE
A cost-benefit analysis provides meaningful data to decision makers. If the benefits of a control outweigh the costs, the control can be implemented to reduce the risk. If the costs are greater than the benefits, then the risk can be accepted.

Additional steps may need to be taken to ensure users are aware of the importance of the control. Even though laptop computers are stolen all the time, users are still very surprised when it happens to them. Policies may need to be created that require the use of the control. Additionally, training may need to be included to reinforce the importance of the control.

Qualitative Risk Assessments

A **qualitative risk assessment** doesn't assign dollar values. Instead, it determines the level of risk based on a more subjective assignment of the **probability** and impact of a risk, unlike a quantitative risk assessment, which is calculated based on cost estimates. These values are determined by gathering the opinions of experts.

Probability and impact are defined as follows:

- **Probability**—The likelihood that a threat will exploit a vulnerability. The risk occurs when a threat exploits a vulnerability. A scale can be used to define the probability that a risk will occur. The scale can be based on word values, such as *low, medium*, or *high*. Then,

---

[2] "(Annual) Data Breach Investigations Report," Verizon Business, https://www.verizon.com/business/resources/reports/dbir/

[3] "CrowdStrike 2025 Global Threat Report," CrowdStrike, https://go.crowdstrike.com/2025-global-threat-report.html

TABLE 5-1 Probability Scale

PROBABILITY	DESCRIPTION
Low	The risk is unlikely to occur. Threats are not active. Vulnerabilities either are not known or have been mitigated.
Medium	A moderate chance exists that the risk will occur. It has occurred in the past, but mitigation controls have reduced recent occurrences.
High	A high probability exists that the risk will occur. It has occurred in the past and will occur again if not mitigated.

percentage values can be assigned to these words. For example, a value of 10% could be assigned to a low probability and 100% to a high probability.

- **Impact**—The negative result if a risk occurs. Impact is used to identify the magnitude of a risk. The risk results in some type of loss. However, instead of quantifying the loss as a dollar amount, an impact assessment could use words, such as *low*, *medium*, or *high*. These categories can also be used to identify probabilities. However, where a probability is expressed as a percentage, impact is expressed as a relative value. For example, low could be 10, medium could be 50, and high could be 100.

> **NOTE**
>
> An important point to realize about the qualitative risk assessment is that the scale must be defined. However, there is no single standard. One company may use three values of low, medium, and high. Another company may use five values of slight, slightly moderate, moderate, moderately severe, and severe. As long as the scale in the risk assessment is defined, any scale can be used.

The risk level can be calculated with the following formula:

$$\text{Risk level} = \text{Probability} \times \text{Impact}$$

TABLES 5-1 and **5-2** show one way the scales can be defined in a risk assessment. The values for each of these scales are assigned based on current known threats and vulnerabilities as well as current controls. Note that the expert assigns the probability and impact as words, such as *low* and *medium*. Later, the person completing the risk assessment converts the words to numbers based on the scale. For example, if the expert assigns a low probability, the risk assessment gives it a value of 10%. The experts won't necessarily know the actual values and ranges. Instead, they make their decisions based on the descriptions. While many people do this, I do not recommend assigning numeric values to qualitative analysis. It can

TABLE 5-2 Impact Scale

IMPACT	DESCRIPTION
Low	If the risk occurs, it will have minimal impact on the company. The attack will not impact any critical data or systems.
Medium	If the risk occurs, it will have a moderate impact on the company. It may affect critical data or systems but not to a large extent.
High	If the risk occurs, it will have a high impact on the company. It will affect critical data or systems and cause substantial losses.

be misleading. If someone notes a 10% in your risk analysis report, they may assume that is based on quantitative data, not a rough qualitative estimate.

A qualitative analysis can be divided into two sections:

- The first section attempts to prioritize the risk.
- The second section evaluates the effectiveness of controls.

Both sections can be performed at the same time. However, for clarity, they are presented as two separate actions in this chapter.

Prioritizing the Risk

The goal of this part of the risk assessment is to identify which risks are most important. Identifying the most important risks is done by assigning probability and impact values to known risks.

For example, a company website sells company products. Because of recent outages, the most important risks to the website need to be identified. A list is derived based on feedback from several experts. These risks now need to be prioritized.

The risk categories are:

- **DoS attack**—Any denial of service (DoS) or distributed DoS (DDoS) attack that results in an outage.
- **Web defacing**—Modification of the website by unauthorized parties.
- **Loss of data from unauthorized access**—Any loss of confidentiality. This loss could be from an attacker accessing customer data or any internal private data. The loss does not include the loss of public data, which is freely available.
- **Loss of website data from hardware failure**—The loss of any website data. This loss can include data used to show the webpages to customers or the website application used to retrieve and format the data into webpages.

The website is typically located behind a web application firewall and protected in a demilitarized zone (DMZ). It is also common, and prudent, that the web server has antivirus software installed. The qualitative analysis survey could be distributed to key experts to determine risks.

These surveys can be conducted in several ways: via surveys that are filled out independently, by interviewing experts, or within a meeting but without discussion. If there is discussion, the boss might say, "Clearly, any loss of data will have a high impact," which may influence subordinates. Some may have thought the value was low but may instead enter it as high or medium.

TABLE 5-3 shows how the results could look. The average probabilities and impacts have been summarized and entered into each box. For example, for the DoS attack, the average

TABLE 5-3 Qualitative analysis survey results

CATEGORY	PROBABILITY (%)	IMPACT	RISK LEVEL
DoS attack	High	High	High
Web defacing	Medium	High	Medium
Loss of data from unauthorized access	Low	High	Medium
Loss of website data from hardware failure	Low	High	Medium

Survey for Determining Risks

We are attempting to identify the most serious risks to our website. Please enter a value of low, medium, or high under each heading in the following table for each category listed. Your decisions should be based on current controls and safeguards. For example, the website is currently placed on the internet and is protected with a host-based firewall. Assume this firewall will remain.

Qualitative Analysis Survey

CATEGORY	PROBABILITY THE RISK WILL OCCUR (LOW, MEDIUM, OR HIGH)	IMPACT IF THE RISK OCCURS (LOW, MEDIUM, OR HIGH)
DoS attack		
Web defacing		
Loss of data from unauthorized access		
Loss of website data from hardware failure		

probability and the impact were both determined to be High. The probability and impact were calculated by averaging each of the inputs by the different experts. The risk level was determined by the formula Probability × Impact. Note some sources use numbers, however since these are usually rough estimates, I use qualitative labels instead.

This data can be presented graphically in many ways. The risk matrix in **FIGURE 5-2** shows one method.

At this point, Table 5-3 shows that the highest risk is from a DoS attack, which has a risk level of 100. The lowest risk level is 3 for the loss of data from unauthorized access.

Loss of data certainly seems as if it would be very important. And indeed that is a critical risk, particularly if your system contains personally identifiable information (PII), financial data, confidential information, etc. However, the probability has been ranked low. In this case it is not that the impact is low (that was actually ranked high). However, a high impact with a low probability is certainly less of a risk than a high impact with a high probability, such as the DoS case.

On the other hand, the risk of a DoS attack clearly rises to the top as the biggest risk. Based on the current controls, the experts agree that the system will be attacked. When it is attacked, they also agree that the impact will be high.

FYI

Having a **redundant array of independent disks (RAID)**, configurations allow a system to continue to run even if a disk drive fails. Sophisticated RAIDs allow a system to operate even if more than one disk drive fails. RAID also provides fault tolerance. A fault can occur, and the disk subsystem can tolerate it, meaning it will continue to operate. While there are other levels, typically one will see a RAID 1 (disk mirroring) or RAID 5 (common for most servers).

FIGURE 5-2

Risk matrix.

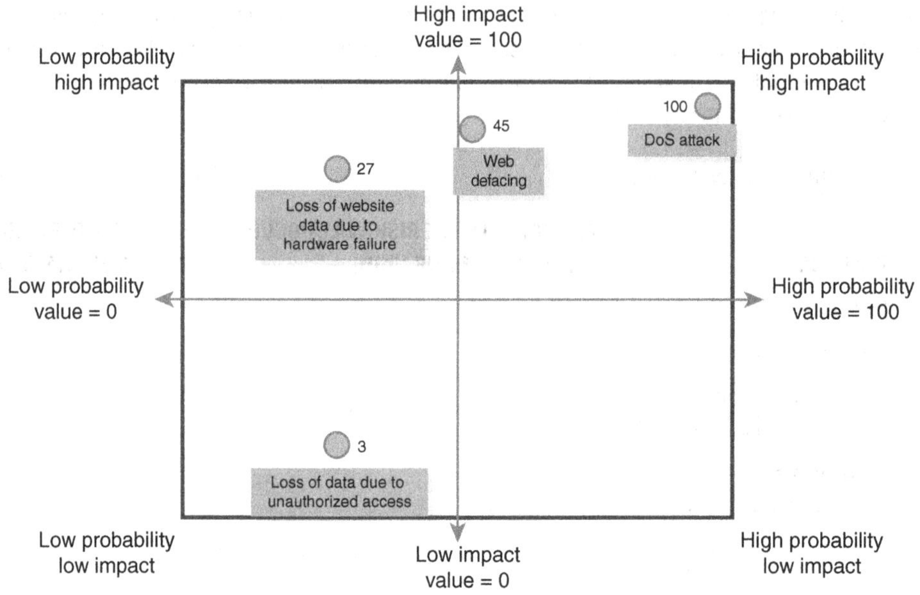

The list of risks from most to least important is:

- **Priority 1**—DoS attack, with a value of high
- **Priority 2**—Web defacing, with a value of medium
- **Priority 3**—Loss of website data from hardware failure, with a value of low
- **Priority 4**—Loss of data from unauthorized access, with a value of medium

Evaluating the Effectiveness of Controls

At this point, which safeguards or controls should be applied for high-impact risks can be determined. A survey could help here also. For example, the mitigation choices survey could be used.

Just as the risks can be summarized, so, too, can the effectiveness of the controls. **TABLE 5-4** shows the presumed results of the survey. As in other surveys, high has a value of 100, medium has a value of 50, and low has a value of 10.

Table 5-4 shows that placing the server in the DMZ will provide the best protection from a DoS attack. Additionally, an IDS will also provide a high level of protection. The table helps to match up the best controls for the individual risks as follows:

- **DoS attack**—Protect with DMZ and/or IDS
- **Web defacing**—Protect with DMZ
- **Loss of website data from unauthorized access**—Encrypt data at rest and implement MFA

Survey for Determining Safeguards or Controls

The following table lists controls in the left column. Across the top, it lists risks. Please enter a value of low, medium, or high under each heading. The value you enter should indicate the value of the control to mitigate the risk. For example, if you think placing the web server in a DMZ will have a high success rate in preventing DoS attacks, enter *high* under this heading. If you think it will have a low success rate, enter *low*.

Mitigation Choices Survey

CONTROL	DOS ATTACK (LOW, MEDIUM, OR HIGH)	WEB DEFACING (LOW, MEDIUM, OR HIGH)	LOSS OF WEBSITE DATA FROM HARDWARE FAILURE (LOW, MEDIUM, OR HIGH)
Place web server in DMZ			
Add IDS			
Add RAID for data			
Create backup plan			
Implement Multi Factor Authentication to access data			
Encrypt data at rest			

Benefits

A qualitative assessment has several primary benefits:

- Uses the opinions of experts
- Is easy to complete
- Uses words, instead of numbers, which are easier to express and understand

TABLE 5-4 Mitigation choices survey results

CONTROL	DOS ATTACK	WEB DEFACING	LOSS OF WEBSITE DATA FROM HARDWARE FAILURE
Place web server in DMZ	High	High	Medium
Add IDS	High	High	Medium
Add RAID for data	Low	Low	Medium
Create backup plan	Low	Low	Medium
Implement Multi Factor Authentication to access data	Low	Medium	Medium
Encrypt data at rest	Low	Low	High

Data is gathered from the experts who know the systems the best. Their combined system knowledge and experience allow them to identify the source of problems quickly. As long as experts are available for gathering data, the risk assessment is easy to complete. They can be provided with surveys to complete at their own pace, and they don't even need to meet together; they can be interviewed separately.

A qualitative risk assessment uses scales, which can easily be adapted to the culture of the organization. The scales allow individuals to understand what the values are by being expressed in everyday words they use, which also makes it easier to involve people who may be experts in their field but are not security or IT experts.

For example, human resources (HR) experts may have significant knowledge about the requirements for HIPAA. They know the dangers from unprotected data and the actual fines

Performing an Assessment With the Delphi Method

One way that is commonly used to perform a qualitative assessment is the Delphi method, which can be used to gather data to create or identify a consensus.

A primary benefit of the Delphi method is that it allows individuals to freely share their opinions without pressure. Instead of all the participants talking through an issue in a meeting, responses are gathered independently.

The Delphi method can be accomplished in several ways. One way is to work through the following steps:

1. **Identifying a problem**—The problem can be with a single IT system or a group of servers. The problem should be within the knowledge of experts who are added to the team. For example, the problem could be related to the website failures and could be stated as "WebServer1 has suffered four failures in the past year resulting in losses."
2. **Gathering input from experts**—The problem is sent to the group of experts, and they are asked to respond. For the web server failure, they could be asked to identify primary risks. If the causes are known, they can be asked to identify the probability and risk. If the highest risks are known, the process can be repeated to identify the best solutions.
3. **Collating the responses**—The responses will be in different forms for different phases. For example, the responses could be a random list of risks, a prioritized list of risks, or a list of controls to mitigate the risk.
4. **Sharing the results**—Sharing the results will take different forms depending on the phase of the project. If a list of risks has just been collated, the team can now be asked to identify the probability and impact of each risk. When work on the controls begins, the process can be repeated. A list of controls to mitigate the risk can be requested. Then, the team can be asked to identify the effectiveness of the different controls for specific risks.
5. **Repeating as necessary**—The process can be repeated until all the data has been gathered.

The Delphi method is very flexible. Today, surveys can often be done via email. Many email programs actually allow surveys to be sent so users need only to click a button. Users could also fill out surveys created on an internal web server, which may take a little time to develop but the results can be quickly collated.

It is important that the data be gathered independently. If the data is gathered in a meeting, participant responses may be slanted based on the opinions of others in the room. A strong participant can sway others and prevent full participation from the team.

that can be assessed or the jail time awarded. HR experts can provide substantial input into a risk assessment.

Limitations

A qualitative assessment has several limitations. These include:

- **Subjective**—The analysis and results are based on opinions more than facts. A different perspective on these opinions could provide a completely different result. If the opinions are gathered in a group, a strong participant could shape the ideas of the entire group.
- **Based on expertise of the experts**—The value of the assessment is only as valuable as the expertise of the experts. If the experts have a solid foundation of knowledge and wide breadth of experience, the results can be valuable. On the other hand, if access to real experts is not available, the results may have very limited value.
- **No CBA**—A qualitative assessment does not include a CBA. The usefulness of the controls isn't as clear as with a quantitative analysis. Although the opinions of the experts are still valuable, the results may not be as clear to management. Management may have a more difficult time deciding which safeguards to use.
- **No real standards**—A company needs to define the scales used in the process. For example, the scale can be as simple as low, medium, and high. However, the scale needs to be developed and defined for the participants, which requires the expertise of someone who understands risk assessments and how the data will be used.

Comparing Quantitative and Qualitative Risk Assessments

As a reminder, neither method is considered superior to the other. They both have benefits and limitations. As a summary, here are a few comparisons between quantitative and qualitative risk assessments.

Quantitative analysis:

- Objective
- Uses numeric values, such as dollar amounts
- Reliably repeatable
- More time consuming
- Requires access to a significant amount of historical data
- Data not always easy to obtain
- Based on SLE, ARO, and ALE formulas
- Shows clear losses and savings with dollar values
- Data can easily be used in a CBA

Qualitative analysis:

- Subjective
- Based on opinions of experts
- Can be done quicker at a lower cost than quantitative analysis
- Uses word values, such as low, medium, and high
- Requires a definition of scales used in the risk assessment

Sample Risk Assessment Outline

A risk assessment ends with a report, which management can then use to decide what controls to implement. Following is a list of topics that are commonly included in a risk assessment report:

- **Introduction**—The introduction provides the purpose and scope of the risk assessment. It includes descriptions of the components, users, and locations for the system considered in the risk assessment.
- **Risk assessment approach**—This section identifies the approach used to complete the risk assessment. It includes details on how the data was collected and who was involved. If a qualitative approach is used, this section will describe the risk scale.
- **System characterization**—This section provides more details on the system. It could include details on the hardware, software, or network connections and may include diagrams to graphically show the assessed system.
- **Threat statement**—This section lists potential threats, threat sources, and threat actions. For example, one threat may be an attacker launching a DoS attack on an internet-facing server.
- **Risk assessment results**—Results can be listed as threat/vulnerability pairs representing a risk. The risk is described with existing security controls. The likelihood of the risk occurring with current controls is listed. How the risks are described depends on which analysis is used. A quantitative method uses terms such as SLE, ARO, and ALE. A qualitative method identifies probability and impact based on a defined scale. All of this data is supported with discussions identifying how the result was obtained.
- **Control recommendations**—A list of recommended safeguards or controls is provided. This list can include comments on the effectiveness of the controls. A quantitative method will often be accompanied by a CBA for each control. A qualitative method will often rank the effectiveness of the controls.
- **Summary**—The summary can be in one or more tables that summarize the results. This format makes it easy for management to see the highest risks based on the risk rating. The summary also makes it easy to approve any of the recommendations.

Risk Assessment Challenges

When completing a risk assessment, several challenges must be addressed and overcome. Many of these challenges are dependent on the type of assessment that was chosen. Both the quantitative and qualitative assessments have their own challenges. These challenges were listed in the previous section as limitations.

Several additional challenges exist. These include:

- Using a static process to evaluate a moving target
- Availability of resources and data
- Data consistency
- Estimating impact effects
- Providing results that support resource allocation and risk acceptance

These challenges are explored in the following sections.

Using a Static Process to Evaluate a Moving Target

As mentioned previously, a risk assessment is a point-in-time assessment. It evaluates the system against known risks at a specific time and considers the risks based on current controls. In other words, the risk assessment is a static process. However, security is not static. Risks can and do change because attackers and attacks are constantly changing.

As attackers become successful at an attack, security experts implement controls. At some point, these attacks are less successful. Attackers then learn new methods of attack. Security experts modify the controls or implement new controls, and the battle continues daily.

Some threats and vulnerabilities look as if they've been mitigated successfully and no longer present a risk. Then, suddenly, they appear as another threat. Domain Name System (DNS) cache poisoning is a good example. DNS cache poisoning can cause a system to resolve a website name to a bogus internet protocol (IP) address. Users may try to access Acme.com with a web browser, but, instead, they are redirected to Malware4u.com. DNS cache poisoning was identified years ago as a significant threat. It was successfully mitigated and fell into disuse. From an IT security perspective, it almost became a historical footnote.

Then, in the summer of 2008, a flaw was discovered and published by Dan Kaminsky. Quick as a flash, DNS cache poisoning was once again an issue. Once the results were published, attackers quickly learned how to exploit the vulnerability. DNS cache poisoning was once again raised as a serious concern. Security controls addressed this flaw, and DNS cache poisoning became rare again.

If a risk assessment was completed in March but a vulnerability is announced in June that affects the system, the validity of the assessment is affected. For this reason, being aware of new risks as they become known is necessary.

FYI

One way to stay informed of vulnerabilities is to subscribe to alerts from the US-Cybersecurity Infrastructure Security Agency CISA. Keeping up with the alerts shows new vulnerabilities are discovered every week. Some of these vulnerabilities represent very serious risks. Signing up to receive emails and alerts from CISA can be done at https://www.cisa.gov/about/contact-us/subscribe-updates-cisa

Availability of Resources and Data

Availability challenges are present in two primary areas. One area relates to the availability of resources, and the other area relates to the availability of data. Both areas are important to address early in the process of the risk assessment. If they are not addressed, they can seriously affect the quality.

Concerning resources, personnel involved in the assessment should be knowledgeable about the system they are assessing. With a higher level of expertise, a higher-quality assessment can be expected. If the risk assessment team does not have the high level of knowledge and experience they need, they may have to resort to guessing.

The risk assessment needs support from upper management. This support will help ensure that management dedicates adequate resources to the team. If a leader of a risk assessment has problems getting support from a specific department, upper management can help. On the other hand, if upper-level support is not available for the project, the leader will likely get less and less support.

As far as data goes, its availability is also important. Data availability will drive the type of assessment that is performed. For example, if a lot of internal historical data related to actual performance and outages is available, it can be used to perform a quantitative risk assessment. This historical data can be used to identify values for SLE and ARO. If this data isn't available, a qualitative risk assessment will probably be done instead.

> **TIP**
> Even having access to historical data, performing a qualitative risk assessment may still be chosen. One of the reasons for choosing to do a qualitative instead of a quantitative risk assessment might be time. A qualitative risk assessment can usually be completed more quickly than a quantitative risk assessment.

Without the availability of the right personnel and the right data, the risk assessment becomes much more difficult to complete. If the issues are addressed early, the chances of success will be better.

Data Consistency

Another challenge with risk assessments is data consistency. Data consistency refers to the accuracy of data. Several issues can affect data consistency. These include:

- Differences in data format
- Changes in data collection
- Changes in the business

Each of these concerns can directly affect the accuracy of the data. However, even having less than 100% accurate data doesn't mean that the data can't be used.

Some risk assessments address the accuracy of data with an **uncertainty level**, which indicates how valid the data is. If all conditions were ideal, the data would be 100% accurate. In this case, the uncertainty level would be 0%. In the real world, however, a 0% uncertainty level is unlikely.

For example, historical data could indicate that a website generates approximately $2,000 of revenue per hour. Current data could indicate this trend is continuing with slight growth. The certainty that the data is accurate could be 80%, or a 20% uncertainty level. When using this sales data to calculate the SLE, the uncertainty level could also be provided.

Differences in Data Format

Data format can affect how data is used, manipulated, and interpreted. In general, a database is more efficient for querying and manipulating large amounts of data. However, data could have originally been created in a word processing document or a spreadsheet. If data was migrated from one format to another, weighing the accuracy of the data differently can be chosen.

For example, data was previously stored in a Microsoft Excel worksheet but is now stored in a Microsoft SQL Server database. When it was stored in the worksheet, it met the needs of the user. However, it wasn't easy to view the data from different perspectives or query it to show different totals and subtotals. In the database, it is now easy to use queries to view the data with multiple perspectives. The data may be very similar, but the database now allows a deeper perspective on the data to be gained.

With this in mind, the users who worked with the Excel worksheets may have drawn accurate conclusions. However, the conclusions may not be as substantial as conclusions drawn from data stored in a database.

If the data is from different sources, recognizing that it may have been interpreted differently is important. This might cause inconsistencies when comparing the data. All of this can affect the uncertainty level of the data.

Changes in Data Collection

Changes in data collection can also affect the accuracy of data. The primary change that is likely to be seen is a change from manual data collection to automated data collection.

There are many wonderful things to say about humans, but the truth is that humans aren't the best at mundane repetitive tasks. Computers are. When people collect and enter data manually, errors should be expected.

Controls and checks help find these errors. Input validation methods verify that the data is valid. For example, a ZIP Code has five digits. An input validation method detects invalid ZIP Code entries of four or six digits. Additionally, one employee can double-check data entered by another employee.

Manual data entry can negatively affect the uncertainty level. Failing to double-check the data for accuracy can also affect the uncertainty level.

On the other hand, if data is collected using automated methods, the predictability of data is much higher. If data is collected, stored, and manipulated using automated methods, the uncertainty level will be much lower.

Changes in the Business

The amount of business a company does this year will usually be different from last year, which is often due to growth. For some businesses, however, changes in the amount of business could be due to loss of market share or some other business reason. The fact is, sales are rarely stagnant. In fact, stagnant sales are perceived negatively.

It is important to understand what happened in the past so that what will happen in the future can be predicted. However, the future is never exactly the same as the past. For example, a website may have had an average of $2,000 per hour in revenue last year. However, the sales over the Christmas season may have doubled over the previous year, and current predictions are that this year's sales may also double. All this together may require the modification of the average sales per hour from $2,000 to $4,000.

Similarly, the company could have lost market share in a certain sales market. The loss may have been because the company allocated less money for research and development or marketing or because of any of a dozen other reasons. So, if sales are decreasing, this fact should be taken into consideration.

> **NOTE**
>
> Change management is a process that ensures that changes are made only after a review process and that the changes are documented. It is an important process covered by the Information Technology Infrastructure Library (ITIL). Many companies use change management processes even if they aren't following ITIL practices directly.

Then again, although sales data may show that sales are decreasing, a new manager may be instituting changes to increase sales, and preliminary signs may be showing an increase. All of these factors could lead to changing the uncertainty level of the numbers used.

Estimating Impact Effects

The potential impact of any risk is difficult to estimate. The most important thing to realize is that the impact is just an estimate. If what will happen in the future could be accurately predicted, working in the IT or cybersecurity field would probably not be an option.

When estimating the impact effects, several factors come into play, which is true even when accurate historical data is available. For example, a website could have been attacked, resulting in an outage of several hours. While troubleshooting the outage, the technicians learn quite a bit. Yes, the primary focus is to resolve this current outage. However, the knowledge and experience gained from it is tucked away. The next time the server suffers an outage, the recovery time may be much quicker.

Even this example is dependent on several variables. A company with a high turnover rate of IT professionals doesn't build up the same experience level as does a company with a low turnover rate. If a system is down for the same reason it was down six months ago but it's the first time a new technician has seen it, the outage will likely be just as long.

On the other hand, previous attacks may have been successful due to vulnerabilities in the system. If these vulnerabilities were discovered, they were likely corrected. However, even if they were corrected, the corrections may not have been documented.

Without the documentation of the previous corrections, everything may appear to be the same today as it was during the previous attack. Instead, several changes may have been implemented that reduced the likelihood of the attack or the impact of the attack. In this example, the uncertainty level may be dependent on changing management practices in the organization.

Providing Results That Support Resource Allocation and Risk Acceptance

The results of a risk assessment need to be useful, which should come as no surprise. However, security professionals can fall into the trap of thinking security must be pursued at all costs, which isn't true. A proper balance between profitability and survivability must constantly be considered.

Two important points to consider are:

- Resource allocation
- Risk acceptance

Resource Allocation

Security teams don't have an unlimited amount of funds or number of personnel. Instead, security will be allocated a finite percentage of resources, an idea that is important to keep in mind when performing the risk assessment.

Any recommendations need to be realistic. They need to consider the culture of the business and the actual potential for the recommendations to be accepted.

Risk Acceptance

Some organizations are willing to accept more risks than others, which is neither right nor wrong; accepting more risk is just the way a business operates. For some businesses, risk taking is an indication of how innovative they can be. When creating a risk assessment, being aware of the business culture is important.

There are two sides to accepting more risk:

1. The greater the risk, the greater the rewards.
2. Greater risks can result in larger losses.

For example, many companies are in existence today that had stock for sale for less than a dollar at one point. Anyone who bought $10,000 of their stock would be a millionaire today. However, few actually bought that $10,000 worth of stock. The reason is that, when the stock was at a low price, no one knew whether the company would survive. Some people took the risk and were greatly rewarded. However, others took similar risks on other companies that have since gone bankrupt. Their risky investment turned out to be a huge loss.

Remembering that senior managers make the big decisions in a company is important. They are responsible for identifying which risks to mitigate, share or transfer, avoid, or accept. Recommendations made to senior managers should be based on and consistent with what residual risk they are expected to accept.

Regardless, the responsibility still exists to present all of the data. If some of the recommendations clearly don't look as if they will be accepted, they can be included in the report but not in the list of actual recommendations.

> **NOTE**
>
> Residual risk is any risk that remains after management has decided to implement controls. Senior management is responsible for making these decisions. Additionally, senior management is responsible for any losses that occur as a result of residual risk.

Best Practices for Risk Assessment

Risk assessments can proceed differently in different organizations. A risk assessment of a web server may look substantially different from an assessment that evaluates HIPAA data. However, several things can be included to help ensure success.

The following list identifies several best practices for risk assessment approaches:

- **Starting with clear goals and a defined scope**—A risk assessment should include a scope statement. The scope statement helps keep the assessment on track and prevents scope creep.
- **Enlisting senior management support**—Senior management needs to be committed to the risk assessment. Without support, the risk assessment loses value. When risk assessment teams realize the risk assessment isn't valued, they put less time and effort into it. An assessment without senior managers' support is almost doomed from the outset.
- **Building a strong risk assessment team**—The value of the risk assessment is based on the competence and expertise of the risk assessment team. Team members should have expertise in the system. For example, in performing a qualitative analysis, if data is gathered from personnel who aren't experts, then their opinions won't be considered as

valuable as data gathered from experts. Team members should also understand the methodology used for the risk assessment.

- **Repeating the risk assessment regularly**—Threats, risks, and vulnerabilities are constantly evolving; therefore, a risk assessment should be repeated on a regular basis. Some federal agencies require risk assessments to be repeated at least every 3 years. Many organizations create a risk assessment policy, which identifies what the organization is expected to do on a recurring basis and defines generic goals for any risk assessments.
- **Defining a methodology to use**—By consistently using the same methodology, people become better at it. For example, a company could decide to use qualitative risk assessments on a regular basis. If this is the case, the scales that are used should be defined. When assessments are done the same way repeatedly, they are easier to accomplish and tend to provide higher-quality results.
- **Providing a report of clear risks and recommendations**—Every risk assessment should end with a report that identifies the findings, which should be clearly stated. Ensuring that the risks are clearly defined is important. Even more important is to ensure that recommendations are clear. The whole purpose of the risk assessment is ultimately to mitigate risks with recommended controls. If the recommendations aren't clear, the report loses a significant amount of its value.

CHAPTER SUMMARY

Risk assessments are used to identify and quantify risks. They do this by identifying threats and vulnerabilities and then applying an assessment methodology to prioritize the risks. Once the risks are quantified, controls and safeguards can be identified. A risk assessment can also be used to identify the best controls to implement.

The two primary risk assessment methods are quantitative and qualitative. A quantitative risk assessment is used when historical data is readily available. This data can be used to derive the ALE from SLE and ARO: ALE = SLE × ARO. A qualitative risk assessment uses the opinions of experts. It doesn't have predefined formulas but instead requires that a scale be created, such as low, medium, and high. The quantitative risk assessment provides a CBA. The qualitative risk assessment, on the other hand, can be accomplished in a shorter period of time.

KEY CONCEPTS AND TERMS

annual loss expectancy (ALE)
annual rate of occurrence (ARO)
exposure factor (EF)
probability
qualitative risk assessment
quantitative risk assessment
redundant array of independent disks (RAID)
safeguard
safeguard value
single loss expectancy (SLE)
single point of failure (SPOF)
uncertainty level

CHAPTER 5 ASSESSMENT

1. What can be used to help quantify risks?
   A. SLE
   B. ARO
   C. Risk assessment
   D. Risk mitigation plan
   E. All of the above
2. ________ describes the loss that will happen to the asset as a result of the threat, which is expressed as a percentage value.
3. Risk assessments are a static process.
   A. True
   B. False
4. A ________ risk assessment uses SLE.
5. What elements are included in a qualitative analysis?
   A. SLE, ALE, and ARO
   B. ALE, ARO, and ARP
   C. Probability and impact
   D. Threats and vulnerabilities
6. What elements are included in a quantitative analysis?
   A. SLE, ALE, and ARO
   B. ALE, ARO, and ARP
   C. Probability and impact
   D. Threats and vulnerabilities
7. Qualitative analysis is less time consuming than quantitative analysis.
   A. True
   B. False
8. A primary benefit of a ________ risk assessment is that it can be completed more quickly than other methods.
9. A primary benefit of a ________ risk assessment is that it includes details for a cost-benefit analysis.
10. What must be defined when performing a qualitative risk assessment?
    A. Formulas used for ALE
    B. Scales used to define probability and impact
    C. Scales used to define SLE and ALE
    D. Acceptable levels of risk
11. A ________ risk assessment is objective. It uses data that can be verified.
12. A ________ risk assessment is subjective. It relies on the opinions of experts.
13. One of the challenges facing risk assessments is getting accurate data. What can be included in the risk assessment report to give an indication of the reliability of the data?
    A. Probability statement
    B. Accuracy scale
    C. Validity level
    D. Uncertainty level
14. An IT security team leader is working on a qualitative risk assessment for her company. She is thinking about the final report. What should the IT security team leader consider when providing the results and recommendations? (Select two.)
    A. Resource allocation
    B. Risk acceptance
    C. SLE and ARO
    D. SLE and ALE
15. Of the following, what would be considered a best practice when performing risk assessments?
    A. Starting with clear goals and a defined scope
    B. Enlisting support of senior management
    C. Repeating the risk assessment regularly
    D. Providing clear recommendations
    E. All of the above

CHAPTER 6

Performing a Risk Assessment

RISK ASSESSMENT IS OFTEN CONSIDERED SYNONYMOUS with risk analysis. It is the process of identifying risks to the operations of a business. Such risks include assets, people, technology, and operations, such as the mission, functions, and reputation of the business. The National Institute of Standards and Technology's (NIST's) Special Publication (SP) 800-37 *Risk Management Framework for Information Systems and Organizations* provides risk management guidelines that include risk assessment, threat and vulnerability analysis, and security controls that serve to mitigate risks. In Chapter 5, we discussed the preparations for risk assessment. In this chapter, we will explore how to actually perform a risk assessment.

There are other risk management approaches, other than NIST SP 800-37, and we will explore some of those in this chapter and in the rest of this book. However, this is such a common methodology that we will use it frequently as an exemplar. Here are the basic steps of the NIST SP 800-37 framework:

Prepare	Essential activities to prepare the organization to manage security and privacy risks
Categorize	Categorize the system and information processed, stored, and transmitted based on an impact analysis
Select	Select the set of NIST SP 800-53 controls to protect the system based on risk assessment(s)
Implement	Implement the controls and document how controls are deployed
Assess	Assess to determine if the controls are in place, operating as intended, and producing the desired results
Authorize	Senior official makes a risk-based decision to authorize the system (to operate)
Monitor	Continuously monitor control implementation and risks to the system

Several steps must be taken to perform a risk assessment. The first step is to clearly define what will be assessed, which involves describing the system. This is somewhat different than defining the scope, which was discussed in Chapter 5. This is more detailed. Specific items are listed. Data is then collected to identify the threats and vulnerabilities, which helps to identify the risks. Next, controls, or countermeasures, to mitigate the risks are identified, and in-place and planned controls are evaluated. The final step of performing the risk assessment is to evaluate and recommend additional controls. These recommendations should be supported with a cost-benefit analysis (CBA).

Chapter 6 Topics

This chapter covers the following topics and concepts:

- What to consider when selecting a risk assessment methodology
- How to identify the management structure
- How to identify assets and activities
- How to identify and evaluate relevant threats
- How to identify and evaluate relevant vulnerabilities
- How to identify and evaluate controls
- How to select a methodology based on the assessment needs
- How to develop mitigating recommendations
- What presenting risk assessment results entails
- What the best practices for performing risk assessments are

Chapter 6 Goals

When you complete this chapter, you will be able to:

- Select an appropriate risk assessment methodology
- Define the operational characteristics and mission of the system to be assessed
- State the importance of reviewing previous findings and status
- Describe the relevance of a management structure to a risk assessment
- Identify the types of assets to include in a risk assessment
- List steps to identify and evaluate threats
- List actions to identify and evaluate vulnerabilities
- List actions to identify and evaluate controls
- Describe the difference between in-place and planned controls
- Describe the process used to assess threats, vulnerabilities, and exploits
- Describe the process used to develop mitigation recommendations
- Describe the results of a risk assessment
- List best practices for performing risk assessments

Selecting a Risk Assessment Methodology

Once the decision has been made to perform a risk assessment, an outline will need to be created to guide the process by deciding what specific steps to take. Performing a risk assessment isn't a project decided on one day and completed the next. It takes time and planning.

The two primary types of risk assessment approaches are *quantitative* and *qualitative*, as you may recall from Chapter 5. This chapter helps to paint the overall picture of both approaches. In Chapter 5, we discussed preparatory steps. In those steps you will have identified assets and threats within the scope of the assessment. Now you will begin actually assessing. In general, a risk assessment involves the following steps:

- Identifying and evaluating existing controls
- Identifying any gaps in existing controls verses identified threats and vulnerabilities
- Evaluating risks
- Developing recommendations to mitigate risks
- Determining residual risk after controls are applied
- Presenting recommendations to management

Before progressing with the risk assessment, two preliminary actions need to be completed. These are:

- Defining the assessment
- Reviewing previous findings

Defining the Assessment

What will be assessed needs to clearly be defined. If a system is to be assessed, then the system needs to be described. This is more detailed than what was described in Chapter 5. An example of a system might be the Human Resource department's (HR's) personnel records database. This should be in as much detail as needed. For example, is this an Oracle database or perhaps Microsoft SQL Server? You should also note if it is an on-premises database, or cloud hosted. If a process is to be assessed, then the process needs to be described. An example of a process would be the finance department's creation of an invoice. Identifying the resources involved in that invoice process could include users inputting data, the servers involved, the applications involved, and perhaps other resources.

When describing the system or process, two primary areas are often the focus:

- Operational characteristics
- Mission of the system

The scope of the risk assessment is also important to define to help prevent uncontrolled changes, which can result in cost overruns and missed deadlines.

NOTE

Scope of risk assessments: According to NIST SP 800-30, "the scope of the risk assessment determines what will be considered in the assessment. Risk assessment scope affects the range of information available to make risk-based decisions and is determined by the organizational official requesting the assessment and the risk management strategy." Similar to "scope creep," when unplanned work gets added to a project, the risk manager needs to define the risk assessment scope to avoid unplanned data gathering and analysis.

Operational Characteristics

Operational characteristics define how the system operates in an environment. Just naming the system, such as "Email server," is not enough; instead, how the system is currently configured and operating needs to be identified.

For example, **FIGURE 6-1** shows a single email server in a network that handles all email to and from the internet. The server also provides email services for all clients in the internal network. But the illustration in Figure 6-1 is old and doesn't reflect the organization's current configuration.

FIGURE 6-2, on the other hand, shows the organization's current network diagram, which has a demilitarized zone (DMZ). The DMZ includes an email server used to send and receive email from the internet and an internal email server that sends and receives email from the DMZ server but does not interact with the internet.

The differences between Figures 6-1 and 6-2 help show the importance of documenting current operational characteristics. What would happen if a risk assessment was begun

FIGURE 6-1

Outdated configuration of email server in the organization's network.

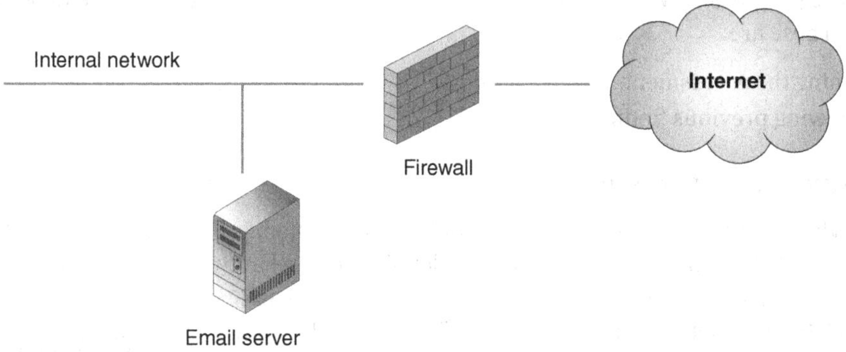

FIGURE 6-2

Upgraded diagram showing an internal email server and an email server in a DMZ.

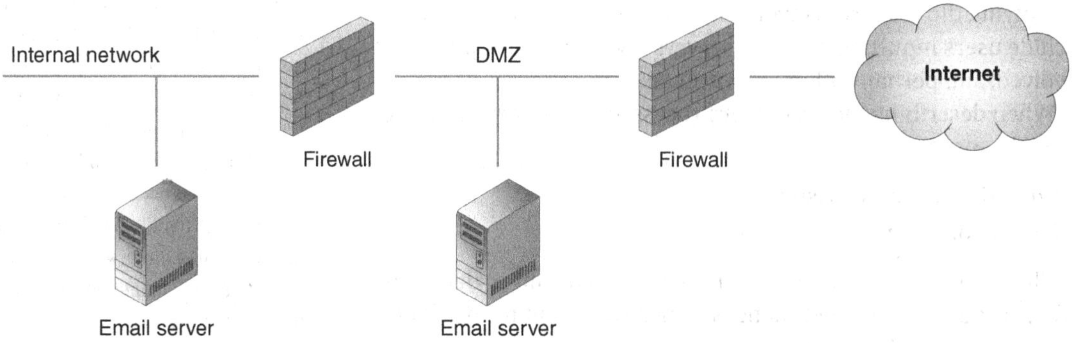

by evaluating the threats against the system in Figure 6-1? The obvious answer is that the information would be outdated and valuable time would be spent on the wrong effort.

The risk assessment needs to be performed against the current system. However, the current configuration isn't always apparent or readily available. Sometimes, discovering the current configuration takes some digging. Here are two simple questions that can be asked:

- Do the diagrams to be used show all of the current systems?
- Does the documentation describe the current systems' configurations?

Mission of the System

The mission of the system defines what the system does. Compared with the operational characteristics of the system, the mission is easy to define. The definition of the mission for any single system can be as short as a paragraph or can consist of simple bullet statements.

For example, an email system could have the following mission: The email server provides all email services for the organization, which include the following functions:

- Routing email between internal clients
- Accepting email from external email servers and routing to internal clients
- Accepting email from internal clients and routing to external email servers
- Scanning all email attachments and removing malware
- Scanning all email for spam and stripping out confirmed spam
- Logging email

Managing Configuration and Change

Configuration management and change management are two important risk management processes, and they also have a direct impact on risk assessments. Sometimes, these two processes are mentioned together, but they are different.

Configuration management (CM) refers to a systematic process for establishing and maintaining consistency of a system's performance and functional attributes with its requirements, design, and operational information. The primary goal is to manage change without negatively impacting system integrity or availability. Configuration management often depends on a configuration management database (CMDB). A CMDB is a centralized repository that stores information on configuration items (CIs) and their relationships. It is vital for impact analysis, incident resolution, and compliance audits.

Change management prevents unapproved changes to systems, thereby reducing risks. All changes are formally requested using a change management process. Technical experts review the requests and then either approve or disapprove them. Change management is critical to allow any proposed changes to be reviewed for new risk. Any proposed changes must be documented, assessed, and approved by the business/process owner. And, if needed, new controls might be included to mitigate any new risk. The goal is to reduce unintended outages that result from changes.

When change management is not implemented, a change to one system can easily cause an outage in another system. For example, a technician in a large organization is troubleshooting a problem with a printer. The printer isn't automatically receiving an Internet Protocol (IP) address, which prevents print jobs from reaching the printer. The technician manually assigns an IP address and verifies the printer is working.

The IP address assigned to the printer is also assigned to a server that other technicians are repairing at the time. After the technicians repair the server and bring it online, it no longer works properly. The printer has the server's IP address, causing an IP address conflict. The technicians have to spend extra time troubleshooting the issue and correcting both problems.

These problems could have been avoided had a change management process been in effect. The printer technician would have submitted the change request for the printer, and the administrator who assigns IP addresses would have easily seen the conflict and denied the request. Therefore, the server wouldn't have had an extended outage.

Additionally, a change management process ensures the correct documentation for changes. Simply put, configuration management is about the arrangement of the components of a system, whereas change management is about the modification of the components.

When an organization has mature processes in place for configuration and change management, risk assessments are easier to perform because identifying the current status of a system is easier and available documentation is more up to date.

Reviewing Previous Findings

If previous audits or risk assessments are available, they should be reviewed. These reports can contain much valuable information to make the job of performing a risk assessment easier.

These reports list assets, threats, and vulnerabilities and should also list controls currently in place. They may provide recommendations for additional controls. Three items especially worth investigating are:

- **Recommendations**—Previous recommendations give insight into several issues. They address threats, vulnerabilities, and controls that were considered relevant at the time. Even though many issues may have changed, some of them may be the same or similar.
- **Current status of accepted recommendations**—Ideally, all previously accepted recommendations are in place. The effectiveness of approved and implemented recommendations can then be measured. However, if an approved recommendation isn't in place, the previous report may help in determining why it wasn't implemented. Perhaps the hardware or software is still in the purchasing pipeline, or the approved recommendation was simply ignored.
- **Unapproved recommendations**—The recommendations that were not approved can also give some insight into the business. They may indicate that the organization is willing to accept a higher level of residual risk or that the organization suffered losses that would have been mitigated by an unapproved control. If the latter is true, then management may be more receptive to the control at this time.

Identifying the Management Structure

The management structure refers to how responsibilities are assigned. When the scope of the risk assessment is defined, keeping the scope within the ownership of a single entity is helpful. Working with one entity allows for easier implementation of recommendations.

A small organization may have a single information technology (IT) division that is responsible for all IT systems and processes. Because its staff members control all IT systems, they can implement recommendations for any of the systems.

However, a larger organization may have several IT divisions. In this case, various managers or management teams oversee different IT systems, and each manager has different responsibilities. For example, an organization may have the following divisions for IT management:

- **Network infrastructure**—This division is responsible for all the routers and switches in the network and may include all the firewalls.
- **User and computer management**—This division performs the day-to-day management of the network and accounts and may also include basic security measures. For example, the **Group Policy** tool can manage accounts in a Microsoft domain, and administrators who manage the Microsoft domain would manage Group Policy.
- **Email servers**—Some larger organizations have 10 or more email servers to manage email and trained personnel who are dedicated to primarily managing these servers. Personnel ensure email delivery and manage spam filtering and malicious attachments.
- **Web servers**—An organization can have dozens of web servers configured in one or more web farms. A web farm can generate a significant amount of revenue and have dedicated personnel to manage it.
- **Database servers**—Many organizations have a large amount of data stored in databases. Large databases are stored on dedicated servers. The knowledge needed to manage these servers is specialized, so some organizations have dedicated database administrators to manage them.
- **Configuration and change management**—This division oversees configuration settings and changes to either all servers or all systems. The team members may be responsible for building new servers, and they coordinate and document all change requests.

> **NOTE**
>
> Group Policy is an automated management tool used in Windows operating systems. A policy can be set once and apply to all users and computers in the domain. For example, a password policy can be set that applies to all users, which can ensure that users use strong passwords and regularly change them.

A small organization may perform a risk assessment for many systems at the same time. However, a larger organization will likely separate the risk assessments. For example, a large organization hosts e-commerce websites. Elements of the websites include web servers, database servers, and firewalls. However, various divisions within the organization manage these different elements. One division manages the web servers; another division manages the database servers; and a third division manages network security, including the firewalls. Performing a single risk assessment on all three elements can be challenging, and this is especially true when implementing recommendations. Managers in the different divisions might have competing goals, schedules, and priorities.

However, if the organization assesses a single division at a time, the results are easier to implement. For example, three separate risk assessments could be performed, one each for the web servers, database servers, and firewalls. Each assessment would have specific recommendations targeted for the owners of the system.

Identifying Assets and Activities Within Risk Assessment Boundaries

Asset valuation is the process of determining the fair market value of an asset, which is one of the first priorities of risk management. The asset value can be determined from the asset replacement value or either what the asset provides to the organization or the cost to recover the asset. The value can also be determined using a combination of both values.

After the values of the assets have been determined, then their importance can be prioritized. If an asset is worth $1,000, it may require one level of protection. If another asset is worth $1 million, that asset may require another level of protection. Keep in mind that assets are not just the physical equipment. Frequently information on the systems is worth more than the cost of the systems themselves.

NOTE

This section introduces assets and activities related to risk assessment.

Only the assets that are within the boundary of the risk assessment should be evaluated. Scope creep occurs when assets outside the scope of the risk assessment are evaluated, a process that results in wasted time and resources.

The value of an asset can be viewed from different perspectives:

- **Replacement value**—The replacement value is the cost to purchase a new asset to replace an existing asset. For example, if a laptop fails or is stolen, the price to purchase a new laptop with similar hardware and software may be $1,500.
- **Recovery value**—The recovery value is the cost to get the asset operational after a failure. For example, if the hard drive on a server fails, the entire server wouldn't be replaced. Instead, just the hard drive would be replaced, and steps would be taken to recover the system, which may require reinstalling the operating system and restoring data from a backup. The time needed to perform the repair would also need to be considered. For example, if a repair requires two hours, the system is not available for two hours. For example, if the system is a web server generating $10,000 an hour in revenue, $20,000 would be included as part of the recovery value.

Several elements need to be considered when determining the value of any asset. These include:

- System access and availability
- System functions
- Hardware and software assets
- Personnel assets
- Data and information assets
- Facilities and supplies

System Access and Availability

Access and availability refer to how and when the asset needs to be available. Some assets need to be available 24 hours a day, 7 days a week. Other assets need to be available only Monday through Friday during business hours. The more available the asset needs to be, the greater are the risks related to outages.

For example, a web server is used to sell products over the internet. Customers may access the website at any time, but, if the website is not operational when the customer tries to access it, the company loses a sale. Moreover, a customer may have been lost.

With this in mind, the risk assessment needs to consider the risks associated with this website going down at any given time, which includes how to perform maintenance on the system without taking the website down. Maintenance includes performing backups of the data and keeping the system up to date.

The web server may be one of many servers in a web farm, or it may be one of several web servers in a failover cluster. Both configurations allow a single server to go down while the website continues to function, but, if a single server is run, an outage can be catastrophic.

On the other hand, a system could have a file server that is used only internally by employees when they are at work between 8:00 a.m. and 5:00 p.m., Monday through Friday. This schedule allows extensive time for performing backups or other maintenance when employees are not at work.

System Functions

The functions of a service-providing system should be considered when determining the asset's value. Of particular importance is how the functions are performed, manually or through automation.

For example, the value of email in an organization is being evaluated. The email system could have several elements, including a spam filter. Studies report that as much as 90% of the email sent through the internet is spam. Spam filters will eliminate some of this spam with a goal of not eliminating any valid emails.

A spam filter that filters out as much as 30% of the spam provides a significant reduction in unwanted email with a high assurance that valid email won't be filtered. **FIGURE 6-3** shows an email server with a spam appliance added to filter spam. In the figure, all email is routed from the internet through the spam appliance. The appliance filters some of the spam and sends the rest of the email to the email server.

FIGURE 6-3

Email server with a spam appliance.

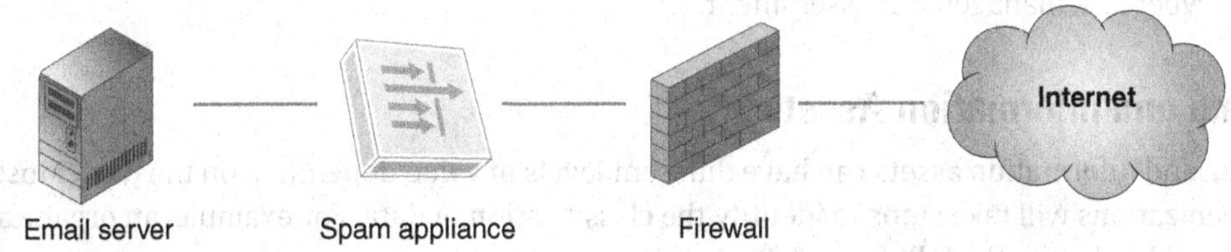

NOTE

Whitelisting means that only those items on the **whitelist** are allowed; all others are denied by default. Blacklisting takes the opposite approach. Everything is allowed unless it has been explicitly added to the **blacklist**. With email, whitelisting can be too restrictive and prohibit ever getting email from new sources. However, regarding deciding what software to allow to be installed, whitelisting can be very effective.

With this in mind, what is the value of the spam filter? It uses an automated process, so the value is simply the value of the appliance. If it breaks or malfunctions, it can be replaced.

However, some spam filters require much more interaction, such as dedicated technicians who are constantly viewing the filtered spam to ensure it doesn't include any valid emails. These technicians could be adding valid email source addresses to whitelists and known spammers to blacklists.

When calculating the value of the manually managed spam appliance, the work done by the administrator also needs to be considered. The value of the asset may be higher if additional labor and expertise are needed to initially configure it as well as manage it.

Hardware and Software Assets

Hardware assets are any assets that can be physically touched, which include computers, such as laptops, workstations, and servers. Hardware assets also include network devices, such as routers, switches, and firewalls.

A wide range of values exist among the devices. A simple desktop PC can cost less than $500. However, a high-end server can cost tens of thousands of dollars.

Software assets include both the operating systems and the applications. The operating system is what allows the computer to operate; an operating system could be a Microsoft system, such as Windows 11 or Windows Server 2025, or it could be a UNIX/Linux or Macintosh system.

Applications allow tasks to be performed. For example, Microsoft Word is an application that allows documents to be created and edited. Similarly, Oracle is a server-level application used to manage databases.

Operating systems and applications can also have a wide range of costs. For example, the operating system and applications for a desktop PC can range in the hundreds of dollars. However, the operating system and applications for a server can easily range in the thousands of dollars.

Personnel Assets

Personnel are obviously important assets to an organization. This is why human resources departments expend substantial efforts to hire and retain qualified personnel. However, assessing the value of the people working for an organization is typically outside the scope of a cyber risk management assessment.

Data and Information Assets

Data and information assets can have different levels of value depending on the data. Most organizations will take steps to identify the classification of data. For example, an organization could identify the following data classifications:

- **Public data**—Public data is freely available to anyone. It may be available via public sources, such as news releases or other publications, or via an organization's website.
- **Private data**—Private data is internal data. It includes data on employees and customers. Because of its delicate nature, personal data should be protected for fear that the information may be abused, for example, for purposes of identity theft. It may also include data on internal processes.
- **Proprietary data**—Proprietary data is highly valuable data and deserves a high level of protection. If this data is lost, it could seriously affect the company's profitability. For example, a company could spend millions of dollars on research and development whose goal is to create a product the company will sell. If a competitor gets this data, it could beat the originating company to market and sell the product itself, resulting in the research and development funds being lost.
- **Trade Secrets**—Trade secrets are a form of proprietary data, but are considered highly valuable and need to be protected accordingly. A trade secret is confidential business information that provides a company with a competitive advantage. This information must be secret (not generally known), have economic value, and be subject to reasonable efforts to maintain its secrecy. Typically, reasonable efforts to maintain its secrecy mean security beyond what is used for non-trade secret information.

Facilities and Supplies

Other items to consider when valuing assets are the facilities and supplies needed to run the business. This information is needed when calculating the company's insurance needs.

Insurance is one of those items that a business always wants to have but never wants to use. It provides a layer of protection if the company suffers a loss. However, the loss is rarely painless. Even if the insurance company covers the loss, the process is difficult.

Some organizations may realize that one of their facilities is so important that it needs redundancy. In this case, *redundancy* is another site that can perform the same functions. The four types of alternate sites are:

- **Hot site**—A location that can take over the operations of another location within a short period of time. A hot site has all the hardware, software, and data needed to perform the critical functions of the original site and is the most expensive of the four types of alternate sites.
- **Cold site**—A building with electricity and running water but little else. Computers and data can be brought to this location to set up operations. A cold site is the least expensive of the four sites. However, it takes the longest time to set up and is the hardest to test.
- **Warm site**—A compromise between a hot site and a cold site. It may include all the hardware, but the data may not be up to date, and it may take as long as one or more days to implement.
- **Mobile site**—A compromise between a warm and a cold site. It has portable structures with necessary hardware and software. The temperature of a mobile site depends on how much infrastructure it has available for use; hence, it could almost function like a warm or cold site.

The type of alternate site chosen depends on the value of the primary location. The supplies that will be stored there need to be considered to ensure the alternate location can perform the same type of work. Of course, an alternate location may not be necessary at all.

Identifying and Evaluating Relevant Threats

A threat is any potential danger to the data, the hardware, or the systems. A threat assessment is the process of identifying threats.

How threats interact with risks as a whole is important to understand. **FIGURE 6-4** shows the relationship between threats, attacks, vulnerabilities, and loss. A threat creates an attack, which exploits a vulnerability. When the threat/vulnerability pair occurs, a loss is incurred.

NOTE

This section introduces threats and activities related to risk assessment.

In the diagram, an attacker is presented as a threat. However, a threat can be anything that can compromise confidentiality, integrity, or availability. Threats can be external or internal, natural or man-made, or intentional or accidental.

One of three primary methods can be used to identify threats. They are:

- Reviewing historical data
- Performing threat modeling
- Performing threat intelligence

Reviewing Historical Data

History often repeats itself, and this is true with IT systems. Much time can be saved by reviewing historical data to identify realistic threats.

When reviewing historical data, the following events are important:

- **Attacks**—If an organization's website has been attacked before, likely it will be attacked again. The success of the next attack depends on the level of protection that was implemented since then, which is true for any type of event.
- **Natural events**—If hurricanes have hit a company's location before, they likely will do so in the future. Most organizations that are in risk zones for natural disasters, such as

FIGURE 6-4

Threats and vulnerabilities.

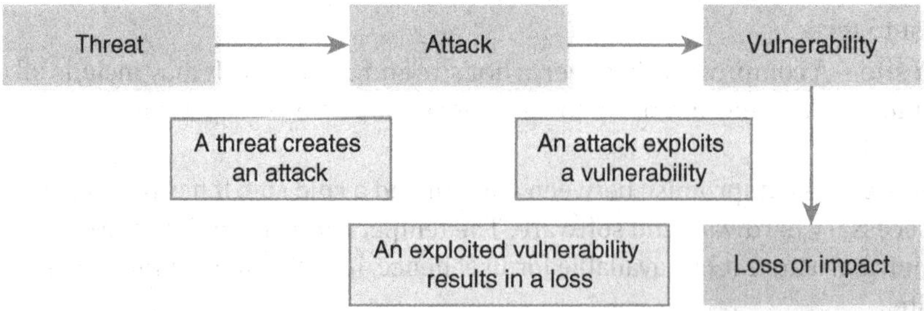

hurricanes, tornadoes, and earthquakes, have disaster recovery and business continuity plans in place. These plans should be reviewed, if not tested, on a regular basis, such as once a year.

- **Accidents**—Accidents can be any accidental event that affects confidentiality, integrity, or availability and includes users accidentally deleting data. Accidents can also include user errors or mishaps in the workplace.
- **Equipment failures**—Equipment failures result in outages, and some systems are more prone to failure than others. Additionally, some failures have a much greater impact on the mission of the business. By analyzing past failures, often, future failures can be predicted. The systems that will benefit from additional redundant hardware should be identified.

Performing Threat Modeling

Threat modeling is a process used to identify possible threats on a system by looking at a system from the attacker's perspective. The result of threat modeling is a document called a threat model.

The threat model provides information on:

- **The system**—Background information on the system is also included.
- **Threat profile**—The threat profile is a list of threats that identifies what the attacker may try to do to the system, including possible goals of the attack. For example, one attack may attempt to take the system down, and another attack may attempt to access data in the system.
- **Threat analysis**—Each threat in the threat profile is analyzed to determine whether an asset is vulnerable. Threat analysis includes reviewing existing controls to determine their effectiveness against the threat.

Threat modeling allows the prioritization of attacks based on their probability of occurring and their potential harm.

Performing Threat Intelligence

Performing cyberthreat intelligence is the process of being aware of current threats that are likely to affect your systems. That can be attacks on systems similar to yours or in your industry. For example, if there is a current attack being executed against Windows Server 2025, and you run Windows Server 2025 instances, then you should be aware of this threat. There are a number of websites that will help you with this.

Alien Vault

Alien Vault Open Threat Exchange provides a platform for exchanging cyberthreat intelligence data. OTX (Open Threat Exchange) is an open-access platform where users can publish and subscribe to indicators of compromise (IOCs), threat actor profiles, attack techniques, and other cybersecurity intelligence. It is free to use and integrates with security tools to enrich threat detection capabilities. You can browse data on their website, https://otx.alienvault.com/, or set up programmatic connections to automatically pull data relevant to you. Their system provides something they call OTX Pulses. Pulses are curated threat intelligence packages that include indicators of compromise (IoC) descriptions of threat actors, and related information.

SANS Storm Center

The SANS Institute has their "Storm Center" which provides information on ongoing threats: https://isc.sans.edu/register.html. The Storm Center is a free, community-driven cybersecurity threat monitoring and alerting service. Operated by the SANS Institute, it functions as a kind of "internet weather report", providing real-time data and analysis on malicious cyberactivity happening across the globe. This site provides real-time threat information and has data such as the most targeted ports, protocol anomalies, and geographic patterns of attacks.

CVE Database

The CVE Database (Common Vulnerabilities and Exposures) is a publicly accessible, standardized list of known cybersecurity vulnerabilities and exposures. It serves as a critical resource for security professionals, IT administrators, and developers by providing a common naming convention and reference for publicly identifying and evaluating relevant vulnerabilities: https://www.cve.org/

Identifying and Evaluating Relevant Vulnerabilities

A vulnerability is a weakness in physical, technical, or operational security. It can be procedural, technical, or physical.

Two things are certainly related to vulnerabilities:

- **All systems have vulnerabilities**—Eliminating all vulnerabilities is just as impossible as eliminating all risks. The goal is to identify the relevant vulnerabilities so controls can be implemented to reduce the weaknesses.
- **Not all vulnerabilities result in a loss**—Only when the threat and vulnerability come together as a threat/vulnerability pair does a loss occur. Only the relevant vulnerabilities need to be identified and evaluated.

One of the ways to identify and evaluate vulnerabilities is through assessments. The two primary assessments are:

- Vulnerability
- Exploit

NOTE

A vulnerability assessment is performed to discover weaknesses. However, realizing that attackers can perform the same steps is important to remember. Many of the popular vulnerability assessment suites include tools that can be used to perform exploit assessments.

Vulnerability Assessments

A **vulnerability assessment** is a process used to discover weaknesses in a system. The assessment will then prioritize the vulnerabilities to determine which weaknesses are relevant.

Vulnerability assessments can be performed internally or externally. An internal assessment attempts to discover weaknesses from within the network, and an external assessment attempts to discover what attackers outside the company may see.

A vulnerability assessment often starts by gathering information, using vulnerability scanners to perform network reconnaissance. A vulnerability assessment is similar to an enemy scouting out a target to evaluate it and identify the best method of attack. A vulnerability assessment may have several goals, such as:

- **Identifying IP addresses**—Ping scanner tools identify which IP addresses are in use. When a system responds to a ping, it is operational with that IP address.
- **Identifying names**—For computers on the internet, "Whois" tools can be used to identify the name of a computer from the IP address.
- **Identifying operating systems**—A fingerprinting tool can identify which operating system is running on an IP address. The tool sends traffic to and receives traffic from the system and then analyzes the traffic to determine which operating system is running. For example, a Microsoft operating system includes unique bits in Internet Control Message Protocol (ICMP) traffic. These bits verify that it is a Microsoft product. Similarly, some UNIX and Linux operating systems include bits in ICMP packets that identify those operating systems.
- **Identifying open ports**—A port scan identifies open ports, which identify which protocols and what services are running. For example, if port 80 is open, the Hypertext Transfer Protocol (HTTP) is running on the system, which indicates it is a web server.
- **Identifying weak passwords**—A password cracker determines the password for one or more accounts. The success of the password cracker largely depends on the strength of the password, which means that a password cracker can discover weak passwords.
- **Capturing data**—Data transferred over the network can be captured and analyzed. If it has been transferred in cleartext or is unencrypted, it can be read.

NOTE

This section introduces the process of identifying and evaluating vulnerabilities.

Several tools are available for performing vulnerability assessments. Some tools perform only a specific function, such as translating an IP address to a name. Other tools include multiple functions, such as Microsoft Office, which includes a full suite of applications.

Some of the commonly used vulnerability assessment tools are:

- **Nmap**—Nmap is a free network mapping tool. It combines a ping scanner, to discover IP addresses, with a port scanner, to determine open ports. It then uses other techniques to discover the operating system and other details of the remote system.
- **Nessus**—Nessus is a commercial product that provides a full suite of tools. As an example, it can run Nmap or one of several other port scanners, can detect common vulnerabilities in the configuration of a system, and includes password crackers. Tenable Network Security sells Nessus, and the company regularly improves the product by publishing new tools in the form of snap-ins.
- **SAINT**—SAINT is an acronym for System Administrator's Integrated Network Tool. Just as Nessus includes a full suite of vulnerability tools, so does SAINT. Saint Corporation sells SAINT and other security tools.

- **Shodan.io**—Shodan.io is a search engine that allows users to discover internet-connected devices across the globe. Unlike traditional search engines like Google that index websites, Shodan indexes the metadata, banners, and services exposed by devices on the internet, such as servers, webcams, routers, industrial control systems (ICS), IoT devices, and more. Shodan (Sentient Hyper-Optimized Data Access Network) is often referred to as the "search engine for the Internet of Things (IoT)" or "Google for hackers" because it reveals the digital footprints of exposed and sometimes vulnerable devices. Developed by John Matherly in 2009, Shodan continuously scans the internet using specialized crawlers that connect to IP addresses and log the responses of devices on various ports: https://www.shodan.io/.

Exploit Assessments

An **exploit assessment** attempts to discover what vulnerabilities an attacker can exploit. These assessments are also referred to as *penetration tests*. An exploit assessment is usually started with a vulnerability assessment. After the weaknesses have been discovered, then the exploit assessment is attempted.

A significant difference exists between an exploit assessment and a vulnerability assessment. Specifically, an exploit assessment is intrusive; its goal is to test the exploit. If the exploit assessment is successful, it can disrupt operations. With this in mind, performing exploit assessments should be done cautiously and never without explicit authorization. Accidentally stopping a production service could bring someone's exploit assessment career to an abrupt end.

Identifying and Evaluating Controls

A **control**, also called a **countermeasure**, is a security measure or a safeguard. A control is implemented to reduce a risk, and a risk can be reduced by reducing vulnerabilities or the impact of the threat.

When identifying and evaluating controls, the following should be considered:

- **In-place controls**—**In-place controls** are those that are currently installed in the operational system.
- **Planned controls**—Planned controls are those that have a specified implementation date.

In-Place and Planned Controls

Before new security controls are considered, the current (in-place) controls should be evaluated. First remember that a control is anything that can mitigate a threat. This obviously includes anti-virus software, firewalls, and similar technology, but also includes policies and training. Before you can accurately assess any potential need for new controls, you will first need a clear understanding of the current controls.

Once you are clear on what controls currently exist, the next step is to evaluate the efficacy of these controls. It is not enough to have controls in place, they must be able to mitigate the threat until the residual risk is below the level that is acceptable for the organization.

There are various ways to evaluate a control's efficacy. For example, if a control is meant to mitigate the threat of malware, one should review the frequency and severity of malware attacks prior to the implementation of that control, and after the implementation.

A **planned control** is one that is not yet implemented but has already been selected and scheduled for implementation. Typically these are unlikely to be changed. However, reviewing the documentation that recommended it is still valuable. The current systems can be evaluated to ensure the original threats and vulnerabilities still exist. Additional tools or techniques may also exist that will allow the enhancement of the original recommendations.

Control Categories

Controls are organized or classified in several ways. One of the popular methods is to define them based on these three categories:

- Administrative/Managerial controls
- Technical controls
- Physical controls

The following sections explain these three categories, but other categories are also used. NIST has published many documents related to information security. SP 800-53 Rev. 4, Security and Privacy Controls for Federal Information Systems and Organizations, was released in April 2013.

TABLE 6-1 shows the current NIST control families.

No matter how the controls are listed, the goals are the same, to protect the confidentiality, integrity, and availability of systems and data.

> **NOTE**
>
> This section introduces the identification and evaluation of controls.

Procedural Controls

Procedural controls, also called managerial, are policies, procedures, and guidelines intended to inform personnel on how to perform actions. Note, that in the past these were called Administrative controls and some sources may still use this terminology.

> **NOTE**
>
> Previous versions of NIST SP 800-53 referred to *procedural controls* as *administrative controls*.

Examples of procedural controls are:

- **Policies and Procedures** —This control may be an organization's security policy. Additionally, it could also be the specific procedures used to back up a server.
- **Security plans**—These plans are comprehensive to help an organization deal with different events. For example, a disaster recovery plan helps an organization plan for a disaster, such as a hurricane or an earthquake.
- **Insurance**—Insurance can reduce the impact of a risk. Common examples include fire insurance and flood insurance. In recent years, cyberbreach insurance has also become common.
- **Personnel checks**—An organization may have policies in place to perform different background checks on personnel.
- **Awareness and training**—Many organizations regularly take steps to raise the security awareness of personnel, which can be done through, for example, formal training, posters, and emails.

TABLE 6-1 NIST Control Families

CONTROL FAMILIES	NUMBER OF CONTROLS
Access Control	23
Awareness and Training	4
Audit and Accountability	16
Security Assessment and Authorization	8
Configuration Management	11
Contingency Planning	12
Identification and Authentication	11
Incident Response	10
Maintenance	6
Media Protection	8
Physical and Environmental Protection	19
Planning	6
Personnel Security	8
Risk Assessment	5
System and Services Acquisition	20
System and Communications Protection	41
System and Information Integrity	16
Program Management	16

- **Rules of behavior**—Many organizations use rules of behavior, also called acceptable use policies (AUPs), to let people know what they can do with computers and systems. An AUP is often a document that users read and sign when they are hired. Commonly, employees are required to review the documents on a regular basis, such as once a year.

Technical Controls

A technical control uses computers or software to protect systems. The benefit of a technical control is that it is automated, which means that it is set once and will consistently enforce the control.

Some examples of technical controls are:

- **Logon identifier**—Users are required to provide credentials before they are granted access to the system, which is also referred to as authentication. Three primary factors of authentication exist:

   - Something the user knows, such as a username and password
   - Something the user has, such as a smart card
   - Something about the user, such as information captured by biometrics
- **Session time-out**—Many systems automatically time out after a period of inactivity. For example, a password-protected screen saver locks a computer after a specific number of minutes. When the time has passed, the screen saver starts, and the user must enter credentials before accessing the system again.
- **System logs**—System logs record activity performed by systems, users, or attackers. For example, a system log can identify when a server was shut down or when specific services were stopped or started. Application logs can record specific application activity.
- **Audit trails**—Many types of audit logs can be used to create an audit trail. A security log can record all access to specific files, and a firewall log can record all traffic entering or leaving a network.
- **Input validation**—Applications can use data range and reasonableness checks to validate data before using it. As a simple example, dividing by zero is impossible. A program that accepts values used in a divide operation can ensure the divisor value is not zero before using it.
- **Firewalls**—Network firewalls can control traffic coming into and out of a network. Host-based firewalls can restrict traffic for individual systems.
- **Encryption**—Data can be encrypted when it is stored on a drive or transmitted over a network, which provides confidentiality of the data.

Physical Controls

A physical control controls the physical environment. Physical controls include locks and guards to restrict physical access and elements to control the environment, such as heating and cooling systems.

Examples of physical controls are:

- **Locked doors**—Server rooms can be locked to protect servers, and wiring closets that host routers and switches can be locked. Proprietary data can also be protected, such as employee files or research data, by locking doors and filing cabinets.
- **Guards and access logs**—Guards can be hired to control access to sensitive areas, such as at the front entrance of a building or in internal areas, and an access log can be used to list individuals who have authorized access. The guard then allows access only to personnel on this list. Access logs can also be used to record individuals who have accessed a room.
- **Video cameras**—Cameras can monitor areas on a continuous basis. Closed-circuit television (CCTV) systems work very well as a deterrent because many CCTV systems can record data from multiple cameras.
- **Fire detection and suppression**—A fire can destroy a significant amount of data and hardware in a very short period of time. Effective detection and suppression systems detect the fire before it gets too big and then quickly extinguish it.

- **Water detection**—Some areas are prone to flooding. When water is detected, pumps can be turned on automatically to remove the water. If the flooding can't be controlled, the detection system can turn off electrical systems to reduce possible damage.
- **Temperature and humidity detection**—Systems need to operate within certain temperature ranges. If they get too hot, electrical components overheat and fail. High humidity can cause condensation on the systems, which can also cause failures. Heating, ventilation, and air-conditioning (HVAC) systems control the temperature and humidity.
- **Electrical grounding and circuit breakers**—Proper grounding ensures that dangerous voltage is routed to ground when electrical systems fail. Grounding protects equipment and personnel, and circuit breakers protect systems and wiring. When a failure results in excess current, the circuit breaker will cut the power before the excess current can start a fire or damage the equipment.

Another Approach to Categorizing Controls

The preceding categories devise security controls based on what the controls address. Another way of categorizing controls is based on what they do. Looking at controls from this viewpoint provides the following categories:

- Preventive—Aim to stop incidents before they occur (e.g., firewalls, policies).
- Detective—Identify and alert to incidents in progress or that have occurred (e.g., SIEM, log monitoring).
- Corrective—Respond to and fix issues after an incident (e.g., backup recovery, patch management).
- Deterrent—Discourage malicious activity through warnings or visible defenses (e.g., warning signs, visible security presence).
- Compensating—Alternative controls put in place when primary controls aren't feasible.

Selecting a Methodology Based on Assessment Needs

Once the elements have been individually identified and evaluated, the associated risk needs to be calculated. These were discussed in Chapter 5 and will now be applied. The two primary methodologies that can be used are:

- Quantitative risk assessment
- Qualitative risk assessment

NOTE

The mean time between failures (MTBF) gives a reliability estimate for hard drives. RAID hard drives often have a higher MTBF than standard hard drives. For simplicity, the ALE after control calculation assumes all the drives have the same MTBF.

Quantitative Method

The quantitative method uses predefined formulas. The collected data is used to identify the following values:

- **Exposure factor (EF)**—The EF describes the loss that will happen to an asset as a result of a threat and is expressed as a percentage value.

- **Single loss expectancy (SLE)**—The SLE is the expected loss for any single incident. It is expressed in monetary terms, such as $1,000. The asset value (AV) multiplied by the EF equals the SLE.
- **Annual rate of occurrence (ARO)**—The ARO is the number of times the loss is expected to occur each year. For example, the risk may have occurred four times last year, so the ARO is four.
- **Annual loss expectancy (ALE)**—The ALE can be calculated as SLE × ARO. For example, the ALE would be $1,000 × 4, or $4,000.
- **Safeguard or control value**—This value is the cost of the control and is expressed in monetary terms.

A control is implemented to reduce a risk. More directly, the control will reduce the ARO. If the ARO was four before the control, the ARO should be less than four after the control. Then, the cost of the control is compared to the savings.

For example, a website generates revenue of $5,000 an hour. In the past two years, it has suffered two hard drive failures. Each year, one of the several hard drives in the system has failed. Each failure has resulted in about three hours of downtime. The hard drive cost was about $300. What is the SLE, ARO, and ALE?

- The SLE is $15,300. The calculation is $5,000 × 3 for the outage. Then, $300 is added for the new hard drive. The SLE includes the AV, which is what the business stands to lose if a threat occurs, multiplied by the EF. If the EF is 1 (i.e., 100% exposure to a threat) and the AV is $15,300, then the SLE is equal to 1 multiplied by $15,300.
- The ARO is 1. Historically, the outage has occurred once a year. If steps are not taken to reduce the risk, it will likely occur once each year.
- The ALE is $15,300. The calculation is $15,300 × 1.

This example doesn't include intangible costs. For example, a customer who visited the website when it was down may never come back. The cost to get this customer back or to get another customer is an intangible cost.

The decision may be made that a hardware redundant array of independent disks (RAID) can eliminate this risk. A hardware RAID that costs $3,000 is identified. It includes several disk drives. If any single drive fails, the RAID can detect the failure and automatically recover, which means that the failure of one drive will not cause the entire system to fail. The RAID will change the ARO from 1 to 0.

Is it cost effective to implement this RAID? This determination can be made by comparing three pieces of information:

- **ALE before control**—$15,300
- **Cost of control**—$3,000
- **ALE after control**—$300, resulting in a savings of $15,000. A hard drive in the RAID might still fail, which would still result in a cost of $300 for the replacement hard drive. However, the RAID would prevent the outage.

If the cost of the control is less than the ALE before the control, the cost is justified. In other words, $3,000 is being spent to save $15,000, which results in a realized savings of $12,000.

On the other hand, if the cost of the control was $50,000, the cost would not be justified based on the existing data: $50,000 would be spent to save $15,000, which puts savings in the hole. If the cost of the control is close to the ALE after the control, the return on investment can also be calculated over several years. The ALE is also impacted by the EF and the AV because both factors determine the SLE. The SLE multiplied by the ARO equals the ALE.

Qualitative Method

In this scenario, the actual costs aren't available or aren't easy to calculate. Instead, a qualitative methodology can be used. A qualitative methodology uses the opinions of experts to determine two primary data points:

- **Probability**—The likelihood that the risk will occur. It can be expressed in words, such as *low*, *medium*, or *high*. It can also be expressed in a percentage, such as 10%, 50%, or 100%.
- **Impact**—Identifies the magnitude of the loss if the risk occurs. It can be expressed in words, such as *low*, *medium*, or *high*. It can also be expressed as a number in a range, such as 1 to 10 or 1 to 100.

The probability and impact allow the risks to be ranked. This ranking allows prioritizing the most and least important risks.

In this example, buffer overflow attacks, SQL injection attacks, and web defacing for a web server are being evaluated. Experts have provided the data shown in **TABLE 6-2**, based on the current controls protecting the server.

Each of these risks can be prioritized:

- **Buffer overflow**—Risk score of 5. The calculation is .10 × 50.
- **SQL injection attacks**—Risk score of 67.5. The calculation is .75 × 90.
- **Web defacing**—Risk score of 6.25. The calculation is .25 × 25.

The information in Table 6-2 clearly shows that the highest risk based on current controls is from SQL injection attacks. Now, controls to mitigate this risk can be identified.

Then, the experts can be queried to identify the controls that will provide the best gain. A similar survey can be used that identifies the probability and impact of a risk after implementation of a control.

TABLE 6-2 Qualitative Analysis Survey With Existing Controls

RISK	PROBABILITY	IMPACT	RISK SCORE
Buffer overflow	10%	50	5
SQL injection	75%	90	67.50
Web defacing	25%	25	6.25

Developing Mitigating Recommendations

After performing the analysis, specific recommendations can be provided to management. These recommendations should mitigate the risks. The data that has been collected can be included to support the recommendations.

Supporting data may include:

- Threat/vulnerability pairs
- Estimate of cost and time to implement
- Estimate of operational impact
- Cost-benefit analysis

Threat/Vulnerability Pairs

The recommended controls should address specific risks. A risk occurs when a threat exploits a vulnerability. If a threat doesn't exist to exploit a vulnerability, a risk doesn't exist. Similarly, if a vulnerability doesn't exist that a threat can exploit, a risk doesn't exist.

For example, malicious software is a very real threat. However, if an isolated system that will never connect to the internet or accept data from other sources is created, it is not vulnerable. In this example, a threat/vulnerability pair doesn't exist because a threat can't be matched to a vulnerability. In contrast, a typical computer system has access to the internet, accepts email, and allows users to connect universal serial bus (USB) devices, all of which make it highly vulnerable.

A control needs to address specific threat/vulnerability pairs. Each recommendation will address one or more threat/vulnerability pairs. If a control can't be associated with a threat/vulnerability pair, the control is not necessary, which becomes an easy check for the validity of the control.

A parallel can also be drawn with physical controls. If a computer laboratory is unlocked, either deliberately or accidentally, then a human threat could exploit the unlocked laboratory to gain access to the computers in it. The risk comes from a threat (human being), exploiting a vulnerability (unlocked door) to harm an asset (laboratory computers and what information they contain). To control this, the door to the laboratory and the computers must be locked and made available only to authorized personnel. Also, CCTV cameras could be installed as an additional control mechanism.

Many controls will address several threat/vulnerability pairs. If the control will mitigate several pairs, each of the pairs should be listed.

Estimate of Cost and Time to Implement

The cost of the control should be included in the recommendation and will be included in the CBA. Accurately identifying this cost by including both direct and indirect costs is important.

The direct cost is simply the purchase of the control. However, indirect costs aren't always easy to identify. For example, the indirect costs could include the labor needed to learn the control as well as the cost of training.

A common mistake is made in underestimating the costs needed to implement a control. For example, a sophisticated firewall may require a trained administrator. If a firewall is acquired but the administrators don't have the knowledge to use it, it will sit idle. Administrators will then need to master it on their own or attend a formal class. In the interim, the firewall sits in the box.

A schedule or time to implement the control should also be included. For simple controls, the time can be negligible. For other controls, the time can be extensive. For example, the decision is made to increase security when users log on. Instead of using usernames and passwords, smart cards are used, which will require a phased approach. A public key infrastructure (PKI) will need to be added to issue certificates, and card readers will need to be added to all systems. Then, smart cards can be issued to users.

Estimate of Operational Impact

Sometimes, controls can consume so many system resources that the system is unable to perform its primary job. If a control has any effect on the system's normal operations, it has an operational impact. The **operational impact** of a control can be identified as negligible, low, medium, high, or overwhelming. Ideally, a control will have very little impact on normal operations. If the impact is too high, the control may not be usable. Considering the operational impact is important while developing recommendations.

Any computer system has four primary resources. If a control has an operational impact, the impact will usually show up in one of these resources:

- **Processor**—The processor performs the majority of the computing work. Desktop PCs usually have a single multicore processor, and servers often have multiple processors. Controls can consume a significant amount of processing power. If the server's processor usage peaks close to 100%, the system slows to a crawl.
- **Memory**—The processor can work only with data that is in memory. The amount of memory in a system is often a limiting factor. If the system is low on memory, it swaps data back and forth between memory and the disk drive. This swapping considerably slows down the system.
- **Disk**—The capacity and speed of the disk subsystem is important to consider. Controls often require a minimum amount of disk space. Additionally, data is stored on the disk until the processor needs it. When the processor needs the data, it swaps the data into the memory. If the speed of the disk is slow, swapping the data may slow down the system.
- **Network interface card (NIC)**—A computer uses a NIC to access resources on the network. If the control being considered will transfer data on the network, the current bandwidth of the NIC should be considered.

Overwhelming Controls

One organization spent over $10,000 to implement a security control it wasn't able to use, but a little planning could have prevented this loss.

As background, a **host-based intrusion detection system (HIDS)** can be used as a security control and is installed on individual systems. A HIDS is used in addition to antivirus software. The software detects and prevents malware attacks, and the HIDS detects intrusion attacks on the system.

An organization had antivirus software installed on its systems. It then purchased and installed the HIDS. The combination of the antivirus software and the HIDS software overwhelmed the resources of the systems. The processor usage started peaking close to 100%, and even simple tasks, such as launching a word processor, took a long time.

The company removed the HIDS from all its systems. Over time, the systems were upgraded, and the HIDS was added onto the newer systems. However, this situation proved embarrassing for the manager who had approved the purchase of the HIDS.

Cost-Benefit Analysis

A CBA should be included to support all recommendations because it shows that the cost is justified. Ideally, the CBA will show that a small amount of money can be spent up front to save a lot of money in the long term. The CBA is an important tool needed by management to justify the cost.

As demonstrated earlier, a quantitative risk assessment includes dollar figures, which can be used in the CBA. A qualitative risk assessment, on the other hand, doesn't include direct dollar figures. Therefore, when using a qualitative risk assessment, additional steps need to be taken to create the CBA.

Presenting Risk Assessment Results

After the risk assessment has been completed, a report documenting the results is created. This report should include two phases.

In the first phase, the recommendations are presented to the managers who are responsible for deciding which recommendations to implement, and they may not approve every recommendation.

Managers may determine that the CBA for a recommendation doesn't justify the cost. For another recommendation, they may decide they want to accept the risk. Any risk that remains after controls have been implemented is a residual risk. Because managers decide which controls to implement, they are also responsible for the residual risks.

In the second phase, the decisions made by the managers are documented. Then, a plan of action and milestones (POAM) is created. The POAM can be used to track and monitor the controls. It helps ensure the controls are implemented and also helps to track the actual costs.

Best Practices for Performing Risk Assessments

To ensure success when performing risk assessments, several steps can be taken. The following list identifies best practices for performing risk assessments:

- **Ensuring systems are fully described**—The description includes both the operational characteristics and the mission of the system. Ensuring that the data is current is important because IT systems change as they are upgraded and improved. If current documentation isn't used, resources are wasted.
- **Reviewing past audits**—If audits have been performed, ensure the results are reviewed. Audits identify vulnerabilities and often include specific recommendations. These recommendations should be either in place or planned.
- **Reviewing past risk assessments**—If a previous risk assessment was performed, it should be reviewed. Some systems are assessed on a regular basis, such as every year or every three years. This information can be reviewed and compared with recent activity. For example, new threats or vulnerabilities may have resulted in outages that weren't previously addressed.
- **Matching the risk assessment to the management structure**—The risk assessment should be performed based on the ownership or responsibility of the system. When the risk assessment crosses management lines, implementing the controls becomes harder than when there is only one owner.
- **Identifying assets within the risk assessment boundaries**—When identifying assets, ensure that only assets within the scope of the risk assessment are included. This will help eliminate scope creep.
- **Identifying and evaluating relevant threats**—Only relevant threats should be evaluated. Historical data can be reviewed to determine what threats have caused problems in the past. Threat modeling can also be used to identify threats.
- **Identifying and evaluating relevant vulnerabilities**—Many weaknesses exist, but not all of them should be included, only those that are relevant to the risk assessment.
- **Identifying and evaluating controls**—Ensure that all controls are directly related to at least one threat/vulnerability pair and that the CBA justifies the cost of the control.
- **Tracking the results**—Document the results of the risk assessment and the approved recommendations, and create a POAM to track the implementation of the recommendations.

CHAPTER SUMMARY

The performance of the risk assessment takes several specific steps. Having a clear definition of the system to be assessed is the first step. Whenever possible, the management structure should be considered to ensure easy implementation of the recommendations.

Next, threats and vulnerabilities are identified. Relevant threat/vulnerability pairs identify actual risks. Then, controls to mitigate these risks are evaluated. These recommendations along with a CBA are presented to management for a decision. Finally, a POAM is used to track the approved recommendations.

KEY CONCEPTS AND TERMS

asset valuation
audit trail
blacklist
change management
configuration management
control
countermeasure
exploit assessment
Group Policy
host-based intrusion detection system (HIDS)
in-place control
operational impact
planned control
procedural control
threat modeling
vulnerability assessment
whitelist

CHAPTER 6 ASSESSMENT

1. A company is beginning a risk assessment for a system. Both the ________ characteristics and the mission of the system should be defined in the early stages of the risk assessment.
   A. Tactical
   B. Strategic
   C. Operational
   D. Visionary

2. Which of the following should be identified during a risk assessment?
   A. Assets
   B. Threats
   C. Vulnerabilities
   D. Controls
   E. All of the above

3. Of the following choices, which would be considered an asset?
   A. Hardware
   B. Software
   C. Personnel
   D. Data and information
   E. All of the above

4. When defining the system for the risk assessment, what should be included?
   A. Only the title of the system
   B. The current configuration of the system
   C. A list of possible attacks
   D. A list of previous risk assessments

5. Which of the following is *not* included in a risk assessment?
   A. Organizational mission
   B. People
   C. Nations
   D. Risk management
   E. None of the above

6. Which type of assessment can be performed to identify weaknesses in a system without exploiting the weaknesses?
   A. Vulnerability assessment
   B. Risk assessment
   C. Exploit assessment
   D. Penetration test

7. An acceptable use policy is an example of a(n) ______ control.

8. An organization requires users to log on with tokens. This is an example of a(n) ______ control.

9. Video cameras are used to monitor the entrance of secure areas of a building. This is an example of a(n) ______ control.

10. Which of the following should be matched with a control to mitigate a relevant risk?
    A. Threats
    B. Vulnerabilities
    C. Threat/vulnerability pair
    D. Residual risk

11. What does a qualitative risk assessment use to prioritize a risk?
    A. Probability and impact
    B. SLE, ARO, and ALE
    C. Safeguard value
    D. Cost-benefit analysis

12. What does a quantitative risk assessment use to prioritize a risk?
    A. Probability and impact
    B. SLE, ARO, and ALE
    C. Safeguard value
    D. Cost-benefit analysis

13. An organization purchased a control and installed it on several servers. This control is consuming too many server resources, and the servers can no longer function. What was not evaluated before the control was purchased?
    A. The cost and time to implement the control
    B. The operational impact of the control
    C. The in-place and planned controls
    D. The impact of the risk

14. What is included in a risk assessment that helps justify the cost of a control?
    A. Probability and impact
    B. ALE
    C. CBA
    D. POAM

15. What is created with a risk assessment to track the implementation of the controls?
    A. CBA
    B. POAM
    C. ALE
    D. SLE

© Yuichiro Chino/Moment/Getty Images

CHAPTER 7

Identifying Assets and Activities to Be Protected

A CRITICAL STEP IN A RISK ASSESSMENT is to identify the assets that need to be assessed, as was discussed in previous chapters. It is also critical to know what functions or activities need to be protected.

After the organization has identified the important assets, it can take steps to protect them. A business impact analysis helps it identify the impact if one of its services fails, and a disaster recovery plan helps it identify the steps needed to restore a failed system. On a larger scale, the organization can use a business continuity plan to help ensure that mission-critical systems continue to operate even after a disaster.

Chapter 7 Topics

This chapter covers the following topics and concepts:

- What system access and availability are
- What manual and automated system functions are
- What hardware and software assets are
- Personnel
- What data and information assets are
- How asset and inventory management are related to the seven domains of a typical information technology (IT) infrastructure
- How to identify facilities and supplies needed to maintain business operations

Chapter 7 Goals

When you complete this chapter, you will be able to:

- Identify the importance of system access and availability
- Differentiate between manual and automated system functions
- Identify hardware assets that need to be protected
- Identify software assets that need to be protected

- Identify personnel assets that need to be protected
- Identify organizational data and information assets
- Identify customer data and information assets
- Identify intellectual property data and information assets
- Identify data warehouse and data mining assets
- Identify asset management and inventory management steps that can be taken for each of the seven domains of an IT infrastructure
- Describe the purpose of identifying mission-critical systems and applications
- Describe the purpose of business impact analysis planning
- Describe the purpose of business continuity planning
- Describe the purpose of disaster recovery planning
- Describe the purpose of business liability insurance planning
- Describe the purpose of asset replacement insurance planning

System Access and Availability

System access and availability refers to when users need a system or service that it is indeed available. How much of the time a system needs to be available will vary from one system to another. Some systems must be operational 99.999% of the time. Other systems must be operational only during business hours, such as between 8:00 a.m. and 5:00 p.m., Monday through Friday.

Five nines, or 99.999% uptime, can be achieved, usually with a cluster or cloud resources. **FIGURE 7-1** shows a database server protected with a two-node **failover cluster**. A failover cluster provides fault tolerance for a server and ensures that a service provided by a server will continue to run even if a server fails. It includes at least two servers, called *nodes*.

In a failover cluster, a user appears to connect to a single database server. Figure 7-1 shows this server as the apparent database server. Nodes 1 and 2 are physical servers that can actually be touched. The apparent database server is just the logical view of the active node.

While node 1 is active, node 2 is inactive. Node 1 will serve all data requests. It accesses the data on an external drive. At this point, node 2's only job is to query node 1 and check its heartbeat as often as every 30 seconds. As long as node 1 is up, node 2 doesn't do anything else.

> **NOTE**
> Five nines, or 99.999% uptime, is sometimes needed for certain services, which equates to about 5.256 minutes of downtime a year. The calculation is 60 minutes × 24 hours × 365 days × .00001.

> **NOTE**
> Failover clusters can, and frequently do, have more than two nodes. For example, multiple services can be protected in an eight-node failover cluster. In an eight-node cluster, two nodes are often inactive, and six are active.

FIGURE 7-1

Database server protected with a failover cluster.

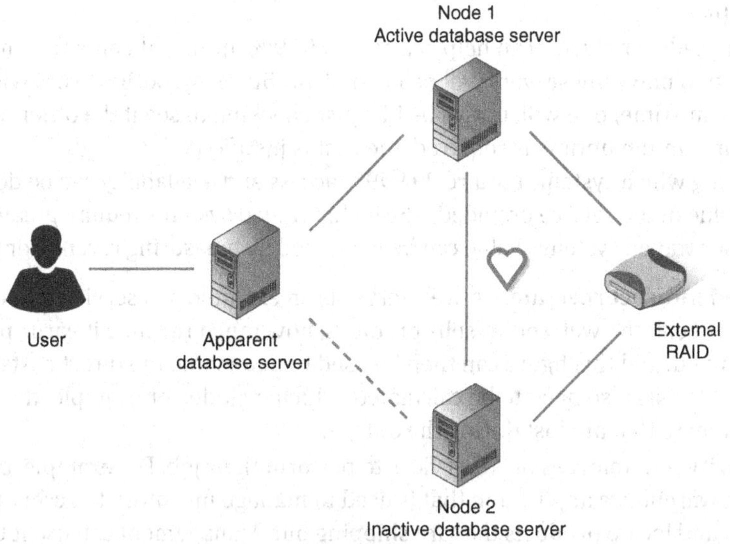

However, if node 1's heartbeat stops, indicating that node 1 has failed, node 2 goes into action by taking over the services of node 1. Because node 2 has access to the same data on the external drive, data isn't lost. The user is still connected to the apparent database server, but data is now served from node 2. The switchover is not apparent to the end user, and, typically, service is not interrupted.

The drive can be a single point of failure (SPOF). An SPOF is any part of a system that can cause an entire system to fail if it fails. A hardware redundant array of independent disks (RAID) is often used to ensure that data isn't lost, even if a drive fails. It is very uncommon to find a server with only a single drive. At least RAID 1 (drive mirroring) is considered a minimum with RAID 5 being more common, as was discussed in Chapter 6.

NOTE

Common RAID levels

RAID 0—Striping (No Redundancy): Data is split evenly across two or more disks (striped), improving performance. This has no redundancy, but improves performance.

RAID 1—Mirroring: Identical data is written to two or more drives. This requires a minimum of two disks.

RAID 2 and RAID 3 are almost never used in practice. RAID 4 is also very uncommon.

RAID 5—Striping with Distributed Parity: Data and parity (error-checking information) are striped across three or more drives. This requires a minimum of three disks.

RAID 6—Striping with Double Parity: Like RAID 5, but with two parity blocks for fault tolerance. This requires a minimum of four disks and can survive two disks failing.

RAID 10 (1+0) —Mirrored Sets in a Striped Set: Combines RAID 1 and RAID 0 by mirroring data and then striping it. This requires a minimum of four disks.

The failover cluster also allows maintenance to be performed without any downtime because maintenance can be performed on the inactive node without affecting users. If the active node needs servicing, the nodes can be switched so that the inactive node becomes active.

Although a failover cluster can help achieve 99.999% uptime, it comes at a high cost. At a minimum, two powerful servers will be needed. Additionally, both servers will never be used at the same time; one will always be idle just checking to see if the other one is up. However, if maximum uptime is required, the cost is justified.

Determining which systems require 99.999% access and availability can be done by identifying the value of the service provided. The highly valued systems require greater protection than the lesser valued systems. Value can be measured by measuring revenue or productivity:

- **Direct and indirect revenue**—A web server is an example of a service that can provide direct revenue. If the web server sells products, how much revenue it earns per hour can be determined, and this figure can then be used to determine the direct costs of the outage. Indirect costs also need to be calculated, which include, for example, the cost to bring back customers that are lost during the outage.
- **Productivity**—Employees need services to perform their job. For example, employees may use a warehouse application that is used to manage inventory to accept products coming in and locate products that are shipping out. Management can use it to determine the value of the current inventory at any time. If this application fails, all shipments may stop. If the failure isn't restored quickly, it may result in delayed shipments, an inaccurate inventory, and other problems. Similarly, many companies consider email a critical service today. If it fails, productivity quickly drops.

Sometimes, the value of system access and availability is underestimated. That is, until it fails. Proactive risk managers will include system access and availability requirements when identifying assets.

How Much Downtime Can the Organization Accept?

Ask a nontechnical manager "How much downtime can the organization accept?" and the answer is often none. But that answer is not always accurate.

Although 99.999% uptime is achievable, it is expensive. It requires multiple servers configured in failover cluster configurations and hardware RAID. It may even require labor to watch the system 24 hours a day, 7 days a week, 365 days a year.

The cost of all of these pieces can be very high. Although a business may not want a system to suffer any downtime, most systems can accept some. When managers understand the cost of five nines, they often reconsider their answer.

System Functions: Manual and Automated

Services are usually provided by combining multiple functions. These functions can be manual, automated, or a mixture of the two. When identifying system assets, understanding the difference between manual and automated is important.

An automated spam appliance used to filter spam is an example of a system function. The spam appliance could also be considered one of many functions used to provide email service. Other functions for email could include the ability to scan for malware and to sign and encrypt messages.

Manual Methods

Some systems use manual instead of technical methods. For example, for a hotel using manual methods, employees can track everything from the initial reservation to checkout using paper logs. Although hard to believe, that's how it was done about 20 years ago. If the process is manual, there are two primary asset values:

- **Written records**—The guest log is a handwritten log that records when guests check in and check out. Managers use this log to bill the customer.
- **Knowledge of the process**—Employees would know how to create the bill from the available records. Once the payment has been received, there would be a separate process to deposit the money. If the hotel is a small mom-and-pop business, possibly only the owners and one or two employees know the entire process.

In this example, the value is the written records and the personnel with the knowledge of the process. Although visiting a hotel today that uses only manual methods is unlikely, working at a company that uses manual internal company processes is possible.

Automated Methods

A hotel may be able to automate many of its processes. Because it is part of a service industry, the hotel will still include some human interaction. The following example shows how a hotel could automate the majority of its processes.

Customers could register online, and many hotels prefer that they do. Some hotels give discounts for users who do register online. Customers would be able to see which days are available and what the costs are for each day. They can pick their days and make deposits or payments. Online registration reduces the cost of labor for the hotel.

The reservation would then be in the system when the customers arrive. They would check in with a friendly receptionist, who would check the details via the automated system. The receptionist would confirm the details, and the customers would soon be on their way to the room, perhaps with the bell staff towing their luggage.

Some hotels offer convenience bars, which are often automated, that include snacks and refreshments. When the customer picks anything up, the convenience bar senses the change in weight, and the front desk is alerted upon checkout that the customer may owe something. The charge for this convenience is often very high. For example, a candy bar purchased for $.75 elsewhere may cost $5.00.

Many hotels often include a TV channel showing the customer's bill. This bill is updated automatically when a customer charges a bill at a restaurant or retrieves a cold bottle of water from the convenience bar. When the customer is ready to check out, they access the TV channel to pay the bill. Soon the customer is heading to the airport and home sweet home.

NOTE

Many laws mandate the protection of personally identifiable information (PII). PII is any data that can be used to identify an individual and can also be medical, financial, or criminal data. The National Institute of Standards and Technology (NIST) published SP 800-122, which is a guideline used to help government entities and public companies protect PII. The European Union recently updated its guideline to reflect what is now known as the **General Data Protection Regulation (GDPR)**. Many states within the United States are enacting their own privacy laws. California has led the way on this with the California Consumer Privacy Act (CCPA) and the California Privacy Rights Act (CPRA).

When evaluating this type of automated method, several other things need to be considered, such as the following:

- **Value to the customers**—These automated methods are often considered valuable to the customers. If the registration process is clear and streamlined, customers are more likely to use it. If the checkout process is error free, the chaos is taken out of checking out. The benefits may be difficult to quantify, but these types of services may result in more return visits and word-of-mouth advertising.
- **Value to the company**—Any process that can be automated requires less labor to use, and less labor results in lower costs and higher profit. The reduced labor needs to be balanced with the cost to implement and maintain the system. Ten lower-paid service people may be replaced with one higher-paid information technology (IT) professional, still saving plenty on salary costs.
- **Ensuring process stays up**—Ensuring the process is available when the customer wants to access it is important, which includes the reservation system available on the internet and the automated customer checkout system.
- **Protecting data**—Instead of just protecting a guest book to check people in and out, large databases will need to be maintained. These databases include personally identifiable information (PII), such as customer names, credit card data, addresses, and phone numbers. If this data is compromised, the company may be liable for customer losses due to identity theft.

The important point to remember is that assets are more than just things. They can also be the processes that provide the services. And of course, the information is an asset.

Hardware Assets

Hardware assets are the assets that can be physically touched. They include any type of computers, such as servers or desktop PCs; networking devices, such as routers and switches; and network appliances, such as firewalls and intrusion detection systems (IDS). Understanding what hardware a company has is important to performing a risk assessment.

NOTE

Most organizations use databases to track hardware assets.

However, much more information than just the number of devices the company owns must be identified. Some of this other information includes:

- Location
- Manufacturer
- Model number
- Hardware components, such as processor and random access memory (RAM)
- Hardware peripherals, such as add-on network interface cards (NICs)

- Basic input/output system (BIOS) version
- Operating System

This list is not exhaustive but rather basic. You may find that in some organizations much more needs to be documented regarding hardware. The preceding list is a good starting place and will be sufficient for many businesses.

Controlling Hardware Purchases

Many organizations have policies to control hardware purchases. Only hardware on the approved hardware list can be purchased. This is often a necessary step to ensure that any hardware purchased for the organization meets certain criteria.

In addition to controlling what hardware can be purchased, configuration management is also important. For example, if all the users have identical desktop PCs, desktop support personnel need to learn the specifics of only one system. Once they master the one system, they can easily troubleshoot all the systems. On the other hand, if the environment has 30 different types of desktop PCs, they can be harder to troubleshoot.

Software Assets

Software assets include the OS and applications. The OS starts the computer. Examples of OSs are Microsoft Windows, Mac OS, and Red Hat Linux. The applications perform specific functions or tasks. Examples of applications are Microsoft Word and Adobe Reader.

Most organizations use a database to track hardware assets. Using the same database to track software assets is common.

When identifying software assets, being specific is important. Listing an OS as just Windows or Linux is insufficient because operating systems (also known as *distros*) have many versions. Similarly, listing an application as just Word is not enough.

OS specifics should include:

- Hardware system where the OS installed
- Name of the OS, such as Microsoft Windows 11 or macOS 26.
- Latest service pack installed

The service pack installed is critical information. This will be necessary in support as well as in managing risk. An accurate listing of OSs can help IT personnel quickly identify whether the OSs are vulnerable to new threats. For example, IT personnel discover a new exploit for Microsoft Windows 11. Knowing how many Windows 11 systems the company has along with the service pack installed and where they are will help them in quickly addressing the exploit.

On the other hand, if IT personnel don't have an accurate listing, their job will be much harder because they will have to check all the systems. Even having to check as few as 50 systems will take time. With 5,000 systems, the task becomes impossible to complete manually, which makes automated asset management necessary.

However, if an accurate inventory is available, the job becomes much easier. A simple look at the inventory will identify how many systems are running Windows 11. Additionally, the inventory will link the OS to the hardware, and IT personnel will know exactly where the Windows 11 systems are located.

FYI

A **service pack (SP)** is a group of updates, patches, and fixes that apply to a specific OS. SPs occasionally include extra capabilities for the OS, and they are usually cumulative. For example, Windows 11 has sub-versions, such as 21H2; 22H2; 23H2; and 24H2. Each version includes service packs up to that date. The recommended and easiest way to get SP updates is to turn on Windows Automatic Update on the computer, and let Windows notify you when the updates that you need are ready to install. For example, Windows 11 automatically downloads and installs the updates that are needed, allowing the device to run efficiently and securely. However, automatic updates also run the risk of an update conflicting with something else on the system. While most home users are advised to have automatic updates turned on, most businesses install updates on a test machine to ensure there are no conflicts, then roll the update out in stages.

Automated Asset Management

Many enterprise tools can be used to automate asset management. These tools can identify all the hardware in the networks, which includes the desktop PCs, servers, and network devices, such as switches and routers.

For example, Microsoft sells the System Center 2025 which provides remote control, patch management, software distribution, OS, deployment, network access protection, and hardware and software inventory. The Microsoft System Center 2025 offers enterprise-class data center management of hybrid cloud environments. System Center can identify all the systems in the network using tools in a Microsoft domain. Once System Center identifies the systems, it methodically queries each system to identify the installed software.

Most systems will reveal their model and serial numbers when queried correctly. Administrators can print out lists of these systems with the software installed on each. Then, they can use these lists to match the supposed inventory against the actual inventory as well as to discover software that has been installed without authorization.

Zabbix is an open source tool similar to Microsoft System Center.[1] Zabbix is a free, open-source enterprise-level monitoring platform designed to monitor various components of IT environments, such as networks, servers, virtual machines (VMs), applications, databases, cloud services, and more. It offers real-time monitoring, visualization, alerting, and automation capabilities.

Prometheus[2] is another open-source systems monitoring and alerting toolkit originally developed by SoundCloud and now part of the Cloud Native Computing Foundation (CNCF) (alongside Kubernetes). It is designed to collect, store, and query time-series data, especially for dynamic and containerized environments.

---

1 "The Universal, Open-Source Observability Solution for IT & OT," Zabbix, https://www.zabbix.com/

2 "Open Source Metrics and Monitoring for Your Systems and Services," Prometheus, https://prometheus.io/

Lists will also help administrators discover two important types of unauthorized software—malware, which can be damaging to the system or the network, and unlicensed software. If a company purchases 100 copies of an application but 200 copies are installed, the company may have unnecessary legal liabilities by violating licensing agreements.

Similarly, the specifics of installed applications should include:

- Name of the application, such as Microsoft Windows Office Professional
- Version number
- Service pack or update information if it is available

All this information is almost impossible to gather manually. However, the process can be automated. Many tools are available that can identify all the hardware and software assets in an organization.

Personnel Assets

Personnel assets are the people working for the company. The success of any organization is due in large part to its personnel. Sometimes, things work best when several key personnel have been trained for any key function, instead of a single person.

When any function or process depends on a single person, that person becomes an SPOF. Although having talented and skilled personnel is desirable, having too much reliance on a single person is not.

Many things can take an employee out of the environment, including illness, accident, family emergency, winning the lottery, a better job, or more money elsewhere. Job conditions and pay can be controlled, but most other things can't.

A hard drive can be an SPOF, and it can be protected with a RAID. As well, a server can be an SPOF, and a failover cluster can be used to protect against its failure.

Similarly, a person can be an SPOF, as previously mentioned. If only one person knows how to maintain a system, that system is at risk. This risk can be reduced by taking certain measures, such as:

- **Hiring additional personnel**—If a critical system is maintained by only one person, hiring additional personnel to help can eliminate the SPOF.
- **Cross-training**—Personnel should be cross-trained in different systems. They will still perform a primary job function, but they will occasionally spend time learning about other job functions. Cross-training helps broaden personnel's understanding of overall operations. They will then be able to step in for short-term emergencies when necessary.
- **Rotating jobs**—Personnel can be rotated into different jobs on a regular basis, such as once a year. Rotating people into different jobs helps them build skills in various technologies and helps ensure that more than one person knows how to maintain any IT system. Job rotation also helps an organization discover dangerous shortcuts or fraudulent activities. Rotating personnel into and out of jobs helps an IT administrator gain more internal oversight into job practices, which ensures that personnel are following rules and policies and reduces the possibility of collusion. Collusion occurs when two or more people engage in secret activity for fraudulent purposes.

Data and Information Assets

Another important asset to consider is data and information held by the company. The value of data can't be overstated. An organization's losing data can have a tragic result.

Data is protected in two ways:

- **Access controls**—Access controls protect data from unauthorized disclosure and help protect the confidentiality of data.
- **Backups**—Backups protect data when it becomes corrupted or accidentally deleted. At least two copies of backups should exist. One copy is kept locally, and another copy is kept in a separate geographic location. The second copy protects against disasters, such as fire or flood. Keeping the only backup of the data with the server means that, if the server room burns in a fire, there will be no backups.

Endless stories abound about companies that failed due to a data loss. For example, a company has been steadily growing, and its data is stored on a single computer, which includes billing data, such as accounts payable and receivable data; customer data; and all the critical data for the company. One day, the hard drive on the computer crashes. None of the data is accessible, and no backups exist. With customer and billing data lost, the company soon fails. Another example is a company that fails to implement two-factor authentication. Unfortunately, a data breach occurs, and millions of customer records are stolen, which compromises customers' identities and the organization's reputation and results in financial loss.

Classification of Data

Most organizations take the time to classify their data. Different classifications warrant different levels of protection.

The government uses classifications, such as Confidential, Secret, and Top Secret. Each classification has a formal definition. For example, Top Secret data includes information whose unauthorized disclosure would pose the gravest threat to national security. Data classified at different levels receive different levels of protection. For example, Top Secret data would receive the highest level of protection.

FIGURE 7-2 shows how an organization can classify its data. In the figure, three classifications are used: Public, Private, and Proprietary.

An organization can define the data in any way that fits. Public data could be defined as any data that is accessible from public sources, such as websites. Private data could be customer or employee data, and Proprietary data could be financial data or data created from research and development.

Organizations can use any classification labels desired. The labels aren't as important as using some method of data classification. In other words, the classifications could be Unclassified, Sensitive, and Privileged instead of Public, Private, and Proprietary. Additionally, an organization can use as many data classifications as it needs to protect its data. However, an organization must consider how easily and readily employees will classify new data as they create it.

FIGURE 7-2

Classification of data.

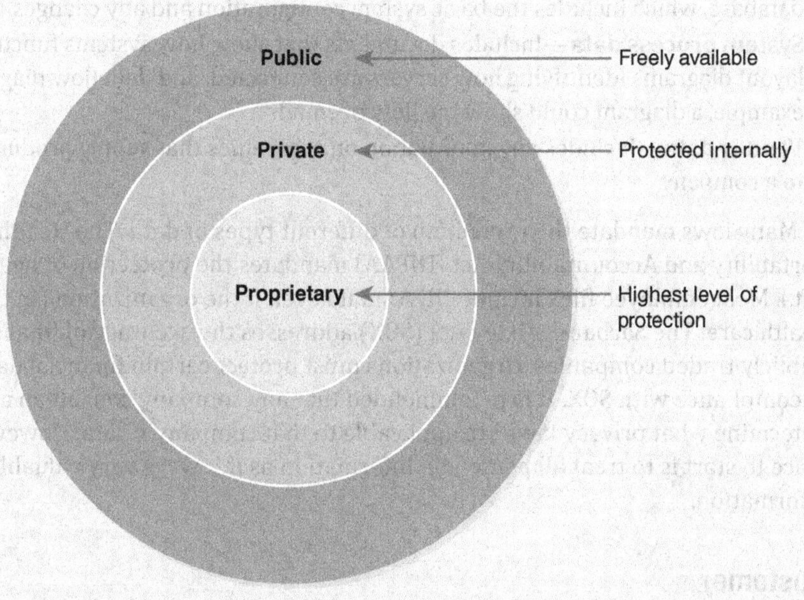

These stories might seem like fiction, but they're not. They repeat for small businesses across the country. Many organizations simply don't recognize the value of their data until it is lost. However, once the data is lost, it's too late to recover it.

After valuable data has been identified, steps need to be taken to protect it, which include backing up the data regularly and protecting it from unauthorized disclosure.

Data and information assets include the following categories:

- Organization
- Customer
- Intellectual property
- Data warehousing
- Data mining

Organization

Organizational data includes any internally used data, and most of it should remain private. However, if a company is publicly held, some of the financial data may be published, which can include:

- **Employee data**—Includes any information held about employees. Most companies have internal human resources (HR) departments that maintain records on employees, which can include personal data, employee reviews, healthcare choices, and more.

- **Billing and financial data**—Includes accounts payable and accounts receivable data and any data related to the financial health of the company, which could include loan data and profit and loss statements.
- **System configuration data**—The configuration of each system is often documented in a database, which includes the basic system configuration and any changes.
- **System process data**—Includes documents that show how systems function, network layout diagrams identifying how servers are connected, and data flow diagrams. For example, a diagram could show the flow of email.
- **Vendor data**—Includes any information on companies that supply products or services to a company.

Many laws mandate the protection of different types of data. The Health Insurance Portability and Accountability Act (HIPAA) mandates the protection of health-related data. Most employee files include HIPAA data even if the organization isn't involved in health care. The Sarbanes-Oxley Act (SOX) addresses the accuracy of financial data for publicly traded companies. Organizations must protect certain financial data to remain in compliance with SOX. It is recommended that any company consult an attorney to determine what privacy laws are applicable to that company's data. However, a good place to start is to treat all personnel information as if it were very valuable, confidential information.

Customer

Customer data includes the data the company holds on customers. How the company chooses to collect and use its customer data determines whether data is only minimal or comprises a full-blown database. For example, a company may want to send out a monthly newsletter via email to customers, which requires only the email addresses. If desired, customer names could be collected to personalize the email.

On the other hand, a company may do extensive sales via a website, which requires collecting as much information as possible. When customers come to the company's site, knowing what they purchased in the past will allow the company to automate advertisements or recommendations for sales based on these past purchases. When customers are ready to purchase, they won't need to reenter credit card data because it's already stored.

Customer data could include:

- Name
- Address
- Phone number
- Email address
- Historical purchases
- Accounts receivable data
- Credit card or banking data
- Account name and password
- Demographic data, such as age and gender

The more data that is stored, the more valuable that collection of data becomes. For example, someone hacking into a system that stores only email addresses and viewing this data isn't necessarily critical. However, if PII is part of that data, several laws mandate that it be protected. Additionally, if credit card data is collected and an attacker gains access to it, the company may be liable for financial losses.

Intellectual Property

Intellectual property data is data created by a person or an organization, which can include inventions, literary and artistic works, symbols, names, and images. The World Intellectual Property Organization (WIPO) divides intellectual property into six categories:

- **Industrial designs**—Industrial designs constitutes the ornamental or aesthetic aspect of an article. A design may consist of three-dimensional features, such as the shape or surface of an article, or of two-dimensional features, such as patterns, lines or color.
- **Copyright**—Includes literary and artistic works, such as books, films, and music, and artistic works, such as paintings and drawings.
- **Patents**—A patent is a legal right granted by a government that gives an inventor the exclusive right to make, use, sell, and license an invention for a certain period of time—typically 20 years from the filing date, in most jurisdictions.
- **Trademark**—A trademark is a legally recognized symbol, word, phrase, design, or combination thereof that identifies and distinguishes the source of goods or services of one party from those of others. It is a type of intellectual property, like patents and copyrights, but it specifically protects branding elements.
- **Trade secret**—A trade secret is a type of intellectual property that consists of confidential business information which provides a company with a competitive advantage. Unlike patents, trademarks, or copyrights, trade secrets are not publicly disclosed and not registered with any government office. Their protection depends entirely on maintaining their secrecy. A trade secret must be not generally known or readily ascertainable by others; it provides actual or potential economic benefit by not being publicly known; and the owner takes reasonable steps to maintain its secrecy (e.g., NDAs, restricted access).
- **Geographical indications**—Geographical indications and appellations of origin are signs used on goods that have a specific geographical origin and possess qualities, a reputation or characteristics that are essentially attributable to that place of origin. Most commonly, a geographical indication includes the name of the place of origin of the goods.

Organizations can have one or both categories of intellectual property, depending on the function of the company. For example, a recording company may focus on copyright intellectual property. However, a medical research company may focus only on industrial property.

Both national and international laws protect intellectual property. However, thieves still steal it. The money invested in the creation of the property can be lost if the data is not protected. For example, a television company could spend several years and millions of dollars developing a new screen that provides a 3D view with vivid colors. About 6 months before the company is ready to go to market, a competitor accesses all the research data and then creates a similar product. Because the competitor doesn't have to recoup the research and development costs, it can actually sell the TV cheaper than the company that created it.

Any organization that has intellectual property needs to protect it. The level of protection depends on its value.

Data Warehousing and Data Mining

Data warehousing and **data mining** techniques combine to retrieve meaningful data from very large databases. Although a database can host huge amounts of data, that data isn't readily useful. The goal is to convert the raw data into useful intelligence, which can be done with data warehousing and data mining:

- **Data warehousing**—The process of gathering data from different databases. The data is retrieved from the source databases and placed in a central database. New relationships between the source databases are created in the central database, which is the data warehouse. Data in a warehouse is not modified. Instead, data is modified in the source databases. Periodically, the data in the data warehouse is refreshed, which brings the data warehouse current with the source data. Refreshing the data warehouse can be very resource-intensive.
- **Data mining**—Data mining is the process of discovering patterns, trends, correlations, or useful information from large sets of data using statistical, mathematical, machine learning, and computational techniques. It is a core step in the Knowledge Discovery in Databases (KDD) process and is widely used in business, science, engineering, and security to extract actionable insights from data.

Most databases are optimized as online transactional processing (OLTP) databases, meaning they can quickly record transactions. A *transaction* is any type of addition, deletion, or modification of data. For example, an OLTP database is effective at recording sales. However, OLTP databases aren't very effective for data analysis. Instead, the OLTP database is reorganized in a data warehouse and can be combined with one or more other OLTP databases. Once the databases are reorganized, data mining can retrieve relevant data.

For example, here are some possible questions a manager may have:

- How many widgets has the organization sold this year?
- What was the peak month for widget sales?
- Who is the top-performing salesperson this quarter?
- Who is the bottom-performing salesperson this quarter?
- What were the sales figures for each of the regions this quarter? How do these figures compare with sales figures for the same quarter last year?

If an organization uses data warehouses, methods need to be established to protect the source databases and the data warehouse. The most important element is to have effective backup strategies. Additionally, extract, transform, and load (ETL) processes often require a great deal of time to develop. Developers create the ETL processes using scripts or tools to identify the steps. The ETL processes should be included in the backup strategy.

Extract, Transform, and Load

Data is moved from a database to a data warehouse using extract, transform, and load (ETL) techniques. The ETL process is an important element of a business intelligence (BI) solution. Database developers identify the data to be retrieved, how to modify it for the target database, and how to load it. The three steps are:

- **Extraction**—The process of retrieving data from existing databases. Not all the data is extracted. Instead, only the data that is relevant to the decision makers is retrieved. For example, some customer sales data can be extracted for analysis. However, other customer data, such as credit card data, may not be needed, so it isn't extracted.
- **Transformation**—The process of converting the data into a common format needed for the data warehouse. For example, one database may identify the male gender as "M," whereas another database uses "Male." Neither "M" nor "Male" is incorrect. However, the designation needs to be consistent in the target database. The transform process will change the data so it is consistent in the data warehouse.
- **Loading**—The process of loading the data into the data warehouse. Data is loaded after it has been transformed to a standard format. Depending on how the data warehouse is configured, loading the same data in different locations is possible. Although this isn't efficient for an OLTP database, it is efficient for data mining.

The ETL process is automated using scripts or other techniques. If necessary, it can be performed regularly on new data, which enables the data warehouse to be kept up to date with the actual source data.

Big data is a newer term that many database specialists use when talking about very large databases. It refers to any set of data that is so large and complex that it is difficult to process with existing database tools. Instead, specialists build new applications to meet the needs of these large data sets, but the goals are the same as those for smaller data sets. Specialists build tools to capture and store the data. They then add tools so that decision makers can query the data to answer specific questions.

Asset and Inventory Management Within the Seven Domains of a Typical IT Infrastructure

Approaching an IT management problem from the perspective of the seven domains of a typical IT infrastructure is useful. These IT management problems include **asset management** and **inventory management**.

The seven domains of a typical IT infrastructure are:

- User Domain
- Workstation Domain
- LAN Domain
- LAN-to-WAN Domain
- WAN Domain
- Remote Access Domain
- System/Application Domain

FIGURE 7-3 shows the seven domains of a typical IT infrastructure.

A difference exists between inventory management and asset management. Basic definitions of the two are:

- **Inventory management**—Used to manage hardware inventories, which includes only the basic data, such as model and serial numbers. It shows what assets are on hand, where they're located, and who owns them. Inventory management is valuable to ensure that the inventory isn't easily lost or stolen.
- **Asset management**—Used to manage all types of assets. It includes much more detailed data than an inventory management system includes. For example, asset management would cover installed components, hardware peripherals, installed software, update versions, and more.

Organizations may decide to use either or both types of management for different areas. For example, an organization may use inventory management for desktop PCs, which ensures the PCs are tracked and the investment is not lost. However, the same organization can also use automated asset management techniques. Asset management ensures the systems are patched correctly.

FIGURE 7-3

The seven domains of a typical IT infrastructure.

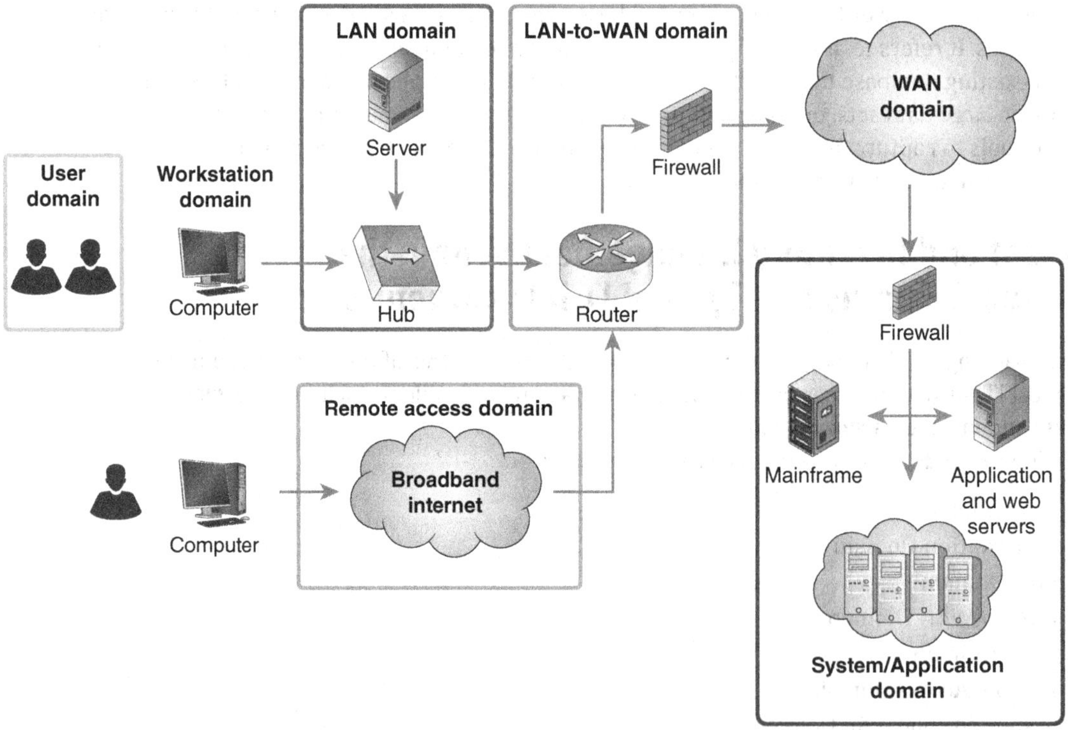

For each of the seven domains, company management needs to determine the answers to two basic questions considering the assets the company has:

- Are the assets valuable to the organization?
- Are they included in any type of inventory or asset management system?

If the assets are valuable, they should be included in either an inventory or an asset management system.

User Domain

The User Domain includes people or employees. An HR department maintains records on employees. These records can be manual records, such as folders held in filing cabinets, or files held on servers.

Data on users includes:

- Personal and contact data
- Employee reviews
- Salary and bonus data
- Healthcare choices

A significant concern with asset management in the User Domain is confidentiality. Data must be protected against unauthorized disclosure. At the very least, the data includes PII that must be protected by law. If any healthcare data is included, HIPAA mandates its protection. If salary and bonus data are leaked, it often results in morale problems.

Workstation Domain

The Workstation Domain includes the PCs used by employees, which could include typical desktop PCs and mobile computers or laptops. Assets in the Workstation Domain have two risks that need to be addressed:

- **Theft**—An organization has a significant investment in these systems and can't afford to allow them to disappear. Inventory management systems include processes whereby each item is manually located on a periodic basis, which verifies the system is still in the organization's control.
- **Updates**—As updates, fixes, and patches are released, they need to be applied to the systems. If the systems are not updated, they become vulnerable to new exploits. Automated asset management systems should be used to keep systems up to date. An automated system will often perform three steps: (1) inspect systems for current updates, (2) apply updates, and (3) verify the updates.

LAN Domain

The LAN Domain includes all the elements used to connect systems and servers together. The local area network (LAN) is internal to the organization. The primary hardware components are hubs, switches, and routers.

NOTE

Switches have replaced hubs in most organizations today. A switch is more efficient because it minimizes traffic to only what's necessary. Moreover, a switch provides an added layer of security by directing network traffic onward to the target system, rather than broadcasting it to all connected systems. An attacker using a protocol analyzer will be able to capture only a limited amount of data when a switch is used in place of a hub.

Having a basic inventory of these devices is important, which includes model number, serial number, and location. Although any network device includes firmware, the more functional network devices, such as routers and switches, have a built-in OS. The version of the OS determines its capabilities, so including the version in the inventory is often useful.

Configuration data should also be included for these devices in an asset management system. For example, scripts can be run to configure routers and switches. These scripts configure the devices to pass or block specific traffic. If a device loses its configuration, the script is run again, which assumes, of course, that the script is available. If the script isn't available, the configuration data will need to be typed in line by line. If no record of the previous configuration data is available, the device will have to be troubleshot until it is restored to its original configuration.

LAN-to-WAN Domain

The LAN-to-WAN Domain is the area in which the internal LAN connects to the wide area network (WAN). In this context, the WAN is often the internet. The primary devices to be concerned with here are firewalls. A single firewall or multiple firewalls to create a demilitarized zone (DMZ), or a buffer area, can separate the LAN from the WAN.

Firewalls in the LAN-to-WAN Domain are hardware firewalls. They can be programmed to allow and block specific traffic. The following information should be included in an asset management system:

- **Hardware information**—Includes basics, such as the model and serial numbers. If the model supports different add-ons, such as additional memory or network interface cards, they should also be included.
- **Configuration data**—A significant amount of time goes into creating a firewall policy, after which firewall rules and exceptions to implementing the policy should be created. At the very least, all these rules and exceptions need to be documented. Whenever possible, to automate the process, scripts should be created and then backed up.

NOTE

Internal computers have access to the internet but not directly. Most organizations direct client traffic through a proxy server to give clients indirect access to the internet. The proxy server has connectivity to the WAN with a public IP address and connectivity to internal clients with a private IP address.

WAN Domain

The WAN Domain includes servers that have direct access to the internet. These servers include all those that have public Internet Protocol (IP) addresses and are public-facing in the DMZ.

Most organizations won't have many servers in the WAN Domain. However, any servers in the WAN have significantly higher risks. Taking extra precautions to ensure these servers are hardened as much as possible is very important.

Inventory and asset management information for WAN-based servers include:

- **Hardware information**—Includes basics, such as the model and serial numbers. Documentation is similar to how servers in the LAN-to-WAN Domain would be documented.
- **Update information**—Servers in the WAN need to be kept up to date, which is an important step to ensure the servers stay secure. As patches, fixes, and updates are released, they need to be evaluated. If the update is needed and testing shows it doesn't have negative effects, it should be applied. Updating of servers can be manual or automated. Either way, having an accurate record of updates installed on servers is important.

Remote Access Domain

Remote access technologies give users access to an internal network via an external location. This process can be done via direct dial-up or a virtual private network (VPN).

When dial-up is used, clients and servers have modems and access to phone lines. When a VPN is used, the VPN server has a public IP address available on the internet. Clients access the internet and then use tunneling protocols to access the VPN server.

Inventory and asset management information needed for servers in the Remote Access Domain is similar to that in the WAN Domain. However, for dial-up remote access servers, the dial-up equipment will also need to be included, which includes both modems and phone branch exchange (PBX) equipment:

NOTE

Hardening a server makes it more secure from the default installation. The first things to do are remove unneeded services and protocols and enable the local firewall. Additionally, the server should be kept up to date by regularly applying updates after testing them.

NOTE

A VPN provides access to a private network over a public network, such as the internet.

- **Modems**—Modems for a remote access server are more sophisticated than a simple modem for a client. They are often configured in banks of several modems and can be programmed to answer calls from more than one line.
- **PBX equipment**—Phone systems are managed using a PBX. PBXs often come as mini servers with full OSs.

System/Application Domain

The System/Application Domain includes servers used to host server applications. Examples of types of application servers include:

- **Email server**—Can be a single email server but also a larger email solution, including both front-end and back-end server configurations.
- **Database server**—Can be an Oracle or Microsoft SQL server as a single server or in a group of servers.
- **Web server**—A web server hosts websites and serves them to web clients. A single web server can host a single website or hundreds of websites.
- **Networking service server**—Includes Domain Name System (DNS) servers and Dynamic Host Configuration Protocol (DHCP) servers.

Inventory and asset management systems should include the following information on any servers in the System/Application Domain:

- **Hardware information**—Includes basics, such as the model and serial numbers, just as a workstation would be inventoried, and an inventory of the hardware components.
- **Update information**—Servers need to be kept up to date, which is especially true if any servers are public facing, such as web servers and some email servers.

Identifying Facilities and Supplies Needed to Maintain Business Operations

Accidents and disasters happen, some of which can be so catastrophic that a business can stop functioning. Ensuring a business can continue to function even after a catastrophe requires planning.

Several steps can be taken in the planning process. These include:

- Mission-critical systems and applications identification
- Business impact analysis planning
- Business continuity planning
- Disaster recovery planning
- Business liability insurance planning
- Asset replacement insurance planning

Mission-Critical Systems and Applications Identification

A primary step in any planning is to identify which systems and applications are mission critical. A mission-critical system is any system that must continue to run to ensure a business continues to function. Similarly, a mission-critical application must also continue to run to ensure a business continues to function.

Determining what is mission critical before first understanding how an organization operates is impossible. For example, salespeople within a company sell products directly to customers, and customers submit orders over the phone or in person. Salespeople then enter the order into an application connected to a back-end database. In this example, the mission-critical elements are the salespeople, the phone, the application, and the back-end database.

On the other hand, a company sells the same products as in the previous example. However, customers are able to place their orders directly through a website. In addition, they can send orders to salespeople via email, and the salespeople then enter the orders into an application. This application is connected to the same database that the website uses. Customers can also phone orders in, but they do so less than 10% of the time. In this example, the organization has more mission-critical systems than in the first example. The salespeople, the phone, the application, and the back-end database are still mission critical, but the website application and email would also be mission critical.

The point to remember here is that the importance of a system is determined by how it's used. One organization may consider a specific system mission critical, whereas another organization may consider the same system disposable.

Business Impact Analysis Planning

A **business impact analysis (BIA)** identifies the impact of a sudden loss of business functions. The impact is often quantified in a cost. Both direct and indirect costs are used to calculate the impact. Direct costs are the immediate loss of sales or the expenses related to recovering from the loss. Indirect costs are related to the loss of customer confidence.

The BIA provides an analysis of the effect of a loss of specific IT services. For example, a BIA can be used to determine the impact of a loss of email or a specific database. The BIA also helps an organization determine the minimum set of services required for the company to continue to operate.

For example, remote users may use VPN technologies to connect to the private network from remote locations. What is the impact on the business if VPN services stop? A BIA could be completed to make that determination.

Other methods may be available for remote users to connect to the company. For example, remote users may still have access to email using a webpage, and remote salespeople may still be able to place orders using the phone. The BIA could determine that, although the VPN services are valuable, their loss would have minimal impact on the overall mission of the company.

On the other hand, a BIA for email services may determine that the loss of email would have a significant impact on the company. Email may be used for customer contact, project tasking, tracking, and other important communications.

When completing a BIA, the following steps would be taken:

- **Defining the scope**—The scope of a BIA is limited to specific IT systems. For example, the BIA could examine the impact of the loss of email or a website. If the scope is limited to loss of email, loss of additional IT services should not be included. The possibility of scope creep is reduced by defining the scope early in the project. Performing a BIA is possible for a total loss of services for a specific location. For example, a company could have multiple locations, one of which could be in an earthquake or hurricane zone. The BIA could determine the impact if a disaster caused a total loss of services from this latter location.
- **Identifying objectives**—BIA objectives are related to the scope of the BIA. The objectives identify specifically what the BIA should achieve. For example, a BIA task may include the following objectives:
  - Determining the direct impact of the loss of email services for one business day
  - Determining the indirect impact of the loss of email services for one business day
  - Calculating the impact of the loss of email services for three business days
  - Calculating the impact of the loss of email services for five business days

- **Identifying mission-critical business functions and processes**—Not all business functions and processes are mission critical. Some functions are convenient and help productivity, but the mission could still survive without them. The BIA separates the critical from the noncritical functions.
- **Mapping business functions and processes to IT systems**—This step can be easy or complex. For example, if the BIA analyzes email services served by one email server, the IT system is the email server. On the other hand, if an organization uses Microsoft SharePoint to increase collaboration among employees, the analysis can be complex. A SharePoint solution can include web servers, file servers, and database servers. Documentation on the IT systems will help in completing this step.

NOTE

The BIA is an important part of a business continuity plan and can also be part of a disaster recovery plan (DRP).

The result of the BIA is a BIA report, which documents the findings of the analysis. It often includes direct and indirect costs, maximum acceptable outage, and materials or resources needed for recovery.

Business Continuity Planning

A **business continuity plan (BCP)** is a document used to help a company plan for a disaster or an emergency. The goal is to ensure that the critical operations of an organization continue to function. The BCP includes procedures and instructions used to restore operations in the event of a disaster.

When completing a BCP, the following steps would be taken:

1. Identifying the scope
2. Identifying key business areas
3. Identifying critical functions
4. Identifying dependencies between key business areas and critical functions
5. Determining acceptable downtime
6. Creating a plan to maintain operations

Details from a BIA report help in the creation of the BCP. The BIA and BCP are commonly completed in conjunction with each other.

The BCP includes specific steps that can be taken for different phases. The content of the phases is dependent on the disaster. For example, plenty of warning is given for a hurricane. One phase might be 72 hours before its arrival, and another phase might be 36 hours before. However, an earthquake or a fire wouldn't include these same phases.

BCP phases include the following:

- **Notification/activation phase**—Assessment teams are activated to respond to the emergency. These teams can be activated before the emergency in some situations, such as with a hurricane. For more immediate emergencies, such as a fire, the notification is done when the emergency occurs. The goal of this phase is to take steps to continue operations.
- **Recovery phase**—During this phase, the damage is assessed. If any losses are incurred, immediate steps can be taken to recover the systems. The focus in this phase is on the mission-critical systems.

- **Reconstitution phase**—During this phase, the organization returns to normal operations. If any mission-critical systems were kept operational using recovery operations, they can be normalized. For example, operations that were moved to an alternate server during the recovery phase can be returned to the original server. Non-mission-critical systems can be returned to operation in this phase.

Disaster Recovery Planning

A **disaster recovery plan (DRP)** includes the details needed to recover a system from a disaster and provides the details necessary to respond immediately to a disaster. A DRP is included as part of a BCP.

Sometimes, the terms *BCP* and *DRP* are used interchangeably. However, they are separate. The differences are worthwhile to note:

- **BCP**—The BCP is an overall plan used for emergency response. It identifies the critical systems for an organization, including acceptable downtimes. The BCP includes BIAs and DRPs for individual IT systems.
- **DRP**—The DRP is a key component of a BCP. It includes the details needed to recover one or more systems after a disaster. For example, a fire may have destroyed several servers in a server room. The DRP identifies the steps needed to recover the servers, including restoring data from backups.

BCP Versus DRP

Some documentation indicates that a BCP and a DRP are the same thing, but they are not. Although they are commonly used together, a BCP and a DRP indeed provide different value.

When studying for the International Information System Security Certification Consortium [(ISC)^2] Certified Information Systems Security Professional (CISSP) and Systems Security Certified Practitioner (SSCP) exams, remembering that a BCP and DRP are not the same is important. One domain of the CISSP exam is Business Continuity and Disaster Recovery Planning, which separates BCP and DRP topics, and the exam taker is expected to know the differences. Similarly, the SSCP exam includes separate objectives for BCP and DRP topics.

NIST published SP 800-34, Contingency Planning Guide for Information Technology Systems, which provides the following definitions:

- **Business continuity plan (BCP)**—A business continuity plan (BCP) is a comprehensive strategy that outlines how an organization will continue operating during and after a disruption or disaster. To ensure full resilience, several supporting and related plans are typically developed alongside the BCP.
- **Disaster recovery plan (DRP)**—Details how to restore critical technology infrastructure (e.g., servers, networks, applications) after a disaster. This plan will include RTO (recovery time objective) and RPO (recovery point objective).
- **Incident response plan (IRP)**—Provides steps for identifying, containing, eradicating, and recovering from cybersecurity breaches or incidents. Proper CMS can help avoid an incident becoming a disaster, at least in some instances.

- **Crisis management plan (CMP)**—This plan will usually be executed alongside a DRP, BCP, or IRP. It covers decision-making structures, stakeholder communication, and media relations.

These definitions show that a BCP has a wider scope than a DRP. A BCP helps an organization continue to operate, and a DRP focuses on recovering one or more systems after a major failure.

Note that a system may be restored but still not be able to perform mission-critical operations. For example, a fire destroys a building. A single database server may be able to be restored, including the data from off-site backups. However, this server won't necessarily restore all the critical operations.

Business Liability Insurance Planning

The primary risk management techniques are avoiding, sharing or transferring, mitigating, and accepting. Risk can be shared or transferred by outsourcing and purchasing insurance. Business liability insurance is used to protect an organization from lawsuits and covers the company for damages from a lawsuit along with legal costs.

Three primary types of business liability insurance exist. The type of insurance needed depends on the function of the business. The types of liability insurance are:

- **General**—Most organizations will purchase general insurance. It provides protection against injury claims and property damages, which provides an overall umbrella of insurance covering most lawsuits. It may be all that an organization needs.
- **Professional**—This type of insurance protects the company if an employee provides faulty or inaccurate advice. It includes protection against malpractice, errors, and negligence. A company providing IT services to other companies may need this.
- **Product**—This type of insurance protects the company if a customer becomes injured because of using its product. For example, batteries in mobile computers can cause risks. This insurance would provide protection if a faulty battery caused a fire.
- **Cyber**—In recent years it has become increasingly common for businesses to have cyberbreach insurance to cover the costs of a cyberbreach.

Asset Replacement Insurance Planning

Another type of insurance that can be purchased is asset replacement insurance, which is intended to replace assets damaged from a disaster. This insurance is usually purchased in conjunction with other steps to prevent a disaster.

For example, an organization may want to protect itself from fire damage. It can install fire suppression equipment and place portable fire extinguishers throughout the building. However, despite best efforts, fires might still occur.

Fire insurance can help a company replace assets if a fire causes damage. Other types of insurance that provide protection for assets include:

- Flood insurance
- Hurricane, wind, tornado, or other weather insurance
- Life insurance for certain people, such as key officers

The insurance purchased depends on many factors, which include the value of the organization's assets. For inexpensive assets, the cost of the insurance isn't justified. The insurance could cost more over several years than replacing the product. The insurance purchased also depends on the relevant risks. For example, hurricane insurance is relevant for coastal states, such as Florida, Louisiana, and Texas, but is not relevant for landlocked states, such as Iowa or Ohio.

CHAPTER SUMMARY

This chapter has provided information on identifying assets. Asset identification is an important first step in any risk identification process. An organization's assets include its hardware and software, data and information assets, and personnel. The seven domains of a typical IT infrastructure can be used to ensure that all the assets are identified.

Once the assets have been identified, they can be protected using various tools. A business impact analysis helps in identifying the impact to the business if a service fails, which helps in prioritizing the most important assets. A disaster recovery plan documents the steps that would need to be taken to restore a failed system. A business continuity plan is broader and is used to help ensure that mission-critical systems continue to operate even after a disaster.

KEY CONCEPTS AND TERMS

asset management
big data
business continuity plan (BCP)
business impact analysis (BIA)
data mining
data warehousing
disaster recovery plan (DRP)
failover cluster
General Data Protection Regulation (GDPR)
inventory management
service pack (SP)

CHAPTER 7 ASSESSMENT

1. Ensuring that a service is operational 99.999% of the time is possible even if a server needs to be regularly rebooted.
   A. True
   B. False

2. What is a single point of failure?
   A. Any single part of a system that can fail
   B. Any single part of a system that can cause the entire system to fail if it fails
   C. Any single part of a system that has been protected with redundancy
   D. Any single part of a system

3. When identifying the assets in an organization, what would be included?
   A. Hardware
   B. Software
   C. Personnel
   D. Only A and B
   E. A, B, and C

4. When identifying hardware assets in an organization, what information should be included?
   A. Model number and manufacturer
   B. Serial number
   C. Location
   D. Only A and C
   E. A, B, and C

5. An organization may use a ______ rotation policy to help discover dangerous shortcuts or fraudulent activity.

6. What type of data should be included when identifying an organization's data or information assets?
   A. Organizational data
   B. Customer data
   C. Intellectual property
   D. A and B only
   E. A, B, and C

7. What is a data warehouse?
   A. A database used in a warehouse
   B. A database used to identify the location of products in a warehouse
   C. A database created by combining multiple databases into a central database
   D. One of several databases used to create a central database for data mining

8. What is data mining?
   A. The process of retrieving relevant data from a data warehouse
   B. A database used in metal mining operations
   C. A database created by combining multiple databases into a central database
   D. A process used to extract, load, and transform a data warehouse

9. What can an asset management system be compared with to ensure an entire organization is covered?
   A. Hardware and software assets
   B. Software assets
   C. Personnel and data assets
   D. The seven domains of a typical IT infrastructure

10. When updating an organization's business continuity plans, only ______ systems should be included.

11. Which of the following is a privacy regulation that may impact data sourced from the European Economic Area?
   A. HIPAA
   B. GDPR
   C. PCI DSS
   D. FOIP

12. What should an organization use if it wants to determine what the impact would be if a specific IT server fails?
   A. BIA
   B. BCP
   C. DRP
   D. BCC

13. What should an organization use if it wants to ensure it can continue mission-critical operations in the event of a disaster?
   A. BIA
   B. BCP
   C. DRP
   D. BCC

14. What should an organization use if it wants to ensure it can recover a system in the event of a disaster?
   A. BIA
   B. BCP
   C. DRP
   D. BCC

15. A BCP and a DRP are two different things.
   A. True
   B. False

CHAPTER 8

Identifying and Analyzing Threats, Vulnerabilities, and Exploits

RISKS are realized when threats are able to exploit vulnerabilities. With this in mind, identifying and analyzing threats, vulnerabilities, and exploits is important. These processes can be done with threat assessments, vulnerability assessments, and exploit assessments.

The purpose of a threat assessment is to identify and rank threats to the network. Without an accurate understanding of threats to a network, it is not possible to perform an adequate job of mitigating those threats.

Weaknesses in a network can be identified by doing a vulnerability scan. There are numerous automated tools to perform vulnerability scanning. Some are free of charge. Whether one uses commercial or free tools for vulnerability scanning, it is recommended that one perform vulnerability scanning with multiple scanners in order to get a complete result. No single tool is infallible, and using multiple tools substantially lowers the risk of missing something.

Chapter 8 Topics

This chapter covers the following topics and concepts:

- What threat assessments are
- What vulnerability assessments are
- What exploit assessments are

Chapter 8 Goals

When you complete this chapter, you will be able to:

- Describe techniques used to identify threats
- List best practices for threat assessments within the seven domains of a typical IT infrastructure
- Describe the value of reviewing documentation for a vulnerability assessment
- Describe the value of reviewing system logs, audit trails, and intrusion detection system outputs for a vulnerability assessment

- Identify tools used to perform vulnerability scans
- Describe the value of performing audits and personnel interviews for a vulnerability assessment
- Describe and contrast process analysis and output analysis within the context of a vulnerability assessment
- Describe the different types of system testing used with vulnerability assessments
- List best practices for performing vulnerability assessments within the seven domains of a typical information technology (IT) infrastructure
- Identify exploits throughout the seven domains of a typical IT infrastructure
- Describe how to mitigate exploits using a gap analysis and remediation plan
- Explain the value of configuration management and change management to mitigate identified exploits
- Describe how to verify and validate that an exploit has been mitigated
- List best practices for performing exploit assessments within a typical IT infrastructure

Threat Assessments

A **threat assessment** identifies and evaluates potential threats. The goal is to identify as many potential threats as possible and then evaluate the threats based on probability and impact if the threat is realized. Let us begin by ensuring you are familiar with basic definitions. A risk is a potential for harm or loss to an organization. A vulnerability is a flaw in the system that would allow a risk to be realized. A threat is a particular actor that could exploit a vulnerability and cause a risk to be realized. Note the tool or technique are what the threat uses to exploit the vulnerability.

NOTE

Identifying every possible threat is likely to be impractical. However, one can strive to identify as many threats as possible, starting with those most likely to occur. As one works through threat identification, starting with likely threats means that anything that is missed will be very unlikely. Certainly, the goal is to identify all threats; just bear in mind that may not be possible.

Risks assessments and threat assessments are closely related. One will normally perform them in sequence or even simultaneously. While it is common for organizations to perform these assessments at specific points in time, a new trend of continuous, ongoing threat and risk assessment is gaining popularity. If resources allow for such ongoing assessment, it is preferred. The reason is the dynamic threat landscape of recent years. New threats are continually emerging, which necessitate new assessments and re-evaluation of risk.

A risk is a potential for harm or loss to an organization. A vulnerability is a flaw in the system that would allow a risk to be realized. A threat is a particular actor that could exploit a vulnerability and cause a risk to be realized.

FIGURE 8-1
Threats to an organization.

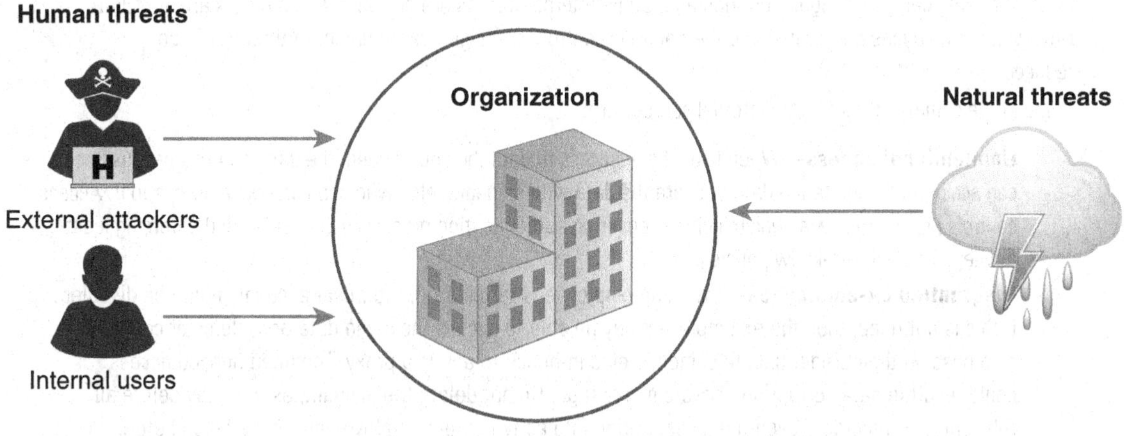

FIGURE 8-1 shows the various threats to an organization. They are generically categorized as either human or natural. Human threats can be internal or external or intentional or unintentional. Natural threats occur from weather or other non–man-made events.

External attackers can be hackers launching denial of service (DoS) attacks on a network; malware writers trying to access, modify, or corrupt an organization's data; or even terrorists launching attacks on buildings or entire cities.

Internal users can also cause damage. A disgruntled employee may be able to access, modify, or corrupt the organization's data. If proper access controls aren't used, other employees may also access, modify, or corrupt data. Although the disgruntled employee's actions will be purposeful, accidental damage can also occur.

According to a 2025 study published by the Ponemon Institute[1] regarding insider threats, 55% were simply due to negligence, 20% due to being outsmarted by outside attackers, and 25% were deliberate. The same study showed that the average time to detect an insider threat is now 81 days, down from 86 days in 2023. Incidents of negligence had an average per incident cost of $676,517, up from $505,113 in 2023. Average cost per incident of malicious insiders was $715,366, up from $701,500 in 2023. The report also stated that sales, HR, and marketing are the top three roles most susceptible to being exploited by an external adversary (47%, 41%, and 40% respectively). This makes sense as these roles are less technical and less likely to be wary of common phishing/social engineering techniques.

[1] "Cost of Insider Risk: Global Report 2025," Ponemon Institute and DTEX, https://www2.dtexsystems.com/l/464342/2025-02-19/583csx/464342/1740000012hNhGjMpn/2025_Cost_of_Insider_Risks_Global_Report_by_Ponemon_and_DTEX.pdf.

Reducing Internal Threats

Internal threats can cause significant damage. Some internal threats are accidental, and others are malicious. However, if employees are trained and their actions controlled, a significant number of threats will be reduced.

Some of the common threats from internal sources are:

- **Unintentional access**—When users have access to data they don't need, the data is at risk because users can accidentally delete the data or share the data with someone else who shouldn't have access to it. Access controls protect the data, which includes ensuring authentication processes are secure and enforcing least privilege and need-to-know policies.
- **Disgruntled ex-employees**—When an employee is terminated, their user account should be disabled. If this is not done, then the ex-employee may be able to access the same data or systems or could also pass on their credentials to someone else in-house to act as a proxy. The unauthorized access could result in data corruption or system sabotage. Do not delete the account, as that may delete all relevant logs/records preventing investigation into activities the employee may have taken before termination.
- **Responding to phishing attacks**—Phishing attacks attempt to get users to give up information or perform an action they wouldn't normally do. Some phishing emails include links to malicious websites. If users click on the link, they can inadvertently install malware on their systems. More sophisticated phishing attempts target specific companies and fool the users. **Spear phishing** is a targeted phishing attempt that looks as if it's coming from someone in the company. Training helps users recognize these attacks.
- **Forwarding viruses**—Users can open infected emails and forward them to coworkers without realizing the danger or bring viruses from home on universal serial bus (USB) flash drives. Up-to-date antivirus software provides protection against known viruses, training helps users understand how viruses are replicated, and technical policies prevent the use of USB flash drives.
- **Lack of laptop control**—Laptops are easily stolen. When users don't exercise physical control over laptops, the computers often disappear, and the organization loses the hardware and software. Moreover, data on the laptop is compromised. Training users on how often laptops are stolen helps them understand the need to secure them.
- **Advanced persistent threat (APT)**—An APT is a sophisticated cyberattack carried out by criminals or nation-states over an extended period of time to either steal data or surveil systems. The criminals or attackers usually have a clear goal in mind, and they spend time and resources to identify vulnerabilities to assets they intend to steal or harm. Given their level of sophistication, they can remain undetected for a long time. Attack methods can take the form of malware, and motives can be financial, political espionage, or control. Examples include the Cobalt Group's attack on financial institutions around the globe, including attacks on automated teller machines (ATMs), card processing systems, payment systems, and Society for Worldwide Interbank Financial Telecommunication (SWIFT) systems. Another example is Mythic Leopard's attack on the Indian Army, specifically using spear phishing attacks on the Central Bureau of Investigation and the Indian Army by impersonating an Indian think tank.

Natural threats include fires and weather events, such as floods, earthquakes, tornadoes, and electrical storms. These are just as important as other types of threats and must be considered in managing risk. The goal of a threat assessment is to identify threats, which can be done by reviewing historical data and using threat modeling. After the threats have been identified, the likelihood of the threats needs to be determined because some threats are more likely to occur than others. Next, the threats are prioritized. Sometimes, threats can be matched with vulnerabilities to determine costs. However, sometimes costs can't be identified without completing a vulnerability assessment. The last step in a threat assessment is to provide a report that lists the findings and includes the threats and their likelihood and any identified costs.

This section on threat assessments includes:

- Techniques for identifying threats
- Best practices for threat assessments within the seven domains of a typical IT infrastructure

Techniques for Identifying Threats

Two primary techniques are used to identify threats: reviewing historical data and performing threat modeling. Which technique is chosen depends largely on the environment and available materials, but both techniques could also be used.

If historical data is available, reviewing this data is often the easier approach. Historical data provides specific information on past threats. However, there is no guarantee that past threats will repeat themselves or that a new threat won't appear. On the other hand, threat modeling is more complex than reviewing historical data because it requires the examination of systems and services from a broader perspective, which can be time consuming.

Reviewing Historical Data

One of the best ways to determine what threats exist is to analyze past incidents. These incidents include those at the organization, at similar organizations, and in the local area:

- **Organization**—A review of past incidents will reveal threats that have resulted in losses.
- **Similar organizations**—Incidents with other organizations in the same business will reveal possible threats to the organization.
- **Local area**—Natural and weather events are likely to occur again in the same area.

This data can be gathered by compiling records and conducting interviews. Data can be compiled from any existing records, including security records; insurance claims; and troubleshooting records, to determine outages and their causes. Interviews can be conducted with management and other employees. Management knows the particular threats that have resulted in significant losses, and employees often know exactly what the problems are and where the threats exist.

An Organization's Historical Data. An organization's historical data can be reviewed to identify past incidents from threats. Past incidents can take many forms, such as those resulting from users accidentally or maliciously causing problems or those coming from external attackers or natural events.

Following are examples of past incidents from threats:

- **Internal users**—Users were granted access to data they didn't need, or they stumbled upon it and shared it with coworkers, which resulted in unauthorized disclosure of confidential data.
- **Disgruntled employee**—An employee was terminated for cause on Monday, and his account was not disabled. The employee accessed his account on Wednesday, and he deleted a significant amount of data. Some of the deleted data had not been backed up and was lost permanently.
- **Equipment failure**—A server crashed after a power spike and remained down for several hours until the power supply was replaced.
- **Software failure**—An ordering database application crashed on a database server, and the server had to be rebuilt from scratch. Administrators reinstalled the operating system and then reinstalled the database application. They then restored the data from backups. This process took over 10 hours, and customers could not place online orders during this time.
- **Data loss**—All users are required to store their data on a central file server, and the data is backed up once a week on Sunday. The file server crashed on Wednesday, and many users lost over two days of work.
- **Attacks**—An email server became infected with a virus, which spread to all the email users' mailboxes. Cleaning the system and returning email services to users took approximately 2 days to complete.

NOTE

An attacker defaces a website by changing the contents. For example, instead of seeing the home page for the website, a user might see the home page for a pornographic site. In addition, attackers often leave a calling card of sorts. Somewhere on the page, an attacker may include text similar to "hacked by xxx." Another variation is "p'wned by xxx." *Pwn* and *p'wned* are slang for own or owned. In other words, attackers are bragging that they conquered the site.

Each of these examples shows only the threat, but various controls could have been implemented to have prevented the threat. For example, if users had access to data they didn't need, the principles of least privilege and need to know could have been implemented. However, the goal at this stage is only to identify the threats.

TIP

The principles of need to know and least privilege specify that users are granted access to only what they need to perform their job. The principle of need to know specifies users have access only to the data they need. The principle of least privilege specifies that users have only the rights and permissions they need to perform their job.

Similar Organizations' Historical Data. Many threats are common to similar organizations. By identifying the threats against similar organizations, possible threats against a specific organization can be identified. For example, attackers like to attack law enforcement websites. Years ago, many instances occurred of such websites being defaced. However, most law enforcement agencies recognize the threat today, and they take additional steps to protect their websites.

Any organization with public-facing servers faces similar threats. Apache is a popular web server product that can be run on UNIX, Linux, and Microsoft platforms. It serves webpages over the internet. Any company that hosts Apache faces the same threats as companies with public-facing servers.

Local Area Data. Primary considerations for the local area are weather conditions and natural disasters. If a location is on the coast and the coast has had hurricanes in the past, it will likely have hurricanes in the future. If a location is in a flood zone, it will likely flood in the future.

Anyone who has lived in the area knows what the natural threats are. Someone new to the area can interview employees or other locals and should get more than one perspective because one person's disaster may be another person's minor inconvenience. Steps should not be taken to resolve problems based on anecdotal evidence alone.

For example, local employees may live in a flood zone. They may relay horrific stories of how flood waters flowed into their homes and destroyed everything on the first floor. While this event was horrific for them, its happening previously doesn't mean your organization will flood in the future. This information should be balanced against other sources, such as flood zone maps, which show exactly the areas that are likely to flood. If the organization is on high ground and not in a flood zone, steps do not need to be taken to protect it from a flood.

Performing Threat Modeling

Threat modeling is more complex than just researching historical data for threats. It is a process used to assess and document an application's or a system's security risks.

Ideally, threat modeling is performed before an application is written or a system is deployed. It is done when security is considered throughout the full life cycle of a product or service. In other words, if security is considered only at the end of the project, it frequently falls short.

When threat modeling is used, the assets to be evaluated first need to be identified. Asset management helps in identifying the assets that are important to an organization, including their value. Steps can then be taken to identify the threats against the valuable assets.

A key part of threat modeling is to think like an adversary, instead of a manager or an administrator. In this context, the adversary can be an external attacker or an internal user. The internal user doesn't have to be malicious to be a threat. However, if the internal user has the potential to accidentally cause harm, the result is the same.

An excellent starting point when performing threat modeling is to use the seven domains of a typical IT infrastructure. The seven domains are presented later in this section with best practices.

When performing threat modeling, here are some of the key questions that should be asked:

- What system needs to be protected?
- Is the system susceptible to attacks?
- Who are the potential adversaries?
- How might a potential adversary attack?
- Is the system susceptible to hardware or software failure?

- Who are the users?
- How might an internal user misuse the system?

Threat modeling for complex systems can become quite extensive. Depending on the system being evaluated, specific objectives may need to be defined to limit the scope of the evaluation.

There are specific threat modeling techniques that can assist you in this process. The STRIDE model is a threat modeling framework developed by Microsoft to help identify and mitigate potential security threats during the design phase of software development. It is a mnemonic that categorizes six types of threats:

S—Spoofing Identity
T—Tampering with Data
R—Repudiation
I—Information Disclosure
D—Denial of Service (DoS)
E—Elevation of Privilege

The idea is to examine each system or subsystem to determine its vulnerability to each of these classifications of attacks/threats. The STRIDE model is typically applied to data flow diagrams (DFDs), examining each element (process, data store, data flow, and external entity) for possible threats in each STRIDE category. This structured approach ensures comprehensive threat identification and supports secure system design from the outset.

Another method of threat modeling is DREAD. The DREAD model is a risk assessment framework used in security threat modeling to quantify and prioritize potential threats based on specific criteria. It complements models like STRIDE by helping evaluate the impact and likelihood of each threat. Originally developed at Microsoft, DREAD is an acronym for the following five categories:

D—Damage Potential: How severe would the damage be if the threat were exploited?
R—Reproducibility: How easy is it to reproduce the attack?
E—Exploitability: How easy is it to launch the attack?
A—Affected Users: What percentage of users would be impacted?
D—Discoverability: How easy is it to discover the vulnerability?

The LINDDUN model is specifically for threat modeling privacy. This model has the following categories:

- Linkability
- Identifiability
- Non-repudiation
- Detectability
- Disclosure of information
- Unawareness
- Non-compliance

The preceding are just three modeling methodologies. There are more. It is not the case where you select just one modeling methodology. It is common to apply multiple methodologies to modeling threats to your organization.

When performing threat assessments, understanding the system or application being evaluated is important. This understanding includes what systems are involved and how data flows into and out of the systems. Without a full understanding of a system, shifting the perspective to that of an attacker is difficult. Understanding a system often requires interviewing the experts and reviewing the documentation on the system.

Best Practices for Threat Assessments Within the Seven Domains of a Typical IT Infrastructure

One method of ensuring that all threats have been addressed is to use the seven domains of a typical IT infrastructure: User Domain, Workstation Domain, LAN Domain, LAN-to-WAN Domain, WAN Domain, Remote Access Domain, and System/Application Domain. **FIGURE 8-2** shows the seven domains.

Methodically going through each of these domains and evaluating the threats allows for the evaluation of potential threats from different perspectives. Here are some best practices that can be used when evaluating these threats:

- Assume nothing, recognizing that things change.
- Verify that systems operate and are controlled as expected.

FIGURE 8-2
The seven domains of a typical IT infrastructure.

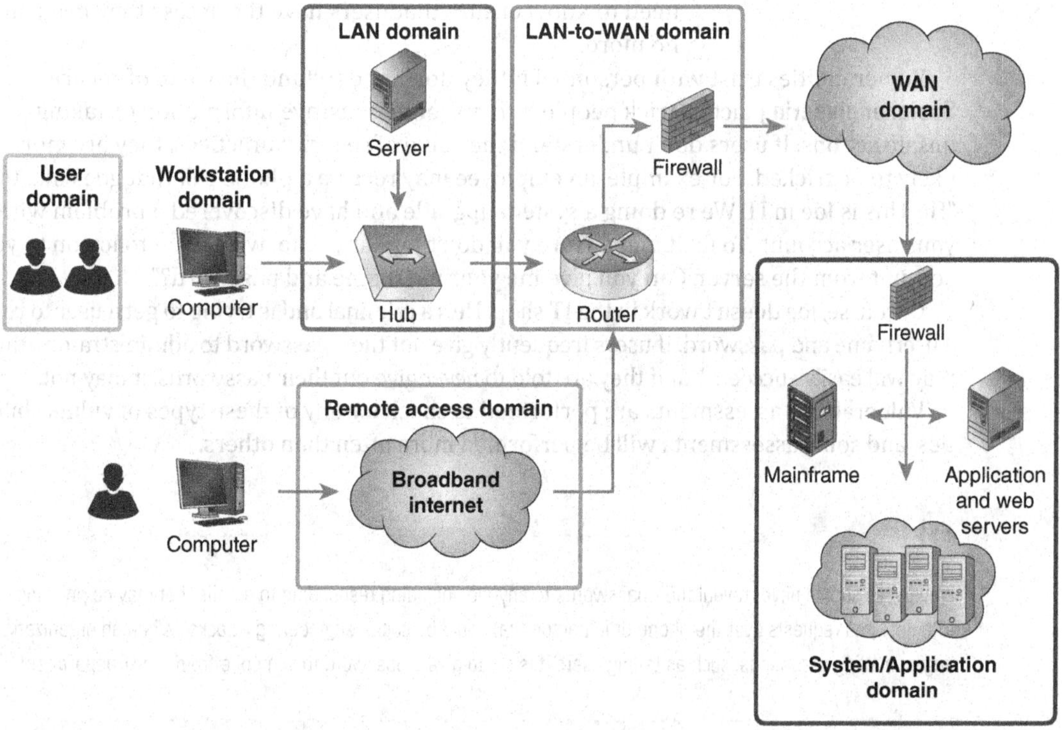

- Limit the scope of the assessment to a single domain at a time.
- Use documentation and flow diagrams to understand the system that's being evaluated.
- Identify all possible entry points for the domain that's being evaluated.
- Consider threats to confidentiality, integrity, and availability.
- Consider internal and external human threats.
- Consider natural threats.

Vulnerability Assessments

A vulnerability assessment is performed to identify vulnerabilities within an organization. Vulnerabilities are any weaknesses in an IT infrastructure. They can exist for a specific server, for entire networks, or with personnel.

For example, a single web server could be vulnerable to a buffer overflow attack. For example, a buffer overflow bug was discovered in May. If the web server is not patched until July, it will remain vulnerable between May and July.

NOTE

A buffer overflow attack occurs when an attacker sends more data or different data than a system or application expects. Buffer overflow vulnerabilities are fixed with updates or patches. If servers aren't patched, the vulnerability remains.

Entire networks can be vulnerable if access controls aren't implemented. For example, if all users are granted the same rights and permissions for a network, no access control exists. All data on the network could be vulnerable to unauthorized disclosure. However, administrative models can be used to implement access controls. The principles of least privilege and need to know ensure that users have the access they need and no more.

Vulnerabilities exist with personnel if they don't understand the value of security. **Social engineering** tactics trick people into revealing sensitive information or taking unsafe actions. If users don't understand the value of security practices, they are more likely to be tricked. For example, an employee may receive a phone call that goes like this: "Hi. This is Joe in IT. We're doing a system upgrade and have discovered a problem with your user account. To fix it and ensure you don't lose any data, we'll need to log on to your account from the server. Can you give me your username and password?"

Of course, Joe doesn't work in the IT shop. He's a criminal and is trying to get a user to reveal a username and password. If users frequently give out their password to administrators, this ploy will easily succeed, but if they are told to *never* give out their passwords, it may not.

Vulnerability assessments are performed to check for any of these types of vulnerabilities, and some assessments will be performed more often than others.

FYI

Employees should never reveal their passwords to anyone, including responding to emails that may be phishing attempts and requests over the phone or in person that could be social engineering attacks. When an organization begins making exceptions, such as telling users it is OK to give a password to someone from the IT department, the users get confused. They may think that the phishing attempt or social engineering attack is another exception. Automated vulnerability scans of systems are usually performed frequently and can be done with assessment tools on a weekly basis. Audits can be performed on an annual basis to see whether security controls are being used as expected. For example, an annual audit can detect whether access controls are still being used as expected. Additionally, tests can be done annually to see whether personnel respond to social engineering tactics. The following website, hosted by the U.S. government, provides helpful tips on avoiding social engineering and phishing attacks: https://www.us-cert.gov/ncas/tips/ST04-014.

An added benefit of a vulnerability assessment is the resulting documentation, which can be used to show compliance with various laws and guidelines. Several laws govern IT, such as the Sarbanes-Oxley Act (SOX), the Gramm-Leach-Bliley Act (GLBA), and the Health Insurance Portability and Accountability Act (HIPAA).

Vulnerability assessment testing can be performed internally or externally:

- **Internal assessments**—Security professionals try to exploit the internal system to see what they can learn about vulnerabilities. Some large companies have dedicated staff who regularly perform assessments. A smaller company could assign internal assessments as an extra task for an IT administrator.
- **External assessments**—Outside consultants are hired to assess the security by exploiting the system to see what they can learn. They provide a fresh look at a company's system and are usually very good at quickly identifying weaknesses.

TIP

If possible, personnel who own the system or are responsible for its security should not perform the assessment. Having an objective view is harder if the personnel have a stake in making the system look good. Being immersed in the details of the system also makes objectivity harder and impedes assessing vulnerabilities with fresh eyes.

Gaining permission to perform any vulnerability assessment is always important and should be done in writing. Security professionals often refer to this written document as the "get out of jail free" contract, which should be signed by someone senior enough to stand behind it. While most vulnerability assessments are nonintrusive and won't affect operations, some vulnerability assessment methods can take a system down or simulate a DoS attack.

This section on vulnerability assessments includes the following topics:

- Review of documentation
- Review of system logs, audit trails, and intrusion detection and prevention system outputs
- Vulnerability scans and other assessment tools
- Audits and personnel interviews
- Process analysis and output analysis
- System testing
- Best practices for performing vulnerability assessments within the seven domains of a typical IT infrastructure

Review of Documentation

One of the steps that can be taken when performing a vulnerability assessment is to review the available documentation from multiple sources, including:

- **Incidents**—If any security incidents have occurred, the documentation from the incident should be reviewed. Often, the cause of an incident is directly related to a vulnerability. For example, a successful buffer overflow attack on an internet-facing server may have resulted in a malware infection, which may indicate that the system is not being updated often enough.
- **Outage reports**—Any outage that has affected the mission of the business can be investigated. If the outage affected the bottom line, a vulnerability can probably be identified.
- **Assessment reports**—Past assessment reports should be reviewed to identify common problems and problems that have not been corrected.

Review of System Logs, Audit Trails, and Intrusion Detection and Prevention System Outputs

In addition to reviewing past assessment reports, other information can be reviewed to determine vulnerabilities. The three common sources of information are system logs, audit trails, and intrusion detection systems (IDSs). There is no particular order in which they should be reviewed. However, if the network has the data available, all of it should be reviewed.

System Logs

All computer systems have some type of system logs. These logs have different names for different operating systems but overall have the same purpose. They log data based on what the system is doing.

For example, Microsoft Windows systems have a log called System. This log is viewed using the Windows Event Viewer. The System log records system events, such as when systems and services start or stop, and errors, warnings, and information events.

What is happening to a system can be determined by reviewing the system logs. Some events, such as warnings and errors, will jump out, indicating obvious problems. Other events need a little more analysis to identify trends.

Audit Trails

An **audit trail** is a series of events recorded in one or more logs, which are referred to as audit logs, but an audit trail can be recorded in many types of logs. For example, Microsoft Windows includes a Security log that records auditable events. Additionally, security applications, such as firewalls, record auditable events.

Any type of audit log attempts to log at least the information about who, what, when, and where. If a user is logged on, the credentials are used to identify who accessed the data. For some logs, such as firewall logs, the "who" may be the source's Internet Protocol (IP) address instead of a username.

Auditable events are any events to be tracked; for example, who has accessed a folder. Auditing on the folder could be enabled so that each time someone accessed any files within the folder, the access would be recorded. The event would include the username, what file was accessed, when it was accessed, and the server or computer where it was accessed.

Many organizations have automated systems that can review audit trails. An automated system is capable of examining logs from multiple sources. Sometimes, these systems are combined with IDSs that can review the events to detect intrusions.

Intrusion Detection and Prevention System Outputs

An intrusion detection and prevention system (IDPS) is able to monitor a network or system, capture network traffic, and send an alert when an intrusion is detected. A host-based IDS is installed on a single system. A network-based IDS has several monitoring agents installed throughout the network that report to a central server. A signature-based IDS detects attacks based on known malicious attack sequences or patterns. An anomaly-based IDS employs machine learning algorithms to detect unknown malware attacks. Most systems use both signature-based and anomaly-based methods. **FIGURE 8-3** shows an example of a network-based IDS with three monitoring agents installed on the network.

One monitoring agent is on the internet side, one is in the demilitarized zone (DMZ), and one is on the internal network. An examination of the output of an IDS will reveal several key points. These three agents work together to identify what type of attacks

NOTE

While intrusion detection systems (IDSs) and intrusion prevention systems (IPSs) are commonly known as intrusion detection and prevention systems (IDPSs), they differ somewhat. An IDS analyzes and monitors network traffic and generates an alert if anomalous activity is noted. An IPS does the same, but also blocks the anomalous activity. Be aware that any system can have false positives. This means that an IPS could mis-identify legitimate activity as being an attack and block that activity.

FIGURE 8-3

Network-based intrusion detection system.

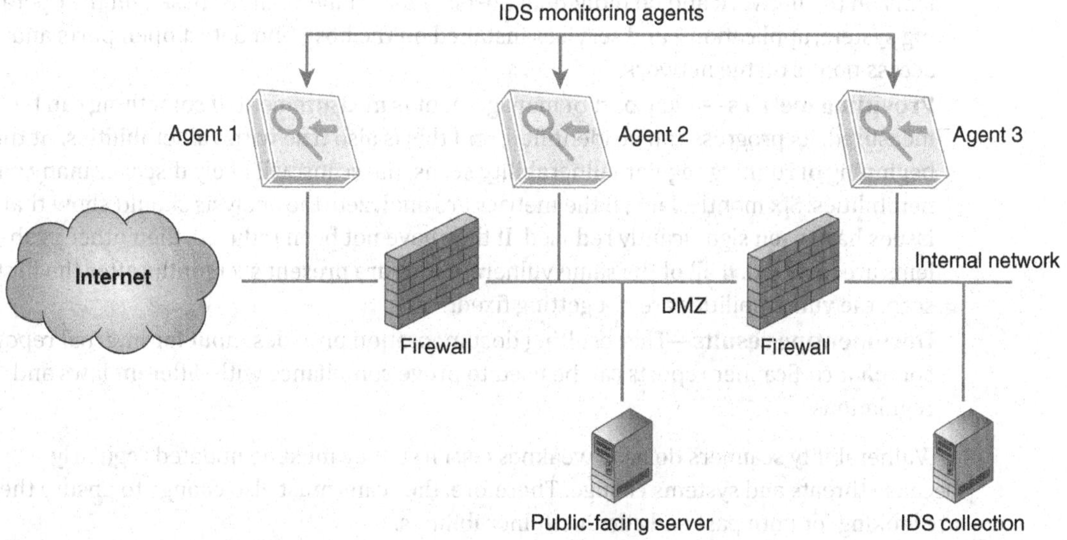

are launched against the network, and they provide insight into the success of different mitigation techniques.

Events from agent 1 show how many attacks are launched against a network from the internet. Events from agent 2 identify the attacks that are able to get through the external firewall, which shows the effectiveness of the firewall against specific types of attacks and helps reveal the vulnerabilities for any public-facing servers in the DMZ. Agent 3 shows the attacks that are able to get through the second firewall of the DMZ. These attacks on an internal network can be very damaging if not addressed.

Although the focus of Figure 8-3 is on attacks from the internet, internal attacks are also possible. The network agent on the internal network monitors for internal attacks. A network having several internal agents installed to monitor an internal network is common.

Internal attacks aren't necessarily from malicious users. They are often from malware that has infected one or more systems on the network. However, the benefit of a network-based IDS is early detection of an infection.

Vulnerability Scans and Other Assessment Tools

TIP

When shopping for a vulnerability assessment scanner, paying attention to how often the scanner is updated is important. A scanner that isn't updated regularly may be useful for only a short period of time, whereas a scanner that is regularly updated might be worth the extra expense.

Many tools are available to perform vulnerability scans within a network. Some of the more commonly used tools include Rapid7 InsightVM; Nessus; OpenVAS, which is an open source alternative to Nessus; OWASP ZAP for website vulnerabilities; and Veracode.

These tools provide several benefits, some of which include:

- **Identifying vulnerabilities**—They provide a fast and easy method to identify vulnerabilities. The scan is run and then the report is analyzed.
- **Scanning systems and network**—Vulnerability scanners can inspect and detect problems on the network and on individual hosts; detect vulnerabilities based on the operating system, applications, and services installed on the host; and detect open ports and access points on the network.
- **Providing metrics**—A key part of management is measurement. If something can be measured, its progress can be identified, and this is also true with vulnerabilities. At the beginning of running regular vulnerability scans, the scans will likely discover many vulnerabilities. Six months later, if the metrics are analyzed, the analysis should show that the issues have been significantly reduced. If they have not been reduced, then other problems are involved. If all of the same vulnerabilities are present six months after the first scan, the vulnerabilities are not getting fixed.
- **Documenting results**—The resulting documentation provides input for internal reports compliance. Scanner reports can be used to prove compliance with different laws and regulations.

Vulnerability scanners do have weaknesses. First, they must be updated regularly because threats and systems change. Therefore, the scans must also change to ensure they are looking for both past and current vulnerabilities.

Second, some scanners may have a high false-positive error rate. In other words, they incorrectly indicate a vulnerability exists. While this can be annoying, it makes sense from a security perspective. If there's a possibility for error, the scanner errs on the side of too many warnings, instead of not enough. Here are two examples:

- A system is vulnerable, but the scans are not detecting the vulnerabilities. This situation can occur from a low false-positive error rate.
- A system is not vulnerable, but the scans keep identifying vulnerabilities. This situation can occur from a high false-positive error rate.

Most security professionals want to avoid the first scenario. They don't want their systems to have unreported vulnerabilities.

Last, some scanners can generate a lot of network traffic, which could interfere with normal operations if the network is already busy.

Audits and Personnel Interviews

Audits are performed to check compliance with rules and guidelines. A vulnerability assessment audit specifically checks an organization's compliance with in-place internal policies.

For example, an organization may have a policy in place related to employees who leave the company. The policy may state that user accounts should be immediately disabled if an employee leaves and, six months later, deleted.

An audit determines whether the policy is being followed. The audit can be quick and automated if the auditor has scripting skills. The auditor could write a script to check for enabled accounts that haven't been used in the past 15 days. The output is then checked with the human resources department to determine whether any of these users are still employed. A similar script could be used to determine whether any accounts exist that haven't been used in the past six months.

Personnel interviews could be completed to gain insight into possible new issues. For example, personnel could be asked what they consider to be current vulnerabilities. Often, employees know what the issues are, but they aren't asked.

In addition, personnel can be interviewed to identify their security knowledge. For example, employees could be asked when it is acceptable to give out their password. A secure organization will have a policy in place stating that users should never give out their password to anyone.

Process Analysis and Output Analysis

Process analysis is performed in some systems to determine whether vulnerabilities exist in their processes. In other words, instead of just looking at the output, the processes used to determine the output are evaluated. Output analysis, on the other hand, is performed by examining the output to determine whether a vulnerability exists.

Neither analysis is superior to the other. However, there are times when one will be preferable over the other. For example, the effectiveness of a firewall may be a concern. Firewalls

FIGURE 8-4

Firewalls control network traffic.

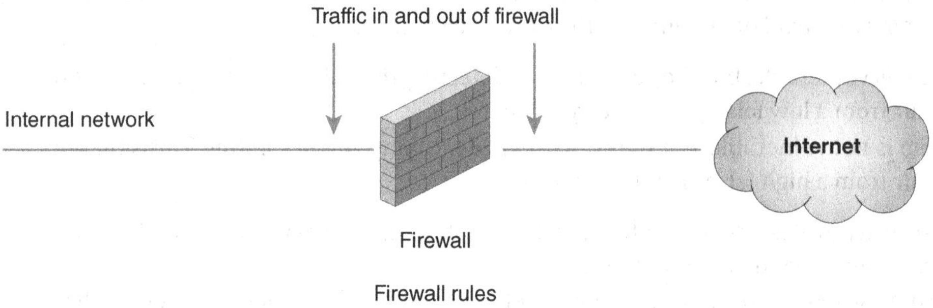

use rules to determine whether traffic is allowed. Either process analysis or output analysis can be used to determine the effectiveness of the firewall.

FIGURE 8-4 shows that the firewall is blocking and allowing traffic into and out of the network. Process analysis requires reviewing all the rules to determine whether they provide the desired security. Output analysis examines the input and output of the firewall to determine whether only desired traffic is allowed through the firewall.

If the firewall has only five rules, process analysis would be completed rather easily. However, if the firewall has over 100 rules, output analysis may be easier to perform.

System Testing

System testing is used to test individual systems for vulnerabilities. These systems include individual servers and individual end-user systems. The primary testing performed on systems is related to patches and updates because the majority of vulnerabilities occur because of bugs that are resolved by patching. For example, a company could have a bank of servers that are running Microsoft Windows Server 2025. Several patches and updates have been released for the servers since they've been installed. System testing queries the servers to determine whether they are up to date.

System testing could be done with traditional management tools, vulnerability assessment tools, or both. Microsoft includes traditional tools, such as Windows Server Update Services (WSUS) and System Center Configuration Manager (ConfigMgr). Each of these server products can query systems in the network and ensure they have all the appropriate updates. If a system doesn't have an update, WSUS or ConfigMgr can push the update to the system and double-check to ensure it has been installed. For example, Microsoft Security Bulletin MS14-011 identified a critical vulnerability in the VBScript scripting engine in Microsoft Windows. This vulnerability could allow remote code execution if a user visited a specially crafted website. The remote code could install malware.

Microsoft has released updates for all affected systems. Any system that doesn't have the update related to MS14-011 is vulnerable. WSUS and ConfigMgr can be used to check clients for the vulnerability and deploy the appropriate updates.

As an additional check, vulnerability assessment tools can verify that systems have appropriate updates, but most of them don't deploy the updates.

Functionality Testing

Functionality testing is primarily used with software development. It helps ensure that a product meets the functional requirements or specifications defined for the product.

One of the problems that can occur with software development is scope creep, which occurs when additional capabilities are added that weren't originally planned. In other words, the add-ons are outside the scope of the original product specifications. While this looks good on the surface, it adds additional security issues.

Each additional line of code that is added to an application represents a potential bug. If additional capabilities are added, they need to be tested. If they are added without being documented, their being tested is highly unlikely.

When an application is developed with the original functions, functional testing ensures that the application works as expected. Functional testing often includes attempts to develop an application.

Edge testing is one technique that can often detect potential buffer overflow errors. For example, if an input between 1 and 100 is expected, edge testing enters numbers on the edges. The numbers 0 and 1 are on the beginning edge of the range. The numbers 100 and 101 are on the outer edge of the range.

Access Controls Testing

Access controls testing verifies user rights and permissions. A *right* grants the authority to perform an action on a system, such as to restart it. A *permission* grants access to a resource, such as a file or printer.

Most organizations have administrative models in place that specify what rights and permissions regular users are granted. These models ensure that users have what they need to perform their job but no more. They help support security principles of least privilege and need to know.

In **FIGURE 8-5**, a company has certain resources that only sales personnel should access and other resources that only IT department personnel should access. Access restrictions are enforced by putting employees into the appropriate groups and assigning permissions to the group.

All members of the sales group automatically have access to the sales resources, and all members of the IT group automatically have access to the IT resources. Members of the sales group do not have access to IT department resources just as members of the IT group do not have access to sales department resources.

Similarly, only certain users within an organization should have administrative rights to systems. Even though from a usability perspective, granting everyone administrative access would be easier to implement, doing so would sacrifice security. It violates the principle of least privilege by giving all users rights to do anything, and it violates the principle of need to know by granting all users access to all data in the organization.

Access controls testing verifies that the users are granted the rights and permissions needed to perform their jobs and no more. It ensures that an administrative model is used as it was designed.

FIGURE 8-5

Access controls applied to users.

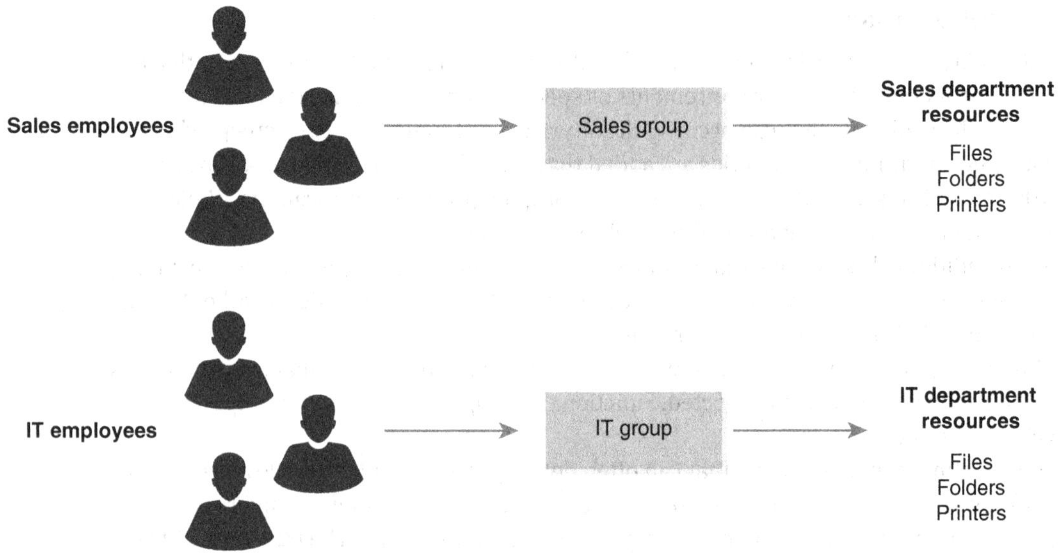

Security or Usability?

A company has grown explosively in a short time and is now faced with some basic technical challenges. The company has a single administrator managing the entire network. Although this administrator managed the network well when the company was smaller, he is now overwhelmed by the company's growth.

He is faced with two competing goals: security and usability. Users request changes to their rights and permissions more and more often. He understands that rights and permissions ensure that users have only what they need to perform their job. He also understands the value of the principles of least privilege and need to know. Instead of just making the changes, he tries to investigate the need. These delays result in complaints to his manager.

The administrator expresses his need to the manager for additional help. He also tries to explain the purpose of access controls to the manager. Unfortunately, he is unable to get any additional help. The manager stresses that he doesn't want to hear any more complaints from users needing additional access.

In this situation, the manager is focused on usability, and the administrator is focused on security. However, the manager is the boss, so what he says goes.

Two things happen. First, the administrator adds all users to administrator accounts, which ensures that all users will always have access to anything they need. It also ensures that the manager will not hear any more complaints about access controls. Second, the administrator begins looking for another job because he understands that it is just a matter of time before these changes will cause problems. At the very least, they will result in a loss of confidentiality.

Penetration Testing

Penetration testing attempts to exploit vulnerabilities. It verifies the effectiveness of controls, or countermeasures. In other words, a vulnerability was discovered, and a control to protect against the vulnerability was implemented, after which a penetration test is performed to see whether the control works.

> **NOTE**
>
> Penetration testing is also referred to as exploit testing. **Exploit testing** is explored later in this chapter.

If the penetration test is successful, then the controls aren't adequate. Additional steps will need to be taken to protect against an attack.

A penetration test is much more invasive than a vulnerability assessment test. Specifically, if a penetration test is successful, it may actually take down a system. With this in mind, the need to be cautious when performing penetration tests is great.

Transaction and Application Testing

Transaction and application testing ensures that an application will function correctly with a back-end database.

A **transaction** in a database is a group of statements that either succeed or fail as a whole. If any single statement fails, the entire transaction fails.

For example, a woman is withdrawing $100 from her ATM. The ATM checks her account and verifies she has the money. It then debits the amount from her account and gives her the money. Once she has the money, it views the transaction as complete and commits the transaction, making it final. However, if the ATM loses power before it gives her the money, the ATM does not commit the transaction. The debit is recognized as part of an incomplete transaction, and it is rolled back. Transaction testing ensures that transactions behave as expected.

> **NOTE**
>
> In an SQL injection attack, the attacker can read sections of a database or the entire database without authorization. SQL injection attacks can also be used to modify data in the database.

Application testing is used to ensure that an application works with the back-end database as expected. A well-known vulnerability with front-end applications that interact with back-end databases is SQL injection. Many tools are available that can automate SQL injection testing on systems.

Best Practices for Performing Vulnerability Assessments Within the Seven Domains of a Typical IT Infrastructure

When performing vulnerability testing, each of the seven domains of a typical IT infrastructure should be considered. These seven domains were mentioned earlier and are shown in Figure 8-2.

Vulnerabilities exist in each of the domains. The focus can be on only one domain at a time, but all seven domains should be examined on a regular basis.

A company may have tools that are focused on only the LAN Domain or the LAN-to-WAN Domain. However, if this is the only vulnerability testing the company does, the testing is missing many other potential problems. For example, social engineering attacks against the User Domain are often successful simply because users don't understand the risks.

The following best practices apply to most of the domains:

- **Identifying assets first**—Asset management helps to identify which resources to protect. Not all assets need vulnerability assessments, only the valuable ones.
- **Ensuring scanners are kept up to date**—Vulnerability scanners need to be updated regularly, which is similar to how antivirus software needs to be updated with malware definitions. An antivirus program that isn't kept up to date is only marginally better than no antivirus program at all, which is also true for a vulnerability scanner.
- **Performing internal and external checks**—Attacks can come from internal and external sources, so vulnerability assessments should be performed from internal and external locations. Check for vulnerabilities behind the firewall; from outside the firewall; and, with a DMZ, from the internet into the DMZ.
- **Documenting the results**—The results of every vulnerability assessment should be documented. This documentation can be used in several ways. Older results can be compared against current results to track progress. Some vulnerability assessments can be used to document compliance with laws and regulations.
- **Providing reports**—Reports that summarize the important findings and provide recommendations are presented to management.

Vulnerability Assessment Report

Although there is no standard format that must be used when completing vulnerability assessment reports, most of these reports include common information. The following information should be considered for inclusion in a vulnerability assessment report:

- **Table of contents**—If the report is lengthy, a table of contents should be included to make finding relevant information easy for the reader.
- **Executive summary**—An executive summary is a short summary of the report. Executive summaries are generally limited to no more than a single page or, for large reports, 10% of the total document.
- **Methods**—This section identifies what tools were used to perform the assessment. It should include enough detail so that someone else is able to reproduce the results. The same person could be performing the same assessment 6 months later, and this section will help ensure that they are performing the same tests.
- **Results**—This section identifies the results of the assessments. It lists discovered vulnerabilities. Whenever possible, this section should also include estimates on the likelihood of the vulnerabilities being exploited.
- **Recommendations**—Some vulnerabilities should be mitigated, whereas others can be ignored. The recommendations section identifies which vulnerabilities are serious and which ones are minor. If available, controls can also be included.

Exploit Assessments

Exploit assessments attempt to exploit vulnerabilities. In other words, they simulate an attack to determine whether the attack can succeed. An exploit test usually starts with a vulnerability test to determine the vulnerabilities, which is followed by an attempt to exploit the vulnerabilities.

Many large organizations have dedicated security teams used to perform exploit assessments. Others hire outside professionals. These personnel spend close to 100% of their work time learning about vulnerabilities and exploits. They learn how to identify the vulnerabilities and how to exploit them. They also learn what is needed to protect an organization from the exploits.

Unless someone is a security professional focused only on vulnerability and exploit assessments, they won't have the detailed knowledge of these teams. However, whether someone works as an IT professional or in IT management, they should understand the basics.

The following sections cover some of the basic topics related to exploit assessments:

- Identifying exploits
- Mitigating exploits with a gap analysis and remediation plan
- Implementing configuration or change management
- Verifying and validating the exploit has been mitigated
- Best practices for performing exploit assessments within an IT infrastructure

Identifying Exploits

The first step in an exploit assessment is to perform a vulnerability test. The vulnerability test will provide a list of potential vulnerabilities that can be exploited. However, knowing that a vulnerability can be exploited is different from knowing how to exploit it.

Some vulnerabilities are easily exploited through existing tools, for which developers have already identified the exploit and written an application. The only thing left for the attacker to do is run the application. These applications are so easy to use that kids can use them, which is the basis for the term *script kiddie*. A script kiddie is someone who has the application but doesn't really know what they are doing.

> **TIP**
>
> The term *script kiddie* conjures up the image of a bored teenager downloading and running applications. The applications are easy to use but can cause significant damage. No matter whether the attack is coming from a script kiddie or a dedicated criminal with IT skills, all attacks need to be protected against.

Other vulnerabilities require the expertise of talented programmers or developers. For example, the Microsoft Security Bulletin MS14-011 was mentioned earlier. Although the documentation indicates what is possible, it doesn't include code identifying what to do or how to do it. Anyone who wants to exploit this vulnerability would need to write code to simulate the attack, which is not an easy task.

When attempting to identify exploits, all seven domains of a typical IT infrastructure should be considered. The following list shows possible items to check in each of the seven domains:

- **User Domain**—Common exploits against users are related to social engineering. Users who can be easily tricked or conned indicate that more training is needed.
- **Workstation Domain**—Two common things to check on workstations are updates and antivirus software. Common exploits occur when systems aren't patched. Additionally, systems need to have updated antivirus software installed to protect against malware.
- **LAN Domain**—This is the private internal network. If attackers are able to install a sniffer on the network, they can capture network traffic. Attackers can then view any data sent as cleartext; therefore, sensitive data should be encrypted. Physical security helps prevent unauthorized access to network resources. Also, training helps employees recognize social

engineering tactics. For example, a social engineer impersonating a phone repair technician might try to gain access to a wiring closet, but trained employees are less likely to be tricked.

- **LAN-to-WAN Domain**—This is the boundary between the public internet and the private network. Attackers attempt to discover holes in the firewall and exploit them. An aggressive policy of allowing only required traffic through the firewall provides the best protection. Additionally, IDSs can detect and mitigate many of the threats.
- **WAN Domain**—This domain includes any internet-facing servers. Common exploits against these systems are buffer overflow attacks. The best defense is to keep the systems updated. Additionally, these servers are commonly protected in a DMZ.
- **Remote Access Domain**—This domain includes dial-up remote access servers and virtual private network (VPN) servers. Common exploits attempt to break through the authentication and authorization process to access the internal network.
- **System/Application Domain**—Exploits in this domain are dependent on the system or application. Database servers have specific exploits, such as SQL injection attacks. Unpatched web servers are commonly vulnerable to buffer overflow attacks, and email servers are vulnerable to spam infected with malware.

Many common exploits exist. Even though they are common, they can still succeed and cause damage. The following sections include details on some of these exploits.

Social Engineering

Social engineering attacks often succeed due to the trusting nature of people. A simple example is piggybacking.

Piggybacking occurs when one person follows another person into a secure area without using a key, badge, or cipher code. For example, a company has restricted access to a building. Personnel are required to use a badge and a personal identification number (PIN) to open a door. However, once the door is open, other people can walk through the door; they are called piggybackers or tailgaters.

> **TIP**
>
> Piggybacking is also known as *tailgating*. Mantraps are commonly used to prevent piggybacking. A *mantrap* allows only a single person to pass through at a time. It can be as simple as a subway-like turnstile that allows only a single person through or a full-sized cage that allows only one person to walk through at a time.

A security consultant was hired to perform a security assessment for a company. She hung back waiting for someone who looked friendly. She loaded her arms up with books, boxes, and briefcases. The person in front of her not only allowed her in without a badge; he actually held the door open for her.

Most people want to be courteous and kind, and slamming the door in front of someone needing assistance conflicts with courtesy. However, in this case, courtesy was a problem. The exploit assessment indicated that the vulnerability could be exploited by exploiting a person's natural courtesy.

MAC Flood Attack

Most organizations replace hubs with switches to prevent unrestricted sniffing attacks. A sniffing attack allows an attacker to connect a network interface card into an unused wall socket and capture data. If a hub is used, an attacker can capture any data traveling through the hub. If a switch is used, the attacker is not able to capture as much data.

However, an attack on the switch can cause it to work like a hub. Switches build tables matching their physical ports to media access control (MAC) addresses. Most systems have only a single MAC address. In this case, the switch matches one physical port to one MAC address.

In a MAC flood attack, attackers send hundreds of packets to the same port. However, these attacks use spoofing techniques to change the MAC address. The result is that the switch sees hundreds of MAC addresses from the same port. At some point, the switch can no longer keep up. It "fails open" and works like a hub.

For example, attackers or testers have access to an unprotected network jack in a conference room. After plugging a computer into the jack, they can launch a MAC flood attack. After a while, the switch goes to "fail open" mode. Attackers then turn on a protocol analyzer and capture all the data going through the switch.

TCP SYN Flood Attack

A TCP SYN flood attack is a common attack against public-facing servers. It helps to understand how a Transmission Control Protocol (TCP) session works to understand this exploit.

NOTE

A TCP SYN flood attack is a specialized type of DoS attack. Any DoS attack attempts to prevent a server or system from responding to normal requests. Hacker tools exist that allow an attacker to enter the IP address of the server to attack and click Go. The tool launches the DoS attack without any additional input needed from the attacker.

FIGURE 8-6 shows the TCP three-way handshake used by TCP to establish a session between two systems. The first system sends a packet with the synchronize (SYN) flag set. The second system responds with a packet that has the SYN and acknowledge (ACK) flags set. The original system then responds with a packet with the ACK flag set. The two systems now have an established session.

This situation is similar to two people starting a conversation. The first person says "Hi" and sticks his hand out. The second person says "Hi" and extends her hand. The two people shake hands and a conversation starts. Admittedly, not everyone starts a conversation by shaking hands. Even if two people do not shake hands, a verbal or nonverbal connection is established between them before the conversation starts.

In a TCP SYN flood attack, the handshake is never completed. In **FIGURE 8-7**, the systems send the first two packets. However, the originating system never sends the third packet. This situation is likened to one person sticking his hand out to shake and then withdrawing it when the other person extends her hand.

8 Identifying and Analyzing Threats, Vulnerabilities

FIGURE 8-6
TCP three-way handshake.

FIGURE 8-7

TCP SYN flood attack withholds third packet in three-way handshake.

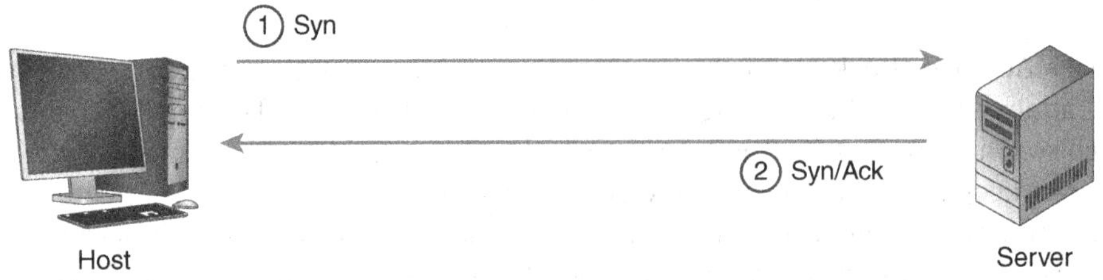

If this happens once, it won't cause a problem. However, in a TCP SYN flood attack, an attacking system may send hundreds of SYN packets to start the TCP session. The attacking system never completes the handshake by sending the last ACK packet. This situation leaves hundreds of open sessions on the server waiting for the ACK packet to complete the handshake. A TCP SYN flood attack consumes resources on a server and can cause the server to crash.

A common way these attacks are mitigated is with an IDS. An IDS can detect the attack and mitigate it. For example, the IDS can close all the open sessions before they become a problem and can change settings so that all packets from the attacking computer are blocked.

Mitigating Exploits With a Gap Analysis and Remediation Plan

> **TIP**
>
> A gap analysis and a remediation plan are often done to satisfy regulatory compliance requirements. For example, if an organization is governed by HIPAA, a gap analysis can identify where the organization stands right now. The remediation plan identifies what steps need to be taken to ensure the organization is in full compliance with HIPAA when the plan has been completed.

An exploit assessment will identify exploits that are mitigated as well as those that are not. The difference between what is mitigated and what is not mitigated represents a gap in the security. A **gap analysis** report documents these differences.

A remediation plan is often included with a gap analysis. It includes details on what would need to be done to close the gap. The goal is to ensure that all serious exploits are mitigated once the remediation plan has been completed.

Using both a gap analysis and a remediation plan for any company that is regulated by HIPAA or SOX is common. This was especially true when the laws were first introduced and companies were taking steps to ensure compliance. In other words, organizations weren't expected to be 100% compliant with the law the day it was enacted. Instead, the organization was expected to take specific steps to become compliant.

Because of the highly technical nature of some of these laws, organizations will often bring in outside consultants to perform the gap analysis. The consultants can often perform the analysis by reviewing existing documentation and procedures combined with interviews of appropriate personnel. If desired, they can also create a remediation plan.

Implementing Configuration or Change Management

Both configuration management and change management can help prevent or remediate exploits. In configuration management, standards are used to ensure that systems are configured similarly. Additionally, compliance auditing is performed to ensure that systems have not been improperly modified.

When configuration management techniques are used, they provide a higher level of confidence that systems are protected against exploits. For example, a well-known exploit can target systems that haven't had an update in three years. Configuration management techniques ensure that an update is always included in any new deployment.

Change management is a process that controls changes to systems. Changes are performed only after they have been reviewed and approved. Change management is an important process because many IT outages occur due to unauthorized changes. Organizations with mature change management processes reduce these outages.

A common example is a well-meaning administrator who makes a change to solve a small problem on a local system. The administrator can inadvertently create a much larger problem on the network. For example, an application may not work with a specific update applied. If the administrator removes the update, the system becomes vulnerable to the exploit.

Verifying and Validating the Exploit Has Been Mitigated

After controls have been deployed to mitigate an exploit, they need to be checked to be sure they work. In other words, the testing needs to be repeated to ensure that the exploit has been mitigated.

Two possibilities exist. One is that the control may not work at all. If this is the case, it needs to be replaced. The other is that the configuration may need to be slightly modified to work completely. For example, certain settings may have been required when the control was first deployed but were missed. These changes can be made, and the control tested again.

The easiest way to verify that an exploit has been mitigated is by using the same way it was originally identified. If a vulnerability scan found the problem, the scan should be run again. If an audit identified the problem, the specifics related to the exploit should be audited.

Best Practices for Performing Exploit Assessments Within an IT Infrastructure

The following list identifies several best practices that can be followed when performing exploit assessments:

- **Getting permission first**—An exploit assessment can take down a system. Ensuring that management understands the risks and approves the process is paramount. Without permission, several issues can arise. If an outside consultant is performing the exploit assessment, they may be liable for damages caused by the outage. Most security professionals will not begin the assessment until they have the permission in writing. Many industry ethics guidelines specifically prohibit any assessment without permission.

- **Identifying as many exploits as possible**—All the tools available should be used with vulnerability assessments to identify possible exploits as well as examining all seven domains of a typical IT infrastructure.
- **Using a gap analysis for regulatory compliance**—In identifying exploits for regulatory compliance, such as for HIPAA, a gap analysis is used. The gap analysis identifies the differences between what is needed and what is in place. This provides formal documentation to show that steps are being taken to become compliant with the law.
- **Verifying that exploits have been mitigated**—After controls have been implemented to mitigate exploits, they must be verified that they work. The same techniques that were originally used to discover the exploit should be used to verify it is mitigated.

CHAPTER SUMMARY

This chapter provided information on threat assessments, vulnerability assessments, and exploit assessments. Each type of assessment can be used to identify potential risk factors in an IT infrastructure. The goal is to identify as many threats, vulnerabilities, and exploits as possible. Once they have been identified, steps can be taken to mitigate them.

Threat assessments aren't expected to be all encompassing or complete. Instead, they are performed to identify the likely threats that will occur. These threats are identified by reviewing historical data and performing threat modeling. Vulnerability assessments identify weaknesses in a network. Some vulnerability assessments can be performed manually. Other vulnerability assessments can be performed using automated tools, such as Nessus, a popular vulnerability scanner tool. Any scanning tool has to ensure that systems have no vulnerabilities and thus must be up to date. An exploit assessment determines whether weaknesses can be exploited. It can be performed before and after a control has been implemented to verify the effectiveness of the control.

KEY CONCEPTS AND TERMS

audit
audit trail
change management
exploit testing
gap analysis
penetration testing
social engineering
spear phishing
threat assessment
transaction

CHAPTER 8 ASSESSMENT

1. The two major categories of threats are human and ______.

2. A threat is any activity that represents a possible danger, with the potential to affect confidentiality, integrity, or accessibility.
   A. True
   B. False

3. Which of the following methods can be used to identify threats?
   A. Reviewing historical data
   B. Performing threat modeling
   C. Both A and B
   D. Neither A nor B

4. What are some sources of internal threats? (Select all that apply.)
   A. Disgruntled employee
   B. Equipment failure
   C. Software failure
   D. Data loss

5. Which of the following choices is *not* considered a best practice when identifying threats?
   A. Verifying systems operate and are controlled as expected
   B. Limiting the scope of the assessment
   C. Considering threats to confidentiality, integrity, and availability
   D. Assuming the systems have *not* changed since the last threat assessment

6. A(n) ______ assessment is used to identify vulnerabilities within an organization.

7. Who should perform vulnerability assessments?
   A. Internal security professionals working as employees
   B. External security professionals hired as consultants
   C. Either internal or external security professionals or both
   D. Only the IT personnel who own the systems

8. What is the name of a common tool used to perform an automated vulnerability assessment scan?
   A. Wireshark
   B. Superscan
   C. Nessus
   D. VA Scanner

9. What is a common drawback or weakness of a vulnerability scanner?
   A. A high false-positive error rate
   B. A high false-negative error rate
   C. A low false-positive error rate
   D. A low false-negative error rate

10. An organization wants to check compliance with internal rules and guidelines to ensure that existing policies are being followed. What should be performed?
    A. Threat assessment
    B. Gap analysis
    C. Audit trail
    D. Audit

11. A business wants to know whether its users are granted the rights and permissions needed to do their job only and no more. A(n) ______ test should be performed.

12. A business wants to identify whether any of the discovered vulnerabilities can be exploited. What should be performed?
    A. Audit
    B. Transaction and applications test
    C. Functionality test
    D. Exploit assessment

13. An organization is governed by HIPAA and wants to know whether it is in compliance. What would document the differences between what is required and what is currently implemented?
    A. Gap analysis
    B. Vulnerability assessment
    C. Threat assessment
    D. Penetration test

14. Which of the following types of IDSs is installed on a single system?
    A. Anomaly-based IDS
    B. Signature-based IDS
    C. Host-based IDS
    D. Network-based IDS

15. An IDS may employ machine learning algorithms to detect unknown malware attacks.
    A. True
    B. False

CHAPTER 9

Identifying and Analyzing Risk Mitigation Security Controls

CONTROLS MITIGATE RISK, which means that a control will either reduce the likelihood of a risk being realized, or reduce the damage caused if a risk is realized. It is important to have overlapping controls for a given threat. One should also be aware that controls need to be reevaluated frequently.

There are hundreds of controls that can be implemented in any environment. When evaluating controls, considering controls in different categories is best. The National Institute of Standards and Technology (NIST) published SP 800-53. This document groups 212 controls into 20 families designated by the acronyms AC for access control, IR for incident response, and CM for configuration management. Controls are ranked low, medium, and high, based on three types, common, custom, and hybrid. Controls are also categorized as procedural (or administrative), technical, and physical. NIST SP 800-53 Rev. 5 emphasizes outcome-based, privacy, and threat intelligence controls.

Chapter 9 Topics

This chapter covers the following topics and concepts:

- What in-place controls are
- What planned controls are
- What the different families of controls defined by NIST are
- What procedural controls are
- What technical controls are
- What physical controls are
- What best practices for risk mitigation security controls are

Chapter 9 Goals

When you complete this chapter, you will be able to:

- Differentiate between in-place and planned controls
- Identify the family a given control belongs to
- Identify and list procedural controls
- Identify and list technical controls
- Identify and list physical controls
- List best practices for risk mitigation security controls

In-Place Controls

When identifying and analyzing risk mitigation security controls, what is in place needs to be identified. Essentially finding out what controls are in place is a necessary first step in determining if there are any additions or changes needed.

Some of these in-place controls may need to be replaced, which depends on whether they meet current goals. For example, an antivirus software may be installed on systems in the network. However, the systems may have been infected by malware in the past year, which prompts the decision to replace it with something considered more reliable or perhaps to add another overlapping, compensating control.

Based on such information, any controls in place should be evaluated for their effectiveness. If a control is determined to be not effective, it can be replaced with an alternative control. Controls, also called countermeasures, will reduce or neutralize threats or vulnerabilities. Controls have three primary objectives:

- Prevent
- Recover
- Detect

As the names suggest, detection controls are meant to detect a possible security breach, Preventive controls are meant to stop a breach. And recovery controls are meant to recover operations. Some controls focus on only one objective, and other controls focus on more than one. However, if a control can't meet one of these objectives adequately, it should be replaced.

Planned Controls

Planned controls are those that have been approved but not yet installed. Planning documents identify what the controls have been purchased for and include supporting documentation. A planned control will have a specified implementation date.

A control might not be implemented yet for various reasons. Perhaps the control has been purchased but hasn't yet arrived. Perhaps the control has arrived but hasn't been installed. The reason a control hasn't been implemented isn't as important as realizing that it will be implemented.

Planned controls should be identified before other controls are approved so that an additional control isn't purchased if one is already planned for purchase that would address the same vulnerability.

The effectiveness of a planned control can still be evaluated, but evaluating it won't be as easy as evaluating a control in place because only the information can be researched. The planned control can't be tested until it has been implemented. However, if a different control is determined to work better, the planned control may be able to be canceled and the other one purchased.

Control Categories

There are hundreds if not thousands of types of security controls. To make these types a little easier to comprehend, risk mitigation security controls are divided into categories. However, the categories are grouped differently depending on who does the categorizing.

Some controls are categorized using either of the following methods:

- **NIST SP 800-53, Security and Privacy Controls for Federal Information Systems and Organizations**—NIST SP 800-53 Rev. 5 identifies 20 families of controls.
- **Implementation method**—Three implementation methods are used to categorize controls: procedural controls, technical controls, and physical controls. This chapter focuses on these three implementation methods.

NIST Control Families

NIST special publications are becoming more and more valuable for IT professionals in the United States. They document security best practices and provide a central source of knowledge for IT security professionals.

NIST released SP 800-53 Rev. 5 in 2020, which provides guidance on more than 200 security controls. These controls handle a wide range of security issues organized into 20 families.

NIST SP 800-53 can be used to review security in any organization. For example, the Physical and Environmental Protection family includes 19 controls. Organizations use these controls for better physical security. They can be reviewed to determine whether they are relevant to an organization. Many of the controls described include additional references that provide more details on how to implement them.

TIP

NIST SP 800-53 Rev. 5, which was released in 2020, puts new emphasis on privacy and expanded security controls and introduces new changes to control categories. Note: NIST released SP 800-53 version 5.2.0 on August 27, 2025, to improve security and reliability of existing software to align with Executive Order 14306.

Functional Controls

Some controls are identified based on the function they perform. These functions are categorized into three broad classes of controls: preventive, detective, and corrective.

Preventive controls attempt to prevent a risk from occurring. For example, many actions taken to harden a server are preventive. These actions include disabling unneeded services and removing unneeded protocols. If the service or protocol is not on the server, it can't be attacked. Similarly, keeping a system updated with patches is preventive. If the update is installed, the attack can't succeed.

Detective controls attempt to detect when a vulnerability is being exploited. Audit logs and audit trails are examples of passive detective controls. When the logs are reviewed, the incident is discovered. An intrusion detection system (IDS) is an example of an active detective control. An IDS can review logs in real time, which allows it to detect an attack when it is occurring.

Corrective controls attempt to reverse the effects of a problem. File recovery and data correction are examples of corrective controls. For example, reliable backups allow data to be restored if they become corrupt. Many corrective controls are also considered recovery controls.

NOTE

Previous revisions of NIST SP 800-53 classified control families as management, operational, or technical. However, the authors removed this classification in NIST SP 800-53 Rev. 4. The reason for removing them is that many control families include controls in two or more of these classes. Further revisions have been made in NIST 800-53 Rev. 5, with control families updated.

Chapter 3 of NIST SP 800-53 Rev. 5 shows a detailed control catalog that documents most of the security and privacy controls in these families. Appendix E documents the controls in the Program Management family. SP 800-53 is a living document, which means the security controls documented in the catalog will change over time. Some controls will be added, some will be removed, and others will be modified.

The following list provides an overview of the control families. The family identifier is a two-letter acronym and is listed in parentheses. The control families include:

- **Access Control (AC)**—This family of 25 controls helps an organization implement effective access control. They ensure that users have the rights and permissions they need to perform their jobs and no more. This family of controls also includes least privilege, separation of duties, and other privileges.
- **Audit and Accountability (AU)**—This family of 16 controls helps an organization implement an effective audit program. Some controls identify what to audit, and other controls provide details on protecting the audit logs. This family also includes information on using audit logs for nonrepudiation.
- **Awareness and Training (AT)**—This family of six controls includes steps that can be implemented to raise the security awareness of all users in the organization. These items help an organization identify needed training and properly document the training.
- **Configuration Management (CM)**—This family of 14 controls addresses both change management and configuration management. Change control practices prevent unauthorized changes,

and configuration management controls stress the use of baselines to configure new systems. The least functionality control documents methods of hardening systems, which include the common method of removing or disabling unneeded protocols and services.

- **Contingency Planning (CP)**—These 13 controls are used to help an organization recover from failures and disasters. They include those related to planning, training, and testing for failures and disasters and those related to alternate sites for storage or processing. NIST SP 800-34 is the primary reference.
- **Identification and Authentication (IA)**—These 12 controls cover different practices for identifying and authenticating users. Each user should be uniquely identified, meaning that each user has one account that is used by only one user. Similarly, device identifiers uniquely identify devices on the network.
- **Incident Response (IR)**—The nine IR controls cover all aspects of security incidents, which include training, testing, handling, monitoring, and reporting. NIST SP 800-84 and SP 800-115 are the primary references.
- **Maintenance (MA)**—The seven MA controls cover security aspects related to maintenance, such as tools, maintenance personnel, and timely maintenance.
- **Media Protection (MP)**—The eight MP controls focus on protection of removable digital media, which include tapes, external hard drives, and USB flash drives. This family of controls also includes nondigital media, such as paper and film, and covers the access, marking, storage, transport, and sanitization of media.
- **Personnel Security (PS)**—The PS family of nine controls covers several aspects related to personnel security, which includes personnel screening, termination, and transfer.
- **Physical and Environmental Protection (PE)**—The PE family provides 23 controls related to physical security, many of which are included in the Physical Control Examples section later in this chapter.
- **Planning (PL)**—The PL family of 11 controls focuses on security plans for systems. It also covers rules of behavior for users. Rules of behavior are also called an acceptable use policy.
- **Program Management (PM)**—This family of 32 controls is driven by the Federal Information Security Management Act (FISMA). It provides controls to ensure compliance with FISMA. These controls complement other controls; they don't replace them. This family is the only one that is not covered in Appendix F of SP 800-53. Instead, it is covered in Appendix G.
- **Risk Assessment (RA)**—This family of 10 controls provides details on risk assessments and vulnerability scanning.
- **Assessment, Authorization, and Monitoring (CA)**—This family of nine controls addresses steps to implement a security and assessment program. It includes controls to ensure only authorized systems are allowed on a network and details on important security concepts, such as continuous monitoring and a plan of action and milestones.
- **System and Communications Protection (SC)**—The SC family is a large group of 51 controls that cover many aspects of protecting systems and communication channels. Controls for denial of service protection, boundary protection, transmission integrity, and confidentiality are included.

NOTE

Previous versions of SP 800-53 labeled the CA family as Certification, Accreditation, and Security Assessment. The CA acronym refers to Certification and Accreditation. Even though NIST changed the name, it will still use the CA acronym. Do not confuse the CA in certification and accreditation with the CA family of controls.

- **System and Information Integrity (SI)**—This family of 23 controls provides information for maintaining the integrity of systems and data. Flaw remediation identifies steps to keep systems updated, and malicious code protection lists steps to protect against malware.
- **System and Services Acquisition (SA)**—The SA family includes 23 controls related to the purchase of products and services. These controls include those related to hardware, software, and protecting the supply chain, and several controls address security issues related to software development.
- **Personally Identifiable Information Processing and Transparency (PT)**—This family includes eight controls. The family addresses the requirements for how personally identifiable information can be processed, or the conditions under which they can be processed.
- **Supply Chain Risk Management (SR)**—This family includes 12 controls. These controls address enterprise-level program management and supply chain risk considerations as they relate to federal mandates.

Appendix E of SP 800-53 Rev. 5 includes a summary of the controls in each of these families. This appendix is close to half the size of the entire document, which is about 440 pages as of this writing. It is an excellent place to start when looking for specific things that can be done in an organization to improve security in any of these areas.

Procedural Control Examples

Procedural controls refer to the procedures performed by individuals. They are often detailed in written documents that an organization uses for security. Procedural controls are directives from senior management on how to address security within the organization. Previous versions of NIST SP 800-53 referred to these controls as administrative controls.

The following sections provide examples of some of the common procedural controls in these categories:

- Policies and procedures
- Security plans
- Insurance and bonding
- Background and financial checks
- Data loss prevention program
- Education, training, and awareness
- Rules of behavior
- Software testing
- Acceptable use policies

NOTE

The actual methods used to protect against loss of data are technical controls. However, the program that identifies which data to protect is a procedural control.

NOTE

Procedural controls must have support from senior management. If management doesn't support the guidelines, their lack of support will soon become apparent to employees. The organization will have two sets of policies: one that is the written set of policies and the other that is the unwritten set of policies that everyone follows.

Policies and Procedures

Policies and procedures are written documents that provide guidelines and rules for an organization. An organization will typically have several policies and procedures. A policy is a high-level document that provides overall direction without details. A procedure provides the detailed steps needed to implement a policy.

Policies have widespread application. They identify the direction management wants to take on a specific topic, meaning they document high-level management decisions. Personnel within the organization can then take steps to implement the policy. Policies also provide authority. This authority can be used to purchase resources in support of a policy. Without the policy in place, a purchase may be more difficult to justify.

Cybersecurity policies are formalized rules, principles, and guidelines established by an organization to protect its digital assets, networks, data, and users from cyberthreats and unauthorized access. These policies define acceptable behavior, outline technical safeguards, and ensure compliance with legal, regulatory, and industry standards. These include access control policies, change management policies, security awareness and training policies, and other policies.

For example, a backup policy would identify what data needs to be backed up, based on its value. The data could include user data, databases, application data on servers, and more. The backup policy would also identify storage and retention requirements. It would specify that copies of backups be stored in a separate location, which provides protection against a disaster, such as a fire.

A backup policy would include a retention policy, which identifies how long backups are to be retained. For example, the retention policy might specify that some data be retained for 3 years and other data be retained for only 30 days. Again, the choices are dependent on management decisions, which are documented in the written policy.

With a backup policy in place, the department responsible for backing up the data can purchase resources to implement the policy. These resources include tape drives, tapes, and software. Backups can get expensive; without a backup policy in place, sometimes managers balk at the cost.

Procedures are narrower in scope and more task-oriented than policies. They identify specific steps needed to implement a policy. Any policy could have multiple procedures.

For example, a backup policy would state that backups need to be performed but not how to perform them. Procedures, on the other hand, state how to perform the backups. Separate procedures could be created for backing up user data, databases, and other application data and transferring tapes to an off-site location.

Examples of policies might be:

- **Acceptable use policy (AUP)**—Defines acceptable use of systems by delineating what a user can and cannot do on a system. Sometimes, an AUP is referred to as rules of behavior.
- **Vulnerability scanning policy**—Provides authority to perform regular scans. It identifies specific goals of the scans and how often the scans are performed.
- **Removable media policy**—Many organizations recognize the risks associated with removable media, such as USB flash drives. By means of a policy, they restrict the use of these drives.
- **Data protection & privacy policy**—Defines how to handle personally identifiable information (PII). This type of policy may reference legal or regulatory requirements, such as HIPAA.

Examples of procedures might be:

- **AUP procedure**—Identifies how users acknowledge the AUP. For example, users may be required to read and acknowledge their understanding of the AUP by signing a document.
- **Vulnerability scanning procedures**—Procedures would be identified for different types of scans and would specify how the scans are to be documented and reported.
- **Removable media enforcement**—Procedures can enforce the restriction of removable media. For example, the basic input/output system (BIOS) could be manipulated to prevent the use of removable media, or third-party software could be purchased to block their use. Microsoft domains allow administrators to restrict the use of removable media with Group Policy.

It should be noted that there are standards that help you to develop policies. ISO 17799 is a standard that provides guidance on developing and writing policies. The standard describes best practices related to control objectives and controls in the following areas of information security management:

- Security policy
- Organization of information security
- Asset management
- Human resources security
- Physical and environmental security
- Communications and operations management
- Access control
- Information systems acquisition, development, and maintenance
- Information security incident management
- Business continuity management
- Compliance

Referencing this standard while developing your policies can help you avoid many common mistakes.

Security Plans

Organizations create separate security plans to address different scenarios. Many of the security plans are common to most organizations. This section covers the following security plans found in many organizations:

- Business continuity plan
- Disaster recovery plan
- Backup plan
- Incident response plan

Disaster Recovery and Business Continuity Plans

A disaster recovery plan (DRP) is a plan you have in place to return business to normal operations after a disaster occurs. The disaster could be a natural disaster, a significant cybersecurity breach, a fire, or anything that disrupts normal business operations. A DRP must include a number of items. It must address personnel issues. That means being able to contact your employees during an emergency. It may also involve finding temporary personnel. A DRP must also include having specific people assigned to specific tasks. Your DRP needs to address who in your organization is tasked with the following:

- Locating alternative facilities and equipment
- Installing and configuring software
- Setting up the network at the new facility
- Contacting staff, vendors, and customers

These are just a few areas that a disaster recovery plan must address. A business continuity plan (BCP) is related but different in focus. A BCP is about getting just essential operations up and running. One way to think about it is that a DRP is designed to fully restore the business to the condition it was in just prior to the disaster. A BCP is concerned with just getting the essentials running in the interim, before you can fully implement the DRP.

Backup Plan

A backup plan, which is derived from a backup policy, is often included as part of a DRP. Data can't be recovered after a disaster unless it previously has been backed up. The backup policy identifies data valuable to the organization and specifies storage and retention requirements. The backup plan includes procedures identifying how this data can be backed up because not all data is backed up the same way.

User data is simple to back up if the data is stored centrally. Often, an organization will require users to store their data on a central server, and the backup plan documents this requirement. Administrators then back up the data on the server. Backing up data on each individual user system is almost impossible.

Databases hosted on database servers require dedicated software to back them up. The same software can't be used to back up both user data and databases. Additionally, many other server applications, such as email servers, require dedicated backup software.

Backup plans also identify how to perform test restores, which verify that backed-up data can be restored. Many horror stories tell of how an organization regularly went through the motions to back up its data but, when the data needed to be restored, technicians discovered that none of the backups were usable. A test restore simply restores a backup media to some test drive to ensure the backup is valid.

While database administrators may use a number of different types of data backups, from a security point of view, there are three primary backup types that you should be familiar with:

- **Full:** All changes
- **Differential:** All changes since last full backup
- **Incremental:** All changes since last backup of any type

To appreciate the differences, it may be helpful to use a scenario. Consider a scenario in which a full backup is done automatically each morning at 2 a.m. But you are concerned about the possibility of a server crash before the next full backup, so you have decided to perform an additional backup every 2 hours. The type backup you choose will determine the efficiency of doing those frequent backups and the time needed to restore. We will consider each type of backup you could be doing every 2 hours and the impact it has.

Full: In this scenario you perform full backups at 4 a.m., 6 a.m., 8 a.m., and 10 a.m., and then the system crashes at 10:15 a.m. Restoration is simple: you simply restore that last full backup. However, running a full backup every 2 hours is very time-consuming and resource-intensive, and it may very well negatively impact your day-to-day data operations.

Differential: In this scenario you perform a differential back up every 2 hours, and then the system crashes at 10:15 a.m. To restore, you will need to restore the last full backup, which was done at 2 a.m., and the most recent differential backup, which was done at 10 a.m. This approach requires only two restorations, rather than the one required when using the full backup strategy. However, those differential backups are going to get larger each time you do them, and you may eventually develop data efficiency issues later in the day.

Incremental: In this scenario you elect to do incremental backups every 2 hours, and then the system crashes at 10:15 a.m. To restore, you need to restore the last full backup, which was done at 2 a.m., and then, in order, restore each incremental backup since that time. This type of restoration is much more complex, but each incremental backup is small and does not take much time or consume many resources.

There is no single approach that is right for every situation. That is one reason there are different approaches. However, you should carefully consider what works best for your organization. You should also consider what frequency of backups is best for your organization. Some organizations are now using continuous live backups. Lastly, there is a well-known backup best practice called the "3-2-1 backup rule." The 3-2-1 rule is a strategy that recommends making 3 copies of the data, storing them on 2 different media, and finally keeping 1 copy off-site. This best practice significantly reduces exposure to all too common, but unexpected bad luck trying to recover from a disaster.

Incident Response Plan

An incident response plan documents how an organization should respond to a security incident. The organization could have multiple incident response plans, depending on the complexity of the organization.

A security incident is any incident that affects the confidentiality, integrity, or availability of systems or data. Security incidents occur when a threat exploits a vulnerability.

For example, a system is infected with malware. The organization's plan could be to take the following steps in response to an infection:

- Disconnect the local area connection cable.
- Leave the system power on.
- Write down any messages that appear.
- Report the incident.

A more complicated problem may occur from a denial of service (DoS) attack on a server, which would require a response from an administrator or security professional. Once the incident has been verified, the administrator could then take steps to isolate the incident and then protect any evidence about the attack.

Insurance and Bonding

A risk can be avoided, shared or transferred, mitigated, or accepted. In cases where the likelihood of damage is very low and the impact is very high, organizations often choose to share or transfer the risk. The primary way the risk is shared or transferred is by the organization's purchasing of insurance.

Most insurance policies specify shared responsibilities between the insurance company and the customer. For example, fire insurance typically covers most but not all damage from fire. It also requires customers to take reasonable precautions to prevent fires. In some cases, the entire risk can be transferred with an insurance policy.

Many types of insurance can be purchased. The goal is to protect a company from a loss. If the risk occurs, the insurance helps pay for the loss, which keeps the risk from bankrupting the company.

Some types of insurance, such as fire and flood insurance, are obvious. Other types of insurance deserve an explanation.

Business interruption insurance can be purchased as an add-on to some policies. For example, a company may add business interruption insurance onto a fire insurance policy. If a fire occurs and the company can't operate normally, the insurance pays for losses until the company opens up again. This insurance usually covers operational expenses, such as rental of equipment, and would also pay for profits that the company would have normally earned.

Errors and omissions insurance, also known as professional liability insurance, is valuable if a company supplies services to other companies. For example, imagine a company performs maintenance on a customer's servers. In the process of performing the maintenance, the technician accidentally plugs in a power supply the wrong way and ruins the server. The customer may take the company to court. This insurance will provide protection.

Similarly, a company may provide consultants to customers. A consultant may help a customer create a backup plan but forget to include off-site storage. Because the consultant is the expert, this is a glaring omission. If the customer suffers a fire and loses all the backups for the organization, the company may sue. Again, the errors and omissions insurance provides protection.

Bonding is a type of insurance that covers against losses by theft, fraud, or dishonesty. A person covered by bonding insurance is referred to as being bonded. Organizations purchase bonding insurance when required by law and to provide a level of security to their customers.

For example, a company provides IT support to customers at their homes. Bonding insurance could be purchased to cover the technicians. If a technician in the company steals from a customer while performing the service, the bonding company would pay for the loss. Bonding insurance is often very narrow. For example, the insurance may not pay unless the employee has been tried and convicted of the theft. Instead of pursuing a conviction against the employee, the customer may just sue the company.

Background and Financial Checks

Many organizations perform background and financial checks on prospective employees, which are completed before the employee is hired.

Background checks commonly include police and FBI checks, which will identify any criminal behavior on the part of a prospective employee. Past mistakes won't automatically stop someone from being hired. However, there are times when past convictions are relevant.

A truck driver is unlikely to be hired if he has a reckless driving conviction on his record. Similarly, an administrator is unlikely to be hired if she's recently been convicted of theft. A shoplifting conviction is enough to prevent a company from hiring an employee in a position of trust.

Most companies also complete financial checks for prospective employees. A person with a poor credit rating may be viewed suspiciously. Employers wonder whether the poor credit rating is a reflection of responsibility and accountability. If a person ignores their debts, does that imply irresponsibility on the job?

Today, internet resources are commonly included in background investigations, which include simple Google or Facebook searches. A person who has fanatically ranted on a topic may be viewed as problematic. More than anything, companies want employees who can work well with others. Someone who has a Facebook page filled with attacks on others may be bypassed for someone who has never had a Facebook page.

Data Loss Prevention Program

A data loss prevention program helps a company prevent data loss. Data loss can be viewed in one of two ways:

- **Loss of confidentiality**—A company loses confidentiality when unauthorized entities view its data. For example, if an unauthorized user views data, confidentiality is lost. Inadequate access controls may allow an unauthorized user to view data, an attacker could hack into an online site and access a back-end database, or a user could lose a laptop that has proprietary information stored on it.
- **Loss due to corruption**—Files can become corrupt through a variety of ways. The disk drive could crash, an application could hiccup when writing a file, or users could accidentally or purposely delete or modify data. How the data is lost isn't as important as preparing for the loss with backups.

An organization can protect against loss of confidentiality using two methods. One method is using access controls. Authentication methods identify and verify users. Permissions then grant authorization to access resources. The principle of least privilege ensures that users have access to only the resources they need and no more.

The other method of protection against loss of confidentiality is encryption. Data can be encrypted while it's at rest or being transferred. At-rest data is any data that is stored on media, such as a hard drive or USB flash drive. Data can also be encrypted when it's transferred over a network.

A data loss prevention program identifies the data that is valuable to an organization. Data can be classified as public, private, or proprietary. The data loss prevention program would then specify the importance of data in each of these categories and would also specify whether the organization wants to protect against loss of confidentiality, loss due to corruption, or both.

Education, Training, and Awareness

An organization can have the best documented security controls on the planet. However, if the employees don't know what they are or how to implement them, the controls simply aren't effective. Education, training, and awareness controls ensure that employees know why having security controls in place is important and how to implement security controls, and are aware of the organization's security standards.

Awareness programs are generic and apply to all personnel. They use different techniques to inform and remind people about security, and they try to have users personalize security. In other words, instead of security being someone else's responsibility, users recognize that security is everyone's responsibility, including theirs. Some examples of how awareness can be raised include:

> **TIP**
>
> NIST published SP 800-50, Building an Information Technology Security Awareness and Training Program, in 2003. It provides details on how to design, develop, and implement an awareness and security training program.

- Logon or welcome banners
- Emails
- Posters

Training is provided for different audiences. Some training is generic and for all personnel. For example, all users should be educated on social engineering tactics. Other training is specialized and targeted at specific groups. For example, training on how to maintain a specific firewall is provided to the administrators who will maintain it. Specific security professionals are trained on how to run and interpret vulnerability scans.

Education generally focuses on the risk of not protecting the organization. It applies to organizational executives and attempts to do a cost-benefit analysis of security controls, standards, and practices.

Rules of Behavior

Rules of behavior let users know what they can and cannot do with systems. Users read this document before being granted access to a system and are often required to sign a document indicating that they have read and understand the rules of behavior.

> **TIP**
>
> Rules of behavior are called an acceptable use policy (AUP) in some organizations. Most private organizations use an AUP. The purpose of rules of behavior and an AUP is the same.

The Office of Management and Budget (OMB) mandates the use of rules of behavior for agencies under OMB jurisdiction. These rules are documented in OMB Circular A-130, Appendix III, which also references the rules of behavior control documented in SP 800-53.

Some common elements in a rules of behavior document are:

- **Privacy**—Many organizations stress that users have no expectation of privacy. If they are using employer resources, they are subject to monitoring, and data can be viewed at any time. This data includes a user's data files, email files, and a history of a user's internet activity. Organizations frequently scan all outgoing transmissions, such as emails, which helps them ensure that personally identifiable information (PII) is not being released.

- **List of restricted activities**—Most systems restrict certain kinds of activities. Organizations will often explicitly restrict access to any sites with sexual or pornographic content. The list of restrictions could also include gaming, gambling, or personal business. Although these restrictions try to avoid offending employees, other restrictions intend to protect resources. For example, some companies restrict any type of audio or video streaming, such as online radio stations, which protects the network from being overloaded with unnecessary traffic.
- **Email usage**—Users are informed of what email can be used for and what restrictions exist. Most companies allow users to send and receive personal email. However, users should not use email for any type of harassment or transmission of objectionable materials.
- **Protection of credentials**—Users are told to protect their credentials, such as username and password, and they are given information on how to create a strong password.
- **Consequences or penalties for noncompliance**—Such consequences could be reprimands or suspension of privileges. Serious offenses could result in the employee's termination.

This list isn't all inclusive. An organization will include the information necessary to ensure that users understand what is expected of them. Some organizations limit this information to a single page, and other organizations make this list longer.

Software Testing

An organization that develops software should take the time to test it, and it should have a policy that mandates software testing. The primary reason to test the software is to reduce the number of undiscovered bugs in the software.

A 2017 study from Tricentis reported annual losses from software failures to be in the $1.7 trillion range. The Consortium for IT Software Quality (CISQ) put its 2018 estimate at roughly $1.1 trillion. These numbers reflect the growing need for and importance of software quality checks through testing.

The types of software testing performed are technical controls. For example, data range and reasonableness checks could be performed. However, creating a policy requiring software testing is the place to start.

Technical Control Examples

Technical controls are tools that automate protection. They include hardware, software, and firmware that enforce security using a technical method. A technical control is significantly different from a procedural control. The procedural control identifies what should be done and often requires a person to intervene and ensure the procedural control is followed.

In contrast, a technical control is enforced using technology. For example, a password enforcement policy can be created on many systems. It could specify that passwords must be strong, which means they have at least eight characters and are a mixture of uppercase and lowercase letters, numbers, and special characters. The policy could also specify changing passwords every 30 days.

The system prompts users to change their password. If they choose not to, the system locks them out until they change it. When they change it, the new password must be strong because the system will reject weak passwords.

This section presents examples of other technical controls, including:

- Logon identifier
- Session time-out
- System logs and audit trails
- Data range and reasonableness checks
- Firewalls and routers
- Encryption
- Public key infrastructure

NOTE

The Data Range and Reasonableness Checks section, later in this chapter, covers these topics in more detail.

Logon Identifier

A logon identifier is another name for a user account. The account is uniquely identified and matched to the user. Every time the user logs on, this account is used, which helps enforce several other controls.

A logon identifier is needed for access control. If every user logged on with an account named "Bob," then every user would have the same access. The user's real name doesn't matter. Permissions granted to "Bob" are granted to all users who log on with the Bob account.

However, if every user logs on with a different account, permissions can be assigned individually. Users who need access to resources are granted the access, and users who don't need access aren't granted the access.

Audit logs, which record who, what, where, and when details, use logon identifiers. The "who" comes from the logon identifier. Users log on with their own account, and any auditable actions are recorded with this account information.

The logon identifier also provides nonrepudiation, which means users cannot believably deny they took an action if it is logged with their logon identifiers.

TIP

In Microsoft systems, the logon identifier is called a security identifier (SID). Every user account has an SID assigned when it is created. This SID is unique and used to grant access to resources.

Session Time-Out

Most systems include session time-out controls, which help ensure that an unauthorized user doesn't have access to a session without providing credentials.

TIP

The default time-out for many websites is 20 minutes, which is a long time. Therefore, someone using a public computer should always log off as soon as they are done. Just walking away and leaving the session open would allow someone else to access the computer 15 minutes later. The intruder would then have access to that session, which would stay open for the intruder as long as they kept it active.

An example of a simple session time-out control is a screen saver. A screen saver can be configured to start after 10 minutes of inactivity and to require users to log on again after the screen saver has started. That way, if a user walks away from a computer without locking it, the screen saver will start after 10 minutes and lock the system.

Many websites include session time-outs. For example, many banking sites will close the session after 20 minutes. After credentials have been provided to log on to the banking site, as long as the user is active on the site, the session remains open. This feature allows different pages to be viewed without logging on again.

However, if the webpage is left open but is inactive for 20 minutes, the time-out control will close the webpage and clear out the session data. To access the page again, logon credentials must be entered again.

Similarly, if a session on a public computer is inactive for 20 minutes, it will close, which helps prevent unauthorized users from accessing the site.

System Logs and Audit Trails

Operating systems and network devices include the capability to record different types of events. Recording events and regularly reviewing the logs can help identify what is occurring. Logs can be used to investigate security events and to troubleshoot problems.

Logs typically record the following details on events:

- Who did it
- What happened
- Where it happened
- When it happened

> **TIP**
> NIST SP 800-53 recommends internal system clocks for timestamps. An internal clock provides a consistent time for all events.

> **TIP**
> Logs need to be reviewed. This action would seem to be obvious, but this step is often overlooked. Administrators become overwhelmed with day-to-day tasks, and the log reviews become less important. Reviewing logs becomes even more difficult when too many events are logged. Many organizations use automated tools to review the logs for key events. These tools provide alerts on key events and track trends.

This information is often shortened to who, what, where, and when. The logon identifier identifies who took the action, the system identifies what happened and where it happened, and a clock provides a timestamp to record when it happened.

Several types of logs are present in any network. Desktop and server operating systems include logs; firewalls include logs to track allowed and blocked traffic; and network server applications, such as Domain Name System (DNS), log events. Logging can be enabled or enhanced on just about any system.

System logging tracks different types of events on the operating system. For example, Microsoft Windows operating systems include the System log to record system events. These events include when services start or stop or when the system starts or stops. These events are categorized as errors, warnings, and information events.

Security logging focuses on security events. Some security events are automatically logged. However, logging can be configured to record additional auditable events. For example, auditing on folders could be enabled to show whether anyone accessed a folder holding sensitive data. This type of auditing would record the details of anyone reading, modifying, or deleting data.

Not all events should be logged, though. Instead, logging should include only what is important. Logging too many events takes up extra resources, which include processing power to capture and log the events and disk space as the log fills up.

Data Range and Reasonableness Checks

Application developers use data range and reasonableness checks to help ensure they are receiving valid data. Developers can't ensure the data is accurate, but they can ensure the data is valid.

> **NOTE**
>
> Data range and reasonableness checks are also referred to as input validation. The data input by the user is checked to ensure it is valid, and invalid data is not used.

Valid data follows a specific format, for example, a text box that expects a five-digit U.S. ZIP Code. The only valid characters are five numbers. If the user enters anything other than five numbers, the data is not valid.

Along the same lines, for example, the user's ZIP Code is 23456. If the user accidentally enters 33456, the application can't tell that the ZIP Code is incorrect. Because 33456 is a valid five-digit number, it will pass the validation test.

Validation checks appear on websites. The user is prompted to enter certain data, such as a name and an email address. If the user misses or enters something incorrectly, the website complains to the user, such as showing a red asterisk with an error explanation. The explanation may say something like "You must enter an email address."

Data range checks ensure data is within a certain range. For example, users may be asked to enter a number between 1 and 100. The data range check ensures the number is between 1 and 100. If the entered data is outside the valid range, it is not used. Instead, the user is prompted to try again.

Similarly, a date range can verify that dates are within a certain range. For example, a birth date could be used to ensure someone is over a certain age. It compares the current date with the birth date. If the user is too young, the website could redirect the user to an error page.

Reasonableness checks ensure that the entered data is reasonable. For example, how many letters would be expected in a first name, and what types of characters are valid in a first name are defined.

> **TIP**
>
> Reasonableness checks can prevent some buffer overflow attacks. A buffer overflow can occur when a webpage receives more data than is expected. If an attacker tries to enter more data than expected into a text box, the validation check can reject it. Because the data is rejected, the buffer overflow doesn't occur.

The parameter might be that a first name can't have more than 25 characters nor contain numbers. Therefore, when a user enters data for a first name, it could be checked against this parameter.

Reasonableness checks can be used for any type of data. The data simply needs to be defined. For example, if a reasonableness check is used for a first name, what constitutes a first name needs to be defined. Thus, five letters as a maximum for a first name isn't acceptable.

Firewalls and Routers

Firewalls and router software are used as technical controls in a network. They control the traffic by allowing some traffic and blocking other traffic.

NOTE

Routers use routing tables to identify how to route traffic. The routing table identifies the best path to get traffic from one point to another. Routers use access control lists (ACLs) to control what traffic gets from one point to another. The ACLs say what kind of traffic can go which direction or from which interface.

Many firewalls and routers use an implicit deny philosophy, meaning all traffic is blocked unless it is explicitly allowed. To identify allowed traffic, firewalls use rules, and routers use access control lists (ACLs).

A router provides basic filtering of traffic, based on:

- Internet protocol (IP) addresses
- Ports
- Some protocols

In **FIGURE 9-1**, the router can be configured to allow traffic from any hosts with IP addresses on subnets 1, 2, or 3. Ports are used to identify protocols. For example, the Hypertext Transfer Protocol (HTTP) uses port 80. An ACL can be configured to allow HTTP traffic to the intranet web server on subnet 1. The Simple Mail Transfer Protocol (SMTP) uses port 25. An ACL can be configured to allow SMTP traffic to the email server on subnet 2.

The firewall starts with basic routing capabilities. However, most firewalls are much more advanced. Router ACLs can evaluate only a single packet at a time. However, a firewall can evaluate the entire conversation. Once a session has been established between two hosts, the firewall can evaluate all the traffic between them, which is referred to as a stateful evaluation.

Rules created on the firewall allow a network to be protected from external attacks. By allowing only specific traffic, the capabilities of attackers from the internet are limited.

FIGURE 9-1

Traffic controlled with routers and firewalls.

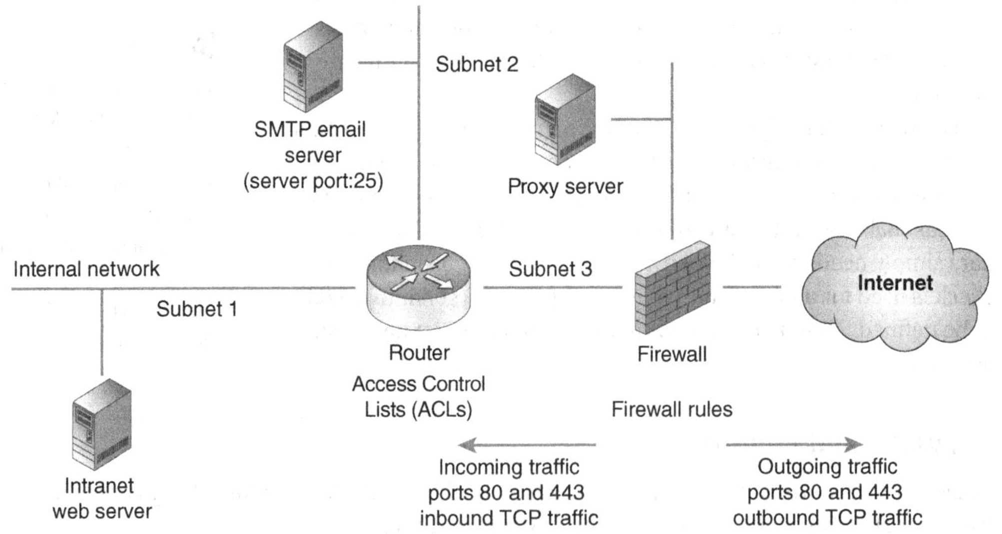

Well-Known Ports

Ports 0 through 1023 are well-known ports. Ports in this range are assigned to specific protocols. When the port is used, an operating system recognizes that it is for the related protocol.

The Internet Assigned Numbers Authority (IANA) assigns well-known ports. The full list of ports can be viewed at http://www.iana.org/assignments/port-numbers.

The well-known port for HTTP is port 80. When a system receives a packet with a destination port of 80, it knows to pass this packet to the service handling the HTTP protocol. A server running the HTTP protocol is normally a web server.

Because port 80 is a well-known port, it doesn't need to be included in the uniform resource locator (URL), but it could be included. The following URL includes the port: https://www.iana.org/assignments/service-names-port-numbers/service-names-port-numbers.xml:8080.

Firewalls and routers use these port numbers to identify allowed traffic. For example, if a firewall wanted to allow HTTP traffic, it would have a rule to allow traffic on port 80. Similarly, a router would allow HTTP traffic with an entry in the ACL.

Encryption

Encryption changes plaintext data into ciphered data. For example, the word *password* is in plaintext, but encrypted it may look like this: *MFIGs3x/$6oOD*.

Data can be encrypted at rest or when transferred. At-rest data is any data stored on media, such as a hard drive or a USB flash drive. If a user stores sensitive data on a laptop computer, the data can be encrypted to protect it. If the laptop is lost or stolen, there is less chance the data will be compromised. Similarly, data stored on a USB flash drive can be encrypted. If the USB drive is lost or stolen, the encrypted data will be difficult for anyone to read.

Attackers and administrators can capture and read data sent over a network. For example, Wireshark is a free packet analyzer that can capture data sent over the network. Once the data has been captured, the process to open and analyze the individual packets is trivial. Wireshark allows individuals to read any data sent over the network in cleartext.

> **TIP**
>
> Encryption provides confidentiality for data and helps prevent unauthorized disclosure. Only users with access to decryption keys can decrypt the data.

Encrypted data is not impossible to decrypt given enough resources and time. However, encryption algorithms are designed to make decryption too difficult and take too much time to make it worthwhile.

> **NOTE**
>
> A packet analyzer that can capture traffic is commonly called a **sniffer**, and capturing packets over the network is called *sniffing*. A patient attacker can sniff network traffic and capture a significant amount of data.

For example, years ago, the Rivest, Shamir, Adelman (RSA) encryption, which was used on the internet, employed 40-bit keys, which, in their time, were secure. However, in 1997, a student at UC Berkeley cracked a 40-bit RSA key in 3.5 hours, and, today, it can be done in minutes. Currently, 1024-, 2048-, or 4096-bit keys are commonly used with RSA. According to RSA, 1024-bit keys have been cracked, and 2048-bit keys can be sufficiently used until 2030. NIST recommends 2048-bit keys for RSA.

Encryption is classified as either:

- **Symmetric**—This encryption uses one key. As a simple example, a key of 53 could be used to both encrypt and then decrypt data. Keys are much more complex than just a two-digit number, however. Strong symmetric algorithms use 256 bits.
- **Asymmetric**—Asymmetric encryption uses two keys. One key is called the public key, and the other key is called the private key. These two keys are matched to each other. Any data encrypted with the public key can be decrypted only with the matching private key. Any data encrypted with the private key can be decrypted only with the public key.

Advanced Encryption Standard (AES) is the primary symmetric encryption protocol used today. In the 1990s, NIST asked for developers to submit cryptographic algorithms for evaluation. After a lengthy evaluation, NIST selected and ratified AES in 2000 as a standard.

AES is fast and efficient. It's quick even when encrypting small amounts of data, such as on USB flash drives, and doesn't need as much processing power as some older encryption algorithms.

Despite its strength, encryption shouldn't be considered foolproof. Encryption algorithms continue to improve, but so do cryptanalysis techniques designed to crack algorithms. The National Security Agency (NSA) has a relevant saying: "Cryptanalysis always gets better. It never gets worse."

Public Key Infrastructure

A public key infrastructure (PKI) is created to provide support for certificates. Even though the PKI has several elements, the purpose of all the elements is centered on certificates. Some of the elements of a PKI are:

- Certificate authority
- Certificates
- Public and private keys
- Web of trust

> **TIP**
>
> A private CA is simply a server running the certificate authority software. A public CA usually refers to a company.

A **certificate authority (CA)** issues and manages certificates and can be public, such as VeriSign. A CA can also be private. A private CA is created within a company, and it issues certificates internally.

Systems have a listing of CAs that they trust. If a system trusts a CA, it automatically trusts any certificates issued by the CA. This situation is similar to driver's licenses issued by a department of motor vehicles (DMV). If a driver's license is presented as identification, people trust it as valid because the DMV is trusted. All driver's licenses issued by the DMV are automatically trusted. Similarly, all certificates issued by a trusted CA are automatically trusted.

Certificates are used for identification and to aid in encryption. Certificates include details on the entity that received the certificate. For example, if the certificate was issued to a server, the certificate would include details on the server, such as its name. The server is able to present the certificate as proof of its identity.

Public and private keys, which are matched, are used with a PKI. Data encrypted with one of the keys can be decrypted only with the matching key. A public key is embedded in the certificate and passed to others. The private key always stays private.

For example, a certificate is issued to a web server. When a user connects to the web server and starts a secure session, the server sends the certificate to the user. The certificate includes a public key. The user can encrypt data with the public key and send it to the server. Because the server holds the private key, it can decrypt the data. Because no other entity has the private key, no one else can decrypt the data.

Certificates are also used with a **digital signature**, which provides authentication, nonrepudiation, and integrity.

For example, an email can be signed with a digital signature. The receiver has verification that it was sent by the signer and not someone trying to impersonate the signer. A digital signature is created in two steps:

- A message hash is created.
- The hash is encrypted with the sender's private key.

FIGURE 9-2 shows that a hash is simply a number created by running an algorithm. For example, a simple hash for the message "Hello" could be 77. No matter how many times the algorithm

FIGURE 9-2
Using digital signatures.

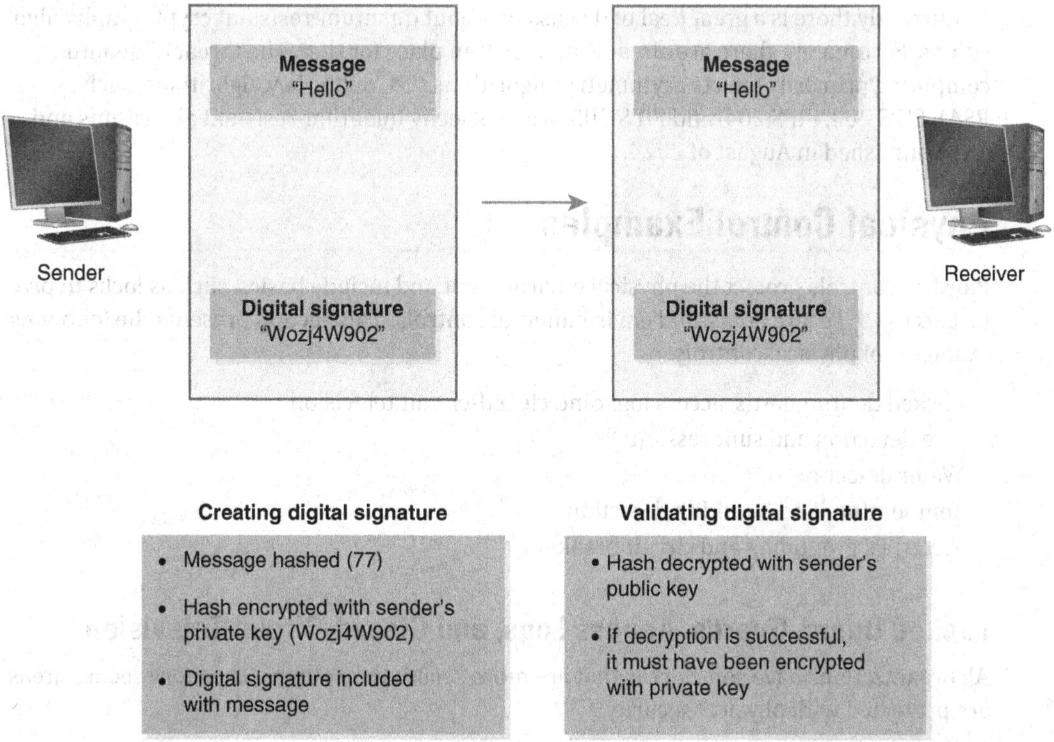

is run, the hash would always be 77. The hash is then encrypted with the sender's private key. The result may be Wozj4W902.

The encrypted hash is sent with the message. The receiver has the public key, which is then used to decrypt the hash. This sequence provides three security benefits:

- **Authentication of the sender**—The matching public key decrypted the hash, which verifies that the message was encrypted with the sender's private key because only the sender has access to the private key.
- **Nonrepudiation**—The sender cannot deny sending the message. Again, only the sender has access to the sender's private key. No one else could have encrypted the hash if the sender's matching public key decrypted it.
- **Integrity**—The recipient can calculate the hash on the message and decrypt the received hash. If both hashes are the same, this verifies that the message was not modified.

> **NOTE**
>
> **Nonrepudiation** techniques prevent someone from denying they took an action. For example, an audit log records who, what, where, and when details for events. If an audit log recorded that a user deleted a file, the user cannot believably deny it. The user logged on, and the audit log recorded the action with the user's logon credentials. The only alternative is that the user gave out their credentials. Digital signatures also provide nonrepudiation.

A digital signature is not possible without a PKI because it requires matching public and private keys. The public key must be able to be packaged into a certificate. A CA is needed to issue the certificates.

A **web of trust** is used in Pretty Good Privacy (PGP)- and OpenPGP-compatible systems to ensure that the binding between a public key and its owner is authentic. It is an alternative to the PKI, which relies on a CA. A web of trust is based on a decentralized trust model, as opposed to a CA's centralized trust model.

Currently there is a great deal of discussion about quantum-resistant cryptography algorithms. Fortunately, there are already standards in place for that. The threat of quantum computing primarily affects asymmetric algorithms (i.e., public key algorithms, such as RSA). FIPS 203, FIPS 204, and FIPS 205, which specify quantum-resistant algorithms and were published in August of 2024.

Physical Control Examples

Physical controls protect the physical environment and include basics, such as locks to protect access to secure areas, and environmental controls. This section presents the following examples of physical controls:

- Locked doors, guards, access logs, and closed-circuit television
- Fire detection and suppression
- Water detection
- Temperature and humidity detection
- Electrical grounding and circuit breakers

Locked Doors, Guards, Access Logs, and Closed-Circuit Television

All organizations have some areas that are more secure than others. The more secure areas are protected with physical security.

For example, a server room holds servers that shouldn't be accessible to just anyone because servers need to be protected. Different types of physical security can be used to protect the servers.

FYI

A proximity card is a small credit card–sized device. It includes electronics that will activate when it is close to a proximity reader. The card sends a signal to the reader identifying it. If the card is authorized, the door will open.

Some credit cards also use this technology. The card is simply waved in front of the credit card reader, which registers it. Unfortunately, proximity card readers are portable. An attacker can put one in a small box or bag and then gather credit card data just by riding up and down on an elevator for a day.

The simplest method of physical security is to simply use locks on doors. The locks could be simple locks with keys or cipher locks for which users need to enter a combination of numbers to gain access, or they could require proximity cards issued to employees. Some proximity cards also require users to enter a personal identification number (PIN).

Guards can also be used to protect secure areas. Guards will often be given a list of authorized personnel, and, as long as individuals are on the access list, the guards will grant them access.

Access logs provide an audit trail of who has entered and exited a building. Access logs can be manually or automatically created. For a manual example, guards can keep a log of all personnel who enter or exit the building. For an automated example, some proximity or badge readers can be automated. Each time a user enters or exits the building, the reader records the user's identity along with the time and date.

Three-Barrier Protection

Many organizations utilize three barriers of protection, which include a main entrance, a more secure employee area, and a more secure computer area. Each of these barriers is layered, meaning the secure computer area is within the employee area and the employee area is within the main entrance.

The main entrance is often open, which allows anyone to come and go. However, main entrances are commonly monitored by video cameras.

Employee areas are a little more secure than the main entrance. Guards may be in place to ensure that only employees or authorized visitors can enter the employee area. Cipher locks could be used requiring employees to tap in codes to gain access, and some organizations issue access cards to employees, which must be used to gain access.

Computer centers are the third barrier. They can be a server room, a wiring closet, or anywhere else that stores secure hardware or data. Only select groups of employees, such as administrators, are allowed access.

Closed-circuit television (CCTV) uses video cameras to monitor areas. Cameras can be stationary as well as pan, tilt, and zoom (PTZ) cameras. PTZ cameras can be controlled by security personnel to focus on any area covered by the camera.

The level of protection for any area is dependent on the importance of the hardware or data stored there. One organization may have a limited number of physical controls, whereas another organization may have extensive physical controls. Neither choice is right or wrong. If the systems or data is valuable, money needs to be spent to protect them, based on their value.

Fire Detection and Suppression

Fire detection and suppression systems provide protection against fires. Fires can start and spread rapidly; therefore, the goal is to have a system that can detect them as quickly as possible. Once the fire has been detected, the suppression system attempts to put the fire out.

Detection systems detect changes in the environment that indicate a fire is burning. These changes include significant changes in heat, smoke, and gases.

Fire suppression systems vary depending on the type of fire. There are five primary classes of fires. In the United States, they are classified as follows:

- **Class A**—Ordinary combustibles, such as wood and paper
- **Class B**—Flammable liquids, such as gasoline
- **Class C**—Electrical fires
- **Class D**—Combustible metals, such as magnesium
- **Class K**—Cooking oils and fats (kitchen fires)

NOTE

The classes of fires are labeled slightly differently in Europe, Africa, Australia, and New Zealand.

TIP

Personnel safety should always be the top priority. If an electrical fire has started, the power should be turned off first.

Different classes of fires are fought differently. For example, a Class A fire can be extinguished with water, but water should never be used to put out a Class C fire because it will damage the equipment. Additionally, if the electricity is still on, it could travel up the stream of water and electrocute the firefighter.

Server rooms are at most risk of Class C fires. A primary way to fight Class C fires is with gas systems, such as carbon dioxide (CO_2) and FM-200. Gas systems flood an area with a gas to displace oxygen and disrupt the chemical reaction causing the fire.

Gas systems can be dangerous to personnel. For example, technicians may be working in a server room when a fire is detected. If the gas is released without warning, it will remove the oxygen. Most gas displacement systems provide a warning to personnel, giving them time to leave the room.

Fire detection and suppression systems are physical controls. However, they work in conjunction with the procedural control of insurance. The insurance provides an added layer of protection by paying for any damage that occurs. Most insurance companies will not provide insurance unless a company has adequate detection and suppression systems.

Water Detection

Some locations are susceptible to flooding. Water damage can be expensive, but there are ways to protect an area. For example, water can be pumped out with water pumps before it rises to a dangerous level.

Water detection systems will detect when water is seeping into an area. The detection system will automatically start the pumps, which will continue until the water is no longer detected.

Temperature and Humidity Detection

High temperatures and humidity levels can damage electrical equipment. When the temperature rises, electrical components can overheat and burn up. If the humidity is too high, moisture can condense on the equipment, and this water causes electrical shorts, which will damage the equipment.

Most server rooms are kept cool to prevent heat damage. Many server rooms use raised flooring to cool the room. **FIGURE 9-3** shows an air-conditioning system in a server room. Chilled air is pumped into the area under the raised floor. Equipment is installed in equipment bays, which have hollow bases and are installed over holes in the raised floor. They also have strong fans at the top of the bays to pull the air from the raised floor through the equipment and out the top of the bays.

Sophisticated server rooms use hot and cold aisles. Bays in alternating rows are reversed. The front of the bays in one row faces the front of the bays in another row. This is the cold aisle. The back of the bays in one row face the back of the bays in another row. This is the hot aisle. Cool air is pumped through perforations in the floor on the cold aisles and is pulled through the front of the bays, and warm air goes out the back.

If the air-conditioning fails, the equipment is at risk. If the temperature gets too hot, electrical components burn out, which causes failures. Temperatures inside electrical equipment are often 10°C warmer than the room temperature. Many organizations have policies in place to turn off equipment if the air-conditioning fails and the area reaches a certain temperature. The short-term loss of the mission is better than the long-term loss of the equipment.

> **TIP**
>
> Heating, ventilation, and air conditioning (HVAC) systems control both the temperature and humidity.

FIGURE 9-3

Air-conditioning system in a server room.

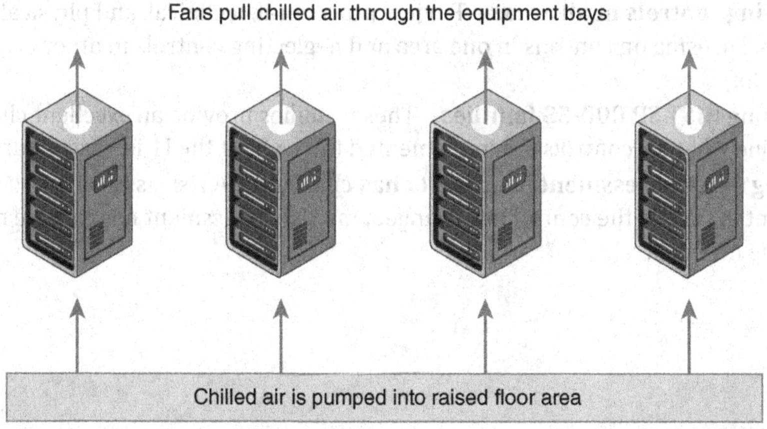

Electrical Grounding and Circuit Breakers

Electrical grounding and circuit breakers protect equipment from electrical damage if a failure occurs. If a short occurs in an electrical system, the short could cause a dangerous voltage to build on the case of the system. If someone touches the case, they could be shocked, and, of course, this is unacceptable. To prevent this scenario from happening, systems are grounded.

An electrical ground is a wire driven into the ground, often with a stake. Access to this ground wire is available throughout a building. Any electrical systems are wired so they can connect to this ground. If a failure occurs, dangerous voltages are sent to the electrical ground, which helps ensure that dangerous voltages don't present a risk to personnel.

Circuit breakers detect changes in heat. If the circuit breaker detects excessive heat, it opens and breaks the circuit, which prevents dangerous conditions that can cause fires.

Here's how a circuit breaker works: Electricity travels down wires, and each wire is rated to carry a certain load of current, which is measured in amperes, or amps. If a wire has excessive current, it can overheat and cause a fire. Instead of allowing this to happen, a circuit breaker is installed on the same line that carries the current. Circuit breakers are also rated for certain loads that are measured as amps. If the load exceeds the rated amps, the circuit breaker opens, and the current flow stops, thus protecting the system.

NOTE

Fuses also function like circuit breakers. If excessive current flows through the fuse, the connection in the fuse will overheat and burn up, which breaks the connection. One important difference between fuses and circuit breakers is that fuses must be replaced, but circuit breakers can simply be reset.

Best Practices for Risk Mitigation Security Controls

The following list identifies several best practices that can be followed when identifying risk mitigation security controls:

- **Ensuring the control is effective**—The control should be able to reduce or eliminate a threat or vulnerability, which it does by preventing, recovering, and/or detecting events.
- **Reviewing controls in all areas**—Review procedural, technical, and physical controls. Focusing on controls in one area and neglecting controls in other areas is easy to do.
- **Reviewing NIST SP 800-53 families**—These families provide an excellent check to determine whether controls are implemented throughout the IT infrastructure.
- **Redoing a risk assessment if a control has changed**—A risk assessment is performed at a point in time. If the control has changed, the risk assessment needs to be redone using the new control.

CHAPTER SUMMARY

This chapter provided information on different types of controls. Effective controls will reduce or neutralize threats or vulnerabilities to an acceptable level. In-place controls are operating. Planned controls have a planned implementation date.

When considering additional controls, they can be evaluated in specific families. NIST SP 800-53 provides detailed guidance on 20 families of controls. Controls can also be considered as procedural, technical, and physical. Evaluating controls in all families and categories is important. For example, technical controls alone cannot address all risks.

KEY CONCEPTS AND TERMS

Advanced Encryption Standard (AES)
certificate
certificate authority (CA)
corrective control
detective control
digital signature
nonrepudiation
preventive control
rules of behavior
sniffer
web of trust

CHAPTER 9 ASSESSMENT

1. A(n) ______ will reduce or eliminate a threat or vulnerability.
2. Controls can be identified based on their function. The functions are preventive, detective, and corrective.
   A. True
   B. False
3. What are the primary objectives of a control?
   A. Prevent, control, and attack
   B. Prevent, respond, and log
   C. Prevent, recover, and detect
   D. Detect, recover, and attack
4. What type of control is an intrusion detection system (IDS)?
   A. Preventive
   B. Detective
   C. Corrective
   D. Recovery
5. Controls are often categorized based on how they are implemented. What are the three common methods of implementing controls?
   A. Preventive, detective, and corrective
   B. Administrative, technical, and operational
   C. Technical, administrative, and environmental
   D. Procedural, technical, and physical
6. A(n) ______ control is used to ensure that users have the rights and permissions they need to perform their jobs and no more.
7. Logon identifiers help ensure that users cannot deny taking a specific action, such as deleting a file. What is this called?
   A. Digital signature
   B. Encryption
   C. Nonrepudiation
   D. PKI

8. What should be used to ensure that users understand what they can and cannot do on systems within the network?
   A. Acceptable use banner
   B. Data range checks
   C. Rules of behavior
   D. Audit trails

9. What can be used to ensure confidentiality of sensitive data?
   A. Encryption
   B. Hashing
   C. Digital signature
   D. Nonrepudiation

10. What should be logged in an audit log?
    A. All system events
    B. All security-related events
    C. The details of what happened for an event
    D. Who, what, when, and where details of an event

11. An organization wants to issue certificates for internal systems, such as an internal web server. A(n) _______ will need to be installed to issue and manage certificates.

12. Which of the following is a procedural control?
    A. Session time-out
    B. Reasonableness check
    C. Water detection
    D. DRP

13. Which of the following is a technical control?
    A. PKI
    B. Awareness and training
    C. Guards
    D. Electrical grounding

14. Which of the following is a physical control?
    A. Logon identifiers
    B. CCTV
    C. Encryption
    D. BCP

15. The web of trust has a centralized trust model.
    A. True
    B. False

CHAPTER 10

Planning Risk Mitigation Throughout an Organization

AFTER COMPLETING THE BASICS of identifying assets, threats, and vulnerabilities, identifying controls can begin. Controls mitigate risk throughout an organization. One of the ways to evaluate controls is to identify critical business operations and functions. Controls should be in place to protect against risks for these critical areas of a business.

Risk mitigation needs to permeate an organization. That means that risk mitigation is an IT function, but it is also a personnel function, an accounting function, a management function, etc. There certainly need to be technical mitigation controls, but also procedural and policy controls. The key is to remember that any organization is only as secure as its weakest link. You may feel you have the most secure network possible, but a user failing to follow policies, or worse yet, not having appropriate policies, can undermine all of your efforts.

Chapter 10 Topics

This chapter covers the following topics and concepts:

- Where an organization should start with risk mitigation
- What the scope of risk management for an organization is
- How to understand and assess the impact of legal and compliance issues on an organization
- How to translate legal and compliance implications for an organization
- How to assess the impact of legal and compliance implications on the seven domains of a typical IT infrastructure
- How to assess how security countermeasures and safeguards can assist with risk mitigation
- What the operational impacts of legal and compliance requirements are
- How to identify risk mitigation and risk reduction elements for an entire organization
- What a cost-benefit analysis is
- What best practices for planning risk mitigation throughout an organization are

Chapter 10 Goals

When you complete this chapter, you will be able to:

- Describe how an organization should start with risk mitigation
- Identify the scope of risk management within an organization
- Apply risk management scope concepts to critical business operations
- Apply risk management scope concepts to customer service delivery
- Apply risk management scope concepts to mission-critical business systems, applications, and data access
- Apply risk management scope concepts to the seven domains of a typical IT infrastructure
- Apply risk management scope concepts to systems security gaps
- Assess the impact of legal and compliance issues within an organization
- List compliance laws, regulations, and mandates that apply to an organization
- Describe legal and compliance implications within an organization
- Describe the impact of legal and compliance implications on the seven domains of a typical IT infrastructure
- Evaluate security countermeasures and safeguards that can assist with risk mitigation
- Describe operational impacts of legal and compliance requirements
- List risk mitigation and risk reduction elements
- Describe a cost-benefit analysis
- List best practices for planning risk mitigation throughout an organization

Where Should an Organization Start With Risk Mitigation?

As has been briefly discussed in previous chapters, risk mitigation will begin by identifying assets. An asset inventory is a first step in determining the value of its systems, services, and data. The value of the assets can be quantified monetarily. At least physical assets have a specific monetary cost. However, that may not accurately describe their worth. For example, a web server may have cost $10,000 but it could be responsible for a large portion of a company's income stream. That would make it worth far more than $10,000. For this reason, qualitative valuations are also used. For example, values, such as high, medium, and low, can be assigned to assets. These values do not necessarily equate only to the cost of equipment, but also include the possible business impact if the assets were damaged, offline, or lost. The value isn't a calculated impact of any particular risk because that value can change dramatically with different issues, and that assessment comes later.

As an example, an asset inventory could have resulted in the following priorities:

- Database servers—High
- File servers—High
- Email servers—High
- Network infrastructure—High
- Web server—Medium
- User desktop systems—Medium
- User laptops—Low

NOTE

This list isn't intended to be a complete list of all assets. Instead, it provides a sample of how an organization may prioritize its assets. Obviously, different organizations will have different valuations.

Next, the threats and vulnerabilities are identified and analyzed, which is done with threat assessments, vulnerability assessments, and exploit assessments. A threat and vulnerability assessment can be performed on each asset. Different assets will have different threats. As one example, given that web servers are public facing, they generally have threats that internal servers do not.

For example, an assessment on the database servers could be done, which could start in several ways. One way is to consider the basics and ask some questions:

- **Loss of confidentiality**—Is the data sensitive? Are access controls in place? Should at-rest data be encrypted? Should data be encrypted when it's transferred?
- **Loss of integrity**—Can the database recover from power loss? Are data versions required? Is configuration of the database documented? Are change management practices followed?
- **Loss of availability**—Are reliable backups performed regularly? Are copies of backups stored off-site? Are backups checked to ensure they can be restored? What are the required hours for data availability? Are redundant drives used? Are failover clusters required?

The questions asked will be different for different assets. For example, the concerns in examining a web server will be different from the concerns in examining confidential data, such as trade secrets; therefore, the questions asked to identify the areas of concern will be different for each asset.

National Institute of Standards and Technology (NIST) Special Publication (SP) 800-53 includes extensive documentation on controls. A good way of ensuring that the right questions are asked is by using SP 800-53 to go through the control families one by one. If the controls apply to the organization, then they should be included in the plan for risk mitigation.

Next, the controls are evaluated to determine which ones should be implemented. A significant part of this step is doing the cost-benefit analysis (CBA), which is covered later in this chapter.

What Is the Scope of Risk Management for an Organization?

The scope of risk management indicates an area of concern, which can also be thought of as an area of control. Some things can be controlled, and others cannot. For example, hurricanes and earthquakes cannot be controlled, but their impact can be reduced by planning how an organization will respond.

FYI

The scope identifies the boundaries of a project. The biggest problem of not identifying the scope is scope creep. Scope creep happens when a project's goals or deliverables grow without control. For example, personnel could spend time and resources on low-value assets at the expense of high-value assets. If the project scope isn't controlled, the project can consume more resources, cost more, and take more time than would have been necessary if the scope had been defined. In the case of risk management, the boundaries may grow beyond the resources or time available to manage the risk, which can result in the organization's not being able to identify or evaluate new risks while evaluated risks go without a response.

TIP

Risk management must be driven by business needs, which means that the risks that are managed are those that have the potential to affect the business. Costs to manage risks outside this scope are not justified.

When considering risk management scope within the organization, consider the following items:

- Critical business operations
- Customer service delivery
- Mission-critical business systems, applications, and data access
- Seven domains of a typical IT infrastructure
- Information systems security gap

The following sections cover these topics.

Critical Business Operations

An early step in risk management is identifying which business operations are critical. These business operations are the ones that must be functional to ensure the organization stays afloat.

A business impact analysis (BIA) is the key tool used in this step. It helps an organization identify the impact on the business if various risks occur.

One of the key elements of the BIA is the identification of both direct and indirect costs. Direct costs reflect the immediate cost of an outage. For example, if a web server fails and cannot process sales, the sales lost during this period are direct costs. Indirect costs include the loss of customer goodwill and the cost to restore that goodwill.

These costs help identify the priority of the service or function. If the costs of an outage are high, then spending money to prevent outages is justified.

BIAs identify the **maximum acceptable outage (MAO)**. The MAO is the maximum amount of time a system or service can be down before the mission is affected. The MAO is also referred to as maximum tolerable outage (MTO) or maximum tolerable period of disruption (MTPOD).

The MAO directly affects the required recovery time. As an example, the MAO is 30 minutes for a system, which means that recovery plans must be able to restore the failed system within 30 minutes.

A large part of the BIA is data collection. Data can be collected by going through available reports and interviewing personnel.

When completing a BIA of a specific service or function, the following key questions should be answered:

- How does this service affect the organization's profitability?
- How does this service affect the organization's survivability?
- How does this service affect the organization's image?
- How will an outage affect employees?
- How will an outage affect customers?
- When does this service need to be available?
- What is the MAO of the service?

Customer Service Delivery

Risk management includes an evaluation of services that the organization provides to its customers. In this context, a customer is any entity that receives a service.

Obvious customers are those that purchase the organization's services. For example, if the organization provides email services to small businesses, these small businesses are the organization's customers. Instead of managing their own email servers, they outsource the service to the organization.

These customers have an expectation related to this service. They could expect that email will be available 24 hours a day, 7 days a week. Alternatively, they may expect access to the email only during their business hours. Either way, identifying their expectations is important.

A **service level agreement (SLA)** is a document that identifies an expected level of performance, which includes the minimum uptime or the maximum downtime. Organizations use SLAs as a contract between a service provider and a customer. An SLA can identify monetary penalties if the terms aren't met.

If an organization has SLAs with other organizations, they should be included in the risk management review and special attention paid to any monetary penalties. For example, an SLA could specify a maximum downtime of 4 hours (i.e., the MAO), after which hourly penalties would start to accrue. Of course, SLAs that promise low levels of downtimes cost more. This extra cost is imposed to pay for the extra controls that are necessary to provide a higher level of service.

A less obvious customer is the internal customer. Any employee or department that receives a service is a customer. Here are some common services provided to internal employees:

- Email services
- Access to the internet
- Network access
- Server applications, such as database servers
- Access to internal servers, such as file servers
- Desktop computer support

NOTE

Entities within an organization often have agreements that are similar to an SLA but are more informal and don't include monetary penalties. For example, a remote office may have an agreement with the main office that virtual private network (VPN) services will be provided during business hours.

Employees won't have SLAs with an IT department, but they will have expectations related to the services. If any of the services fails for too long, the downtime will begin to affect the employees' ability to perform their jobs, which in turn impacts the organization's mission. By identifying the time frame when the outage affects the mission, the MAO can be identified.

Just because a service doesn't have an external customer doesn't mean it should be ignored. Many services are required for internal customers.

Mission-Critical Business Systems, Applications, and Data Access

Many organizations have mission-critical systems, applications, and data. When any of these critical assets are not available, the mission is affected. Therefore, identifying and reviewing these assets is important when reviewing risk management and risk mitigation plans.

Mission-critical business systems are any systems or processes integral to the organization. A deep understanding of the business is necessary to identify these systems, which can be aided by first identifying the organization's **critical business functions (CBFs)** and **critical success factors (CSFs)**.

A CBF is any function considered vital to an organization. If the CBF fails, the organization will lose the ability to perform essential operations, such as sales to customers. If the organization cannot perform the function, it will lose money through either lost revenue or indirect losses.

A CSF is any element necessary to perform the mission of an organization. An organization will have a few elements that must succeed for the organization to succeed. For example, a reliable network infrastructure may be considered a CSF for many companies today. If the network infrastructure fails, communication can stop.

CBFs are supported by several elements. For example, an organization sells products on the internet. Figures 10-1, 10-2, and 10-3 show the different supporting elements in a complete transaction. By analyzing these elements, the CBFs can be identified.

In **FIGURE 10-1**, the customer makes the purchase. In this example, the customer is purchasing the product from an internet web server, and a back-end database server records the transaction.

FIGURE 10-1

Critical business functions: making the purchase.

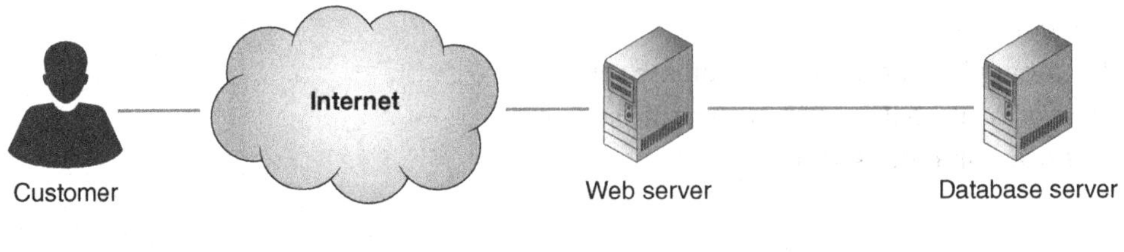

The CBFs here are:

- **Internet access**—The web server must have reliable internet access. If internet access fails, the customer can't access the web server.
- **Web server availability**—The web server must be operational, which includes the web server and the web application. If the web server fails, the customer can't complete the purchase.
- **Database server availability**—A database server records the transaction, which includes details on the customer, the product purchased, and payment information. If the database server fails, the web application cannot complete the transaction.

FIGURE 10-2 shows how a payment is received. Although payment processing will often occur as part of the transaction, here it's separated for clarity. Credit card transactions are common on the internet, and the organization using them must comply with the Payment Card Industry Data Security Standard (PCI DSS) to process them. The web application uses data in the database to identify details for the credit card payment and then sends a request to the appropriate bank for payment.

> **NOTE**
>
> PCI DSS is discussed later in this chapter in the Legal Requirements, Compliance Laws, Regulations, and Mandates section.

This step requires the same CBFs as the purchase step and one additional element. PCI DSS compliance is required, which ensures the organization is meeting minimum security standards for credit card data. If the organization is not compliant with PCI DSS, it can lose the ability to process credit cards as well as be assessed fines.

FIGURE 10-3 shows the last step in the process, in which workers use a warehouse application to identify products to ship. This application interacts with a database server, which

FIGURE 10-2

Critical business functions: receiving funds.

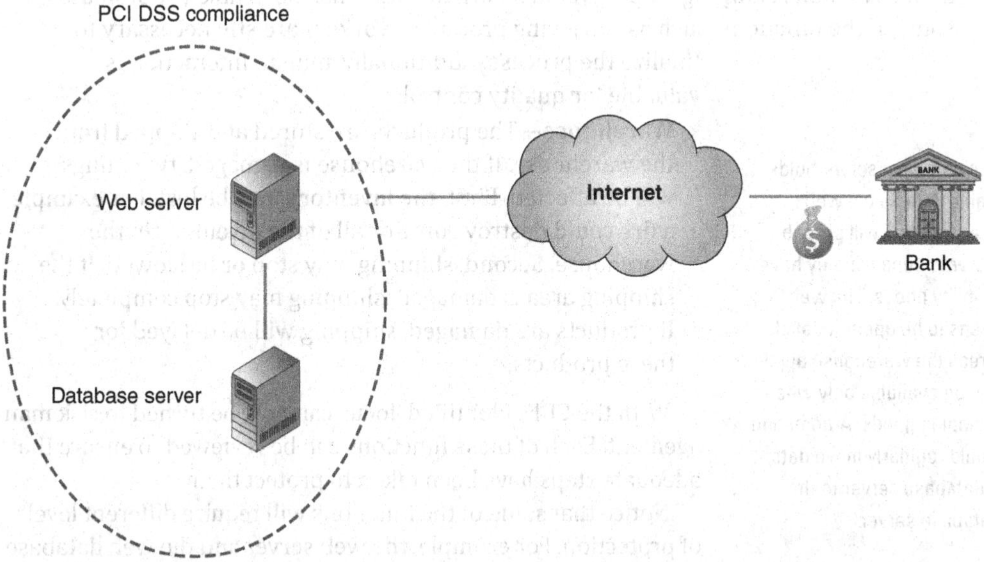

FIGURE 10-3

Critical business functions: shipping the product.

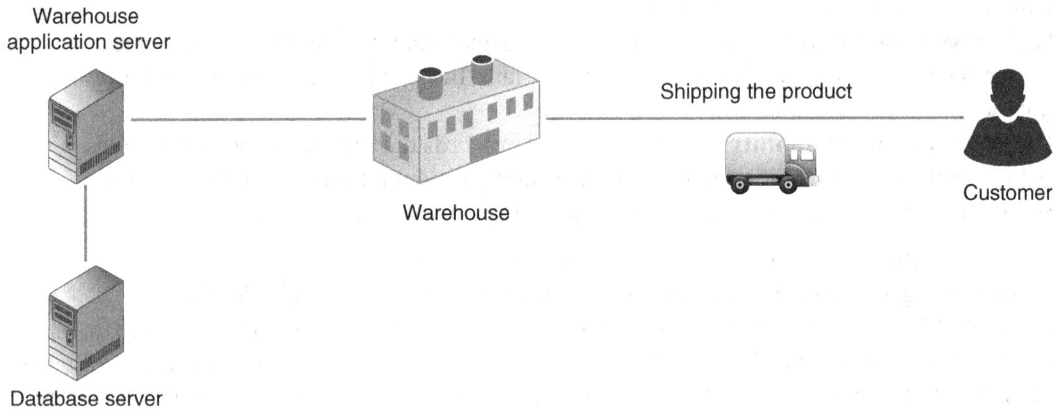

has details on purchased products, customers, and product locations. The warehouse workers then ship the product to the customer.

This step has several additional CBFs:

- **Warehouse application server**—This application must be available to the workers and able to interact with the database server. If the application is not available, the workers won't be able to identify products to ship, and thus shipping will stop.
- **Database server**—The database server is needed to identify which products to ship and details on where to ship them. If the data from this server is not available, shipping will stop.
- **Workers**—The workers pack and ship the purchased products. If the workers aren't available, shipping stops. Even if an organization has been able to automate some of the functions, such as retrieving products, workers are still necessary to finalize the process. Additionally, human interaction is valuable for quality control.
- **Warehouse**—The products are stored and shipped from the warehouse. If the warehouse is damaged, two things will be affected. First, the inventory may be lost. For example, a fire could destroy some or all of the inventory in the warehouse. Second, shipping may stop or be slowed. If the shipping area is damaged, shipping may stop completely. If products are damaged, shipping will be delayed for these products.

> **TIP**
>
> The warehouse database server holds much of the same data as the web database server, but they will probably be separate servers because they have different availability needs. The web application needs to be operational all the time, whereas the warehouse application needs to be available only when workers are shipping goods. Automation techniques would regularly move data from the web database server to the warehouse database server.

With the CBFs identified, focus can now be turned to risk management. Each of these functions can be reviewed to ensure that adequate steps have been taken to protect them.

Notice that some of the functions will require different levels of protection. For example, the web server and the web database server need to be operational all the time, which makes their MAOs short. The servers may require failover clusters to ensure the services continue to run even if a server fails. However, shipping may occur only 6 days a week during the daytime, which means the warehouse server won't need the same level of protection as the web server and the web database server. The MAO for this server would be significantly longer.

Seven Domains of a Typical IT Infrastructure

The seven domains of a typical IT infrastructure can also be reviewed to identify risks. By looking at each of these domains, the scope of risk management needed for the organization can be identified. **FIGURE 10-4** shows the seven domains of a typical IT infrastructure.

User Domain

Every organization has users; in fact the users are the reason we have computers. The computers facilitate the work of users. Therefore, looking at the risks associated with the User Domain is important. On of the risks associated with users are related to social engineering, which involves a social engineer trying to trick a user into giving up information or performing an unsafe action.

FIGURE 10-4

The seven domains of a typical IT infrastructure.

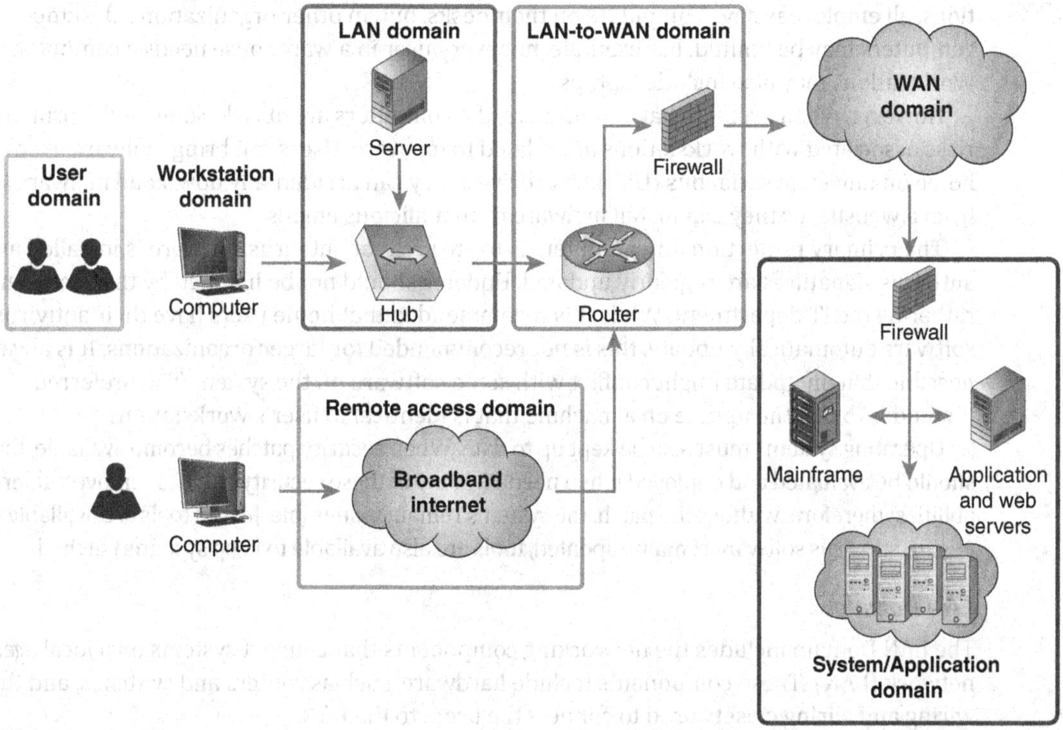

Social engineering risks can be mitigated by raising user awareness. Raising user awareness can include instituting an acceptable use policy (AUP), which helps ensure users know what they should and shouldn't do; using logon banners to remind users of the AUP; sending out occasional emails with security tidbits to keep security awareness on users' minds; and posting signs in employee areas to help raise awareness.

Another risk in the User Domain is simple carelessness. Even with training, robust technology, and other security measures, a careless employee can undermine all of that. This can be quite difficult to mitigate. Awareness training that emphasizes the need for taking due care can be part of your mitigation strategy.

A third risk in the User Domain is malicious intent. One does not like to consider one's colleagues as potential threats, but it does happen. Insider threats are a serious issue. These are mitigated by several processes. The first is adhering to fundamental security principles of *least privileges* and *separation of duties.* Least privileges means that any employee (or any process/service) has only just enough privileges to perform required duties and no more. This will not stop misuses, but will mitigate the damage. Separation of duties means that any action which could have a critical impact on the organization cannot be done by a single user. Two or more users need to collaborate to take action. Finally, monitoring user activity can help mitigate this threat. Is a user accessing files they do not normally access? Is that user downloading excessive amounts of data, or visiting suspicious IP addresses/domains? These can all be indicators of malicious activity.

Workstation Domain

The Workstation Domain comprises the computers that users will use. In some organizations, all employees have computers on their desks, but, in other organizations, desktop computers may be limited. For example, not every user in a warehouse needs a computer. Workstations may also include laptops.

However, when users do have computers, the computers are at risk. Some of the primary risks associated with workstations are related to malware. Users can bring malware from home on universal serial bus (USB) flash drives, they can accidentally download malware from a website, or they can install malware from malicious emails.

The primary protection for computers is to ensure that antivirus software is installed and antivirus signatures are regularly updated. Updates should not be handled by the users, but rather by the IT department. While it is recommended that home users have their antivirus software automatically update, this is not recommended for larger organizations. It is always possible that an update might conflict with some software on the system. The preferred method is to test the update on a machine that is identical to user's workstations.

Operating systems must also be kept up to date. When security patches become available, they should be evaluated and deployed when needed. Many of these security patches remove vulnerabilities; therefore, without the patch, the systems remain vulnerable. Just as tools are available to ensure antivirus software remains updated, tools are also available to keep systems patched.

LAN Domain

The LAN Domain includes the networking components that connect systems on a local area network (LAN). These components include hardware, such as routers and switches, and the wiring and wiring closets used to connect the users to the LAN.

Computers typically access network resources via servers. For example, in a Microsoft environment, clients are connected in a Microsoft domain, which includes at least one server acting as a domain controller. In a Microsoft domain, every user must have an account to log on to the domain, and every computer must have an account on the domain.

The LAN Domain is subject to significant risks. Routers have access control lists (ACLs) used to control what traffic is allowed through them, and switches can be programmed for specific functionality.

Routers and switches are commonly located in a wiring closet or server room, which helps ensure they are protected with physical security. If an attacker has unrestricted access to these devices, the ACLs could be modified, or an attacker could connect a wireless access point to capture and transmit all the traffic going through any of these devices.

Many organizations also practice port security as an added control. Port security ensures that only specific computers are able to attach to the network device, which means that, if an attacker brings in a computer, they will not be able to connect the computer to the network.

An important aspect of LAN security is network segmentation. Networks should be segmented based on data sensitivity. For example, you might have sales people on one network segment, and software developers on another. This way, should an intruder or malware affect one network segment, it is not automatically granted access to the entire network.

LAN-to-WAN Domain

The LAN-to-WAN Domain marks the boundary where the private network meets the public network. In this context, the public network is the internet.

Several types of attacks come from the internet. The primary protection here is the use of one or more firewalls. Firewalls can examine traffic as it passes through and allow or block traffic based on rules.

Although most organizations have firewalls in place, the major concern here is the management of the firewalls. A common problem is improperly configured firewall rules. It can be a challenge to find the right mix of allowing sufficient traffic to facilitate business needs while blocking unwanted traffic.

WAN Domain

The WAN Domain includes all systems that are accessible over a wide area network (WAN). These systems primarily refer to servers accessible over the internet. Servers available on the internet have public Internet Protocol (IP) addresses. They can be reached from any system on the internet, which makes them easy targets.

A primary method of protection for systems in the WAN Domain is the use of a demilitarized zone (DMZ). A DMZ uses two firewalls, one of which has direct access to the internet and the other direct access to the internal network. The area between the two firewalls is called the DMZ.

Although the DMZ won't stop an attacker from accessing a server, it can limit the attacker's access. For example, a web server

NOTE

The WAN Domain can also include systems that are accessible over a WAN link, which is semiprivate. For example, an organization can lease lines from a telecommunications company that other customers share. These lines aren't as public as the internet, but the organization's systems are still susceptible to attacks from the other customers leasing the same lines.

NOTE

A DMZ typically uses two firewalls. Public-facing servers are configured in the DMZ between the two firewalls. Most modern routers have a DMZ built in. That means you plug into one port for your WAN traffic and another for your LAN, and yet a third port for the DMZ.

can be placed in the DMZ to host a website. Both unsecured and secured web servers use the Hypertext Transfer Protocol (HTTP). The well-known ports for HTTP and Hypertext Transfer Protocol Secure (HTTPS) are 80 and 443, respectively. The DMZ can be configured to allow traffic to the web server using only ports 80 and 443 and to block all other traffic.

These servers also need to be kept up to date. When security patches are released, they should be evaluated as soon as possible and then tested to ensure they don't have any negative impacts, after which they can be deployed to the servers.

Remote Access Domain

The Remote Access Domain allows remote users to access the private network. Typically this means using a VPN, which allows a user to access the private network over a public network, such as the internet.

Several different controls can be used to protect servers in the Remote Access Domain. Automatic callback is one method used with dial-in remote access servers, although this method is rarely used today. For example, Sally works from home. Her account information includes her phone number. When she dials in, she is prompted to log on. As soon as she logs on, the remote server hangs up and calls her home number.

Remote access policies are another control used with remote access. Policies are used to specify several conditions to ensure the connection is secure. For example, a policy could specify that only IPSec connections are allowed.

Remote access monitoring is another control used with remote access. It reports remote user activities, including their status during VPN connections. A monitoring console is used to track client connections, including the quantity and duration of connections across various types of server configurations.

System/Application Domain

The System/Application Domain comprises any server-based applications, including email servers and database servers, and any server or system that has a dedicated application.

For example, Oracle Database hosts databases on a server, Microsoft Exchange is a popular email server, and Apache hosts web applications on web servers. Each of these applications is specialized, and each has its unique risks. They often require specialized knowledge to manage and configure. Moreover, they require attention to detail to keep them secure.

A primary requirement to keep these systems secure is to ensure administrators have adequate training and knowledge. Additionally, configuration and change management practices are helpful. Configuration management ensures the systems are configured using sound security practices, and change management ensures that the configuration is not modified without adequate review.

System applications often have bugs, and vendors release security patches when they have identified the bugs. Administrators of these systems need to stay in tune with the vendor so that they're aware when patches are released. Unfortunately, some patches cause other problems, such as system crashes; thus, administrators typically test patches to ensure they do not have any negative effects and then apply the patches only after testing. Additionally, they often use software to verify that systems have current patches. When systems are not up to date, the software sends alerts to administrators. In some organizations, network access control (NAC) software isolates unpatched systems. Access to these systems are limited, until the software is up to date.

Information Systems Security Gap

The information systems security gap refers to the difference between the controls that are in place and the controls that are needed. In a perfect world, the in-place controls would address all threats and vulnerabilities. However, threats and vulnerabilities are constantly changing.

Defense in Depth

Even if you have aggressive risk management and risk mitigation plans, security gaps will usually still exist. Having 100% secure systems 100% of the time is impossible. However, **defense in depth** is a security practice that adds multiple layers of overlapping protection. Even if a gap occurs in one layer of a system, chances are greater that it will still be protected from another layer.

As an example, antivirus protection often uses a three-pronged approach. Antivirus software is installed at the firewall to scan incoming data, on the email server to scan for malicious attachments or scripts, and on all workstations and servers.

Why should antivirus software be installed on desktop systems if the firewall and email server already scan for malware? The reason is that users could transmit a virus from a CD, DVD, or USB flash drive.

In addition, although antivirus software protects desktop systems, additional antivirus software is needed to scan email attachments. Malware is most commonly sent through email; therefore, if antivirus software hasn't been installed on the email server, the email server will forward malware to clients. If a single system isn't up to date or malfunctions with the antivirus software, it will be infected, and this infection could quickly spread.

Defense in depth is more expensive in the short run, but it closes more security gaps and, in the long run, saves money.

A risk assessment provides a point-in-time report. It can be used to compare the existing threats and vulnerabilities against the in-place controls. Even if the last risk assessment was perfect, it wouldn't be able to address the threats and vulnerabilities that emerged after the risk assessment had been completed.

Gap analysis reports are often used when dealing with legal compliance. For example, a gap analysis report can be used when reviewing compliance with the Health Insurance Portability and Accountability Act (HIPAA) or the Sarbanes-Oxley Act (SOX). The gap analysis report documents the security gap.

The gap analysis report should be combined with a remediation plan, which identifies how the security gap is closed, meaning it provides recommendations on what controls to implement.

Understanding and Assessing the Impact of Legal and Compliance Issues on an Organization

An organization must know what laws and regulations apply to it because noncompliance can have serious consequences. Some laws assess hefty fines on an organization, some laws can result in jail time, and some laws can negatively affect an organization's ability to do business. Once pertinent laws and regulations have been identified, the organization needs to ensure that it is in compliance.

In this context, compliance is a mitigation control. Controls are implemented to mitigate risk, which they do by reducing or neutralizing threats or vulnerabilities to an acceptable level.

For example, Health Insurance Portability and Accountability Act (HIPAA) fines can be as high as $25,000 a year for mistakes, and General Data Protection Regulation (GDPR) fines can be as high as $22 million or 4% of a business's annual global turnover, whichever is greater. An internal compliance program can ensure that these costly mistakes don't happen. When assessing the impact of compliance issues in an organization, two distinct steps need to be taken. The first step is to identify what compliance issues apply to the organization, and the second step is to assess the impact of these issues on the organization's business operations. These two topics are presented in the following sections.

The Growth of Compliance Laws

Compliance has become more prominent in the past few decades. In the 1960s, General Electric and Westinghouse were convicted of several antitrust regulations. They were part of a widespread bid rigging and price fixing conspiracy. Congress responded with the Foreign Corrupt Practices Act (FCPA) in 1977.

In 1991, the U.S. Federal Sentencing Guidelines for Organizational Ethics legislation was passed. It included provisions to punish organizations for criminal actions and deterrence incentives to detect and prevent crime.

The Enron scandal occurred in 2001. A group of executives used a variety of tactics over several years to hide billions of dollars in debt from failed deals and projects. When they were exposed, Enron's stock price went from $90 per share to less than $1, resulting in about $11 billion in losses to investors. Several executives were indicted and sentenced to prison.

WorldCom executives also used a variety of tactics over several years to artificially inflate the company's value by around $11 billion. When the chief executive officer (CEO) was ousted in April 2002, things began to fall apart, and, in June 2002, the fraud was discovered. WorldCom filed for bankruptcy in July 2002 and never repaid most of its creditors. Several of WorldCom's executives were also indicted and sentenced to prison.

Congress responded to these scandals with laws to expand the reliability of financial reporting for public companies. The Sarbanes-Oxley Act was one such law. It increased penalties for defrauding shareholders and imposed more stringent requirements for internal controls.

Then, in 2006, the U.S. housing bubble burst, driving down home prices. Unfortunately, many homes were financed with shady subprime mortgages, resulting in a high number of foreclosures in 2007. More than 25 subprime lenders went bankrupt in 2007. This situation reached a critical stage in 2008 when Lehman Brothers, a huge global bank, went bankrupt. These events helped trigger a worldwide recession, commonly called the Great Recession.

Many banks bought insurance to cover their losses from insurance giant AIG. However, AIG was not able to cover these losses and was at risk of going bankrupt too. The U.S. government rescued AIG from bankruptcy with an $85 billion bailout in 2008. Later, the U.S. government gave AIG an additional $37.8 billion. Congress passed the Troubled Asset Relief Program (TARP) in late 2008. TARP rescued many other financial companies. Congress authorized $700 billion in expenditures through TARP, but the government disbursed only $431 billion. As of December 2012, the U.S. government had recouped more than $405 billion of this money.

Congress responded to the subprime mortgage debacle with the Dodd-Frank Wall Street Reform and Consumer Protection Act. Many experts believed that a lack of financial regulation allowed the Great Recession to occur. One of the goals of the Dodd-Frank law is to prevent similar financial crises. While Dodd-Frank doesn't directly affect IT resources as much as Sarbanes-Oxley does, it does apply to IT resources in financial organizations.

These events certainly do not represent a complete history because there has been much more fraud and many more scandals. However, they do provide a partial view of how corruption can grow and how Congress reacts.

Corporate compliance has become so important in some organizations that they have created a new position, the chief compliance officer (CCO). Some companies use the title of chief ethics compliance officer (CECO) or ethics compliance officer (ECO).

Legal Requirements, Compliance Laws, Regulations, and Mandates

Although there are many laws and regulations that apply to IT, they don't all apply to IT. Therefore, one of the important issues to understand first is which laws apply to an organization.

As a reminder, some of the key laws that apply to organizations are:

- Health Insurance Portability and Accountability Act (HIPAA, enacted 1996)
- Sarbanes-Oxley Act (SOX, enacted 2002)
- Federal Information Security Management Act (FISMA, enacted 2002)
- Federal Information Security Modernization Act (FISMA, enacted 2014)
- Family Educational Rights and Privacy Act (FERPA, enacted 1974)
- Children's Internet Protection Act (CIPA, enacted 2000)
- Payment Card Industry Data Security Standard (PCI DSS, enacted 2004)
- Gramm-Leach-Bliley Act (GLBA, enacted 1999)
- General Data Protection Regulation (GDPR, enacted 2018)

The following sections identify how an organization can determine whether a law applies to it. Some laws are specific and narrow in scope, whereas others, such as HIPAA, apply to a wide range of organizations.

Health Insurance Portability and Accountability Act (HIPAA)

HIPAA applies to any organization that handles health information. The obvious organizations that handle health information are hospitals and doctor's offices. However, HIPAA reaches much further than the medical industry.

Health information includes any data that relates to the health of an individual. This data includes a person's past, present, and future health; condition, physical health, or mental health; and any past, present, or future payments for health care. If an organization creates or receives health information, it must comply with HIPAA, and this includes employers, health plan sponsors, healthcare providers, public health authorities, and more. If an organization isn't involved in health care but does provide a health plan, it falls under HIPAA. HIPAA has been augmented by HITECH (Health Information Technology for Economic and Clinical Health Act).

Sarbanes-Oxley Act (SOX)

SOX applies to any business that is required to be registered with the Securities and Exchange Commission, which include all publicly traded companies. In other words, if someone can buy stock in the company, then SOX applies.

SOX establishes a set of standards. Even if they don't apply directly to private businesses, private businesses can use these same standards. If the organization faces legal issues later, it can point to its actions as good faith efforts to avoid the problems.

Federal Information Security Management Act (FISMA)

FISMA applies to all U.S. federal agencies. Its goal is to ensure that federal agencies take steps to protect their data.

The National Institute of Standards and Technology (NIST) is tasked by FISMA to develop standards, guidelines, and best practices to support FISMA. Special publications created by NIST for FISMA are available at http://csrc.nist.gov/publications/sp.

Family Educational Rights and Privacy Act (FERPA)

FERPA applies to all education institutions and agencies that receive funding under any program administered by the U.S. Department of Education (ED).

The obvious examples are any public schools from grades kindergarten through 12. However, many other entities can receive funding from the ED, which include any school or agency offering preschool programs, and any institution of higher education, such as colleges and universities.

Funding is often indirect. Although public grade schools receive their funding directly from the ED, other institutions receive their funding indirectly. The ED provides student aid and grants for college. If a student receives this funding and uses the money to pay for college, the college is receiving ED funding.

The ED updated FERPA in 2012. Amendments allow for greater disclosures of student personal information and student information in the school's directory. They also regulate student IDs and email addresses.

Children's Internet Protection Act (CIPA)

CIPA applies to any school or library that receives funding from the U.S. E-Rate program, which is sponsored by the Federal Communications Commission (FCC). It provides discounts for internet access.

Schools and libraries are not required to use the E-Rate program, but, if they choose to take advantage of the discounts, schools and libraries are governed by CIPA. The annual E-Rate application requires schools and libraries to certify that they are complying with CIPA.

Payment Card Industry Data Security Standard (PCI DSS)

PCI DSS is not a law. Instead, it is a standard that was jointly created by several credit card companies and is overseen by the Payment Card Industry (PCI) Security Standards Council. Any organization that accepts credit card payments must comply.

Many credit card companies support PCI DSS. They include Visa International, MasterCard Worldwide, American Express, Discover Financial Services, and JCB International. The PCI Security Standards Council includes employees of these companies.

Smaller companies can certify that they are compliant by completing a self-assessment questionnaire, and large organizations are independently audited by a qualified security assessor.

The PCI Security Standards Council released PCI DSS v4.1 in June 2024.

> **TIP**
>
> PCI compliance and PCI DSS compliance mean the same thing.

General Data Protection Regulation (GDPR)

The GDPR is a European Union regulation regarding data and privacy protection. The law addresses the transfer of personal information of EU and European Economic Area (EEA) residents outside their region. The law seeks to give control to individuals of this region over their own personal data and information, especially as it pertains to international organizations trading outside of the EU and EEA. The law applies to any business, regardless of its location and the citizenship of the data subject.

The law differentiates a data controller from a data processor. The data controller is the business or individual who determines the purpose of the personal data that is collected and how it is processed. The processor, on the other hand, is the business or individual who acts on behalf of the controller, excluding the controller's employees. The law is supported by a number of privacy protection principles. The GDPR is the major reason for all websites asking permission to use cookies, which allow them to track a visit.

Assessing the Impact of Legal and Compliance Issues on an Organization's Business Operations

Once the compliance requirements for an organization have been determined, the next step is to determine the impact that these requirements have on the organization. The impact can be significantly different depending on the law or standard being applied.

The following sections present potential impacts for some of the common laws and standards.

Health Insurance Portability and Accountability Act (HIPAA)

HIPAA affects a wide spectrum of a business, and the cost of noncompliance is high. The steps required to comply can be complex, depending on how much health-related information an organization handles.

First, the penalties are severe if the rules aren't being followed. Organizations can be fined $100 per violation and up to $25,000 per year for mistakes. If someone knowingly obtains or releases data they shouldn't, the penalties can be as high as $50,000 and 1 year in prison. If data is obtained or disclosed under false pretenses, penalties can be as high as $100,000 and 5 years in prison. If data is obtained or disclosed for personal gain or malicious harm, penalties can be as high as $250,000 and 10 years in prison.

However, compliance can also be expensive. Organizations that handle health data must take specific steps to protect it, which include protecting any data that they create, receive, or send and protecting any of the systems that handle health data.

The responsibility to keep the data secure rests with the organization. The data must be protected while at rest, which means that, if it is stored on a hard drive or in a filing cabinet, it must be protected. Protecting data at rest can be done through access controls or physical security, depending on the type of data.

Use of health information is restricted. Employees who handle and review health information must be trained so they know the requirements. As an example, data cannot be released to a third party without the written consent of the patient.

Data must also be protected when transmitted. When any health data is transmitted, it must be transmitted in a specific format. The good news is that health plan providers are well versed in HIPAA. A company that outsources a health plan can also outsource handling of the health data. For example, a health plan provider can be contracted to provide insurance to employees, and employees can then be directed to the health plan provider's website to enroll. When a health plan is managed in this manner, the provider hosts almost all the information. The originating company has very little data, and its risks are limited.

Sarbanes-Oxley Act (SOX)

The business impact of SOX is a high liability for the accuracy of data. High-level officers, such as CEOs and chief financial officers (CFOs), must personally verify and attest to the accuracy of financial data. The goal is to avoid mega scandals, such as the loss of $11 billion by Enron's investors.

Because of this high liability, organizations are required to take extra steps to ensure the accuracy and integrity of the data, which includes implementing internal controls and requiring both internal and external audits to verify compliance. Two key benefits are that SOX increased executives' accountability to act in their shareholders' interest and its required monitoring helped provide better control of internal costs.

Some opponents of SOX have argued that the costs of compliance are excessive. However, the costs for most organizations are manageable according to a 2013 survey by Protiviti.

Federal Information Security Management Act (FISMA)

Because FISMA applies only to federal agencies, it does not affect the revenue of any organization. However, it can have a significant effect on operations.

A core requirement of FISMA is to identify, certify as compliant, and authorize for operation all IT systems in the organization, a process that can be lengthy. One of the primary problems is the slow implementation of new systems.

FISMA encourages the use of baselines. As long as a system follows the same baseline as another system, it can be certified and authorized quickly.

NOTE

A baseline is any known starting point. A baseline for an IT system represents the same hardware, software, and configuration as another system's. For example, if one server has been authorized using a baseline, another server can be authorized much more quickly by using the same baseline.

Cyber Incident Reporting for Critical Infrastructure Act of 2022 (CIRCIA)

The Cyber Incident Reporting for Critical Infrastructure Act of 2022 (CIRCIA) mandates that certain critical infrastructure entities report significant cyberincidents and ransomware payments to the Cybersecurity and Infrastructure Security Agency (CISA). This act aims to enhance national cybersecurity by improving information sharing and response capabilities. Covered entities must report covered cyberincidents (substantial cyberincidents) to CISA within 72 hours of reasonably believing the incident occurred.

IoT Cybersecurity Improvement Act of 2020

The IoT Cybersecurity Improvement Act of 2020 requires the National Institute of Standards and Technology (NIST) and the Office of Management and Budget (OMB) to take steps to increase cybersecurity for Internet of Things (IoT) devices used by the federal government, including developing standards and guidelines.

Family Educational Rights and Privacy Act (FERPA)

FERPA requires covered organizations to share student records with students or their parents. If a student or a parent makes the request, the school must comply.

Students or parents can request the correction of errors in the student's record, and the school has an obligation to consider the request. However, the school isn't required to make all the changes a student asks for. For example, if a student requests a poor grade to be removed from a record but the grade is accurate, the school isn't required to remove it.

Students can grant access to their record to specific third parties. For example, a student may grant access when applying for admission to a college or university. Some specific third parties are automatically granted access to the records. Many school officials, for instance, do not need student permission to view the record.

The biggest impact FERPA has on business operations is ensuring that employees know the rules, which can be done with training. If a student under 18 requests access to their record, the employee should know the right belongs to the parent. If a parent of a 20-year-old requests access, the employee should know the right belongs to the student. Similarly, if a third party requests access, the employee should know whether access should be granted.

> **TIP**
>
> FERPA grants specific rights to parents of students under 18. However, when the student turns 18, these rights transfer to the student, and the parents no longer have rights to the information without the student's knowledge and consent.

Children's Internet Protection Act (CIPA)

CIPA imposes several technical requirements on schools and libraries. They must be able to filter offensive content to ensure that minors aren't exposed to it. If the school or library cannot comply with CIPA, it risks losing all E-Rate discounts.

E-Rate funding provides discounts to schools and libraries for internet access. Any school or library that requests discounts under the E-Rate program is required to certify that it complies with CIPA rules.

The first challenge in complying with CIPA is identifying offensive content. CIPA allows the school or library to define *offensive* using local standards, which means that what is deemed offensive content in a library in one area of the country may be acceptable in a library in another area of the country.

FIGURE 10-5

Proxy server used as a TPM.

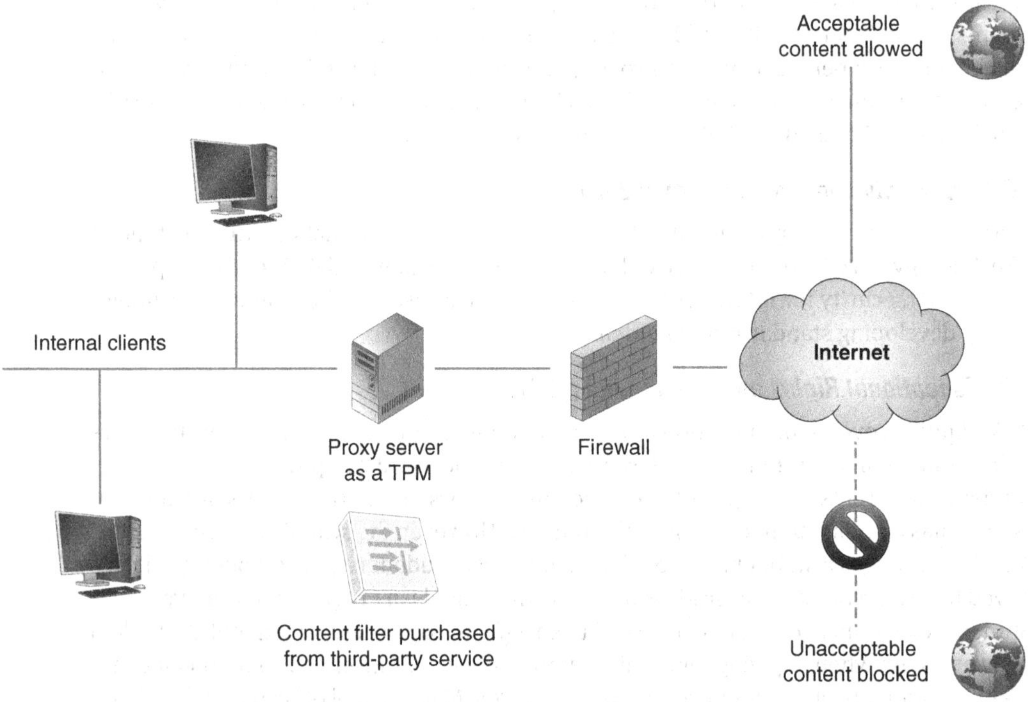

Schools and libraries filter the content with a **technology protection measure (TPM).** **FIGURE 10-5** shows an example of a **proxy server** used as a TPM. A proxy server receives requests from clients for webpages, retrieves the webpages, and then serves the webpages to the clients. It can also filter the requests to block content requests.

Users are able to access the internet through the proxy server. All content requests are filtered using the content filter. If the content is acceptable, the page is retrieved and sent to the client. If the content is unacceptable, the content is blocked.

A proxy server commonly works with data provided by a third-party service, which provides a list of content to filter. The list is often in the format of specific website Uniform Resource Locators, or URLs. The proxy server uses this list to prevent the content from reaching the requesting computer.

CIPA defines a *minor* as anyone under the age of 17. Their access should be restricted by the TPM. However, anyone 17 years old or over should be able to use the computer without restrictions. For example, if an adult wants to use it, they can request that the TPM filter be removed. An administrator or librarian should be able to remove the filter in a timely manner.

General Data Protection Regulation (GDPR)

The GDPR requires data controllers and processors to put appropriate technical and organizational measures in place to protect the privacy of EU/EEA citizens. The GDPR is built around the following principles:

- Principles relating to the processing of personal data
- Lawfulness of processing
- Conditions of consent
- Conditions applicable to a child's consent in relation to information society services
- Processing of special categories of personal data
- Processing of personal data relating to criminal convictions and offenses
- Processing that does not require identification

Payment Card Industry Data Security Standard (PCI DSS)

PCI DSS is built around the following six principles and 12 requirements:

- **Build and Maintain a Secure Network**
  - Requirement 1: Install and maintain a firewall.
  - Requirement 2: Do not use defaults, such as default passwords.
- **Protect Cardholder Data**
  - Requirement 3: Protect stored data.
  - Requirement 4: Encrypt transmissions.
- **Maintain a Vulnerability Management Program**
  - Requirement 5: Use and update antivirus software.
  - Requirement 6: Develop and maintain secure systems.
- **Implement Strong Access Control Measures**
  - Requirement 7: Restrict access to data.
  - Requirement 8: Use unique logons for each user. Don't share usernames and passwords.
  - Requirement 9: Restrict physical access.
- **Regularly Monitor and Test Networks**
  - Requirement 10: Track and monitor all access to systems and data.
  - Requirement 11: Regularly test security.
- **Maintain an Information Security Policy**
- Requirement 12: Maintain a security policy.

All of the principles and requirements are IT related, but they also reflect many common best practices. If an organization is already using best practices, PCI DSS won't have much effect on its business operations. However, if an organization is not currently using common security practices, PCI DSS compliance may affect its budget and operations.

Translating Legal and Compliance Implications for an Organization

Compliance implications can have far-reaching effects. Just as with other threats and vulnerabilities, losses can be both direct and indirect. For example, if an organization is fined $10,000 for mistakes related to HIPAA, the direct loss is $10,000. However, once this information hits the news, the organization will experience indirect losses.

The media may report that a company mishandled health data. If customers have health data stored with that organization, they may leave. Even if customers don't have health data stored with that organization, they may be suspicious of how it handles other data. Similarly, employees may realize their data is being mishandled and leave the company.

Sometimes, a public relations (PR) campaign can restore an organization's good name. PR isn't cheap, though. Creating effective campaigns takes talent and money to implement. However, proactively spending money on PR campaigns can reduce the effects of an incident, which will ultimately save money for the organization.

Assessing the Impact of Legal and Compliance Implications on the Seven Domains of a Typical IT Infrastructure

The seven domains of a typical IT infrastructure were presented earlier in this chapter. When evaluating legal and compliance implications, the impact on each of these domains should be examined:

- **User Domain**—Most compliance issues affect the User Domain in some way. Users need to be trained to ensure they comply with the procedures. For example, HIPAA requires users to understand what data they can give out, CIPA requires librarians to know how to turn off the TPM for an adult, and PCI DSS requires users to have unique logons.
- **Workstation Domain**—If employees will access covered data with their workstations, the workstations need to be examined. If HIPAA or SOX data is stored on the systems, that data needs to be protected with access controls. Many small companies use desktop PCs as point-of-sale (POS) systems. A POS system is an electronic cashier, and it needs to be compliant with PCI DSS guidelines. Any desktop system needs antivirus software installed.
- **LAN Domain**—The LAN needs to be secure to prevent attackers from capturing data, which includes HIPAA, SOX, and PCI DSS data. Encryption technologies may be required to ensure transmitted data is secure and is especially true if the organization uses wireless networks. In the past, attackers captured details of wireless transactions while sitting in the parking lot of the business.
- **LAN-to-WAN Domain**—A firewall protects a LAN from potential WAN attacks, and PCI DSS specifically requires a firewall. A library may use a proxy server as a TPM to comply with CIPA. A proxy server has access to the internet and the intranet and therefore would need additional security to protect it from external attacks.
- **WAN Domain**—Some PCI DSS systems may have direct access to the internet to transmit transaction data; therefore, they need additional protection. For example, transmissions need to be encrypted, and the systems need to be protected from attackers who may try to access stored data.
- **Remote Access Domain**—Many organizations use VPNs to connect a main and a remote office. Many laws mandate protection of data transmissions. If users transmit sensitive

data over the VPN, the VPN must be verified to be secure. For example, if users transmit HIPAA data over the VPN, the data should be encrypted.

- **System/Application Domain**—Both health data and financial data that are governed by HIPAA and SOX are often hosted on database servers, which need to be examined to ensure they comply with these laws. Access controls should ensure that least privilege principles are implemented. Proxy servers used as TPMs to meet CIPA requirements must include a method to disable the TPM when adults use the service.

Assessing How Security Countermeasures, Controls, and Safeguards Can Assist With Risk Mitigation

The primary purpose of controls, countermeasures, and safeguards is to mitigate risk. Controls are implemented at a point in time to reduce the risks at that time. However, threats and vulnerabilities change, and, because they do, the effectiveness of the controls can change. Therefore, regularly assessing controls to ensure they are effective is important.

> **TIP**
>
> The terms *countermeasure*, *safeguard*, and *control* are used interchangeably. Each is used to mitigate risk.

The effectiveness of a control can be measured by determining how well it meets its goals. A control will attempt to mitigate risk by:

- **Reducing the impact of threats to an acceptable level**—For example, the threat of a hurricane can't be stopped, but a business continuity plan that identifies an alternate location for the business can reduce the threat.
- **Reducing a vulnerability to an acceptable level**—For example, some denial of service (DoS) attacks can take down unpatched servers. By keeping servers up to date with current patches, they are less vulnerable to known DoS attacks.

A risk assessment will evaluate the threats and vulnerabilities at a specific time and recommend controls based on the known risks when the assessment is performed. It should be repeated periodically.

Additionally, a risk assessment should be repeated if the control is changed. For example, if a hardware firewall is replaced with a different model, the original risk assessment is no longer valid and should be redone with the new firewall.

Understanding the Operational Implications of Legal and Compliance Requirements

Compliance requirements will often affect how systems operate. When considering the legal and compliance requirements, how compliance may affect operations needs to be considered. Here are some examples:

- **HIPAA**—HIPAA requires the protection of all health-related data. When this data is stored electronically, it becomes easier to control using standard access controls in a network. A company may choose to switch from paper-based to computer-based records, which will affect how employees access data and represent a change in operational procedures.

- **SOX**—SOX requires the protection of financial data, which may be stored on a database server. If so, the database server is subject to additional controls that may not be required for other database servers. Administrators may need to take additional steps to protect the data and users to access the data.
- **FISMA**—FISMA requires specific procedures for government agencies to purchase and deploy systems. If a company purchases systems outside of the norm, the process to get them certified and authorized can be lengthy, and this delay may affect the agency's ability to field new systems in a timely manner.
- **FERPA**—FERPA mandates access to educational records by students or parents. If the school has a large volume of these requests, its regular operations could be affected. To avoid this situation, the school could choose to limit when access to records is granted.
- **CIPA**—CIPA requires that minors be protected from offensive content but adults should be able to have unrestricted access. Librarians may not have had to manage systems in the past. However, they may need to be trained on how to turn off the TPM for adult access.
- **PCI DSS**—If an organization is already conducting standard security practices, PCI DSS has little effect on normal operations. However, if the organization has weak security practices, PCI DSS standards could drastically change operations. Although this is good in the long run, it may be uncomfortable for users to get used to in the short term.
- **GDPR**—GDPR differentiates the duties and responsibilities of data controllers from data processors. Data controllers have an obligation to engage only processors that provide sufficient guarantees to implement appropriate technical and organizational measures that protect the rights of data subjects. The processors must also follow all applicable measures to protect the personal data of data subjects.

Identifying Risk Mitigation and Risk Reduction Elements for the Entire Organization

Although looking at individual systems and functions for possible risks is important, so too is taking a broader view. A macro view of the organization identifies how all the pieces fit together.

Most organizations have a security policy created by senior management. It lays out the philosophy of security in the organization and identifies big-picture security goals. Security controls are implemented based on direction from the security policy.

Some of the controls that have a macro view of the organization include:

- **Account management controls**—These controls ensure that account management is secure. With account management controls, each user is given a separate account, which is disabled if the user leaves, and password management policies are used for the accounts.
- **Access controls**—Although access controls are applied to individual systems, they are created using a global system. For example, Microsoft domains use Active Directory Domain Services as the basis for assigning permissions and controlling access. Most organizations create an administrative model that defines how to use groups to organize users. Then, access permissions are granted to the groups, instead of individual users. Least privilege is a core principle enforced with access controls.

- **Physical access**—An attacker's breaking into a system is just a matter of time if they have unrestricted physical access to the system. Therefore, physical access controls are necessary to protect the valuable assets by restricting physical access to them. They can include key locks, cipher locks, proximity cards, and closed-circuit television (CCTV) systems.
- **Personnel policies**—Personnel policies, such as separation of duties and mandatory vacations, are used to help prevent fraud. These policies aren't targeted at individuals but rather at positions, such as accounting positions where personnel have access to organizational monies.
- **Security awareness and training**—Some training is targeted for specific groups, such as managers or administrators, and other training is given to all personnel. Regardless, training and awareness programs can be used to raise the security awareness of all personnel.

Many additional controls are available for review. The most important point here is that an organization's controls should not be focused solely on individual systems. A sound security program will have a mix of both broad and narrow security controls.

Performing a Cost-Benefit Analysis

Creating a cost-benefit analysis (CBA) is a significant step when evaluating a control. In a CBA, the cost of the control is compared to the cost of the risk should it occur. If the control costs more to implement than the risk would cost, then the control isn't cost effective.

Two pieces of data are necessary to perform an effective CBA: the cost of the control and the projected benefits of the control. The projected benefits can be calculated with the following formula:

Loss before control – Loss after control = Projected benefits

Then, determining whether the control should be used can be calculated with this formula:

Projected benefits – Cost of control = Control value

If the result is a positive value, the control is worthwhile, but, if the result is negative, the control costs more than the benefits and it shouldn't be purchased.

For example, an organization has a database server that is hosting a large database, and backups are completed regularly. However, a risk assessment determines that backup copies are stored in the same room that the backup server is in. The risk in this example is that a fire could destroy the server and all the backup tapes. By storing a copy of the backup tape at an off-site location, the risk can be eliminated.

The first step in performing the CBA is to identify the value of the data. If this database is a primary database for the organization, the value could easily be in the millions of dollars. For this example, the value is $1 million, which means a complete loss before the control is $1 million.

NOTE

Although fire insurance provides some protection from data losses, the insurance company might not pay if an organization is found negligent. In other words, if an organization doesn't take the precaution of storing backups at an off-site location, the insurance company may not pay for the value of the data. The insurance company would pay for the hardware lost but probably not pay for the data lost.

TIP

A CBA normally looks at benefits and costs for a single year. If the benefits and costs of a control are close to each other, the **return on investment (ROI)** of purchasing the control can be calculated. An ROI will indicate the value of a control over its lifetime and determine the monetary benefits of investing in the control.

An external company can pick up the tapes weekly and store them at an off-site location. The external company can also rotate tapes in and out based on the client company's needs. The cost for this service is $100 a month, or $1,200 a year.

Subscribing to this service means that the most data that can be lost is 7 days' worth. If a fire destroys the client's building right before the most recent backup tape has been picked up, the last 7 days of its data will be lost. The value of that week's worth of data is $10,000.

With this information, all the necessary numbers have been determined and can now be plugged into the formulas: The loss before the control is $1 million, the loss after the control is $10,000, and the cost of the control is $1,200.

$$\text{Loss before control} - \text{Loss after control} = \text{Projected benefits}$$
$$\$1{,}000{,}000 - \$10{,}000 = \$990{,}000$$
$$\text{Projected benefits} - \text{Cost of control} = \text{Control value}$$
$$\$990{,}000 - \$1{,}200 = \$988{,}800$$

These figures show the value of storing data off-site and will be important when trying to get support to approve the purchase of the control. If a request is made to spend $1,200 annually without justification, the request may be denied. However, a request submitted to prevent a potential $990,000 loss by investing $1,200 will more than likely be approved.

Best Practices for Planning Risk Mitigation Throughout an Organization

When planning risk mitigation strategies for an organization, several best practices can be used. These include:

- **Reviewing historical documentation**—Historical documentation includes previous documentation of risk assessments and BIAs, policies and procedures, and security incidents. Although the risks may have changed, many of the threats and vulnerabilities will have stayed the same.
- **Including both a narrow and a broad focus**—Specific risks and mitigation strategies for specific systems and functions can be identified, which represents a narrow focus. However, the focus must also be broadened to include the entire organization. For example, training and awareness programs help ensure the entire organization recognizes the importance of security.
- **Ensuring that governing laws have been identified**—Taking the time to understand the laws is important to determining compliance within the organization. If a law does apply to the organization, the organization needs to implement the steps necessary to ensure it is compliant.
- **Redoing risk assessments when a control changes**—Risk assessments are completed at a point in time. Therefore, if the control changes, the risk assessment is no longer valid.
- **Including a CBA**—CBAs provide justification for controls and help to determine their value. CBAs clearly demonstrate that a control should be purchased or that a control isn't worth its cost.

CHAPTER SUMMARY

This chapter covered important elements of risk mitigation throughout an organization. Controls are implemented to mitigate risk by reducing the impact of threats or reducing vulnerabilities, and the effectiveness of the controls can be measured against those two requirements. They should be most effective at preventing risk for any critical business operations in an organization.

Legal compliance issues for IT have grown important in recent years. More laws and regulations apply, and the cost for noncompliance can be expensive. Therefore, taking the time to identify relevant laws and guidelines is important because regulations can have varying impacts on an organization and they should be considered when implementing supporting controls.

KEY CONCEPTS AND TERMS

critical business function (CBF)
critical success factor (CSF)
defense in depth
E-Rate funding
maximum acceptable outage (MAO)
proxy server
return on investment (ROI)
service level agreement (SLA)
technology protection measure (TPM)

CHAPTER 10 ASSESSMENT

1. A(n) ______ is used to identify the impact on an organization if a risk occurs.

2. MAO is the minimal acceptable outage that a system or service can experience before its mission is affected.

   A. True
   B. False

3. An organization wants to have an agreement with a vendor for an expected level of performance for a service that includes ensuring that monetary penalties are assessed if the minimum uptime requirements are not met. What should you use?

   A. MAO
   B. BIA
   C. SLA
   D. IDS

4. What would be used to identify mission-critical systems?

   A. Critical outage times
   B. Critical business functions
   C. PCI DSS review
   D. Disaster recovery plan

5. What can an organization use to remind users of an AUP's contents?

   A. Logon banners
   B. Posters
   C. Emails
   D. All of the above

6. Organizations that violate GDPR rules may be fined ________ or ________ of their annual global turnover, whichever is greater.

7. Which of the following strategies helps reduce security gaps even if a security control fails?
   A. Access control implementation
   B. Critical business factor analysis
   C. Defense in depth
   D. Business impact analysis

8. How much can an organization be fined in a year for HIPAA-related mistakes?
   A. $100
   B. $1,000
   C. $25,000
   D. $250,000

9. What determines whether an organization is governed by FISMA?
   A. Whether it is registered with the Securities and Exchange Commission
   B. Whether its employees handle health-related information
   C. Whether it receives E-Rate funding
   D. Whether it is a federal agency

10. What determines whether an organization is governed by HIPAA?
   A. Whether it is registered with the Securities and Exchange Commission
   B. Whether its employees handle health-related information
   C. Whether it receives E-Rate funding
   D. Whether it is a federal agency

11. What determines whether an organization is governed by SOX?
   A. Whether it is registered with the Securities and Exchange Commission
   B. Whether its employees handle health-related information
   C. Whether it receives E-Rate funding
   D. Whether it is a federal agency

12. What determines whether an organization is governed by CIPA?
   A. Whether it is registered with the Securities and Exchange Commission
   B. Whether its employees handle health-related information
   C. Whether it receives E-Rate funding
   D. Whether it is a federal agency

13. A CBA has been performed on a prospective control. The CBA indicates the cost of the control is about the same as the control's projected benefits. What should be done?
   A. Identify the ROI
   B. Purchase the control
   C. Cancel the purchase of the control
   D. Redo the CBA

14. Which of the following is a valid formula used to identify the projected benefits of a control?
   A. Loss after control – Loss before control
   B. Loss before control – Loss after control
   C. Cost of control + Losses
   D. Cost of control/12

15. A CBA can be used to justify the purchase of a control.
   A. True
   B. False

CHAPTER 11

Turning a Risk Assessment Into a Risk Mitigation Plan

ONCE THE RISK ASSESSMENT HAS BEEN COMPLETED and approved, the next step is to create a risk mitigation plan. This describes the approved countermeasures and how to implement them. If much time has passed since the risk assessment was completed, the findings should be checked to ensure they are still valid. For example, some threats or vulnerabilities may have disappeared. Ideally, the risk mitigation plan will follow quickly after the risk assessment.

A significant part of the risk mitigation plan is the identification of costs. Ideally, the risk assessment will already have identified the costs, but some hidden costs may have been overlooked. If additional costs are discovered, the cost-benefit analysis will need to be recalculated. Lastly, it's important to follow up on the risk mitigation plan, which includes ensuring that all the approved countermeasures are implemented and the countermeasures mitigate the risks as expected. It should be obvious that costs are not the ***only*** factor in risk mitigation, but they must be ***a*** factor.

Chapter 11 Topics

This chapter covers the following topics and concepts:

- What a review of a risk assessment is
- What translating a risk assessment into a risk mitigation plan entails
- How to prioritize risk elements
- What the verification of risk elements entails
- What a cost-benefit analysis for risk elements includes
- What implementing a risk mitigation plan includes
- How to follow up on a risk mitigation plan
- What best practices for enabling a risk mitigation plan are

Chapter 11 Goals

When you complete this chapter, you will be able to:

- Evaluate a risk assessment created for the IT infrastructure
- Describe the process to translate a risk assessment into a risk mitigation plan
- Discuss the importance of prioritizing risk elements
- Describe the process to verify what risk elements can be mitigated
- Perform a cost-benefit analysis for risk elements
- Describe the process of implementing a risk mitigation plan
- Describe the process to follow up on a risk mitigation plan
- List best practices for enabling a risk mitigation plan from a risk assessment

Reviewing the Risk Assessment for the IT Infrastructure

Once a risk assessment has been completed and approved, it can be reviewed for the IT infrastructure. What you are doing is reviewing how far the current status deviates from the risk assessment. In other words, how effective are current controls in mitigating the issues identified during the risk assessment. This is important to help you determine how many new mitigation measures are needed. A risk assessment includes the following high-level steps:

- Identify and evaluate relevant threats.
- Identify and evaluate relevant vulnerabilities.
- Identify and evaluate countermeasures.
- Develop mitigating recommendations.

Next, management reviews the risk assessment. Management can approve, reject, or modify the recommendations. The management decisions are then documented and included in a plan of action and milestones document.

The following step is for the purpose of translating the risk assessment into an actual risk mitigation plan. Before jumping into this, the risk assessment should be reviewed, paying special attention to the following key items:

- **In-place countermeasures**—The risk assessment may have addressed some of the countermeasures that are already being used. Some of the countermeasures may need to be upgraded or reconfigured, and some may need to be replaced completely. If a countermeasure is to be replaced, the original countermeasure shouldn't be removed until the new one has been installed. It should not be a surprise that some of the current countermeasures are sufficient. It would certainly be a surprise if one discovered that all current countermeasures are ineffective.

- **Planned countermeasures**—A planned countermeasure is one that has been approved and has a date for implementation. Planned countermeasures are documented in the risk assessment. These countermeasures should be reviewed to determine their status. A countermeasure may have been installed since the risk assessment was published. The date a planned countermeasure will be implemented might also affect the timeline for an approved countermeasure. These countermeasures should be documented in the plan of action and milestones.
- **Approved countermeasures**—Approved countermeasures are the controls previously approved by management. They need to be added into the implementation pipeline. Some of them will be easy to implement, whereas others may be complex and require extra steps. They may need to be purchased or delegated. All of them need to be tracked for completion.

Overlapping Countermeasures

Another important consideration when reviewing the plan is to determine whether there is any overlap among the countermeasures. One countermeasure may reduce or resolve more than one risk. Additionally, some risks may be mitigated by more than one countermeasure. Overlapping countermeasures are actually highly desirable. Having more than one mitigation process for a given threat is a key to good security.

One example of overlapping countermeasures is the issue of mitigating malware. You should certainly use antivirus software on the workstations. You should also have policies and training advising users about the dangers of downloading programs, clicking on links, or inserting a USB drive. You may also have a separate antivirus at the firewall. This would be an instance of three overlapping controls. This is a preferred scenario. You cannot depend on a single control to mitigate significant threats.

Attacks Ignored for a Full Weekend

A large network operations center had several countermeasures in place to detect attacks. These countermeasures provided notification to network operations center personnel on a large monitor viewable by all personnel. During one weekend, an IDS sent alerts on a potential attack. One of the administrators investigated and realized it was a false alert. Three more alerts occurred in the next hour, and other administrators investigated. Each time they were false alerts. These false alerts continued, but, at some point in the next few hours, an actual attack started, which also caused alerts. However, the administrators began to expect false alerts, and they gave all the alerts less and less attention. The IDS had become the IDS that cries wolf. When the real wolf was at the door, no one believed it, and none of the alerts were recognized as valid. This is often referred to as alert fatigue.

When administrators came on duty Monday morning, they completed a review of activity and detected the actual attack. Luckily, the attack didn't take down any systems, but the attacker did gather reconnaissance data.

False alerts should be minimized if possible. Personnel can get accustomed to seeing alerts and dismiss them without investigation. This activity of reducing false alerts is called "tuning the IDS." Without tuning, personnel may dismiss a live attack before even investigating it. This is why rules for an IDS have to be adjusted until one finds the proper level for a given organization.

Risk Assessments: Understanding Threats and Vulnerabilities

One of the methods that can be used to determine whether countermeasures overlap is to conduct a risk assessment, which maps the countermeasure to threats, vulnerabilities, and the assets being protected. This helps to paint a complete picture of risk, which is often represented with the following formula:

Risk = Threat × Vulnerability × Asset

A vulnerability is a weakness; by itself, it doesn't present a risk. Similarly, threats by themselves don't present a risk. Risk is the probability of a threat taking advantage of a vulnerability to cause loss, damage, or harm to an asset. Countermeasures either reduce or eliminate the impact of the threat or the vulnerability on the asset.

According to NIST 800-30, a risk assessment is used to identify, estimate, and prioritize risk to the operations of a business or organization. The risk assessment helps decision makers in these organizations identify and evaluate how these threats impact them and what countermeasures can be implemented to reduce vulnerabilities and harm to their assets. The eventual outcome is a determination of risk.

NOTE

Risk = Threat × Vulnerability × Asset need not be a quantifiable mathematical formula. In other words, numerical values are not necessarily assigned to threats and vulnerabilities to determine a numerical value for risk. Instead, the formula shows that risks occur when both threats and vulnerabilities are combined to harm an asset. If one has actual numbers, that is great. However, one will often simply use qualitative measurements.

FYI

Nonrepudiation prevents individuals from denying they took an action. By logging usernames, audit logs include details on who performed an action. Because the activity is logged, users can't deny they took the action. Effective nonrepudiation is lost if one user can use another user's account. The same goes for shared accounts where all team members use, for example, "admin." Some logs include Internet Protocol (IP) addresses and computer names. This audit trail helps an investigator determine what actually happened.

For example, consider user accounts of terminated employees. As a best practice, accounts should be disabled but not deleted when the employee leaves. If necessary, administrators can enable the account later with a different password. This allows a supervisor to access the ex-employee's data. After the supervisor reviews and copies important data, administrators delete the ex-employee's account.

Imagine that a company doesn't do anything to old accounts. As long as the account is enabled, anyone can access it. If an employee had remote access, then that employee can still access the systems remotely even if they have no malicious intent. They are certainly not maintaining accounts for an organization they no longer work at. That means you might change your password requirements to require longer and more complex passwords, but these 'ghost' accounts are not going to be updated.

Perhaps a previous employee still has friends on the job. The previous employee could give their credentials to a friend, and the friend could log on using the ex-employee's credentials. At this point, nonrepudiation is lost. If any of the activity is logged, it looks as if the ex-employee is taking the action. For example, Bob is an ex-employee, but Sally learns his username and password. With that information, Sally can log on as Bob. Audit logs may record what Sally does, but they record Bob's username. This might send security personnel on a wild goose chase trying to determine how Bob gained access to the network.

In this situation, the vulnerability is that inactive accounts are still enabled. User accounts aren't managed, leaving them available even if they aren't needed. The threat is that a previous employee or someone else may log on and access the account. The assets that could be lost, damaged, or harmed include valuable company information in the accounts.

Identifying Countermeasures

Risks are mitigated by adding countermeasures. The following countermeasures could be implemented to mitigate the risks from not disabling inactive accounts:

- **Creating an account management policy**—An **account management policy** is a written policy that spells out exactly what should be done with accounts. The policy may cover much more than just ex-employee accounts. It should also include rules for requesting and obtaining management approval for new accounts. Account management should also include establishing a robust plan for recovering access in case of lost passwords or other account issues.
- **Creating a script to check account usage**—Administrators could be tasked with writing a script to identify inactive accounts. An organization might define an inactive account as any account that hasn't been used in the past 30 days. The script would scan accounts and automatically disable inactive accounts. Administrators could schedule the script to run once a week, log the results, and email the results to interested personnel.
- **Controlling physical access to employee areas**—Access to employee-only areas could be controlled. Limiting access can be as simple as posting signs to discourage nonemployees from entering or as involved as using physical locks, cipher locks, badges, or proximity cards.

Similarly, the risk assessment may determine that users are not using strong passwords or changing their passwords regularly. The vulnerability is that the passwords are weak because password-cracking tools can easily crack weak passwords. The threat is that an attacker may use one of the many tools available to crack the weak password. Attackers can then use the cracked passwords to log on to a system or network.

The solution is to implement a **password policy**. A password policy is often part of an overall account management policy. Password policies can be enforced using technical means. For example, Microsoft domains allow IT administrators to enforce strong password practices with Group Policy.

> **TIP**
> Group Policy settings allow an administrator to configure a setting once in a domain. This setting will then apply to all users and computers in the domain. If desired, the administrator can also configure a Group Policy Object to apply to specific users and computers. Once configured, Group Policy works the same in a network with 5 users and computers as it does in a network with 50,000 users and computers.

A password policy would specify the following:

- **Password length**—Common recommended lengths are at least 8 characters for regular users and at least 15 characters for administrators. Although 15-character passwords may seem outrageous to an administrator who hasn't used them, they are used. However, passphrases are commonly used instead of passwords. For example, a password could be !LoveCh33s3burg3rsFromBurg3rk!ng. This is a complex 32-character password, but it isn't hard to remember.

- **Complexity**—The complexity refers to the mixture of characters. Complex passwords commonly have a mixture of at least three of the four character types. Character types are uppercase letters, lowercase letters, numbers, and special characters. Some requirements specify all four character types must be used. A complex password is more difficult to crack than a simple password.
- **Maximum age**—The maximum age identifies when the password must be changed. For example, a maximum age of 45 indicates the password must be changed at least every 45 days. Once the maximum age passes, the user is unable to log on until the password has been changed.
- **Password history**—Some users will try to use one or two passwords. They use password 1 until they are forced to change the password, and then they switch to password 2. When they are forced to change the password again, they switch back to password 1. They constantly swap back and forth between password 1 and password 2. However, when password history is used, users are prevented from using a password they used before. For example, the past 24 passwords for Windows domain systems can be remembered, which means that users are prevented from reusing passwords until they have used 24 other passwords.
- **Minimum age**—Establishing a minimum age prevents users from changing their passwords until a minimum amount of time has passed. Administrators commonly use 1 day as a minimum password age, which works with the password history to prevent users from changing their passwords right away to get back to their original passwords. With a password history set to 24 and the minimum age set to 1 day, users would have to change their passwords every day for the next 25 days to get back to the original password, which makes circumventing the intended policy too difficult for the users. Users will instead comply with the intention of the policy, which is to change the password to a new password.

> **TIP**
>
> NIST 800-63B shares valuable tips on passwords:
>
> - Having an eight-character minimum when the password is set by individuals
> - Having a six-character minimum when the password is set by a system
> - Supporting at least 64 characters maximum length
> - Allowing at least 10 password attempts before lockout
> - Checking chosen passwords against known dictionaries
>
> NIST also recommends you block the following passwords:
>
> - Passwords obtained from previous breach corpuses. This term simply means data that was released in previous breaches.
> - Dictionary words.
> - Repetitive or sequential characters (e.g. 'aaaaaa,' '1234abcd').
> - Context-specific words, such as the name of the service, the username, and derivatives thereof.
>
> This list is not exhaustive but is worth reviewing. Furthermore, two-factor authentication is now quite commonplace and there is no reason that every organization should not implement it. Multi-factor authentication apps are common, including Microsoft Authenticator, Okta, Duo, and others.

At this point, the countermeasures can be matched with the threat/vulnerability pairs. **TABLE 11-1** shows the threat/vulnerability pairs matched to recommended countermeasures.

The information in the table shows that the account management policy is addressing two threat/vulnerability pairs. This information can be valuable. If administrators recognize that a single countermeasure is addressing multiple risks, they may decide to increase the priority of the countermeasure. While the threat/vulnerability pairing is effective in evaluating threats and vulnerabilities, NIST 800-30's risk assessment approach is also an effective alternative.

TABLE 11-1 Matching Threat/Vulnerability Pairs With Countermeasures

THREAT	VULNERABILITY	COUNTERMEASURE(S)
Previous employee	Inactive accounts not disabled	Implement account management policy Write script to deactivate accounts Restrict access to employees only
Weak passwords	Password-cracking tools launched by attacker	Implement account management policy Implement Group Policy password policy

Scripting as a Technical Countermeasure

Technical countermeasures don't have to be expensive. Some can be created at no cost with scripts if administrators have the expertise.

The difference between good administrators and great administrators is often the ability to write administrative scripts. Good administrators can get tasks done, but they often take longer. This is especially true for repetitive tasks. Great administrators can accomplish tasks much more quickly and with little effort. One of the great benefits of scripts is that they can be automated. For example, an administrator wants to disable inactive accounts. The administrator could write a script to identify and disable accounts that haven't been used in the past 30 days and then schedule that script to run every Saturday night. All accounts would be automatically examined on a weekly basis and inactive accounts disabled without any additional administrative effort. Compare this with the administrator who can't script. The same tasks could still be accomplished, but they would take time each week.

As administrators become more proficient with scripts, they can add additional bells and whistles. For example, a script can log results or send an email. After the script has located and disabled inactive accounts, it can email a list of accounts that were disabled.

Scripts can meet most administrative needs. A common saying among scripting administrators is "If you can envision it, you can script it."

Translating a Risk Assessment Into a Risk Mitigation Plan

The next step is to translate the risk assessment into a risk mitigation plan. The mitigation plan will include the details on how and when to implement the countermeasures.

Here are three important considerations when developing the mitigation plan:

- Cost to implement the countermeasures
- Time to implement the countermeasures
- Operational impact of the countermeasures

Cost to Implement

Many of the countermeasures to be implemented will need to be purchased. Therefore, being able to accurately identify the costs of these countermeasures is important. On the surface, the cost of the countermeasure may be simple to calculate. However, there are frequently hidden costs.

Costs can include the following items:

- Initial purchase cost
- Facility costs
- Installation costs
- Training costs

FYI

If hidden costs are discovered, they may affect the decision to implement the countermeasure. If the difference between the original estimate and the actual cost is significant, the countermeasure may no longer be cost effective. In that case, a cost-benefit analysis should be redone. If the results show that the countermeasure changes the original cost-benefit analysis, the data should be presented to management. Management could decide to still go forward or stop the purchase of the countermeasure.

One of the common problems that creeps up in this stage is a lack of money. Ideally, the risk assessment should accurately identify the cost of the countermeasure, but, if new costs are discovered, they may cause problems. The new cost may be beyond the original budgeted amount, which may move the cost of the countermeasure from a budgeted item to an unfunded requirement. Unfunded requirements may simply have to wait until the next year for implementation.

Initial Purchase Cost

The cost of the initial purchase is the price of the product. For software, such as a software vulnerability scanner, the cost is the retail price minus any discounts given to the organization. For hardware, such as a router or server, the initial purchase cost is the price of the hardware.

Some countermeasures may be developed internally. For example, this chapter has mentioned scripts used as a countermeasure. If the organization has a talented administrator, they may be able to easily write the script. Writing the script won't take much time or prevent the completion of other tasks.

On the other hand, if scripting is a new function for the administrator, the decision may be made to calculate the labor costs. The administrator will take a significant amount of time to write the first script but will spend less and less time on subsequent scripts because they will become easier and easier to complete. The initial purchase price is usually identified accurately in the risk assessment. If a product is being purchased, the price can be verified with the vendor.

Facility Costs

Facility requirements include space, power, and air-conditioning, but sometimes these requirements are overlooked. If they're needed but not identified, they can cause significant problems with the schedule and may even affect the accuracy of the cost-benefit analysis.

Many people have the impression that a server room has unlimited space, but that's rarely the case. Servers are usually mounted in equipment bays, which are about the width and

FIGURE 11-1

Equipment bays hosting servers and other components.

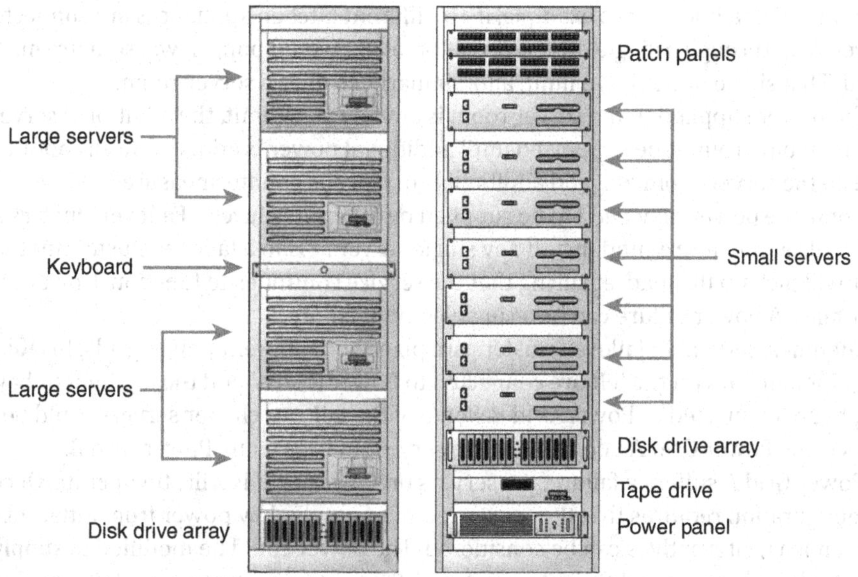

depth of a home refrigerator and about six feet tall. **FIGURE 11-1** shows how equipment is mounted in an equipment bay.

The bay on the left has four large servers. They could be large 32-processor systems with 2 terabytes (TB) of memory. The bay on the right has seven smaller servers. These could be smaller 4-processor systems with 32 gigabytes (GB) of random access memory (RAM). The applications hosted on the servers dictate the size. For example, a database server hosting a very large database requires more resources than a file server used to host user files.

Equipment bays commonly host other components, as can be seen in Figure 11-1, which shows patch panels, disk drive arrays, a tape drive, and more.

As an example of facility costs, the mitigation plan calls for adding two additional servers to an existing server room that has only two bays. They won't fit into the existing bays. Either equipment has to be removed from these bays or another bay added. If this requirement wasn't identified before, it will add additional cost for the countermeasure.

> **NOTE**
>
> Figure 11-1 shows spaces between the servers, but they are illustrated only so the various components can be seen. However, in an actual bay, these spaces wouldn't be there. Either the server and components would be mounted right on top of each other, or metal plates, which help counteract the airflow through the bay, would be installed to cover the spaces.

Besides space, air-conditioning and power requirements should also be considered. Air-conditioning units provide a certain level of cooling power. For example, the air-conditioning unit needed to keep a 1,000-square-foot home cool is much smaller than one needed to keep a 3,000-square-foot home cool. Similarly, the air-conditioning unit used to keep two bays cool may not be able to keep three bays cool.

Power is another consideration. Regarding power, two things need to be considered—power capacity and power source.

First, the server room must be able to support the additional power. Using the power requirements of a home as an example, if 15 different kitchen appliances are connected into a power strip through a single outlet, circuit breakers would pop, or, worse, a fire may be started. That single outlet has a limit, and, similarly, so does a server room.

If the power supplied to the server room is already at its limit, the additional servers and equipment bays cannot be supported until additional power is added. Routing additional power to the server room will add additional cost for the countermeasure.

Second, the power may need to be supplied by different sources. Failover clusters add additional servers for redundancy. If any single server fails in a failover cluster, another server will pick up the load, ensuring that the service continues to function. However, what if power fails? A power failure can be a single point of failure.

Sometimes, servers in failover clusters are placed on different power grids. In **FIGURE 11-2**, the equipment bays on the left are connected to Power Grid A, and the equipment bays on the right are connected to Power Grid B. Some of the failover cluster servers could be placed in bays using Power Grid A and some of the servers in bays using Power Grid B.

If Power Grid A suffers a failure, the servers on Power Grid B will still operate. Of course, this configuration requires that the server room be supplied by power from different power grids. If it isn't, alternatives can be considered. The power could be modified to supply power to the room from a different power grid. Some organizations place failover cluster servers in different locations to ensure that each server is on a different power grid.

Another method of providing alternative sources is using a different **uninterruptible power supply (UPS)**. A UPS can be a simple portable unit used on a home computer or a room filled with banks of batteries.

If power fails, the UPS will provide power for a short amount of time. For some less-critical systems, a UPS allows a system to shut down logically. For critical systems, a UPS provides time for generators to power on and stabilize. After the generators have stabilized, power is switched from the UPS system to the generators, which provide long-term power.

FIGURE 11-2

Failover cluster servers connected to different power grids.

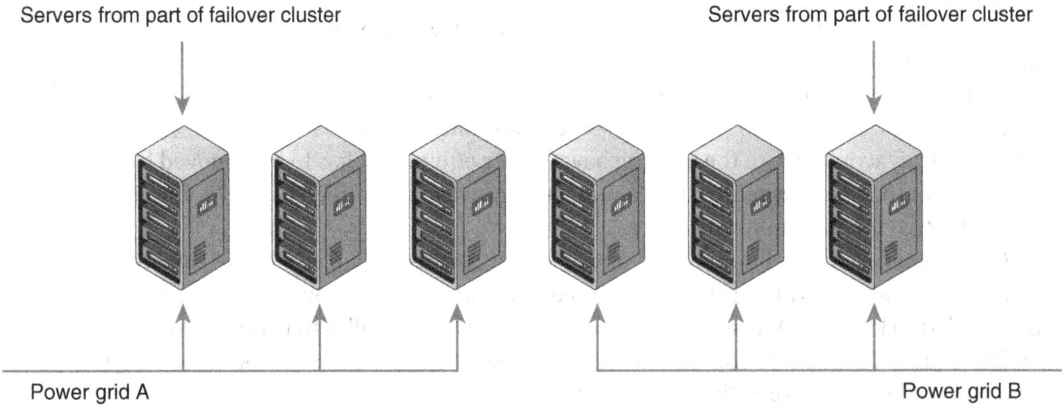

Most countermeasures won't require additional facility costs. However, if facility costs are required, the overall costs for the countermeasure will increase significantly. These additional costs may be so high that the cost-benefit analysis shows that adding the countermeasure no longer makes fiscal sense.

Installation Costs

In-house administrators will install most countermeasures. However, some sophisticated countermeasures may require outside help. Occasionally, the extra expense is warranted to have the vendor install and configure the countermeasure to be sure it has been installed correctly. This decision is often dependent on the level of expertise of staff.

As an example, a small school with a library has not received any E-Rate funding discounts from the Federal Communications Commission (FCC) in the past. These discounts subsidize the cost of internet access. However, the library wants to apply for the discounts. It must comply with the Children's Internet Protection Act (CIPA) to filter the content to ensure that children are protected from offensive content.

The library could decide to purchase a proxy server to comply. The proxy server can be used with a subscription to filter offensive content. However, the school may not have the expertise to install and configure the proxy server easily. Instead of taking the chance of making mistakes and being on the wrong side of the CIPA law, the school could decide to outsource this.

In this example, the installation costs will add to the cost of the countermeasure.

Training Costs

Another overlooked cost is training. The new countermeasure may be the greatest thing since the invention of the personal computer, but, if no one knows how to operate it, it will sit in the corner gathering dust. Technical training can be expensive, costing as much as $6,500 to send a single administrator to a weeklong training session.

Many companies will host training on location. Costs may be as much as $40,000 to send a trainer to the company to train 15 or so people.

Obviously, technical training costs can quickly add up, and, as with other costs, they can significantly add to the total cost of a countermeasure. In addition to the final cost, they may also affect the schedule. Implementation of the countermeasure may need to be delayed until personnel have been trained.

Time to Implement

The time to implement the countermeasure can vary widely. Some implementations can be completed within days or weeks, whereas some may take months. Considering the entire process is important when identifying timelines.

For example, creating a written account management policy may seem like a simple and quick procedure, and a security expert could probably draft an account management policy within a day. However, that policy is not the IT account management policy. All policies need senior management approval and buy-in; therefore, the draft needs to be routed to senior management for review.

> **TIP**
>
> A risk assessment includes a plan of action and milestones (POAM), which is a valuable tracking tool, especially for complex projects. Once the time and schedule for a countermeasure have been identified, the POAM will need to be updated with this data.

FIGURE 11-3

Web server with back-end database server.

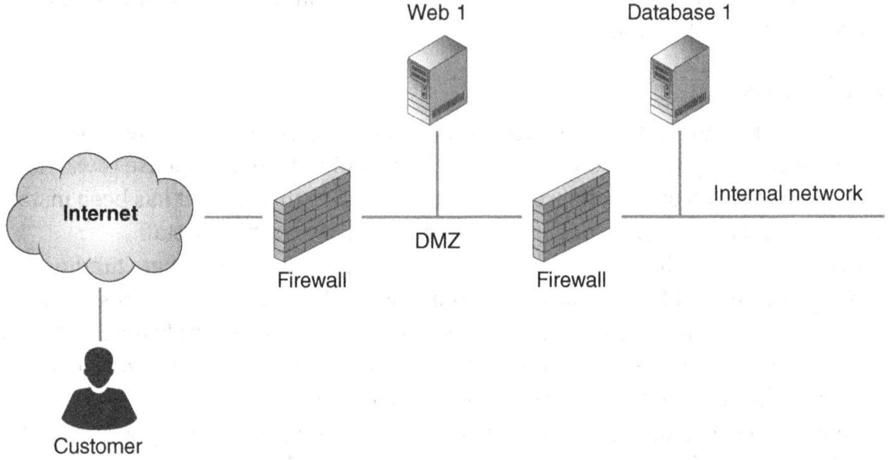

Management will more than likely want changes, some of which may be stylistic and some of which may be content related. To get managers' buy-in, the policy needs to be their policy. The more changes they make, the more they own it. If a policy isn't edited at least once, perhaps management really isn't buying into it.

A policy owned by management will be supported by management. If management doesn't support the policy, no one will.

Just because management's review of a policy may take only 20 minutes doesn't mean the policy will be done in the 20 minutes after completion of the first draft. Unless there's been a recent high-level security incident, a written security policy is not likely to be a top priority. It will take time to rise to the top of the managers' in pile.

With all of this in mind, an estimate of 30 days may be made for the completion of the policy. Routing the policy through proper management personnel may take a couple of weeks. Changes will be made to the policy; then, it will be resubmitted for final approval and signature, which may take another week or so.

Some timelines could be much more complex. For example, **FIGURE 11-3** represents a company's current web server configuration. The web server is in the demilitarized zone (DMZ) and accesses a back-end database hosted on a different server. The server supports an online business that has enjoyed explosive growth in the past 2 years and is currently generating millions of dollars in revenue a year.

A recent outage resulted in tens of thousands of dollars in lost sales. Combined with indirect costs, management estimates the company lost over $100,000. Managers want to prevent outages like this in the future. However, even after engineers identify a solution, its implementation will take much longer than 30 days.

TIP

Tracking countermeasures is important and doesn't have to be complex, just accurate. For example, if a policy is submitted to the chief information officer (CIO) for review, a comment can be made in the POAM or other tracking document to that effect and can be as simple as "submitted draft to CIO on April 14."

FIGURE 11-4

Here, a single web server has been replaced by a web farm.

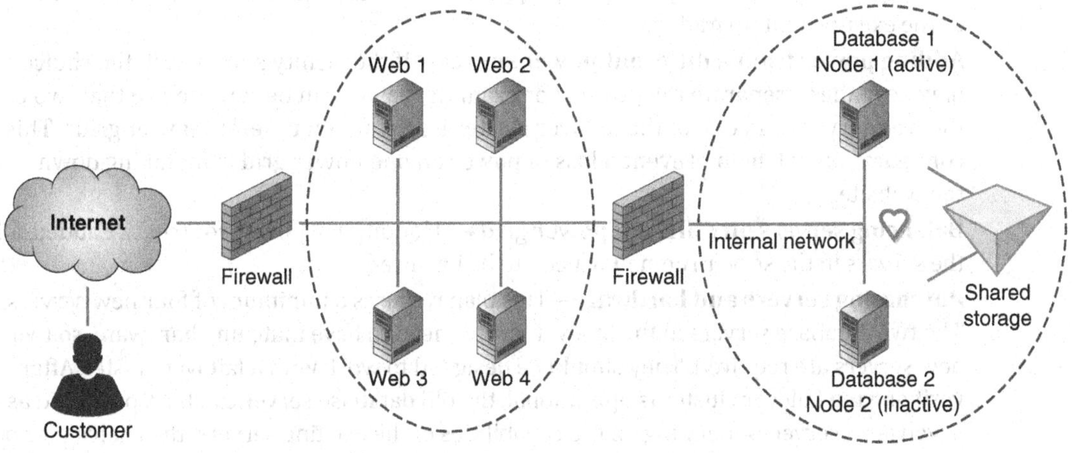

After management has approved the solution, additional servers need to be purchased to create the configuration shown in **FIGURE 11-4**. This plan expands the web server into a **web farm**. The back-end database server will be protected with a failover cluster.

A web farm consists of multiple servers using **network load balancing**. The first client connects to web 1, the next client connects to web 2, and so on. At any given time, each of the servers has about the same load. Web farms allow an organization to easily scale out by adding additional servers. For example, an administrator can add a server to the web farm if there is a surge in demand. Additionally, if one of the servers in the web farm fails, network load balancing ensures that clients aren't directed to the failed server.

A failover cluster provides fault tolerance for the database server. Node 1 is active, and node 2 is inactive. Node 2 monitors the health of node 1 by monitoring its heartbeat. If node 1 fails, node 2 takes over.

Clearly, there are differences between Figures 11-3 and 11-4. The new configuration adds four servers and two different technologies. It will require much more planning than the implementation of a written account policy.

Several things need to be considered in the new configuration: the server room may not have equipment bay space, the added servers may exceed the power capabilities of the room, or air-conditioning capacity may need to be added. The timeline could include the following steps:

> **TIP**
>
> A system or service should be able to be scaled up or scaled out when demand is increased. **Scale up** means that additional resources are added to a server. For example, the processor could be upgraded or additional RAM added. **Scale out** means that additional servers are added to the service. A web farm with network load balancing supports scaling out without changing the core application. In this case, the core application is the web application hosted on the web servers.

- **Adding an additional equipment bay**—The bay should be the same size as other bays and be installed the same way, which ensures that it takes full advantage of the existing air-conditioning. Adding another bay assumes the room will support it. If it won't, then the problem may be bigger.

- **Adding additional air-conditioning capacity**—An additional unit may need to be added or the existing unit upgraded.
- **Adding power from a different power source**—If the facility supports it, the choice may be made to separate the power. For example, power can be rerouted so that two of the web servers and one of the failover cluster nodes are on different power grids. This configuration will help prevent a loss of power on one power grid from taking down the website.
- **Balancing servers on different power grids**—If additional power sources are added, all the servers in the server room may need to be balanced.
- **Purchasing servers and hardware**—This plan requires a minimum of four new servers. The two database servers in the failover cluster need to have matching hardware, so two new servers are required. They should be designed to work with a failover cluster. After verifying the failover cluster is operational, the old database server can be repurposed as a web farm server. Depending on the capabilities of the existing servers, the choice may be made to replace the old servers with six new servers.
- **Providing training to administrators**—Configuring and administering failover clusters can become complex. If administrators haven't worked with a failover cluster before, they will need training. Network load balancing is easy to work with, but administrators might need training for this, too.
- **Installing and configuring servers**—This step depends on the experience of the administrators. For example, the installation and configuration of the failover clusters could be outsourced. Many of the companies that sell failover cluster solutions also provide installation support.
- **Testing**—Before the system goes live, the web farm and failover cluster need to be tested to verify that they will work as expected because every system will have technical issues that need to be resolved.
- **Implementing**—The original configuration is switched over to the new configuration, sometimes in a phased implementation. For example, the failover cluster may be implemented first; once it's stable, the web farm can be implemented.

> **TIP**
>
> Implementing the new configuration is time consuming and expensive, but the cost is justified based on the loss of over $100,000 during a recent outage. Moreover, these countermeasures are needed to ensure the availability of the website to help ensure that it continues to generate revenue.

It should be noted that cloud resources significantly reduce the cost of implementation as well as time to implement. Anything that is hosted in a cloud environment you can readily spin up new services to and decommission them if no longer needed. This is one reason more and more organizations are virtualizing some or all of their environment.

Operational Impact

On one hand, the more secure a system is, the harder it is to use. On the other hand, the easier it is to use, the less secure it is. In short, any countermeasure can have an impact on normal operations.

Operational impact should be identified as early as possible so steps can be taken to minimize it. For example, the goal is to minimize the traffic allowed through the firewall, which could be realized through the implementation of an implicit deny philosophy.

An **implicit deny** philosophy starts by blocking all traffic and then adding rules to identify allowed traffic. The firewall allows traffic that matches an explicit rule and blocks all other traffic. Even if the firewall doesn't have a rule to explicitly deny certain traffic, it is implicitly denied.

The challenge is to identify what traffic is allowed. One way would be to block all traffic and wait until people complain, but that method would be sure to impact operations.

A better method would be to enable extensive logging on the existing firewall. The log can then be analyzed to determine what traffic the firewall currently allows. Most logs can be imported into other tools for better analysis. For example, a text log can be imported into a database, which makes analyzing the data much easier than if it were in a text file.

Just because traffic is going through the network doesn't mean it should be. For example, the written security policy may state that Network News Transfer Protocol (NNTP) traffic is restricted. NNTP uses Transmission Control Protocol (TCP) port 119. A review of the traffic log may show a substantial amount of traffic using this port. This situation should be investigated to see whether the security policy is out of date or perhaps someone made an unauthorized change on the firewall to allow this traffic.

Traffic that looks unfamiliar should be investigated and not just blocked without consideration. For example, a company may have a line of business (LOB) application used for ordering parts and supplies from vendors that is using port 5678. If this port is blocked, the application will be blocked, and employees will no longer be able to use the LOB application to order parts and supplies. Clearly, that will have a detrimental effect on operations.

Prioritizing Risk Elements That Require Risk Mitigation

One of the ways that the most important countermeasures can be identified is by prioritizing the risk elements. Risks occur when a threat exploits a vulnerability. The importance of a risk can be determined by estimating its likelihood and impact.

The likelihood of a risk is a reflection of how likely it is that a threat will exploit a vulnerability, and the impact identifies the damage to the organization. Risks that are highly likely to occur and will have a high impact are the most important.

> **NOTE**
>
> Phishing is a form of social engineering cybercrime whereby the phisher attacks its targets by posing as a trusted source, often luring the targets to provide sensitive data; for example, their bank details. Phishing can also be used to deliver malware. Individuals who are not educated in recognizing threats of this nature often lose out, especially when the attackers are able to access their personally identifiable information.

Using a Threat Likelihood/Impact Matrix

Threats can negatively affect confidentiality, integrity, or availability. The severity of a threat is evaluated by identifying the likelihood that a threat will affect one of these elements, and the impact is evaluated by determining the extent to which it will be affected.

TABLE 11-2 shows a sample threat likelihood/impact matrix. This matrix can be used to determine the priority of various threats. Threats with a 0% to 10% likelihood of occurring would

TABLE 11-2 A Threat Likelihood/Impact Matrix

	LOW IMPACT (10)	MEDIUM IMPACT (50)	HIGH IMPACT (100)
High threat likelihood 100% (1.0)	10 × 1 = 10	50 × 1 = 50	100 × 1 = 100
Medium threat likelihood 50% (.50)	10 × .5 = 5	50 × .5 = 25	100 × .5 = 50
Low threat likelihood 10% (.10)	10 × .1 = 1	50 × .1 = 5	100 × .1 = 10

be assigned a value of 10%, threats with a likelihood between 11% and 50% would have a value of 50%, and threats with a likelihood between 51% and 100% would have a value of 100%. Similarly, impact values of 10, 50, or 100 would be assigned, depending on the impact to the organization.

Prioritizing Countermeasures

A threat likelihood/impact matrix can be used to prioritize risks and countermeasures. Risks with higher scores would result in a higher loss and should be addressed before risks with lower scores.

Risks are evaluated based on current in-place countermeasures. For example, if an organization was not using antivirus software, the likelihood would be high that systems could become infected. If several systems became infected, the impact would also be high. A high likelihood of 100% times a high impact of 100 equals a score of 100.

In another example, the company has antivirus software installed on all its systems, and, in the past year, only one malware incident had caused problems after a single user had disabled the antivirus software. The malware tried to spread but was quickly detected by antivirus software on other systems. In this example, both the likelihood and impact are low, giving the occurrence of the threat a score of 1.

FYI

The numerical values assigned to the word values can be different if desired. For example, a low impact could be assigned a value of 0 instead of 10. A high likelihood could be assigned a value of 90% instead of 100%. Additionally, there can be more than three data points, and different names can be used, such as low, moderately low, moderate, moderately severe, and severe. **TABLE 11-3** shows an example of how the threat likelihood/impact matrix can be used to prioritize threats. Each of the threats is assigned a likelihood and impact based on current countermeasures.

The information from Table 11-3 shows that the greatest current threats are the two with a score of 50:

- Attacks on DMZ servers
- Loss of data on a key database server

These two threats would probably be given high priority for addressing their recommended countermeasures.

TABLE 11-3 Threat Scores Used to Prioritize Threats

THREAT	LIKELIHOOD	IMPACT	SCORE
Attacks on DMZ servers Servers in the DMZ are currently updated only once every 6 months.	High value of 100%	Medium value of 50	50
Loss of data on key database server Backups are currently done on the database server daily, but recent restore attempts have not been successful.	Medium value of 50%	High value of 100	50
Loss of data due to fire Backups are done regularly but stored in the server room.	Low value of 10%	High value of 100	10
Malware infection Antivirus software is currently installed on all systems.	Low value of 10%	Low value of 10	1

The attacks on DMZ servers are a threat because these servers are updated only once every 6 months. These updates are intended to fix bugs and vulnerabilities that have been discovered since the software was released. If the bugs aren't fixed, the servers are vulnerable. Many attackers look for servers that do not have recent patches installed, giving this risk a high likelihood.

In this case, the solution is simple. A countermeasure would be implemented to ensure that the servers are up to date. Several ways are available to do this, but, if a risk assessment recommended a specific countermeasure and it was approved, it should be used.

Similarly, Table 11-3 indicates holes in the backup procedures. First, backups aren't reliable. Their unreliability could be because there is no backup plan or no backup procedures, or test restores are never done to test the backups. A common countermeasure to establish the reliability of backups is to develop a backup plan and backup procedures. The plan could include a requirement to perform test restores on a weekly basis.

Test Restores as Part of a Backup Plan

A common management saying is that what can't be measured can't be managed, and this includes the effectiveness of backups. However, it is relatively easy to measure the effectiveness of backups by regularly performing test restores and tracking the success rate.

Test restores are frequently mandated as part of a backup plan. A test restore simply retrieves a backup media and attempts to restore data from it. If the data can be restored, the test was successful. If the data cannot be restored, the test was not successful. An unsuccessful test should be investigated.

A test may be unsuccessful due to many reasons:

- **The medium could be old or corrupt**—The length of time media are kept in rotation should be reevaluated, or higher-quality tapes should be purchased.
- **The medium could be faulty**—The problem needs to be fixed as soon as possible. If the drive is faulty, all the backups are suspect.
- **The backup procedures could be faulty**—The procedures should be reviewed and corrected. If the procedures are incorrect, all the backups could have problems.

Whatever the problem, the good news is that a test restore discovers it before a crisis. If actual data were lost and couldn't be restored, the problem would be much more serious.

Companies that measure backups often strive for a success rate of over 95%. Companies that don't measure the effectiveness of their backups could have a success rate anywhere from 0% to 100%. They just don't know until data is lost whether the data can be restored.

The threat scores aren't necessarily perfect. They do take a little human interaction to ensure that the organization's needs are met. For example, the threat of "loss of data due to a fire" has a score of 10. Just because this score is less than the two scores of 50 doesn't mean it can't be addressed earlier.

Management may decide that, even though the score is low, the impact is sufficiently high that it needs to be addressed as soon as possible. The countermeasure for this threat is simple. Store a copy of backup media off-site.

Verifying Risk Elements and How They Can Be Mitigated

When converting the risk assessment into a risk mitigation plan, the risk elements may need to be verified because the risk assessment is a point-in-time assessment and the threats and vulnerabilities may have changed. Additionally, the approved countermeasure needs to be verified to ensure it can still mitigate the current risk.

The same steps used in the risk assessment can be used to verify the risk elements. For example, the risk assessment may have used a vulnerability scanner that discovered an SQL injection vulnerability, and a penetration test could have been used to verify that the vulnerability could be exploited.

Then, 3 months pass before the risk assessment is approved. The same vulnerability scan could then be performed to see whether the vulnerability remained. If the vulnerability still exists, the penetration test could be rerun. If the vulnerability can be exploited, then the risk remains.

However, in this example, application and database developers may have taken immediate steps to resolve the problem. Many simple programming techniques can mitigate this risk. A common reason application developers omit them is because the developers are unaware of the risks. Based on this scenario, reevaluating the risk and the solution would be worthwhile. The application developers can be interviewed to determine what they did to resolve the vulnerability, and then the solution can be evaluated to determine its effectiveness.

The IT administrator may even decide to recommend this solution as a countermeasure. They would write a policy to ensure that all code that is vulnerable to SQL injection attackers use this countermeasure and that all applications be tested for SQL injection vulnerability before being released.

Perhaps the original solution was to purchase a product. However, if the risk is no longer present, money shouldn't be spent on the countermeasure.

Performing a Cost-Benefit Analysis on the Identified Risk Elements

A **cost-benefit analysis (CBA)** helps determine whether a countermeasure should be used. If the benefits of a countermeasure are more than the costs, the countermeasure provides benefits, whereas, if the benefits of the countermeasure are less than the cost of the countermeasure, the countermeasure does not provide benefits.

If two possible countermeasures that will mitigate the same risk are available, two CBAs can be completed to determine which one provides the better benefits. That countermeasure can then be implemented.

> **NOTE**
>
> If the turnaround between approval of the risk assessment and the start of the mitigation plan is quick, this step is less important. The risk assessment would have identified the risk elements and recommended steps to mitigate them. Management then approves these steps.

Calculating the CBA

When performing a CBA, the starting point is to identify the losses that are expected without the countermeasure in place and the losses that are expected after the countermeasure has been implemented. This calculation determines the projected benefits. The formula is:

Loss before countermeasure − Loss after countermeasure = Projected benefits

Next, the cost of the countermeasure is identified. The formula is:

Projected benefits − Cost of countermeasure = Countermeasure value

If the result is a positive value, the countermeasure provides cost benefits, whereas, if the cost of the countermeasure is more than the benefits, the countermeasure doesn't provide cost benefits. If the values are close to each other, the return on investment (ROI) can be calculated. An ROI calculates the countermeasure's value over its lifetime.

> **TIP**
>
> One way to prevent SQL injection attacks is to use stored procedures to validate input. A stored procedure is a type of script or mini program used within a database application. Instead of using data entered by users directly, data is passed to a stored procedure. The stored procedure validates the data before using it. The stored procedure rejects invalid data commonly used in an SQL injection attack.

The most important part of this process is identifying the costs and benefits. The goal is to identify both tangible and intangible values. If the costs and benefits are not accurately identified, the CBA loses its value and may need to be redone.

A significant amount of time might be needed to complete an accurate CBA. Because of this time requirement, a CBA would not be performed on every possible recommended countermeasure. For example, if a skilled administrator can write a script to mitigate a risk, the countermeasure has almost zero cost. Therefore, performing a CBA wouldn't be necessary. On the other hand, a failover cluster can be very expensive because servers must be added, which can require added facility costs to accommodate them.

A CBA Report

CBA reports can be presented in any number of formats. However, creating the CBAs consistently, especially within the same project, is valuable. For example, two CBAs may need to be created for two countermeasures that will mitigate the same risk. The managers don't want to purchase both countermeasures, so they determine which countermeasure will provide the greater benefit. If both CBAs are completed using the same methods and format, comparing the two and choosing the more valuable control is easier.

The following elements are commonly included in any CBA report for a countermeasure:

- **Recommended countermeasure**—The countermeasure is identified in as much detail as possible. For example, a risk assessment recommends a failover cluster. Details on the cluster might include the cost of the two matched servers and other failover cluster hardware and the cost of administrator training or the cost to outsource the installation of the failover cluster.
- **Risk to be mitigated**—Details of the threat/vulnerability pair that results in the risk are provided. The likelihood and impact of the threat is included if a threat matrix method was used to prioritize the risk. If the countermeasure is eliminating a vulnerability, an overview of how it does so is included. If the countermeasure is reducing a vulnerability, an estimate of the success is included. For example, if the countermeasure is expected to reduce incidents from 10 a year to 1 a year, that would be stated here.

> **NOTE**
> A quantitative risk assessment includes an estimate of the annual loss expectancy (ALE) due to a risk. The ALE can be used as the "loss before countermeasure."

- **Annual projected benefits**—Direct and indirect benefits are calculated as an annual monetary value. The benefits are determined by calculating losses with and without the control. For example, currently, a 25% chance of a service failing once a year exists. When it fails, it results in a loss of $20,000. A countermeasure can reduce this risk to zero. The loss without the countermeasure is $20,000 × .25, or $5,000, and the loss with the countermeasure is zero, which indicates that the projected benefits are $5,000 annually.
- **Initial costs**—The initial costs, which would include the purchase price and any indirect costs to implement the countermeasure, are stated here. Indirect costs include training and the cost to modify the environment, which may include adding power capability, upgrading air-conditioning, or improving physical access countermeasures.
- **Annual or recurring costs**—Some countermeasures require ongoing costs to maintain them. For example, a proxy server could be used to block access to gambling sites. Manually identifying all the gambling sites and entering them into the proxy server is very time

consuming. However, content filter companies maintain lists of sites in many categories, such as gambling sites. Instead of entering this information manually, organizations pay for the subscription services as an ongoing cost.

- **A comparison of the costs and benefits**—This is the primary purpose of the report. If the costs are less than the benefits, the countermeasure provides a benefit, whereas, if the costs are greater than the benefits, then the costs do not provide a benefit. If the results are close, an ROI can be calculated.
- **Recommendation**—The countermeasure is recommended only if it provides a benefit.

Implementing a Risk Mitigation Plan

The next step is to implement the risk mitigation plan, which is when the countermeasures are put into place. The two primary goals when implementing a risk mitigation plan are:

- Staying within budget
- Staying on schedule

Any project will have unknowns and surprises, and this is especially true for complex countermeasures. However, advance planning will reduce these unknowns to a minimum. Without adequate planning, the project may go overbudget or be frequently delayed.

Either problem could cause management to change its mind on the value of the countermeasure. If it costs too much or takes too long to implement, management will question the value of the countermeasure.

Staying Within Budget

In the example of the addition of the web farm and failover cluster presented earlier in the chapter, after they are implemented, they will decrease outages and increase availability of the website. These are examples of complex countermeasures.

If all the costs to implement the plan have been identified, the project will go smoothly, but, if some of the costs were not identified, the project will have problems. These problems could appear in any of the following areas:

- **Initial purchase costs**—The equipment is expensive, and servers used in a failover cluster have specific technical requirements. If someone decides to cut costs and buy cheaper servers at the expense of the failover cluster requirements, additional problems may be encountered. Extensive testing may be necessary to ultimately determine whether the cheaper servers would be reliable in the failover cluster. Worse, the cheaper servers might not work in a failover cluster, and more servers would need to be purchased.
- **Facility costs**—The new servers may not fit in the existing equipment bays, which would require facility costs to accommodate them. As well, the addition of the servers may overload the power fed to the room and cause circuit breakers to pop, which could result in outages for other servers. The air-conditioning may be inadequate to sufficiently cool the room, which could overheat and result in equipment damage to existing servers. Any of these problems could be substantial if they were not addressed earlier.

- **Installation costs**—If the in-house personnel don't have the expertise to install the countermeasure, additional expenses will be incurred for a professional installation, and the project will be delayed. In-house technicians, without the necessary expertise, trying to but failing to do the install and configuration will expend valuable labor hours, and, worse, their efforts may actually damage the countermeasure.
- **Training costs**—If technicians don't know how to operate the countermeasure, it may just sit in the corner gathering dust. Yes, it is a fancy new server that can do great and wonderful things. But, if no one knows how to use it, it may stay in the box or be powered down after technicians install it, and a delay in implementation will occur until personnel receive adequate training.

Any of these additional costs could easily bust the budget. If the cost of the countermeasure exceeds the allocated budget, management could decide to pull the plug on the countermeasure. Moreover, each time an additional cost is identified, the CBA needs to be reevaluated because the original decision to implement the countermeasure was based on the original costs. As the costs go up, the value of the countermeasure goes down.

Staying on Schedule

An important consideration for any project is the schedule. Tasks should be planned to ensure they occur in a specific order, which means that, if any task is delayed, other tasks may also be delayed, and these delays may affect the actual implementation date.

One of the tools that can be used for staying on schedule is a milestone chart. **FIGURE 11-5** shows a sample milestone chart for the web server upgrade discussed in this chapter. Project managers typically use project management software that automates the creation of these charts.

When using project management software, the milestone dates and the length of any specific tasks can be entered. The software then allows for the displaying of the data in multiple formats.

For example, **FIGURE 11-6** shows the same project in a Gantt chart format. Once the data have been entered into the project management software, showing the data in an alternate format is relatively easy. Often, changing the format requires only a few clicks of the mouse.

Some tasks are dependent on each other. For example, new equipment bays need to be installed before power can be run to the bays, and the timing of the training is important. If training is provided too early, it won't be fresh when the technicians need to install the equipment, whereas, if it's provided too late, they may need to install the equipment without the training or the project schedule could slip.

A critical path chart shows dependencies, as shown in **FIGURE 11-7**. If any of the items in the critical path slip, the entire project will be delayed. Managers must pay close attention to critical path items to ensure the project stays on schedule.

For example, milestones 2 and 5 are not on the critical path. The purchase of the servers and hardware and the addition of air-conditioning to the room can be delayed. Of course, they can't be delayed indefinitely. When it's time to install and configure the servers, these milestones must be met. However, managers can give milestones 2 and 5 less attention early in the project as they focus on critical path milestones.

FIGURE 11-5
Milestone plan chart.

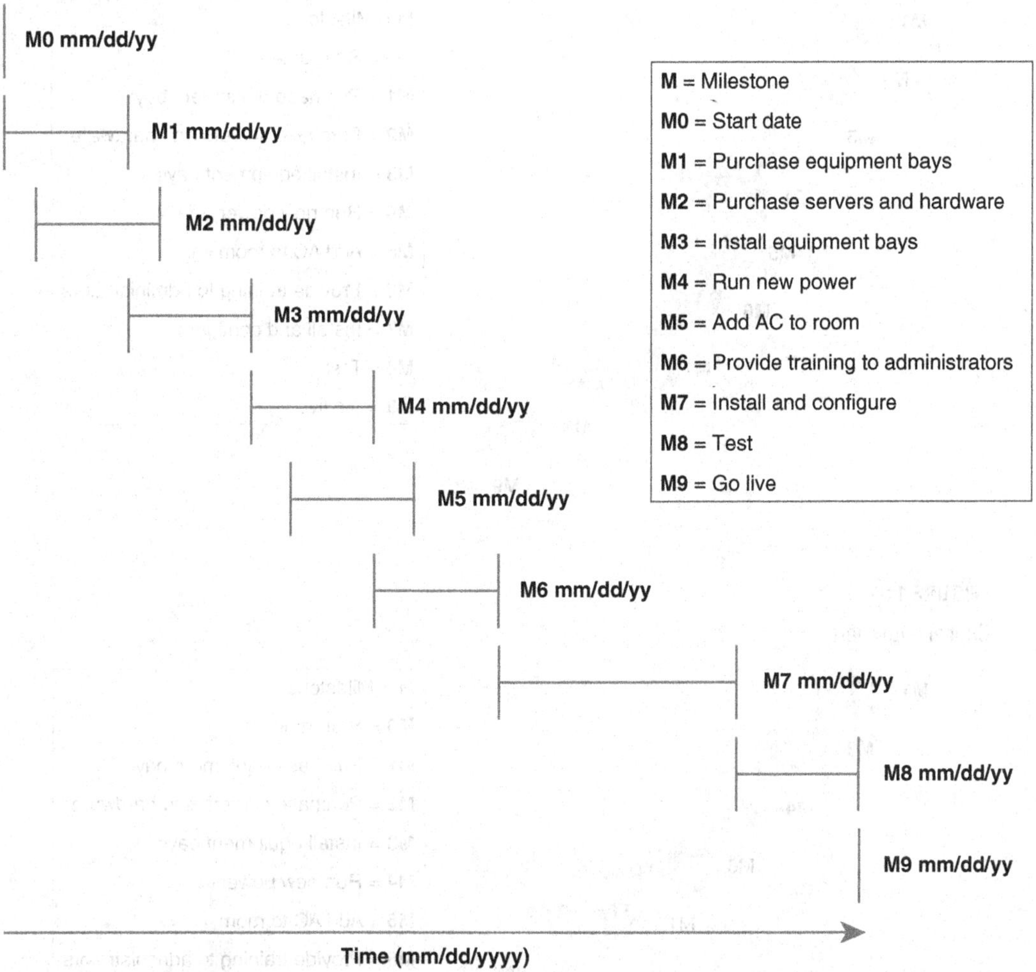

The tools used aren't as important as realizing that they are available. For simple projects, the schedule may simply be sketched out on a napkin, but larger projects would benefit from the more sophisticated project management tools that are available.

Following Up on the Risk Mitigation Plan

An important part of management is follow-up to ensure that plans are implemented as expected, and the risk management plan is no exception. When following up on risk mitigation plans, the following two elements should be included:

- Ensuring countermeasures have been implemented
- Ensuring security gaps have been closed

FIGURE 11-6

Gantt chart.

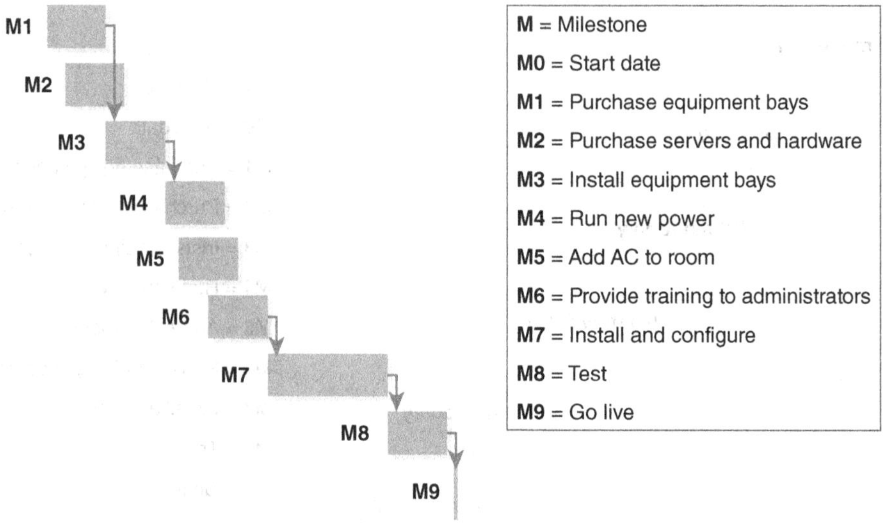

FIGURE 11-7

Critical path chart.

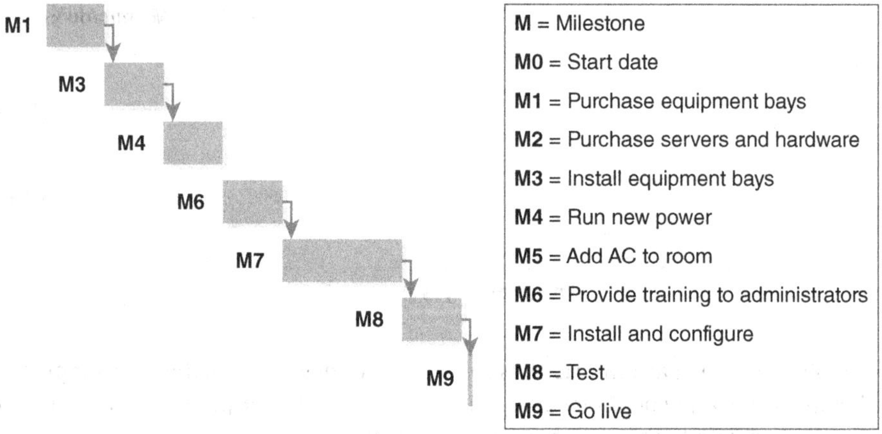

Ensuring Countermeasures Have Been Implemented

The primary tool used to ensure countermeasures are implemented is the POAM. The POAM is created with the risk assessment, but it is a living document because managers update it regularly. As the risk assessment transforms into a risk mitigation plan, the POAM document expands.

The POAM includes all the approved countermeasures and their timelines. A simple countermeasure may have only one or two milestones, whereas a complex countermeasure could have multiple milestones. If the milestones are met as expected, chances are better of ensuring the schedule is met. In other words, focusing on the final date is not as important as focusing on the milestone dates.

If a single milestone is missed, the entire project may be delayed. As mentioned previously, the critical path chart is invaluable in determining which milestones must be met to ensure the project stays on schedule.

When project management software is used, a quick glance at the display will often show whether the implementation of a countermeasure is on schedule. Project management software uses color-coded status symbols. For example, a green circle could indicate the project is on schedule; a yellow circle, the project is slightly delayed; and a red circle, a severe delay. Many project managers use lingo in reports indicating that a project is "in the green" or "in the red." "In the green" indicates it is on schedule, and "in the red" indicates it is severely delayed, which often alerts senior management.

NOTE

A separate POAM can be created exclusively for the risk mitigation plan. For example, the POAM in the risk assessment may require the creation of a risk mitigation plan by a specific date. Regardless of what is used to track the plan's progress, the point is that it must be tracked.

Ensuring Security Gaps Have Been Closed

Countermeasures must be checked to be sure they are working as expected. Because the purpose of a countermeasure is to mitigate a risk, it should either reduce the impact of a threat or reduce a vulnerability.

The same is true of any product; it should work as expected. Watching an infomercial may convince people that an advertised product will help them lose weight, make them rich, or improve their health. However, when they receive it and it doesn't perform up to their expectations, they realize they wasted their money.

Similarly, not all countermeasures perform as expected. The only way their performance will be discovered is to test and evaluate them, and some countermeasures are easier to evaluate than others. For example, a vulnerability scanner has detected a vulnerability, and the risk assessment recommends a countermeasure to eliminate the vulnerability. After the countermeasure has been implemented, the same vulnerability scan is run. If the scan doesn't detect the risk, then clearly the countermeasure has closed the security gap. However, if the scan still detects the risk, then clearly the security gap remains open, and additional steps will need to be taken. The risk assessment doesn't necessarily have to be redone from the beginning, but the gap should be addressed.

In the web farm and failover cluster example, the goal was to eliminate outages and increase availability. An outage will show that the solution isn't working. However, an outage will cost money in lost revenue. Instead of waiting for an outage, testing can be performed to measure the countermeasure's performance. Some tests and measurements that can be used are:

- **Measuring the load on the web farm**—During normal operation, the load should be balanced among servers and can be measured using load-balancing software. The resources on each individual server can also be measured. If the servers have similar hardware, the processor, memory, network card, and disk usage of each server should be about equal.

- **Removing a server from the web farm**—Removing a server simulates the failure of a server in the web farm and should not affect the entire farm. In other words, if a server is removed from the web farm, the other servers should pick up the load. Additionally, new clients should not be referred to the nonexistent server.
- **Adding a server to the web farm**—If the website experiences more growth, it should be able to handle another web server being added to the web farm, which allows the web farm to scale out. The network load balancing software should then balance the load with the new server. Therefore, additional clients can be added to the web service without changing the actual service.
- **Transferring nodes on the failover cluster logically**—Failover clusters include software that can logically swap nodes. For example, it can be used to logically switch node 2 from inactive to active and node 1 from active to inactive. If this switch fails during testing, it doesn't cause an outage, but it does indicate the cluster will not prevent an outage during an actual failure.
- **Shutting down the active node on the failover cluster**—If logical transfers work, an actual failure of the active node can be simulated. Failover clusters usually identify a specific procedure used to simulate a failure. The inactive node should sense the failure and take over as the active node. If the test fails, the system can quickly be switched back with minimal impact on the operations. This type of failover testing can affect the service provided by the failover cluster. Therefore, testing should be done during a slow period and with much forethought and planning. One of the primary considerations is the ability to return the system to normal if it fails.

The goal of any testing and evaluation is to ensure that the countermeasure has acceptably closed the security gap. But, if the security gap hasn't been closed, managers need to be informed of the remaining, or residual, risk, and they may decide that the gap has been closed satisfactorily. Managers may also decide that an additional countermeasure needs to be identified to further mitigate the risk.

Best Practices for Enabling a Risk Mitigation Plan from the Risk Assessment

The following list identifies several best practices that can be followed when enabling a risk mitigation plan from a risk assessment:

- **Staying within the scope**—The mitigation plan is derived from the risk assessment, which means the scope of the mitigation plan should not go outside the scope of the risk assessment. If the scope isn't managed, then the costs can easily get out of control.
- **Redoing CBAs if new costs are identified**—Completing a cost-benefit analysis for a countermeasure is commonly part of the risk assessment. If additional costs are identified later, then the CBA will need to be redone with the accurate costs.
- **Prioritizing countermeasures**—Countermeasures should be prioritized based on their importance. A common way to identify the priority of countermeasures is to score them

with a threat likelihood/impact matrix; the high-priority countermeasures should be implemented first.

- **Including current countermeasures in analysis**—When scoring countermeasures, the current countermeasures must be considered. For example, a threat may have a high impact, but an in-place countermeasure has reduced it to a low impact. When evaluating a threat, the in-place countermeasure should be considered and a low impact assigned to the threat.
- **Controlling costs**—Costs should stay within the allocated budget. Any change in the costs can affect the CBA. If additional costs are too high, the value of the countermeasure may be significantly reduced.
- **Controlling the schedule**—Costs frequently go up when the schedule is delayed, and the longer the implementation is delayed, the longer the organization remains at risk.
- **Following up**—Approved countermeasures should be checked to be sure they have been implemented and that they have mitigated the risk as expected.

> **TIP**
>
> Nodes can regularly be swapped during the lifetime of a failover cluster. A common reason to do so is for maintenance. For example, node 2 can be updated while node 1 is active. Later, node 2 can be brought online and activated, which will allow node 1 to be taken down to update it.

CHAPTER SUMMARY

This chapter covered many of the details that should be considered when turning a risk assessment into a risk mitigation plan. The starting point is to thoroughly review the countermeasures, a process that often includes matching threats with vulnerabilities and identifying all the costs associated with them, including any hidden costs. If the costs change, the cost-benefit analysis may need to be redone.

If much time has passed since the risk assessment was approved, the existence of the risk elements and the effectiveness of the countermeasures in mitigating the risks must be verified. Two key goals while executing the plan are to stay within budget and on schedule. Last, a follow-up should be done to ensure that the approved countermeasures are implemented and that they actually mitigate the risks as expected.

KEY CONCEPTS AND TERMS

account management policy
cost-benefit analysis (CBA)
implicit deny
network load balancing
password policy
scale out
scale up
uninterruptible power supply (UPS)
web farm

CHAPTER 11 ASSESSMENT

1. A(n) ________ countermeasure is one that has been approved and has a date for implementation.
2. A single risk can be mitigated by more than one countermeasure.
   A. True
   B. False
3. The formula for risk is Risk = ________.
4. What would an account management policy include?
   A. Details on how to create accounts
   B. Details on when accounts should be disabled
   C. Password policy
   D. A and B only
   E. A, B, and C
5. What could a password policy include?
   A. Length of password
   B. List of required passwords
   C. User profiles
   D. All of the above
6. The ________ plan will include details on how and when to implement approved countermeasures.
7. A countermeasure is being reviewed to be added to the mitigation plan. What costs should be considered?
   A. Initial purchase costs
   B. Facility costs
   C. Installation costs
   D. Training costs
   E. All of the above
8. Which of the following items are considered facility costs for the implementation of a countermeasure?
   A. Installation and air-conditioning
   B. Installation and training
   C. Power and air-conditioning
   D. Power and training
9. What's a reasonable amount of time for an account management policy to be completed and approved?
   A. Twenty minutes
   B. One day
   C. One month
   D. One year
10. What can be used to determine the priority of countermeasures?
    A. Cost-benefit analysis
    B. Threat likelihood/impact matrix
    C. Disaster recovery plan
    D. Best guess method
11. A risk assessment was completed 3 months ago and has recently been approved. What should be done first to implement a mitigation plan?
    A. Verify risk elements
    B. Purchase countermeasures
    C. Redo risk assessment
    D. Redo the CBA
12. Two possible countermeasures are being evaluated to mitigate a risk, but management wants to purchase only one. What can be used to determine which countermeasure provides the better cost benefits?
    A. Threat likelihood/impact matrix
    B. Threat score
    C. CBA
    D. CIA
13. A cost-benefit analysis is being performed to determine whether a countermeasure should be used. Which of the following formulas should be applied?
    A. Loss before countermeasure – Loss after countermeasure
    B. Loss after countermeasure – Loss before countermeasure
    C. Projected benefits – Cost of countermeasure
    D. Cost of countermeasure – Projected benefits
14. Of the following items, what one(s) should be included in a cost-benefit analysis report?
    A. Recommended countermeasure
    B. Risk to be mitigated
    C. Costs
    D. Annual projected benefits
    E. A and C only
    F. A, B, C, and D
15. NIST 800-63 provides guidance on risk management strategies and policies.
    A. True
    B. False

PART THREE

Risk Mitigation Plans

CHAPTER 12 Mitigating Risk With a Business Impact Analysis 311

CHAPTER 13 Mitigating Risk With a Business Continuity Plan 335

CHAPTER 14 Mitigating Risk With a Disaster Recovery Plan 361

CHAPTER 15 Mitigating Risk With a Computer Incident Response Team Plan 389

CHAPTER 12

Mitigating Risk With a Business Impact Analysis

AN IMPORTANT PART of a business continuity plan (BCP) is a business impact analysis (BIA). The business impact analysis is a combination of collecting data and analyzing in order to rank the importance of various systems and subsystems.

After the data has been collected, it can be analyzed to identify the critical functions and resources, after which acceptable outage times can be determined. The maximum acceptable outage (MAO) for a resource drives the recovery objectives, the two primary ones being recovery time objectives (RTOs) and recovery point objectives (RPOs).

Chapter 12 Topics

This chapter covers the following topics and concepts:

- What a business impact analysis is
- What the scope of a business impact analysis is
- What the objectives of a business impact analysis are
- What the steps of a business impact analysis are
- What mission-critical business functions and processes are
- How business functions and processes map to information technology (IT) systems
- What best practices for performing a business impact analysis are

Chapter 12 Goals

When you complete this chapter, you will be able to:

- Define a business impact analysis
- Identify the scope for a business impact analysis
- Identify objectives for a business impact analysis
- Identify mission-critical business functions and processes
- Map business functions and processes to IT systems
- List best practices for performing a business impact analysis

What Is a Business Impact Analysis?

A **business impact analysis (BIA)** is a study used to identify the impact that can result from disruptions in the business. It focuses on the failure of one or more critical information technology (IT) functions.

> **TIP**
>
> The BIA includes systems critical to the company's survivability. However, lesser systems can also be included. In other words, a company may have significant problems if email capabilities are lost for a week, but the company wouldn't necessarily fail. Still, email may be considered important enough to include in a BIA.

Another way of thinking of a BIA is that it helps with identifying the systems critical to the survival of an organization. As a reminder, survivability is the ability of a company to survive loss due to a risk. Some losses are so severe that they can cause the business to fail if they aren't managed.

A basic understanding of the following terms is necessary when working with BIAs:

- **Maximum acceptable outage**—The **maximum acceptable outage (MAO)** identifies the maximum acceptable downtime for a system. If an outage exceeds the MAO time, it negatively affects the organization's mission. The MAO directly affects the recovery time.
- **Critical business functions**—**Critical business functions (CBFs)** include those considered vital to an organization. If a CBF fails, the organization will lose the ability to perform essential operations, such as sell products to customers. If the organization cannot perform the function, it will lose money.
- **Critical success factors**—**Critical success factors (CSFs)** include elements necessary to perform the mission of an organization. An organization will have a few elements that must succeed for the organization to succeed. For example, a reliable network infrastructure may be considered a CSF for many companies today. If the network infrastructure fails, all other business functions may stop.

The BIA isn't intended to include all IT functions, only the critical IT systems and components, which are identified by identifying the CBFs. Systems and components that support CBFs are critical.

> **TIP**
>
> A *stakeholder* is any individual or group that has a stake or interest in the success of a project. Stakeholders include executives and managers who have a stake in the success of their department or division, meaning they want to ensure success in their area of responsibility.

What makes a business function critical? Any stakeholder can determine that a business function is critical. If the stakeholder determines that the loss of the function will cause an unacceptable loss, it is a critical function. The stakeholder makes this decision based on experience and opinion, and it is not made lightly. Once the function has been designated as critical, the stakeholder needs to dedicate resources (money and personnel) to protect it.

Additionally, a law can dictate that a function be considered critical. For example, the Health Insurance Portability and Accountability Act (HIPAA) mandates the protection of health-related information. Access controls and other protection measures are critical components required to maintain HIPAA compliance.

The BIA is largely a data-gathering process. Input is received from stakeholders, users, process owners, and others in the organization. Data can be gathered from interviews, questionnaires, and surveys or by reviewing available reports; any method that provides information on the target system can be used.

The BIA doesn't provide solutions but rather is part of a larger business continuity plan (BCP) and provides input into the BCP, whereas the BCP does include solutions. For example, the BCP may provide recommendations for controls to reduce the impact of an outage.

Comparing a BIA against a risk assessment is helpful in understanding the purpose of a BIA. A risk assessment looks at threats and vulnerabilities. When a threat exploits a vulnerability to harm an asset, a risk occurs, and the primary goal of a risk assessment is to reduce the risk by reducing or eliminating the vulnerability or reducing the impact of the threat and its harm on the asset.

On the other hand, a BIA doesn't address threats or vulnerabilities like the risk assessment does. Instead, it looks at the effect of an outage. Although the focus of a BIA is primarily on business continuity, a BIA can also be used in a risk assessment. In other words, if the goal is to determine what systems need to be evaluated with a risk assessment, a BIA can be considered for identifying and prioritizing the critical systems.

Similarly, if a risk assessment has already been completed, that data can be used to help in creating the BIA. One of the first steps in doing a risk assessment is to identify assets, which can help in identifying the assets that are important to the organization.

Collecting Data

Several methods are available for gathering the data in the BIA data-gathering process. One of these methods is to conduct interviews with key personnel. To improve the quality of the data gathered from these interviews, they should be planned, such as ensuring that the people to be interviewed have the time to answer the questions and that the right questions have been prepared. These questions should focus on CBFs and the MAO of supporting resources.

Another method is to use either paper- or computer-based questionnaires, forms, or surveys that are limited and focused; in other words, focused on only one process at a time. For example, a SharePoint website could be used to gather and compile the data. If the form is too long, people may not have the time needed to answer it, whereas a shorter form can elicit more usable information.

Another method of collecting input is to host meetings or conference calls. A benefit of this format is that people can interact with each other, which can provide richer results. However, gaining consensus may be difficult, which is especially true in trying to identify the priority of different systems.

Seven Steps of Contingency Planning

The National Institute of Standards and Technology (NIST) published Special Publication (SP) 800-34 Rev. 1, Contingency Planning Guide for Federal Information Systems. Contingency planning helps an organization identify measures to recover services after an emergency or disaster. SP 800-34 Rev. 1 includes information on BIAs. Even though SP 800-34 Rev. 1 is focused on federal information systems, it can also be used for private companies.

SP 800-34 Rev. 1 identifies seven steps to contingency planning. The seven steps are:

1. Developing the contingency planning policy statement
2. Conducting the business impact analysis

3. Identifying preventive controls
4. Creating contingency strategies
5. Developing an information system contingency plan
6. Ensuring plan testing, training, and exercises
7. Ensuring plan maintenance

As can be seen from the second step, the BIA drives much of contingency planning. Contingencies need to be planned only for systems that the BIA identifies as critical.

Varying Data Collection Methods

Various data collection methods can be used. For example, because some people may have a lot of information, an interview may be appropriate. But just because one person is interviewed does not mean everyone should be interviewed.

If people are already weighed down with a large number of meetings, they may resent another meeting for a BIA. On the other hand, they may welcome the opportunity to fill out an online form at their leisure.

Defining the Scope of the Business Impact Analysis

As with any project, defining the scope, or the boundaries, of a BIA early in the process is important. Defining the scope helps ensure that the BIA is focused and that the correct functions are analyzed.

The scope is affected by the size of the organization. For a small organization, the scope of the BIA could include the entire organization. For larger organizations, the scope may include only certain areas. For example, one BIA may include only the online sales division of a large business, and other BIAs would examine other areas of the business.

FIGURE 12-1 shows an online web server with a back-end database used for e-commerce. The BIA could focus only on the critical functions needed to support this web server. Based

FIGURE 12-1

Online web server with back-end database.

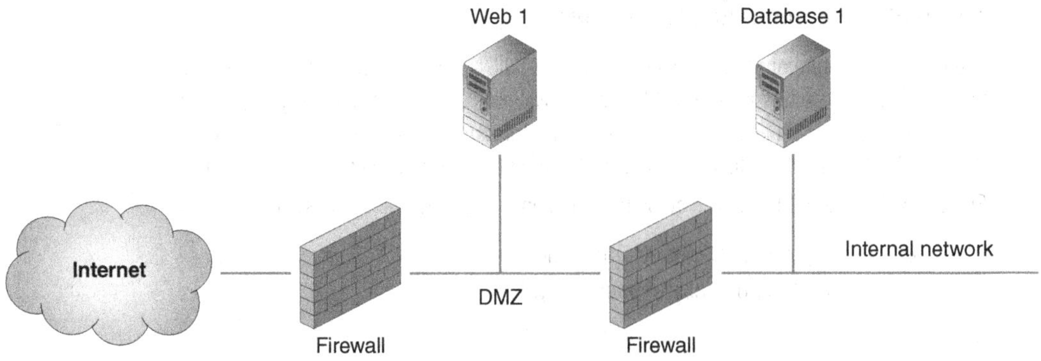

FIGURE 12-2
Product shipment phase.

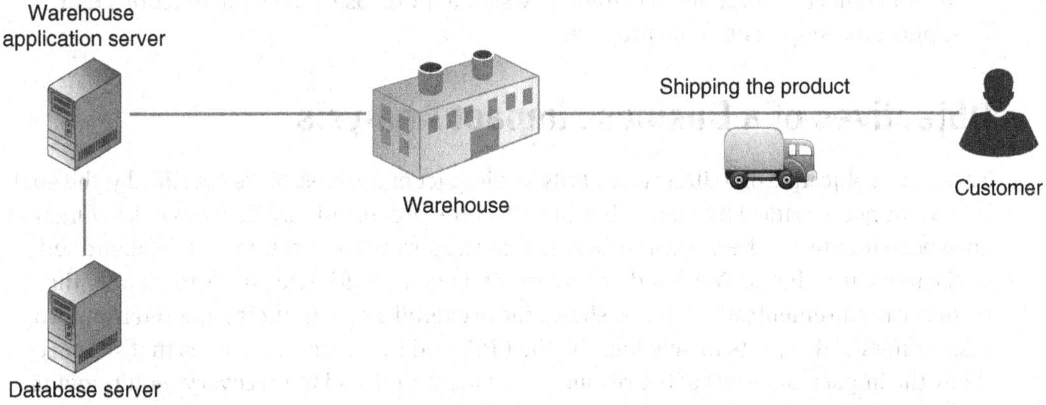

on the figure, the systems needed to support online sales are the web server, the firewalls, and the database server, representing the phase when a customer purchases a product. It doesn't include other phases, such as the shipment of the product, which is shown in **FIGURE 12-2**. The functions needed for these two phases are distinctly different and so is the MAO of each. The MAO for the website is much shorter than the MAO for the shipping function.

> **TIP**
>
> The budget should also be considered when identifying the scope. If the organization is large enough, a security consultant can be hired to assist with the BIA, whereas, if the budget is limited, hiring a security consultant may not be possible.

For example, if the website is down at the time a customer is ready to purchase a product, then the sale is lost, regardless of how long it was down. Similarly, if a point-of-sale system is down and a customer can pay with only a credit or debit card, then the sale is lost.

On the other hand, if an outage occurs at the shipping end, its impact isn't immediate. Even if it lasted a full day, it might result in only a slight delay in a shipment, which isn't critical.

Just because the impact of an outage is not critical in the shipping phase doesn't mean it shouldn't be included in the BIA. Instead, the point is that the scope should be specifically identified. Here is an example of a vague scope statement:

> The scope of the BIA will cover the functions of the website.

One person conducting a BIA may interpret this scope to mean only the purchase phase. If the intent of the BIA is to include both the purchase and shipment phases, the BIA would then be incomplete. Another person may interpret it to mean both the purchase and shipment phases. If the intent is to have the BIA cover only the purchase phase, money would be wasted doing both.

The following scope statement is clearer:

> The scope of the BIA will cover the functions of the website during the customer purchase phase, which includes all the functions that support a customer's visit and purchase. The shipment phase is not included in this BIA.

If the shipment phase is to be included, the scope statement could be modified as follows:

> The scope of the BIA will cover all functions of the online website, which includes all the functions that support a customer's visit and purchase and all the functions that support the shipment of the product.

Objectives of a Business Impact Analysis

The overall objective of a BIA is to identify the impact of outages. More specifically, the goal is to identify the critical functions that can affect the organization. After the critical functions have been identified, the critical resources that support these functions can be identified.

Each resource has an MAO and an impact if it fails. The ultimate goal is to identify the recovery requirements. **FIGURE 12-3** shows these overall steps: Input is gathered from process owners and experts to help identify the CBFs and the critical resources that support them, the impact and MAO of the resources are identified, and the recovery requirements from the MAO are determined.

An indirect objective of the BIA is to justify funding. After the recovery requirements in the BIA have been identified, controls to support these requirements in the BCP are identified. If the impact is high, spending money to prevent the outage would be cost effective.

NIST SP 800-34 Rev. 1 includes a diagram similar to that in **FIGURE 12-4**. It shows the relationship between costs and the time of an outage. The line labeled Cost of Disruption indicates that the cost of a disruption is very low immediately after an outage occurs. However, as the outage time increases, the cost of the disruption also increases. The other line identifies the Cost to Recover from an outage. To be able to recover from an outage almost immediately, the costs are high. However, if a longer outage time is acceptable, the costs to recover are lower.

FIGURE 12-3
Objectives of a BIA.

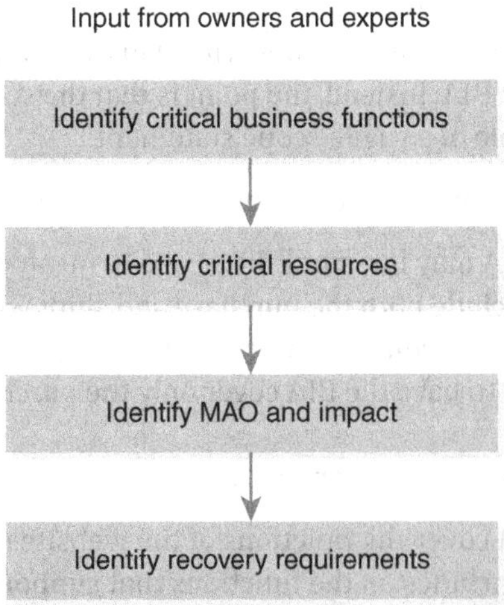

FIGURE 12-4

Relationship of costs.

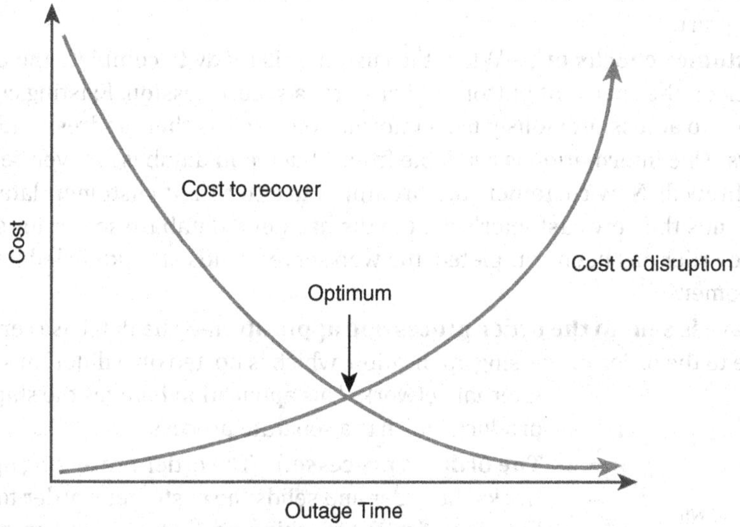

For example, if a website that sells products online fails for 60 seconds, the cost of the disruption would be very low, whereas, if the outage lasts for days, the cost of the disruption would be very high. Controls can be implemented that allow the website to recover immediately from a 60-second outage, but the cost would be very high. In contrast, spending very little money on recovery controls would result in a longer outage time.

These considerations help to identify the optimum cost point. At this point, the company would spend the minimum amount on recovery controls while still minimizing the costs of disruption.

The following sections cover the objectives of a BIA in more detail.

Identifying Critical Business Functions

To an IT specialist, the CBFs are not always apparent. For example, a security expert may not know the CBFs of a website. To the security expert, the web server would be an obvious component, but there are others.

Interviewing or surveying the experts can help in gaining insight into all the components that support the web server, and identifying the underlying steps of CBFs is often useful. For example, the following list details the steps of an online website purchase:

1. **The customer visits the website**—The customer accesses the website using a web browser. The website is hosted on a web server located in the organization's demilitarized zone (DMZ), and a firewall provides security while also providing access to the web server.
2. **The customer browses the product catalog**—The website sends queries to a back-end database when users search for specific products. The database server is on the internal

network behind a second firewall. The web server uses the database query results to build a webpage, which it sends back to the customer.

3. **The customer picks a product**—While browsing, the customer can add products into a shopping cart.
4. **The customer checks out**—When the customer is ready to complete the purchase, they click on the checkout button, which starts a secure session. Existing customers can log on to access previously used information, such as their address and credit card numbers. This information is available from a back-end database server behind the second firewall. New customers are prompted to enter their customer data. The web server sends the new customer's data to the back-end database server for storage. After the order has been completed, the web server sends an acknowledgment email to the customer.
5. **A message is sent to the order processing application**—The database server sends a message to the order processing application, which is hosted on a different server in the internal network. This application handles the shipment of the product, which is a separate process.
6. **The order is processed**—The order processing application tracks the order and sends the customer's order to a warehouse application for shipping. It also accepts status data from the warehouse application. Warehouse personnel ship the order and enter information into the warehouse application. The order processing application sends emails to customers letting them know the status of their orders, which includes when an order ships and follow-up emails for shipment problems, such as delays.

> **TIP**
>
> Identifying CBFs first is a top-down approach followed by identifying the critical IT services and infrastructure that support the CBFs. A bottom-up approach would likely miss important elements; for example, trying to determine what functions a server supports.

In this example, the CBFs are:

- The customer's accessing the website
- The web server's accessing the database server
- The order processing application's tracking the order

With this information, the critical resources can be identified.

Identifying Critical Resources

Critical resources are those that are required to support the CBFs. Once the CBFs have been identified, they can be analyzed to determine the critical resources for each.

The example of the website shows how to identify critical resources from the CBFs. One of the website CBFs is the customer's accessing the website. The following IT resources are required to support this function:

- Internet access
- Web server
- Web application

- Network connectivity
- Firewall on the internet side of the DMZ

The second CBF is the web server's ability to access the database server. The database server hosts both product and customer information. The customer information is used when a customer makes a purchase and to target advertising for the returning customer. The following IT resources are required to support this function:

- Web server
- Web application
- Database server
- Network connectivity
- Firewall on the internal side of the DMZ

NOTE

This isn't the only way the process could be designed. The product database could be hosted on a server in the DMZ so that data could be retrieved more quickly, and the customer database could be hosted separately in the internal network. The DMZ could be designed differently too. Many design possibilities exist, which is why asking the experts is important. They will know how the process is configured.

The third CBF is the order processing application's tracking of the order. It needs to receive orders from the database server and be able to track the order until delivery. The following IT resources are required to support this function:

- Order processing application
- Server hosting the order processing application
- Database server
- Warehouse application
- Network connectivity
- Internet access

Recovery Without a BIA

Imagine the recovery steps after a disaster in an organization that hasn't performed a BIA. What systems should administrators restore first? What CBFs should they restore first? If they don't have any guidance, there probably won't be any order to the recovery.

Administrators will likely be more knowledgeable about some systems and try to start them first. Of course, while they're doing that, managers may redirect them to their pet projects to bring them up first, or executives may redirect them yet again to bring up their favorite systems first. Even though none of these systems may be critical to the survivability of the organization, without a BIA, administrators might still focus on these noncritical systems.

In contrast, a BIA identifies the CBFs and helps everyone within the organization understand what is important to the organization. More specifically, it helps administrators understand which systems they should start first.

Therefore, the time to perform a BIA is before a disaster happens so that employees will know the priorities, which are specified in writing in the BIA. Without documentation, anything can happen, but one thing is certain—cool heads will not prevail during the disaster.

In many instances, the critical resources will overlap. In other words, a critical resource required for one function may also be required for another function. For example, the web server is required for two of the functions, and facility support (e.g., power, heating, and air-conditioning) is required for all of them.

A resource can be listed one time for all the functions or with each function. In the case of IT resources, listing each of the resources with each of the functions is the better idea. For example, all IT resources require facility support. They could be listed one time as follows:

- **Power**—Uninterruptible power supplies and generators are required to ensure systems remain operational during power outages.
- **Heating and air-conditioning**—Heating and air-conditioning are required to ensure that all systems can operate.

Identifying the MAO and Impact

Once the CBFs and IT resources that support them have been identified, the next item to consider is the MAO and impact. The MAO is also referred to as the **maximum tolerable period of disruption (MTPD)**. The MAO helps to determine which CBFs need to be recovered and restarted as soon as possible after a disaster, identifies the specific resources needed to restart the CBF, and helps to determine how soon these systems need to be recovered.

The other consideration in this process is the impact on the business, which is monetary but doesn't need to be expressed as money. Instead, the impact is often expressed as a relative value, such as high, medium, or low, but it can also be expressed as a number, such as 1 through 4.

Once the impact level has been identified, it can be matched with an MAO. **TABLE 12-1** shows an example of how impact value levels can be defined in an organization. Each level is matched to the MAO to identify how long the system can be down before the impact is felt.

TABLE 12-1 Sample Impact Levels

IMPACT VALUE LEVEL	MAXIMUM ACCEPTABLE OUTAGE AND IMPACT
Level 1	2 hours
Business functions must be available during all business hours. Online systems must be available 24 hours a day, 7 days a week.	Any outage will have an almost immediate impact on the business.
Level 2	1 day
Business processes can survive without the business function for a short time.	If the outage lasts more than a day, it will have an impact on the business.
Level 3	3 days
Business processes can survive without the business functions for 1 or more days.	The outage won't have an impact on the business if the outage lasts as long as 3 days.
Level 4	1 week
Business processes can survive without the business functions for extended periods.	The outage won't have a significant impact on the business unless it lasts longer than a week.

When calculating the MAO for an organization, both direct and indirect costs must be considered.

Direct Costs

The direct costs are usually easier to calculate than the indirect costs. Some of these costs are readily apparent, and others are not. The following list shows some of the direct costs:

- **Loss of immediate sales and cash flow**—This is the most obvious loss. During the outage, the company won't be able to sell its products or services, and it loses the normal cash flow from these sales.
- **Equipment replacement costs**—If equipment is damaged, it needs to be repaired or replaced. Depending on the equipment, these costs can be substantial.
- **Building replacement costs**—If a building is lost due to a fire or natural disaster, it needs to be rebuilt or replaced. Although insurance covers most of the costs, it rarely covers all of them, and the organization must make up the difference.
- **Penalty costs for late delivery**—Service level agreements (SLAs) specify expected levels of service and often impose penalties if the service is not met, which should be calculated as direct costs for an outage.
- **Penalty costs for noncompliance issues**—Some laws impose penalty costs for noncompliance. If a failure results in noncompliance with a law, this cost should be included.
- **Costs to re-create or recover data**—Data lost during an outage needs to be re-created or restored. Some data may need to be re-created manually, whereas other data may be recoverable using existing backups. Labor costs may be associated with recovering data.
- **Salaries paid to staff who are idled due to outage**—If an outage prevents normal work, workers will still be on the clock, which means they will still be paid to perform jobs they can't perform.

> **NOTE**
>
> The MAO values are assigned internally by each organization, which means that the values and recovery objectives used by one organization can be completely different from those used by another organization.

Loss of Share Value After a Disaster

If an organization is a publicly traded company, the share price should also be considered. Millions of investor dollars can be lost in a short time.

A 2020 article on the website of Capitol Technology University states "Share prices of breached companies hit a low point approximately 14 market days following a breach. Share prices fall 7.27% on average, and underperform the NASDAQ by -4.18%"(https://www.captechu.edu/blog/cybersecurity-breaches-and-their-impact-on-stock-prices).

Organizations that recover decisively also see their stocks recover. Within 100 days, these stocks not only regain their price, but often show gains of about 10% to 15%. Organizations that do not recover well often find that their stock rallies about 75 days after the disaster but then settles at about 15% below its before-disaster level.

The organizations that recover are better prepared for the disasters, but their successful recovery doesn't happen by accident: They have talented leaders and comprehensive disaster preparedness plans.

Indirect Costs

Identifying indirect costs is more difficult than identifying direct costs, but they must be identified because their value also affects the impact value. The following list shows some of the indirect costs that need to be considered:

- **Loss of customers**—Customers who can't purchase from the company may purchase from a competitor, and, in doing so, they may find the experience satisfying and never come back. Attracting new customers to replace those lost costs a significant amount of money.
- **Loss of public goodwill**—The outage may cause the organization to look less desirable to the public. For example, if an outage results in the compromise of customers' personally identifiable information, they may begin to distrust the organization, and, if their credit card data is compromised, they may no longer do business with the organization.
- **Costs to regain market share**—When customers and goodwill are lost, the company loses market share, which its competitors gain. Most companies realize that keeping a customer is much easier than attracting a new one.
- **Costs to regain positive brand image**—If the company's brand is tarnished, the company must take steps to repair it. Repairing a tarnished reputation takes a lot of advertising money, and some companies never recover.
- **Loss of credit or higher costs for credit**—When an outage affects a company's cash flow, it can also affect the company's credit rating. A lower credit rating results in higher costs, and, worse, a company may lose its existing credit.
- **Lost opportunities during recovery**—While an organization is dealing with the outage, employees spend their time addressing it. These same employees may have been working on projects to attract new business, which means the new business becomes a lost opportunity.

Identifying Recovery Requirements

The recovery requirements establish the time frame in which systems must be recoverable and identify the data that must be recovered. For example, some data loss might be acceptable, whereas other data loss is not.

Two primary terms related to recovery requirements are **recovery time objective (RTO)** and **recovery point objective (RPO)**. Although the RTO applies to systems or functions, the RPO applies only to data. More specifically, the RPO addresses data housed in databases.

The RTO is the time in which the system or function must be recovered and would be equal to or less than the MAO. For example, if the MAO is 1 hour, the RTO needs to be 1 hour or less.

The RPOs identify the maximum amount of data loss an organization can accept, which is the acceptable data latency. For example, a database may record hundreds of sales transactions a minute. The organization may need to recover this data up to the moment of failure, which would be an expensive process, but, because each transaction represents revenue, the cost is justified. On the other hand, another database may import data only once a week; to ensure nothing is lost, the only data that would need to be restored would be the data that had been added since the last import, which is a much less expensive process.

RTO can also be thought of as time critical and RPO as mission critical. The RTO identifies the time when the system is restored, and the RPO identifies data that is mission critical. Some processes must be restored in a timely manner, which requires a short RTO. Restoration of other processes can be delayed as long as all the data is recovered.

After the MAO has been identified, identifying the recovery time objectives becomes easy. **TABLE 12-2** adds an additional column, the recovery objectives, to Table 12-1 and shows that the recovery objective is directly related to the MAO.

Looking at impact value level 4, the question could be asked: if an organization can do without a function for up to a week, why include it in the BIA at all? This level can be thought of as encompassing minor desirable functions. Although the organization won't fail without them, it would be able to operate with fewer problems with them functional. For example, an organization may not use internet access for mission-critical tasks, but having internet access may make it easier for employees to perform other jobs.

> **TIP**
>
> Although lower RTOs are achievable, they are much more expensive. Therefore, when interviewing stakeholders, connecting the cost with the RTO is important. For example, ensuring that a database is recoverable up to the moment of failure is possible, even after major disasters, such as earthquakes, but would require a separate site, separate servers, and immediate data replication, all of which are expensive. Once stakeholders recognize the costs, they may decide on a different RTO.

TABLE 12-2 Sample Recovery Objectives

IMPACT VALUE LEVEL	MAXIMUM ACCEPTABLE OUTAGE	RECOVERY OBJECTIVE
Level 1	2 hours	2 hours or less
Business functions must be available during all business hours. Online systems must be available 24 hours a day, 7 days a week.	Any outage will have an almost immediate impact on the business.	Functions in this category must be recovered in less than 2 hours.
Level 2	1 day	24 hours or less
Business processes can survive without the business function for a short amount of time.	If the outage lasts more than a day, it will have an impact on the business.	Functions in this category must be recovered within 24 hours.
Level 3	3 days	72 hours or less
Business processes can survive without the business functions for 1 or more days.	The outage won't have an impact on the business if the outage lasts as long as 3 days.	Functions in this category must be recovered within 72 hours.
Level 4	1 week	7 days or less
Business processes can survive without the business functions for extended periods.	The outage won't have a significant impact on the business unless it lasts longer than a week.	Functions in this category must be recovered within 1 week.

Recovering Databases

When determining recovery options for a database, several options are available. Some RPOs require recovering the data up to a moment in time, whereas others require recovering data from only a week ago. It depends on how the data is used and updated.

For example, a database used for online transaction processing (OLTP) records sales. As a back-end database for a busy online web server, every minute of data is important. Databases use transaction logs to record transactions. These transaction logs and regular backups can be used to restore data up to the moment of failure.

Advanced recovery models replicate data from one server to another. The transaction log updates the database on one server and is then copied to the other server. The copied log updates the database on the second server. Even if the primary server becomes corrupt, the second server has all the data since the last copied transaction log. To ensure that no more than 5 minutes of data would be lost, the log to the other server would be copied every 5 minutes.

As another example, a database holds product data and is updated with new data and backed up once a week. If the database becomes corrupt, it can be restored from the week-old backup, which has all the data to date. Even if it were backed up before the import, the data could easily be imported after the database has been restored to recover all the data.

The RPO isn't calculated directly from the MAO. Instead, personnel will need to be interviewed to determine what data loss is acceptable, which would vary in different types of databases. Commonly, acceptable data loss is measured in minutes, such as 15 minutes.

A database used to record sales can't accept much data loss because every minute of data loss represents lost sales revenue. On the other hand, other databases may not change as much, and their changes may be manually reproduced. If there aren't many changes and they can easily be reproduced, more data loss can be accepted. For example, a database is manually updated about five times a week, and the updates have a paper trail that shows what needs to be reproduced. Therefore, data loss of a week could easily be accepted in the database. Because the updates have a paper trail, the database can be restored and the updates reproduced.

Steps of a Business Impact Analysis Process

The majority of the work of a BIA is gathering the data surrounding the CBFs within the scope of the BIA. After the data has been gathered, it is analyzed. The end stage is the publication of the BIA report. Some organizations may want to include recommendations to meet recovery times, but that is not technically part of a BIA. Normally, recommendations for controls come after the BIA.

The overall steps of a BIA are:

1. Identifying the environment
2. Identifying stakeholders
3. Identifying CBFs
4. Identifying critical resources

5. Identifying the MAO
6. Identifying recovery priorities
7. Developing the BIA report

Although these steps identify the actions to take, they can be combined or ordered differently. The most important point to remember is that the goal of the BIA is to identify the critical resources and recovery priorities. The actual steps to get there can be different from one organization to another.

Identifying the Environment

The first step is to identify the overall IT environment, which means having a thorough understanding of the business function. If the business generates sales revenue, knowing the sales amounts, which include the number of customers and transactions, is important. Sales revenue translates to lost sales during an outage.

A BIA is possible to perform on a CBF that doesn't generate sales revenue. For example, an email system is a CBF for many organizations. It may serve 5,000 employees and pass tens of thousands of emails daily. Even though it doesn't generate any direct sales revenue, most organizations would identify it as a CBF.

Identifying the environment may include determining what is critical, including getting a big picture of the IT systems within the scope of the BIA. Depending on the scope, this step could include collecting diagrams and technical documentation, which would help to determine which components are critical.

A BIA can be completed on an entire organization or only portions of it. For example, for a small company with less than 100 users, a BIA could be completed on the entire company. On the other hand, a company with several offices spread throughout the country may require several BIAs, instead of just one enormous BIA. Individual BIAs could be done for any of the small offices and for different functions within the organization. For example, a single BIA could be done for online sales and another one for database support.

After completing this step, the administrator will have a better idea of what systems to include in the BIA and will also be able to identify the stakeholders.

> **TIP**
> The BIA is not concerned with identifying or implementing recovery methods but is an important prerequisite. An administrator can't begin looking for recovery methods until they know what needs to be recovered.

Identifying Stakeholders

Stakeholders are those individuals or groups that have a direct stake or interest in the success of a project. For example, a vice president of sales would have a direct stake in the success of sales. Stakeholders know the CBFs.

A stakeholder can help ensure that adequate resources are available, which includes simple matters, such as ensuring personnel are available for interviews for the BIA, and larger issues, such as identifying the MAO.

Individual stakeholders can identify any system or function as critical because they are responsible for losses due to outages. They are also responsible for dedicating resources to protect the systems. Because these are their responsibilities, the stakeholders' opinions matter the most.

Identifying Critical Business Functions

Some BIAs are designed to focus on a specific CBF from the beginning. For example, a BIA could be commissioned specifically for an online website. Thus, the processes involved are the only thing left to identify.

Another BIA could be focused on a remote office, so the first thing that would need to be done is to identify what functions are done at the remote office. For example, the majority of the work at the remote office may be done offline, such as providing presentations to client sites on a regular basis. Based on this scenario, the people there could still do these presentations even if they lost all IT functions for a week or more. In this case, none of the functions would be considered critical.

On the other hand, a remote office may sell products or services, which means the office needs constant connectivity with the main office during business hours. If the remote office loses connectivity, employees can't close a sale. If these employees generate a lot of revenue, the organization might consider connectivity as a critical function.

Identifying Critical Resources

Critical resources are the resources needed to support the CBFs and processes. They could include hardware, such as servers or routers, and software, such as the operating system and applications.

When identifying critical resources, the supporting infrastructure must be included. For example, a web server must be operational 24 hours a day, 7 days a week and needs facility support, which could include power, heating, and air-conditioning. If a critical system requires support personnel for operations, food, potable water, and other items should be included as critical resources.

Identifying critical personnel is also important. Any system has several key personnel integral to its success, such as executives, managers, supervisors, administrators, or key customers or vendors.

In the example presented earlier of the online web server with the back-end database, the following systems would be included:

- Web server
- Database server
- Internal firewall
- External firewall

Interviewing the experts is important to identify critical systems that support any CBF. For example, in an email service within a Microsoft domain, the obvious systems are any of the email servers. However, within a Microsoft domain, several additional servers are critical, which include a domain controller (DC), a DC that's also a global catalog server, and a Domain Name System (DNS) server used to locate servers within the domain. If any of these servers are unavailable, the email service will not work.

Identifying the MAO

Once the critical resources have been identified, the MAO for each of them can be identified. Each of these resources supports a CBF. If the MAO of a resource isn't clear, the MAO of the CBF it supports must be identified, which is also the MAO of the resource.

In addition to identifying an MAO, an impact statement, which identifies the effect of the loss, should be included. The impact can be directly stated by identifying what cannot be done in case of a loss, or it can be stated in monetary terms.

For example, email services may be critical. However, the organization may be able to continue to operate for as long as 8 hours before suffering a serious impact. On the other hand, a web server generating $60,000 in revenue an hour loses as much as $1,000 in direct sales a minute. The organization can identify the MAO for this web server as 5 minutes.

TABLE 12-3 shows a sample output for this step.

Identifying Recovery Priorities

This part of the BIA identifies the most and the least important critical systems. The highest priorities are assigned based on the shortest MAOs. For example, in comparing a system that impacts operations after 5 minutes of downtime with another system that can be down for 8 hours before an impact occurs, clearly, the system with a 5-minute MAO should be recovered first.

The output of the BIA at this stage can be as simple as a list of the critical systems with designated priorities, such as 1, 2, and 3. The priorities could also be categorized. For example, the most important systems could be categorized as high, and the other categories could be listed as medium or low.

TABLE 12-4 shows how recovery priorities could be listed for an organization's systems. This table uses a scale of 1 to 5 with 1 as the highest priority. Desktop PCs are added as the lowest priority.

TABLE 12-3 MAO and Impact for Specific Resources

RESOURCE	MAO	IMPACT
Web server	5 minutes	Loss of significant direct sales revenue and indirect losses. 5 minutes of downtime results in a loss of about $5,000 in direct sales.
Database server	5 minutes	Loss of significant direct sales revenue and indirect losses. Users will still be able to browse the website. 5 minutes of downtime results in a loss of about $5,000 in direct sales.
Email server	8 hours	Loss of primary communications within the company. Loss of primary communications with vendors and customers.

TABLE 12-4 Recovery Priorities

SYSTEM	PRIORITY
Web server	1
Database server	1
Email server	2
Desktop PCs	5

Developing the BIA Report

The BIA report compiles the data that has been collected. No specific format is required, but it usually includes the following sections:

- **Preliminary system information**—The preliminary system information includes generic information, such as the organization, system name, and system documentation.
- **System points of contact (POCs)**—POCs are the system experts and stakeholders who provided the input into the BIA. They can also be queried with any follow-up questions. Both internal and external POCs may be included, depending on the scope of the BIA.
- **System resources**—The specific resources are listed in this section, which include the hardware and software and any personnel or other resources.
- **Critical roles**—Some POCs may have critical roles related to a system. If so, they can be identified in this section, which will make following up with them easier.
- **Table linking critical roles to critical resources**—This table matches the personnel to the systems. For example, if email services are considered critical, the email POC would be matched with this system.
- **Table identifying resources, outage impact, and MAO**—This table lists each critical resource that was identified in the BIA. For each resource, the impact of an outage and the MAO are included. This table is one of the most important elements of the BIA.
- **Table identifying recovery priority of key resources**—This table lists the internally developed recovery priority, designated by numbers, such as 1, 2, and 3, or words, such as high, medium, or low.

BIA Reports Are Popular

Once the BIA has been completed, many people may want to see it, which is especially true if the BIA looks at more than one function. The BIA provides an overall picture of the organization that isn't commonly available.

Disaster recovery and security personnel often have more knowledge of the details of a business than others within the organization, executives have a good overall view, and managers and employees often know their area well but don't have a good understanding of other areas. Thus, the BIA is important to all of them because it ties everything together.

Because of the BIA's comprehensive overview of the organization, executives often classify it as confidential. So before distributing it to anyone, obtaining permission is important.

Identifying Mission-Critical Business Functions and Processes

An important step in developing the BIA is identifying the mission-critical business functions and processes, a task that is not always easy. Two of the most important points to remember about this process is that the experts have the key information, and using different data collection methods to get this information will be necessary.

Mission-critical business functions are those that are considered vital to an organization. They are derived from critical success factors, or CSFs. CSFs are the elements necessary to perform the mission and are required for the success of the organization.

FIGURE 12-5 shows that processes are the underlying actions that contribute to the CSFs. In other words, certain processes result in achieving CSFs. Successful CSFs result in performing CBFs.

For example, a company generates the majority of its revenue from online sales. Thus, selling products from the website is a CBF. However, to say the company needs to sell products to be successful isn't enough. The underlying factors and processes that are needed to sell the products must be identified.

For example, a company sells widgets online. Some of its underlying CSFs could be:

- Best widgets available
- Motivated employees
- Customer satisfaction
- Effective advertising

Different processes support each of these CSFs. For example, some of the processes that support customer satisfaction are:

- Satisfying buying experience
- Competitive pricing
- On-time delivery

Many companies document these processes with workflows. If workflows exist, they can easily be used to determine the steps in the processes. If they don't exist, the steps in a process should still be able to be documented.

On-time delivery is an important process that supports customer satisfaction, and it includes several steps. Documenting the steps makes identifying the critical resources needed to ensure on-time delivery easier.

FIGURE 12-5

Key processes, CSFs, and CBFs.

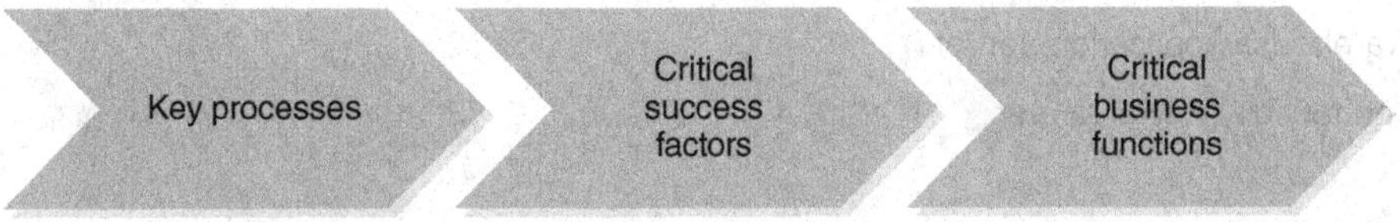

Figure 12-2, presented earlier in the chapter, shows the elements involved in the product shipment phase. The actual workflow could be:

1. The web server sends orders to the warehouse database.
2. The warehouse application identifies new orders.
3. The application notifies warehouse workers of new orders, including the location of the product.
4. Warehouse workers retrieve the product.
5. Warehouse workers package and ship the product.

With this knowledge, the critical resources required for on-time delivery can now be identified. They include:

- The database server hosting the warehouse database
- Communication between the database server and the web server
- The application server hosting the warehouse application
- Employees in the warehouse
- Shipping supplies and shipment method

Mapping Business Functions and Processes to IT Systems

Once the CBFs and processes have been identified, they need to be mapped to the actual IT systems. Then, the recovery options can be determined.

In the example of the shipment of products, three primary systems are involved. First, employees access the warehouse application, and, second, the warehouse application accesses the warehouse database. If either of these systems fails, the employees can't identify the products to ship. The third system is a link between the web server accepting the orders and the database server. If this system fails, new orders can't be identified or shipped.

The priority of these systems must then be identified, as shown in **TABLE 12-5**. The same scale as mentioned in Table 12-4 is used. A priority of 1 is the highest and 5 is the lowest. Shipments can't occur if the database server or the warehouse application server fails. However, some delay in shipments is acceptable, so these systems are assigned a priority of 2.

If the connection with the web server is broken, new orders can't be passed to the warehouse, but the warehouse workers can still process existing orders. Therefore, a priority of 3 is assigned to this connection.

TABLE 12-5 Critical Business System Priorities

SYSTEM	PRIORITY
Database server	2
Warehouse application server	2
Connection to web server	3

Best Practices for Performing a BIA for an Organization

When performing BIAs, several best practices can be used. Following is a list of some of them:

- **Starting with clear objectives**—Everyone involved with the BIA must understand its scope, which is best defined in writing. Many projects get off track simply because individuals have varying understandings of the requirements.
- **Not losing sight of the objectives**—The purpose of the BIA is to identify the critical functions, critical systems, and MAO. This data is used to determine the recovery priorities.
- **Using a top-down approach**—Starting with the CBFs and drilling down to the IT services that support them is the top-down approach, whereas by starting with the servers, important elements that are needed for the success of the CBFs will be missed.
- **Varying data collection methods**—When collecting data, the method used must be matched with the organization's practices. Solid data may be obtainable from individual interviews with some people, but access to other people for individual interviews may not be available. In this case, questionnaires can be used. Group discussions are often useful when collecting BIA data, and such discussions can be coordinated in conference calls, meetings, and workshops.
- **Planning interviews and meetings in advance**—Data gathering is an important part of the BIA, so ensuring that the attendees have enough time to provide the data needed is important. If they're rushed or aren't prepared, the data that's needed may not be provided.
- **Not looking for the quick solution**—The BIA is time consuming especially in data collection, evaluation, and the identification of priorities. Shortcuts are likely to overlook critical functions or processes.
- **Considering the BIA as a project**—All normal project management practices apply. Milestones should be set and progress tracked.
- **Considering using tools**—Many tools that are available that can assist with the completion of disaster preparedness projects can also help with developing a BIA.

Considering Using Tools

Tools are available that can assist in completing the BIA. For example, BIA Professional is one of several tools sold by Sungard Availability Services. It includes tools that can help with gathering and compiling information and guides the user through the process from beginning to end.

The tool includes web-based surveys. The questions can be designed so that they branch off users' answers. In other words, users who don't have direct knowledge of a specific process won't be asked questions about the process. Once the questions have been created, links to the surveys can be sent to the experts, who can answer the questions from anywhere via the internet.

BIA Professional is a part of Sungard's overall Continuity Management Solution suite of tools. Alternative tools available include BlockSim by ReliaSoft and BCM by Factonomy.

CHAPTER SUMMARY

The BIA is a valuable tool that can help identify critical systems and resources. Once they have been identified, the MAO time for resources can then be identified. The impact of the outage and the MAO is then used to determine recovery priorities. Some systems may need to be up and operational almost immediately after a disaster, whereas other systems can be down for days at a time.

Two important terms related to the BIA are the recovery time objective (RTO) and recovery point objective (RPO). The RTO helps identify systems that are time critical, and the RPO helps identify systems that hold data that is mission critical.

KEY CONCEPTS AND TERMS

business impact analysis (BIA)
critical business function (CBF)
critical success factor (CSF)
maximum acceptable outage (MAO)
maximum tolerable period of disruption (MTPD)
recovery point objective (RPO)
recovery time objective (RTO)

CHAPTER 12 ASSESSMENT

1. The ________ identifies the maximum acceptable downtime for a system.
2. Which of the following can determine what functions are considered critical business functions?
   A. Clients
   B. Stakeholders
   C. Project team
   D. Chief technology officer
3. The BIA is a part of the ________.
4. What defines the boundaries of a business impact analysis?
   A. MAO
   B. BCP
   C. Recovery objectives
   D. Scope
5. What are two objectives of a BIA? (Select two.)
   A. Identifying minimum acceptable outage
   B. Documenting new policy
   C. Identifying critical resources
   D. Identifying critical business functions
6. In developing a BIA, when calculating the costs to determine the impact of an outage for a specific system, both the direct and ________ costs should be calculated.
7. In a BIA, the maximum amount of data loss an organization can accept is called what?
   A. BIA time
   B. Maximum acceptable outage
   C. Recovery time objectives
   D. Recovery point objectives

8. What is the time required for a system to be recovered called?
   A. BIA time
   B. Maximum acceptable outage
   C. Recovery time objectives
   D. Recovery point objectives
9. Which of the following statements is true?
   A. The RPO applies to any systems or functions, whereas the RTO refers only to data housed in databases.
   B. The RTO applies to any systems or functions, whereas the RPO refers only to data housed in databases.
   C. Both the RTO and RPO apply to any systems or functions.
   D. Both the RTO and RPO apply to data housed in databases.
10. In a BIA, which one of the following is a direct cost of the impact of an outage for a specific system?
   A. Loss of customers
   B. Loss of public goodwill
   C. Loss of sales
   D. Lost opportunities
11. What type of approach does a BIA use?
   A. Bottom-up approach in which servers or services are examined first
   B. Top-down approach in which CBFs are examined first
   C. Middle-tier approach
   D. Best-guess approach
12. Mission-critical business functions are considered vital to an organization. What are they derived from?
   A. Critical success factors
   B. Critical IT resources
   C. Executive leadership
   D. Employees
13. In developing a BIA, what should the critical business functions be mapped to?
   A. Personnel
   B. Revenue
   C. Replacement costs
   D. IT systems
14. Of the following choices, which is (are) considered best practice(s) related to a BIA?
   A. Starting with clear objectives
   B. Using different data collection methods
   C. Mitigating identified risks
   D. A and B only
   E. All of the above
15. A cost-benefit analysis is an important part of a BIA.
   A. True
   B. False

CHAPTER 13

Mitigating Risk With a Business Continuity Plan

BUSINESS CONTINUITY PLANS (BCPs) are an important element of risk management. They help an organization plan for a major disruption or disaster and ensure that critical business functions (CBFs) continue to operate. The business impact analysis (BIA) sets the stage for the BCP by identifying CBFs. The BCP coordinator then develops the BCP to support these CBFs. The BCP coordinator receives assistance from one or more BCP teams and team leads.

Activities happen in different phases if a disruption occurs. The first phase is the notification/activation phase, called by the BCP coordinator. The second phase is the recovery phase, where CBFs are recovered and returned to full operation. The final phase is the reconstitution phase, where the organization returns to normal operations. For a BCP to succeed, personnel need to be trained, and the BCP needs to be tested and exercised. Additionally, the BCP needs to be reviewed regularly and kept up to date.

Chapter 13 Topics

This chapter covers the following topics and concepts:

- What a business continuity plan (BCP) is
- What the elements of a BCP are
- How a BCP mitigates an organization's risk
- What best practices for implementing a BCP are

Chapter 13 Goals

When you complete this chapter, you will be able to:

- Define a BCP
- Identify the elements of a BCP
- Describe the purpose of a BCP and the sections a BCP often includes
- Identify key responsibilities of personnel related to a BCP
- Describe the procedures in the notification and activation phase of a BCP

- Describe the procedures in the recovery phase of a BCP
- Describe the procedures in the reconstitution phase of a BCP
- Identify the different types of testing and exercises used for a BCP
- Identify different steps used to maintain the BCP
- Describe how a BCP mitigates an organization's risk
- List best practices for enabling a risk mitigation plan from a risk assessment

What Is a Business Continuity Plan?

A business continuity plan (BCP) is a plan designed to help an organization continue to operate during and after a disruption. The disruption can be an intentional attack or a natural disaster. The goal is a continuation of operations. This is different than a disaster recovery plan which seeks to fully recover from some disruption. A business continuity plan seeks to maintain essential business functions until such a complete recovery can occur.

BCPs can address any type of disruption or disaster. Organizations that operate near a Southern U.S. coast plan for hurricanes, businesses in the heartland's "tornado alley" plan for tornadoes, Californians plan for earthquakes, and everyone plans for fires.

Disruptions can also be from attacks or failures. A critical server going down could have been caused by an attacker through the internet, a malware infection, or a hardware or software failure. If the server provides a CBF, the BCP needs to ensure that plans are in place to get it operational as soon as possible.

> **TIP**
>
> The scope of the BCP can be limited to certain parts of an organization. For example, it could include just a specific location or specific CBFs. However, the BCP is focused on the overall business functions rather than just the individual IT systems.

The scope of the BCP includes a global view of the organization and the information technology (IT) systems, the facilities, and the personnel, which is not to say that all elements of an organization must continue to operate during a disruption. Instead, this means that the BCP examines all elements and then identifies the elements that are mission-critical and need to continue to operate. Non–mission-critical elements that do not need to continue aren't addressed by the BCP.

Mission-critical systems are those identified as critical to the mission of the organization to keep the organization functioning. The term *mission critical* can also apply to functions or processes.

A business impact analysis (BIA) is included as part of a BCP. The BIA has several key objectives that directly support the BCP. These include:

- **Identifying critical business functions (CBFs)**—A CBF is any function considered vital to an organization. If the CBF fails, the organization will lose the ability to perform mission-critical operations.
- **Identifying critical processes supporting the CBFs**—The critical processes are the steps or actions taken to support the CBFs.

- **Identifying critical IT services supporting the CBFs, including any dependencies**—These services include the servers and other hardware necessary to support critical processes. Many services have dependencies. For example, an application server may need a database server to remain operational.
- **Determining acceptable downtimes for CBFs, processes, and IT services**—The BIA defines this downtime as the maximum acceptable outage (MAO). When considering the BCP, whether there are different MAOs for different times of the year should also be determined. For example, a database server may be critical for end-of-year processing but not critical at other times.

All of these objectives come together in the BCP to align the organization's priorities. The BIA identifies the mission-critical systems, applications, and operations, and the BCP provides the plan to ensure that they continue to operate even if a disaster strikes.

Similarly, the BCP includes disaster recovery plans (DRPs), which help the organization restore IT services after the disaster. Any organization can create its BCP using procedures that match its needs. However, the overall steps of a BCP are:

- Chartering the BCP and creating BCP scope statements
- Completing the BIA
- Identifying countermeasures and controls
- Developing individual DRPs
- Providing training
- Testing and exercising plans
- Maintaining and updating plans

Elements of a BCP

BCPs are large, comprehensive documents. They include many elements and often cover many contingencies. A single format will not cover all requirements for all organizations. However, some guides suggest the inclusion of certain elements.

Business Continuity Versus Disaster Recovery

The terms **business continuity (BC)** and **disaster recovery (DR)** are not synonymous but rather two separate but related processes, even though some people confuse them and use the terms interchangeably. BC covers all functions of a business to ensure that the entire business can continue to operate in the event of a disruption and includes a BIA and DRP as attachments to the BCP. DR is largely a function of IT and includes the elements necessary to recover from a disaster, such as backups, recoveries, and restores. DR can also be broader and include alternate sites and other elements. However, the DRP is a part of the larger BCP.

For example, a bank operates on a coast threatened by hurricanes. Customers use the bank's website to do online banking. If a hurricane hits, the bank wants to ensure that its website will continue to be available. Therefore, the BCP could include a DRP that includes the steps needed to recover the website at an alternate location.

Weather services provide warnings at certain hourly periods, such as a warning being issued when a hurricane is expected to hit within 72 hours. The BCP could designate specific steps at 72 hours, 48 hours, and 24 hours, and the DRP would provide details on how to move the website to an alternate location.

The BCP may address other nontechnical elements of the hurricane. For example, when should the bank close? When should the vault be locked? Should guards remain inside? Are any other security precautions necessary?

After the disaster has passed, the BCP and the DRP would have different goals, but they would work together. Again, the BCP is focused on getting the overall business functions back to normal, and the DRP is focused on restoring and recovering IT functions.

For example, the following sections are often included in a BCP:

- Purpose
- Scope
- Assumptions and planning principles
- System description and architecture
- Responsibilities
- Notification and activation phase
- Recovery phase
- Reconstitution phase
- Plan training, testing, and exercises
- Plan maintenance

The following sections describe the contents of these sections.

Purpose

The purpose of the BCP is to ensure that mission-critical elements of an organization continue to operate after a disruption, which can be any event that has the potential to stop operations. The BCP is implemented when a disruption occurs or is imminent. The BCP then stays in place until the restoration of normal operations.

Only CBFs are maintained during the disruption, which means doing business as usual does not continue during a disaster. The BIA identifies the CBFs and their priorities, and the BCP ensures that all the elements are in place to maintain those CBFs.

The BIA also includes acceptable outage times. Some CBFs may need to be kept operational with minimal outage, whereas other CBFs may have lower priorities. Depending on the recovery time objectives identified in the BIA, these lower-priority CBFs may be down for hours or even days.

Scope

Just as with any project, the scope of the BCP needs to be defined because the success of the project is dependent on personnel understanding the tasks. If there is no scope statement, two problems can occur. First, the desired tasks won't be finished, which means the BCP will be incomplete. Second, scope creep can occur. Scope creep happens when the project keeps taking on additional tasking. For example, the intended scope may cover a single location, but instead the BCP includes research and recommendations for five locations.

The scope statement can include several key items, such as the location, the systems, the employees, and the vendors. Only the critical systems identified in the BIA should be included. Employees who are necessary to support the critical systems should be included and identified by title or position, rather than name. If parts or supplies can be obtained from a specific source only, then the vendor should be included in the BCP.

Although a BCP will take a global view of the organization, it doesn't have to cover the entire organization. The BCP could cover only specific locations. For example, a company has a main office in Atlanta and regional offices in Chicago, Los Angeles, and Miami. It could create four separate BCPs, one for each location.

Individual departments or divisions may have smaller threats that need to be addressed from a business continuity perspective, but, generally, these departments use contingency planning or redundancy measures. The smaller threats wouldn't be addressed with separate BCPs.

Assumptions and Planning Principles

Every BCP needs to include some basic assumptions and planning principles that are very helpful in the initial development of the BCP and also useful in the implementation phases.

A key planning principle is the length of time that the company is expected to continue operations under the BCP before returning to normal operations. For example, a company could plan on continuing operations under the BCP for 7 days following a hurricane. Seven days then becomes a guiding principle for many other elements, such as 7 days of supplies, 7 days of fuel for generators, or 7 days of food and water for personnel.

> **TIP**
>
> These assumptions and principles will drive much of the decision-making process, so they need to be accurate. For example, if the company assumes that it will never lose power, it won't plan for alternate power sources. However, if a disruption does result in a power loss, the rest of the plan would be useless.

Assumptions and principles can be reviewed and assessed in several different categories, which include the incidents to be addressed in the plan, strategy, priorities, required support, and other elements. The following sections provide guidance for these areas.

Incidents to Be Included and Excluded

Many BCPs identify specific incidents that are included and excluded. For example, the BCP may be designed to address specific disruptions due to hurricanes or earthquakes or to address generic incidents, such as power loss from any cause.

As an example, an organization is in a hurricane-prone area. It will have many hours if not days of advance notice before the hurricane hits. Safety precautions and preparedness steps are well known for hurricanes, such as securing anything that can blow away, preparing for wind damage, and, for some areas, flooding.

Now, compare this organization to one in an area prone to earthquakes. The organization doesn't receive any notice that an earthquake is about to hit. One moment everything is calm, and the next, buildings are collapsing. Depending on the severity of the quake, damage can range from very little to mass destruction.

The responses to each of these incidents are very different. Therefore, knowing what incidents the BCP will be used to respond to will provide a better idea of what steps to include.

On the other hand, some incidents are generic. For example, the BCP could include plans to provide backup generator power to the organization if power is lost, which could be used no matter how the power is lost. Plans could also be included to relocate to another location if one location is not usable. Again, why the location is unusable doesn't matter. The cause could be a fire, a flood, a tornado, an earthquake, or something else.

Strategy

The strategy of the BCP identifies some of the key elements of the plan, which could include location, notification, and transportation.

If an organization is in a single location, the strategy would be to address this single location, whereas, if the organization is in several locations, a strategy would need to be identified for each one. For example, an organization may decide that key IT resources will be centrally located and maintained, such as in a large university that has many buildings spread across an expansive campus. Instead of maintaining operations at each building, the BCP could identify specific resources to be maintained at one or more central buildings.

If an incident has occurred or is imminent, BCP team members will need to be notified. Therefore, identifying how to notify all key players is important. One such way is using a phone tree. With a phone tree, one person starts the process by calling several key people, such as team leads. Then, the teams leads call people on their lists and so on until, eventually, everyone has been notified.

Transportation may be a concern. If members will need transportation from one area to another, the BCP should address it. For example, company vehicles could be designated for shuttling personnel as needed. Or, if equipment needs to be moved, how that will happen should be identified in the BCP.

Supplies are an important concern if they are needed for continued operation. For example, if the company will need supplies to continue producing a product, they must be available. Utilities, such as water, power, and gas, are needed. If the strategy is to continue to operate on the BCP plan for 7 days, the company will need to provide its own utilities for 7 days.

Communications is another concern because typical communications are often interrupted during a disruption. Land-based phone lines may not function and, in some situations, neither will cell-based phones. Many organizations use push-to-talk cell phones, which work as cell phones and walkie-talkies. Even if the cell phone functions stop working during an emergency, the walkie-talkie function still works.

The benefit of the push-to-talk phones is that they don't require external resources for the walkie-talkie functions because they simply broadcast on a frequency. As long as the other cell phone is in reach, it receives the message. One approach is to purchase many of these push-to-talk phones and issue them to key players during the first phase of the plan.

Priorities

The BIA identifies CBFs and critical resources and their priorities. Generally, the BCP reaffirms these priorities and will ensure that efforts focus on returning the top-priority systems first. These top-priority systems will have the most resources dedicated to restoring them.

Required Support

The BCP requires support during every phase, most importantly, management's support. Without this support, the required input and support from personnel and the required funding will not be available. Therefore, the BCP is doomed to fail without the support from top-level management.

Later in this chapter, responsibilities are listed for individuals and teams. Clearly, these teams must provide support to the BCP and be supported in their endeavors.

During the notification and activation phase, all personnel need to respond as quickly as possible. Some personnel may be identified as mission-critical, and they will need to remain at the site during the emergency.

> **TIP**
>
> Having supplies on hand for continued production may conflict with other organizational principles. For example, many organizations use a just-in-time philosophy, in which parts and supplies arrive when needed. Stocking 7 days of supplies at all times for the BCP ties up funds in inventory. In addition, some supplies need to be rotated to ensure they don't expire or become outdated.

System Description and Architecture

The BCP identifies CBFs that need to remain operational during the disruption. Each of these CBFs has individual systems that support it. Therefore, having current descriptions and documentation on these systems is important. This documentation needs to be detailed enough to identify the critical system and the supporting architecture. If the documentation isn't available or is out of date, maintaining and recovering the CBFs becomes much more difficult.

While the CBF systems are being documented for the BCP, elements that need to be addressed in the recovery plan can be identified. For example, documentation may show that a system must maintain connectivity via a wide area network (WAN) link to stay operational. If the plan doesn't include an alternative, this WAN link becomes a single point of failure. For example, **FIGURE 13-1** shows a WAN link connecting a database server at the headquarters office to a remote location. If the WAN link fails, the CBF fails. Therefore, the WAN link must stay operational to support the CBF.

FIGURE 13-1
Database servers connected via a WAN link.

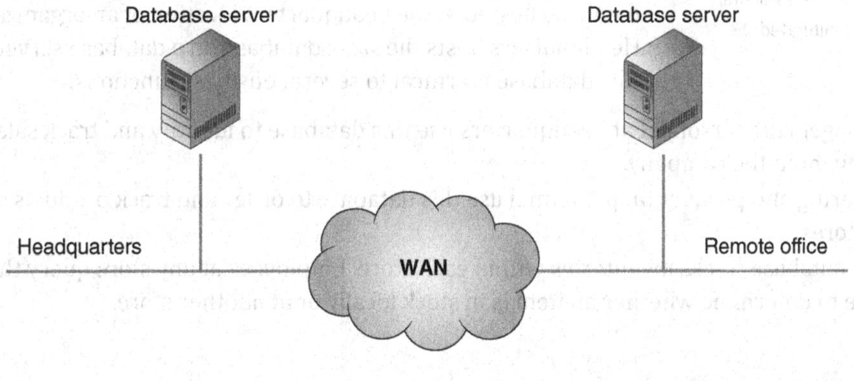

FIGURE 13-2

Database servers with primary and alternate connection methods.

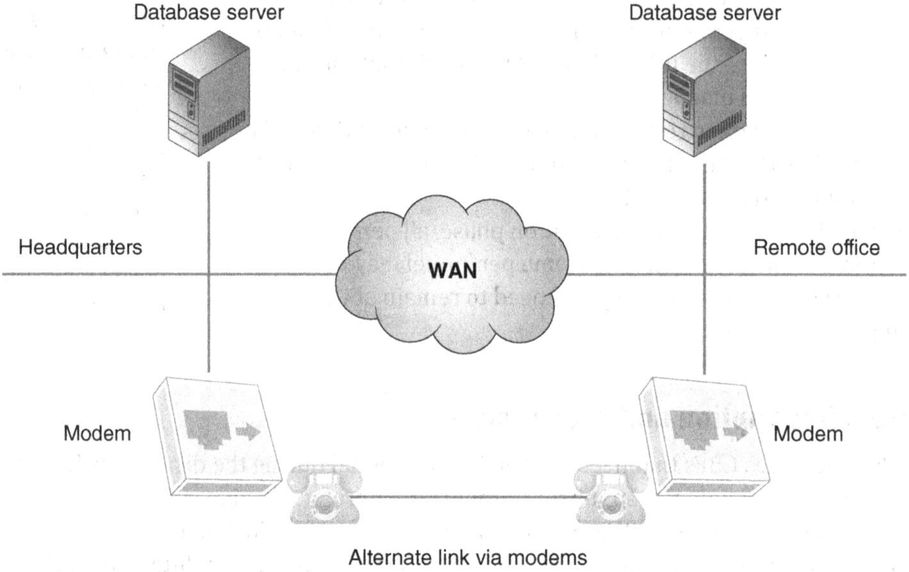

> **TIP**
>
> Ensure steps are taken to provide for families of employees, which is especially true if employees need to stay on-site during the disruption. Employees should never have to choose between taking care of their families or the organization in an emergency. At one time discussions of issues such as pandemics seemd academic. However, now in the post-COVID 19 world, we should all realize that this is yet another risk that must be evaluated and mitigated.

FIGURE 13-2 shows the same two servers with a backup method of communication. The servers communicate via the WAN link the majority of the time. If it fails, the servers communicate via the modems. Although the modem link is substantially slower than the WAN link, it can still meet the organization's needs during a disruption.

The following sections identify some common documentation that needs to be included with the BCP.

Overview

The overview section provides a description of a CBF in big-picture terms. For example, following is a description of a critical database hosted at the headquarters location of an organization. Headquarters hosts the sales database on a database server, and this database is critical to several business functions:

- Management personnel at headquarters use this database to identify and track sales throughout the company.
- Ordering and production personnel use this database to order and track products shipped to stores.
- The database tracks inventories within each store. Employees at any store query the database to determine whether an item is in stock locally or at another store.

Each store has a local database server that hosts a database for the store and records store sales, and the store databases synchronize with the headquarters database server once an hour. This information doesn't provide details but does provide enough information to understand the big picture.

Functional Description

The functional description builds on the overview by providing more details of the systems.

Many systems interact with other critical systems, so including figures is valuable whenever possible. As an example, **FIGURE 13-3** shows a diagram for the database described in the overview section that displays how each of the outlying stores connects to headquarters over the WAN links.

> **NOTE**
>
> In this example, the database server hosted at headquarters is critical. As described, no indication is given that the store database servers are critical, which means that a store database server could fail without affecting the headquarters database. However, in another company, the database server at each store location may be critical. In that case, all of them could be included in the same BCP, or a BCP for each store could be created.

FIGURE 13-3

Database servers connected between stores and headquarters.

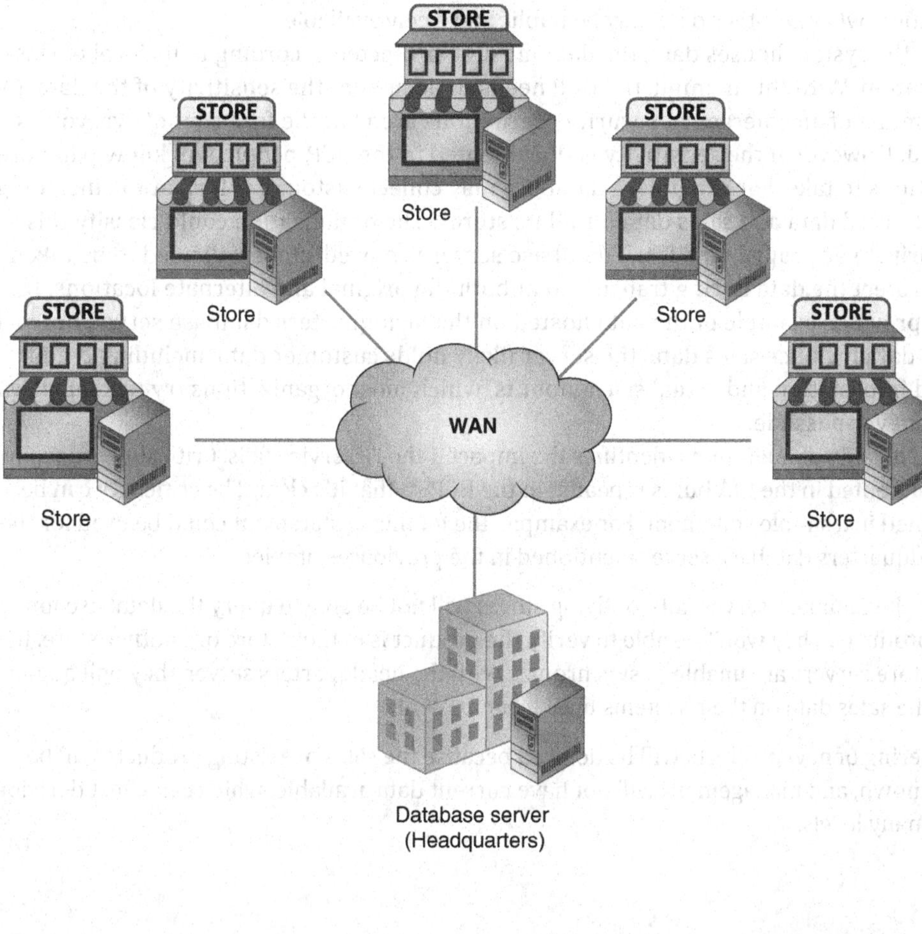

The description would provide more details. For example, it would include the store names and the store locations and details on the WAN links, and, if there were redundant WAN links, it would describe them.

Details on the headquarters server are also important. This description should include the server name, the operating system, and the database application used. For example, the server could be running Windows Server 2019 with SQL Server 2019.

If the server includes any fault-tolerance capabilities, they would be mentioned here. For example, the database server might be in a failover cluster and include a redundant array of independent disk (RAID) subsystem. A two-node failover cluster allows one server to fail without affecting the services provided by the database. With RAID, a system will continue to operate even if a drive fails.

Sensitivity of Data and Criticality of Operations

The BCP includes information on the sensitivity of the system's data and details on the criticality of the system operations.

Any organization will have some secret or proprietary data. The organization must define classifications for this data because the classification determines the level of protection required for the data. Some data may be classified as private and used only within the organization, whereas other data may be public and freely available.

If the system houses data, the data must be protected according to its level of classification. With this in mind, the BCP needs to document the sensitivity of the data. In the midst of an emergency, security precautions aren't at the forefront of everyone's mind. However, if the sensitivity is documented in the BCP, people will know what precautions to take. For example, a database may collect customer information, including credit card data and sales data for all its stores. The organization could classify this data as private or proprietary. If the database server is moved, steps will need to be taken to protect the data during transit and at both the original and alternate locations. In the previous example of the data hosted on the headquarters database server, because this data includes sales data, the server likely holds customer data, including credit card information and actual sale amounts, which most organizations try to keep private whenever possible.

Criticality of operations identifies the impact if the IT service fails. Criticality is usually documented in the BIA but is repeated in the BCP so that it's clear. The criticality can be defined in a simple statement. For example, the following statement could be used for the headquarters database server mentioned in the previous example:

> If the database server fails, outlying stores will not be able to query the database for products. They won't be able to verify the product is in their store or another store. If store servers are unable to synchronize with the headquarters server, they will queue the sales data on their systems until it can be sent.

Ordering of new products will be delayed because the sales of existing products will be unknown, and management will not have current data available, which can affect decisions on many levels.

Identifying Critical Equipment, Software, Data, Documents, and Supplies

> **TIP**
> The primary objective of a security system is to protect confidentiality, integrity, and availability. The loss of any of these should be considered when documenting this section in the BCP. For example, what will happen if the organization loses the availability of data or a system?

The BCP should list all the critical components for the system for the following reasons: First, the BCP states clearly which components are needed for the CBF, and second, it provides a list that can be used to restore the system from scratch.

This list includes any equipment, such as servers, switches, and routers. Because the servers may need to be rebuilt from scratch, the BCP should list the operating system and any applications needed to support the system. If an image is used to rebuild servers, it will list the version number.

Items on the list can include a database hosted on the system; any type of files, such as documents or spreadsheets; and any needed supplies. These supplies can be as simple as office supplies, such as printer paper and toner. For some systems, the list can include technical supplies, such as special oils for machinery or tools needed for maintenance.

Whenever possible, the location of these items should be included. Some organizations create "crash carts" that include all the components needed to rebuild a system. They include CDs or DVDs for operating systems, applications, or images and basic instructions for building or rebuilding systems.

Telecommunications

Required connectivity with other systems is an important element to document in the BCP. Connectivity can be from the internal network, the internet, dedicated WAN lines, or phone lines.

External connections often use lines from telecommunications companies. Internet service providers (ISPs) typically provide more than just access to the internet. They can also lease lines used for WANs and virtual private networks (VPNs).

Any required communication links should be documented. For example, if a database receives updates from other databases using VPN lines, that information should be included. Some systems have multiple communication lines for redundancy. If the system can operate without specific telecommunication lines, they should be identified along with the redundant connection.

Responsibilities

Responsibilities within a BCP should be assigned. Assigning responsibilities makes things clear to everyone concerned. When tasking has not been completed or is behind schedule, getting the project back on track is easier when those responsible are known.

Employees in the organization will fill specific roles in a BCP. These roles include the BCP program manager, the BCP coordinator, BCP team leads, and BCP team members.

The next section covers these roles and responsibilities and some of the other key personnel who may be included in the BCP.

BCP Program Manager

A BCP program manager (PM) usually manages multiple BCP projects within a large organization. For example, a large organization could have several locations and BCPs for each one. A BCP coordinator manages a single BCP and reports to the BCP PM. The BCP PM ensures that each BCP is progressing as expected. The PM can use traditional project management skills to manage these BCPs. For example, every BCP has a start date, milestones, and an end date for the development stage and will include dates for the reviews to start. These reviews will also have milestones and end dates.

The BCP PM is responsible for ensuring that each of the BCPs is on track. Depending on the hierarchy of the organization, the BCP PM may not have any authority over the individual BCP coordinators, which makes it necessary for the PM to have exceptional communication skills.

Other organizations may have a specific department of PMs who have specialized project management skills. Lead PMs oversee several other PMs. In this situation, the BCP PMs have direct authority over the BCP coordinators.

BCP Coordinator

The BCP coordinator is in charge of a specific BCP. This individual can have two roles depending on the stage of the BCP:

- Before the BCP has been completed, this person is responsible for developing and completing it.
- When the BCP has been completed, the BCP coordinator is responsible for declaring the emergency and activating the BCP.

When an emergency is declared, the BCP coordinator contacts appropriate teams or team leads. For example, if an emergency management team is used, the BCP coordinator will contact the emergency management team lead.

BCP Teams

A BCP can't be planned, implemented, and executed by a single person. Instead, teams are put together to help in the process.

If the organization is small, it may have a single BCP team that has the responsibilities of all the individual teams mentioned in the following sections. Members have different levels of expertise. Some members will be more active during different phases than others. Larger organizations have multiple teams with different goals and responsibilities.

Although different teams have different goals, members need some common skills and abilities. Most importantly, they need to work together. One member who can work with others and get the job done is better than numerous "experts" who excel at finding fault with others but rarely complete their own tasks.

> **TIP**
>
> Smaller organizations may use a single team for the BCP, which would include one or more senior management employees to fulfill the role of the executive management team, personnel who could survey and assess the damage of the critical resources, and members who can recover the critical resources.

Three commonly used teams are the **emergency management team (EMT)**, the **damage assessment team (DAT)**, and the **technical recovery team (TRT)**. These teams are described as follows:

- **Emergency management team**—This team is composed of senior managers. They have overall authority for the recovery of the system but also work closely with the BCP coordinator. At this point, there is a potential for a conflict. Who's in charge? The BCP coordinator or the EMT lead? To avoid this conflict, the BCP identifies who makes the ultimate decisions. For example, the BCP coordinator may be in charge until the EMT lead shows up, and then authority passes to the EMT lead. Either way, the EMT works closely with the DAT to identify damage. The EMT also works closely with the BCP coordinator to determine the response.

- **Damage assessment team**—This team assesses the damage and declares the severity of the incident. The members primarily collect and report data but don't take action. The exception is if they identify personnel who need assistance.

  Preserving the health and safety of personnel is always a top priority. The team can include IT personnel, facility personnel, and any other personnel overseeing resources. Team members report to the EMT. The BCP may designate specific forms to be used by this team to report their findings. For example, a damage assessment form would allow the members to document the location and severity of damage they discover.
- **Technical recovery team**—This team is responsible for recovering the critical IT resources. During the disruption only the IT resources identified in the BIA will be recovered and restored. The members of the TRT will need skills directly related to the resource they are recovering. For example, if team members need to restore a database server, they need knowledge of how to do so.

Key Personnel

The BCP may identify additional personnel who have other responsibilities. These personnel would vary from one organization to another. They could include:

- **Critical vendors**—If specific supplies or other resources are needed from a critical vendor, the BCP would identify its responsibilities. A critical vendor could be a vendor that is the sole source for a specific part or product that is sold. It could also be a vendor that will deliver emergency supplies within a certain time. For example, a company could contract with a vendor to deliver potable water to the site anytime a hurricane is within 36 hours of striking. Service level agreements (SLAs) may be in place with the vendor to ensure it provided the service when needed.
- **Critical contractors**—Many companies have contractors on staff in addition to full-time employees. Contractors can be full-time workers supplementing the staff or part-time workers fulfilling a specific need. If contractors are expected to have specific roles in the BCP, they should be identified. For example, some contractor positions may be mission-critical, which would require the workers to work on-site through any type of disruption. The specific responsibilities of these contractors should be identified in the BCP.
- **Telecommuters**—Telecommuters often work from home. Working from home is effective as long as the organization is fully operational. However, during a disruption, the telecommuters may not be able to access the organization's resources so that they cannot accomplish any work. The organization may want these employees to access resources at a different location. Alternately, these workers may have skills that will help the organization get through the disruption, and they may need to report to the work site. The BCP documents what the organization expects of these workers during a disruption.

Order of Succession and Delegation of Authority

In some disasters, the key personnel may not be available. For example, the chief executive officer (CEO) may want to be informed by the BCP coordinator before the BCP is activated. However, what if the CEO is on vacation and can't be reached? Whom should the BCP coordinator notify instead?

The BCP would include an order of succession, or chain of command, to address these types of situations. An organization could designate the order of succession as follows:

- CEO
- Chief information officer (CIO)
- Vice presidents (VPs) in the following order: service delivery, sales, and marketing
- Department directors in the following order: service delivery, sales, and marketing

If the CEO or the CIO were on site, they would be contacted first. If the CEO or CIO isn't there, the VP of service delivery would be contacted. Notice that, if both the VPs of service delivery and sales are there, the order of succession specifies that the VP of service delivery is first.

Similarly, identifying what authority can be delegated may be included in the BCP. Decisions made during a major crisis can affect the organization for years afterward. The BCP may specify that either the CEO or CIO must make some decisions, even if they aren't on site. If the CEO or CIO isn't reachable, these decisions can then be delegated based on the order of succession. If the BCP doesn't delegate authority and personnel on site cannot reach an executive, they won't be able to make decisions. The inaction may cause more damage than making a decision that is less than perfect.

Notification and Activation Phase

The BCP coordinator declares the notification and activation phase, which is when the disruption has occurred or is imminent. Comparing hurricanes and earthquakes shows how this phase can differ depending on the disruption.

Weather forecasters are able to give warnings several days in advance for many hurricanes. Although the forecasts aren't 100% accurate, they do provide advance warning for an organization to prepare in case it does hit. The BCP can be written so that different steps are taken at different stages. For example, **TABLE 13-1** shows what actions to take at different times when a hurricane is approaching. In the table, the time frames are identified with a specific stage or level code. This stage is internal and indicates what actions to take when that code is reached. This is not a complete list, but it does provide an idea of how different actions are taken at different times.

> **NOTE**
>
> Sometimes, time frames are reported differently by different sources. For example, one TV station says a hurricane will make landfall in 75 hours, whereas another TV station says it will hit in 72 hours. The BCP coordinator is the authority to declare when a specific hurricane stage has been reached.

In contrast, an earthquake doesn't give any notification. Instead, it just hits. What's more, after a major earthquake hits, many aftershocks can be expected.

With this in mind, the BCP for an earthquake will have a much different notification and activation phase. The BCP could even be written so that personnel are required to take specific actions

TABLE 13-1 Hurricane Checklist

TIME FRAME	ACTIONS
96 hours Hurricane stage 4	Inform all personnel that a hurricane can hit within 96 hours. Begin general cleanup outside to ensure that materials that can become projectiles in hurricane-force winds are moved inside. Review steps and responsibilities for other stages.
72 hours Hurricane stage 3	Review supply list. Ensure that all needed supplies are on hand. For buildings susceptible to flooding, begin sandbagging activities. Review steps and responsibilities for other stages.
48 hours Hurricane stage 2	Release nonessential personnel to take care of their homes and families. Test backup generators. Notify the hurricane crew that they are on call and when they should report to the site.
24 hours Hurricane stage 1	Bring in the hurricane crew that will stay throughout the hurricane. Release all other personnel.

when it hits, without being formally notified. For example, the response team members could immediately report to their lead for direction.

The BCP coordinator will still activate the BCP, which ensures that everyone is notified. However, if an earthquake hits, what happened will be obvious to anyone in the area.

Notification Procedures

Notification procedures can vary from one organization to another. However, the most important step is to ensure that the BCP coordinator is notified of any disruption or disaster covered by the BCP. If a disruption or disaster occurs during working hours, the BCP coordinator will probably be on the scene quickly. If it happens after hours, the BCP coordinator should be tracked down and contacted.

Using some type of phone tree to notify the teams and team members is common. For example, the BCP coordinator could notify the team leads for the EMT, DAT, and TRT. Team leads could then notify all the members of their teams.

> **TIP**
> Issuing the BCP coordinator a cell phone is a justifiable expense in this instance. The BCP coordinator should be reachable at any time of day or night to respond to major disruptions or disasters.

Damage Assessment Procedures

The DAT is responsible for assessing the damage and reporting it to the BCP coordinator. The team's primary goal is to identify the extent of the damage as quickly as possible.

Again, the time when the DAT goes into action is dependent on the disruption. If it's a hurricane, the members will assess the damage inside the building as the storm hits. For example, they will assess internal flooding and leaks due to storm damage as they occur. When the storm has passed and people can safely go outside, the DAT will assess the damage externally. If the disruption is an immediate disaster, such as an earthquake, the DAT will go into action as the members arrive on the scene.

Data is passed to the EMT team lead and the BCP coordinator. They work together to determine the extent of the damage based on all the reports.

The EMT team lead will then make a determination on what to do. If critical operations can continue to operate on-site, the TRT will begin recovery operations. If damage is extensive and critical operations cannot continue in the same location, operations may need to be moved to an alternate location.

Plan Activation

The BCP coordinator is responsible for activating the BCP but does so based on predefined criteria. In other words, the BCP coordinator doesn't just make the decision based on a hunch.

For example, the following items are valid reasons to activate the BCP:

- Safety of personnel
- Damage to the building affecting CBFs
- Loss of operations affecting one or more CBFs
- Specific criteria identified in the BCP, such as a hurricane warning or an earthquake

Specific responsibilities when the plan is activated include:

- **BCP coordinator**—The BCP coordinator's primary responsibility after activating the plan is ensuring everyone is aware that it's activated, which includes anyone involved in the plan. The BCP coordinator will notify team leads. The coordinator's responsibility also includes notifying senior management personnel, such as the CEO or CIO.
- **EMT lead**—The EMT lead coordinates the actions of the EMT. The team lead also works closely with the DAT lead and the BCP coordinator.
- **EMT**—The EMT works with the DAT and the TRT as directed by the EMT lead. Members of this team also interact with personnel outside the organization. For example, a member of this team will talk to the press and ensure the organization presents an image of being "in control" as much as possible. If the organization looks as if it is in chaos, it might lose public trust, which will affect the goodwill of the company for years to come.
- **DAT lead**—The DAT lead coordinates the actions of the DAT and works closely with the EMT lead and the BCP coordinator.
- **DAT**—The DAT gathers all the information on the disruption or disaster. Its goal is to provide specific details on what is damaged and the extent of the damage. Whenever possible, the team tries to determine whether the site is recoverable and reports its findings to the DAT lead.

TIP

BCPs identify alternate locations, which include hot sites, warm sites, and cold sites.

If the site is not recoverable within a certain period of time, operations may need to move to an alternate location. The BCP coordinator, EMT lead, and DAT lead work together to determine possible recovery solutions based on available data.

Alternate Assessment Procedures

In some instances, the DAT may not be able to assess the damage directly. If necessary, the team can do an indirect assessment based on the available information.

For example, when Hurricane Barry hit the U.S. state of Louisiana in 2019, many organizations had to evacuate, and personnel were not able to return immediately. However, TV images showed the extent of the damage in the area. Executives may not have seen their buildings, but they saw the damage to nearby buildings and knew that they weren't returning to operations in the original buildings anytime soon.

Personnel Location Control Form

Many organizations use a notification roster. This form identifies the name and contact information of appropriate personnel. It can be used in many different ways, but the primary purpose is to contact personnel when necessary.

For example, consider an organization that is activating a BCP due to an incoming hurricane. Employees can use this form to notify all appropriate personnel. This same form can be used by the BCP coordinator to locate and talk to any of the team leads. Similarly, the team leads can use it to contact personnel on their teams. The format can be as simple as that shown in **TABLE 13-2**.

Recovery Phase

The step after the notification and activation phase is the recovery phase. This phase is when the TRT members go to work. They have several goals, including:

- Restoring temporary operations to critical systems
- Repairing damage done to original systems
- Recovering damage to original systems

Once the TRT has completed its job, the critical operations will function. The TRT does not focus on recovering and restoring all operations but instead focuses only on the CBFs identified in the BIA.

TRT members commonly use specific DRPs to recover individual systems. For example, the BCP may designate a website and a database server as critical. A DRP could be included as an attachment to the BCP, showing how to recover and restore these services.

Recovery Planning

The success of the recovery phase is based on the recovery planning that was done beforehand. As someone once said, "It wasn't raining when Noah built the Ark," meaning it's too late to plan when the disaster strikes. The plans must be made earlier.

Recovery planning often takes the format of a DRP, which will identify the steps and procedures to restore and recover systems after an incident.

TABLE 13-2 Personnel Location Control Form

NAME	PHONES		EMAIL
Darril Gibson	Cell	xxx-xxx-xxxx	Darril@darrilgibson.com
	Home	xxx-xxx-xxxx	
	Work	xxx-xxx-xxxx	

Recovery Goal

The recovery goal is dependent on several factors. The goal could be to recover a portion of the functionality of a CBF. For example, a database may need to be operational so that it can accept some updates and queries. However, it may not need to be able to support the full load of normal operations.

On the other hand, the recovery goal could be much more complete. For example, an organization may have services provided at one location. When a disaster strikes, it may need to restore all functionality at another location.

The TRT will perform the work to achieve the recovery goals. The DRP guides the work, but it is possible that the work will be in phases, depending on the depth of the recovery. This is especially true when operations have to be relocated to a different location.

Technical Recovery Team Lead

The TRT lead oversees the work done by the TRT. This team lead needs to be very familiar with existing DRPs and may even have authored them. The team lead also keeps the EMT lead and BCP coordinator informed of the progress.

Technical Recovery Team

The TRT performs the recovery work. The scope of its work will depend on the extent of the damage and whether operations are moved. For example, a hurricane could have caused water damage in the server room. On-site personnel may have limited the amount of damage by quickly killing the power and moving the servers before the water reached them, which could make the recovery as simple as cleaning up the water damage and moving the servers back and rebooting them.

On the other hand, an earthquake could have destroyed the building and buried the servers beneath the rubble, which makes recovery much more complex. The TRT members must restore the servers at an alternate location, which means they will need to retrieve the off-site backups and ship them to the alternate location, after which they will need to restore and configure the data on them.

The success of the TRT is often dependent on the advance work it has done with the DRP. Ideally, appropriate personnel had tested the DRP and kept it up to date. If not, the TRT will likely have unforeseen problems. Additionally, moving operations from one location to another is a huge project, and problems should be expected. But, if personnel had never tested the DRP, even more problems can be expected.

Reconstitution Phase (Return to Normal Operations)

The last phase is the reconstitution phase, which is when both the critical and noncritical functions are returned to normal. This phase begins when one of two things occurs:

- The damage at the original location is repaired.
- Management decides to move operations permanently to an alternate location.

Move Least Critical Functions First

When moving CBFs from an alternate back to an original location, the least critical functions should be moved first, which will help ensure that the most critical functions aren't interrupted.

When functions are restored at the original location, the process may not go smoothly at first, but, if the least critical functions are moved first, only they will be affected. After the kinks have been worked out of the process, then the more critical functions can be moved.

Original or New-Site Restoration

If damage at the original location is extensive, management may decide to move operations, a decision that will involve many factors. For example, a fire damaged a primary company building. In response, the TRT recovered critical business operations at a regional office. Later, the DAT determined that the fire damage was so extensive that the company needed to rebuild the original building. Now, management must decide where to relocate these operations.

Even though critical operations are at the alternate location, they may not be able to support the noncritical operations. Management could decide to move all operations to a new site and restore them there. On the other hand, the damage could have been only minor, and the critical operations would then need to be moved from the alternate back to the original location. Either way, the TRT will perform the primary work because it is most familiar with the DRPs and the steps that need to be taken to restore the functions.

Concurrent Processing

Concurrent processing means that operations are running at two separate locations at the same time. For example, a disruption has caused operations to be moved to an alternate location, after which the systems will be rebuilt at the primary location. In this situation, many experts recommend operating from both locations for 3 to 5 days to be sure that the primary location systems are running smoothly before shutting down the operations in the alternate location.

NOTE

Not all systems will support concurrent processing. Some of them may present technical challenges that prevent running both systems at the same time.

Plan Deactivation

A few things still need to be considered at this stage. First, just returning the original site to operations doesn't necessarily mean that everything has been normalized. For example, if operations have been moved to an alternate location, that location must be cleaned up.

It may have had all the equipment that was needed already in place, but, if it didn't, multiple servers, routers, and switches might have been shipped there. Now, the goal is to return the alternate location to how it was before the disruption or even better.

Another important consideration is data. Sometimes, after a major disaster, management decides to leave some hardware staged at the alternate location. However, if data is left on these systems, it presents an unnecessary risk because it could be retrieved by anyone who has physical access to the alternate location.

Again, the TRT will be responsible for completing these steps. Including a checklist in the BCP is worthwhile to ensure that nothing critical is overlooked. Once everything has been normalized, the BCP can be deactivated.

Plan Training, Testing, and Exercises

Although creating the BCP is a huge step, its creation is not enough. Steps need to be taken to teach personnel about the plan. The plan also needs to be tested, and exercises demonstrating that it will work need to be performed. The overall goals of these steps are:

- **Training**—Teaching people details about the BCP
- **Testing**—Verifying that the BCP will work as planned
- **Exercises**—Demonstrating how the BCP will work

BCP Training

The BCP coordinator is responsible for ensuring all personnel are trained, of whom the most important are the members of the teams. They should have a good understanding of what their actual responsibilities are when the BCP is activated.

Each of the BCP teams has different responsibilities, but not all the teams need to be trained on all their responsibilities at the same time. Several training sessions can be held as follows:

- **Training session for all teams**—This training gives everyone an overall idea of the plan and how each team fits into its success.
- **EMT training**—This training is targeted at members of the EMT and identifies their specific responsibilities.
- **DAT training**—This training is targeted at members of the DAT. It stresses the importance of the assessment and identifies tools or checklists to use.
- **TRT training**—This training is targeted at members of the TRT. It includes reviews of each of the individual disaster recovery plans.

> **TIP**
>
> Because team leads will need to interact with each other, all of them should attend all team training. For example, the DAT lead should attend not only the DAT training but also the EMT and TRT training.

Training should be conducted at least annually unless the BCP or systems change, in which case, training will need to be done more often. For example, if a critical system identified in the BCP is replaced, the BCP needs to be modified. Subject matter experts update the DRP, and, if it is changed, members of the TRT will then need training on the new DRP.

BCP Testing

BCP testing should be completed at least annually. The goal of the testing is to show that the steps within the BCP are achievable, and it provides team members an opportunity to walk through the steps of the plan.

Testing may include the following steps:

- **Testing individual steps within each phase of the BCP**—This testing requires a line-by-line review of the BCP. Procedures, such as performing a recall, can be tested only by retrieving the recall roster and calling people on it.
- **Testing all disaster recovery plans**—This testing ensures that the steps in the DRP can be completed as written. For example, a DRP may identify steps for rebuilding and recovering a database server. An administrator will follow the DRP on an offline system to determine whether the steps succeed.
- **Locating and testing alternate resources**—If the plan identifies alternate locations or resources, they need to be tested. For example, if the plan identifies an alternate location, test the alternate location to see whether it can actually support the CBFs.

Testing should reveal any problems or deficiencies with the plan, which includes any problems with the steps, resources, or personnel, and they should be resolved as soon as possible.

BCP Test Exercises

The primary purpose of BCP exercises is to show how the BCP will work. These exercises should be challenging but realistic and should present problems that are solvable.

In addition to testing the capabilities of the BCP, an exercise will also build participants' confidence. If an actual emergency occurs, people will be able to think back to the exercise. If everything failed, they won't feel very confident about the plan during the emergency and may even abandon or try to circumvent it during an emergency.

Many organizations use a phased approach toward exercising a plan. Instead of doing full-scale exercises at first, they perform tabletop and functional exercises.

> **TIP**
>
> BCP exercises should not affect normal mission operations. Any steps that will affect operations can be tested with a simulation. Multiple scenarios can be done as tabletop exercises. For example, one scenario may be a weather-related event, such as a hurricane. The BCP coordinator can identify the stage, and team leads or members can respond by identifying what they would do. Another scenario can be more immediate, such as a fire that occurs in the middle of the night. Documenting and evaluating the exercise is important and can be done by someone who isn't a member of any of the BCP teams. Having this outside perspective can be valuable in ensuring that all the issues are addressed.

Tabletop Exercises. A tabletop exercise brings all the members together to talk through the process. In such an exercise, all the team members sit around a conference room table, and the BCP coordinator then presents a scenario to them.

Team members identify what they'd do to respond to the scenario. At this point, the BCP has been written and approved so that ideally the team members' responses would match what the BCP says. However, in this setting, participants may place themselves in the actual situation and identify different problems.

Functional Exercises. A functional exercise evaluates specific functions within the BCP. For example, the BCP identifies an alternate location for some critical functions. A functional exercise can be performed to restore and recover all the critical resources at the alternate location.

Functional exercises can be less dramatic and resource intensive. For example, simply initiating the recall roster can verify that it is accurate and identify how much time the recall will take to complete.

Just as with a tabletop exercise, documenting the results of the functional exercise is important. The BCP coordinator or someone who isn't a member of any of the BCP teams can do this.

Full-Scale Exercises. A full-scale exercise is more realistic than either tabletop or functional exercises because it simulates an actual disruption of CBFs. Team members aren't sitting around a table discussing what they'd do, but instead they take action.

Completing full-scale exercises requires many resources, the primary one being personnel. However, full-scale exercises provide the most realistic view of how team members will respond to an actual emergency.

Just as with other exercises, documenting the results is important. Depending on the breadth of the plan, several outside observers documenting what they see may be beneficial, and gathering input from the team members after the exercise has been completed is important. They will likely have insight into what elements of the BCP worked and how to improve the BCP.

A single report can then be compiled to document this data. At this time, any issues should be addressed, which may require modifying the BCP.

NOTE

The primary difference between testing and a functional exercise is that testing is done without a time frame. Team members can be given advanced notice to perform a test and all the time they need to perform it. On the other hand, a functional exercise is more immediate because team members do not require any advanced notice. The amount of time it takes to complete the functional exercise should be documented.

Plan Maintenance

The BCP coordinator is responsible for the BCP plan, which includes reviews and updates of the BCP. There are several specific reasons to update the BCP, such as:

- Changes to the IT infrastructure
- Regular updating, such as annually
- After testing or exercises

BCP Plan Revisions Tracking

All revisions to the BCP need to be documented. This ensures that people can easily tell if the document has been modified and they have the most up-to-date version. Many organizations use a simple version control page. For example, **TABLE 13-3** shows an example of a version control page.

In addition to the change being documented in the version control page, all relevant parties must be apprised about the change. For example, if changes directly affect the EMT members, they should know what those changes are.

TABLE 13-3 BCP Version Control Page

DATE	AUTHOR	VERSION	COMMENTS
xx / xx / xx	Individual or group making the change	Current version of the document, such as 1.1, 2.0, and so on	Comments about the changes made to the document

BCP Updates Based on Changes Within the IT Infrastructure

The BCP should be reviewed when any substantial changes occur within the IT infrastructure, which is especially true after any changes have been made to critical systems.

For example, a single server hosts a web server and a database for online sales. The BCP includes a DRP to recover this server if a disaster occurs. If this system is upgraded to a four-node web farm with back-end database servers in a two-node failover cluster, the change is substantial, but the original BCP and DRP don't address this new configuration. If these servers are moved to an alternate location, the original BCP and DRP simply won't provide much help. Therefore, the appropriate thing to do is review the BCP and then upgrade the BCP and DRP to reflect the changes.

Organizations that have change management procedures in place make this review much easier. The BCP coordinator can simply review approved change requests periodically to determine when changes have occurred. Another suggestion is to include a check item in the change management review. For example, the TRT lead may be required to verify that the change won't affect the BCP or any DRPs. Because many changes are inconsequential, they don't require a change to the BCP.

BCP Annual Updates and Content Refreshment

The BCP coordinator is responsible for reviewing the BCP at least annually, even if there are no known changes. This review ensures the BCP still addresses and meets all the organization's requirements. It includes a review of the BIA to ensure that CBFs haven't been modified and are still considered critical; operational and security requirements; and a review of any of the individual processes, such as recalls, and more technical procedures, such as DRPs.

The review process can be separate from the rewriting process. For example, a member of the TRT can be tasked to review a specific DRP that is included as an attachment of the BCP. The review may identify changes to the system that make the DRP out of date. The TRT member should report the results of the review back to the BCP coordinator, and then the BCP coordinator would have the TRT lead update the DRP.

The BCP coordinator should route changes through appropriate personnel. If a change directly affects the TRT, the changes should be routed through the TRT lead for input. Additionally, all affected personnel should be notified of the change when it has been completed. For example, either the TRT lead or the BCP coordinator should notify all TRT members of the change.

BCP Testing

The review of the BCP should also include reviewing information from training, testing, and exercises. Much valuable information can be learned during each of these activities, such as determining that some of the procedures in the BCP will work well and that others will need to be improved by updating the BCP.

Ideally, the BCP would be updated soon after the report from these events has been completed. However, a review of these reports can also be included in the annual review of the BCP, which ensures that all the issues identified in the training, testing, and exercises are resolved.

How Does a BCP Mitigate an Organization's Risk?

BCPs mitigate an organization's risk by ensuring that the organization is better prepared for disasters. If a disaster occurs, the organization will meet it with the benefit of forethought and planning. On the other hand, if an organization doesn't have a BCP, managers must make spur-of-the-moment decisions.

Pilots are often praised for their ability to react coolly in the face of disaster. For example, Captain Chesley "Sully" Sullenberger realized his best option was to land a jetliner in the Hudson River in 2009, which prompted him to calmly say into the microphone, "We're gonna be in the Hudson."

Why was he so calm? Because pilots train for disasters so many times that they know what needs to be done. Even in the midst of a crisis, they calmly identify the best steps to take to reduce the impact of disasters.

On the other hand, if a pilot had never trained for a disaster, and then suddenly he had two jet engines go dead, he'd be tempted to try anything to get things going again. Much of his energy would be wasted on attempting actions that couldn't succeed or would make matters worse.

Similarly, the BCP helps an organization plan and train for disasters so that if one does occur, the organization is much better prepared to address it.

> **TIP**
>
> Serious losses have caused entire companies to fail when they didn't have a BCP. In his *The Definitive Handbook of Business Continuity Management*, Andrew Hiles wrote that between 60% and 90% of companies that lost a key facility but didn't have a BCP completely failed within 24 months. The BCP is like insurance. A company always wants to have it but never wants to use it.

Best Practices for Implementing a BCP for an Organization

When implementing a BCP, several best practices can be used. Following is a list of many of these:

- **Completing the BIA early**—The BIA should be done early in the process for the BCP. Without the BIA, no one would know what systems are critical or what priority to use to recover the systems.
- **Exercising caution when returning functionality from alternate locations**—When restoring functionality from an alternate location to the primary location, these best practices should be considered:
  - **Restoring least critical functions first**—This allows for getting the bugs out of the process without affecting critical functions.
  - **Using concurrent processing after a disruption**—If systems have been rebuilt at the primary location, they should be run for 3 to 5 days before cutting off the services at the alternate location.
- **Reviewing and updating the BCP regularly**—The BCP coordinator should review and update the BCP at least annually. If critical systems are changed or modified between annual reviews, the BCP should be reviewed when those changes or modifications occur.

- **Testing all the individual pieces of the plan**—This testing includes basic procedures, such as recalls, and the more detailed procedures documented in DRPs.
- **Exercising the plan**—The plan should be verified that it works by performing test exercises. These exercises should not affect normal operations.

CHAPTER SUMMARY

This chapter covered the details on BCPs. The primary purpose of a BCP is to ensure that an organization can continue to operate after a disruption or disaster. The BCP includes details on the CBFs, including what needs to be done to keep them operating. Many individuals and teams share responsibilities. The BCP program manager oversees all BCPs, and the BCP coordinator manages one or more BCPs. Multiple teams with individual team leads also provide support to the BCP coordinator during development and implementation of a BCP.

A BCP has three primary phases. In the notification and activation phase, the BCP coordinator initiates the activity; in the recovery phase, critical systems are recovered and restored; and in the reconstitution phase, normal operations are restored when the disaster has passed. All BCP team members and leads should be trained on the BCP, and it should be tested and exercises done to ensure its completeness. The BCP coordinator is responsible for regularly updating the BCP, which includes regular updates and additional ones when warranted.

KEY CONCEPTS AND TERMS

business continuity (BC)
disaster recovery (DR)
damage assessment team (DAT)
emergency management team (EMT)
mission-critical
technical recovery team (TRT)

CHAPTER 13 ASSESSMENT

1. A(n) ________ is a plan that helps an organization continue to operate during and after a disruption or disaster.
2. Business continuity and disaster recovery are the same thing.
   A. True
   B. False
3. A BCP includes specific locations, systems, employees, and vendors, and these requirements are identified in the ________ statement.
4. What is the purpose of a BCP?
   A. To identify CBFs
   B. To reduce or eliminate threats
   C. To ensure mission-critical elements of an organization continue to operate after a disruption
   D. All of the above

5. What does a BCP help to protect during and after a disruption or disaster?
   A. Confidentiality, information, and authentication
   B. Certifications, identities, and accreditations
   C. Mission-critical and non–mission-critical CBFs
   D. Confidentiality, integrity, and availability

6. The ________ is responsible for declaring an emergency and activating the BCP.

7. After a BCP has been activated, who has overall authority for the recovery of systems?
   A. EMT
   B. DAT
   C. TRT
   D. CAT

8. After a BCP has been activated, who will assess the damages?
   A. BCP coordinator
   B. EMT
   C. DAT
   D. TRT

9. After a BCP has been activated, who will recover and restore critical IT services?
   A. BCP coordinator
   B. EMT
   C. DAT
   D. TRT

10. What are the three phases of a BCP?
   A. Notification and activation, transfer, and recovery
   B. Notification and activation, recovery, and reconstitution
   C. Recovery, renewal, and reconstitution
   D. Transfer, recovery, and notification

11. A major disruption has forced a company to move operations to an alternate location. The disruption is over, and now the process of normalizing operations needs to begin. What operations should be moved back to the original location first?
   A. Least CBFs
   B. Most CBFs
   C. Non–mission-critical personnel
   D. Mission-critical personnel

12. A major disruption has forced a company to move operations to an alternate location. The disruption is over, and now the process of normalizing operations needs to begin. Several servers have been rebuilt at the primary location. What should be done?
   A. Test the servers and then turn off the servers at the alternate location.
   B. Bring the servers online and turn off the alternate location servers.
   C. Run the servers concurrently with the alternate location for 3 to 5 days.
   D. Test the servers for 3 to 5 days before bringing them online.

13. What can be done to show that the BCP will work as planned?
   A. BCP planning
   B. BCP training
   C. BCP testing
   D. BCP exercises

14. What types of exercises can demonstrate a BCP in action? (Select three.)
   A. Tabletop exercises
   B. Functional exercises
   C. Pull-the-plug exercises
   D. Full-scale exercises

15. Once a BCP has been developed, it should be reviewed and updated on a regular basis, such as annually.
   A. True
   B. False

CHAPTER 14

Mitigating Risk With a Disaster Recovery Plan

THE ENTIRE REASON for disaster recovery planning is because disasters can and do occur. These can be natural disasters, such as a major storm, flood, or earthquake. Disasters can also be a substantial data breach or failure of key technology. The purpose of a disaster recovery plan is to guide an organization into fully recovering IT operations. In Chapter 13, we discussed business continuity planning and getting essential operations functioning. In this chapter we will dive into specifically the IT systems. There is certainly overlap between DRP and BCP; both depend on business impact analysis and look at the same data. The difference is in the end goal of each plan. Essentially BCP is broader than DRP.

When developing a DRP, several factors that are critical to its success need to be considered. These factors include elements that must be provided by management, what the DRP developers need, and an understanding of several primary concerns. These primary concerns include recovery time objectives (RTOs), the need for alternate locations, and having a budget. Without funding, the DRP is sure to fail.

There are several standards that can assist you in developing an effective disaster recovery plan. ISO/IEC 27031:2011 — *Guidelines for information and communication technology readiness for business continuity* can also be applied to disaster recovery. NIST Special Publication 800-34 Revision 1, titled "Contingency Planning Guide for Federal Information Systems," provides comprehensive guidance for creating effective contingency plans for federal information systems. Although targeted at U.S. federal agencies, the principles are broadly applicable to any organization seeking to improve its IT continuity and disaster recovery capabilities. This standard is also applicable to both business continuity planning and disaster recovery. This standard covers the following types of plans:

- **Business Continuity Plan (BCP)** – Ensures mission/business continuity.
- **Disaster Recovery Plan (DRP)** – Restores IT operations at alternate locations.
- **Incident Response Plan (IRP)** – Addresses cyberincidents.
- **Occupant Emergency Plan (OEP)** – Handles physical facility incidents.
- **Continuity of Operations Plan (COOP)** – Maintains essential functions during a wide range of emergencies.
- **Crisis Communications Plan** – Manages internal and external communication.

Individual DRPs can vary in the elements within them, but overall, several elements are commonly included. All DRPs start by defining their purpose and scope and what disasters they will address. They include detailed steps and procedures that identify how to recover the organization in response to a disaster. Once they have been written, they need to be tested and regularly reviewed and updated.

Chapter 14 Topics

This chapter covers the following topics and concepts:

- What a disaster recovery plan (DRP) is
- What critical success factors (CSFs) are
- What the elements of a DRP are
- How a DRP mitigates an organization's risk
- What best practices for implementing a DRP are

Chapter 14 Goals

When you complete this chapter, you will be able to:

- Describe the need for and purpose of a DRP
- Define CSFs for a DRP
- Identify what management must provide to ensure the success of the DRP
- Identify what DRP developers need to ensure the success of the DRP
- Describe RTOs as they are used in the DRP
- Define and contrast cold sites, hot sites, warm sites, and mobile sites
- Define a redundant backup site
- Describe the access concerns when planning for an alternate location
- Describe the purpose of the disaster recovery financial budget
- Identify the elements of a DRP
- Describe the contents of recovery steps and procedures used in the DRP
- Identify the types of testing used for a DRP
- Identify the steps used to maintain the DRP
- Describe how a DRP mitigates an organization's risk
- List best practices for implementing a DRP

What Is a Disaster Recovery Plan?

A **disaster recovery plan (DRP)** is a plan to restore IT systems to full operation after a disaster. This will often be full operations at an alternate location; in fact, some standards and textbooks assume one will be restoring operations at an alternate location. The key point, however, is the focus is restoring the IT systems.

The DRP can also be used to rebuild systems after hardware or software failures. If a critical system crashes, operations stop. Although this isn't as big a disaster as an earthquake, it is a disaster for this system.

Disaster recovery occurs after a disaster. It will bring a system back into service after it has failed. The specific steps and procedures for disaster recovery are documented in the DRP. One or more DRPs are included in the BCP.

> **TIP**
>
> **Business continuity plans (BCPs)** are developed for the overall business. In comparison, the DRP targets specific systems and is an element of the BCP.

Fault Tolerance Is Not Disaster Recovery

Many organizations provide fault tolerance for systems. It helps ensure systems continue to operate even after a failure of a component. However, fault tolerance and disaster recovery are not the same thing. To be completely clear, fault tolerant systems are quite important. But simply having fault tolerant systems is not sufficient for disaster recovery.

For example, a redundant array of independent disks (RAID) provides fault tolerance for disks. If a disk in the system fails, the fault is tolerated, and the system continues to operate. However, if a disaster destroys the server, the fault-tolerant RAID system can't overcome this failure. The server must be able to be rebuilt and the lost data restored for disaster recovery.

Similarly, fault tolerance doesn't negate the need for backups. If a server is protected by a RAID system, backups still need to be done. The RAID protects against the failure of a single disk, but, if the server catches fire or a catastrophic failure destroys all disks, data on the RAID will be lost. Therefore, without a backup, the data will be lost forever.

Both fault tolerance and disaster recovery techniques are necessary. Fault tolerance increases the availability of systems even when an isolated outage occurs, whereas disaster recovery provides the procedures to recover systems from outages after a major failure.

Disaster recovery planning may be described by many terms, but they all mean essentially the same thing. Instead of the term *disaster recovery planning*, the following terms may be used:

- Contingency planning
- Emergency management procedures
- Business resumption planning
- Corporate contingency planning

- Business interruption planning
- Disaster preparedness

When working with DRPs, understanding several DRP-related terms is important. These include:

- **Critical business functions (CBFs)**—CBFs are any functions considered vital to an organization. These vital functions must be restored in the event of a disruption to protect the assets of the organization. If the CBF fails, the organization will lose the capability to perform critical operations necessary to meet its obligations and even continue to survive. Individual information technology (IT) systems and services support CBFs.
- **Continuity of operations planning (COOP)**—This is the U.S. government term for both BCP and DRP.
- **Maximum acceptable outage**—**Maximum acceptable outage (MAO)**, also called the maximum tolerable downtime (MTD), is the maximum amount of time a system or service can be down before it affects the organization's objectives or survival. The MAO directly affects the required recovery time because a system must be recoverable before the MAO time is reached. This term is also sometimes known by other names: maximum tolerable period of disruption (MTPoD) or maximum tolerable outage (MTO).
- **Recovery time objective**—**Recovery time objective (RTO)** is the time when a system or function must be recovered to avoid unacceptable business consequences. The RTO is equal to or less than the MAO. For example, if the MAO is 10 minutes, the RTO is 10 minutes or less. Unlike the MAO, the RTO does not necessarily impact the survivability of the business.
- **Business impact analysis**—A **business impact analysis (BIA)** is a study that identifies the CBFs and MAOs, the impact to the business if one or more IT functions fails, and the priority of different critical systems.
- **Business continuity plan (BCP)**—A BCP is a comprehensive plan that helps an organization prepare for different types of emergencies. Its goal is to ensure that mission-critical functions continue to operate even after a disruption or disaster happens. The BCP includes a BIA and one or more DRPs.
- **Minimum business continuity objective**—The **minimum business continuity objective (MBCO)** is the minimum level of services that is acceptable to an organization to meet its business needs and objectives during a disaster.
- **Recovery time actual (RTA)** —Once business continuity and/or disaster recovery plans are tested, there will be actual times for recovery. If all goes well, then the RTA should be equal to or less than the RTO. If not, then additional work is required.

Need for a DRP

Every organization that has a critical mission needs to plan for disasters. If the operations that support the mission stop, the business stops. Unless an organization can do without critical business systems for any period of time, it needs a DRP.

The time to plan for a disaster is before the disaster, not during it. Once the disaster occurs, it's too late to determine which systems are critical, which critical systems are more important than others, and which methods are the best to restore and recover the most important systems.

However, if the BCP identifies the critical systems and the DRP provides details on how to recover these systems, the organization is ready to respond. Without the DRP, the organization may not be able to recover.

Purpose of a DRP

Most DRPs include a purpose statement to help identify the goals of the DRP, which are often multiple. These include:

- **Saving lives**—The protection and safety of personnel is always important. If any steps are required to protect personnel, the DRP will identify them. These steps include what to do to prepare for an impending disaster, such as a hurricane, and what to do as it is occurring and after it has passed.
- **Ensuring business continuity**—The DRP includes procedures to restore CBFs if a disaster occurs. The purpose of these procedures is to ensure that mission-critical operations continue to function during and after a disaster.
- **Recovering after a disaster**—The DRP addresses processes to recover the organization after the disaster has passed, which include normalizing any CBFs moved to an alternate location and normalizing noncritical functions.

DRPs are often divided to reflect different phases of a disaster. One phase identifies the steps and procedures to restore CBFs as soon as a disaster strikes, which may include moving CBFs to an alternate location. Another phase identifies the steps and procedures for normalizing operations. This phase returns operations to the original location. A single DRP can address each of the phases.

Eight Tiers of Disaster Recovery

SHARE Inc. is a volunteer-run user group for IBM mainframe computers that was founded in 1955 by Los Angeles area users of the IBM 704 computer system. They created a model they called the seven tiers of disaster recovery which was published in 1992. This model was updated in 2012 by IBM to be an eight-tier model. The eight tiers are shown in the following table:

TIER	DESCRIPTION	KEY FEATURE	RECOVERY SPEED
0	No off-site backup	No plan	None
1	Off-site backup only	Manual recovery	Very slow
2	Backup + hot site	Preconfigured recovery site	Slow
3	Electronic vaulting	Automated data transfer	Moderate
4	Point-in-time copies	Snapshot-based recovery	Faster
5	Transaction integrity	Consistent recovery state	Fast
6	Real-time replication	Minimal data loss	Very fast
7	Fully automated and integrated recovery solution	Orchestrated and immediate recovery	Near instant

Critical Success Factors

The success of a DRP depends on several **critical success factors (CSFs)**. A CSF is an element necessary for the plan's success. For example, any organization has several CSFs that must be successful to ensure the success of the organization. Similarly, DRPs have CSFs. Without these factors included in the DRP, it has less chance to succeed.

Elements that are critical to the success of a DRP include:

- Management support
- Knowledge and authority for DRP developers
- Identification of primary concerns, such as RTOs and alternate location needs
- A disaster recovery budget

> **TIP**
>
> A key success factor in a disaster recovery plan is management support. Management, particularly upper-level executives, must support the plan for it to succeed. Resources will be needed to create an effective BCP or DRP, and without strong management support, those resources may not be allocated. One could argue that the stronger the managerial support, the more successful the DRP is likely to be.

The following sections explore these disaster recovery plan CSFs in more depth.

What Management Must Provide

Like risk management and security plans, DRPs require the support of management. Some support can be as simple as publicly endorsing the plan, whereas other support can be much more material, such as providing funds.

Resources

The primary resource that management provides is personnel, who are needed to create, test, and update the DRP. They can be in-house employees or outside consultants who are specialists in disaster recovery. It is also important that the right people be allocated to this task. As an example, if the person working on the database portion of the DRP is new and does not have deep knowledge of your organizations database(s), this will lead to a flawed DRP.

Financial support from management is also necessary. For example, if the company needs an alternate location, one will be secured only with financial support. If backups are needed, funding will be necessary to purchase backup tapes or other backup media.

Leadership

Management must also provide leadership to support any DRP. Leaders understand the importance of the DRP and know that its success can be achieved only with combined teamwork. Leaders help disaster recovery and business continuity teams recognize the value of the DRP.

What DRP Developers Need

The developers of the DRP need some specific knowledge and authority to succeed. Any system subject matter expert (SME) can't just be tasked with and expected to be able to write a DRP. Neither can some disaster recovery experts be expected to be able to write a DRP.

Instead, personnel with combined skills are needed. The DRP developers need to have an understanding of disaster recovery and how the organization functions. They can often work with individual SMEs to identify specific steps for systems.

Knowledge of Disaster Recovery

The DRP team must have an understanding of disaster recovery in general and specifically what a BIA is, what a BCP is, and how a DRP fits in with a BIA and a BCP. This would likely include knowledge of relevant disaster recovery standards.

As a reminder, the BIA identifies the critical systems and prioritizes them. The business impact analysis therefore, forms the basis for both business continuity plans and disaster recovery plans (See **FIGURE 14-1**).

Knowledge of How the Organization Functions

Understanding how the organization functions is critical to writing an effective DRP. For example, are the organization's normal operations 24 hours a day, 7 days a week, or typical 9 a.m. to 5 p.m. Monday to Friday? This will make a substantial impact in disaster recovery planning.

In addition to the operating hours, any organization has specific processes in place that the DRP developer needs to understand, and some of them are critical. Either the DRP supports these processes or the DRP can assume that they will remain operational. Other processes are not critical and should not be relied on for the DRP.

> **TIP**
>
> Many companies hire outside consultants to help with the development of DRPs and BCPs. These consultants can work with management and the SMEs to ensure that the DRPs meet the needs of the organization.

For example, one organization may have both uninterruptible power supplies (UPSs) and generators in place. These units provide continuous power to critical systems even if commercial power is lost. The DRP may include steps to ensure that fuel is on hand to last a specific amount of time when a disaster occurs.

FIGURE 14-1

Risk management: BIA, DRP, and BCP.

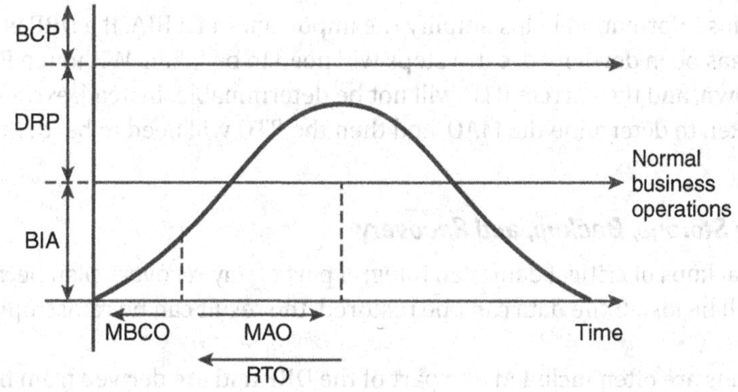

Another organization may use cloud computing for some CBFs, such as data services. If so, service level agreements (SLAs) will be in place to ensure that a third-party vendor keeps these operational, so the DRP doesn't need to address these services.

Authority

DRP developers need some authority when creating the DRP. For example, a DRP developer needs to gather data before writing the DRP. This is especially true if the developer is not an SME. To succeed, the DRP developer needs authority to interview experts who understand the systems.

If the DRP crosses departmental lines, the DRP author needs to make decisions that can affect multiple departments. With this in mind, the DRP author needs management support to make the initial decisions. It is important to ensure that the DRP team has the authority to make decisions relevant to creating an effective DRP.

Primary Concerns

The DRP should address several primary concerns, and the DRP developer should have a clear idea of what they are before writing the DRP. One important concern is recovery time objectives (RTO), which identify the critical nature of the DRP. Some systems need to be restored almost immediately, whereas others can be offline for days before they are recovered.

Having knowledge about required off-site resources is also important. At a minimum, a copy of backups needs to be stored off-site. The DRP may also address the use of alternate locations for operations. All of these topics are explored in other sections in this chapter.

Recovery Time Objectives

The RTOs identify when a system must be recovered and is derived from the MAO identified in the BIA. Outages longer than the MAO will have a significant negative effect on the organization, which means that, if the outage isn't resolved within the RTO, it will impact the mission.

An MAO could be 60 minutes, 24 hours, or something different. However, this number drives the RTO. For example, if the MAO is 60 minutes, the DRP needs to be written to meet an RTO of less than 60 minutes. If the MAO is 24 hours, the RTO needs to be less than 24 hours.

Knowing this information helps amplify the importance of a BIA. If a DRP is being written before a BIA has been developed, extra steps will need to be taken. Without a BIA, the MAO will be unknown, and the correct RTO will not be determinable. Instead, extra steps will need to be taken to determine the MAO, and then the RTO will need to be identified and the DRP written.

Off-Site Data Storage, Backup, and Recovery

Performing backups of critical data is an integral part of any recovery plan because inevitably data will be lost. If the data can't be restored, the result can be catastrophic to the organization.

Backup plans are often included as a part of the DRP and are derived from backup policies. The backup policy identifies details, such as what data should be backed up and how long the backup data should be kept. The backup plan identifies the steps to take to back up and restore the data.

Restore Failures

The goal of backing up data is to be able to restore it, so it would seem obvious that the data on the backups should be restorable. However, it is always possible that the backup media has failed, or perhaps the backup process itself was flawed. This is why it is critical to perform test restorations. The frequency of that test restore will depend on organizational policies. The process is relatively simple: take the backup media and restore it to a device, then examine the restored data to ensure it is intact and not corrupted. At a minimum this test restoration should be done when you first begin a new backup process or plan, then at least once per year. More frequently would certainly be better.

If one does not test backup media, then it is not possible to know if your backups are correct until a disaster occurs and you attempt to restore the data at that point. If, at that time, you discover the backups are corrupt, incomplete, or incorrect, then you have not only failed to mitigate the disaster, you have in fact exacerbated it. It is difficult to overstate that backups of data are critical for disaster recovery but such backups must be tested and verified.

One method to avoid unexpected discovery of bad backup media is adopting a commonly accepted backup strategy known as the "3-2-1 rule." The 3-2-1 rule is the recommended strategy of having 3 copies of your data, stored on 2 different media, with at least 1 copy being stored off-site. So, by having a copy off-site, you avoid localized or facility disasters. And by utilizing 2 different media, you mitigate the risk of having technology-specific faults or incidents.

When one thinks of backups, it is typical to think of data. However, in some situations, programs may need to be backed up. For example, if the organization develops applications, their backups must be available. Naturally, the source code should be kept secure, but backups will also be needed of this source code. Typically, source code is kept in a source code repository, and that repository can be part of the regular backup.

Another critical element of backups is ensuring that copies of backups are stored off-site. Not all the backups should be stored in the same location as the servers. If a fire destroys the building, it destroys the servers and all the backups, whereas, if copies of backups are stored in a separate location, they can always be used to restore the data even if a fire completely destroys the building.

Traditional backups don't always need to be performed to ensure copies of the data are available. Other technical processes can be used too. For example, database applications, such as Oracle and Microsoft SQL Server, support data replication.

FIGURE 14-2 shows that users access a primary database server for data and that this primary server is also replicating data to a secondary server, which has up-to-date data each time replication occurs. If the primary server fails, the secondary server can be brought online to take over for the primary server. How often replication occurs can also be controlled, which ensures that the RTO for the system can be met.

The following two terms identify different types of redundant transfers, which are often used as part of an overall disaster recovery plan:

- **Electronic vaulting**—This method transfers the backup data to an off-site location over wide area network (WAN) links or tunnels through the internet.

FIGURE 14-2

Data backups from data replication.

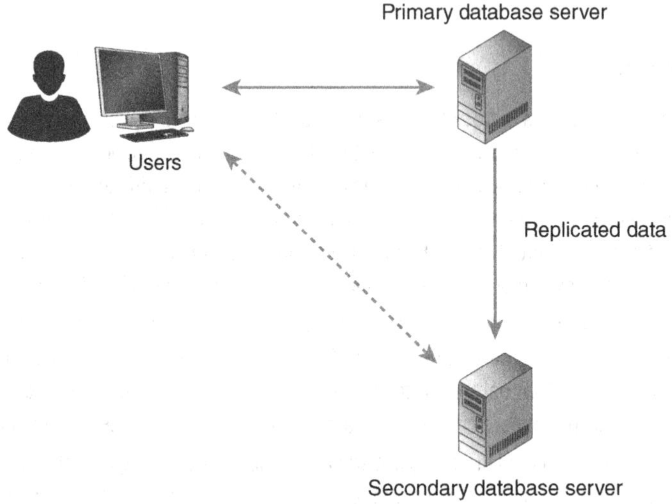

- **Remote journaling**—This method starts with full copies of the data at the remote location and then sends a log of the changes from the primary location to the secondary location. These changes are applied as a batch to the secondary location. After they have been applied, the secondary location is up to date.

> **TIP**
> Several methods of replicating data from one database server to another are available. Mirrored servers can be created, and both of them can be online; standby servers can be created with one online and the other offline to accept the replicated data; and complex replication models can be created with distributors, publishers, and subscribers.

Slight variations of remote journaling are possible with databases. These variations include database mirroring and database shadowing techniques.

Alternate Locations

Many companies need to ensure that their businesses stay in operation even if a significant disruption occurs. For example, businesses working along the San Andreas fault in California have an almost constant threat of an earthquake. If an earthquake hits, the business may not be able to function in the same location.

One or more alternate locations need to be identified if an organization must continue to operate even if a major disaster occurs. These alternate locations can be in different buildings, different cities, or even different states, which depends on the type of disaster being prepared for. For example, if a fire destroys a building, an alternate location in the same city will work, but, if an earthquake is being prepared for, an alternate location in a different city or possibly in a different state would be needed.

Four types of alternate locations are available: cold sites, warm sites, hot sites, and mobile sites. Each site must have the capability to host the critical data and programs of the primary location. However, each site has different costs and initial capabilities. As an introduction, **TABLE 14-1** provides an overview of cold-, warm-, hot-, and mobile-site capabilities.

TABLE 14-1 Comparison of Cold, Warm, Hot, and Mobile Sites

CAPABILITIES AND COSTS	COLD SITE	WARM SITE	HOT SITE	MOBILE SITE
Time to bring the site online	Longest	Balanced	Shortest; minutes or hours	Within 36 to 72 hours
Equipment located at the site	None; only facilities, such as space and power	Most equipment needed to support the CBFs	Most if not all of the equipment needed to support the CBFs	Mobile equipment
Expense to maintain the site	Lowest cost	Balanced	Highest cost	Moderate cost
Testing capabilities of the site	Hardest to test	Balanced	Easiest to test	Relatively easy

Cold Site. A **cold site** is an available building that has electricity, running water, and restrooms but none of the equipment, data, or applications needed for critical operations. It may have raised floors if needed to support a server environment.

For example, an organization could rent space in a different building to prepare for a major disaster. If a disaster occurs, they would move the equipment and data to this location and set up the CBFs there. Obviously, it would take a lot of work to move and set up the equipment.

Cold sites are inexpensive to maintain because they are just empty buildings. However, it is difficult and costly to test a cold site.

> **NOTE**
>
> When renting space in a different building for a cold site, it's important to ensure this space isn't rented to others. For example, some businesses rent out available space to two or more organizations. When a disaster hits, several organizations might try to move into the same space.

Hot Site. A **hot site** includes all the equipment and data necessary to take over business functions. A hot site will be able to assume operations within hours and sometimes within minutes. It usually has personnel at the location 24 hours a day, seven days a week.

Hot sites are expensive to maintain. However, some newer technologies make them a little easier to manage. **Cloud computing** and **virtualization** are two newer technologies that are sometimes used with hot sites. Cloud computing is a general term for anything that involves hosting services over a public network, such as the internet.

As shown in **FIGURE 14-3**, several services are hosted using cloud computing. Each of these services is accessible over the internet, so the physical location of the services doesn't matter. As long as users are able to access the internet, they are able to access the services.

This can be useful for hot sites. For example, if critical operations need to be managed from a regional office instead of from

> **TIP**
>
> Organizations often contract with third-party vendors to provide services via cloud computing. The organization doesn't need to manage the service; rather it has an SLA with the vendor that provides the service.

FIGURE 14-3
Cloud computing.

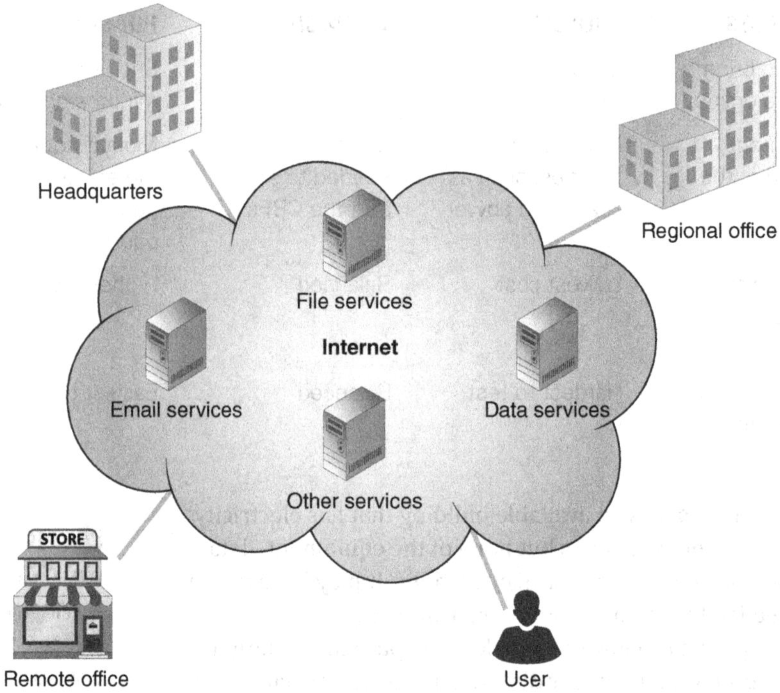

headquarters, the transfer can be almost seamless. Both locations already have access to the critical services. The only thing that may need to be moved to the regional office is personnel.

Time Clock Services Provided via Cloud Computing

Many organizations have switched to cloud computing for tracking employee work hours. An internet-based web server hosts a time clock application, and employees then use a web browser to log on and record hours.

Some of these services allow employees to record the number of hours worked for any given day, whereas others require employees to log on when they report to work and "punch in." Before they leave, employees log on and "punch out." These websites are often configured so that they are accessible only from the employees' location, which prevents employees from punching in and out from home.

At the end of the pay period, a supervisor approves the hours, and the data is then turned over to accounting to process paychecks.

Time clock services significantly reduce the time that an organization spends managing payroll, and, because this is a primary function of the company providing the service, it is able to do it efficiently and for a low cost.

FIGURE 14-4

One physical server hosting four virtual servers.

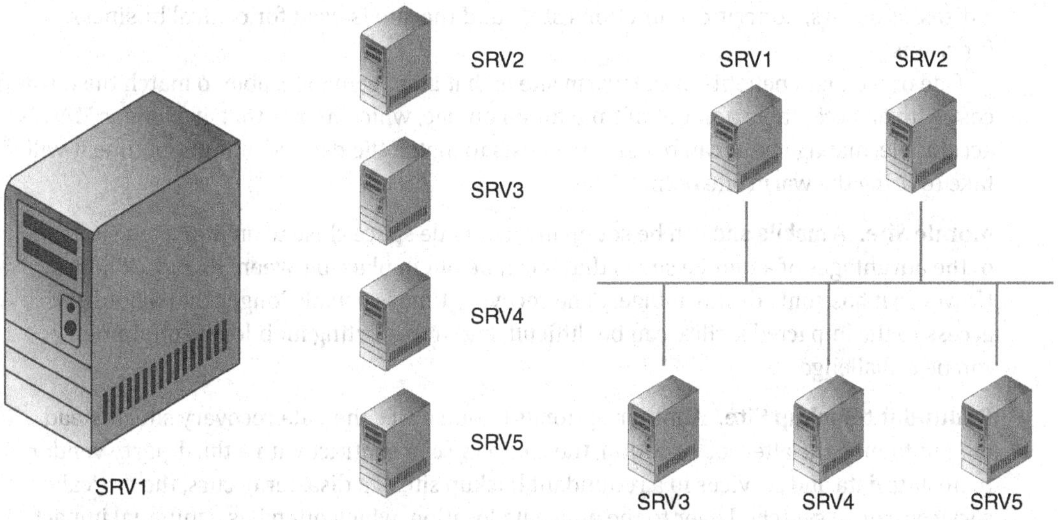

Virtualization is another technology that can be useful for hot sites. Several virtual servers can be hosted on a network within a single physical server. Each virtual server runs on the network just as if it's a physical server.

In **FIGURE 14-4**, SRV1 is the physical server, and it is hosting four servers named SRV2, SRV3, SRV4, and SRV5. All five servers operate as if they are on the network as separate servers. SRV1 would have more resources than a typical server because it would have multiple processors, a significant amount of random access memory (RAM), and fast hard drives. Administrators would allocate some of these resources to each virtual server.

Once a virtual server has been created, it can easily be moved from one physical server to another. The virtual server consists of a group of files stored on the physical server. Admittedly, these files are quite large. However, the virtual server can be shut down, the files copied to another physical server, and the virtual server started there.

Virtual server files can be transferred over a WAN link if the bandwidth is adequate. If not, a high-capacity universal serial bus (USB) drive is an option. Just copy the virtual server files to the USB drive, plug it in to a new physical server, and copy the files to the physical server. The process of copying these files varies depending on the virtualization software. For example, in Microsoft's Hyper-V, the files are exported from the original server and then imported into the new server.

Virtual servers also require less facility support. If four servers are being hosted on a single physical server, not as much physical space is needed as would be necessary for five physical servers. Additionally, this single physical server draws less power and requires less air-conditioning than five physical servers.

Warm Site. A **warm site** is a compromise between a cold and a hot site. It includes most or all of the equipment needed, but data is not usually kept up to date. The equipment is maintained in an operational state. If a disaster occurs, the systems are updated with current data and brought online.

Warm sites are often fully functioning sites for noncritical business functions. When a disaster occurs, noncritical functions stop, and the site is used for critical business functions.

One of the main benefits of the warm site is that management is able to match the desired cost with an acceptable amount of time for an outage, which means that, if a longer MAO is acceptable, management can balance the costs to match the desired amount of time it will take to bring the warm site online.

Mobile Site. A **mobile site** can be set up in an outside space close to an impacted site. One of the advantages of a mobile site is that it can be put in place between 36 and 72 hours. However, it has some disadvantages. The recovery time is usually longer that a hot site, access to the impacted facility can be difficult, and transporting mobile-site equipment can be a challenge.

Redundant Backup Site. Another option is to outsource the data recovery site. Instead of maintaining the alternate location, the company can contract with a third-party vendor to host its data and services in a redundant backup site. If a disaster occurs, the critical services can be switched over to the alternate location, which often has a minimal impact on operations.

Fully redundant backup sites have the ability to host all the data and services, and they can be used as both the primary and secondary environments. In this scenario, all of the data and services are outsourced to the third-party vendor's primary location. If a disaster occurs, the vendor is responsible for switching over to the secondary environment. It is also becoming common to have real-time ongoing backup. This means that data is being constantly copied to an off-site location. This is often done with third-party backup services.

User Access. Users must have access to data and services if the operations are moved to an alternate location. In this situation, what is needed for them to have access depends on how they are using the data and services.

If users access services over the internet, then the alternate location must include internet access with the required bandwidth. However, users may normally access the services internally or via private WAN links. If this is the case, then the alternate location must have the capacity to get the data to the users, which may require additional WAN links.

Management Access. Management may also need access to data and services during the disaster, and, in many instances, management represents just another user. If users have access, then management also has access.

However, in some instances, management may have specific needs, such as for time-sensitive data. For example, if the end of the fiscal year is close, certain data must be accessible to management for reporting requirements. These specific management needs must be identified. When they are addressed, the DRP can meet them.

Customer Access. Customers must have the access they require. Customer access needs vary from one organization to another depending on how customers normally access the organization's network and what customer expectations are during a disaster.

For example, with a local bank, the majority of banking may be done at the bank's location. However, more and more customers use online banking today. If a disaster hits, customers can use the online site for many of their banking needs. The DRP should ensure that the bank's website continues to function even if a major disruption affects the physical location of the bank.

Today, many organizations have websites, and most of them outsource their website hosting, which means that the website isn't hosted on a server at the organization's location. Instead, organizations rent space on a web server, and the hosting provider hosts the website. In this example, the hosting provider is responsible for disaster recovery.

However, this doesn't mean that the website shouldn't be considered. What if a disaster affected the website hosting provider? How would this situation affect the organization? Low-cost hosting providers often don't have significant disaster recovery processes in place, and both minor and major disruptions take down websites on a regular basis.

Disaster Recovery Financial Budget

The last CSF to consider for a DRP is money. A DRP cannot be successfully developed and implemented without a budget because money is necessary to pay for preparation and executing a DRP if a disaster strikes.

There are several costs to consider when preparing for disasters. These include:

- **Backups**—Although most operating systems include backup software, it usually does only the basics. Most organizations purchase third-party backup software that is easier to use and has more capabilities. Additionally, backup media, such as multiple backup tapes, can be expensive. The cost increases when larger amounts of data need to be backed up.
- **Alternate locations**—Any type of alternate location costs additional money. As mentioned previously, hot sites are the most expensive, whereas cold sites are the least expensive. The site that is chosen depends on several factors, including the available budget.
- **Fuel costs during a disaster**—If an organization needs to be able to generate power for extended periods, someone must purchase fuel for the generators. The BCP identifies assumptions, such as how long critical operations need to function without outside support, such as commercial power. This information helps determine how much fuel to purchase.
- **Food and water during a disaster**—If personnel need to support the systems during the disaster, they need food and water. The amount needed depends on how many people will stay at the location and how many days they are expected to stay.
- **Emergency funds right after a disaster**—Funds are often needed right after a disaster for unforeseen circumstances. The budget should include funding for these expenses if needed. Additionally, these funds need to be accessible when the disaster hits.

In addition to establishing the budget, the people who can release the funds need to be identified, which is especially true for any monies needed during and immediately after the disaster. These people can be identified in the DRP or the BCP.

Elements of a DRP

No specific rules identify what must be in a DRP. Sections and elements can be added and removed to meet the company's needs. However, many elements are commonly included. These are:

- Purpose
- Scope
- Disaster/emergency declaration
- Communications
- Emergency response
- Activities
- Recovery procedures
- Critical operations, customer service, and operations recovery
- Restoration and normalization

Eight Rs of Disaster Recovery (DR) Planning

Some DR experts list the eight Rs of recovery planning, which provide a good overview of the recovery planning process. The eight Rs are:

- **Reason for planning**—The scope and purpose sections address the reasons for the DR and personnel safety and the CBFs.
- **Recognition**—When the disaster is recognized, it is "declared." Personnel are notified, and a decision is made to activate the plan.
- **Reaction**—Management and DR personnel respond to the emergency by assessing damage and deciding which steps to take next.
- **Recovery**—DR personnel follow procedures to recover critical systems. If necessary, they activate alternate locations.
- **Restoration**—DR personnel restore CBFs to full operation, which can include restoration of facility resources, such as power; connectivity, such as local area network (LAN) and WAN connections; and the systems that support the CBFs.
- **Return to normal**—After the disaster has passed, DR personnel return the systems to normal operations, which could include moving from generator power to commercial power and moving functions from the alternate location back to the primary location.
- **Rest and relax**—DRP responders need to have time off after the incident and to be thanked for helping the organization survive the disaster.
- **Reevaluate and redocument**—Identify the things that went well and the things that can be improved. Document any lessons learned. Review any weaknesses or deficiencies in the plan. Use this data to update the plan.

The DRP should also be tested and maintained. Testing verifies that the procedures are valid. Additionally, the DRP should regularly be reviewed and updated to ensure it stays current. The following sections explore these elements in greater depth.

Purpose

The DRP starts with a simple statement identifying its purpose. DRPs are often written to support an individual function, service, or system. A DRP could be written to restore a single database server to functionality after a disaster. It would include the steps necessary to recover the database server after the failure.

The DRP could also be written to restore several servers that work together to host a service. For example, a website could be supported by several elements, which could include several web servers in a web farm and several database servers in a failover cluster. If a disaster took the website down, the DRP would include steps to either restore or recover all of these elements.

Either way, the purpose of the DRP needs to be defined early in the process and included in the final product. When defining the purpose, the following activities should be considered:

- **Recovery**—Immediately after a disruption in services, a system should be recoverable, which would include a complete system rebuild if necessary and recovery of all the data. The RTO defines the maximum length of time this process should take.
- **Sustaining business operations**—CBFs need to continue to operate even during a disaster. Several methods can be used to ensure these CBFs can continue, which could include a fully redundant data center, alternate locations, or redundant data sites. The method used should match the needs of the service and the available budget.
- **Normalization**—Once the disaster has passed, the systems need to be normalized, which means different things depending on what was done to sustain business operations. For example, if alternate locations were used, normalization includes moving the CBFs back to the original location.

Scope

The scope of any project helps identify the boundaries. It helps all parties understand what is and is not covered. Without an identified scope, well-meaning people can cause the project to grow and expand, which is commonly known as scope creep.

The purpose of the DRP drives the scope. Based on the purpose of the DRP, elements that should be included and those that should not can be identified. Although the included elements may be obvious to some, they would still need to be identified in the DRP.

When developing the scope, the following areas should be considered:

- **Hardware**—Hardware includes servers and network devices necessary to support them. Replacement servers and support equipment, such as office equipment or spare parts for the critical servers, should be available on-site or at another location.
- **Software**—All software needed to support the CBFs needs to be considered, which includes operating systems and applications. Many organizations use imaging technologies. An *image* is an exact replica of a computer's operating system, applications, settings, and other files. IT personnel might capture an image of a generic server every few months. Then, when a system crashes, IT personnel can use this image to quickly restore a server's operations.

- **Data**—Data considerations are essential to include in the scope of the plan. These considerations include a backup plan that identifies backup requirements if data is needed for CBFs. The recovery point objectives (RPOs) identify the amount of data loss that is acceptable, which depends on the value of the data.
- **Connectivity**—Connectivity to the service consumers should also be included, which could be connectivity for users, managers, and customers, depending on who the consumers are. Connectivity could be redundant internet service provider (ISP) links to the internet or redundant WAN links.

Disaster/Emergency Declaration

When a disaster or emergency occurs or is imminent, the DRP is implemented. Usually, the overall BCP is activated first, and then, based on what the DRP does, the DRP is activated to support the BCP.

As an example, a hurricane is approaching. The BCP coordinator could activate the BCP when the hurricane is 96 hours out. The DRP might specify that, when the hurricane is 48 hours out, a recovery team deploys to an alternate location to prepare systems to take over operations. In this example, the DRP is not activated immediately with the BCP. The BCP might specify other actions to take immediately, but they are separate from this DRP. Instead, this DRP is activated when the hurricane is within 48 hours of striking.

The point is that the DRP should clearly state what causes it to be activated. Activation could result in the recall of personnel and the movement of equipment. When the time comes to take these steps, then do so. However, taking these steps before they are necessary can result in spending money needlessly.

Consider the hurricane again. Hurricanes don't always travel in a straight line. A hurricane that is 96 hours away from striking can easily turn or weaken. Instead of hurricane-force winds, the location might just get some rain, in which case, the DRP shouldn't be activated.

Communications

Several communications elements are important to the success of a DRP. These include:

- **Recall**—The DRP should identify all personnel who should be notified when the DRP is activated. They include any personnel who have any responsibilities within the DRP and senior management personnel. Phone trees are often included as part of the BCP and can be used for this purpose.
- **Users**—Users may need to be notified whether the DRP affects them. For example, critical business operations may not include some routine functions that users expect. They should be notified about what services are not available due to the disaster. This notification can be done before the disaster. Later, the users can be sent a reminder about these services.
- **Customers**—If the disruption affects customers, they should be notified. For example, an online website may be moved to an alternate location, causing it to be down for a short period. The website could post a single page indicating that the DRP is being implemented in response to a disaster and that the website will be operational again within a specific time. Customers will understand and appreciate this. In contrast, if the website is

unreachable and displays an error message, it indicates the organization was unprepared for the disaster.

- **Communications plan**—DRPs often include both primary and alternate communications plans to ensure that personnel are able to communicate during an outage. The plans may be IT based, such as email or instant messaging, or cell phones or walkie-talkies could be used. They could even include specific meeting times in a central location set up as a "war room" instead of using electronic communications.

Emergency Response

The DRP could include an emergency response element that is used for short-fused disasters. For example, an earthquake will strike without warning, and tornadoes strike with very little warning. Similarly, a fire could result in a disaster that requires an emergency response.

Emergency response steps could include:

- Recall and notification of personnel
- Damage assessment
- Plan activation
- Implementation of specific steps and procedures

Depending on the location of the organization, the DRP could be written to address specific disasters. For example, many organizations on the East Coast of the United States have DRPs that cover hurricanes. The DRP would include many preparation steps, but the emergency response steps wouldn't appear until much later in the plan, after the hurricane strikes.

Activities

The emergency response section identifies several emergency response steps to take, such as recalling personnel and assessing the damage. The DRP also identifies other activities to take in response to the disaster.

A primary activity of any DRP is ensuring that personnel safety has been addressed. Ensuring personnel safety and the protection of life should always be at the forefront of any DRP. In other words, the clear message should be *people* first, *things* next.

Activities defined in the DRP depend on the purpose and scope of the DRP. If the DRP addresses the recovery of a single system, the activities are limited and focused. If it addresses a large, complex system, many more activities will be required.

If advance warning of the disaster is given, activities may include preparing the environment. This is possible with weather-related events, such as hurricanes and other serious storms. However, many other disasters don't provide any warning.

When alternate locations are used, a primary activity is preparing the alternate location. A cold site requires the most work. All the required equipment will need to be moved to the alternate location, set up, and configured, which will result in a flurry of activity to prepare. The activity section for a cold site will be quite extensive.

On the other hand, activities required to set up a hot site will be minimal. Personnel may be designated in a flyaway team to go to the hot site to take over operations. How and when operations will cut over to the hot site will need to be identified.

A warm site is a compromise between a hot site and a cold site. The activities to get the warm site up and operational depend on how much equipment and data are normally staged at the alternate location. The activity section can be quite extensive if the warm site is more of a cold site than a hot site. Mobile sites can also be expensive, although cheaper than a hot site. Equipment needs to be transported, and recovery time is usually a few days longer than for a hot site.

Recovery Procedures

> **TIP**
>
> Recovery operations begin after activating the DRP and assessing the damage. Recovery focuses on measures necessary to restore IT capabilities and repair damage. The goal is to restore the mission-critical capabilities at either the original location or an alternate location.

The recovery steps and procedures describe all the specific actions required to recover systems or functions. This section often includes multiple procedures. For example, each critical function could have a separate procedure. Different personnel will be recovering separate systems, so the procedures could all be implemented at the same time.

Recovery procedures should also consider contingencies. For example, if certain recovery steps don't work, the procedures should provide guidance for the recovery personnel. Additionally, procedures should address dependencies. If a server requires specific access to the internet or another server, the procedure should state these requirements.

Recovering Systems

Recovery procedures identify steps for rebuilding and recovering a system after a disaster. They often include steps for recovering a system from scratch, which includes installing the operating system and all applications. If data is needed, the plan specifies how to restore the data.

For example, a database server could be running an Oracle database on a Microsoft Windows Server operating system. The recovery procedure would start with instructions for installing the Windows operating system. After installation, the procedure would describe how to install Oracle, and, last, the procedure would describe how to restore the database.

The recovery plan should be clear as to which steps must be completed before moving on to the next step. In other words, data shouldn't be restored to a server until after the operating system and application have been successfully installed.

> **TIP**
>
> If servers have been imaged, the image may need to be recaptured periodically. For example, if the operating system or application has been updated or modified, the original image won't have the changes. Either the image must be recaptured after a change has been made or the changes must be verified to have been reapplied after the image is restored on a server.

Capturing an image of a server hosting Oracle is possible. If the server crashes, the image can be installed on a system. It will include the operating system, the fully configured Oracle application, and the data that was on the system when the image was captured. IT personnel will have to update the data from a recent backup. Restoring the image is much quicker than reinstalling everything from scratch.

A DRP could include specific recovery procedures for several servers and services. Separate written documents can be created for each procedure. The DRP can reference these procedures as separate appendixes.

These procedures are one of the most important elements of the DRP to test. Although many of the steps in the DRP may be generic in nature, these recovery procedures are often very technical.

During a disaster, the best administrators may not be available. Instead, junior technicians might be recovering systems. With this in mind, be sure that the procedural steps are clear and easy to follow.

Backup Plans

If data needs to be restored, an effective backup plan must be in place. One of the first steps in developing a backup plan is to identify critical data. Critical data is data that supports CBFs. Such data can be large databases or any other types of files that are critical.

The backup plan identifies several elements, including:

- The data to back up
- Backup procedures for data
- Length of time to keep the data
- Types of backups, such as regular, electronic vaulting, or remote journaling
- Frequency of backups
- Off-site storage location, including how to retrieve a backup during a disaster
- Testing of restore procedures and schedules
- Disaster restore procedures

The RPOs identify the amount of data loss that is acceptable for any data. Therefore, the RPO is considered in the backup plan. If the RPO is a short period of time, such as minutes instead of hours or days, backups must be performed more frequently. If the RPO is a longer time, backups can be scheduled less often.

For example, with a high-volume database, the RPO could be 10 minutes, indicating that no more than 10 minutes of data loss is acceptable. The transaction log for the database can be backed up every 10 minutes to ensure that the last 10 minutes of data can be restored. This transaction log backup is restored after the other database backups are restored.

Mission-Critical Operations

A DRP addresses mission-critical operations. CBFs support these operations, and specific servers and services support the CBFs. Because a CBF is any function that is considered vital to the organization, if the organization loses the ability to perform the CBF, it loses the ability to perform mission-critical operations. By addressing CBFs, the DRP helps ensure that the critical servers and services continue.

> **TIP**
>
> A DRP ensures that backup plans exist for critical data. However, an organization may have backup plans that protect other data in the organization.

As an example, **FIGURE 14-5** shows a web farm connected to a back-end database. The web servers in the web farm host an application that sells products online. In this example, the mission-critical operation is sales of products.

Several CBFs support the sale of products. First, the web farm hosts the web application. One CBF serves webpages to clients. Users access the website, and one of the servers in the web farm sends webpages to the clients. Additionally, the back-end database server hosts databases, including the product database. Web servers query the database server and populate webpages with product data.

Once a customer decides to buy, an additional CBF comes into play. Existing customer data is retrieved from the customer database. The database also stores new customer

FIGURE 14-5
Web farm with back-end database.

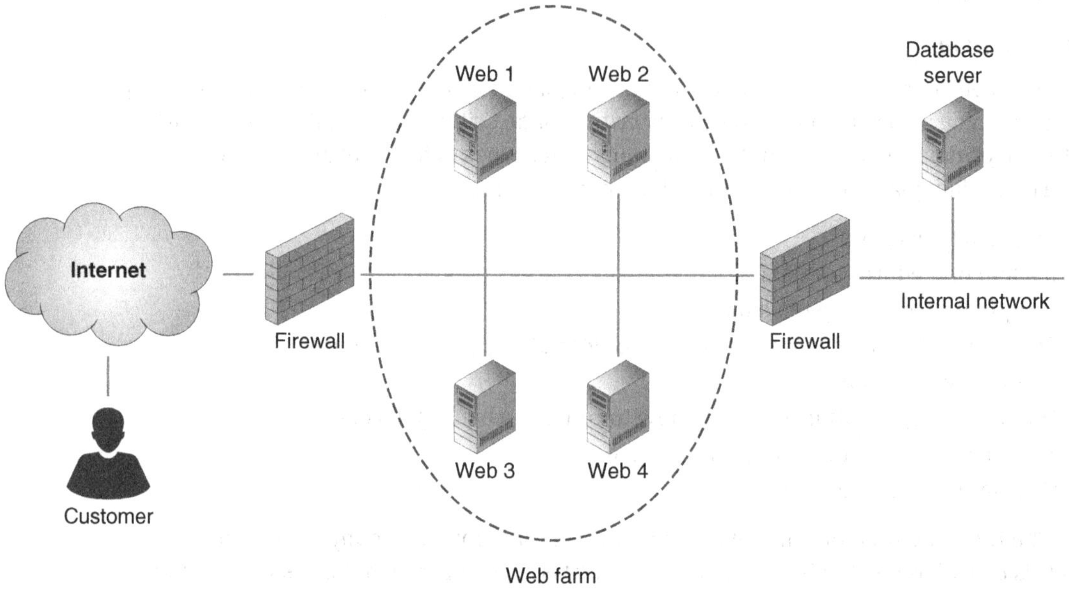

data after a sale. Once a customer purchases the product, another CBF handles payment processes. Another CBF ensures that the product is shipped. All of these CBFs support the mission-critical operation of product sales.

Figure 14-5 shows that several servers are needed to support some of these CBFs. Specifically, both the web servers in the web farm and the back-end database server are needed. The DRP would ensure that these servers are included.

Critical Operations, Customer Service, and Operations Recovery

The DRP identifies mission-critical operations and CBFs to support. However, specifying steps for other elements of the business is often important.

For example, will customer service activities be stopped when a disaster occurs? Alternatively, will customer service activities move? If customer service is provided via phone, the functions may be easily switched to another location. On the other hand, if the organization does little customer service, it may not consider recovering during the disaster critical enough. Customers could be provided a simple notification. For example, a notification could be posted on the organization's webpage or a short message recorded on the phone system.

Similarly, the company may have other operations that need to be recovered, which may not necessarily be considered a part of any CBF, but management may still consider them important enough to recover. For example, some personnel may be working on critical research projects. Although the research isn't critical for current cash flow, management may want to ensure it can continue to operate. In this situation, the systems and services for research will need to be recovered.

This section can also provide another look at normal operations. While preparing the DRP, what is considered a CBF and what is not should be reviewed. Some operations may appear critical, yet initially excluded from the DRP when looking at daily activities. These operations should be added.

Restoration and Normalization

Once the disaster has passed, personnel shift their focus to restoration and normalization. Some DRPs refer to this as the reconstitution phase. The BCP coordinator is typically the authority who announces when normalization begins. It might start after damage at the original location has been repaired. Management might also decide to start normalization earlier, based on other considerations.

Personnel return all mission-critical and non–mission-critical functions to normal during this phase. However, they are not all done at the same time. The DRP specifies the order in which they occur.

Unforeseen problems can be expected during the normalization phase. Because of these problems, normalizing the least critical functions first is important, especially if functions were moved to another location. Doing this ensures that the most critical functions aren't interrupted as problems arise.

In some situations, the DRP might require concurrent processing. For example, as critical functions are normalized in the primary location, the recovered systems are kept operating in the alternate location. If problems affect the primary location, the load can easily be shifted back to the alternate location.

Testing

Testing DRPs is important to ensure they perform as expected. Because the DRP is written to restore CBFs, testing of the DRP should not affect operations of these CBFs. The goal of the tests is to identify any problems or omissions in the DRP.

Like a BCP, different testing methods can be used to test a DRP. The following are common testing methods:

- **Desktop exercise**—In a desktop exercise, participants meet in a conference room setting. Participants talk through the steps of the DRP. The desktop exercise is similar to a tabletop exercise used in a BCP.
- **Simulation**—A simulation goes through the steps and procedures in a controlled manner. The goal is to ensure that the DRP can be completed in the order presented. Simulations may test portions of the DRP without testing them all. For example, only the data at an alternate location could be restored to ensure this procedure works.
- **Parallel**—The backup systems are brought online but the live systems are still online. This will allow you to evaluate whether the backup systems worked, but still have the primary systems providing services.
- **Fail-Over**—The fail-over test takes the main systems offline and lets the backup systems take over. If there is a failure of the backup system, it will readily become apparent. Clearly, this sort of test could cause an interruption of service. Accordingly, this level of

TABLE 14-2 Recovery Times Checklist

STEP	START TIME	END TIME
Locate server and install operating system		
Install applications on server		
Locate backup tape and restore data		
Notify DRP coordinator of completion		

testing should only be done after the previous levels have been executed successfully, and it should also be done at a time that will cause the least disruption to service.

The results of all tests should be thoroughly documented and include any lessons learned, mistakes, or weaknesses uncovered during testing. This documentation can then be used to improve the DRP. Updating the DRP is commonly done if testing identifies any deficiencies.

One of the benefits of testing is that it will give an accurate time frame for recovery. For example, with a database server, one administrator may think a technician can rebuild and restore it in 30 minutes, and another administrator may estimate it will take as long as 4 hours. Actually rebuilding and restoring the server will give an accurate time of how long it takes. A checklist is helpful for tracking the time frame for individual steps. The checklist may look similar to **TABLE 14-2**.

Maintenance and DRP Update

The DRP needs to be regularly reviewed and updated. Doing so ensures that it will be ready when needed. IT systems are regularly updated and upgraded, and any of these changes could affect the usability of the DRP.

Most organizations have change management processes in place. These processes ensure that changes to systems are reviewed before the change occurs and that changes are documented. DRP developers should be involved in this process to ensure that they are aware of system changes. When a change is proposed, the DRP developer should review the change to determine whether it affects the DRP.

The DRP review should include the following elements:

- **Systems**—Verify that the systems covered by the DRP have not been changed since the last review. These changes include any significant changes that may affect how the systems are recovered. Even smaller changes should be investigated to determine whether the DRP is affected.
- **Critical business functions**—Verify that the DRP covers the CBFs and that priorities have not changed. An organization can change, resulting in some CBFs becoming more important than others.
- **Alternate sites**—If the DRP requires alternate sites, ensure that the designated sites still support the DRP and that changes to the alternate sites don't adversely affect the DRP. If possible, these alternate sites should be visited while the DRP is being reviewed to determine whether they still meet the needs of the company.

- **Contacts**—Contact information must be accurate. Contact information includes contact information for management personnel who need to be notified and recall information used in the phone trees.

Just as with other documents, tracking changes to the DRP is important. The DRP should include a change page or version control page, which identifies the change, when the change was made, and who made the change.

> **NOTE**
>
> A *phone tree* is a method to facilitate calling a large group of people. The phone tree is a contact list shaped like a pyramid. To start, the person at the top calls a few people, who then each call a few people assigned to them. This process continues until all contacts have been notified.

How Does a DRP Mitigate an Organization's Risk?

DRPs reduce risk by reducing the impact of disasters. The disaster, such as an earthquake, a tornado, or a hurricane, is the threat, which can't be stopped. However, the impact of the threat can be reduced by being prepared, and the DRP helps with this preparation to mitigate both the short- and long-term damage.

For example, the DRP can help reduce the length of an outage after a disaster. Organizations that have a DRP in place are able to handle disasters much more easily than organizations without DRPs. Of course, the existence of a DRP doesn't guarantee success.

With a disaster recovery plan, the company will be much better prepared to recover CBFs. A cold site takes a lot of work to put together in its planning stage. All the equipment must be moved, set up, and configured. With some extra resources and preplanning, the company could plan to use a warm site. However, with no planning, the job will be twice as hard.

In addition to being more difficult to recover without a DRP, more errors and problems will be experienced. The DRP helps with applying critical thinking to problems before they occur and encourages logical thinking about what should be done to minimize them. Experts can be consulted to help with solving problems, and the plan can be tested. Without a DRP, the company will be thrown into the middle of a crisis without any of these benefits. With luck, the disaster won't destroy the business. However, most executives don't want to depend on luck.

Best Practices for Implementing a DRP for an Organization

When implementing DRPs, several best practices can be implemented. Following is a list of many of these best practices:

- **Ensuring BIAs have been completed**—BIAs identify CBFs, which are used to identify the critical business operations and critical servers and services.
- **Starting with a clear purpose and scope**—The purpose and scope statements help ensure the DRP stays focused. Resources are wasted when steps and procedures are taken that are outside the scope of the DRP.
- **Reviewing and updating the DRP regularly**—The DRP should be reviewed at least annually. If critical systems covered by the DRP are changed, the DRP should be reviewed to determine whether the changes affect it.
- **Testing the DRP**—Testing ensures that the DRP can be implemented as expected. While testing the DRP, normal operations should not be affected.

Employing a checklist is often worthwhile to ensure that all the relevant concerns have been addressed. The following checklist can be used before, during, and after the creation of a DRP to identify the company's preparedness:

- Is the organization's BIA up to date? If the BIA is more than 1 year old, it must be updated first.
- Have any systems covered by the BIA changed since the BIA was completed? If so, the BIA needs to be revised.
- Are critical business functions defined? Is it clear what systems need to be recovered first?
- Does the DRP specify the level of service to provide for the CBFs? In other words, if the business must continue to operate during a disaster, does the DRP identify which services need to be restored?
- Are specific responsibilities assigned? Do departments or individuals know what is expected of them at different times during an emergency?
- Is it clear what hardware, software, and data should be recovered? Does the DRP include any necessary support equipment needed to support the CBFs?
- Does the DRP include a backup plan? Does this backup plan include a testing element for test restores? Does the DRP include steps to use for data restores?
- Are backups stored off-site? Are the off-site backups easily accessible if a disaster occurs?
- Is there a communication plan? Does it have alternate methods of communication?
- Are alternate sites required? What type of alternate site is desired? Does the budget allow for the desired site?
- Are facility needs considered? This category includes UPSs, backup power, and heating and air-conditioning systems.
- Have support services been addressed? For example, if backup generators will be needed, is enough fuel on hand to support the organization during the disaster? Is there enough food and water to support on-site personnel during the disaster?
- Are personnel trained on the DRP? Do they know what their responsibilities are before, during, and after a disaster?
- Has the DRP been tested? Have the procedures been tested to verify that they work as expected?
- Is the DRP reviewed at least annually? Is it updated as needed when elements within it are affected?
- Are changes to the DRP tracked?

CHAPTER SUMMARY

This chapter covered important elements of risk mitigation with a disaster recovery plan. It defined a DRP, including its purpose. Several factors are critical to the success of a DRP. Management must provide both resources and leadership. DRP developers need to understand disaster recovery concepts and how an organization operates. The DRP must address several primary concerns. The RTOs identify the time by which a

CBF must be returned to operation. When necessary, CBFs can be moved to alternate locations. A hot site can be used within minutes or hours but is the most expensive to implement. A cold site is simply a building with electricity, water, and other facility support. It's the least expensive but the most difficult to test. A warm site is a compromise between the two. A mobile site is a site that can be set up close to an impacted facility. Another critical success factor is a budget. DRPs must have funding to succeed.

DRPs can include different elements. Starting with purpose and scope statements is common to ensure they are clear to all parties. Identifying the scope helps prevent scope creep. DRPs will include specific steps and procedures. When the disaster strikes, use the steps and procedures in the DRP to recover the systems. DRPs should be tested to verify they work as planned, and they need to be updated periodically and in response to changes.

KEY CONCEPTS AND TERMS

Business continuity plan (BCP)
Business impact analysis (BIA)
Cloud computing
Cold site
Critical success factor (CSF)
Disaster recovery plan (DRP)
Hot site
Maximum acceptable outage (MAO)
Minimum business continuity objective (MBCO)
Mobile site
Recovery time objective (RTO)
Virtualization
Warm site

CHAPTER 14 ASSESSMENT

1. A(n) ________ is a plan used to restore critical business functions to operation after a disruption or disaster.
2. A DRP has multiple purposes, which include saving lives, ensuring business continuity, and recovering after a disaster.
   A. True
   B. False
3. Disaster recovery and fault tolerance are the same thing.
   A. True
   B. False
4. A(n) ________ is an element necessary for success. For example, the success of a DRP depends on management support, a disaster recovery budget and other elements.
5. A business impact analysis (BIA) includes a maximum acceptable outage (MAO). The MAO is used to determine the amount of time in which a system must be recovered. What term is used in the DRP instead of the MAO?
   A. Critical business function (CBF)
   B. DRP action item (DRPAI)
   C. Recovery action item (RAI)
   D. Recovery time objective (RTO)
6. A certain DRP covers a system that hosts a large database. To ensure that the data is copied to an off-site location, what could be used?
   A. Data replication
   B. Electronic vaulting
   C. Remote journaling
   D. All of the above

7. A copy of backups should be stored ________ to ensure the organization can survive a catastrophic disaster to the primary location.

8. An alternate location is being considered for a DRP, and the costs need to be minimized. What type of site would be chosen?
   A. Cold site
   B. Warm site
   C. Hot site
   D. Mobile site

9. An alternate location is being considered for a DRP, and it must be brought online as quickly as possible. What type of site would be chosen?
   A. Cold site
   B. Warm site
   C. Hot site
   D. DRP site

10. An alternate location is being considered for a DRP, and it needs to be a business location that is already running noncritical business functions. This location has most of the equipment needed. What type of site is this?
    A. Cold site
    B. Warm site
    C. Hot site
    D. DRP site

11. Which of the following elements are commonly included in a DRP?
    A. BCP, BIA, communications, and recovery procedures
    B. BCP, backup plans, and recovery procedures
    C. Purpose, scope, communications, and recovery procedures
    D. Purpose, scope, CIRT activation, and recovery procedures

12. A hot site is being considered as an alternate location. Various technologies are also being considered to keep the data updated and decrease the time that will be necessary for the hot site to become operational. What are some technologies that may help?
    A. Data replication
    B. Cloud computing
    C. Virtualization
    D. All of the above
    E. A and B only

13. Of the following, what is critical for any DRP?
    A. Third-party backup software
    B. Budget
    C. Alternate locations
    D. Fuel for generators

14. An organization has created a DRP, but it hasn't been tested. Which of the following methods can be used to test it?
    A. Desktop testing
    B. Simulation testing
    C. Full-blown DRP testing
    D. All of the above

15. Once a DRP has been created, it doesn't need to be updated.
    A. True
    B. False

CHAPTER 15

Mitigating Risk With a Computer Incident Response Team Plan

COMPUTER SECURITY incidents can result in the loss of confidentiality, integrity, or availability of data or services. Attackers will attack, and incidents will happen. Unfortunately, computer security incidents are increasingly common. Anyone who even casually glances at the news periodically will note numerous breaches. However, an organization can be prepared with computer incident response teams (CIRTs). These teams are trained and have the knowledge and expertise to reduce the damage resulting from attacks. Their actions are guided by a CIRT plan.

The primary purpose of a CIRT plan is to help an organization prepare for incidents and mitigate the damage. The plan identifies members based on their roles and responsibilities. It includes policy statements related to incidents, how to contain the incident, and perhaps how to forensically examine the breach.

Chapter 15 Topics

This chapter covers the following topics and concepts:

- What a computer incident response team (CIRT) plan is
- What the purpose of a CIRT plan is
- What the elements of a CIRT plan are
- How a CIRT plan can mitigate an organization's risk
- What best practices for implementing a CIRT plan are

Chapter 15 Goals

When you complete this chapter, you will be able to:

- Define a CIRT
- Define a CIRT plan
- Describe the roles and responsibilities of CIRT members

- Describe CIRT policies
- Define a computer incident
- Describe the incident handling process
- Describe communication escalation procedures
- Describe incident handling procedures
- Describe how a CIRT plan can mitigate an organization's risk
- List best practices for implementing a CIRT plan for an organization

What Is a Computer Incident Response Team Plan?

> **TIP**
>
> An organization may define a security incident internally. This definition is more specific and may be slightly different depending on the needs of the organization.

A **computer incident** is a violation or imminent threat of a violation of a security policy or security practice. It includes any adverse event or activity that affects the security of computer systems or networks. These adverse events affect the organization's security and may result in loss of confidentiality, integrity, or availability. Computer security incidents can range from minor policy violations that merely represent a potential breach, to malicious hackers gaining full access to the computer systems, exfiltrating data, and causing substantial damage.

The terms *computer incident* and *computer security incident* are synonymous. For example, some organizations have computer security incident response teams (CSIRTs) and CSIRT plans instead of computer incident response teams (CIRTs) and CIRT plans.

> **FYI**
>
> Sometimes, the term CERT (formally an acronym for computer emergency response team) is used in place of CIRT. CERT® is a registered trademark and refers to the federally funded CERT Coordination Center (CERT/CC). CERT/CC is a part of Carnegie Mellon University (CMU). CERT/CC is different from the United States-CERT (US-CERT), which coordinates defense and responses to cyberattacks in the United States. If an organization uses the term *CERT*, it is infringing on CMU's trademark. The terms CIRT, incident response team (IRT), and CSIRT are more commonly used.

An imminent threat of violation is an incident that is about to occur. This term commonly refers to emerging threats, such as viruses or worms that are rapidly spreading. Even if the organization isn't infected now, it will be if action is not taken quickly. For example, an organization may become aware of a virus that has been affecting Windows Server 2025. This virus may not have yet infected the organization's Windows Servers, but the potential is there, and steps must be taken to mitigate this threat. In fact, if an organization will respond to potential threats expeditiously, this can reduce the probability of the threat being realized.

In the context of this chapter, an event is any observable occurrence within a system or network, which includes any activity on the network, such as users accessing files, or data transmitted over the network. Not all events are incidents. Adverse events are those with a negative result. They can include any types of attacks on systems or networks.

Multiple types of computer incidents affect organizations, including:

- **Denial of service (DoS) attack**—A DoS attack is an attack that prevents a system from providing a service. A DoS attack comes from a single attacker. A distributed denial of service (DDoS) attack comes from multiple systems.
- **Malicious code**—Malicious code is any type of malicious software or **malware**, which includes viruses, worms, Trojan horses, and other types of software intended to infect a system. Viruses and other malware that are replicating and causing harm to computers are "in the wild."
- **Ransomware**—Ransomware is certainly a type of malicious code; however, it has become such a substantial problem that it warrants its own category. Ransomware is a type of malicious software (malware) that blocks access to data or systems, typically by encrypting files, and demands a ransom payment from the victim to restore access.
- **Unauthorized access**—Unauthorized access occurs any time an attacker is able to access data without authorization. Unauthorized access can be gained from different types of social engineering attacks and from technical attacks used to gain access or control to systems. Unauthorized access often results in loss of confidentiality.
- **Inappropriate usage**—Inappropriate usage occurs when employees or internal users violate acceptable use policies (AUPs) or other internal policies. It can be as simple as a user going to a malicious website identified as off limits in the AUP, a user copying proprietary data from a secure system to an insecure system, or a user installing peer-to-peer (P2P) software on their system when it is prohibited in the AUP.
- **Multiple component**—Multiple component is an incident that includes two or more incidents at the same time. For example, malware could infect a system and then be used to launch a DoS attack on other systems.

A **computer incident response team (CIRT)** is a group of people who respond to incidents. The CIRT team can be designated in advance or formed as needed. For example, a large organization may have a group of security professionals designated as the CIRT. When an incident occurs, the CIRT responds. A smaller organization may not have a formal CIRT. Instead, when an incident occurs, information technology (IT) professionals respond to the incident as an informal CIRT.

The **CIRT plan** is a formal document that outlines an organization's response to computer incidents. It formally defines a security incident and may also designate the CIRT team. The following sections outline the purpose and elements of a CIRT plan.

Purpose of a CIRT Plan

The purpose of a CIRT plan is to help organizations identify and prepare for computer incidents. Security personnel can then identify the best responses to reduce the potential damage. This allows the team to respond quickly and efficiently. If one waits until an incident occurs to derive a plan, that makes it very likely the plan will not be successful. Furthermore, a plan means that whomever is tasked with responding to an incident has an outline of how to respond, and responses can be consistent.

The purpose of the CIRT plan is similar to the purpose of a disaster recovery plan (DRP). By taking the time to create a plan, critical thinking can be applied to potential problems, the advice of experts can be sought, and the best types of responses can be researched. Putting thought into how one will respond, absent the pressure of an actual ongoing incident, facilitates better decision making.

However, if a plan is not in place, these benefits are not available to responders when the incident occurs, which leaves them no choice but to use trial-and-error techniques. These impromptu techniques may succeed, but, on the other hand, they may allow the attacker to continue and cause significantly more damage to the organization.

A CIRT plan outlines the purpose of the response effort, which is, in general, to identify the incident as fully as possible and then contain it. Answering the five Ws is a good starting point. They are *what*, *where*, *who*, *when*, and *why*. For good measure, *how* it occurred can be added.

The *what* identifies what type of attack occurred. It could be a DoS attack, a malware attack, unauthorized access, or inappropriate usage. Understanding what happened helps to determine the impact and prioritize the response. CIRT plans often include tools to determine the impact and the priority of the attack.

NOTE

The Incident Handling Procedures section that appears later in this chapter shows examples of tools used to determine the impact and priority of incidents. Table 15-1 shows an example of effect rating definitions, Table 15-2 shows an example of criticality rating definitions, and Table 15-3 shows an example of incident impact ratings.

Next, the *where* identifies where the attack occurred. Symptoms will be noticeable on at least one system that raised the alarm. However, other systems should also be checked to see whether they were affected. If more than one system was affected, the impact and priority may need to be reassessed.

If possible, *who* launched the attack should be identified. One useful means of determining who launched the attack is checking logs. Audit logs for systems and firewall and router logs can be checked. If the user authenticated, the logs will identify the user account used for the attack. If the attack was from an external source, the logs will identify an external Internet Protocol (IP) address, which can be blocked to stop the attack.

Technical TIP

Attackers often hijack other systems to launch attacks. For example, attackers controlling botnets send commands to zombies, which then launch attacks, or an attacker can simply drive around until an open wireless network is located, which the attacker can then use to launch the attack. Attacks traced back to this wireless network won't identify the actual attacker but will identify the wireless network. By the time the attack is traced back to the IP address, the actual attacker may be untraceable.

The Growth of Incidents

In November 1988, a computer being attacked on the internet made the news when the Morris worm hit. CERT was created at CMU to respond, and it began counting incidents.

FIGURE 15-1 shows the growth of incidents over the years. In 1988, eight incidents occurred; in 1998, 3,734; and in 2003, 137,529. The last year that CERT at CMU reported the number of incidents was in 2003. If the number of incidents were still being tracked and reported today, they would be off the chart. Unless a computer is never turned on or is kept completely isolated, it will be attacked. Cybercrime worldwide is expected to reach $15.63 trillion by 2029. Ransomware costs victims an average of $1.85 million per incident, with attacks rising by 13% over a five-year period.[1]

FIGURE 15-1

History of incidents tracked by CERT.

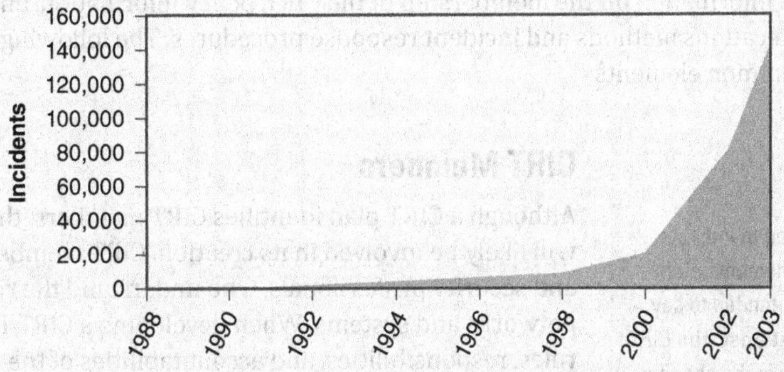

The names of these incidents have morphed over the years. The terms *cyberattack* and *cyberbreach* are commonly used, and both incidents are significant threats on the internet today.

Identifying *when* an attack occurred is much more than just identifying when the symptoms were discovered. Attackers often perform reconnaissance before an attack, and log entries may show that the reconnaissance attacks occurred several times over the past week from the same source. When did the attacker first begin scanning the system in preparation for breaching it?

Answering *why* attackers attack helps to understand their motive. Attackers can have a range of motives. Financial gain has increasingly become the common motive. However, attackers may have a grievance against the organization and that can be the motivation. There are also nation-state threat actors that have political motivation.

As an example, one famous set of attackers regularly stole credit card data, which they used to create fake credit cards. Then, they hired women to shop at malls using these cards. These women bought as much as they could in a lavish shopping spree, spending tens of thousands of dollars, after which they took the goods out to a truck in the mall's

[1] Viking Cloud, "207 Cybersecurity Stats and Facts for 2026," https://www.vikingcloud.com/blog/cybersecurity-statistics.

parking lot, where a *fence* bought the goods at reduced prices and then promptly sold them elsewhere.

Attackers may also be motivated by espionage. Both corporate espionage and international espionage are vigorously alive on the internet today. Spies regularly try to gather as much data about competing organizations or other countries as possible.

Last, *how* the attack occurred must be identified, which in turn helps to identify the vulnerabilities that exist in the system that was attacked. Once the determination has been made of how the attack succeeded, how to prevent it in the future can be identified. In other words, identifying how the attack succeeded helps with identifying controls or countermeasures to prevent future attacks.

Elements of a CIRT Plan

CIRT plans can vary in the elements that are included. However, a CIRT plan commonly includes information on the membership of the CIRT, policy information, and details on communications methods and incident response procedures. The following sections outline these common elements.

CIRT Members

NOTE

This section isn't intended to indicate that these are the only elements of the CIRT plan. Neither is it intended to say that these elements must exist. The CIRT plan will meet the needs of the specific organization, and organizations differ widely.

Although a CIRT plan identifies CIRT members, these members will likely be involved in its creation. CIRT members include IT and security professionals, who understand the risks that threaten networks and systems. When developing a CIRT, identifying the roles, responsibilities, and accountabilities of the team members is important.

Different models can be used for developing a CIRT. The National Institute of Standards and Technology (NIST) regularly releases special publications (SPs). NIST SP 800-61 Rev. 2 identifies the following team models:

- **Central incident response team**—Organizations in a single location can use a single team, which will respond to all incidents. A single team may even cover multiple locations, and all members will have remote access to all of them. They will also be available at any time to provide flyaway support, if needed.
- **Distributed incident response teams**—If the organization has major computing facilities in multiple locations, it might choose to have a single team in each location with all teams centrally managed. For example, if the organization has multiple regional locations with teams at each location, personnel at the headquarters location will still centrally manage the teams.
- **Coordinating team**—This team includes knowledgeable personnel who provide advice to other teams. Team members don't have any authority over the other teams. However, when incidents occur at outlying locations, team members provide assistance as needed.

NOTE

The members of the CIRT are usually identified by title, rather than by name, within the plan.

- **Investigation team**—In addition to responding to the incident, a forensic investigation should be a part of the response. This may provide evidence for criminal or civil proceedings, but even in the absence of such proceedings, only a forensic investigation can provide details of how the incident occurred.

Roles

A CIRT needs a balanced set of skills. The overall goal is to ensure that the team has members with a variety of skills from different areas of the organization. Team members might fill a single role or multiple roles. Some of the roles held by the team members are:

- **Team leader**—The team leader is responsible for the team's actions and is usually a senior manager with expertise in security. However, some CIRTs identify the team leader as the first team member who arrives on the scene. This person takes charge of the incident and directs other member activities.
- **Information security members**—These individuals could be experts on boundary protection, which includes firewalls and routers on the edge of the network. They are able to identify the source of breaches and recommend solutions. These members could also be experts in intrusion detection systems (IDSs) and other systems that include audit logs and audit trails.
- **Network administrators**—Network administrators understand the details of a network, such as what systems are connected and how they're connected and what systems are accessible from the internet. They know what normal traffic flow is and can recognize abnormal traffic.
- **Physical security**—Because attackers can be social engineers and might be on company property, physical security personnel need to be on the team. They know what physical security controls the organization uses, where they are located, and their purpose. They also know the different types of surveillance methods used within the organization, such as video cameras and their capabilities.
- **Legal**—Legal personnel provide advice on the organization's legal responsibilities and legal remedies before, during, and after an incident. Legal personnel understand what legal actions are possible against the attackers and the requirements necessary to pursue legal actions.
- **Human resources (HR)**—If the attack originated from an employee, HR needs to be involved because HR understands the organization's policies and is aware of the available enforcement methods. For example, if an employee violates the AUP, the first offense may result in a formal written warning, and a second or third offense may result in termination. HR personnel would know whether the employee had been previously warned.
- **Communications**—Public relations (PR) personnel become the face of the organization if the incident becomes public. They help to present an image of resolve, even if everything is not quite under control. If PR reps aren't used, team members might express frustration or confusion about the attack, which can present a poor image to customers, vendors, and stockholders of the organization.
- **Forensic Investigator**—Digital forensics is a sub-discipline of cybersecurity, but requires significant training. Forensic investigation can provide details on how the

breach occurred, and thus guide how to improve the system's cybersecurity, thus mitigating or preventing future attacks.

Responsibilities

The CIRT has several responsibilities, such as helping to develop the plan, respond to incidents, and document the incidents. Each member of the team has special skills and responsibilities to the team. However, the team as a whole also has specific responsibilities.

Some of the primary responsibilities of the CIRT include:

- **Developing incident response procedures**—These procedures can be generic procedures to respond to any type of incident or detailed checklists for different types of incidents. For example, malware infections and DoS attacks may each have its own checklist.
- **Investigating incidents**—When an incident occurs, the CIRT is responsible for responding to and investigating it. Depending on the priority and impact of the incident, a single team member may respond. For high-priority, high-impact incidents, the entire team may respond.
- **Determining the cause of incidents**—One of the goals of an investigation is to determine the cause because, by understanding the cause, the CIRT is better able to determine the best response. For example, a user brings in an infected universal serial bus (USB) flash drive from home. After plugging it into the system, the antivirus software detects and quarantines it. Thus, the cause was from the user transferring the virus from home to the work computer via the USB drive. Luckily, the antivirus software detected it, but, unfortunately, some viruses bypass the antivirus software. This type of incident has caused many organizations to outlaw USB flash drives on their networks.
- **Recommending controls to prevent future incidents**—CIRT members often know the best solution to prevent the same incident again. Even if they don't know it already, they have the expertise and experience to identify a control, which may be as simple as upgrading the security policy or more complex and require the purchase and installation of hardware or software. Either way, the CIRT members provide the recommendation.
- **Protecting collected evidence**—Evidence should not be modified when it's collected. For example, police officers don't walk through the blood at a crime scene because doing so would affect the evidence. Similarly, CIRT members should not modify the evidence, such as accessing files or turning off the computers, unless they've captured the RAM content if that is desired. They use bit copy tools to copy hard drives to get a complete copy without modifying the data.
- **Using a chain of custody**—CIRT members are responsible for managing the evidence as soon as they collect it. A *chain of custody* helps ensure that the evidence presented later is the same evidence that was originally collected. It should be established when evidence is seized and maintained throughout the life of the evidence. The chain of custody log documents who had the evidence at any moment and when the evidence has been secured in a semi-permanent storage location.

The CIRT plan at any organization may spell out the previously listed responsibilities, and it could list additional responsibilities of the CIRT, based on its needs or expectations. For

Computer Forensics

What was once called computer forensics is now referred to as digital forensics, cyberforensics, and other names. Given that computing devices are more diverse, these different names make sense. The goal of cyberforensics is to examine computer devices (laptops, servers, cell phones, tablets, and so on) using scientific methods to extract evidence in such a way that such evidence can be presented in a court. Now, there are certainly times when you will use forensics in scenarios that will never go to court. But the techniques were designed to satisfy the evidentiary requirements of courts. A computer forensics investigation generally has three phases:

- **Acquiring the evidence**—In this phase, toolkits are used to capture data on systems without modifying it. For example, a forensic imaging tool can create a complete image of a hard drive without modifying a single bit on the hard drive. Also, to keep data from being modified, first responders must not access any files or turn the system off. It is important that evidence be acquired in a forensically sound method.
- **Authenticating the evidence**—Chain of custody forms track the evidence to document that the data is protected and controlled after it has been collected, which verifies that the evidence is trustworthy. If a chain of custody is not used, the evidence may not be admissible in court because it is considered to be tainted. Furthermore, when imaging evidence, forensic imaging tools use cryptographic hashes to validate the copy.
- **Analyzing the evidence**—Data is inspected and viewed in this phase. If the data includes files on a disk, a copy of the disk is analyzed. If the original data needs to be verified, investigators create another copy, a forensically sound one, from the original disk and analyze it.

Computer forensics is a growing field among computer professionals. Many IT professionals expand their security knowledge and become experts in computer forensics.

example, members may be expected to subscribe to different security bulletins or take other steps to ensure that they stay aware of current risks.

Accountabilities

The CIRT is also accountable to the organization to provide a proactive response to any incident. Although incidents can't be avoided, the team is expected to minimize the impact of any incident.

Organizations often invest a lot of time and money in team members. The goal is to ensure they are trained and capable of handling the incidents. However, serious incidents don't happen often, which doesn't mean that team members don't think about security very often. The team members are expected to keep up to date on security threats and possible responses, which requires dedication on the part of each of the team members.

CIRT Policies

A CIRT plan also includes CIRT policies. These policies may be simple statements or contained in appendixes at the end of the plan. They provide the team with guidance in the midst of any incident.

One of the primary policies to consider is whether or not CIRT members can attack back. In other words, during the investigation of an incident, team members may have the opportunity to launch an attack on the attacker. Should they?

The answer is almost always a resounding no. First, legal ramifications may exist. Even though thieves steal from a company, the company can't use that as an excuse to steal from them because, if the company is caught, it can be prosecuted. A defense of "but he did it first" won't impress a judge. Similarly, even if the attacker broke laws attacking the company's network, no justification exists for the company to break laws to attack back. Attacking back is reserved for nation-states, not companies or private organizations. Perhaps the exception to that 'rule' would be organized crime.

If a company attacks back, it also runs the risk of escalating an incident between itself and the attacker. For example, if a person bumps into another person on a busy street, both of them could say excuse me, and the incident is over. Even if one person is rude and purposely bumps into another person, if the person bumped says excuse me and moves on, the incident is over. However, the incident is not over if the person bumped turns on the other person and flails their arms, pushes, and yells. Instead, the incident is escalated into a conflict, the result of which may depend on which party is willing to cause the most harm to the other.

Similarly, if an attacker attacks a company's network and fails, they might just move on to an easier target. However, if the company attacks the attacker, the incident will be escalated. The attacker might now consider the company's attack as being personal, and they become intent on breaking into the network and causing as much damage as possible.

With this in mind, considering how many work hours an attacker may spend attacking is worthwhile. If personal gains are at stake, such as millions of dollars, 12-hour days or 80-hour workweeks are doable in the short term. Similarly, if the attacker has a personal vendetta against an organization that had the audacity to attack back, they might devote all of their waking time to satisfying the vendetta.

In short, the best practice is not to escalate an attack into a two-sided conflict. Leave any retribution to law enforcement. Attackers can inflict higher damage and costs to an organization than the organization can to the attacker, leaving little reason for an organization to invite more of the same. This is not to say that an organization should never attack back. Government and military agencies may have specific units that are trained to attack to gather evidence on criminal activities or to carry out purposeful cyberwarfare against a government's enemies. However, if this isn't the organization's mission, refrain from attacking back.

Other policies included in the CIRT plan may include those related to evidence, communications, and safety. Evidence collected during an investigation may need to be used to prosecute people in the future. However, specific rules exist that govern the collection and storage of evidence, and the CIRT plan can include policies to define these rules.

Communications with media can be challenging for anyone who doesn't have experience in this area. However, a CIRT should have a PR person. A simple policy may state that the only person who may talk to the media about any incident is the PR person. If the media query anyone else, the response is to refer the query to the public relations office or a specific PR person.

Although computer incidents aren't as dangerous as disasters, such as hurricanes or earthquakes, some danger could be involved. A CIRT plan often states that the safety of personnel is most important and that actions should not be taken that risk the safety of any personnel.

FIGURE 15-2

Incident response life cycle.

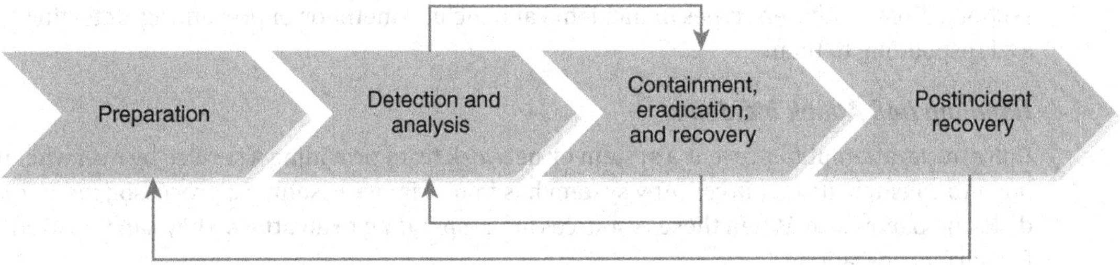

Incident Handling Process

A CIRT plan identifies the incident handling process, which can be a large part of the plan, depending on its detail. NIST SP 800-61 Rev. 3 was published in April 2025,[2] Incident Response Recommendations and Considerations for Cybersecurity Risk Management, and outlines four phases of an incident. **FIGURE 15-2** shows these four phases as an incident response life cycle.

The four phases outlined in NIST SP 800-61 Rev. 3 are described as follows:

- **Preparation**—Preparation involves creating a CIRT plan, defining incidents, and creating CIRTs. The team members are trained and have specific roles and responsibilities. They know how to recognize, contain, and mitigate incidents.
- **Detection and analysis**—This phase uses various controls to detect incidents, which include IDSs and antivirus software. Because some detected events may not actually be incidents, they need to be investigated and analyzed to determine whether they are actual incidents or false positives.
- **Containment, eradication, and recovery**—After an incident has been detected, it needs to be contained as quickly as possible. This containment can be as simple as removing the cable from the network interface card (NIC) on the affected system, which removes the source of the attack. For example, if a system is infected with malware, the malware should be quarantined or removed. Then, the system can be returned to normal operations. Attacks often include several elements. After eradicating one element, the detection and analysis step must often be repeated. This process is repeated until verification has been obtained that all the malicious elements have been eradicated. Only then is the post-incident recovery phase initiated.
- **Postincident Activity**—This phase includes an after-action review, whereby the incident and the response are examined to determine where the response could be improved. When warranted, the CIRT plan is modified accordingly. Learning from the incident is an excellent way to improve an organization's cybersecurity.

[2] Nelson, Alexander, et al., "NIST SP 800-61 Rev. 3
Incident Response Recommendations and Considerations for Cybersecurity Risk Management: A CSF 2.0 Community Profile," National Institute of Standards and Technology, April 2025, https://csrc.nist.gov/pubs/sp/800/61/r3/final.

The preparation phase is the same for any type of incident in that personnel within the organization take the time to plan and prepare. Similarly, the postincident recovery phase is the same for any incident. However, the two middle phases are often different. The following sections discuss different types of incidents and include methods of preventing, detecting, and responding to them.

Handling DoS Attack Incidents

DoS attacks attempt to prevent a system or network from providing a service by overwhelming it to consume its resources. Any system has four primary resources: processor, memory, disk, and bandwidth. When these resources are responding to an attack, they can't be used for normal operations.

A DDoS attack is launched from multiple systems, and these systems are often controlled in a botnet. **FIGURE 15-3** shows multiple zombies, or clone computers, that have been infected by malware and are now controlled by an attacker from a command-and-control center. When the attacker issues a command, the zombies attack.

DoS attacks attack a single system. There are several indications that a DoS attack is occurring. These include:

- User reports of system unavailability
- IDS alerts on the attack
- Increased resource usage on the attacked system

> **NOTE**
>
> Botnets often include tens of thousands of computers. Cybercriminals manage the botnets and rent access to them to other criminals. For example, an attacker can rent access to launch a DDoS attack on a specific server.

FIGURE 15-3

DDoS attack launched from a botnet.

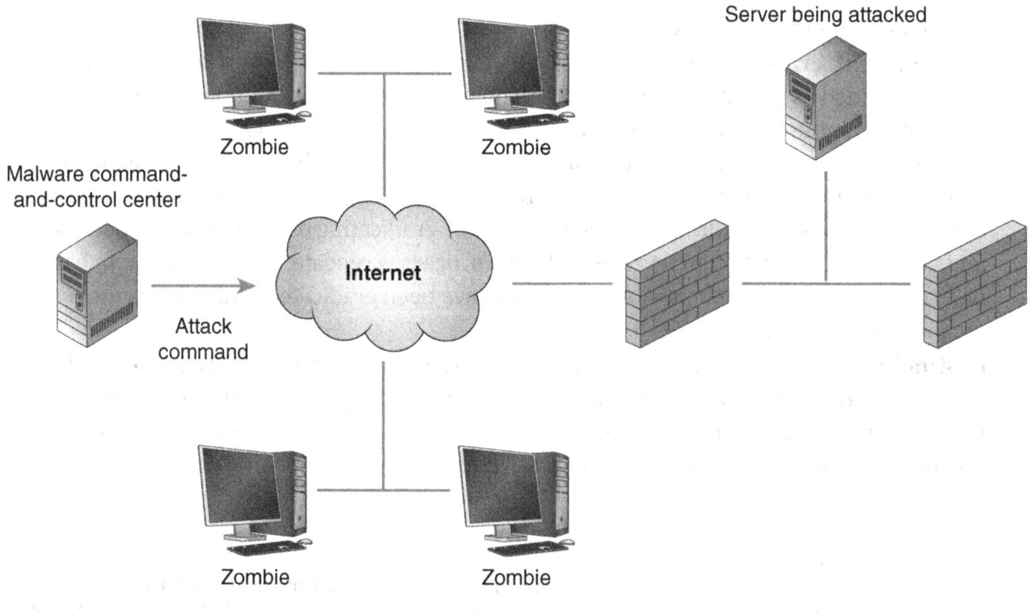

- Increased traffic through the firewall to the attacked system
- Unexplained connection losses
- Unexplained system crashes

A suspected attack can be confirmed by reviewing available logs. System logs include information on system activity, firewall logs can show network traffic to the system, and logs gathered by the IDS can identify many specific types of attacks.

The response depends on the type of attack. If the attack is due to a vulnerability, such as an unpatched system, the primary response should be to fix the vulnerability; in this case, patch the system. Many attacks can be blocked at the network firewall, and other attacks can be blocked at the system firewall.

Many IDSs include automated response capabilities, such as changing firewall rules to block specific types of traffic. An IDS that responds is called an intrusion prevention system (IPS). For example, if the attack is Internet Control Message Protocol (ICMP) based, the IDS can configure the firewall to block ICMP traffic. If the attack is a synchronized (SYN) flood attack that is withholding the third packet of a Transmission Control Protocol (TCP) handshake, the IDS can configure the firewall to block traffic from the attacking IP.

NOTE

Although the SYN flood attack is an older DoS attack, it is a good illustration of how a DoS occurs. Put another way, you will not encounter this attack in modern times; however, it is easy to understand the process. Attackers launch SYN flood attacks via the internet.

If an IDS system doesn't automatically respond to the attack, changes can be made manually. The goal is to identify the source of the attack and modify the firewall rules to block the traffic. Basic packet-filtering rules can be modified on routers or firewalls. Traffic can be blocked based on IP addresses; ports; and some protocols, such as ICMP.

The internet service provider (ISP) can also be recruited to assist with the response by filtering the traffic so the attack doesn't even reach the network.

Handling Malware Incidents

Malware incidents are the result of any malicious software, such as viruses and worms. Many types of malware exist, and new ones appear daily. Some of the varieties include:

- **Malware**—Malware is a broad term for any malicious software. That includes computer viruses and worms, spyware, ransomware, backdoors, Trojan horses, and literally any software that can have a deleterious impact on the target systems.
- **Identify Theft**—ID theft may depend on malware or other attacks to get the personally identifiable information (PII); however, the ID theft also involves the attacker using the information. This is usually a law enforcement issue, but becomes an organization issue if the organization's systems were the source of the PII.
- **Malicious mobile code**—Mobile code includes different types of malware that execute when a user visits a website or opens an email. Some of the languages and methods used are Java, ActiveX, JavaScript, and VBScript.

TIP

NIST SP 800-83 Rev. 1, Guide to Malware Incident Prevention and Handling for Desktops and Laptops, includes details on how to address malware incidents.

FYI

Trojan horses are named after the wooden horse in Greek mythology. This wooden horse looked like a gift from the gods to the people of Troy, so the residents of Troy rolled the horse through the gates to the city and partied all day and night celebrating their good fortune. But, when the city slept, hidden attackers climbed out of the horse and opened the gates to let the attacking army in, which promptly sacked the city of Troy. The lesson is the same today as it was then: Beware of gifts from unknown sources.

The primary protection against malware is antivirus software, and many organizations use it in a three-pronged approach. First, antivirus software is installed on all the systems in the organization; second, it is installed on email servers, which blocks malware delivered via email; and third, it is often installed at the boundary of the network, which is where the intranet meets the internet and can filter all traffic for potential malware.

Additionally, signature files on the antivirus software must be updated regularly. Most organizations use automated techniques to install the antivirus software, and these automated techniques also update the signatures regularly.

A secondary protection is to train and educate users because many of them are unaware of how malware is delivered, and they don't recognize the extent of damage possible from it. Routine training educates users about the types of malware threats and what to do if malware infects their system.

Some organizations create checklists that identify what users should do if their systems are infected, and they post them where users can regularly see them. The first step after identifying the virus is to contain the threat, perhaps by removing the NIC.

If malware infects an email server, isolating the email server is the best thing to do until the malware can be contained. Depending on the extent of the malware, this may require IT personnel to shut down the email server and rebuild it. It could also mean simply removing the cable at the NIC until the malware has been removed. Restoring systems from known un-infected backups is often a part of the restoration process.

Moreover, many organizations configure web browsers and email readers to prevent the execution of malicious mobile code. For example, Microsoft domains can use Group Policy to configure all the systems in the network. Group Policy settings can be set once to restrict execution of scripts or unsigned ActiveX controls on all user systems.

Handling Unauthorized Access Incidents

An unauthorized access incident occurs when a person gains access to resources even though that person does not have authorized access. Sometimes, unauthorized access can be gained accidentally. For example, if an administrator grants a user too many privileges, the user might stumble upon classified data. However, the focus in this section is on attackers gaining unauthorized access, which they can do by gaining access through social engineering or technical attacks.

Once they have gained access, attackers try to exploit it, often by using privilege escalation techniques to gain additional access. Examples of unauthorized access incidents include:

- Attacking and defacing a web server
- Uploading data to or downloading data from a File Transfer Protocol (FTP) server
- Using an unattended workstation without permission
- Viewing or copying sensitive data without authorization
- Using social engineering techniques to collect organization data
- Guessing or cracking passwords and logging on with these credentials
- Running a packet sniffer, such as Wireshark, to capture data transmitted on the network

The majority of these types of attacks originate from attackers outside the organization. Because internet-facing servers are the most vulnerable to internet-based attacks, attackers often access servers or other internal resources through the internet.

One of the basic protection steps that can be taken is to ensure that all servers are hardened. Steps to harden a server include:

- **Reducing the attack surface**—If services are not used, disable them. If protocols are not used, remove them. If an attacker launches an attack using a protocol that isn't installed on the server, the server is protected.
- **Keeping systems up to date**—Software vendors release patches and updates to eliminate bugs that cause security vulnerabilities. These updates must be applied regularly to protect the systems.
- **Enabling firewalls**—Firewalls filter all traffic to ensure that unwanted traffic does not reach vulnerable systems. Network-based firewalls provide one layer of protection for the computers in the network, and host-based firewalls provide another layer of protection. Therefore, both types of firewalls should be enabled.
- **Enabling IDSs**—IDSs detect attacks either passively or actively. A passive IDS detects the attack and then provides notification, whereas an active IDS (also called an IPS) can modify the environment and stop attackers before any damage is done.

Moreover, basic access controls also provide protection. These controls ensure that all users authenticate on the network before gaining access to resources. Additionally, the principle of least privilege ensures that users have access to only the data they need and no more.

Without credentials to authenticate on the network, outside attackers won't have any success gaining access. However, their lack of access doesn't prevent them from using social engineering tactics to discover network credentials by tricking or conning users into giving up valuable information, such as their usernames and passwords, which they can then use to launch an attack.

Unauthorized access incidents can be detected through several methods. IDSs often provide warnings about reconnaissance activity before an attack. For example, an attacker may scan a server for open ports to determine what protocols are running. The data thus gained in the reconnaissance attack is then later used in the access attack. A System Information Event Monitoring tool (SIEM) aggregates logs and alerts from many systems and provides both administrative alerts to suspicious activity and a centralized location from which to analyze a suspected breach.

Another important tool is Security Orchestration, Automation, and Response (SOAR), which integrates disparate tools like SIEMs, firewalls, endpoint protection, ticketing systems, etc. These can be used to coordinate automated workflows across multiple platforms (e.g., if an IP is flagged as malicious, block it on the firewall and update the SIEM).

Educated users can detect social engineering attempts by recognizing the conning and trickery that a social engineer uses to get them to give up their secrets. Once users recognize these attempts, they can then report them to administrators. Of course, uneducated users often give up their secrets without realizing what they've done because most people are helpful by nature, and this trait is exploited by social engineers.

Some attacks are not detected, though, because an attacker can access data in a database and disappear before anyone even notices. Even if the access is logged, the actual event may go undetected. Oftentimes, the realization that the unauthorized access has occurred isn't discovered until later when a problem is noticed. The stolen data may have been research and development data, which is now being used by a competitor, or customer credit card information. This can be mitigated by appropriate monitoring of logs and SIEM. Failure to notice a breach is often indicative of flaws in the organization's cybersecurity.

The response depends on the attack, but the most important element of any attack is containment. If the attack is detected in progress, the goal is to isolate the affected system, but not necessarily from all users. Instead, the system can be isolated from only the attacker. For example, firewall rules can be modified to block the attacker's IP address.

If the problem is from a compromised account, the account can be disabled, but, if the account is an elevated account, such as one with elevated permissions, other accounts may have been created with it. For example, an attacker may steal the credentials of an administrator account, and, right after logging on, they create another account with administrative permissions. Therefore, even if the first account is locked out, the attacker can still use the second account.

Handling Inappropriate Usage Incidents

Inappropriate usage incidents occur when users violate internal policies, but these incidents usually aren't as serious as external ones. However, depending on the activity, the incidents can be quite serious and result in loss of money for the organization.

Examples of inappropriate usage include users who:

- Spam coworkers
- Access websites that are prohibited
- Purposely circumvent security policies
- Use file sharing or P2P programs
- Send files with sensitive data outside the organization
- Launch attacks from within the organization against other computers

TIP

Attackers commonly scan systems to determine which ports are open because many protocols use well-known ports. If the port is open, the attacker realizes the associated protocol is probably running on the server. For example, if port 80 is open, Hypertext Transfer Protocol (HTTP) is most likely running on the server, which indicates that the server is most likely a web server.

A security policy helps prevent many of these incidents and often requires an AUP, which identifies what is and is not acceptable usage. For example, the AUP may specify that using email to advertise a personal business or using the internet to access gambling or pornographic sites is prohibited. Similarly, the policy often prohibits the use of anonymizer sites. Most proxy servers can detect and block access to anonymizers. Organizations commonly reprimand users who violate AUPs.

AUPs typically restrict the use of P2P software, which people often use to download and share pirated music, videos, and applications. However, one of the main problems with P2P software is **data leakage**, which occurs when the P2P software shares user data without the user's knowledge. For example, users might have files with personal data, such as passwords or credit card information, on their computers, and the P2P software might include steps to protect these files. But, if users don't protect these files, the P2P program might share the files with anyone else using the same P2P program. Similarly, the user could be sharing proprietary data if a P2P program is installed on the user's computer.

Technical TIP

An **anonymizer** site attempts to hide a user's activity. When a user visits the anonymizer site and then visits other sites through it, the anonymizer retrieves the webpages but serves them as if they had originated from it. For example, a user could visit a gambling site via the anonymizer, and, if the internal proxy server tracked the user's activity, it would identify the traffic from the anonymizer but not the traffic from the gambling site. Just the use of an anonymizer alone is considered to be a serious offense by many organizations.

Inappropriate usage incidents can be discovered through several methods, which include alerts, log reviews, and reports by other users. Because firewalls and proxy servers log all the traffic going through them, they can be scanned to determine whether users are violating the policies. Additionally, an IDS can be configured to automatically detect and report prohibited activities.

Many organizations also use data loss prevention (DLP) software, which administrators can configure with keywords associated with proprietary data and to look for personally identifiable information (PII). For example, Social Security numbers include nine numbers and two dashes. A DLP scanner can look for text matching a mask like this: ###-##-####. It scans all traffic going in and out of a network, and, when it detects a match, it sends an alert.

Another way to detect inappropriate usage is through other users. For example, employees may receive spam from another employee advertising a business or promoting a religion, or they may view inappropriate images on an offender's computer. The organization responds to these incidents when the employees report them.

The primary response is based on the existing policies, which include the security policy and the AUP. If policies don't exist, they need to be created. If an employee violates the policy, the employee is at fault, but, if a policy doesn't exist, the organization may be at fault.

Chinese Cyber Espionage

In early 2025 it was revealed that Chinese hackers had breached a U.S. government office that reviews investments to determine if they have national security risks.[3] The breach was part of a broader incursion by the hackers into the Treasury Department's unclassified system, specifically the Committee on Foreign Investment in the US (CFIUS). Data that was revealed included real estate sales near U.S. military bases. This is part of a broader campaign of cyber-attacks by China. Dakota Cary of the Atlantic Council Global China Hub describes this moment as China's golden age of hacking.[4]

In addition to having policies, it's worth stating the obvious: They must be enforced. Some organizations go through the motions of creating policies, but, when it comes time to enforce them, they look the other way. In this situation, employees quickly realize that there are dual policies: one is written but not followed, and the other is unwritten and is the norm.

Handling Multiple Component Incidents

A multiple component incident is a single incident that includes two or more other incidents, which are related to each other but not always immediately apparent. For example, in the first incident of a multiple component incident, a user in an organization receives an email with a malware attachment, and, when it is opened, it infects the user's system.

The malware has three objectives. First, it releases a worm component that seeks out computers on the organization's network and infects them. This is the second incident.

Next, the malware contacts a server on the internet that is managing a botnet. In this role, the organization's infected system acts as a zombie. It waits for a command from the botnet control server and then does whatever it's commanded to do.

Because the organization's infected system has infected other systems on the network, multiple systems could easily be infected, and each of these systems is looking for other systems to infect. They are also acting as zombies in the botnet.

Next, the botnet control server issues a command to all the infected systems, directing them to launch an attack on an internet server. All the zombies in the infected network then attack, which is the third incident.

TIP

A behavior-based IDS is the same as an anomaly-based IDS. Both systems start with a baseline of regular activity, which is monitored and compared with intrusion activities.

[3] Sean Lyngaas, "Chinese hackers breached US government office that assesses foreign investments for national security risks," CNN, January 10, 2025, https://www.cnn.com/2025/01/10/politics/chinese-hackers-breach-committee-on-foreign-investment-in-the-us.

[4] Pfeiffer, Sacha and Kai McNamee, "Why this is China's golden age of hacking," July 19, 2025, https://www.npr.org/2025/07/19/nx-s1-5471340/why-this-is-chinas-golden-age-of-hacking.

From the perspective of the attacked server, the infected organization looks like it is attacking. The party being attacked may query the infected organization's ISP and report the attacks. The ISP may then threaten to discontinue the infected organization's service. Notice that the ISP contact may be the first indication that the infected organization has a problem because the problem may not have been noticeable before then.

In this case, the primary protection is antivirus software and ensuring the antivirus software is up to date. Up-to-date antivirus software reduces the likelihood that systems will be infected. However, up-to-date antivirus software doesn't guarantee that a system won't be infected. It simply reduces the likelihood. A system is always susceptible to new and emerging threats.

Anomaly-based IDSs may notice the increased activity on the network. It starts with a baseline of normal activity, and, when activity increases outside the established threshold, the IDS alerts on the anomaly.

When a multiple component incident is discovered, the root cause must be identified, which, in the preceding example, is the initial malware. If the root cause can be removed, the other issues may be eliminated. However, any one of the individual components in a multiple component incident can take on a life of its own and can launch another multiple component incident.

NOTE

Sentinel One highlights that security trends matter because attacks are becoming more sophisticated, using stealthy, multi-stage techniques that are harder to detect. Breaches can severely damage organizational reputation and erode trust among customers, partners, and investors. Increasingly strict regulations like GDPR and HIPAA impose heavy penalties for poor data protection. The rise of remote work has expanded attack surfaces, heightening risks such as phishing and endpoint compromise. Cyber incidents also carry growing financial consequences, including ransomware losses and long-term brand damage. Finally, delayed patching and weak vulnerability management leave critical security gaps exposed.

Data from SentinelOne. (2026, January 16). 10 cyber security trends for 2026. SentinelOne. https://www.sentinelone.com/cybersecurity-101/cybersecurity/cyber-security-trends/

Communication Escalation Procedures

When someone determines an event is an incident, they declare it to be so, which is known as escalation. One of the first steps to take when declaring an incident is to recall one or more CIRT members, which can be done by a phone tree or any other type of traditional recall.

But incidents can get worse. For example, the initial report may have been a virus on a single computer, but a CIRT member may discover that the malware is being delivered from the email server to every client in the network. What looked like a small problem now has the potential to become catastrophic. In this case, the CIRT member can escalate the response, and, if necessary, the organization can activate the full CIRT.

Communication is very important during the incident, but it may be hampered. For example, email or instant messaging systems might not be available. If these are the primary methods of communication with no backup plan, communication will be challenging.

DRPs often include solutions for potential communication problems, which can also be used for computer incidents. For example, CIRT members can be issued push-to-talk phones or walkie-talkies, or a war room can be set up for face-to-face communications. The war room could be staffed constantly, and team members could report findings to personnel there.

The Organization's Reputation

Communication outside the organization is important to address. If media outlets hear about an incident, they'll start asking questions. How people within the organization respond to these questions affects its reputation. Even if the organization is responding to the incident admirably, negative publicity can result if the response to the media is confused or contradictory.

The best choice is to enlist the help of PR specialists, and, ideally, the CIRT will include a PR person. All personnel should understand that all media queries should go through this PR person.

PR specialists know how to communicate to the media effectively. Even in the midst of a major incident, they are able to present the organization in a favorable light, which is not to say that they know or give all the answers, but they do know how to give honest, positive ones.

A technician may say something like "This worm hammered us. I've never seen so many servers down before, and I don't know how we'll get them back up."

The PR person may say, "We have been attacked. We have several controls in place, but the attack appears to have been very sophisticated and simultaneously hit several elements of our network. Our computer incident response team is on the scene. Even as we speak, they are investigating the source of the problems and resolving them."

Both statements are accurate, but the first statement presents an image of chaos, or being out of control. Although the technician's statement may be accurate, it has the potential to adversely affect the organization's reputation. On the other hand, the PR statement is also accurate, but it preserves the organization's reputation.

NOTE

The checklists in this section are derived from information in NIST SP 800-61 Rev. 2, Computer Security Incident Handling Guide.

Incident Handling Procedures

When an incident is suspected, checklists can be used to guide actions. They can be included in the CIRT plan as procedures to use in response to incidents. IT professionals and CIRT members can use the checklists when responding to incidents.

Although checklists can't be created to respond to every possible incident, they can be tailored to the different types of incidents. For example, a generic checklist can be created to match most incidents, and then, other checklists can be created to identify what do for the different types of incidents.

Calculating the Impact and Priority

One of the important steps when handling an incident is to identify its impact and priority, and the CIRT plan can include tools to help personnel determine both. Members can then refer to these tools for clarification during the incident.

For example, data in **TABLE 15-1** identifies the effect of an attack. A CIRT member compares the actual effect of the risk to the definition, which provides a value or a rating. For example, an organization has multiple locations spread around the country. No effect on any location is a minimal effect. A severe effect on a single location is a medium effect.

TABLE 15-1 Effect Rating Definitions

DEFINITION	RATING	VALUE
No effect on any locations or the critical infrastructure	Minimal	10
Severe effect on a single location or minimal effect on multiple locations	Medium	50
Severe effect on multiple locations	Critical	90

A severe effect on multiple locations is considered critical. Each of these ratings is assigned a numerical value.

The values in Table 15-1 are used to determine both current and projected effects. For example, a DoS attack may be launched against one of several web servers in a web farm. The effect may be minimal as long as only one server is being attacked. However, if the attack isn't resolved soon, it may affect all the servers in the web farm. The projected effect may be considered medium.

TABLE 15-2 can be used to determine how critical the attack is, which is determined by the importance, or criticality, of the systems.

Next, the ratings from Tables 15-1 and 15-2 are used to determine an overall score. Whenever possible, the current and the projected effect should be determined:

- **Current effect rating**—Minimal because the attack is currently affecting only one web server in the web farm. Score of 10. This rating will be used for 25%, or one-quarter, of the overall impact score (10 × .25 = 2.5).
- **Projected effect rating**—Medium because the attack has the potential to spread to more web servers in the web farm. Score of 50. This rating will be used for 25%, or one-quarter, of the overall impact score (50 × .25 = 12.5).
- **Criticality rating**—Medium because the web server does affect a mission-critical system in a single location. Score of 50. This rating will be used for 50%, or one-half, of the overall impact score (50 × .50 = 25).

NOTE

The definitions, values, and ratings used in these examples can be expanded to fit any organization. For example, an organization could have five values and ratings instead of three. Different values, ratings, and even definitions, based on the organization's needs, can also be used.

TABLE 15-2 Criticality Rating Definitions

DEFINITION	RATING	VALUE
Noncritical systems	Minimal	10
Systems that are mission-critical to a single location	Medium	50
Systems that are mission-critical to multiple locations	Critical	90

TABLE 15-3 Incident Impact Rating

SCORE	RATING AND PRIORITY
0 to 25	Minimal, low priority
26 to 50	Medium, medium priority
51 to 100	Critical, high priority

The following formula can then be used to determine the impact:

$$(\text{Current effect rating} \times .25) + (\text{Projected effect rating} \times .25) + (\text{Criticality rating} \times .50)$$

$$(10 \times .25) + (50 \times .25) + (50 \times .50)$$

$$2.5 + 12.5 + 25$$

$$\text{Incident impact score} = 40$$

After the incident impact score has been identified, then the impact of the incident can be rated. **TABLE 15-3** shows a sample incident rating table. Note that a score of 40 indicates that the incident has a medium impact rating.

These numbers can be confusing, especially during a crisis, but a tool can be created to automate the calculation. For example, a spreadsheet can be created with check boxes next to the ratings. Creating the ratings requires doing some underlying calculations, but they can be hidden and locked. A CIRT member then only needs to open the spreadsheet and select the appropriate check boxes.

Using a Generic Checklist

Once the calculation for the impact and priority has been identified, then the checklists can be created. The following checklist is a sample generic checklist:

- **Verifying that an incident has occurred**—This verification ensures that the event is an actual incident and not just a false positive. For example, some IDSs send an alert on unusual activity when the activity is not an actual incident.
- **Determining the type of incident**—Whether the incident is a DoS, malware, unauthorized access, inappropriate usage, or a multiple type of incident is determined. If a checklist exists for an incident, retrieve it from the CIRT plan. Some incidents may require specialists, and, if they do, the appropriate specialists must be recalled.
- **Determining the impact or potential impact of the incident**—The extent of the attack is determined. For example, the attack could be a virus that has affected a single workstation, a worm that has affected multiple servers, or a DoS attack that has taken down a primary web server that is generating over $20,000 an hour in revenue. If the impact is high, the resulting response will be a high priority.
- **Reporting the incident**—If the person reporting the incident isn't a member of the CIRT, they should report the incident to a member of the CIRT. The impact and severity of the incident should be included if possible and the incident reported to management. High-impact incidents should be reported as soon as possible, and lower-priority incidents can be reported after they have been contained.

- **Acquiring any available evidence on the incident**—Evidence must be preserved. Therefore, establishing a chain of custody should begin as soon as evidence has been collected. The chain of custody log should include the time, date, and name of the person who is receiving the evidence. If the evidence is passed from one person to another or into storage, the chain of custody log must be updated, and the evidence must not be modified. No files should be accessed or any system turned off because accessing files modifies the evidence and turning off a system deletes data in its memory.
- **Containing the incident**—The incident must be kept from spreading to other systems and the system isolated, which can be done by removing the NIC from the system or disabling it. If multiple systems are affected, the network must be isolated, which can be done by isolating all the systems on the network or isolating the network devices. For example, a router could be turned off or reconfigured to isolate a subnet.
- **Eradicating the incident**—The exploited vulnerabilities must be identified and the steps necessary to reduce the weaknesses determined. If malware was involved, it must be completely removed. If the attack was on a public-facing server, the server must be hardened to prevent another attack.
- **Recovering from the incident**—Once the incident has been eradicated, systems can be returned to normal operation. Depending on the system and the damage, the system may simply need to be rebooted, or it may need to be completely rebuilt or a system image reapplied. If the system is rebuilt, it must be patched and up to date before and then verified to be operating normally after it has been returned to operation.
- **Documenting the incident**—Documentation includes many elements, one of which is an after-action report describing the incident, which includes all the details gathered during the incident and all the steps taken to eradicate and recover from the incident. If a chain of custody was created, it must be maintained with any collected evidence, which may be needed later.

The following sections show information that can be used in checklists for other types of incidents. CIRT members can use either the generic checklist or the specific type of checklist when responding to an incident.

Handling DoS Attack Incidents

If the attack is a DoS attack, a checklist designed to address DoS attacks can be used. The checklist can be designed to stand alone or to be used in conjunction with the generic checklist.

The following items should be considered when creating a checklist for DoS attacks:

- **Containment**—The DoS attack must be halted as soon as possible. One way to do this is to add filters at routers or firewalls to block the traffic based on the IP address, port, or protocol used in the attack. If the attack cannot be blocked in the network, the ISP may be able to help. Only as a last resort should the server be disconnected. Once it has been disconnected, the service is stopped, which is the primary objective of the DoS attack.
- **Eradication**—Vulnerabilities that allowed the DoS attack must be identified. For example, the vulnerability may have stemmed from a server that wasn't adequately hardened because unused protocols may have been enabled on the system or the server may not

have had up-to-date patches. After the vulnerabilities have been identified, steps need to be taken to mitigate them.

- **Recovery**—If the server has suffered long-term damage, it must be repaired. Because the attack may have installed malware, performing a malware scan with updated antivirus software would be advisable. After recovery, the system must be tested to ensure it is operating normally.

Handling Malware Incidents

If an incident was the result of malicious software, several additional steps can be taken, which are in addition to the steps in the generic checklist. If desired, a specific checklist can be created for malware incidents, or they could be combined into the generic checklist.

> **NOTE**
>
> A *multipartite virus* is a virus that uses multiple infection methods. It often requires more steps or complex procedures to eradicate than simpler malware.

Consider the following items when creating a checklist for malware incidents:

- **Containment**—All the infected systems must be identified and disconnected from the network, and the reason the antivirus software didn't detect the malware must be determined. For example, the antivirus software may have been disabled, or the antivirus signatures may have been out of date. Therefore, the antivirus signatures must be updated and the software enabled. If necessary, the firewall or router rules must be configured to block the malware from being transmitted to or from the infected system.
- **Eradication**—Full scans on the systems must be run. Antivirus software vendors, such as Symantec and McAfee, often host pages that show detailed steps for removing multipartite viruses and other advanced malware. If necessary, individual steps must be performed to remove all elements of the malware from the system, and infected files must be disinfected, quarantined, or deleted.
- **Recovery**—Any files that were deleted or quarantined and are needed for system operation must be replaced, and the system must be verified that it is no longer infected. If multiple steps were required to clean the system, running another full scan before returning the system to operation should be considered.

Handling Unauthorized Access Incidents

Several steps can be taken in response to unauthorized access incidents. Just as with other types of incidents, separate checklists can be created to cover unauthorized access incidents, and the generic checklist can be supplemented with a checklist for unauthorized access incidents.

The following items should be considered when creating a checklist for unauthorized access incidents:

- **Containment**—If an in-progress attack is discovered, the attacked system must be identified and isolated from the network, which can be done by pulling the NIC cable or disabling the NIC. A host-based firewall can be used to block all traffic while logging all attempts to connect. If the incident was from an internal account, the account must be disabled and verified to have been under the principle of least privilege. The determination should be made as to whether an attacker hijacked the account as well and whether other systems were attacked, because attackers who succeed when attacking one system will usually try to attack other systems in the same network. Other systems can then be contained if necessary.

- **Eradication**—The weaknesses that allowed the attack to succeed must be identified, and all the steps to harden the server must be verified to have been completed and that they haven't been modified. Strong passwords must be used and may need to be changed on the system. If additional accounts were created during the attack, they must be disabled and perhaps deleted.
- **Recovery**—After resolving the vulnerabilities, the systems can be reconnected and verified that they are operational. The systems should be tested to ensure they are operating as expected. Adding additional monitoring, such as an IDS, to identify future incidents as soon as possible may need to be considered.

When creating a follow-up report of unauthorized access, the data that was accessed during the attack needs to be considered. If it was private customer data, such as credit card data, the organization may have specific liabilities associated with the incident, which need to be determined and included in the report. Management will be responsible for determining how to handle these liabilities.

Handling Inappropriate Usage Incidents

Inappropriate usage incidents need specific responses to mitigate their effects. The steps to mitigate their effects can be combined with the steps in a generic checklist, or a separate checklist can be created to address inappropriate usage incidents individually.

As a reminder, an inappropriate usage incident occurs when an internal user violates the organization's policies. The following items should be considered when creating a checklist for inappropriate usage incidents:

- **Containment**—The user's account may be disabled until management takes action. For example, if a user is sending religious materials to everyone in the organization, the user's email access can be disabled. Because an employee is unable to perform regular work duties if the user's network access is disabled, immediacy is brought to the problem for both the user and the user's supervisor.
- **Eradication**—Some organizations require users to complete specific training before their access is returned, and other organizations require supervisors to document the activity in the employee's record. If the employee is a repeat offender or the incident is considered severe enough, the employee may be terminated. For example, if a user installed P2P software on an employer-owned computer that resulted in the loss of valuable research and development data through data leakage, the employer may terminate the employee immediately.
- **Recovery**—If the account was disabled, it would be enabled after the appropriate action has been completed, for example, after the employee completes training or HR has documented the incident. If the employee is terminated, the account should be disabled or deleted, based on the organization's policy.

How Does a CIRT Plan Mitigate an Organization's Risk?

The CIRT plan helps an organization prepare for incidents. When the organization is prepared, it responds to incidents much quicker and with focused action. One of the primary benefits of the CIRT plan is the identification of CIRT members so that the organization knows who they are and the individuals on the team know their roles and responsibilities. Once the plan and the members have been identified, the organization has a better understanding of the skills needed to support the requirements, and the members can be trained to ensure that they do.

Without the plan, IT and security professionals don't have the benefit of time to analyze their response. They may pull the NIC cable to stop a DoS attack on a server, and, although doing this will stop the attack, it will also prevent the server from performing the expected service. Uninformed administrators may leave an infected system on the network, which would allow it to infect other systems, or a well-meaning administrator may launch an attack back on an attacker, which may be detected and result in the attacker launching a series of stronger attacks.

Best Practices for Implementing a CIRT Plan for an Organization

When implementing a CIRT plan for an organization, several best practices can be used. Following is a list of some of these:

- **Defining a computer security incident**—Incidents are interpreted differently by different organizations. When incidents are defined in the CIRT plan, all parties are clear as to which events are incidents.
- **Including policies in the CIRT plan to guide CIRT members**—These policies can be related to CIRT members attacking back at attackers and can include statements regarding the use of chain of custody or otherwise protecting evidence and policies related to communications and safety, which depend on what is important to the organization.
- **Providing training**—CIRT members and end users must be trained. The CIRT members should understand their responsibilities and know the best way to respond to different types of incidents, and all personnel should understand the threats as well as basic steps they can take to mitigate them.
- **Including checklists**—The checklists can be formal step-by-step instructions that must be performed in a specific order or informal bullet statements designed to help ensure the CIRT members don't overlook key data. Generic checklists or checklists targeted toward specific types of incidents can be included.
- **Subscribing to security notifications**—Many security bulletins that describe different types of threats, including new emerging threats, are available through email subscriptions. US-CISA regularly sends out emails and alerts. Go https://www.cisa.gov/news-events/cybersecurity-advisories to sign up to receive these emails.

CHAPTER SUMMARY

This chapter covered computer incident response teams (CIRTs) and CIRT plans. Organizations should expect attacks that result in computer security incidents, and several types of incidents exist. Denial of service attacks try to prevent a system from providing a service. Malicious software attacks include viruses, worms, Trojan horses, and other types of malware. Unauthorized access incidents result when individuals gain access to data that they shouldn't have access to. Unauthorized access can be from technical attacks or social engineering tactics. Inappropriate usage incidents result when employees or internal users violate the organization's policies. Some incidents have multiple components.

A CIRT can respond to the attack and mitigate the effects. The CIRT plan identifies organizational policies. For example, a policy may explain the conditions when a CIRT member can attack the attacker. It will certainly include procedures or checklists to use when responding to different types of incidents. Through preparation and training, the CIRT plan helps an organization mitigate the risks associated with incidents.

KEY CONCEPTS AND TERMS

anonymizer
CIRT plan
computer incident
computer incident response team (CIRT)
data leakage
malware

CHAPTER 15 ASSESSMENT

1. A(n) _____________ is a violation of a security policy or security practice.

2. All events on a system or network are considered computer security incidents.

   A. True
   B. False

3. An administrator has discovered that a web server is responding slowly. Investigation shows that the processor, memory, and network resources are being consumed by outside attackers. This is a(n) _____________ attack.

4. A user has installed P2P software on a system, and the organization's policy specifically states that this is unauthorized. An administrator discovers the software on the user's system. Is this a computer security incident? If so, what type?

   A. This is not a computer security incident.
   B. This is a form of inappropriate usage.
   C. This is a form of unauthorized access.
   D. This is a form of malware.

5. Some malware can execute on a user's system after the user accesses a website. The malware executes from within the web browser. What type of malware is this?
   A. Virus
   B. Worm
   C. Trojan horse
   D. Mobile code

6. A malicious virus is replicating and causing damage to computers. How do security professionals refer to the virus?
   A. In the open
   B. In the containment field
   C. In the jungle
   D. In the wild

7. What is the greatest risk to an organization when peer-to-peer software is installed on a user's system?
   A. Loss of copyrights
   B. Piracy of the organization's copyrighted material
   C. Data leakage
   D. DoS attacks

8. Only police or other law enforcement personnel are allowed to do computer forensics investigations.
   A. True
   B. False

9. A log shows that a user has copied proprietary data to his computer. The organization wants to take legal action against him, so it seizes the computer as evidence. What should be established as soon as the computer is seized?
   A. Chain of command
   B. Forensic chain
   C. Permission from the user
   D. Chain of custody
   E. All of the above

10. Many steps are taken before, during, and after an incident. Of the following choices, what accurately identifies the incident response life cycle?
   A. Preparation, deletion and analysis, eradication and recovery, and postincident recovery
   B. Detection and analysis, containment, backup and eradication, and postincident recovery
   C. Preparation, detection and analysis, containment, eradication and recovery, and postincident recovery
   D. Preparation, detection, deletion and analysis, containment and recovery, and postincident recovery

11. In general, members of a CIRT taking actions to attack attackers is acceptable because this is one of the normal responsibilities of a CIRT.
   A. True
   B. False

12. After an incident has been verified, it must be kept from spreading to other systems. What is this called?
   A. Spread avoidance
   B. Containment
   C. Incident response
   D. Impact and priority calculation

13. Which of the following may be included in a CIRT plan?
   A. Policies
   B. Definition of incidents
   C. CIRT member responsibilities
   D. Incident-handling procedures
   E. All of the above
   F. C and D only

14. Attackers attempt a DoS attack on servers in an organization. The CIRT responds and mitigates the attack. What should be the last step that the CIRT completes in response to this incident?
    A. Attacking the attacker
    B. Containing the threat
    C. Documenting the incident
    D. Reporting the incident

15. Several types of malicious code exist. Malware that appears to be one thing but is actually something else is ______________.

APPENDIX A

Answer Key

CHAPTER 1 Risk Management Fundamentals

1. D 2. B 3. A 4. A and C 5. intangible value 6. control 7. B 8. D 9. CVE 10. A 11. CBA, or cost-benefit analysis 12. transfer 13. A, B, and C 14. D 15. C

CHAPTER 2 Managing Risk: Threats, Vulnerabilities, and Exploits

1. D 2. A 3. B 4. C 5. D 6. C 7. B 8. A 9. A 10. E 11. A 12. C 13. C 14. the MITRE Corporation 15. A

CHAPTER 3 Understanding and Maintaining Compliance

1. C 2. D 3. A 4. C 5. B 6. A 7. D 8. A 9. C 10. A 11. B 12. C 13. D 14. 5 15. D

CHAPTER 4 Developing a Risk Management Plan

1. E 2. E 3. D 4. C 5. B 6. A 7. A and B 8. B 9. D 10. A 11. C 12. A 13. C 14. B 15. C

CHAPTER 5 Defining Risk Assessment Approaches

1. E 2. Exposure factor (EF) 3. B 4. quantitative 5. C 6. A 7. B 8. qualitative 9. quantitative 10. B 11. quantitative 12. qualitative 13. D 14. A and B 15. E

CHAPTER 6 Performing a Risk Assessment

1. C 2. E 3. E 4. B 5. D 6. A 7. administrative 8. technical 9. physical 10. C 11. A 12. B 13. B 14. C 15. B

CHAPTER 7 Identifying Assets and Activities to Be Protected

1. A 2. B 3. E 4. E 5. job 6. E 7. C 8. A 9. D 10. mission-critical 11. B 12. A 13. B 14. C 15. A

CHAPTER 8 Identifying and Analyzing Threats, Vulnerabilities, and Exploits

1. natural 2. A 3. C 4. A, B, C, and D 5. D 6. vulnerability 7. C 8. C 9. A 10. D 11. access controls 12. D 13. A 14. C 15. A

CHAPTER 9 Identifying and Analyzing Risk Mitigation Security Controls

1. control, or countermeasure 2. A 3. C 4. B 5. D 6. access 7. C 8. C 9. A 10. D 11. certificate authority (CA) 12. D 13. A 14. B 15. B

CHAPTER 10 Planning Risk Mitigation Throughout an Organization

1. business impact analysis (BIA) 2. B 3. C 4. B 5. D 6. $22 million; 4 percent 7. C 8. C 9. D 10. B 11. A 12. C 13. A 14. B 15. B

CHAPTER 11 Turning a Risk Assessment Into a Risk Mitigation Plan

1. in-place 2. A 3. Threat × Vulnerability 4. E 5. A 6. mitigation 7. E 8. C 9. C 10. B 11. A 12. C 13. C 14. F 15. B

CHAPTER 12 Mitigating Risk With a Business Impact Analysis

1. maximum acceptable outage (MAO) 2. B 3. business continuity plan (BCP) 4. D 5. C and D 6. indirect 7. D 8. C 9. B 10. C 11. B 12. A 13. D 14. D 15. B

CHAPTER 13 Mitigating Risk With a Business Continuity Plan

1. BCP, or business continuity plan 2. B 3. scope 4. C 5. D 6. BCP coordinator 7. A 8. C 9. D 10. B 11. A 12. C 13. C 14. A, B, and D 15. A

CHAPTER 14 Mitigating Risk With a Disaster Recovery Plan

1. disaster recovery plan (DRP) 2. A 3. B 4. critical success factor (CSF) 5. D 6. D 7. off-site 8. A 9. C 10. B 11. C 12. D 13. B 14. D 15. B

CHAPTER 15 Mitigating Risk With a Computer Incident Response Team Plan

1. computer incident or computer security incident 2. B 3. denial of service (DoS) or distributed DoS (DDoS) 4. B 5. D 6. D 7. C 8. B 9. D 10. C 11. B 12. B 13. E 14. C 15. a Trojan horse

© Yuichiro Chino/Moment/Getty Images

APPENDIX B

Standard Acronyms

ACK	acknowledge
ACL	access control list
AES	Advanced Encryption Standard
AG	attorney general
AI	artificial intelligence
ALE	annual loss expectancy
APT	advanced persistent threat
ARO	annual rate of occurrence
ATM	automated teller machine
ATO	authorization to operate
AUP	acceptable use policy
AV	asset value
BC	business continuity
BCP	business continuity plan
BI	business intelligence
BIA	business impact analysis
BIOS	basic input/output system
CA	certificate authority
CAP	Certification and Accreditation Professional
CBA	cost-benefit analysis
CBF	critical business function
CCB	change control board
CCO	chief compliance officer
CCTV	closed circuit TV
CECO	chief ethics compliance officer
CEO	chief executive officer
CERT	Computer Emergency Response Team
CFO	chief financial officer
C-I-A	confidentiality-integrity-availability
CIO	chief information officer
CIPA	Children's Internet Protection Act
CIRT	computer incident response team
CISO	chief information security officer
CISQ	Consortium for IT Software Quality
CISSP	Certified Information Systems Security Professional
CMMI	Capability Maturity Model Integration
COBIT	Control Objectives for Information and Related Technologies
COPPA	Children's Online Privacy Protection Act
CSF	critical success factor
CSIRT	computer security incident response team
CSO	chief security officer
CTO	chief technology officer
CVE	Common Vulnerabilities and Exposures
CVRF	Common Vulnerability Reporting Framework
DAT	damage assessment team
DC	domain controller
DDoS	distributed denial of service
DHCP	Dynamic Host Configuration Protocol
DHS	Department of Homeland Security
DIACAP	Department of Defense Information Assurance Certification and Accreditation Process
DISA	Defense Information Systems Agency
DLP	data loss prevention
DMZ	demilitarized zone
DNS	Domain Name Service or Domain Name System
DoD	Department of Defense

DOJ	Department of Justice
DoS	denial of service
DR	disaster recovery
DRP	disaster recovery plan
ECO	ethics compliance officer
EEA	European Economic Area
EF	exposure factor
EMT	emergency management team
ETL	extract, transform, and load
FCC	Federal Communications Commission
FCPA	Foreign Corrupt Practices Act
FDIC	Federal Deposit Insurance Corporation
FERPA	Family Educational Rights and Privacy Act
FFRDC	Federally Funded Research and Development Center
FISMA	Federal Information Security Modernization Act
FTC	Federal Trade Commission
FTP	File Transfer Protocol
GAAP	generally accepted accounting principles
GAISP	Generally Accepted Information Security Principles
GASSP	Generally Accepted System Security Principles
GB	gigabyte
GDPR	General Data Protection Regulation
GLBA	Gramm-Leach-Bliley Act
HIDS	host-based intrusion detection system
HIMSS	Healthcare Information and Management Systems Society
HIPAA	Health Insurance Portability and Accountability Act
HR	human resources
HTTP	Hypertext Transfer Protocol
HTTPS	Hypertext Transfer Protocol Secure
HVAC	heating and air-conditioning
IA	information assurance
IANA	Internet Assigned Numbers Authority
ICMP	Internet Control Message Protocol
ICS-CERT	Industrial Control Systems Cyber Emergency Response Team
IDPS	intrusion detection and prevention system
IDS	intrusion detection system
IEC	International Electrotechnical Commission
IP	intellectual property or Internet Protocol
IPS	intrusion prevention system
IPSec	Internet Protocol Security
IS	information security
(ISC)^2	International Information System Security Certification Consortium
ISO	International Organization for Standardization
ISP	internet service provider
ISSA	Information Systems Security Association
IT	information technology
ITG	information technology governance
ITIL	Information Technology Infrastructure Library
ITL	Information Technology Laboratory
L2TP	Layer 2 Tunneling Protocol
LAN	local area network
LOB	line of business
MAC	media access control
MAO	maximum acceptable outage
MBCO	minimum business continuity objective
MTBF	mean time between failures
MTD	maximum tolerable downtime
MTO	maximum tolerable outage
MTPD	maximum tolerable period of disruption
NAC	network access control
NCCIC	National Cybersecurity and Communications Integration Center
NCUA	National Credit Union Administration
NIC	network interface card
NIDS	network-based intrusion detection system

NIST	National Institute of Standards and Technology
NNTP	Network News Transfer Protocol
NSA	National Security Agency
NVD	National Vulnerability Database
OLTP	online transaction processing
OMB	Office of Management and Budget
OS	operating system
P2P	peer to peer
PBX	phone branch exchange
PCI	Payment Card Industry
PCI DSS	Payment Card Industry Data Security Standard
PGP	Pretty Good Privacy
PHI	protected health information
PII	personally identifiable information
PIN	personal identification number
PKI	public key infrastructure
PM	project manager
POAM	plan of action and milestones
POC	point of contact
POS	point of sale
PR	public relations
PTZ	pan, tilt, zoom
RAID	redundant array of independent disks
RAM	random access memory
RAT	remote access tool
RMF	Risk Management Framework
ROI	return on investment
RPO	recovery point objective
RSA	Rivest, Shamir, and Adelman (algorithm)
RTO	recovery time objective
SEC	Securities and Exchange Commission
SID	security identifier
SIEM	security information and event management
SLA	service level agreement
SLE	single loss expectancy
SME	subject matter expert
SMTP	Simple Mail Transfer Protocol
SOX	Sarbanes-Oxley Act of 2002 (also Sarbox)
SP	service pack or special publication
SPOF	single point of failure
SQL	Structured Query Language
SSCP	Systems Security Certified Practitioner
SWIFT	Society for Worldwide Interbank Financial Telecommunications
SYN	synchronize
TARP	Troubled Asset Relief Program
TB	terabyte
TCP	Transmission Control Protocol
TPM	technology protection measure or trusted platform module
TRT	technical recovery team
UPS	uninterruptible power supply
URL	Universal Resource Locator
USB	Universal Serial Bus
US-CERT	United States Computer Emergency Readiness Team
VoIP	Voice over Internet Protocol
VP	vice president
VPN	virtual private network
WAN	wide area network
WEP	wired equivalent privacy
Wi-Fi	wireless fidelity
WIPO	World Intellectual Property Organization
WLAN	wireless local area network
WPA	Wi-Fi Protected Access
WPA2	Wi-Fi Protected Access 2
XSS	cross-site scripting

Glossary

A

acceptable use policy (AUP) | Policy that defines acceptable use for IT systems and data.

accepting (a risk) | A way to manage a risk by evaluating it, understanding the potential loss, and choosing to accept it, which is commonly done when the cost of the control outweighs the potential loss.

account management policy | Written policy that spells out exactly what should be done with accounts that access IT systems.

Advanced Encryption Standard (AES) | The primary symmetric encryption protocol used today. NIST selected and ratified AES in 2000 as a standard.

affinity diagram | A diagram that groups the ideas of a problem to solve, usually threats, vulnerabilities, and recommendations. These groups may then be divided into subcategories.

annual loss expectancy (ALE) | The expected loss to one or more assets for a year. It is calculated by multiplying the single loss expectancy (SLE) by the annual rate of occurrence (ARO).

annual rate of occurrence (ARO) | Number of times an incident is expected to occur in a year.

anonymizer | A site that attempts to hide a user's activity. When a user visits the anonymizer site and then visits other sites through it, the anonymizer retrieves the webpages but serves them as if they had originated from it.

asset | A thing of value worth protecting.

asset management | Management of all types of assets, including much more detailed data than an inventory management system includes; for example, installed components, hardware peripherals, installed software, update versions, and more.

asset valuation | The process of determining the fair market value of an asset. The asset value can be determined from the asset replacement value or either what the asset provides to the organization, the cost to recover the asset, or a combination of those two values.

attack surface | How many services can be attacked on a server.

attorney general (AG) | Primary legal advisor for a state, and, for many states, the AG is also the chief law enforcement officer.

audit | The checking of systems and processes to verify that a company complies with existing rules and laws.

audit trail | A sequential record of access to and traffic in and out of a network, using many types of audit logs. A security log can record all access to specific files, and a firewall log can record all traffic entering or leaving a network.

availability | Ensuring data and services are available when needed.

avoiding (a risk) | A way to manage a risk by eliminating the source of the risk or eliminating the exposure of assets to the risk.

B

big data | Any set of data that is so large and complex that it is difficult to process with existing database tools. Instead, specialists build new applications to capture and store these large data sets.

blacklist | A list that a filter (such as an email spam filter) reads to determine the items that are excluded from a system; all items not on the list are allowed by default.

brainstorming | A method of generating ideas in which participants are encouraged to mention anything that comes to mind. All ideas are written down without judgment.

buffer overflow | A common type of exploit in which an attacker sends more data or different data than a system or application expects.

business continuity plan (BCP) | A document used to help a company plan for a disaster or an emergency. The goal is to ensure that the critical operations of an organization continue to function.

business function | An activity a business performs to sell products or services.

business impact analysis (BIA) | Analysis that identifies the impact of a sudden loss of business functions, often quantified in direct and/or indirect costs.

C

Capability Maturity Model Integration (CMMI) | A process improvement approach to management that uses different levels to determine the maturity of a process.

cause and effect diagram | A diagram illustrating the links between the risk management findings of a problem: causes, criteria, and effects.

certificate | Electronic document used for identification and to aid in encryption. It includes details on the entity that received the certificate. The entity is able to present the certificate as proof of its identity.

certificate authority (CA) | A trusted third party that issues and manages certificates. It can be public or private. If a system trusts a CA, it automatically trusts any certificates issued by the CA.

change management | The practice of preventing unapproved changes to systems by having all changes formally requested using a change management process. Technical experts review the requests and then either approve or disapprove them.

Children's Internet Protection Act (CIPA) | An act passed in 2000 that is designed to limit access to offensive content from school and library computers.

Children's Online Privacy Protection Act (COPPA) | An act passed in 1998 that is designed to protect the privacy of children under 13.

computer incident response team (CIRT) plan | A formal document that outlines an organization's response to computer incidents.

cloud computing | A general term for anything that involves hosting services over a public network, such as the internet.

cold site | An available building serving as an alternate site that has electricity, running water, and restrooms but none of the equipment, data, or applications needed for critical operations.

Common Vulnerabilities and Exposures (CVE) | The MITRE Corporation catalog of more than 40,000 common vulnerabilities in IT systems.

compliance | Adherence to government regulations.

computer incident | A violation or imminent threat of a violation of a security policy or security practice. It includes any adverse event or activity that affects the security of computer systems or networks.

computer incident response team (CIRT) | A group of people who respond to incidents.

confidentiality | Preventing unauthorized disclosure of information that should be available only to authorized users.

configuration management | The process of maintaining systems, such as computer hardware and software, in a desired state. Management is optimized with standard configuration for all systems (baselines).

continuous monitoring | The process of ongoing mitigation of risks to systems.

control | Any action or change put into place to reduce a weakness or potential loss.

Control Objectives for Information and Related Technologies (COBIT) | A set of practices that apply to IT management and governance.

corrective control | An attempt to reverse the effects of a problem. File recovery and data correction are examples of corrective controls. For example, reliable backups allow data to be restored if they become corrupt.

cost-benefit analysis (CBA) | The comparison of a business impact with the cost to implement a control.

countermeasure | Any action or change put into place to reduce a weakness or potential loss.

critical business function (CBF) | Any function considered vital to an organization. If the CBF fails, the organization will lose the ability to perform essential operations, such as sales to customers.

critical path chart | A chart that shows a list of project tasks that must be completed on time.

critical success factor (CSF) | Any element necessary to perform the mission of an organization, such as a reliable network infrastructure. If the network infrastructure fails, communication can stop.

D

damage assessment team (DAT) | A team that assesses damage and declares the severity of the incident. The members primarily collect and report data but don't take action.

dark web | A part of the World Wide Web accessible only by using special software. Professional hackers use the dark web to share vulnerabilities and ways to exploit applications.

data leakage | The sharing of user or proprietary data, such as passwords or credit card information, by P2P software without the user's knowledge. If a user doesn't protect the data, the P2P software might share the files with anyone else using the same P2P software.

data mining | The process of discovering patterns, trends, correlations, or useful information from large sets of data using statistical, mathematical, machine learning, and computational techniques.

data warehousing | The process of gathering data from different databases. The data is retrieved from the source databases and placed in a central database. New relationships between the source databases are created in the central database, which is the data warehouse.

deep web | The part of the World Wide Web that is not indexed by standard search engines. It includes email, online banking, and private databases accessible with logins.

defense in depth | A security practice that adds multiple layers of overlapping protection. Even if a gap occurs in one layer of a system, chances are greater that it will still be protected from another layer.

demilitarized zone (DMZ) | The area within two firewalls that public-facing servers are often placed in a network. Also known as a buffer area or a perimeter zone.

denial of service (DoS) attack | A purposeful launching of excessive inbound traffic into an organization that is unrelated to business objectives, such as a flood of network packets or emails.

Department of Defense Information Assurance Certification and Accreditation Process (DIACAP) | A risk management process that applies to IT systems used by the U.S. Department of Defense (DoD).

Department of Homeland Security | The agency responsible for protecting the United States from threats and emergencies, including terrorist attacks, and for responding to natural disasters, such as hurricanes and earthquakes.

detective control | A risk control that tries to detect activity that may result in a loss. Examples include antivirus software and intrusion detection systems.

digital signature | Cryptographic method that provides authentication, nonrepudiation, and integrity. The receiver of a message with a digital signature has verification that it was sent by the signer and not someone trying to impersonate the signer.

disaster recovery plan (DRP) | A plan that includes the details needed to recover a system from a disaster and provides the details necessary to respond immediately to a disaster. A DRP is included as part of a BCP.

distributed denial of service (DDoS) attack | A denial of service (DoS) attack that comes from multiple sources.

due care | Reasonable steps taken by a fiduciary to protect against risks.

due diligence | A reasonable amount of time and effort for a fiduciary to identify risks.

E

E-Rate funding | A program that provides discounts to schools and libraries for internet access.

emergency management team (EMT) | A team composed of senior managers that have overall authority for the recovery of a system but also work closely with the BCP coordinator.

exploit | The method used to take advantage of a vulnerability.

exploit assessment | A process used to discover what vulnerabilities an attacker can exploit. These assessments are also referred to as penetration tests.

exploit testing | Another term for penetration testing.

Exploit Wednesday | The day after Patch Tuesday, in which attackers reverse-engineer the patches to discover their vulnerabilities.

exposure factor (EF) | The loss that will happen to an asset as a result of a threat, expressed as a percentage value.

F

failover cluster | A group of interconnected servers that provides fault tolerance for a server and ensures that a service provided by a server will continue to run even if a server fails. It includes at least two servers, called nodes.

Family Educational Rights and Privacy Act (FERPA) | An act passed in 1974 whose goal is to protect the privacy of student records, including education and health data.

Federal Deposit Insurance Corporation (FDIC) | A federal agency whose primary goal is to promote confidence in U.S. banks. Funds in all banks insured by the FDIC are guaranteed.

Federal Information Security Modernization Act (FISMA) | An act whose purpose is to ensure that federal agencies protect their data by assigning specific responsibilities to them.

Federal Trade Commission (FTC) | A federal agency created in 1914 to promote consumer protection, but that goal has changed over the years.

Federally Funded Research and Development Centers (FFRDCs) | The FFRDCs conduct research for several major departments of the U.S. government.

fiduciary responsibility | A relationship between an entity that has an interest to protect (such as an asset holder or a defendant on trial) and an entity that is trusted to protect that interest (such as a holder of power of attorney or defense attorney). The trusted entity is the fiduciary.

firewall | A hardware and software system that filters network traffic.

firewall appliance | A device that provides a self-contained firewall solution, including both hardware and software that provide protection for a network.

firewall policy | A policy that identifies what traffic to allow past a firewall. It is a written document and is based on the content of the firewall logs.

G

Gantt chart | A chart that shows a project schedule that is commonly used in project management. It generally shows more detail than a milestone plan chart.

gap analysis | A report that documents the differences between exploits that are mitigated and those that are not mitigated; that is, the gap in security.

General Data Protection Regulation (GDPR) | The primary European Union (EU) law regulating how companies protect the personal data of EU citizens. It was designed as a legal framework that sets guidelines to collect and process the personal information of individuals who live in the EU and the European Economic Area (EEA).

goodwill | The generally acceptable accounting principles (GAAP) definition of client confidence.

Gramm-Leach-Bliley Act (GLBA) | An act passed in 1999 that relates to how banking and insurance institutions can merge. In particular, it includes a Financial Privacy Rule and a Safeguards Rule.

Group Policy | An automated management tool used in Windows operating systems. A policy can be set once and apply to all users and computers in the domain.

guideline | Optional recommendation that provides guidance on specific behavior. For example, guidelines are written on how to create a strong password.

H

hardening a server | The mitigation steps needed to protect a vulnerable server.

Health Insurance Portability and Accountability Act (HIPAA) | An law passed in 1996 that ensures that health information data is protected.

host-based intrusion detection system (HIDS) | A security control installed on individual systems that is used in addition to antivirus software.

hot site | An alternate site that includes all the equipment and data necessary to take over business functions.

I

impact of loss | A loss resulting in a compromise to business functions or assets.

implicit deny | A practice in which a firewall blocks all traffic by default and rules are added to identify allowed traffic. The firewall allows traffic that matches an explicit rule and blocks all other traffic.

in-place control | A control that is currently installed in the operational system.

Industrial Control Systems Cyber Emergency Response Team (ICS-CERT) | A group within NCCIC that works to reduce risks to critical infrastructure sectors, including roads, water, communications, energy, and more.

information technology governance (ITG) | The processes that ensure IT resources are enabling an organization to achieve its goals.

Information Technology Infrastructure Library (ITIL) | A group of five books developed by the United Kingdom's Office of Government Commerce (OGC). Among the goals is to document the differences between companies succeeding and companies failing that were using similar information technologies.

intangible value | Value that cannot be measured by cost, such as client confidence or company reputation.

integrity | Ensuring data or an IT system is not modified or destroyed unless authorized.

intellectual property (IP) | Any intangible property that is the result of creativity and is produced by a person or company.

intentional threat | Act that is hostile to an organization.

International Electrotechnical Commission (IEC) | An international standards organization that prepares and publishes standards for electrical, electronic, and related technologies.

International Organization for Standardization (ISO) | An organization that develops and publishes standards.

intrusion detection system (IDS) | A system designed to detect threats, not prevent threats. A passive IDS will log the event and may provide an alert. An active IDS may modify the environment to block the attack after it has been detected.

intrusion prevention system (IPS) | A system placed in-line with network traffic that detects and blocks malicious traffic to prevent attacks from reaching the internal network.

inventory management | Management of hardware inventories, which includes only the basic data, such as model and serial numbers. It shows what assets are on hand, where they're located, and who owns them.

J

job rotation | The transfer of an employee to a new job so that their past transactions are reviewed and examined for suspicious activity.

M

malware | Malicious code, including viruses, worms, Trojan horses, and other types of software, intended to infect a system.

mandatory vacation | Required vacation taken by an employee to reduce fraud or embezzlement by discovering the illegal activity in the employee's absence.

maximum acceptable outage (MAO) | The maximum amount of time a system or service can be down before the mission is affected.

maximum tolerable period of disruption (MTPD) | Alternate name for maximum acceptable outage.

milestone | A scheduled event. It indicates the completion of a major task or group of tasks.

milestone plan chart | A simple graphic representation of major milestones, showing them laid out in a graphic format.

minimum business continuity objective (MBCO) | The minimum level of services that is acceptable to an organization to meet its business needs and objectives during a disaster.

mission-critical | Describes systems, functions, or processes that are critical to the mission of an organization to keep the organization functioning.

mitigating (a risk) | A way to manage a risk by reducing its vulnerabilities through implementing controls.

mobile site | An alternate site that can be set up in an outside space close to an impacted site. One of the advantages of a mobile site is that it can be put in place quickly, somewhere between 36 and 72 hours, but the recovery time is usually longer than that for a hot site.

N

National Cybersecurity and Communications Integration Center (NCCIC) | The central point of contact for cybersecurity within DHS.

National Institute of Standards and Technology | A division of the U.S. Department of Commerce whose mission is to promote U.S. innovation and industrial competitiveness.

National Institute of Standards and Technology Risk Management Framework (RMF) | An informative guide to use when implementing a risk management plan. The RMF is a process that combines security and risk management as part of a systems development life cycle.

network load balancing | A practice in which clients interacting with a web farm will not encounter a failed server. At any given time, each of the servers has about the same load.

nonrepudiation | Type of technique that prevents someone from denying they took an action.

O

operational impact | The effect of a control on a system's normal operations. It can be identified as negligible, low, medium, high, or overwhelming.

P

password policy | Written and technically enforced policy on password length, complexity, minimum and maximum age, number of previously used passwords, and/or other password conditions.

patch management | The continuous understanding, testing, and rolling out of patches to systems and clients. It should include compliance audits to verify that clients are current and can also include the ability to quarantine unpatched clients.

Patch Tuesday | The second Tuesday of every month in which Microsoft releases patches.

Payment Card Industry Data Security Standard (PCI DSS) | An international security standard whose purpose is to enhance security of credit card data.

penetration testing | A process of verifying the effectiveness of controls applied to a discovered vulnerability. If the penetration test is successful, then the controls aren't adequate. Also known as exploit testing.

physical controls | Measures that prevent unauthorized personnel from having physical access to areas or systems.

plan of action and milestones (POAM) | A document used to track progress, used in many types of project management. A POAM is used to assign responsibility and to allow management to follow up on a project.

planned control | A control that is not yet implemented but has already been selected and scheduled for implementation.

policy | A formal statement that is issued directly by an organization's leaders, such as an acceptable use policy, which describes both acceptable and unacceptable behavior when using company-owned computers and network resources.

preventive control | A risk control that attempts to prevent the risk from occurring. Examples include increasing physical security and training personnel.

principle of least privilege | The concept of granting users only the rights and permissions they need to perform their job and no more.

principle of need to know | The concept of granting users access only to the data they need to perform their job and no more.

principle of proportionality | The concept that the amount spent on controls should be proportional to the risk.

probability | The likelihood that a threat will exploit a vulnerability. A scale can be used to define the probability that a risk will occur. The scale can be based on word values, such as low, medium, or high.

procedural control | A policy, procedure, or guideline intended to inform personnel on how to perform actions.

profitability | The ability of a company to make a profit. It is calculated as revenues minus costs.

proxy server | A server that receives requests from clients for webpages, retrieves the webpages, and then serves the webpages to the clients. It can also filter the requests to block content requests.

Q

qualitative risk assessment | A risk assessment method that doesn't assign dollar values, but determines the level of risk based on a more subjective assignment of the probability and impact of a risk. These values are determined by gathering the opinions of experts.

quantitative risk assessment | A risk assessment method that uses numbers, such as dollar values. Data is gathered and then entered into standard formulas.

R

reasonableness | A test that can be applied to risk management to determine whether the risk should be managed.

recovery point objective (RPO) | Identifies the maximum amount of data loss an organization can accept, which is the acceptable data latency. In other words, it identifies mission-critical data.

recovery time objective (RTO) | Time in which a system or function must be recovered.

redundant array of independent disks (RAID) | A technology that combines multiple physical hard drives or solid-state drives into a single logical unit to enhance data redundancy, improve performance, or both. By using techniques like stripping, mirroring, or parity, it ensures data remains available even if a drive fails.

residual risk | The risk that remains after controls have been applied.

return on investment (ROI) | Indicates the value of a control over its lifetime and determines the monetary benefits of investing in the control.

risk | The likelihood or probability that something negative is going to occur.

risk assessment | The first step in risk management, which identifies the assets, threats, vulnerabilities, likelihood of exploitation of vulnerabilities, and risk impacts.

risk management | The practice of identifying, assessing, controlling, and mitigating risks.

risk statement | Summarization of a risk management plan report. It is used to communicate a risk and the resulting impact.

rules of behavior | Rules that let users know what they can and cannot do with systems.

S

safeguard | Any action or change put into place to reduce a weakness or potential loss.

safeguard value | The cost of a control.

Sarbanes-Oxley Act (SOX) | A law passed in 2002 that applies to all publicly traded companies, designed to hold company executives and board members personally responsible for financial data.

scale out | To add new servers to a service.

scale up | To add new resources, such as an upgraded processor or more RAM to a server.

scope | Identification of the boundaries of a risk management plan.

scope creep | Addition of uncontrolled changes that expand the scope of a risk management plan.

script kiddie | An attacker with little or limited knowledge of computers.

Securities and Exchange Commission (SEC) | A federal agency charged with regulating the securities industry, which includes all sales or trades of securities.

security policy | High-level overview of the goals of security but not the details of how to implement the security techniques. Managers use a security policy to identify resources and create plans to implement it.

separation of duties | Principle that ensures that no single person controls all the functions of a critical process. The principle is designed to prevent fraud, theft, and errors.

service level agreement (SLA) | A document that identifies an expected level of performance, which includes the minimum uptime or the maximum downtime.

service pack (SP) | A group of updates, patches, and fixes that apply to a specific OS.

sharing (a risk) | A way to manage a risk by shifting a portion of the responsibility or liability to another party.

single loss expectancy (SLE) | The total loss expected from a single incident to a single asset, calculated as the value of the affected asset multiplied by the exposure factor (EF).

single point of failure (SPOF) | Any single part of a system that, if it fails, causes the entire system to stop functioning. For example, any piece of hardware in a web server whose failure can take down the website the server is hosting is a single point of failure.

sniffer | A packet analyzer that can capture traffic.

social engineering | The art of manipulating people into performing actions or divulging confidential information, often by exploiting psychological vulnerabilities rather than technical weaknesses.

spear phishing | A targeted phishing attempt that looks as if it's coming from someone in the company.

SQL injection attack | A SQL command that is added to a poorly-validated user field, which can compromise the database.

stakeholder | An individual or a group that has a stake, or interest, in the success of a project.

standard | A mandatory rule written to support or at least provide some direction to policies. For example, a password standard could follow an acceptable use policy.

survivability | The ability of a company to survive a loss due to a risk.

SYN flood attack | A TCP communication between a host and a server in which the host does not respond with the ACK flag, prompting the server to continually send SYN packets until it consumes the server's resources and can cause it to crash.

T

tangible value | The actual cost of an asset, which can be expressed in monetary terms.

technical control | Measure that uses technology to reduce vulnerabilities.

technical recovery team (TRT) | A team that is responsible for recovering critical IT resources after a disruption.

technology protection measure (TPM) | A digital tool to control access to digital content, often to protect copyrighted content. In the context of compliance with CIPA, libraries use TPMs as filters of offensive content.

threat | Any actor or activity that represents a possible danger.

threat assessment | The identification and evaluation of potential threats.

threat modeling | A process used to identify possible threats on a system by looking at a system from the attacker's perspective.

threat/vulnerability pair | Situation in which a loss occurs when a threat exploits a vulnerability.

transaction | A group of statements in a database that either succeed or fail as a whole. If any single statement fails, the entire transaction fails.

transferring (a risk) | A way to manage a risk by transferring the entire responsibility or liability to another party.

U

uncertainty level | A numerical indicator of how valid or accurate risk assessment data are. If a set of data is estimated to be 80% accurate, the uncertainty level is 20%.

unintentional threat | A threat that doesn't have a perpetrator, such as a natural event or disaster.

uninterruptible power supply (UPS) | Hardware, as small as a portable unit or as large as a room full of banks of batteries, that provides power to a system when normal power fails, for a short amount of time. For some less-critical systems, a UPS allows a system to shut down logically. For critical systems, a UPS provides time for generators to power on and stabilize.

U.S. Computer Emergency Readiness Team (US-CERT) | A part of the NCCIC, its primary mission is to provide response support and defense against cyberattacks. Its focus is on providing support for the federal civil executive branch of government, but also collaborates and shares information with several other entities.

U.S. Attorney General (U.S. AG) | The head of the United States Department of Justice (DOJ). Many actions that the U.S. AG takes fall into the arena of IT; for example, establishing an intellectual property task force.

V

version control | System in which changes made to data and applications that are shared among several people are properly tracked.

virtualization | A technology that creates simulated, virtual instances of computing resources (servers, storage, networks) on a single physical machine. By abstracting software from hardware, it allows multiple operating systems and applications to run independently on one server.

vulnerability | A weakness.

vulnerability assessment | A process used to discover weaknesses in a system.

W

warm site | A compromise alternate site between a cold and a hot site. It includes most or all of the equipment needed, but data is not usually kept up to date.

web farm | A set of web servers that enables an organization to scale out with the addition of new servers, while compensating for the failure of a server with network load balancing.

web of trust | An alternative to the PKI, which relies on a CA. A web of trust is based on a decentralized trust model, as opposed to a CA's centralized trust model.

whitelist | A list that a filter (such as an email spam filter) reads to determine the items that are allowed on a system; all items not on the list are denied by default.

Index

Note: Page numbers followed by *f* and *t* indicate figures and tables, respectively.

A

acceptable use policy (AUP), 72, 231
acceptance of risk, 24
access control (AC) family, 228
access control lists (ACLs), 242
access controls, 180, 236, 276
access controls testing, 213, 214*f*
access logs, 161, 246–248
accidents, 32, 155
account management controls, 276
account management policy, 285, 291
account usage, 285
accountabilities, 394
active detective controls, 228
active node, 306
activists, 34
ad hoc, 82
administrative controls, 159
administrative scripts, 287
administrators, 294
Advanced Encryption Standard (AES), 244
advanced persistent threats (APTs), 33–34, 200
affinity diagram, 97, 98*f*
AG. *See* Attorney General; State Attorney General
alerts, false, 283
alternate assessment procedures, 350–351
alternate locations, 153
alternate locations/sites, 370–375, 384
annual loss expectancy (ALE), 124, 125, 163, 164
annual or recurring costs, 300–301
annual rate of occurrence (ARO), 124, 163, 164
annual updates, BCP, 357
anomaly-based intrusion detection systems, 406, 407
anonymizer site, 405
antivirus protection, 265
antivirus software, 35, 49, 265
application developers, 94
application testing, 215
approved countermeasures, 283
architecture, BCP, 341–345
ARO. *See* annual rate of occurrence
assessment, 63, 145, 208
assessment, authorization, and monitoring (CA) family, 229
asset management, 185, 186
asset replacement insurance, 194–195
asset valuation, 150
assumptions and planning principles, BCP, 339–341
asymmetric encryption, 244
attack surface, 44, 49, 403
attackers, 25, 33, 46, 135
attacks, 154, 200, 202
Attorney General (AG), 70
audit and accountability (AU) family, 228
audit logs, 228, 239, 284–285
audit trails, 161, 208–209, 240–241
audits, 16, 207, 211
AUP. *See* acceptable use policy
AUP procedure, 232
automated asset management, 178, 186
automated methods, 175–176
automation, 35
availability, 7, 7*f*, 15, 135–136, 172–174, 255
avoidance of risk, 24
awareness, 159
awareness and training (AT) family, 228
awareness and training controls, 237

B

back-end database, 314*f*
background checks, 236
backup plan, 25, 233–234, 368–370, 381
backups, 180, 375
balancing risk and cost, 18–19
BCP. *See* business continuity plan
behavior-based IDS, 406

benefits, 104, 126–127, 131–133, 300
BIA. *See* business impact analysis
BIA Professional, 331
BIA report, 328
Big Data, 185
billing and financial data, 182
black-hat hackers, 34
blacklist, 152
blogs, 47
bonding insurance, 235
botnets, 17, 400, 400*f*, 406
bottom-up approach, 318
boundary protection, 35
brainstorming, 16, 97
budget for risk mitigation, 301–302
buffer overflow, 43, 44, 206, 241
building replacement costs, 321
business assets, 5, 8–9, 30
business changes, 137–138
business continuity (BC), 336–337
business continuity plan (BCP), 192–193, 194, 232–233, 313, 335–359, 361, 363, 364
business functions, 5–6, 317–318, 326, 329–330
business impact analysis (BIA), 191–192, 256, 311–332, 335, 336, 364
business intelligence (BI), 185
business liability insurance planning, 194
business operations, 190–195, 256–257, 269–273, 377
business risks, 10–15, 11*f*, 13*f*
business system priorities, 330*t*

C

cameras, 247
Capability Maturity Model Integration (CMMI), 82–83
cause and effect diagram, 102–103, 103*f*
CBA. *See* cost-benefit analysis
CBFs. *See* critical business functions
central incident response team, 394
CERT Coordination Center (CERT/CC), 390
certificate authority (CA), 244
certificates, 244
certification and accreditation records, 16
Certified Information Systems Security Professional (CISSP), 124
chain of custody, 396
change management, 147–148, 221, 384
Children's Internet Protection Act (CIPA), 65, 267, 268, 271–272, 276, 291
Children's Online Privacy Protection Act (COPPA), 66–67
Chinese cyber espionage, 406
CIPA. *See* Children's Internet Protection Act
circuit breakers, 162, 250
CIRT plan, 389–415
CISSP. *See* Certified Information Systems Security Professional
Class A fires, 248
Class C fires, 248
classification of data, 344
client and stakeholder confidence, 23
closed-circuit television (CCTV), 246–248
cloud computing, 371, 372*f*, 373
CM. *See* configuration management
CMMI. *See* Capability Maturity Model Integration
COBIT. *See* Control Objectives for Information and related Technology
cold site, 153, 371, 371*t*
Common Vulnerabilities and Exposures (CVE), 18, 47, 54–56
communication escalation procedures, 407
communications, 378–379
compliance, 60, 72, 266–273
Computer Emergency Response Team (CERT), 390
computer forensics, 397
computer incident, 390
computer incident response teams (CIRTs), 389–415
computer security incident, 390, 414
computer systems, 8
concurrent processing, 353
confidentiality, 7, 7*f*, 15, 202, 236, 255
configuration and change management section, 147–148
configuration data, 188
configuration management (CM), 40, 49, 147, 221, 228–229
connectivity to service customers, 378
content refreshment, BCP, 357
contingency planning, 313–314
contingency planning (CP) family, 229
Contingency Planning Guide, 193
Continual Service Improvement, 81
continuous monitoring, 41, 63
contractors, 347
control, 158
control categories, 159–162, 227
control costs, 307
Control Objectives for Information and related Technology (COBIT), 76–77
control value, 163

controls, 21, 25, 41, 130–131
coordinating team, 394
coordinator, BCP, 346, 350, 354, 357
COPPA. *See* Children's Online Privacy Protection Act
copyright, 183
corrective controls, 228
corruption of file, 236
cost estimates, 105
cost-benefit analysis (CBA), 21–22, 92, 93, 104–105, 167, 277–278, 299–301
costs, 165–166, 256, 287–291, 316, 317*f*
countermeasures, 21, 158, 282–307, 287*t*
crackers, 34
crash carts, 345
credentials protection, 238
credit card transaction, 72
credit loss, 322
criminals, 33
crisis management plan (CMP), 194
critical business functions (CBFs), 258, 258*f*–260*f*, 312, 317–318, 326, 329–330, 329*f*, 336, 364, 384
critical path chart, 110–111, 110*f*, 302, 304*f*
critical resources identification, 318–320, 326
critical roles to critical resources, 328
critical success factors (CSFs), 258, 312, 329, 329*f*, 366–375
critical system components, 345
criticality of operations, 344
criticality rating, 409*t*
cross-training, 179
current activity updates, 53–54
customer access, 374–375
customer checks out, 318
customer data, 182–183
customer influence, 9
customer information, 319
customer service, 257–258, 382–383
customers loss, 322
CVE. *See* Common Vulnerabilities and Exposures
cyber liability insurance, 194
cyberattacks, 390, 406
cyberbreach, 393
cybersecurity, 53
cyberspace, 52
cyberthreat intelligence, 122

D

Damage Assessment Team (DAT), 346, 347
dark web, 48
data, 8
data and information assets, 152–153, 180–185
data classification, 180, 181*f*, 344
data collection, 137, 313–314, 331
data consistency, 136–138
data format, 136–137
data leakage, 405
data loss, 202
data loss prevention program, 236
data mining, 184
data range and reasonableness checks, 241
data recovery costs, 321
data warehousing, 184
database recovery, 324
database servers, 121*f*, 122, 149–150, 189, 255, 258–261, 317–318, 327*t*, 341*f*–343*f*
defaced Web sites, 202
defaults, 49
defense in depth, 265
delegation of authority, 348
Delphi Method, 132
demilitarized zone (DMZ), 43, 105, 209, 263
denial of service (DoS) attacks, 5, 16, 45, 99, 128, 219, 391, 400–401, 411–412
Department of Defense (DoD) Information Assurance Certification and Accreditation Process (DIACAP), 84–85
Department of Homeland Security (DHS), 50, 69
desire to damage, 33
detective controls, 21, 228
developers, 11
DHS. *See* Department of Homeland Security
digital signature, 245, 245*f*
direct costs, 97, 166, 256, 321
direct revenue, 174
disaster preparedness plans, 321
disaster recovery (DR), 12, 337–338
disaster recovery plan (DRP), 193, 194, 232–233, 361–387
disaster/emergency declaration, 378
disasters, 336, 385
disgruntled employees, 34, 199, 200
disk, 166
disk subsystem, 166
distributed denial of service (DDoS) attacks, 5, 45
distributed incident response team, 394
distros, 177
divide-by-zero error, 44
DMZ. *See* demilitarized zone
documentation, 40
domain controller (DC), 326
domain name system (DNS) cache poisoning, 135

domains of IT infrastructure, 13–15, 17–18, 185–190, 205–206, 205*f*, 215–216, 261–265, 261*f*, 274–275
doors, locked, 161
DoS attacks. *See* denial of service attacks
downtime, 174, 337
DRP. *See* disaster recovery plan
due care, 72
due diligence, 72

E

edge testing, 213
education, 237
effect, 101
effect rating, 409*t*
eight Rs of recovery planning, 376
eight tiers of disaster recovery, 365
electrical grounding, 162, 250
electronic vaulting, 369
elements of BCP, 337–358
e-mail servers, 146, 146*f*, 147, 149, 151, 151*f*, 189, 327*t*, 328*t*
e-mail usage, 238
emergency funds, 375
Emergency Management Team (EMT), 346–347, 350
employee data, 181
employee training, 25
encryption, 161, 243–244, 274
end users, 11–12
Enron, 64, 266
environment identification, 325
environmental threats, 31, 32
equipment, 155, 202, 288–291, 289*f*, 321. *See also* hardware
E-Rate funding, 271
E-Rate program, 65
escalation, 407
ethical hackers, 34
exercises, BCP, 355–356
exploit assessment, 158, 216–222
exploit testing, 215
Exploit Wednesday, 48
exploits, 8, 42–49, 216–222
exposure factor (EF), 124, 162
external attackers, 199
external threats, 15
external vulnerability assessments, 207
extract process, 185
extract, transform, and load (ETL) process, 185
extraction process, 185
EY Global Information Security Survey, 36

F

facilities, 153–154, 190–195, 288–291, 301
failover clusters, 25, 172, 173*f*, 174, 290, 290*f*, 293, 294, 306, 307
fail-over testing, 383–384
failures, 32
false alerts, 283
Family Educational Rights and Privacy Act (FERPA), 64–65, 267, 268, 271, 276
fault tolerance, 25, 344, 363
FCC. *See* Federal Communications Commission
FDIC. *See* Federal Deposit Insurance Corporation
Federal Communications Commission (FCC), 65
Federal Deposit Insurance Corporation (FDIC), 68
Federal Information Security Management Act (FISMA), 61, 62, 229, 267, 268, 270, 276
Federal Trade Commission (FTC), 69
Federally Funded Research and Development Centers (FFRDCs), 54
FERPA. *See* Family Educational Rights and Privacy Act
FFRDCs. *See* Federally Funded Research and Development Centers
fiduciary responsibility, 71
financial checks, 235–236
financial data, 182
Financial Privacy Rule, 64
fire detection and suppression, 161, 248
fire insurance, 277
firewall appliance, 99
firewall policy, 99
firewalls, 49, 91, 98, 99, 161, 188, 208, 210, 212*f*, 241–242, 242*f*, 263, 403
firewalls control network traffic, 212*f*
fishbone diagram, 102
FISMA. *See* Federal Information Security Management Act
formjacking, 33
forums, 47
FTC. *See* Federal Trade Commission
functional controls, 228
functional description of systems, 343–344, 344*f*
functional exercises, 355–356
functionality testing, 213
funds, emergency, 375
fuses, 250
future costs, 23

G

GAISP. *See* Generally Accepted Information Security Principles

Gantt chart, 109–110, 110*f*, 302, 304*f*
gap analysis, 220, 222, 265
gas systems, 248
GDPR. *See* General Data Protection Regulation
General Data Protection Regulation (GDPR), 83–84, 119, 176, 266, 267, 269, 272–273, 276
general liability insurance, 194
Generally Accepted Information Security Principles (GAISP), 75
geographical indications, 183
GLBA. *See* Gramm-Leach-Bliley Act
goodwill, 9
Gramm-Leach-Bliley Act (GLBA), 64, 207
greed, 32
Group Policy settings, 285
Group Policy tool, 149
guards, 161, 247
guidelines, 12
guidelines for compliance, 72–73

H

hackers, 34, 199
hardening a server, 48, 49, 189
hardware, 124, 128, 152, 188, 190, 377
hardware assets, 176–177
headquarters server, 344
Health Insurance Portability and Accountability Act (HIPAA), 61–63, 91–93, 95–100, 119, 182, 207, 265, 266, 267, 269–270, 312
heating, ventilation, and air conditioning (HVAC) systems, 162, 249
hidden costs, 288
HIDS. *See* host-based intrusion detection systems
high impact, 10, 19
HIPAA. *See* Health Insurance Portability and Accountability Act
hire additional personnel, 179
historical data review, 154–155, 201–203
historical documentation review, 278
HITECH, 119
host-based intrusion detection systems (HIDS), 41, 167
hot site, 153, 371–373, 371*t*
hubs, 188
human threats, 15, 32, 199
humidity detection, 162, 249
Hurricane checklist, 349*t*

I

identification and authentication (IA) family, 229
identify theft, 401
IDS. *See* intrusion detection system
IEC. *See* International Electrotechnical Commission
IIS. *See* Internet Information Services
image servers, 377
impact, 9–10, 18–20, 19*t*, 96, 127, 138, 164
impact level, MAO, 320, 320*t*
implicit deny philosophy, 295
inactive node, 306
inappropriate usage, 392, 404–406
incident response (IR), 17, 41, 229, 234
incident response plan (IRP), 193
incidents, 208, 339–340, 393, 400–401, 406–407
indirect costs, 92, 165–166, 256, 322
indirect revenue, 174
industrial designs, 183
industrial property, 183
information assets, 152–153, 180–185
information security vulnerability names, 54–55
information systems security gap, 265
Information Technology Infrastructure Library (ITIL), 50, 79–82, 137
information technology (IT) laws, 60–67
Information Technology Laboratory (ITL), 50–51, 75
initial costs, 300
initial purchase cost, 288, 301
in-place controls, 158–159, 226
in-place countermeasures, 282
input validation, 35, 161, 241
installation costs, 291, 302
insurance, 23, 34, 63, 159, 235, 248
intangible value, 9
integrity, 7, 7*f*, 15, 246, 255
intellectual property data, 183–184
intellectual property (IP), 71
intentional threats, 16, 32–34
internal firewall, 122
internal system clocks, 240
internal threats, 15, 200
internal users, 199, 202
internal vulnerability assessments, 207
International Electrotechnical Commission (IEC), 79
International Organization for Standardization (ISO), 77–79
Internet, 18
Internet access, 259
Internet Assigned Numbers Authority (IANA), 243
Internet Information Services (IIS), 46
Internet service providers (ISPs), 345
intrusion detection and prevention system (IDPS), 209–210

intrusion detection system (IDS), 41, 49, 209, 209*f*, 228, 283, 395
intrusion prevention system (IPS), 49, 209
inventory management, 185, 186
IP. *See* intellectual property
IPS. *See* intrusion prevention system
IR. *See* incident response
Ishikawa diagram, 102
ISO. *See* International Organization for Standardization
IT infrastructure changes, 357
IT infrastructure domains, 185–190, 205–206, 205*f*, 215–216, 261–265, 261*f*, 274–275
IT systems, 192, 330
ITIL. *See* Information Technology Infrastructure Library
ITL. *See* Information Technology Laboratory

J

job rotation, 72, 179
just-in-time philosophy, 341

K

Kaminsk, Dan, 135
key personnel, 347
knowledge of disaster recovery, 367, 367*f*
knowledge of process, 175

L

LAN. *See* local area network
LAN Domain, 14, 18, 187–188, 217, 262–263, 274
LAN-to-WAN Domain, 14, 18, 188, 218, 263, 274
laptop control, 200
late delivery penalty costs, 321
laws and regulations, 60–67, 267–269
leaders, 11
leadership from management, 366
legal and compliance requirements, 275–276
liability insurance, 194
likelihood, 18–20, 19*t*
load process, 185
local area data, 203
local area network (LAN), 187, 262–263
locked doors, 161, 246–248
log reviews, 240
logon identifier, 160–161, 239
loss, 5, 15, 153
lost opportunity costs, 23
lost revenue, 9
low impact, 10, 19

M

MAC flood attack, 218–219
maintenance (MA) family, 229
malicious code, 391
malicious hackers, 34
malicious mobile code, 401
malware, 17, 199, 391, 401–402, 412
management, 105, 149–150, 374
management, resources, 366
management support, 139, 341, 366
managers, 11
mandatory vacations, 72
man-made threats, 15
mantraps, 218
manual methods, 175
map business functions, 192
market share, 322
maximum acceptable outage (MAO), 256, 312, 320–322, 320*t*, 323*t*, 337, 364
maximum age of passwords, 286
maximum tolerable period of disruption (MTPD), 320
mean time between failures (MTBF), 162
Media Access Control (MAC), 219
media protection (MP) family, 229
medium impact, 10, 19
memory, 166
metrics for vulnerabilities, 210
Microsoft Office Project, 108
milestone plan chart, 108–109, 302, 303*f*
milestones, 107
minimum age of passwords, 286
minimum business continuity objective (MBCO), 364
mission-critical business functions and processes, 192, 329–330
mission-critical operations, 381–382, 382*f*
mission-critical systems, 190–191, 258–261, 336
mitigation, 23–24, 37–42, 48–49, 131, 165–167
MITRE Corporation, 18, 50, 54–56
mobile code, 401
mobile site, 153, 374
modeling, 155
modems, 189
Morris worm, 393
multipartite virus, 412
multiple component incidents, 391, 406–407

N

names of computers, 157
National Cybersecurity and Communications Integration Center (NCCIC), 52–53

National Institute of Standards and Technology (NIST), 50–53, 75, 159, 176, 193, 227–230, 255, 268, 271, 313, 316
National Institute of Standards and Technology Risk Management Framework (RMF), 111
natural events, 154–155
natural threats, 15, 199, 201
NCCIC. *See* National Cybersecurity and Communications Integration Center
Nessus tool suite, 157
network components, 8
network firewall, 92
network infrastructure section, 149
network interface card (NIC), 166
network load balancing, 293
networking service server, 189
NIST. *See* National Institute of Standards and Technology
NIST SP 800-53, 227
Nmap network mapping tool, 157
nodes, 172, 173
noncompliance costs, 93, 321
nonrepudiation techniques, 228, 246, 284
normalization, 377
notification/activation phase of BCP, 192, 348–351, 349*t*

O

objectives, 90–93, 191
objectives of BIA, 316–324
offensive content, 271
Office of Government Commerce (OGC), 79
Office of Management and Budget (OMB), 237
off-site data storage, 368–370
OGC. *See* Office of Government Commerce
online transactional processing (OLTP) databases, 184, 324
online website purchase, 317–318
open ports, 157
OpenPGP, 246
operating system (OS), 152, 157, 177
operational characteristics, 146–147
operational impact, 166, 294–295
operations recovery, 382–383
order of succession, 348
order processing application, 318
organization functions knowledge, 367–368
organization historical data, 201, 202
organizational data, 181–182
organizational policies, 71–72
organizations risk, 385
OS. *See* operating system
outage, 92
outage reports, 208
output analysis, 211–212
outsourcing, 23
overlapping countermeasures, 283

P

pan, tilt, and zoom (PTZ) cameras, 247
parallel testing, 383
passive detective controls, 228
password policy, 285
passwords, 157, 206, 285–286
patch management, 41
Patch Tuesday, 41
patches, 48, 264–265
patents, 183
Payment Card Industry Data Security Standard (PCI DSS), 73–75, 119, 259, 267, 269, 273, 276
PBX equipment, 189
PCI DSS. *See* Payment Card Industry Data Security Standard
penetration testing, 215
permissions, 35, 213, 214, 221
perpetrators, 45–48
personally identifiable information (PII), 65, 176
personally identifiable information processing and transparency (PT) family, 230
personnel, 152, 159
personnel assets, 152, 179
personnel interviews, 211
personnel location control form, 351, 351*t*
personnel policies, 277
personnel security (PS) family, 229
phishing attempts, 200
phone branch exchange (PBX), 189
phone tree, 385
physical access, 277
physical and environment protection (PE) family, 229
physical controls, 41, 161–162, 246–250
physical environment, 25
piggybacking, 218
PII. *See* personally identifiable information
pirated files, 18
plan deactivation, 353–354
plan maintenance, BCP, 356–357
plan of action and milestones (POAM), 91, 92, 101, 106–108, 166, 291, 304, 305
planned controls, 158, 159, 226–230
planned countermeasures, 283
planning (PL) family, 229

POAM. *See* plan of action and milestones
policies, 12, 39–40, 159, 230–232
positive brand image, 322
power grids, 290, 290*f*
preliminary system information, 328
Pretty Good Privacy (PGP), 246
preventive controls, 21, 228
principle of least privilege, 35, 202
principle of need to know, 35, 202
principle of proportionality, 21
prior events, 17
priorities in BCP, 340
priority of an incident, 408–410
privacy, 237
privacy standards (HIPAA), 62
private CA, 244
private data, 153, 180
private key, 244
probability of risk, 126–127, 164
procedural controls, 159–160, 230–238
procedures, 39–40, 99, 159, 230–232
process analysis, 211–212
processor, 166
product liability insurance, 194
product shipment phase, 315*f*
productivity, 174
professional liability insurance, 194, 235
profitability, 22–23
program management (PM) family, 229
program manager (PM), BCP, 346
programmers, 46
project management software, 108, 302, 305
project scope, 256
proprietary data, 153, 180
protection barriers, 247
proximity card, 247
proxy servers, 66, 188, 272, 272*f*
public data, 153, 180
public goodwill, 322
public key, 244
public key infrastructure (PKI), 244–246, 245*f*
public relations (PR), 274, 395
public server discovery, 46
publicly traded company, 68
purchase costs, 301
purpose of BCP, 338

Q

qualitative analysis survey results, 128, 128*t*
qualitative methodology, 164
qualitative risk assessments, 123, 126–133
quantitative risk assessments, 123–126, 136

R

RA. *See* risk assessment
RAID. *See* redundant array of independent disks
ransomware, 33
reasonableness, 19*t*, 20
reasonableness checks, 241
recommendations to mitigate risks, 92
recommended countermeasures, 286, 287*t*, 296
reconstitution phase, BCP, 193, 352–354
recovering databases, 324
recovery activities, 377
recovery goal, 352
recovery models, 324
recovery objectives, 323*t*
recovery of lost opportunities, 322
recovery phase, BCP, 192
recovery planning, 351, 376, 380–381
recovery point objective (RPO), 322
recovery priorities identification, 327, 328*t*
recovery procedures, 380–382, 382*f*
recovery requirements identification, 316, 322–324
recovery steps and procedures in a DRP, 380–382
recovery time actual (RTA), 364
recovery time objective (RTO), 322, 364, 368
recovery value, 150
recovery without BIA, 319
redundancy, 153, 374
redundant array of independent disks (RAID), 129, 344, 363
regulations, 68–71
relationship of costs, 317*f*
remediation plan, 220
Remote Access Domain, 14, 18, 189, 218, 264, 274–275
remote journaling, 370
removable media, 232
repair costs, 9
replacement value, 150
report, BIA, 328
reporting, 96, 100–106
reputation, 9
reputation of an organization, 408
residual risk, 25–26, 38, 139
resource allocation, 138
responsibilities, 92, 95–98, 345–348, 396–397
restore failures, 369
restricted activities, 238
return on investment (ROI), 277

reverse engineering, 48
review process for BCP, 357
rights, 35
risk acceptance, 139
risk analysis, 63
risk assessment (RA), 20, 50, 96, 145–148, 167–168, 229, 265, 275, 282–295, 313
challenges, 134–139
components of, 121–123
importance, 119–120
overview, 118–119
practices, 139–140
purpose, 120
types, 123–133
risk elements, 299–301
risk identification, 15–20, 96
risk level calculation, 127
risk management, 20–23, 50–56, 96, 255–265
risk mitigation, 96, 253–279, 358, 414
risk mitigation plan, 281–307
risk mitigation security controls, 250
risk prioritization, 128–130, 295–298
risk response identification, 21
risk statements, 105
risk-handling strategies, 23–25
risks, 4, 5
risks posed by lack of process, 12–13
risks posed by people, 10–12
risks posed by technology, 13–15, 13*f*
rogueware, 33
rotating jobs, 179
routers, 241–242, 242*f*, 263
rules of behavior, 160, 237–238

S

saboteurs, 34
safeguard value, 124, 125, 163
safeguards, 64, 118, 275
SAINT. *See* System Administrator's Integrated Network Tool
sales and cash flow loss, 321
Sarbanes-Oxley Act (SOX), 64, 182, 207, 265, 266, 267, 268
scale out, 293
scale up, 293
scaling out/up, 293
scope, 93–95, 121–122, 191, 256
scope creep, 93, 94, 213, 256, 377–378
scope of BCP, 338–339
scope of BIA, 314–316
scope statement, 139, 339
script checking account usage, 285
script kiddies, 45, 217
SEC. *See* Securities and Exchange Commission
Securities and Exchange Commission (SEC), 68
security, 11, 11*f*, 47, 62, 159, 214, 232–234, 275, 277, 305–306
Security and Privacy Controls for Federal Information Systems and Organizations, 227
security identifier (SID), 239
security policy, 34, 277
senior management support, 139
sensitivity of data, 344
separation of duties, 40, 72
server fingerprinting, 46
server rooms, 249, 249*f*
servers, 43, 263, 288–291, 292*f*, 294, 341*f*–343*f*
Service Design, 80
service level agreement (SLA), 257
Service Operation, 80
service pack (SP), 178
services, 79–82
session timeout, 161, 239–240
share value loss, 321
Shodan.io, 158
simulation, 383
single loss expectancy (SLE), 124, 163, 164
single point of failure (SPOF), 122, 173, 179
site restoration, 353
SLE. *See* single loss expectancy
sniffer, 243
sniffing attacks, 218
social engineering, 5–6, 206, 218
social engineering attacks, 218
software, 91, 152, 202, 377
software applications, 8
software assets, 177–179
software testing, 238
SOX. *See* Sarbanes-Oxley Act
spear phishing, 200
SPOF. *See* single point of failure
SQL. *See* Structured Query Language
SQL injection attack, 18, 44–45, 215, 299
SSCP. *See* Systems Security Certified Practitioner
stakeholders, 93, 312, 325–326
standards, 12
standards for compliance, 72–85
State Attorney General (AG), 70
stored procedures, 299
strategy of BCP, 340
Structured Query Language (SQL), 45

supplies, 153–154, 190–195
supply chain risk management (SR) family, 230
surveys, 128, 129, 131
survivability, 22–23
switches, 187, 188, 218, 219, 263
symmetric encryption, 244
SYN flood attack, 45
system, 155
system access, 151, 172–174
system administrators, 11
System Administrators Integrated Network Tool (SAINT), 157
system and communications protection (SC) family, 229
system and information integrity (SI) family, 230
system and services acquisition (SA) family, 230
system availability, 151
System Center Configuration Manager (SCCM), 212
system configuration data, 182
system description, BCP, 341–345
system functions, 151–152, 174–176
system logs, 16–17, 161, 208, 240–241
system points of contact (POCs), 328
system process data, 182
system resources, 328
system testing, 212–215
System/Application Domain, 14–15, 18, 189–190, 218, 264–265, 275
Systems Security Certified Practitioner (SSCP), 85, 124

T

tabletop exercises, 355
tailgating, 218
tangible value, 8
TCP SYN flood attack, 219–220, 220*f*
teams, BCP, 346–347
technical controls, 41, 160–161, 238–246
technical environment, 25
Technical Recovery Team (TRT), 346, 347, 352
Technology Infrastructure Library (ITIL), 137
technology protection measure (TPM), 272, 272*f*
telecommunications, 345
telecommuters, 347
temperature detection, 162, 249
test restores, 233, 297–298
testing, BCP, 354–355
testing exercise, 355-356
theft of assets, 187
threat assessment, 198–206, 199*f*
threat modeling, 155, 203–205
threat profile, 155
threats, 4–7, 7*f*, 15–16, 30–36, 90, 91, 96, 154–156, 284–285, 295–296, 296*t*
threat/vulnerability pairs, 37–38, 37*f*, 38*t*, 42, 165, 286, 287*t*
3-2-1 rule, 369
three-barrier protection, 247
time clock services via cloud computing, 372
time to implement, 291–294
toolkits, 397
Top Secret data, 180
top-down approach, 318, 331
total cost of security, 23
total risk, 26
total tangible value, 9
trade secret, 153, 183
trademark, 183
training, 35, 40, 159, 354
training costs, 291, 302
transaction testing, 215
transactions, 184, 215
transferring risk, 23
transform process, 185
Transmission Control Protocol (TCP), 219
Trojan horses, 391
trouble reports, 17

U

unapproved recommendations, 148
unauthorized access, 128, 391, 402–404, 412–413
uncertainty level, 136
unintentional access, 200
unintentional threats, 31–32
uninterruptible power supply (UPS), 20, 290
United States Computer Emergency Readiness Team (US-CERT), 50, 53–54
universal serial bus (USB) drive, 373
update information, 189, 190
UPS. *See* uninterruptible power supply
U.S. Federal Sentencing Guidelines for Organizational Ethics, 266
usability, 10, 11*f*, 214
US-CERT. *See* United States Computer Emergency Readiness Team
US-Cybersecurity Infrastructure Security Agency CISA, 135
use access controls, 35
user access, 374
user and computer management section, 149
User Domain, 13, 17, 187, 217, 261–262, 274

V

vandals, 34
VAs. *See* vulnerability assessments
vendor data, 182
vendors, 347
version control, 40
video cameras, 161
virtual private networks (VPNs), 14, 189, 218, 258, 264, 275, 345
virtualization, 371, 373
viruses, 200
VPNs. *See* virtual private networks
vulnerabilities, 4, 6, 8, 17–18, 37–42, 46, 90, 91, 97, 156–158, 231, 284–285
vulnerability assessments (VAs), 42, 50, 156–158, 206–216
vulnerability scans, 210–211

W

WAN. *See* wide area network
WAN Domain, 14, 18, 188–189, 218, 263–264, 274
WAN link, 341–342, 341*f*
WAN traffic, 264
warehouse, 260
warm site, 153, 373–374, 380
water detection, 162, 248–249
weak passwords, 157
web application firewall (WAF), 122
Web defacing, 128
Web farm, 293, 293*f*, 305, 381, 382*f*
web of trust, 246
Web servers, 121*f*, 122, 149, 189, 259, 327*t*, 328*t*, 381
Web site purchase, online, 317–318
Web sites, 202
Website, 91, 95–97, 99–100
well-known ports, 243, 264, 404
white-hat hackers, 34
whitelist, 152
whois tool, 157
wide area network (WAN), 14, 263, 341–342, 341*f*
WIPO. *See* World Intellectual Property Organization
workers, 260
Workstation Domain, 14, 17, 187, 217, 263–264, 274
World Intellectual Property Organization (WIPO), 183
WorldCom, 266
written records, 175

Z

zombies, 17, 392, 400, 406